GLOBAL  STUDIES

AFRICA

FIFTH EDITION

STAFF

Ian A. Nielsen	Publisher
Brenda S. Filley	Production Manager
Lisa M. Clyde	Developmental Editor
Charles Vitelli	Designer
Cheryl Greenleaf	Permissions Coordinator
Shawn Callahan	Graphics
Lara M. Johnson	Graphics Assistant
Lisa Holmes-Doebrick	Administrative Coordinator
Libra Ann Cusack	Typesetting Supervisor
Juliana Arbo	Typesetter
Diane Barker	Editorial Assistant

GLOBAL  STUDIES

AFRICA

FIFTH EDITION

Dr. F. Jeffress Ramsay

The Dushkin Publishing Group, Inc., Sluice Dock, Guilford, Connecticut 06437

Africa

OTHER BOOKS IN THE GLOBAL STUDIES SERIES

China
The Commonwealth of Independent States
   and Eastern Europe
India and South Asia
Japan and the Pacific Rim
Latin America
The Middle East
Western Europe

Library of Congress Cataloging in Publication Data
Main entry under title: Global studies: Africa.
    1. Africa—History—1960–. I. Title: Africa. II. Ramsey, Jeffress F., *comp.*
ISBN 1–56134–224–6   960.3   91–71258

Fifth Edition

Printed in the United States of America

Africa

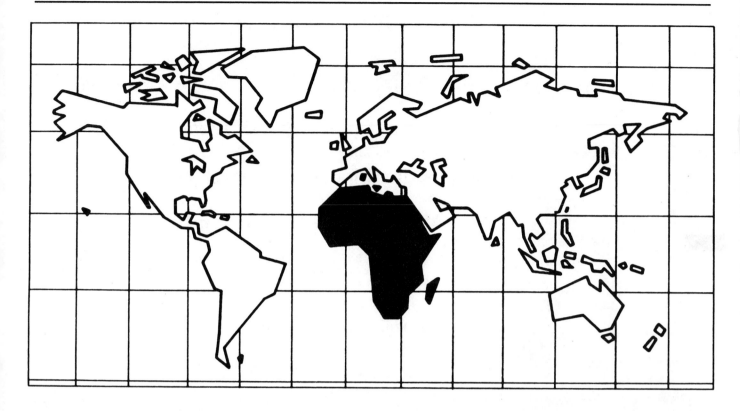

Dr. F. Jeffress Ramsay

Dr. F. Jeffress ("Jeff") Ramsay, the author/editor of *Global Studies: Africa, Fifth Edition,* obtained his Ph.D. in African history from Boston University. He has extensive experience in secondary as well as tertiary education in the United States and in Botswana, where he is currently resident. Dr. Ramsay recently left the Tonota College of Education to become the head of the Social Sciences Department of Legae Academy. In Botswana, he also writes for the *MMEGI* ("Reporter") newspaper, contributes to other popular as well as academic publications, and has been involved in the development of regional museums. Along with Fred Morton and Andrew Murray, he is the coauthor of *Historical Dictionary of Botswana, New Edition* (The Scarecrow Press, 1989), and he collaborated with Fred Morton on *The Birth of Botswana, A History of Bechuanaland Protectorate from 1910 to 1966* (Longman Botswana, 1987).

This revised and updated edition draws on essays and country reports written by Dr. Jane Martin, the author/editor for the first edition, and Dr. Jo Sullivan, the past director of the Outreach Program at the African Studies Center and the author/editor for the second and third editions.

SERIES CONSULTANT

H. Thomas Collins
PROJECT LINKS
George Washington University

Contents

Global Studies: Africa, Fifth Edition

North Africa   Page 14

West Africa   Page 20

Central Africa   Page 69

East Africa   Page 96

Southern Africa   Page 140

Africa: Articles

Introduction

THE GLOBAL AGE

As we approach the end of the twentieth century, it is clear that the future we face will be considerably more international in nature than was ever believed possible in the past. Each day, print and broadcast journalists make us aware that our world is becoming increasingly smaller and substantially more interdependent.

The environmental crisis, world food shortages, nuclear weaponry, and regional conflicts that threaten to involve us all—all make it clear that the distinctions between domestic and foreign problems are all too often artificial, that many seemingly domestic problems no longer stop at national boundaries. As Rene Dubos, the 1969 Pulitzer Prize recipient, stated: ". . . [I]t becomes obvious that each [of us] has two countries, [our] own and planet earth." As global interdependence has become a reality, it has become vital for the citizens of this world to develop literacy in global matters.

THE GLOBAL STUDIES SERIES

It is the aim of this Global Studies series to help readers acquire a basic knowledge and understanding of the regions and countries in the world. Each volume provides a foundation of information—geographic, cultural, economic, political, historical, artistic, and religious—which will allow readers better to understand the current and future problems within these countries and regions and to comprehend how events there might affect their own well-being. In short, these volumes attempt to provide the background information necessary to respond to the realities of our global age.

Author/Editor
Each of the volumes in the Global Studies series is crafted under the careful direction of an author/editor—an expert in the area under study. The author/editors teach and conduct research and have traveled extensively through the regions about which they are writing.

The author/editor for each volume has written the umbrella essay introducing the area. For the fifth edition of *Global Studies: Africa*, the author/editor has extensively revised and updated the regional essays and country reports. In addition, he has overseen the gathering of statistical information for each country and has been instrumental in the selection of the world press articles that appear at the end of the book.

Contents and Features
The Global Studies volumes are organized to provide concise information and current world press articles on the regions and countries within those areas under study.

Area and Regional Essays
Global Studies: Africa, Fifth Edition, covers North Africa, West Africa, Central Africa, East Africa, and Southern Africa. Each of these regions is discussed in a regional essay focusing on the geographical, cultural, sociopolitical and economic aspects of the countries and people of that area. The purpose of the regional essays is to provide the reader with a sense of the diversity of the area as well as an understanding of its common cultural and historical backgrounds. Accompanying each of the regional narratives is a full-page map showing the political boundaries of the countries within the region. In addition to these regional essays, the author/editor has provided a narrative essay on the African continent as a whole. This area essay examines a number of broad themes in an attempt to define what constitutes "Africa."

A Special Note on the Regions of Africa
The countries of Africa do not fall into clear-cut regions. Many of the political divisions that exist today are the product of Africa's colonial heritage, and often they do not reflect cultural, religious, or historical connections. This has created tensions within and among nations, and it makes abstract divisions somewhat arbitrary. Nations that share geographical aspects with one group of countries may share a cultural history with a different group. The regional essays provide explanations for how countries have been grouped in this volume. Readers may encounter different arrangements in other sources. The regional essays should be read carefully to understand why the author/editor chose the divisions made here.

North Africa
North Africa is a special case in relation to the rest of the African continent. Culturally, geopolitically, and economically, the Muslim countries of North Africa are often major players on the Middle Eastern stage as well as on the African scene. For this reason, we have included a regional essay for North Africa in this volume, but the individual country reports and the world press articles for that region appear as part of the expanded coverage of North Africa in *The Middle East* volume of the Global Studies series.

Country Reports
Concise reports on each of the regions with the exception of North Africa follow the regional essays. These reports are the heart of each Global Studies volume. *Global Studies: Africa, Fifth Edition*, contains 47 country reports.

The country reports are composed of five standard elements. Each report contains a map which positions the country among its neighboring states; a summary of statistical information; a current essay providing important historical, geographical, political, cultural, and economic information; a historical timeline offering a convenient visual survey of some key historical events; and, at the end of each report, four graphic indicators with summary statements about the country in terms of development, freedom, health/welfare, and achievements.

A Note on the Statistical Summaries
The statistical information provided for each country has been drawn from a wide range of sources. The most frequently referenced are listed on page 272. Every effort has been made to provide the most current and accurate information available. However, occasionally the information cited by sources differs significantly; and, all too often, the most current information available for some countries is quite dated. Aside from these difficulties, the statistical summary of each country is generally complete and reasonably current. Care should be taken, however, in using these statistics (or, for that matter, any published statistics) in making hard comparisons among countries.

World Press Articles
Within each Global Studies volume is reprinted a number of articles carefully selected by our editorial staff and the author/editor from a broad range of international periodicals and newspapers. The articles have been chosen for currency, interest, and the differing perspectives that they give to a particular region. There are 27 articles in this edition of *Global Studies: Africa.* The article section is preceded by a topic guide. The purpose of this guide is to indicate the main theme or themes of the articles. Readers wishing to focus on a particular theme, say, religion, may refer to the topic guide to find those articles.

Spelling
In many instances, articles from foreign sources may use forms of spelling that are different from the American style. Many Third World publications reflect the European usage. In order to retain the flavor of the articles and to make the point that our system is not the only one, spellings have not been altered to conform to the U.S. system.

Glossary, Bibliography, Index
At the back of each Global Studies volume, readers will find a glossary of terms and abbreviations, which provides a quick reference to the specialized vocabulary of the area under study and to the standard abbreviations (IMF, OAU, ANC, etc.) used throughout the volume.

Following the glossary is a bibliography. The bibliography is organized into general-reference volumes, national and regional histories, novels in translation, current events publications, and periodicals that provide regular coverage on Africa.

The index at the end of the volume is an accurate reference to the contents of the volume. Readers seeking specific information and citations should consult this standard index.

Currency and Usefulness
This fifth edition of *Global Studies: Africa,* like other Global Studies volumes, is intended to provide the most current and useful information available necessary to understanding the events that are shaping the cultures of Africa today.

We plan to revise this volume on a continuing basis. The statistics will be updated, regional essays rewritten, country reports revised, and articles replaced as new and current information becomes available. In order to accomplish this task, we will turn to our author/editor, and—hopefully—to you, the users of this volume. Your comments are more than welcome. If you have an idea that you think will make the volume more useful, an article or bit of information that will make it more current, or a general comment on its organization, content, or features that you would like to share with us, please send it in for serious consideration for the next edition.

(Oxfam photo)

We must understand the hopes, problems, and cultures of the people of other nations in order to understand our own future.

The United States of America

Comparing statistics on the various countries in this volume should not be done without recognizing that the figures are within the timeframe of our publishing date. Nevertheless, comparisons can and will be made, so to enable you to put the statistics of different countries into perspective, we have included comparable statistics on the United States. These statistics are drawn from the same sources that were consulted for developing the statistical information for each country report.

The United States is unique. It has some of the most fertile land in the world, which, coupled with a high level of technology, allows the production of an abundance of food products—an abundance that makes possible the export of enormous quantities of basic foodstuffs to many other parts of the world. The use of this technology also permits the manufacture of goods and services that exceed what is possible in a majority of the rest of the world. In the United States are some of the most important urban centers in the world focusing on trade, investment, and commerce as well as art, music, and theater.

GEOGRAPHY

Area in Square Kilometers (Miles):
9,327,614 (3,540,939)
Capital (Population): Washington, DC
(606,900)
Climate: mostly temperate, but varies
from tropical (Hawaii) to arctic
(Alaska); arid to semiarid in west

PEOPLE

Population

Total: 252,502,000
Annual Growth Rate: 0.8%
Rural/Urban Population Ratio: 21/79
Ethnic Makeup of Population: 80.3%
white; 12.1% black; 9% Hispanic;
2.9% Asian and Pacific Islander; 0.8%
American Indian, Eskimo, and Aleut
(total exceeds 100% due to Hispanic
people being of different races)
Languages: predominantly English;
sizable Spanish-speaking minority

Health

Life Expectancy at Birth: 72 years
(male); 79 years (female)
Infant Mortality Rate (Ratio): 10/1,000
Average Caloric Intake: 138% of FAO
minimum
Physicians Available (Ratio): 1/404

Religion(s)

61% Protestant (21% Baptist, 12%
Methodist, 8% Lutheran, 4%
Presbyterian, 3% Episcopalian, 13%
other Protestant); 25% Roman
Catholic; 2% Jewish; 5% other; 7%
none

Education

Adult Literacy Rate: 97% (official)
(estimates vary widely)

COMMUNICATION

Telephones: 182,558,000
Newspapers: 3,286 with 62,327,962
circulation

TRANSPORTATION

Highways—Kilometers (Miles):
6,365,590 (3,946,667)
Railroads—Kilometers (Miles):
270,312 (167,974)
Usable Airfields: 12,417

GOVERNMENT

Type: federal republic
Independence Date: July 4, 1776
Head of State: President William
("Bill") Jefferson Clinton
Political Parties: Democratic Party;

Republican Party; others of minor
political significance
Suffrage: universal at 18

MILITARY

Number of Armed Forces: 2,013,600
*Military Expenditures (% of Central
Government Expenditures):* $312.9
billion (22.6%)
Current Hostilities: none

ECONOMY

Per Capita Income/GNP: $21,800
Gross National Product (GNP):
$5.465 trillion
Inflation Rate: 3.5%
Natural Resources: metallic and
nonmetallic minerals; petroleum;
arable land
Agriculture: food grains; feed crops;
oil-bearing crops; livestock; dairy
products; fish
Industry: leading industrial power in
the world, highly diversified;
petroleum, steel, motor vehicles,
aerospace, telecommunicationns,
chemicals, electronics, food
processing, consumer goods, fishing,
lumber, mining

FOREIGN TRADE

Exports: $393.9 billion
Imports: $516.2 billion

U.S. (Alaska)

Canada

North
Atlantic
Ocean

United States

U.S. (Hawaii)

Mexico

U.S.

The
Bahamas

Colombia   Venezuela   Suriname
Guyana   French Guiana

Ecuador

Cuba

Brazil

Mexico

Peru

Haiti   Dominican   Puerto Rico
Republic

Antigua
and
Barbuda

Bolivia

Belize

Jamaica

St. Christopher and Nevis

Dominica

Paraguay

Guatemala

Honduras

Chile

El Salvador

Nicaragua

Saint Lucia
Saint Vincent
and the Grenadines   Barbados
Grenada
Trinidad and Tobago

Uruguay

Costa Rica

Argentina

South
Atlantic
Ocean

Panama

Colombia

Venezuela

South Pacific Ocean

N

W   E

S

This map of the world highlights the nations of Africa that are discussed in this volume. Regional essays and country reports are written from a cultural perspective in order to give a frame of reference to the current events in that region. All of the essays are designed to present the most current and useful information available today. Other volumes in the Global Studies series cover different areas of the globe and examine the current state of affairs of the countries within those regions.

Africa

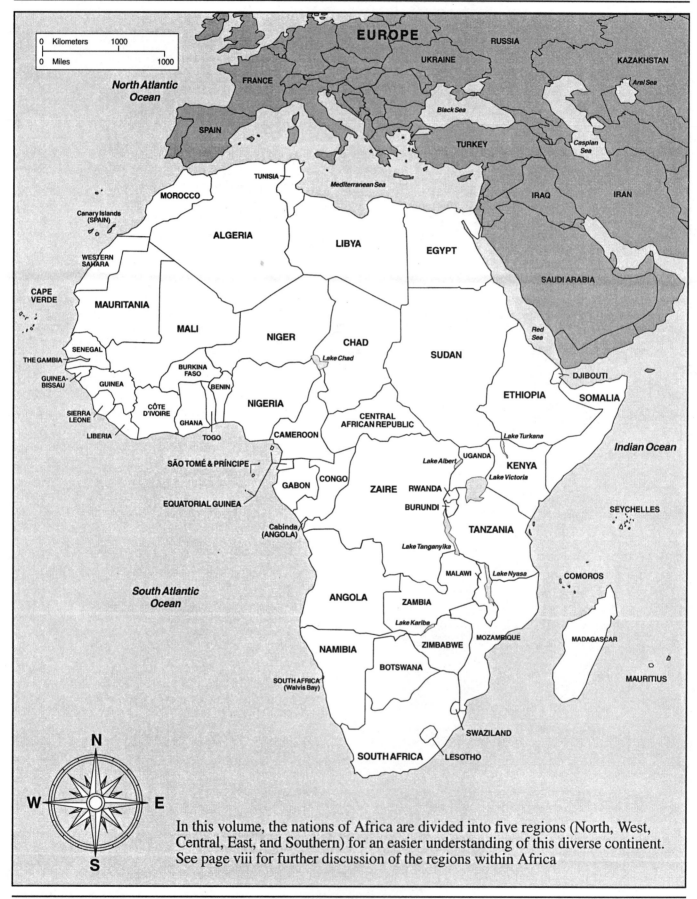

0 Kilometers 1000
0 Miles 1000

EUROPE
RUSSIA
UKRAINE
KAZAKHSTAN
FRANCE
Aral Sea
North Atlantic Ocean
SPAIN
Black Sea
TURKEY
Caspian Sea
TUNISIA
Mediterranean Sea
IRAQ
IRAN
MOROCCO
Canary Islands (SPAIN)
ALGERIA
LIBYA
EGYPT
WESTERN SAHARA
SAUDI ARABIA
CAPE VERDE
MAURITANIA
Red Sea
MALI
NIGER
CHAD
SUDAN
THE GAMBIA
SENEGAL
Lake Chad
DJIBOUTI
GUINEA-BISSAU
BURKINA FASO
GUINEA
BENIN
ETHIOPIA
SOMALIA
SIERRA LEONE
CÔTE D'IVOIRE
NIGERIA
CENTRAL AFRICAN REPUBLIC
Lake Turkana
LIBERIA
GHANA
TOGO
CAMEROON
Indian Ocean
SÃO TOMÉ & PRÍNCIPE
Lake Albert
UGANDA
KENYA
EQUATORIAL GUINEA
GABON
CONGO
ZAIRE
RWANDA
Lake Victoria
Cabinda (ANGOLA)
BURUNDI
SEYCHELLES
TANZANIA
Lake Tanganyika
MALAWI
Lake Nyasa
COMOROS
South Atlantic Ocean
ANGOLA
ZAMBIA
Lake Kariba
MOZAMBIQUE
MADAGASCAR
NAMIBIA
ZIMBABWE
BOTSWANA
MAURITIUS
SOUTH AFRICA (Walvis Bay)
SWAZILAND
SOUTH AFRICA
LESOTHO

N
W   E
S

In this volume, the nations of Africa are divided into five regions (North, West, Central, East, and Southern) for an easier understanding of this diverse continent. See page viii for further discussion of the regions within Africa

Africa: The Struggle for Development

In 1960, 17 African nations gained their independence, liberating most of the continent of colonial rule. The times were electric. In country after country, the flags of Britain, Belgium, France, and the United Nations were replaced by the banners of new states, whose leaders offered idealistic promises to remake the continent and thus the world. Hopes were high, and the most ambitious of goals seemed obtainable. Even non-Africans spoke of the resource-rich continent as being on the verge of a developmental takeoff. Some of the old, racist myths about Africa were at last being questioned.

Yet today, more than 3 decades after the great freedom year, conditions throughout Africa are sobering rather than euphoric. For most Africans independence has been more of a desperate struggle for survival rather than an exhilarating path to development. Now Africa is often described in the global media as "a continent in crisis," "a region in turmoil," "on a precipice," and "suffering"—phrases that echo the sensationalist writings of nineteenth-century missionaries eager to convince others of the continent's need for

(World Bank photo by Pamela Johnson)

This is an electrical transformer at the Volta Aluminum Company in Terna, Ghana. Modern technology and new sources of power are among the factors that contribute to economic development in Africa.

salvation. But the modern headlines are far more accurate than the mission tracts of yesteryear. Today millions of Africans are indeed seeking some form of salvation, from the grinding poverty, pestilence, and, in many areas, wars that afflict their lives. Perhaps this hunger is why contemporary African evangelists are so much more successful in swelling their congregations than were their brethren in the past. It is certainly not for lack of competition; Africa is a continent of many, often overlapping, faiths. In addition to Islam and other spiritual paths, Africans have embraced a myriad of secular ideologies: Marxism, African socialism, people's capitalism, structural adjustment, pan-Africanism, authenticity, nonracialism, the one-party state, and the multiparty state. The list is endless, but salvation seems ever more distant.

Africa's current circumstances are indeed difficult, yet it is also true that the years have brought progress as well as problems. The goals so optimistically pronounced at independence have, for the most part, not been abandoned. Even when the states have faltered, the societies they encompass have remained dynamic and adaptable to shifting opportunities. The support of strong families continues to allow most Africans to overcome enormous adversity. Today there are starving children in Africa, but there are also many more in school uniforms studying to make their future dreams a reality.

A DIVERSE CONTINENT

Africa, which is almost 4 times the size of the United States (excluding Alaska), ranks just below Asia as the world's biggest continent. Well over one-quarter of the membership of the United Nations consists of African states—more than 50 in all. Such facts are worth noting, for even educated outsiders often lose sight of Africa's continental scope when they discuss its problems and prospects.

Not only is the African continent vast but, according to archaeologists, it was also the cradle of human civilization. It should therefore not be surprising that the 600 million or so contemporary Africans maintain extraordinarily diverse ways of life. They speak more than a thousand languages and live their lives according to a rich variety of household arrangements, kinship systems, and religious beliefs. The art and music styles of the continent are as varied as its people.

Given its diversity, it is not easy to generalize about Africa, for each statement there is the exception. However, one aspect that is constant to all African societies is that they have always been changing, albeit in modern times at an ever-increasing rate. Cities have grown and people have moved back and forth between village and town, giving rise to new social groups, institutions, occupations, religions, and forms of communication that make their mark in the countryside as well as in the urban centers. All Africans, whether they be urban computer programmers or hunter-

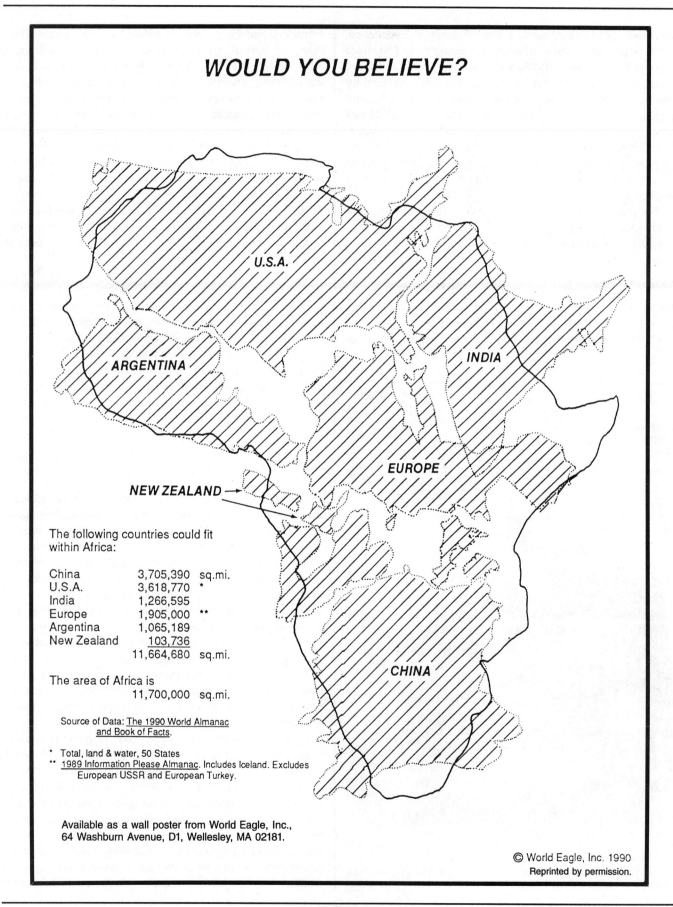

WOULD YOU BELIEVE?

The following countries could fit within Africa:

China	3,705,390	sq.mi.
U.S.A.	3,618,770	*
India	1,266,595	
Europe	1,905,000	**
Argentina	1,065,189	
New Zealand	103,736	
	11,664,680	sq.mi.

The area of Africa is
        11,700,000 sq.mi.

Source of Data: The 1990 World Almanac and Book of Facts.

* Total, land & water, 50 States
** 1989 Information Please Almanac. Includes Iceland. Excludes European USSR and European Turkey.

Available as a wall poster from World Eagle, Inc., 64 Washburn Avenue, D1, Wellesley, MA 02181.

gatherers living in the remote corners of the Kalahari Desert, have taken on new practices, interests, and burdens yet have maintained their African identity. Uniquely African institutions, values, and histories underlie contemporary life-styles throughout the continent.

Memories of past civilizations are a source of pride and community. The medieval Mali and Ghana empires, the glory of Pharaonic Egypt, the Fulani caliphate of northern Nigeria, the knights of Kanem and Bornu, the Great Zimbabwe, and the Kingdom of the Kongo, among others, are all remembered. The past is connected to the present through the generations and by ties to the land. In a continent where the majority of peoples are still farmers, land remains "the mother that never dies." It is valued for its fruits and because it is the place to which the ancestors came and were buried.

The art of personal relationships continues to be important. People typically live in large families. Children are precious, and large families are still desired for social as well as economic reasons. Elders are an important part of a household; nursing homes and retirement communities generally do not exist. People are not supposed to be loners. "I am because we are" remains a valued precept. In this age of nation-states, the "we" may refer to one's ethnic community, while obligations to one's extended family often take precedence over other loyalties.

Most Africans, like the majority of other peoples, believe in a spiritual as well as material world. The continent contains a rich variety of indigenous belief systems, which often coexist with the larger religions of Islam and various Christian sects. Many families believe that their lives are influenced by their ancestors. Africans from all walks of life will seek the services of professional "traditional" healers to explain an illness or suggest remedies for such things as sterility or bad fortune. But this common pattern of behavior does not preclude one from turning to scientific medicine; all African governments face strong popular demands for better access to modern health facilities.

Islam has long been a strong force in Africa. Today the religion rivals Christianity as the fastest-growing faith on the continent. The followers of both religions often accommodate their faith to local traditions and values. People may also join new religious movements and churches, such as the Brotherhood of the Cross and Star in Nigeria or the Church of Simon Kimbangu in Zaire, that link Christian and indigenous beliefs with new ideas and rituals. Like other institutions in the towns and cities, the churches and mosques provide their followers with social networks.

Local art, like local religion, often reflects the influence of the changing world. An airplane is featured on a Nigerian gelede mask, the Apollo space mission inspires a Burkinabe carver, and a Ndebele dance wand is a beaded electric pole.

THE TROUBLED PRESENT

Some of the crises in Africa today threaten its peoples' traditional resiliency. The facts are grim: in material terms, the average African is poorer today than at independence, and it is predicted that poverty will only increase in the near future. In the 1980s widespread famine occurred in 22 African nations; while in 1992, 6 countries were suffering from severe famine, with many others at least partially dependent on outside food aid. Drought conditions have led to food shortages in every African region. The Food and Agricultural Organization (FAO) of the United Nations (UN) estimated that 70 percent of all Africans did not have enough to eat in the mid-1980s. An outpouring of assistance and relief efforts at the time saved as many as 35 million lives. Although agricultural output rose in most areas during the late 1980s, providing enough food promises to be a long-term crisis. In many areas, marginal advances in agricultural production, through better incentives to farmers, have been counterbalanced by declining commodity prices on world markets, population growth, the recurrence of severe drought in Eastern and Southern Africa, and infestations of locusts. Problems of climate irregularity, transport, obtaining needed inputs, and storage require continued assistance and long-range planning.

Wood, the average person's source of energy, grows scarcer every year, and most governments have had to contend with the rising cost of imported fuels. Meanwhile, diseases that once were believed to have been conquered have reappeared: rinderpest has been discovered among cattle and cholera has been found among populations where they have not been seen for generations. The spread of Acquired Immune Deficiency Syndrome (AIDS) also threatens lives and long-term productivity.

Armed conflicts have devastated portions of Africa. The current travails of Liberia, Mozambique, Somalia, and the Sudan, due to internal strife to greater or lesser degrees encouraged by outside forces, place them in a distinct class of suffering—a class that until recently (and may yet again) also included Angola, Ethiopia, Chad, and Uganda. More than a million people have died in these countries over the past decade, while millions more have become refugees. Except for scattered enclaves, normal economic activities have been greatly disrupted or ceased altogether.

Almost all African governments are in debt. In 1991 the foreign debt owed by all the sub-Saharan African countries except South Africa stood at about $175 billion. Although smaller in its absolute amount than that of Latin America, as a percentage of its economic output the continent's debt is the highest in the world and rising swiftly. The combined gross national product (GNP) for the same countries, whose total populations are in excess of 500 million, was less than $150 billion, a figure that represents only 1.2 percent of the global GNP and is about equal to the GNP of Belgium, a country of 10 million people. In Zambia, an extreme example, the per capita foreign debt theoretically owed by each of its citizens is nearly $1,000, while its annual per capita income is less than $300.

A factor that helps to account for Africa's relative poverty is the low levels of industrial output of all but a few of its countries. While the majority of Africans are engaged in food production, not enough food is produced in most countries to feed their citizens. The decline of many commodity prices on the world market has further reduced national incomes. As a result, the foreign exchange needed to import food, machinery, fuel, and other goods is very limited in most African countries. The continent's economy in 1987 grew by only 0.8 percent, far below its annual population growth rate of about 3.2 percent. In the same year cereal production declined 8 percent and overall agricultural production grew by only 0.5 percent. There has been some modest improvement in recent years. But more recent estimates put the economic growth rate at 1.5 percent, still the world's lowest and far below that of the population growth rate.

In order to obtain money to meet debts and pay for their running expenses, many African governments have been obliged to accept the stringent terms of global lending agencies, most notably the World Bank and the International Monetary Fund (IMF). These terms have led to great popular hardship, especially in the urban areas, through austerity measures such as the abandonment of price controls on basic foodstuffs and the freezing of wages. African governments and some experts are questioning both the justice and practicality of these terms: in 1986, some 16 African countries transferred 350 percent more money to the IMF than they received from it in 1985.

THE EVOLUTION OF AFRICA'S ECONOMIES

Africa has seldom been rich, although it has vast potential resources and some rulers and elites have become very wealthy. In earlier centuries the horror of the slave trade greatly contributed to limiting economic development in many African regions. During the period of European exploration and colonialism, Africa's involvement in the world economy greatly increased with the emergence of new forms of "legitimate" commerce. But colonial-era policies and practices assured that this development was of little long-term benefit to most of the continent's peoples.

During the 70 or so years of European colonial rule throughout most of Africa, its nations' economies were shaped to the advantage of the imperialists. Cash crops such as cocoa, coffee, and rubber began to be grown for the European market. Some African farmers benefited from these crops, but the cash-crop economy also involved large foreign-run plantations. It also encouraged the trends toward use of migrant labor and the decline in food production.

Many people became dependent for their livelihood on the forces of the world market, which, like the weather, were beyond their immediate control.

Mining also increased during colonial times, again for the benefit of the colonial rulers. The ores were extracted from African soil by European companies. African labor was employed, but the machinery came from abroad. The copper, diamonds, gold, iron ore, and uranium were shipped overseas to be processed and marketed in the Western economies. Upon independence African governments received a varying percentage of the take through taxation and consortium agreements. But mining remained an enclave industry, sometimes described as a "state within a state" because such industries were run by outsiders who established communities that used imported machinery and technicians and exported the products to industrialized countries.

Inflationary conditions in other parts of the world have had adverse effects on Africa. Today the raw materials that Africans produce often receive low prices on the world market, while the manufactured goods that African countries import are expensive. Local African industries lack spare parts and machinery, and farmers frequently cannot afford to transport crops to market. As a result, the whole economy slows down. Thus, Africa, because of the policies of former colonial powers and current independent governments, is tied into the world economy in ways that do not always serve its best interests.

THE PROBLEMS OF GOVERNMENT

Outside forces are not the only cause of Africa's current crises. In general, Africa is a misgoverned continent. After independence the idealism that characterized various nationalist movements, with their promises of popular self-determination, gave way in most states to cynical authoritarian regimes. By 1989 only Botswana, Mauritius, soon-to-be-independent Namibia, and arguably The Gambia and Senegal could reasonably claim that their governments were elected in genuinely free and fair elections.

The government of Robert Mugabe in Zimbabwe undoubtedly enjoyed majority support, but political life in that state had been seriously marred by violence and intimidation aimed mostly at the opposition. Past multiparty contests in the North African nations of Egypt, Morocco, and Tunisia, as well as Liberia, had been manipulated to assure that the ruling establishments remained unchallenged. Elsewhere the continent was divided between military and/or one-party regimes, which often combined the seemingly contradictory characteristics of weakness and absolutism at the top. While a few of the one-party states, most notably Tanzania, have offered people genuine, if limited, choices of leadership, to a greater or lesser degree most have simply been vehicles of personal rule.

"There is no wealth where there are no children" is an African saying.

But since 1990 there has been a democratic reawakening in Africa, which has toppled the political status quo in some areas and threatened its survival throughout the continent. Whereas in 1989 some 35 nations were governed as single-party states, by 1992 the Banda regime in Malawi stood alone in its unequivocal commitment to the system. In a number of countries—Benin, Cape Verde, the Congo, Mali, São Tomé and Príncipe, and Zambia—the old orders have been decisively rejected in multiparty elections. Elections in other areas have led to a greater sharing of power between the old regimes and their formerly suppressed oppositions. In many countries the democratic transformation is still ongoing and remains fragile. There have been accusations against those in power of manipulation and vote fraud in a number of countries, but so far only in Algeria has the will of the electorate been overtly overridden through a military coup.

Military regimes have not been immune to the winds of change sweeping the continent. In Nigeria, Africa's most populous country, General Ibrahim Babangida has long been committed to a transition back to civilian control. His administration's hope to move the nation smoothly to a guided democracy—in which only two government-created and -defined parties will be allowed to compete for power—remains on target, but rising dissent and repression, coupled with electoral irregularities, have called the process into question.

Events in Benin have most closely paralleled the recent changes of Eastern Europe. Benin's military-based Marxist-Leninist regime of Mathieu Kérékou was pressured into relinquishing power to a transitional civilian government made up of technocrats and former dissidents. Television broadcasts of this "civilian coup" have enjoyed large audiences in neighboring countries. In several other countries, such as Equatorial Guinea, Togo, and Zaire, mounting opposition has resulted in promises of free elections by long-ruling military autocrats. But there remains deep skepticism as to whether these pledges will be properly fulfilled, especially since human-rights abuses have continued. If not, these countries may soon experience turmoil similar to that which has engulfed Ethiopia, Liberia, and Somalia, where military autocrats have been overthrown by armed rebels.

Why did most postcolonial African governments, until recently, take on autocratic forms? And why are these forms now being so widely challenged? There are no definitive answers to either of these questions. One common explanation for authoritarianism in Africa has been the weakness of the states themselves. Most African governments have faced the difficult task of maintaining national unity with diverse, ethnically divided citizenries. Although the states of Africa may overlay and overlap historic kingdoms, most are products of colonialism. Their boundaries were fashioned during the late-nineteenth-century European partition of the continent, which divided and joined ethnic groups by lines drawn in Europe. The successful leaders of African independence movements worked within the colonial boundaries; and when they joined together in the Organization of African Unity (OAU), they agreed to respect the territorial status quo.

While the need to stem interethnic and regional conflict has been one justification for placing limits on popular self-determination, another explanation can be found in the administrative systems that the nationalist leaderships inherited. All the European colonies in Africa functioned as police states. Not only were various forms of opposition curtailed, but intrusive security establishments were created to watch over and control the indigenous populations. Although headed by Europeans, most colonial security services employed local staff members who were prepared to assume leadership roles at independence. A wave of military coups swept across West Africa during the 1960s, while elsewhere aspiring dictators like so-called Life President Ngwazi Hastings Banda of Malawi were quick to appreciate the value of the inherited instruments of control.

Africa's economic difficulties have also frequently been cited as contributing to its political underdevelopment. On one hand, Nigeria's last civilian government, for example, was certainly undermined in part by the economic crisis that engulfed it due to falling oil revenues. On the other hand, in a pattern reminiscent of recent changes in Latin America, current economic difficulties resulting in high rates of inflation and indebtedness seem to be tempting some African militaries, such as Benin's, to return to the barracks and allow civilian politicians to assume responsibility for the implementation of inevitably harsh austerity programs.

External powers have long sustained African dictatorships, through their grants of military and economic aid and, on occasion, direct intervention. For example, a local attempt in 1964 to restore constitutional rule in Gabon was thwarted by French paratroopers, while Joseph Desiré Mobutu's kleptocratic hold over Zaire has from the very beginning relied on overt and covert assistance from the U.S. and other Western states.

The former Soviet bloc and China in the past also helped to support their share of unsavory African allies, in places like Ethiopia, Equatorial Guinea, and Burundi. But the end of the cold war has led to a reduced desire on the part of outside powers to prop up their unpopular African allies. At the same time the major international lending agencies have increasingly concerned themselves with the perceived need to adjust the political as well as economic structures of debtor nations. This new emphasis is justified in part by the alleged linkage between political unaccountability and economic corruption and mismanagement.

The ongoing decline of socialism on the continent is also having a significant political effect. Some regimes have professed a Marxist orientation, while others have felt that a special African socialism could be built on the communal and cooperative traditions of their societies. In countries such as Guinea-Bissau and Mozambique, a revolutionary socialist orientation was introduced at the grass-roots level during the struggles for independence, within areas liberated from colonialism. The various socialist governments have not been free of personality cults, nor from corruption and oppressive measures. At the same time many governments that have eschewed the socialist label have, nonetheless, developed public corporations and central-planning methods, similar to those that openly professed Marxism. In recent years virtually all of Africa's governments, partly in line with IMF and World Bank requirements but also because of the inefficiency and losses of many of their public corporations, have placed greater emphasis on private-sector development.

REASONS FOR OPTIMISM

Although the problems facing African countries have grown since independence, so have the countries' achievements. The number of persons who can read and write in local languages as well as English, French, or Portuguese has increased enormously. More people can peruse newspapers, follow instructions for fertilizers, and read the labels on medicine bottles. Professionals trained in modern technology who, for example, plan electrification schemes, organize large office staffs, or develop medical facilities are more available because of the large number of African universities that have developed in the past 3 decades. Health care has also expanded and improved in most areas. Outside of the areas that have been ravaged by war, life expectancy has generally increased and infant mortality rates have declined.

Despite the terrible wars that are being waged in a few nations, mostly in the form of civil wars, postcolonial African governments have been notably successful in avoiding armed conflict with one another. The principal exception to this rule has been the apartheid regime in South Africa, which has launched numerous acts of aggression against neighboring Southern African states. Even here, however, there is reason for hoping that the South African government's recent withdrawal from Namibia and the opening of a dialogue with its internal opponents will bring its campaign of regional destabilization to a true end.

Another positive development is the increasing attention that African governments and intra-African agencies are giving to women. The pivotal role of women in agriculture and other activities is being recognized and supported. In many countries prenatal and hospital care for mothers and their babies have increased, conditions for women workers in factories have improved, and new cooperatives for women's activities have been developed. Women have also played an increasingly prominent role in the political life of many countries.

The advances that have been made in Africa are important ones, but they could be undercut by continued economic decline. Africa needs debt relief and outside aid just to maintain the gains that have been made. Yet, as the African proverb observes, "someone else's legs will do you no good in traveling." Africa, as the individual country reports in this volume reveal, is a continent of many and varied resources. There are mineral riches and a vast agricultural potential. However, the continent's people, the youths who make up more than half the population and the elders whose wisdom is revered, are its greatest resource. The rest of the world, which has benefited from the continent's material resources, can also learn from the social strengths of African families and communities.

North Africa

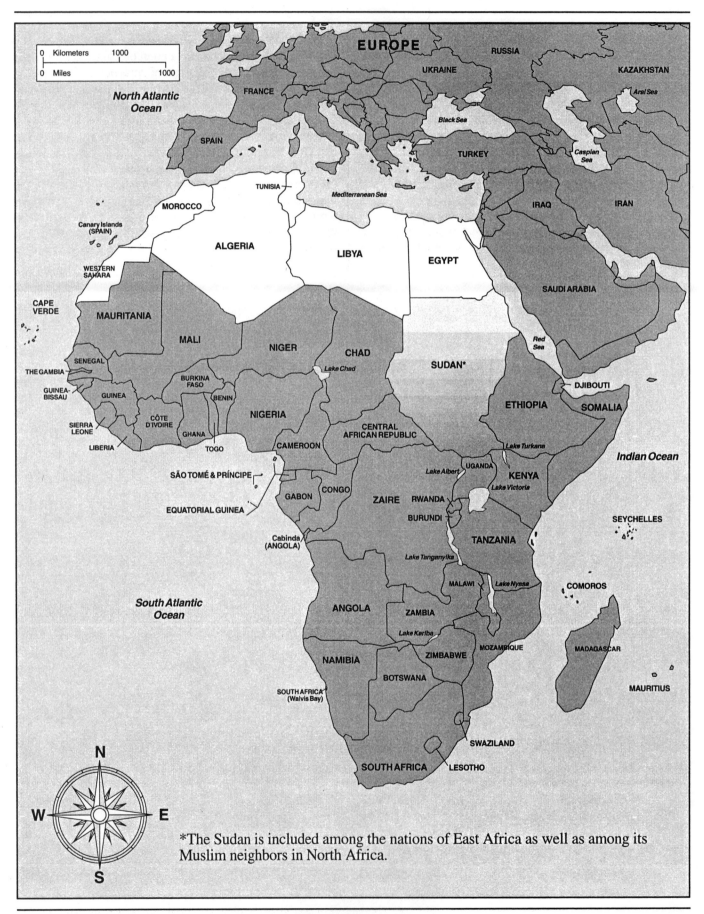

*The Sudan is included among the nations of East Africa as well as among its Muslim neighbors in North Africa.

North Africa: The Crossroads of the Continent

Located at the geographical and cultural crossroads between Europe, Asia, and the rest of the Africa, North Africa has served since ancient times as a link between the civilizations of sub-Saharan Africa and the rest of the world. Traders historically carried the continent's products northward, either across the Sahara or up the Nile River and Red Sea, to the great port cities of the region's Mediterranean coast. Goods also flowed southward. In addition, the trade networks carried ideas. Islam spread from coastal North Africa across much of the rest of the continent to become the religion of at least one-third of all Africans.

North Africa's role as the continent's principal window to the world gradually declined after the year 1500 A.D., as the trans-Atlantic trade increased (the history of East Africa's participation in Indian Ocean trade goes back much further). However, the countries of North Africa have continued to play an important role in the greater continent's development.

The countries of North Africa—Morocco, Algeria, Tunisia, Libya, and Egypt—and their millions of people differ from one another, but they share a predominant, overarching Arab-Islamic culture that both distinguishes them from the rest of Africa and unites them with the Arabic-speaking nations of the Middle East. To understand the societies of North Africa and their role in the rest of the continent, it is helpful to examine the area's geography. The region's diverse environment has long encouraged its inhabitants to engage in a broad variety of economic activities: pastoralism, agriculture, trading, crafts, and, later, industry.

GEOGRAPHY AND POPULATION

Except for Tunisia, which is relatively small, the countries of North Africa are sprawling nations. Algeria, Libya, and Egypt are among the biggest countries on the continent, and Morocco is not far behind. Their size can be misleading, for much of their territories are encompassed by the largely barren Sahara Desert. The populations of the 5 states today range from Egypt's 54 million people to Libya's 4 million; Morocco has 26 million, Algeria 26 million, and Tunisia 8 million citizens. All these populations are increasing at a rapid rate; indeed, well over half the region's citizens are under age 21.

Due to its scarcity, water is the region's most precious resource, so most people live either in valleys near the Mediterranean coast or along the Nile. The latter courses through the desert for thousands of miles, creating a narrow green ribbon that is the home of 95 percent of Egypt's population who live within 12 miles of its banks. More than 90 percent of the people of Algeria, Libya, Morocco, and Tunisia live within 200 miles of either the Mediterranean or, in the case of Morocco, the Atlantic coast.

(United Nations photo)

Land has been less of a barrier to regional cohesiveness in North Africa than have politics and ideology.

Besides determining where people live, the temperate, if often too dry, climate of North Africa has always influenced local economies and life-styles. There is intensive agriculture along the coasts and rivers. Algeria, Morocco, and Tunisia are well known for their tree and vine crops, notably citrus fruits, olives, and wine grapes. The intensively irrigated Nile Valley has, since the time of the American Civil War, which temporarily removed U.S.-produced fiber from the world market, been a leading source of high-quality cotton as well as locally consumed foodstuffs. In the oases that dot the Sahara Desert, date palms are grown for their sweet fruits, which are almost a regional staple. Throughout the steppe lands, between the fertile coasts and the desert, pastoralists follow flocks of sheep and goats or herds of cattle and camels in constant search of pasture. Although now few in number, it was these nomads who in the past developed the trans-Saharan trade. As paved roads and airports have replaced their caravan routes, long-distance

(United Nations photo by Y. Nagata)

Oil and gas discoveries in North Africa produced wide-ranging economic effects.

nomadism has declined. But the traditions it bred, including a love of independence, remain an important part of North Africa's cultural heritage.

Urban culture has flourished in North Africa since the ancient times of the Egyptian pharaohs and the mercantilist rulers of Carthage. Supported by trade and local industries, the region's medieval cities, such as Cairo, Fez, and Kairouan, were the administrative centers of great Islamic empires, whose civilizations shined during Europe's dark ages. In the modern era the urban areas are bustling industrial centers, ports, and political capitals.

Geography, or, more precisely, geology, has helped to fuel economic growth in recent decades. Although agriculture continues to provide employment in Algeria and Libya for as much as a third of the labor force, discoveries of oil and natural gas in the 1950s dramatically altered these two nations' economic structures. Between 1960 and 1980 Libya's annual per capita income jumped from $50 to almost $10,000, transforming it from among the poorest to among the richest countries in the world. Today Libya is the richest country in Africa. Although less dramatically than Libya, Algeria has also greatly benefited from the exploitation of hydrocarbons. Egypt and Tunisia have developed much smaller oil industries, which nonetheless provide for their domestic energy needs and generate much needed foreign exchange. The decline in oil prices during the 1980s, however, reduced revenues, increased unemployment, and contributed to unrest, especially in Algeria. While it has no oil, Morocco profits from its possession of much of the world's phosphate production.

CULTURAL AND POLITICAL HERITAGES

The vast majority of the inhabitants of North Africa are Arabic-speaking Muslims. Islam and Arabic both became established in the region between the sixth and eleventh centuries A.D. Thus, by the time of the Crusades in the eastern Mediterranean, the societies of North Africa were thoroughly incorporated into the Muslim world, even though the area had earlier been the home of many early Christian scholars, such as St. Augustine. Except for Egypt, where about 6 percent of the population remain loyal to the Coptic Church, there is virtually no Christianity among modern North Africans. Until recently, important Jewish communities have existed in all of the region's countries, but their numbers have dwindled as a result of mass immigration to Israel.

With Islam came Arabic, the language of the Koran. Today Egypt and Libya are almost exclusively Arabic-speaking. In Algeria, Morocco, and Tunisia, Arabic coexists with various local minority languages, which are collectively known as Berber (from which the term "Barbary," as in Barbary Coast, was derived). As many as a third of the Moroccans speak a form of Berber as their first language. Centuries of interaction between the Arabs and Berbers as well as their common adherence to Islam have promoted a sense of cultural unity between the two communities, although ethnic disputes have developed in Algeria and Morocco over demands that Berber be included in local school curriculums. As is the case almost everywhere else on the continent, the linguistic situation in North Africa was further complicated by the introduction of European languages during the colonial era. Today French is particularly important as a language of technology and administration in Algeria, Morocco, and Tunisia.

Early in the nineteenth century all the countries of North Africa, except Morocco, were autonomous provinces of the Ottoman Empire, which was based in present-day Turkey and also incorporated most of the Middle East. Morocco was an independent state; indeed, it was one of the earliest to recognize the independence of the United States from England. From 1830 the European powers gradually encroached upon the Ottoman Empire's North African realm. Thus, like most of their sub-Saharan counterparts, all the states of North Africa fell under European imperial control. Algeria's conquest by the French began in 1830 but took decades to accomplish, due to fierce local resistance. France also seized Tunisia in 1881 and, along with Spain, partitioned Morocco in 1912. Britain occupied Egypt in 1882, and Italy invaded Libya in 1911, although anti-Italian resistance continued until World War II, when the area was liberated by Allied troops.

The differing natures of their European occupations has influenced the political and social characters of each North African state. Algeria, which was directly incorporated into France as a province for 120 years, did not win its independence until 1962, after a protracted and violent revolution. Morocco, by contrast, was accorded independence in 1956, after only 44 years of Franco-Spanish administration, during which the local monarchy continued to reign. Tunisia's 75 years of French rule also ended in 1956, as a strong nationalist party took the reins of power. Egypt, although formally independent of Britain, did not win genuine self-determination until 1952, when a group of nationalist army officers came to power by overthrowing the British-supported monarchy. Libya became a temporary ward of the United Nations after Italy was deprived of its colonial empire during World War II. The nation was granted independence by the UN in 1951, under a monarch whose religious followers had led much of the anti-Italian resistance.

NATIONAL POLITICS

Egypt

Egypt reemerged as an important actor on the world stage soon after Gamal Abdel Nasser came to power, in the aftermath of the overthrow of the monarchy. One of the major figures in the post-World War II Nonaligned Move-

ment, Nasser gave voice to the aspirations of millions in the Arab world and Africa, through his championing of pan-Arab and pan-African antiimperialist sentiments. Faced with the problems of his nation's burgeoning population and limited natural resources, Nasser nonetheless refused to let his government become dependent on a single foreign power. Domestically he adopted a policy of developmental socialism.

Because of mounting debts, spurred by enormous military spending, and increasing economic problems, many Egyptians had already begun to reassess some aspects of Nasser's policies by the time of his death in 1970. His successor, Anwar al-Sadat, reopened Egypt to foreign investment in hopes of attracting much-needed capital and technology. Eventually Sadat drew Egypt closer to the United States by signing, in 1979, the Camp David Accords, which ended

(United Nations photo by Y. Nagata)

The Egyptian president, Hosni Mubarak, continues the legacy of his predecessor, Anwar al-Sadat.

more than 3 decades of war with Israel. Egypt has since been one of the largest recipients of U.S. economic and military aid.

Sadat's increasingly authoritarian rule, as well as his abandonment of socialism and foreign-policy initiatives, made him a target of domestic discontent, and in 1981 he was assassinated. His successor, Hosni Mubarak, has modestly liberalized Egyptian politics and pursued what are essentially moderate internal and external policies. While maintaining peace with Israel, Mubarak has succeeded in reconciling Egypt with other Arab countries, which had strongly objected to the Camp David agreement. In 1990–1991 he took a leading role among the majority of

Arab leaders opposed to Iraq's seizure of Kuwait. However, rapid urbanization, declining per capita revenues, debt, and unemployment, all linked to explosive population growth, have continued to strain the Egyptian economy and fuel popular discontent. Some of this discontent has in recent years been channeled into violence by Islamic extremist groups, which now threaten to destroy the traditional tolerence that has existed between Egypt's Muslim majority and Christian minority.

Libya

For years Libya was ruled by a pious, autocratic king whose domestic legitimacy was always in question. After 1963 the

(United Nations photo by Bill Graham)

Nomadic traditions, including loyalty to family and love of independence, are still integral to the culture of North Africa.

nation came under the heavy influence of foreign oil companies, which discovered and produced the country's only substantial resource. In 1969 members of the military, led by Colonel Muammar al-Qadhafi, overthrew the monarchy. Believed to be about 27 at the time of the coup, Qadhafi was an ardent admirer of Nasser's vision of pan-Arab nationalism and antiimperialism. Qadhafi invested billions of dollars, earned from oil, in ambitious domestic development projects, successfully ensuring universal health care, housing, and education for his people by the end of the 1970s. He also spent billions more on military equipment and aid to what he deemed "nationalist movements" throughout the world. Considered a maverick, he has come into conflict with many African and Arab rulers, as well as with outside powers like the United States. Despite Qadhafi's persistent efforts to forge regional alliances, political differences and the expulsion of expatriate workers (due to declining oil revenues), have increased tensions between Libya and its neighbors as well as between the country's own military and middle class.

Strained relations between Libya and the United States, over Qadhafi's activist foreign policy and support for international terrorists, culminated in a U.S. air raid on Tripoli in 1986. The United States has also required American businesses and citizens to leave Libya and has sought other ways to undermine Qadhafi's ambitions. With the support of the United States and other powers, in 1987 the Hissére Habré government of Chad was able to expel the Libyan military from its northern provinces. In 1991 Libya came under greater international pressure when the UN Security Council backed American and British demands for the extradition of two alleged Libyan agents suspected of complicity in the 1987 blowing up of a Pan Am passenger jet over Scotland. The Qadhafi government's failure to submit to this decision has led to the imposition of international sanctions barring other countries from maintaining air-links or selling arms to Libya.

Tunisia

Although having the fewest natural resources of the North African countries, Tunisia enjoyed a high degree of political stability and economic development during the 3 decades that immediately followed the restoration of its independence, in 1956. Habib Bourguiba, leader of the local nationalist party known as the Neo-Destour, led the country to independence while retaining cordial economic and political ties with France as well as other Western countries. Bourguiba's government was a model of pragmatic approaches to both economic growth and foreign policy. A mixed economy was developed, and education's contribution to development was emphasized. The nation's Mediterranean coast was transformed into a vacation spot for European tourists.

However, in the 1980s, amidst economic recession and after 30 years of single-party rule, Tunisians became in-

creasingly impatient with their aging leader's refusal to recognize opposition political parties. Strikes, demonstrations, and opposition from Muslim fundamentalists as well as underground secular movements were the context for Bourguiba's forced retirement in 1987. He was succeeded by his prime minister, Zine al-Abidine ben Ali, whose efforts in 1988 to release jailed Muslim activists and to open political dialogue led to a period of optimism and widespread support. By the middle of that year he had replaced most of the cabinet ministers who had served under Bourguiba. Multiparty elections were held in 1989 but were marred by opposition charges of fraud. There is growing unemployment among Tunisia's youthful, rapidly expanding population.

Algeria

Algeria, wracked by the long and destructive revolution that preceded independence in 1962, has been ruled by a coalition of military and civilian leaders who rose to power as revolutionary partisans of the National Liberation Front (FNL) during the war. Although FNL leaders have differed over what policies and programs to emphasize, in the past

(United Nations photo by Saw Lwin)

Morocco's King Hassan II is a leader whose influence is often pivotal in North African regional planning.

they were able to forge a governing consensus in favor of secularism (but with respect for Islam's special status), a socialist domestic economy, and a foreign policy based on nonalignment. The country's substantial oil and gas revenues were invested in large-scale industrial projects, which were carried out by the state sector. But by the end of the 1970s serious declines in agricultural productivity and growing urban unemployment, partially due to the country's high overall rate of population growth, have sent hundreds of thousands of Algerian workers to France in search of jobs. As a result, cautious encouragement began to be given to private-sector development.

In 1988 rising bread prices led to severe rioting, which left more than 100 people dead. In the aftermath the FNL's long period of one-party rule came to an end, with the legalization of opposition parties. In the 1990 local elections the Islamic Salvation Front (FIS), a coalition group of Muslim fundamentalists, managed to take control of about 80 percent of the country's municipal and departmental councils. This triumph was followed by FIS success in the first round of voting for a new National Assembly in December 1991; the Front captured 187 out of 230 seats. But, just before a second round of voting could be held, in January 1992, the military seized power in a coup. A state of emergency was declared, and thousands of FIS supporters and other opponents of the new regime were detained. In response, some have turned to armed resistance. In June 1992 the political temperature was raised further by the mysterious assassination of Mohamed Boudiaf, a veteran nationalist who had been installed by the military's High State Committee as the president.

Internationally Algeria has been known for its troubleshooting role in difficult diplomatic negotiations. In 1980 it mediated the release of the U.S. hostages held in Iran. After years of tension, largely over the war in Western Sahara, Algeria resumed diplomatic relations with its western neighbor, Morocco, in 1988.

Morocco

Morocco is ruled by King Hassan II, who came to power in 1961 when his highly respected father, King Muhammad V, died. The political parties that developed during the struggle against French rule have continued to contest elections. However, Hassan has rarely permitted them to have a genuine influence in policy-making, preferring to reserve the role for himself and his advisers. As in Tunisia, Moroccan agricultural development has been based on technological innovations rather than on land reform. The latter, while it could raise productivity, would likely anger the propertied supporters of the king. Elites also oppose business-tax

(United Nations photo by J. Slaughter)

Creating an economic and political integration of North African countries has been a goal for a number of years. Economic unification would have the benefits of wider markets, diversified products, and expanded employment; political unification, however, is more problematic, due to the historical and cultural diversity of the area. The Moroccan port of Casablanca, pictured above, is clearly an economic asset to the region.

reforms, yet the government needs revenues to repay its multibillion-dollar debt. Much of the country's economic development has been left to the private sector. High birth rates and unemployment have led many Moroccans to join the Algerians and Tunisians in seeking employment in Europe.

Morocco's 17-year war to retain control of phosphate-rich Western Sahara, a former Spanish colony whose independence is being fought for by a local nationalist movement known as Polisario, has been a persistent drain on the country's treasury (the war costs Morocco about $1 billion a year). Despite major military and economic assistance from the United States, France, and Saudi Arabia, Morocco has been unable to crush Polisario resistance, although its defensive tactics in recent years have proved effective in frustrating guerrilla infiltration throughout most of the territory. A UN peace plan calling for a referendum over the territory's future was agreed to by both sides in 1990. But, although the two parties have generally maintained a ceasefire since 1991, other provisions of the plan have not been implemented, largely as a result of continued Moroccan intransigence.

REGIONAL AND CONTINENTAL LINKS

Since the 1950s there have been many calls for greater regional integration in North Africa. Under Nasser, Egypt was the leader of the pan-Arab movement; it even joined Syria in a brief political union, from 1958 to 1961. Others have attempted to create a union of the countries of the Maghrib (Arabic for "west") region—that is, Algeria, Morocco, and Tunisia. Recently these three countries, along with the adjacent states of Libya and Mauritania, have agreed to work toward an economic community, but they continue to be politically divided. At one time or another

Qadhafi has been accused of subverting all the region's governments; Algeria and Morocco have disagreed over the disposition of the Western Sahara; and each country has at one point or another closed its borders to its neighbors' citizens. Still, the logic of closer political and economic links and the example of increasing European unity on the other side of the Mediterranean will likely keep the issue of regional unity alive.

Both as members of the Organization of African Unity and as individual states, the North African countries have had strong diplomatic and political ties to the rest of the continent. They are, however, also deeply involved in regional affairs outside Africa, particularly those of the Arab and Mediterranean worlds. There have also been some modest tensions across the Sahara. Requests by the North African nations that other OAU countries break diplomatic relations with Israel were promptly met in the aftermath of the 1974 Arab-Israeli War. Many sub-Saharan countries hoped that, in return for their solidarity, the Arab nations would extend development aid to help them, in particular to cope with rising oil prices. Although some aid was forthcoming (mostly from the Gulf countries rather than the North African oil producers), it was less generous than many had expected. During the 1980s a number of sub-Saharan countries resumed diplomatic relations with Israel.

Border disputes, ideological differences, and internal conflicts have caused additional tensions. The Polisario cause in Western Sahara, for example, has badly divided the OAU. When the Organization recognized the Polisario's exiled government, in 1984, Morocco, along with Zaire, withdrew from membership in the body. However, the OAU has also had its regional successes. In 1974 its mediation led to a settlement of a long-standing border dispute between Algeria and Morocco.

West Africa

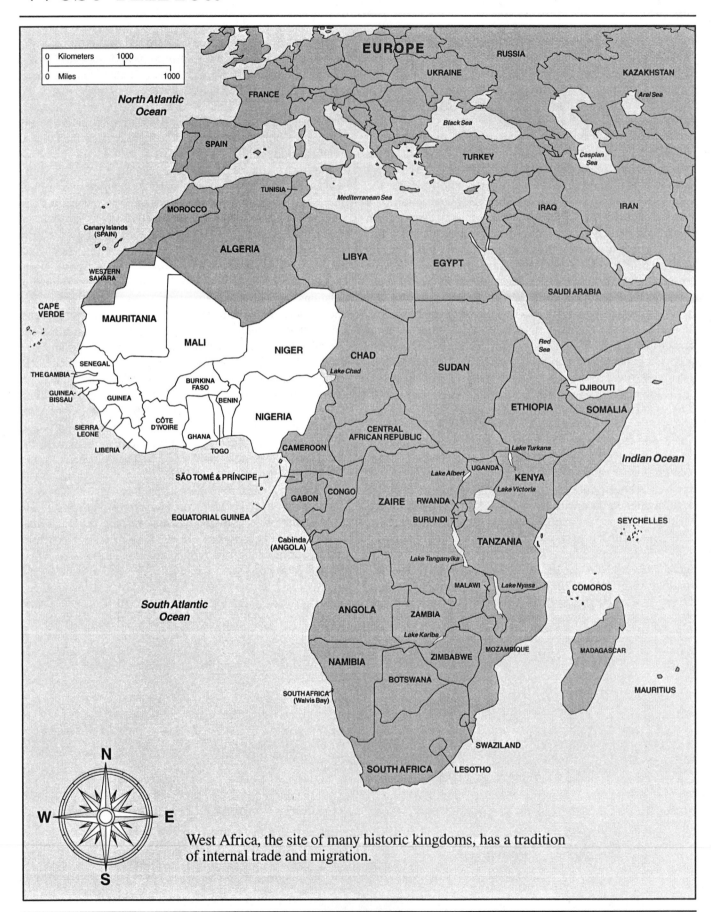

| 0 | Kilometers | 1000 |
| 0 | Miles | 1000 |

North Atlantic Ocean

EUROPE

RUSSIA

UKRAINE

KAZAKHSTAN

FRANCE

Aral Sea

SPAIN

Black Sea

Caspian Sea

TURKEY

TUNISIA

Mediterranean Sea

MOROCCO

IRAQ

IRAN

Canary Islands
(SPAIN)

ALGERIA

LIBYA

EGYPT

WESTERN SAHARA

SAUDI ARABIA

CAPE VERDE

MAURITANIA

MALI

NIGER

CHAD

SUDAN

Red Sea

THE GAMBIA

SENEGAL

Lake Chad

DJIBOUTI

GUINEA-BISSAU

BURKINA FASO

ETHIOPIA

SOMALIA

GUINEA

BENIN

SIERRA LEONE

CÔTE D'IVOIRE

NIGERIA

CENTRAL AFRICAN REPUBLIC

Lake Turkana

LIBERIA

GHANA

TOGO

CAMEROON

Lake Albert

UGANDA

KENYA

Indian Ocean

SÃO TOMÉ & PRÍNCIPE

Lake Victoria

GABON

CONGO

ZAIRE

RWANDA

SEYCHELLES

EQUATORIAL GUINEA

BURUNDI

Cabinda
(ANGOLA)

TANZANIA

Lake Tanganyika

South Atlantic Ocean

MALAWI

Lake Nyasa

COMOROS

ANGOLA

ZAMBIA

Lake Kariba

MOZAMBIQUE

MADAGASCAR

NAMIBIA

ZIMBABWE

MAURITIUS

BOTSWANA

SOUTH AFRICA
(Walvis Bay)

SWAZILAND

SOUTH AFRICA

LESOTHO

N

W E

S

West Africa, the site of many historic kingdoms, has a tradition
of internal trade and migration.

West Africa: Seeking Unity in Diversity

Anyone looking at a map of Africa will identify West Africa as the great bulge on the western coast of the continent. It is a region bound by the Sahara Desert to the north, the Atlantic Ocean to the south and west, and, in part, by the Cameroonian Mountains to the east. Each of these boundaries has historically been a bridge rather than a barrier, in that the region has long been linked through trade to the rest of the world.

At first glance West Africa's great variety is more striking than any of its unifying features. It contains the environmental extremes of desert and rain forest. While most of its people rely on agriculture, every type of occupation can be found, from herders to factory workers. Hundreds of different languages are spoken; some are as different from one another as English is from Arabic or Japanese. Local cultural traditions and the societies that practice them are also myriad.

Yet the more one examines West Africa, the more one is impressed with the features that give the nations of the region a degree of coherence and unity. Some of the common characteristics and cross-cutting features of West Africa as a whole include the vegetation belts that stretch across the region from west to east, creating a similar environmental mix among the region's polities; the constant movement of peoples across local and national boundaries; and efforts being made by West African governments toward greater integration in the region, primarily through economic organizations. West Africans also share elements of a common history.

With the exception of Liberia, all the contemporary states of West Africa were the creations of competing European colonial powers—France, Germany, Britain, and Portugal—that divided most of the area during the late nineteenth century. Before this partition, however, much of the region was linked by the spread of Islam and patterns of trade, including the legacy of intensive involvement between the sixteenth and nineteenth centuries in the trans-Atlantic slave trade. From ancient times great kingdoms expanded and contracted across the West African savanna and forest, giving rise to sophisticated civilizations.

WEST AFRICAN VEGETATION AND CLIMATE ZONES

Traveling north from the coastlines of such states as Nigeria, Ghana, and Côte d'Ivoire, one encounters tropical rain forests, which give way first to woodland savanna and then to drier, more open plains. In Mali, Niger, and other landlocked countries to the north, the savanna gives way to the still drier Sahel environment, between the savanna and the Sahara Desert, and finally to the desert itself.

Whatever their ethnicity or nationality, the peoples living within each of these vegetation zones generally share the benefits and problems of similar livelihoods. For instance, cocoa, coffee, yams, and cassava are among the cash and food crops planted in the cleared forest and woodland zones, which stretch from Guinea to Nigeria. Groundnuts, sorghum, and millet are commonly harvested in the savanna belt that runs from Senegal to northern Nigeria. Herders in the Sahel, who historically could not go too far south with their cattle because of the presence of the deadly tsetse fly in the forest, continue to cross state boundaries in search of pasture.

People throughout West African have periodically suffered from drought, whose effects have often been aggravated in recent years by greater population pressures on the land. These factors have contributed to environmental changes. The condition of the Sahel in particular has deteriorated through a process of desertification, leading to large-scale relocations among many of its inhabitants. The eight Sahelian countries—Cape Verde, The Gambia, Burkina Faso, Mali, Senegal, Niger, Chad (in Central Africa), and Mauritania—have formed a coordinating Committee for Struggle Against Drought in the Sahel (CILSS).

Farther to the south, large areas of woodland savanna have turned into grasslands as their forests have been cut down by land-hungry farmers. Drought has also resulted in widespread brushfires in Ghana, Côte d'Ivoire, Togo, and Benin, which have transformed forests into savannas and savannas into deserts. Due to the depletion of forest, the Harmattan, a dry wind that blows in from the Sahara during January and February, now reaches many parts of the coast that in the recent past did not feel its breath. Its dust and haze have become a sign of the new year—and of new agricultural problems—throughout much of West Africa.

The great rivers of West Africa, such as The Gambia, Niger, Senegal, and Volta, along with their tributaries, have become increasingly important both as avenues of travel and trade and for the water they provide. Countries have joined together in large-scale projects designed to harness their waters for irrigation and hydroelectric power through regional organizations, like the Mano River grouping of Guinea, Liberia, and Sierra Leone and the Organization for the Development of the Senegal River, composed of Mali, Mauritania, and Senegal.

THE LINKS OF HISTORY AND TRADE

The peoples of West Africa have never been united as members of a single political unit. Yet some of the pre-colonial kingdoms that expanded across the region have great symbolic importance for those seeking to enhance interstate cooperation. The Mali empire of the thirteenth to fifteenth centuries, the Songhai empire of the sixteenth century, and the nineteenth-century Fulani caliphate of Sokoto, all based in the savanna, are widely remembered as examples of past supranational glory. The kingdoms of the southern forests, such as the Asante Confederation, the

Dahomey kingdom, and the Yoruba city-states, were smaller than the great savanna empires to their north. Although generally later in origin and different in character from the northern states, the forest kingdoms are, nonetheless, also sources of greater regional identity.

The precolonial states of West Africa gave rise to great urban centers, which were interlinked through extensive trade networks. This development was probably the result of the area's agricultural productivity, which supported a relatively high population density from early times. Many modern settlements have long histories. Present-day Timbuctu and Gao, in Mali, were important centers of learning and commerce in medieval times. Some other examples include Ouagadougou, Ibadan, Benin, and Kumasi, all in the forest zone. These southern centers prospered in the past by sending gold, kola, leather goods, cloth, and slaves to the northern savanna and southern coast.

The cities of the savannas linked West Africa to North Africa. From the eleventh century the ruling groups of the savanna increasingly turned to the universal vision of Islam. While Islam also spread to the forests, the southernmost areas were ultimately more strongly influenced by Christianity, which was introduced by Europeans, who became active along the West African coast in the fifteenth century. For centuries the major commercial link among Europe, the Americas, and West Africa was the trans-Atlantic slave trade, but during the nineteenth century so-called legitimate commerce in palm oil and other tropical products replaced it. New cities such as Dakar, Freetown, and Lagos developed rapidly as centers of the Atlantic trade.

THE MOVEMENT OF PEOPLES

Despite the incorrect view of many who see Africa as being a continent made up of isolated groups, one constant characteristic of West Africa has been the transregional migration of its people. Herders have moved east and west across the savanna and south into the forests. Since colonial times many professionals as well as laborers have sought employment outside their home areas.

Some peoples of West Africa, such as the Malinke, Fulani, Hausa, and Mossi, have developed especially well-established heritages of mobility. In the past the Malinke journeyed from their early center in Mali to the coastal areas in Guinea, Senegal, and The Gambia. Other Malinke traders also made their way to Burkina Faso, Liberia, and Sierra Leone, where they came to be known as Mandingoes.

The Fulani have developed their own patterns of seasonal movement. They herd their cattle south across the savanna during the dry season, and return to the north during the rainy season. Urbanized Fulani groups have historically journeyed from west to east, often serving as agents of Islamization as well as promoters of trade. More recently many Fulani have been forced to move southward as a result of the deterioration of their grazing lands. The Hausa, who mostly live in northern Nigeria and Niger, are also found

(IFC/World Bank photo by Ray Witkin)

A worker cuts cloth at a textile mill in the Côte d'Ivoire. The patterns are similar to traditional patterns. Most of the cloth will be exported.

throughout much of West Africa. Indeed, their trading presence is so widespread that some have suggested that the Hausa language be promoted as a common *lingua franca* for West Africa.

Millions of migrant laborers are regularly attracted to Côte d'Ivoire and Ghana from the poorer inland states of Burkina Faso, Mali, and Niger, thus promoting economic interdependence between these states. Similar large-scale migrations also occur elsewhere. The drastic expulsion of aliens by the Nigerian government in 1983 was startling to the outside world, in part because few had realized that so many Ghanaians, Nigeriens, Togolese, Beninois, and Cameroonians had taken up residence in Nigeria. Such immigration is not new, though its scale into Nigeria was greatly increased by that country's oil boom. Peoples such as the Yoruba, Ewe, and Vai, who were divided by colonialism, have often ignored modern state boundaries in order to maintain their ethnic ties. Other migrations also have roots in the colonial past. Sierra Leonians worked as clerks and craftspeople throughout the coastal areas of British West Africa, while Igbo were recruited to serve in northern Nigeria. Similarly, Beninois became the assistants of French administrators in other parts of French West Africa, while Cape Verdians occupied intermediate positions in Portugal's mainland colonies.

THE PROGRESS OF WEST AFRICAN INTEGRATION

Many West Africans recognize the weaknesses inherent in the region's national divisions. The peoples of the region would benefit from greater multilateral political cooperation and economic integration. Yet there are many obstacles blocking the growth of pan-regional development. National identity is probably even stronger today than it was in the days when Kwame Nkrumah, the charismatic Ghanaian leader, pushed for African unity but was frustrated by parochial interests. The larger and more prosperous states, such as Nigeria and Côte d'Ivoire, are reluctant to share their relative wealth with smaller countries, which, in turn, fear being swallowed.

One-party rule and more overt forms of dictatorship have recently been abandoned throughout West Africa. However, for the moment the region is still politically divided between those states that have made the transition to multiparty constitutional systems of government and those still under effective military control. Overlapping ethnicity is also sometimes more a source of suspicion rather than unity between states. Because the countries were under the rule of different colonial powers, French, English, and Portuguese serve as official languages of the different nations, which also inherited different administrative traditions. Moreover, during colonial times independent infrastructures were developed in each country; these continue to orient economic activities toward the coast and Europe rather than encouraging links among West African countries.

Political changes also affect regional cooperation and domestic development. The now-defunct confederation of Senegal and The Gambia (Senegambia) was dominated by Senegal and resented by many Gambians. The civil war in Liberia has also led to division between the supporters and opponents of the intervention of a multinational peacekeeping force.

Despite the many roadblocks to unity, multinational organizations have developed in West Africa, stimulated in large part by the severity of the common problems that the countries face. The West African countries have a good record of cooperating in the avoidance of armed conflict and the settlement of their occasional border disputes. In addition to the multilateral agencies previously cited that are coordinating the struggle against drought and the development of various river basins, there are also a number of regional commodity cartels, such as the five-member Groundnut Council. The West African Examinations Council standardizes secondary-school examinations in most of the countries where English is an official language, and most of the Francophonic states share a common currency.

The most ambitious and encompassing organization in the region is the Economic Organization of West African States (ECOWAS), which includes all the states incorporated in the West African section of this text. Established in 1975 by the Treaty of Lagos, ECOWAS aims to promote trade, cooperation, and self-reliance. The progress of the organization in these areas has thus far been limited. But ECOWAS can point to some achievements. Several joint ventures have been developed; steps toward tariff reduction are being taken; competition between ECOWAS and the Economic Community of West Africa (CEAO), an economic organization of former French colonies, has been lessened by limiting CEAO; and ECOWAS members have agreed in principle to establish a common currency. Some members of ECOWAS are currently seeking to have the organization play a political role in settling the bloody Liberian conflict, but the success of this effort, along with that of the already dispatched West African peacekeeping force, is uncertain. There is hope that ECOWAS will become more effective in developing West African solutions to the problems of the region's balkanized economies.

Benin (People's Republic of Benin)

GEOGRAPHY
Area in Square Kilometers (Miles):
112,620 (43,483) (slightly smaller than
Pennsylvania)
Capital (Population): official: Porto-
Novo (330,000); de facto: Cotonou
(487,000)
Climate: tropical

PEOPLE

Population
Total: 4,832,000
Annual Growth Rate: 2.9%
Rural/Urban Population Ratio: 62/38
Languages: official: French; others
spoken: Fon, Yoruba, Adja, Bariba,
others

Health
Life Expectancy at Birth: 49 years
(male); 52 years (female)
Infant Mortality Rate (Ratio):
119/1,000
Average Caloric Intake: 100% of FAO
minimum
Physicians Available (Ratio): 1/15,940

Religion(s)
70% traditional indigenous; 15%
Muslim; 15% Christian

Education
Adult Literacy Rate: 23%

COMMUNICATION
Telephones: 8,650
Newspapers: 31

THE DAHOMEY KINGDOM

The Dahomey kingdom, established in the early eighteenth century by
the Fon people, was a highly organized state. The kings had a standing
army, which included women; a centralized administration, whose
officers kept census and tax records and organized the slave trade and,
later, the oil trade; and a sophisticated artistic tradition. Benin, like
Togo, has important links with Brazil that date back to the time of the
Dahomey kingdom. Current Beninois families—such as the da Souzas,
the da Silvas, and the Rodriguezes—are descendants of Brazilians who
settled on the coast in the mid-nineteenth century. Some were descended from former slaves, who may have been taken from Dahomey
long before. They became the first teachers in Western-oriented public
schools and continued in higher education themselves. In Brazil,
Yoruba religious cults, which developed from those of the Yoruba in
Benin and Nigeria, have become increasingly popular in recent years.

TRANSPORTATION
Highways—Kilometers (Miles): 7,445
(4,616)
Railroads—Kilometers (Miles): 579
(360)
Usable Airports: 4

GOVERNMENT
Type: Pluralist democracy
Independence Date: August 1, 1960
Head of State: President Nicephore
Soglo
Political Parties: Coalition of
Democratic Forces; Movement for
Democracy and Social Progress;
Popular Revolutionary Party of Benin;
others
Suffrage: universal for adults

MILITARY
Number of Armed Forces: 4,350
*Military Expenditures (% of Central
Government Expenditures):* 2.3%
Current Hostilities: none

ECONOMY
Currency ($ U.S. Equivalent): 278
CFA francs = $1
Per Capita Income/GDP: $360/$1.7
billion
Inflation Rate: 1.9%
Natural Resources: none known in
commercial quantities
Agriculture: palm products; cotton;
corn; yams; cassava; cocoa; coffee;
groundnuts
Industry: shoes; beer; textiles; cement;
processed palm oil

FOREIGN TRADE
Exports: $250 million
Imports: $442 million

BENIN

In March 1991 Nicephore Soglo was elected as Benin's new president, defeating the incumbent, Mathieu Kérékou. A month earlier, in the country's first multiparty ballot in more than 20 years, Soglo's Coalition of Democratic Forces (RFD) secured a plurality of seats in the new National Assembly. As a result, the former sole party, Kérékou's Popular Revolutionary Party of Benin (PRPB), was reduced to the role of one among a number of opposition groups. The two elections were the culmination of just over a year of dramatic political change in which Benin was transformed from a military-dominated, one-party regime with a self-proclaimed Marxist-Leninist orientation into a functioning multiparty democracy under a government committed to greater reliance on market economics.

THE OLD ORDER FALLS

Former President Kérékou's 17 years of dictatorial rule began to unravel in late 1989. Unable to pay its bills, his government found itself increasingly vulnerable to mounting internal opposition and, to a lesser extent, to external pressure to institute sweeping political and economic reforms.

A wave of strikes and mass demonstrations swept through Cotonou, the country's largest city, in December 1989. This upsurge in prodemocracy agitation was partially inspired by the overthrow of Eastern Europe's Marxist-Leninist regimes; ironically, the Stalinist underground, Communist Party of Dahomey (PCD) also played a role in organizing much of the unrest. Attempts to quell the demonstrations with force only increased public anger toward the authorities.

In an attempt to defuse the crisis, the PRPB's state structures were forced to give up their monopoly of power by allowing a representative gathering to convene with the task of drawing up a new constitution. For 10 days in February 1990 the Beninois gathered around their television sets and radios to listen to live broadcasts of the National Conference of Active Forces of the Nation. The conference quickly turned into a public trial of Kérékou and his PRPB. With the eyes and ears of the nation tuned in, critics of the regime, who had until recently been exiled, were able to pressure Kérékou into handing over effective power to transitional government. The major task of this new, civilian administration was to prepare Benin for multiparty elections while trying to stabilize the deteriorating economy.

The political success of Benin's "civilian coup d'etat" has placed the nation in the forefront of the democratization process currently sweeping Africa. But, having inherited a nearly bankrupt state, President Soglo will need all his skills as a former World Bank economist to meet the hopes and needs of his mostly impoverished electorate.

A COUNTRY OF MIGRANTS

Benin is one of the least developed countries in the world. Having for decades experienced only limited economic growth, in recent years the nation's real gross domestic product has actually declined.

(United Nations photo)

Benin is one of the least developed countries in the world. In recent years, the nation's real gross domestic product has declined. Natives must often fend for themselves in innovative ways. This peddler, pictured here, moves among the lake dwellings of a fishing village selling cigarettes, spices, rice, and other commodities.

| The kingdom of Dahomey is established **1625** | The French conquer Dahomey and declare a French protectorate **1892** | Dahomey becomes independent **1960** | Mathieu Kérékou comes to power in the sixth attempted military coup since independence **1972** | The name of Dahomey is changed to Benin **1975** | An attempted coup involves exiles, mercenaries, and implicates Gabon, Morocco, and France **1977** | 1980s–1990s |

Kérékou announces the abandonment of Marxism-Leninism as Benin's guiding ideology

Unrest, strikes, and escapes by political prisoners lead to the promise of multiparty elections

Multiparty elections are held; Kérékou loses power to Nicephore Soglo

Emigration has become a way of life for many. The migration of Beninois in search of opportunities in neighboring states is not a new phenomenon. Before 1960, educated people from the then-French colony of Dahomey (as Benin was called until 1975) were prominent in junior administrative positions throughout other parts of French West Africa. But as the region's newly independent states began to localize their civil-service staffs, most of the Beninois expatriates lost their jobs. Their return increased bureaucratic competition within Benin, which, in turn, led to heightened political rivalry among ethnic and regional groups. Such local antagonisms contributed to a series of military coups between 1963 and 1972. These culminated in Kérékou's seizure of power.

While Beninois professionals can be found in many parts of West Africa, the destination of most recent emigrants has been Nigeria. The movement from Benin to Nigeria is facilitated by the close links that exist among the large Yoruba-speaking communities on both sides of the border. After Nigeria, the most popular destination has been Côte d'Ivoire. Economic recession in both of these states, however, has led to heightened hostility against the migrants.

THE ECONOMY

Nigeria's urban areas have also been major markets for food. This has encouraged Beninois farmers to switch from cash crops (such as cotton, palm oil, cocoa, and coffee) to food crops (such as yams and cassava), which are smuggled across the border to Nigeria. The emergence of this parallel export economy has been encouraged by the former regime's practice of paying its farmers among the lowest official produce prices in the region. Given that agriculture, in terms of both employment and income generation, forms the largest sector of the Beninois economy, the rise in smuggling activities has inevitably contributed to a growth of graft and corruption.

Benin's small industrial sector is primarily geared toward processing primary products, such as palm oil and cotton, for export. It has thus been adversely affected by the shift away from producing these cash crops for the local market. Small-scale manufacturing has centered around the production of basic consumer goods and construction materials. The biggest enterprises are state-owned cement plants. One source of hope is that, with privatization and new exploration, the country's currently small oil industry will undergo expansion.

Transport and trade are another important activity. Many Beninois find legal as well as illegal employment carrying goods. Due to the relative absence of rain forest (an impediment to travel), Benin's territory has historically served as a trade corridor between the coastal and inland savanna regions of West Africa. Today the nation's roads are comparatively well developed, and the railroad carries goods from the port at Cotonou to northern areas of the country. An extension of the railroad will reach Niamey, the capital of Niger. The government has also tried, with little success, to attract tourists in recent years, through such gambits as selling itself as "the home of voodoo."

POLITICAL PROBLEMS

One of the difficulties facing the current government is President Soglo's lack of a firm majority of supporters in the National Assembly, although most of the parties share his belief that the nation's past failures can be attributed to the previous regime's legacy of "Marxist-Beninism." Nevertheless, there still exists substantial support, especially in the urban areas, for the hard-line Communist Party, which was active as an underground movement during the Kérékou. Should the new government's free-market reforms fail to improve the lives of ordinary Beninois, these "true Communists" may gain support. Another potential source of opposition is the army, which, having retired gracefully from power, may be tempted to make a political comeback. Under Kérékou Benin's oversized military was largely recruited from the former president's home region, which has remained loyal to the PRPB. This fact is a cause for concern.

DEVELOPMENT

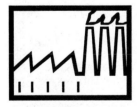

Palm-oil plantations were established in Benin by Africans in the mid-nineteenth century. They have continued to be African-owned and capitalist-oriented. Today there are some 30 million trees, and palm-oil products are a major export used for cooking, lighting, soap, margarine, and lubricants.

FREEDOM

Since 1990 political restrictions have been lifted and prisoners of conscience freed. Recently a number of people have been arrested for supposedly inciting people against the government and encouraging them not to pay taxes.

HEALTH/WELFARE

One-third of the national budget of Benin goes to education, and the number of students receiving primary education has risen to 50% of the school-age population. College graduates serve as temporary teachers through the National Service System, but more teachers and higher salaries are needed.

ACHIEVEMENTS

Fon appliqued cloths have been described as "one of the gayest and liveliest of the contemporary African art forms." Formerly these cloths were made and used by the Dahomeyan kings. Now they are sold to tourists, but they still portray the motifs and symbols of past rulers and the society they ruled.

Burkina Faso

GEOGRAPHY

Area in Square Kilometers (Miles):
274,500 (106,000) (about the size of
Colorado)
Capital (Population): Ouagadougou
(442,000)
Climate: tropical to arid

PEOPLE

Population
Total: 9,360,000
Annual Growth Rate: 2.9%
Rural/Urban Population Ratio: 91/9
Languages: official: French; others
spoken: Mossi, Senufo, Fula, Bobo,
Mande, Gurunsi, Lobi, others

Health
Life Expectancy at Birth: 52 years
(male); 53 years (female)
Infant Mortality Rate (Ratio):
134/1,000
Average Caloric Intake: 100% of FAO
minimum
Physicians Available (Ratio): 1/57,180

Religion(s)
65% traditional indigenous; 25%
Muslim; 10% Christian

Education
Adult Literacy Rate: 18%

DR. OUEDRAOGO AND THE NAAM MOVEMENT

In 1989 Dr. Bernard Ledea Ouedraogo was awarded the Hunger
Project's third annual Africa Prize for Leadership for the Sustainable
End of Hunger, an honor bestowed in recognition of his important
contribution in raising rural living standards throughout West Africa.
During the 1960s Ouedraogo became disillusioned with the top-down
methods then employed by the Burkinabe government and international
aid groups when trying to mobilize local peasants for development
projects. His response was to organize the Naam movement, originally
as a support network for the *naam*, the traditional Burkinabe village
cooperatives. The movement assisted the naam in establishing their
own development projects. Naam has since grown to become the largest
peasant movement in Africa, with more than 4,000 affiliated grass-roots
groups in Chad, The Gambia, Guinea-Bissau, Mali, Mauritania, Niger,
Senegal, and Togo, as well as in Burkina Faso.

COMMUNICATION
Telephones: 13,900
Newspapers: 4

TRANSPORTATION
Highways—Kilometers (Miles): 16,500
(10,230)
Railroads—Kilometers (Miles): 622
(385)
Usable Airports: 43

GOVERNMENT
Type: republic under control of a
military council
Independence Date: August 5, 1960
Head of State: Blaise Compaore
Political Parties: Popular Democratic
Organization-Workers Movement;
dozens of opposition parties
Suffrage: universal for adults

MILITARY
Number of Armed Forces: 7,200
*Military Expenditures (% of Central
Government Expenditures):* 2.7%
Current Hostilities: none

ECONOMY
Currency ($ U.S. Equivalent): 278
CFA francs = $1
Per Capita Income/GDP: $330/n/a
Inflation Rate: 4.5%
Natural Resources: manganese;
limestone; marble; gold; uranium;
bauxite; copper
Agriculture: millet; sorghum; corn;
rice; livestock; peanuts; shea nuts;
sugarcane; cotton; sesame
Industry: agricultural processing;
brewing; light industry

FOREIGN TRADE
Exports: $262 million
Imports: $619 million

BURKINA FASO

Despite the recent introduction of the trappings of multiparty democracy, politics in Burkina Faso continues to be dominated by its president, Blaise Compaore. For half a decade Compaore has survived in a chronically unstable political environment. In December 1991 he sought to legitimize his position through the ballot box—however, he ran unopposed. The May 1992 legislative elections were also won by the president's Popular Democratic Organization–Worker's Movement (ODP–MT). But 35 parties opposed to the ODP–MT boycotted the poll, and only 3 of the participating opposition parties contested seats nationwide.

Compaore rose to power through a series of coups, the last of which resulted in the overthrow and assassination of the charismatic and controversial Thomas Sankara. A man of immense populist appeal, by 1987 Sankara's radical leadership had become the focus of a great deal of internal and external opposition as well as support.

Of the three men responsible for Sankara's toppling, two—Boukari Lingani

and Henri Zongo—were soon executed following a power struggle with the third, Compaore. Such sanguinary competition has aggravated the severe economic and social difficulties of the Burkinabe. (For decades successive military and civilian regimes have faced a daunting task in trying to cope with the challenge of developing the nation's fragile, underdeveloped economy.) It also has called into question the current government's commitment to political pluralism.

DEBILITATING DROUGHTS

At the time of its independence from France, in 1960, the landlocked country then known as the Republic of Upper Volta inherited little in the way of colonial infrastructure. Since independence progress has been hampered by prolonged periods of severe drought. As a result, much of the country has been forced at times to depend on international food aid. To counteract some of the negative effects of this circumstance, efforts have been made to integrate relief donations into local development schemes. Of particular note have been projects instituted by the traditional

rural cooperatives known as *naam,* which have been responsible for such small-scale but often invaluable local improvements as new wells and pumps, better grinding mills, and distribution tools and medical supplies.

Despite such community action, the effects of drought have been devastating. Particularly hard-hit has been pastoral production, which has long been a mainstay of the local economy, especially in the north. It is estimated that the most recent drought destroyed about 90 percent of the livestock in Burkina Faso.

Most Burkinabe continue to survive as agriculturalists and herders, but many are dependent on wage labor. In the urban centers, there exists a significant working-class population who support the nation's politically powerful trade union movement. The division between this urban community and rural population is not absolute, for it is common for individuals to combine wage labor with farming activities. Another population category—whose numbers exceed those of the local wage-labor force—are individuals who seek employment outside of the country. At least 1 million work as migrant laborers

(United Nations photo by John Isaac)

Since Burkina Faso gained its independence from France in 1960, progress has been hampered by prolonged periods of drought. Local cooperatives have been responsible for small-scale improvements such as the construction of this water barrage or barricade as pictured above. Despite such community action, the effects of drought have been devastating.

| The first Mossi kingdom is founded **1313** | The French finally overcome Mossi resistance and claim Upper Volta **1896** | Upper Volta is divided among adjoining French colonies **1932** | Upper Volta is reconstituted as a colony **1947** | Independence under President Maurice Yameogo **1960** | Lieutenant Colonel Laminzana succeeds Yameogo, who resigns after rioting in the country **1966** | **1980s–1990s** |

Captain Thomas Sankara seizes power and changes the country's name to Burkina (Mossi for "land of honest men") Faso (Dioula for "democratic republic")

Sankara is assassinated in a coup; Blaise Compaore succeeds as head of state

Compaore introduces multipartyism, but his critics call the reforms a "shamocracy"

in other parts of West Africa, part of a pattern that dates back to the early twentieth century. Approximately 700,000 of these workers regularly migrate to Côte d'Ivoire. Returning workers have infused the rural areas with consumer goods and a working-class consciousness.

UNIONS FORCE CHANGE

As is the case in much of Africa, it is the salaried urban population who, at least next to the army, have exercised the greatest influence over successive Burkinabe regimes. Trade-union leaders representing these workers have been instrumental in forcing changes in government. They have spoken out vigorously against government efforts to ban strikes and restrain unions. They have also demanded that they be shielded from downturns in the local economy. Although many unionists have championed various shades of Marxist-Leninist ideology, they, along with their natural allies in the civil service, arguably constitute a conservative element within the local society. During the mid-1980s they became increasingly concerned about the dynamic Sankara's efforts to promote a nationwide network of grass-roots Committees for the Defense of the Revolution (CDRs) as vehicles for empowering the nation's largely rural masses.

To many unionists, the mobilization and arming of the CDRs was perceived as a direct challenge to their own status. This threat seemed all the more apparent when Sankara began to cut urban salaries, in the name of a more equitable flow of revenue to the rural areas. When several union

leaders challenged this move, they were arrested on charges of sedition. Sankara's subsequent overthrow thus had strong backing from within organized labor and the civil service. These groups, along with the military, remain the principal supporters of Compaore's ODP–MT and its policy of "national rectification." Yet, despite this support base, the government has moved to restructure the until recently all-encompassing public sector of the economy by reducing its wage bill. This effort has impressed international creditors.

Beyond its core of support, ODP–MT government has generally been met with sentiments ranging from hostility to indifference. While Compaore claimed, with some justification, that Sankara's rule had become too arbitrary and that he had resisted forming a party with a set of rules, many people mourned the fallen leader's death. The widespread use of a new cloth pattern, known locally as "homage to Sankara," in the aftermath of the coup became an informal barometer of popular dissatisfaction. Compaore has also been challenged by the high regard that has been accorded Sankara outside Burkina Faso, as a symbol of a new generation of African radicalism.

Although Compaore, like Sankara, has sometimes turned to sharp antiimperialist rhetoric, his government has generally sought to cultivate good relations with France and the major international financial institutions. But he has alienated himself from many of his fellow West African leaders as well as from the Euro-American diplomatic consensus, through his aggressive support of Charles Taylor's National

Patriotic Front in Liberia. Compaore admits to having sent troops to Liberia to help topple its former leader Samuel Doe—"It was a moral duty to save Liberians from the wrath of a ruthless dictator"—but claims that such support ended in April 1991. (Others in the region are skeptical of this claim.) In 1992 Compaore was also accused of harboring Gambian dissidents, a charge he denies. To many outsiders, as well as Burkinabe, the course of Compaore's government remains ambiguous.

DEVELOPMENT

Despite political turbulence, Burkina Faso's economy has recorded positive, albeit modest, annual growth rates for more than a decade. Most of the growth has been in agriculture. New hydroelectric projects should reduce dependence on imported energy.

FREEDOM

There has been a surprisingly strong tradition of pluralism despite the circumscribed nature of human rights under successive military regimes. Freedom of speech and association are still curtailed and political detentions are common. The Burkinabe Movement for Human Rights has challenged the government.

HEALTH/WELFARE

The inadequacy of public health is reflected in the low Burkinabe life expectancy. Mass immunization campaigns have been successfully carried out, but in an era of structural adjustment, the prospects for a dramatic improvement in health appear bleak.

ACHIEVEMENTS

The biannual Pan-African Film Festival is held in Ouagadougou. This festival has contributed significantly to the development of the film industry in Africa. Burkina Faso has nationalized its movie houses, and the government has encouraged the showing of films by African filmmakers.

Cape Verde (Republic of Cape Verde)

GEOGRAPHY

Area in Square Kilometers (Miles):
4,033 (1,557) (a bit larger than Rhode Island)
Capital (Population): Praia (37,670)
Climate: temperate

PEOPLE

Population
Total: 386,500
Annual Growth Rate: 3%
Rural/Urban Population Ratio: 71/29
Languages: official: Portuguese and Kriolu

Health
Life Expectancy at Birth: 60 years (male); 63 years (female)
Infant Mortality Rate (Ratio): 40/1,000
Average Caloric Intake: 133% of FAO minimum
Physicians Available (Ratio): 1/6,862

Religion(s)
80% Catholic; 20% traditional indigenous

Education
Adult Literacy Rate: 66%

CAPE VERDEANS IN THE UNITED STATES

Large-scale immigration of Cape Verdeans to the United States began in the nineteenth century. Today the Cape Verdean-American community is larger than the population of Cape Verde itself; it is concentrated in southern New England. Most early immigrants arrived in the region aboard whaling and packet ships. The 1980 United States census was the first to count Cape Verdeans as a separate ethnic group.

The community has, on the whole, prospered, and is currently better educated than the U.S. national norm. Cape Verdeans in the United States maintain close ties with their homeland, assisting in local development projects.

COMMUNICATION

Telephones: 1,740
Newspapers: 7 weeklies

TRANSPORTATION

Highways—Kilometers (Miles): 2,250 (1,395)
Railroads—Kilometers (Miles): none
Usable Airports: 6

GOVERNMENT

Type: republic
Independence Date: July 5, 1975
Head of State: President Antonio Mascarenhas Monteiro
Political Parties: Movement for Democracy; African Party for the Independence of Cape Verde
Suffrage: universal over 18

MILITARY

Number of Armed Forces: 1,300
Military Expenditures (% of Central Government Expenditures): 11%
Current Hostilities: none

ECONOMY

Currency ($ U.S. Equivalent): 70 escudos = $1
Per Capita Income/GDP: $740/$286 million
Inflation Rate: 8.2%
Natural Resources: fish; agricultural land; salt deposits
Agriculture: corn; beans; manioc; sweet potatoes; bananas
Industry: fishing; flour mills; salt

FOREIGN TRADE

Exports: $10.9 million
Imports: $107.8 million

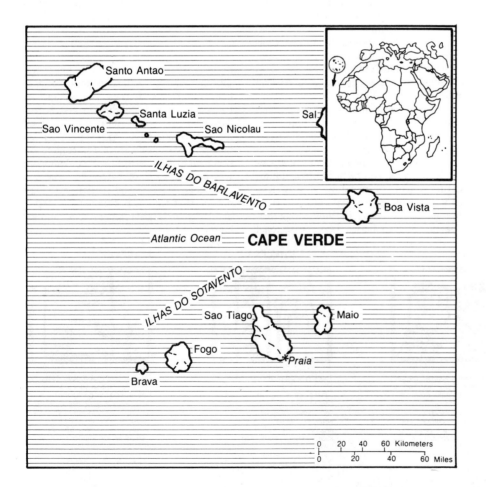

| Cape Verdean settlement begins 1462 | Slavery is abolished 1869 | Thousands of Cape Verdeans die of starvation during World War II 1940s | The PAIGC is founded 1956 | Warfare begins in Guinea-Bissau; Amilcar Cabral is assassinated 1973 | A coup in Lisbon initiates the Portuguese decolonization process 1974 | Independence 1975 | 1980s–1990s |

The 2nd PAICV conference endorses moves toward private-sector development

The PAICV is defeated by the MPD in the country's first multiparty elections

Antonio Mascarenhas Monteiro defeats Aristides Pereira to become Cape Verde's second president

THE REPUBLIC OF CAPE VERDE

After 15 years of single-party rule by the African Party for the Independence of Cape Verde (PAICV), rising agitation led to the legalization of opposition groups in 1990. In January 1991 a quickly assembled antigovernment coalition, the Movement for Democracy (MPD), stunned the political establishment by gaining 68 percent of the votes and 56 out of 79 National Assembly seats. A month later the MPD candidate, Antonio Mascarenhas Monteiro, defeated the long-serving incumbent, Aristides Pereira, in the presidential election. It is a credit to both the outgoing administration and its opponents that this dramatic political transformation occurred without significant violence or rancor. And despite its rejection in the polls, the PAICV was able to claim a solid record of achievements. The PAICV government oversaw an impressive expansion in social services, particularly in the areas of health and education. The Republic of Cape Verde is an archipelago located about 400 miles west of the Senegalese Cape Verde, or "Green Cape," after which it is named. Unfortunately, green is a color that is often absent in the lives of the islands' citizens. Throughout its history Cape Verde has suffered from periods of prolonged drought, which before the twentieth century were often accompanied by extremely high mortality rates (up to 50 percent). The last severe drought lasted from 1968 to 1984. Even in normal years rainfall is often inadequate and irregular.

When the country gained independence, in 1975, there was little in the way of nonagricultural production. As a result, for its survival the new nation had to rely on foreign aid and the remittances of Cape Verdeans working abroad. Despite the continuance of this pattern of dependence, the postindependence period has been marked by a genuine improvement in the lives of most Cape Verdeans.

Cape Verde was ruled by Portugal for nearly 500 years. Most of the islanders are the descendants of Portuguese colonists, many of whom arrived as convicts, and African slaves who began to settle on the islands shortly after their discovery by Portuguese mariners in 1456. The merging of these two groups gave rise to the distinct Cape Verdean Kriolu language (which is also spoken in Guinea-Bissau). Under Portuguese rule, Cape Verdeans were generally treated as second-class citizens, although a few rose to positions of prominence in other parts of the Portuguese empire. Economic stagnation, exacerbated by cycles of severe drought, caused many islanders to emigrate elsewhere in Africa, Western Europe, and the Americas. Today the largest concentration of this emigrant community is found in the United States.

In 1956 the African Party for the Independence of Guinea-Bissau and Cape Verde (PAIGC) was formed under the dynamic leadership of Amilcar Cabral, a Cape Verdean revolutionary who, with his followers, hoped to see the two then-Portuguese colonies form a united nation. Between 1963 and 1974 PAIGC waged a successful war of liberation in Guinea-Bissau, which led to the independence of both territories. Although Cabral was assassinated by the Portuguese in 1973, his vision was preserved during the late 1970s by his successors, who, while ruling the two countries separately, maintained the unity of the PAIGC. This arrangement, however, began to break down in the aftermath of a 1980 coup in Guinea-Bissau, which resulted in the party's division along national lines. In 1981 the Cape Verdean PAIGC formally renounced its Guinean links, becoming the PAICV.

Since independence the PAIGC/CV government has been challenged by the colonial legacy of economic underdevelopment, exacerbated by drought. In contemporary times massive famine has been warded off through a reliance on imported foodstuffs, mostly received as aid. The government has attempted to strengthen local food production and assist the 70 percent of the local population engaged in subsistence agriculture, by drilling for underground water, terracing, irrigating, and building a water-desalinization plant with U.S. assistance. Major efforts have also been devoted to tree-planting schemes as a way to cut back on erosion and eventually make the country self-sufficient in wood fuel. With no more than 15 percent of the islands' territory potentially suitable for cultivation, the prospect of Cape Verde developing self-sufficiency in food appears remote.

The few factories that exist on Cape Verde are small-scale operations catering to local needs. Only textiles have enjoyed modest success as an export. Another promising area is fishing.

DEVELOPMENT

In a move designed to attract greater investment from overseas, especially from Cape Verdean-Americans, the country has recently joined the International Finance Corporation. Efforts are underway to promote the islands as an offshore banking center for the West African (ECOWAS) region.

FREEDOM

A new constitution should entrench the country's recent political liberalization. Opposition publications have emerged to complement the state- and Catholic Church-sponsored media.

HEALTH/WELFARE

Greater access to health facilities has resulted in a sharp drop in infant mortality and a rise in life expectancy. Clinics have begun to encourage family planning. Since independence great progress has taken place in social services, particularly education. Nutrition levels have been raised, and basic health care is now provided to the population as a whole.

ACHIEVEMENTS

Cape Verdean Kriolu culture has a rich literary and musical tradition. With emigrant support, Cape Verde bands have acquired modest followings in Western Europe, Lusophone Africa, Brazil, and the United States. Local drama, poetry, and music are showcased on the national television service.

Côte d'Ivoire (Republic of Côte d'Ivoire)

GEOGRAPHY

Area in Square Kilometers (Miles):
323,750 (124,503) (slightly larger than New Mexico)
Capital (Population): Abidjan (economic) (1,850,000); Yamoussoukro (political) (120,000)
Climate: tropical

PEOPLE

Population

Total: 12,978,000
Annual Growth Rate: 3.5%
Rural/Urban Population Ratio: 53/47
Languages: official: French; others spoken: Dioula, Agni, Baoulé, Kru, Senufo, Mandinka, others

Health

Life Expectancy at Birth: 52 years (male); 56 years (female)
Infant Morality Rate (Ratio): 97/1,000
Average Caloric Intake: 112% of FAO minimum
Physicians Available (Ratio): 1/24,696

Religion(s)

63% traditional indigenous; 25% Muslim; 12% Christian

Education

Adult Literacy Rate: 54%

COMMUNICATION

Telephones: 87,700
Newspapers: 1

THE ARTS OF COTE d'IVOIRE

The arts of Côte d'Ivoire, including music, weaving, dance, and sculpture, have flourished. The wood carvings of the Senufo, Dan, and Baoulé peoples are famous the world over for their beauty and intricate design. Masks are particularly valued and admired by outsiders, but many collectors have never met the Ivoirian people for whom the art has social and religious significance. The Dan mask, for example, is not only beautiful—it also performs a spiritual function. When worn as part of a masquerade performance, it represents religious authority, settling of disputes, enforcing the laws of the community, and respect for tradition.

TRANSPORTATION

Highways—Kilometers (Miles): 46,600 (28,892)
Railroads—Kilometers (Miles): 657 (408)
Usable Airports: 41

GOVERNMENT

Type: republic
Independence Date: August 7, 1960
Head of State: President Félix Houphouët-Boigny
Political Parties: Democratic Party of Côte d'Ivoire; opposition groups
Suffrage: universal over 21

MILITARY

Number of Armed Forces: 14,900
Military Expenditures (% of Central Government Expenditures): 2.3%
Current Hostilities: none

ECONOMY

Currency ($ U.S. Equivalent): 279 CFA francs = $1
Per Capita Income/GDP: $750/$9.7 billion
Inflation Rate: 1.5%
Natural Resources: agricultural lands; timber
Agriculture: coffee; cocoa; bananas; pineapples; palm oil; corn; millet; cotton; rubber
Industry: food and lumber processing; oil refinery; textiles; soap; automobile assembly

FOREIGN TRADE

Exports: $2.5 billion
Imports: $1.4 billion

COTE d'IVOIRE

The first half of 1992 was a period of political disillusionment for many citizens of Côte d'Ivoire (French for "Ivory Coast"). In January, Félix Houphouët-Boigny, the country's octogenarian first president, whose paternalistic rule has lasted for more than 3 decades, rejected his own commission's findings that the army chief of staff, General Robert Guei, was responsible for atrocities committed by his troops at Yopougon University campus in May 1991. "Le Vieux" ("The Old Man"), as the president is known by friend and foe alike, then left for what turned out to be a 4-month "private visit" to Europe. In February 1992 a mass demonstration, called by the main opposition parties (the Ivoirian Popular Front [FPI] and the Ivoirian Human Rights League) to protest against the refusal to sack Guei, turned into a riot, when a small group of hooligans, whose identities remain a matter of dispute, broke off from what had been a peaceful procession.

REFORM AND REPRESSION

The violence provided the government with a pretext to jail the heads of the FPI, Professor Lauret Gbagbo, and the Human Rights League, Professor Degny Segui. Also jailed were dozens of other prominent political and community leaders, including members of another opposition movement, the Ivoirian Workers Party (PIT), as well as journalists and students. Gbagbo, Segui, and 10 other codefendants were subsequently convicted of being "responsible" for "acts of violence," although their prosecution acknowledged that they had not been personally involved in any criminal activity. Others have been imprisoned on charges ranging from "harboring criminals" to putting forward "outrageous arguments." Denouncing what was characterized as an "undeclared state of siege," the FPI withdrew from the National Assembly, making the chamber once more the sole preserve of Houphouët-Boigny's Democratic Party of Côte d'Ivoire (PDCI). Meanwhile Le Vieux himself continued to run the affairs of state by telephone from one of his allegedly numerous European mansions.

Recent events are especially disappointing, given that in 1990 the political life of Côte d'Ivoire seemed to be entering a new phase. Months of mounting prodemocracy protests and labor unrest have led to the legalization of opposition parties, previously banned under the country's single-party government, and the emergence within the PDCI itself of a strong pro-

gressive wing seemingly committed to the liberalization process. Although the first multiparty presidential and legislative elections, in October 1990, were widely regarded as having been less than free and fair by outside observers as well as the opposition, many believed that the path was open for further reform. In November the outgoing National Assembly passed a constitutional amendment to allow its speaker to take over the presidency in the event of a vacancy. This move had raised the prospect that Le Vieux was preparing to step aside in favor of the younger Konan Bedie. Another amendment provided for the naming of a prime minister, a post that has since been filled by Alassane Ouattara, an able technocrat.

ECONOMIC DOWNTURN

Reform and repression have been taking place against the backdrop of a prolonged deterioration in Côte d'Ivoire's once vibrant economy. The primary explanation for this downturn is the decline in revenue from cocoa and coffee, which have long been the country's principal export earners. This has led to mounting state debt, which in turn has pressured the government to adopt unpopular austerity measures. The economy's current problems and prospects are best understood in the context of its past performance.

During its first 2 decades of independence Côte d'Ivoire enjoyed one of the highest economic growth rates in the world. This growth was all the more notable in that, in contrast to many other Third World "success stories" during the same period, it had been fueled by the expansion of commercial agriculture. The nation became the world's leading producer of cocoa and the third-largest producer of coffee. Although prosperity gave way to recession during the 1980s, the average per capita income of the country is still one of Africa's highest. Statistics also indicate that Ivoirians on average live longer and better than their counterparts in many neighboring states. But the creation of a productive, market-oriented economy has not eliminated the reality of widespread poverty, leading some to question whether the majority of Ivoirians have derived reasonable benefit from their nation's wealth.

To the dismay of many young Ivoirians struggling to enter the country's tight job market, much of the political and economic life of Côte d'Ivoire is controlled by its large expatriate population, largely comprised of French and Lebanese. The size of these communities has multiplied since independence. Many foreigners are now quasi-permanent residents who have

thrived managing plantations, factories, and commercial enterprises. Others can be found in senior civil-service positions.

Commercial farmers, who include millions of medium- and small-scale producers, also have prospered. About two-thirds of the work force are employed in agriculture, with coffee alone being the principal source of income for some 2.5 million people, including those who provide services for the industry. In addition to cocoa and coffee, Ivoirian planters grow bananas, pineapples, sugar, cotton, palm oil, and other cash crops for export. While some of these farmers (including the nation's "No. 1 Peasant," Houphouët-Boigny) are quite wealthy, most have only modest incomes.

In recent years the circumstance of Ivoirian coffee and cocoa planters has become much more precarious, due to fluctuations in the prices paid for their commodities on the world market. In this respect, the growers, along with their colleagues elsewhere, are to some extent victims of their own success. Their productivity, in response to international demand, has been a factor in depressing prices through increased supply. In 1988 Houphouët-Boigny held cocoa in storage in an attempt to force a price rise, but the effort failed, aggravating the nation's economic downturn. As a result, the government has taken a new approach, scrapping plans for future expansion in cocoa production in favor of promoting food crops such as yams, corn, and plantains, for which there is a regional as well as domestic market.

Ivoirian planters often hire low-paid laborers who come from other West African countries. There are about 2 million migrant laborers in Côte d'Ivoire, employed throughout the economy. Their presence is not a new phenomenon but goes back to colonial times. Burkina Faso, where many laborers come from, was actually once a part of Côte d'Ivoire. Today Burkinabe as well as citizens of other former colonies of French West Africa have the advantage of being paid in a regional currency, the CFA franc, as well as sharing the colonial vernacular. A good road system and the Ivoirian railroad (which extends to the Burkinabe capital of Ouagadougou) facilitate the travel of migrant workers to rural as well as urban areas.

DEBT AND DISCONTENT

Other factors may determine how much an Ivoirian benefits from the country's development. Residents of Abidjan, the capital, and its environs near the coast receive more services than do citizens of interior areas. Professionals in the cities make bet-

Agni and Baoulé
peoples migrate
to the Ivory
Coast from the
East
1700s

The Ivory Coast
officially becomes
a French colony
1893

Samori Touré, a
Malinke Muslim
leader and an
empire builder, is
defeated by the
French
1898

The final French
pacification of the
country takes
place
1915

Côte d'Ivoire
becomes
independent
under Félix
Houphouët-
Boigny's
leadership
1960

1980s–1990s

The PDCI
approves a plan
to move the
capital from
Abidjan to
Yamoussoukro

Prodemocracy
demonstrations
lead to multiparty
elections; the
pope consecrates
the
Yamoussoukro
basilica

Opposition leaders
are arrested in po-
litical crackdown;
Houphouët-Boigny
bestows his Prize
for Peace Re-
search on F. W.
de Klerk and
Nelson Mandela

ter salaries than do laborers on farms or in small industries. Yet inflation and recession have made daily life difficult for the middle class as well as poorer peasants and workers. This has led to rising discontent. In 1983 teachers went on strike to protest the discontinuance of their housing subsidies. The government refused to yield and banned the teachers' union: the teachers went back to work. The ban has been lifted, but the causes of discontent remain, for no teacher can afford the high rents in the cities. Moreover, teachers deeply resent the fact that other civil servants, ministers, and French cooperants (helpers on the Peace Corps model) did not have their subsidies cut back, and they demand a more even "distribution of sacrifices." In 1987 teachers' leaders were detained by the government.

Conditions for most Ivoirians will get worse before they get better. The non-agricultural sectors of the national economy have also been experiencing difficulties. Many state industries are unable to make a profit due to their heavy indebtedness. Serious brush fires, mismanagement, and the clearing of forests for cash-crop plantations have put the nation's once-sizable timber industry in jeopardy. Ten-and-a-half million hectares of forest, out of a former total of 12 million, have been lost. Plans for expansion of offshore oil production have not been implemented because of an inability to raise the billions of dollars needed for investment.

Côte d'Ivoire's inability to raise capital for its oil industry is a reflection of the debt crisis that has plagued the country since the collapse of its cocoa and coffee earnings. Finding itself in the desperate situation of being forced to borrow to pay interest on its previous loans, the government suspended most debt repayments in 1987. Subsequent rescheduling negotiations with international creditors resulted in an IMF- and World Bank-approved Structural Adjustment Plan. This plan has resulted in a reduction in the prices paid to Ivoirian farmers and a drastic curtailment in public spending, leading to severe salary cuts for public and parastatal workers. Recent pressure on the part of the lending agencies for the Ivoirian government to cut back further on its commitment to cash crops is particularly ironic, given the praise that they bestowed on the same policies in the not-too-distant past. Despite such mounting sacrifices, a long-term crisis is expected.

THE SEARCH FOR STABILITY

The government's ability to gain popular acceptance for its austerity measures has been compromised by corruption and extravagance at the top. A notorious example of the latter is the basilica that was recently constructed at Yamoussoukro, the home village of Houphouët-Boigny, which is to become the nation's new capital city. This air-conditioned structure, patterned after the papal seat of St. Peter's in Rome, is the largest Christian church building in the world. Supposedly a personal gift from Houphouët-Boigny to the Vatican (a most reluctant recipient), its construction is believed to have cost hundreds of millions of dollars.

Côte d'Ivoire's current political upheaval comes after years of stability under what had been a mildly authoritarian one-party regime. To his credit, Houphouët-Boigny has in the past proved himself to be adept at striking a balance among the country's various regional and ethnic groups. He has also generally preferred to deal with internal opponents by emphasizing the carrot rather than the stick. While popular opinion seems to favor new leadership, it may not be easy for any successor to emerge from the shadow of La Vieux, should he step down or be pushed aside.

The course of domestic conflict in Côte d'Ivoire is being watched elsewhere. For decades Houphouët-Boigny has acted as the doyen of the more conservative, pro-Western leaders in Africa. Hostile to Libya and receptive to both Israel and to "dialogue" with South Africa, Côte d'Ivoire has remained especially close to France, which maintains a military presence in the country. Rumors that the French informed Houphouët-Boigny that they were no longer willing to commit their troops to his regime's survival may have been a factor in the (now-compromised) 1990 reforms, which some dubbed "Paristroika."

DEVELOPMENT

It has been said that the Côte d'Ivoire is "power hungry." The Soubre Dam, being developed on the Sassandra River, is the sixth and largest hydroelectric project in the Côte d'Ivoire. It will serve the eastern area of the country. Another dam is planned on the Cavalla River, between the Côte d'Ivoire and Liberia.

FREEDOM

The leader of the Ivoirian Human Rights League is among those who have recently been imprisoned for nonviolent opposition. Appeals by Amnesty International on their behalf and criticism in such international forums as the European parliament have been dismissed by the government.

HEALTH/WELFARE

Côte d'Ivoire has one of the lowest soldier-to-teacher ratios in Africa, while education absorbs about 40% of the national budget. The National Commission to Combat AIDS has reported significant success in its campaign to promote condom use, by targeting especially vulnerable groups.

ACHIEVEMENTS

Ivoirian textiles are varied and prized. Block printing and dyeing produce brilliant designs; woven cloths made strip by strip and sewn together include the white Korhogo tapestries, covered with Ivoirian figures, birds, and symbols drawn in black. The Ivoirian singer Alpha Blondy has become an international superstar as the leading exponent of West African reggae.

The Gambia (Republic of The Gambia)

GEOGRAPHY

Area in Square Kilometers (Miles):
11,295 (4,361) (smaller than
Connecticut)
Capital (Population): Banjul (49,200)
Climate: subtropical

PEOPLE

Population
Total: 874,000
Annual Growth Rate: 3.2%
Rural/Urban Population Ratio: 79/21
Languages: official: English; others
spoken: Mandinka, Wolof, Fula,
Sarakola, Diula, others

Health
Life Expectancy at Birth: 47 years
(male); 51 years (female)
Infant Mortality Rate (Ratio):
138/1,000
Average Caloric Intake: 97% of FAO
minimum
Physicians Available (Ratio): 1/10,588

Religion(s)
90% Muslim; 9% Christian; 1%
traditional indigenous

Education
Adult Literacy Rate: 27%

HALEY'S *ROOTS*

"Kambay Bolong" and "Kunte Kinte" were two of the unfamiliar
terms that Alex Haley's grandmother repeated as she told him of their
"furthest back" ancestor, the African. When Haley started the search
for his roots, he consulted linguists as well as Africans about these
words. "Kambay Bolong" was identified as the Gambia River and
"Kinte" as one of the major Mandinka lineages or large families. Thus
began Haley's association with The Gambia, which culminated in his
visit to the town of Juffure in Gambia's interior. There Haley heard the
history of the Kinte clan from a *griot,* or bard, and identified his past
ancestor. Today many Americans and others who have read or heard of
Haley's story are among the tourists who visit The Gambia. Alex Haley
died in 1992.

COMMUNICATION

Telephones: 11,000
Newspapers: 6

TRANSPORTATION

Highways—Kilometers (Miles): 3,083
(1,911)
Railroads—Kilometers (Miles): none
Usable Airports: n/a

GOVERNMENT

Type: republic
Independence Date: February 18, 1965

Head of State: President (Sir) Alhaji
Dawda Kairaba Jawara
Political Parties: People's Progressive
Party; National Convention Party;
Gambia People's Party; others
Suffrage: universal for adults

MILITARY

Number of Armed Forces: 950
*Military Expenditures (% of Central
Government Expenditures):* 0.7%
Current Hostilities: internal conflicts

ECONOMY

Currency ($ U.S. Equivalent): 8.88
dalasis = $1
Per Capita Income/GDP: $230/$210
million
Inflation Rate: 10.1%
Natural Resources: fish; ilmenite;
zircon; rutile
Agriculture: peanuts; rice; cotton;
millet; sorghum; fish; palm kernels;
livestock; rutile
Industry: peanuts; brewing; soft
drinks; agricultural machinery
assembly; wood- and metalworking;
clothing; tourism

FOREIGN TRADE

Exports: $122.2 million
Imports: $155.2 million

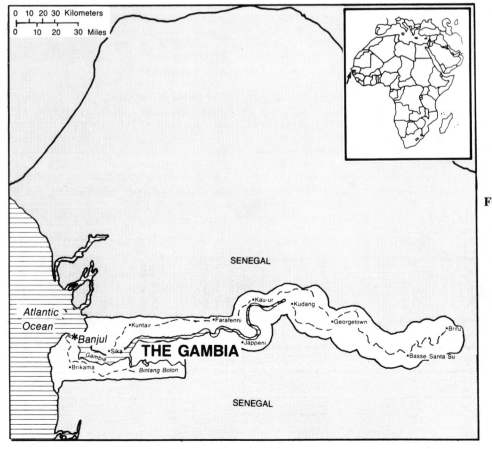

The British build
Fort James at
the current site of
Banjul, on the
Gambia River
1618

The Gambia is
ruled by the
United Kingdom
through Sierra
Leone
1807

Independence
1965

1980s–1990s

An attempted
coup against
President Dawda
Jawara

The rise and fall
of the
Senegambia
Confederation

An era of political
rebuilding and
economic
restructuring

THE GAMBIA

In April 1992 Sir Dawda Jawara won his fifth consecutive 5-year term as president of The Gambia, winning 59 percent of the vote. (His nearest rival received 22 percent.) The president's People's Progressive Party (PPP) was also returned to power, with a reduced majority. Before the election the 69-year-old Jawara had expressed a desire to retire; he agreed to run only in the face of strong PPP and popular pressure. He is now expected to step down in midterm. Most Gambians are proud of their country's record of multiparty politics under Jawara, and some are uneasy about what will be the nation's course when he leaves the stage. Yet despite economic difficulties, a bloody 1981 coup attempt, and chronic fears of external meddling, The Gambia should continue to be a model of political stability and tolerance in an era when much of Africa is seeking to follow its footsteps toward multipartyism.

The Gambia is Africa's smallest noninsular nation. Except for a small seacoast, it is entirely surrounded by its much larger neighbor, Senegal. The two nations' separate existence is rooted in the activities of British slave traders who, in 1618, established a fort at the mouth of The Gambia River, from which they gradually spread their commercial and, later, political dominance upstream. Gambians have much in common with Senegalese. The Gambia's three major ethnolinguistic groups—Mandinka, Wolof, and Fula or Peul—are found on both sides of the border. The Wolof language serves as a *lingua franca* in both the Gambian capital of Banjul and the urban areas of Senegal. Islam is the major religion of both countries, while each also

has a substantial Christian minority. The economies of the two countries are also similar, with each being heavily reliant on the cultivation of groundnuts as a cash crop. Finally, both states have survived as multiparty democracies in a region where authoritarian military and/or single-party regimes have been the norm.

In 1981 the Gambian and Senegalese governments were drawn closer together by an attempted coup in Banjul. While Jawara was absent in London, dissident elements within his Paramilitary Field Force joined in a coup attempt with members of two small, self-styled revolutionary parties. Based on a 1965 mutual-defense agreement, Jawara received assistance from Senegal in putting down the rebels. Constitutional rule was restored, but the killing of 400 to 500 persons during the uprising and the subsequent mass arrest of suspected accomplices left Gambians bitter and divided.

In the immediate aftermath of the coup, The Gambia agreed to join Senegal in a loose confederation, which some hoped would lead to a full political union. But from the beginning the Senegambia Confederation was marred by the circumstances of its formation. The continued presence of Senegalese soldiers in their country led Gambians to speak of a "shotgun wedding." Beyond fears of losing their local identity, many believed that proposals for closer economic integration, through a proposed monetary and customs union, would be to The Gambia's disadvantage. Underlying this concern was the role played by Gambian traders in providing imports to Senegal's market. Other squabbles, such as a long-standing dispute over the financing of a bridge across The Gambia River, finally led to the Confeder-

ation's formal demise in 1989. But the two countries still recognize a need to develop alternative forms of cooperation.

The Gambia has been more successful at rebuilding its politics in the aftermath of the coup attempt. In the 1987 and 1992 elections, opposition parties, most notably Dibba's National Convention Party (NCP), significantly increased their share of the vote, while the PPP has retained majority support.

The government has used its electoral mandate to implement its Economic Recovery Program, which includes austerity measures. The Gambia has always been an economically poor country. During the 1980s conditions worsened as a result of bad harvests and falling prices for groundnuts, which usually account for some 50 percent of the nation's export earnings. The tourist industry was also disrupted by the coup attempt.

In addition to the stresses of economic restructuring, Gambian authorities contend that social stability has been threatened by foreign conspiracies. In 1988 and again in 1992 they accused Libya, and in the latter case also Burkina Faso, of complicity in thwarted exile plots to overthrow their administration. But many among The Gambia's opposition maintain that official corruption has become the greatest threat to future political stability.

DEVELOPMENT

Since independence The Gambia has developed a tourist industry. Whereas in 1966 only 300 individuals were recorded as having visited the country, the figure for 1988–1989 was over 112,000. Tourism is now the second biggest sector of the economy, accounting for 10% of the gross domestic product.

FREEDOM

Despite the imposition of martial law in the aftermath of the 1982 coup, The Gambia has a strong record of respect for individual liberty and human rights. Banjul is the headquarters of the Organization of African Unity's Commission for Human and People's Rights.

HEALTH/WELFARE

School enrollment has expanded greatly since The Gambia's achievement of independence, but 40% of Gambian children remain outside the primary school setup. The Economic Recovery Program austerity has made it harder for the government to achieve its goal of education for all.

ACHIEVEMENTS

Gambian *griots*—hereditary bards and musicians such as Banna and Dembo Kanute—have maintained a traditional art. Formerly, griots were attached to ruling families; now they perform over Radio Gambia and are popular throughout West Africa.

Ghana (Republic of Ghana)

GEOGRAPHY

Area in Square Kilometers (Miles):
238,538 (92,100) (slightly smaller than Oregon)
Capital (Population): Accra (965,000)
Climate: tropical to semiarid

PEOPLE

Population
Total: 15,617,000
Annual Growth Rate: 3.1%
Rural/Urban Population Ratio: 67/33
Languages: official: English; others spoken: Akan (including Fanti, Asante, Twi), Ewe, Ga, Hausa, others

Health
Life Expectancy at Birth: 53 years (male); 56 years (female)
Infant Mortality Rate (Ratio): 86/1,000
Average Caloric Intake: 100% of FAO minimum
Physicians Available (Ratio): 1/2,602

Religion(s)
38% traditional indigenous; 30% Muslim; 24% Christian; 8% others

---

THE KING OF HIGHLIFE

E. T. Mensah is widely credited with having been the creator of modern Highlife, the popular music style, which, during his 5-decade career, he helped spread from Ghana throughout Africa and the rest of the world. During the 1930s Mensah's band, The Tempos, began to experiment with the then-popular dance music of big-band jazz by introducing Ghanaian rhythms and indigenous instruments and lyrics into their repertoire. A new sound quickly emerged, which, while drawing inspiration from the traditional rural environment, reflected the fast pace and sophistication of Ghana's emerging urban centers. Recording contracts and tours allowed the so-called King of Highlife to spread his reign across West Africa in the 1940s. By the next decade the music had become identified with the nationalist struggle. During the 1960s Mensah often accompanied Nkrumah on foreign visits, becoming known as "the Musical Ambassador of Ghana."

Education
Adult Literacy Rate: 60%

COMMUNICATION
Telephones: 38,000
Newspapers: 3

TRANSPORTATION
Highways—Kilometers (Miles): 28,300 (17,546)
Railroads—Kilometers (Miles): 953 (592)
Usable Airports: 9

GOVERNMENT
Type: military; governed by the Provisional National Defense Council
Independence Date: March 6, 1957
Head of State: Flight Lieutenant Jerry Rawlings (chair of the Provisional National Defense Council)
Political Parties: dozens of political parties formed in 1992
Suffrage: none

MILITARY
Number of Armed Forces: 11,900
Military Expenditures (% of Central Government Expenditures): 0.5%
Current Hostilities: internal conflicts

ECONOMY
Currency ($ U.S. Equivalent): 389 cedis = $1
Per Capita Income/GDP: $380/$5.9 billion
Inflation Rate: 50%
Natural Resources: gold; diamonds; bauxite; manganese; fish; timber; oil
Agriculture: cocoa; coconuts; coffee; subsistence crops; rubber
Industry: mining, lumber; light manufacturing; fishing; aluminum

FOREIGN TRADE
Exports: $826 million
Imports: $1.2 billion

GHANA

On March 5, 1992, Ghana's head of state, Jerry Rawlings, marked the 35th anniversary of his nation's independence by reluctantly announcing an accelerated return to multiparty rule. In presidential elections held in November 1992, Rawlings was elected leader of Ghana's Fourth Republic. It was a decisive victory for the man who has ruled since 1981, when he and other junior military officers seized power as the Provisional National Defense Council (PNDC). In the name of ending corruption, they overthrew Ghana's last freely elected government after it had been in office for less than 2 years. Rawlings was, at that time, dismissive of elections: "What does it mean to stuff paper into boxes?" Perhaps success has now swayed his opinion.

PAST DISAPPOINTMENTS

At its independence, in 1957, Ghana assumed a leadership role in the struggle against colonial rule elsewhere on the continent. Both its citizens and many outside observers were optimistic about the country's future. As compared to many other former colonies, the country seemed to have a sound infrastructure for future progress. Unfortunately, economic development and political democracy have since proved to be elusive goals.

The First Republic, led by the charismatic Kwame Nkrumah, degenerated into a bankrupt and increasingly authoritarian one-party state. Nkrumah had pinned his hopes on an ambitious policy of industrial development. When substantial overseas investment failed to materialize, he turned to socialism. His efforts led to a modest rise in local manufacturing, but the sector's productivity was compromised by inefficient planning, limited resources, expensive inputs, and mounting government corruption. The new state enterprises ended up being largely financed from the export earnings of cocoa, which had emerged as the principal cash crop during the colonial period. Following colonial precedent, Nkrumah had resorted to paying local cocoa farmers well below the world market price for their output in order to expand state revenues.

Nkrumah was overthrown by the military in 1966. Despite his regime's shortcomings, he is still revered by many as the leading Pan-African Nationalist of his generation, whose warnings about the dangers of neoimperialism have proved prophetic. Since Nkrumah's fall the army has been Ghana's dominant political institution, although there were brief returns to civilian control in 1969–1972 and again in 1979–1981. Although both the officers and civilians abandoned much of Nkrumah's socialist commitment, for years they continued his policy of squeezing the cocoa farmers, with the long-term result of encouraging planters both to cut back on their production and to attempt to circumvent the official prices through smuggling. This trend, coupled with falling cocoa prices on the world market and rising import costs, helped to push Ghana into a state of severe economic depression dur-

(United Nations photo)

Economic development in Ghana has proved to be disappointing in recent years. The importance of harvesting the sea is shown in the picture above. This form of fishing demands both power and skill; the men in the surf have to throw the weighted net far out in the water.

| A Portuguese fort is built at Elmina **1482** | The establishment of the Asante Confederation under Osei Tutu **1690s** | The "Bonds" of 1844 signed by British officials and Fante chiefs as equals **1844** | The British finally conquer the Asante, a final step in British control of the region **1901** | Ghana is the first of the colonial territories in sub-Saharan Africa to become independent **1957** | Nkrumah is overthrown by a military coup **1966** | The first coup of Flight Lieutenant Rawlings **1979** | **1980s–1990s** |

The second coup by Rawlings: the PNDC is formed

Rawlings accepts World Bank and IMF austerity measures

Prodemocracy agitation leads to a transition to multiparty rule

ing the 1970s, when it is estimated that real wages fell by some 80 percent. Ghana's crisis was then aggravated by an unwillingness on the part of successive governments to devalue the local currency, the cedi, which encouraged black-market trading.

RAWLINGS'S RENEWAL

By 1981 many Ghanaians welcomed the PNDC, seeing in Rawlings's populist rhetoric the promise of change after years of corruption and stagnation. The PNDC initially tried to rule through People's Defense Committees, which were formed throughout the country to act as both official watchdogs and instruments of mass mobilization. Motivated by a combination of idealism and frustration with the status quo, the vigilantism of these institutions threatened the country with anarchy until, in 1983, they were reined in. Also in 1983 the country faced a new crisis, when the Nigerian government suddenly expelled nearly a million Ghanaian expatriates, who had to be resettled quickly.

Faced with an increasingly desperate situation, the PNDC, in a move that surprised many, given its leftist leanings, began to implement a comprehensive, IMF-supported program to reduce the size and economic role of the state. As a result of this Economic Recovery Program (ERP), some 100,000 public and parastatal employees were retrenched, the cedi was progressively devalued, and wages and prices began to reflect more nearly their market value. These steps have led to

economic growth, while annually attracting some $500 million in foreign aid and soft loans, and perhaps double that amount in cash remittances from the more than 1 million Ghanaians living abroad. But the human costs of ERP have been a source of criticism. Many ordinary Ghanaians, especially urban salary-earners, have suffered from falling wages coupled with rising inflation. Unemployment has also increased in many areas. Yet a recent survey found surprisingly strong support among "urban lower income groups" for ERP and the government in general. In the countryside, farmers have benefited from higher crop prices and investments in rural infrastructure, while there has been a countrywide boom in legitimate retailing.

While ERP continues to have its critics, it now enjoys substantial support from politicians aligned with Ghana's three principal political tendencies: the Nkrumahists, loyal to the first president's Pan-African socialist vision; the Danquah-Busia grouping, named after two past statesmen who struggled against Nkrumah for more liberal economic and political policies; and those loyal to the PNDC. Rawlings's success in the 1992 presidential contest may encourage the formation of a grand anti-PNDC coalition between the Nkrumahists, who are plagued by internal divisions, and Danquah-Busia groups. There is also a body of opinion that is critical of all three tendencies, which are sometimes characterized as fronts for power-hungry men fighting yesterday's battles. During the April 1992 referendum to approve the new

constitution, more than half the registered electorate (many Ghanaians have complained that they have been denied registration) failed to participate, despite the government and opposition's joint call for a large "Yes" vote. But the current democratization timetable allows little time for the emergence of new voices.

DEVELOPMENT

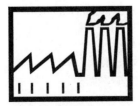

In the 1960s Ghana invested heavily in schooling, resulting in perhaps the best-educated population in Africa. Today hundreds of thousands of professionals, who began their schooling under Nkrumah, work overseas, annually remitting an estimated $1 billion into the economy.

FREEDOM

The move to multipartyism has promoted freedom of speech and assembly. Dozens of independent periodicals have emerged. But people opposed to the transition process have been arrested and harassed, and many continue to fear the National Security Chief Kojo Tsikata and the Bureau of National Investigations.

HEALTH/WELFARE

In 1991 the African Commission of Health and Human Rights Promoters established a branch in Accra to help rehabilitate victims of human-rights violations from throughout Anglophone Africa. The staff deals with both the psychological and physiological aftereffects of abused ex-detainees.

ACHIEVEMENTS

In 1988 Ghana celebrated the 25th anniversary of the School of the Performing Arts at the University of Legon. Integrating the world of dance, drama, and music, the school has trained a generation of artists committed to Ghanaian, African, and international traditions in the arts.

Guinea (Republic of Guinea)

GEOGRAPHY

Area in Square Kilometers (Miles):
246,048 (95,000) (slightly larger than Oregon)
Capital (Population): Conakry (656,000)
Climate: tropical

PEOPLE

Population

Total: 7,456,000
Annual Growth Rate: 2.8%
Rural/Urban Population Ratio: 74/26
Languages: official: French; others spoken: Fula, Mandinka, Susu, Malinke, others

Health

Life Expectancy at Birth: 41 years (male); 45 years (female)
Infant Mortality Rate (Ratio): 144/1,000
Average Caloric Intake: 100% of FAO minimum
Physicians Available (Ratio): 1/26,916

Religion(s)

85% Muslim; 8% Christian; 7% traditional indigenous

Education

Adult Literacy Rate: 24%

COMMUNICATION

Telephones: 10,000
Newspapers: 1

TRANSPORTATION

Highways—Kilometers (Miles): 30,100 (10,662)

Railroads—Kilometers (Miles): 1,045 (648)
Usable Airports: 16

GOVERNMENT

Type: republic, under military regime
Independence Date: October 2, 1958
Head of State: President (General) Lansana Conté
Political Parties: dozens of new parties formed in 1992
Suffrage: none

MILITARY

Number of Armed Forces: 9,700
Military Expenditures (% of Central Government Expenditures): n/a
Current Hostilities: none

ECONOMY

Currency ($ U.S. Equivalent): 811 francs = $1
Per Capita Income/GDP: $380/$2.8 billion
Inflation Rate: 28.2%
Natural Resources: bauxite; iron ore; diamonds; gold; water power
Agriculture: rice; cassava; millet; corn; coffee; bananas; palm products; pineapples
Industry: bauxite; alumina; light manufacturing and processing

FOREIGN TRADE

Exports: $645 million
Imports: $551 million

SAMORI TOURÉ

In the late nineteenth century Malinke leader Samori Touré established a powerful state in the interior of Guinea and Côte d'Ivoire. Samori, called "the Napoleon of the Sudan," was a Muslim who converted many of the areas that he conquered, but he was not a jihadist. His state was based on modern military organization and tactics; this enabled him to resist the European conquest longer and more effectively than any other West African leader. Through alliances, sieges, control of the arms trade, and, ultimately, manufacture of guns and ammunition, Samori fought the French and resisted conquest throughout the 1890s. Manipulating African competition and people's fear of Samori, the French allied with African leaders and prevented a unified resistance to their rule.

| A major Islamic kingdom is established in the Futa Djalon **1700s** | Samori Touré, the leader of a state in the Guinea and Ivory Coast interior, is defeated by the French **1898** | Led by Sekou Touré, Guineans reject continued membership in the French Community; an independent republic is formed **1958** | French President Giscard d'Estaing visits Guinea: the beginning of a reconciliation between France and Guinea **1978** | **1980s–1990s** |

| Sekou Touré's death is followed by a military coup | The introduction of SAP leads to urban unrest | President Lansana Conté begins to establish a multiparty democracy |

GUINEA

Like many African countries, Guinea has recently embarked on a political transition toward a multiparty democracy. In April 1992 President Lansana Conté announced that the new Constitution, guaranteeing freedom of association, would take immediate effect and that legislative elections would be held by the end of the year. Within a month more than 30 parties had been formed. Many see the transformation as a political second chance for a nation whose potential was mismanaged for decades under the dictatorial rule of its first president, Sekou Touré.

From his early years as a radical trade-union activist in the late 1940s until his death in office in 1984, Sekou Touré was Guinea's dominant personality. A descendent of the nineteenth-century Malinke hero Samori Touré, who fiercely resisted the imposition of French rule, Sekou Touré was a charismatic but repressive leader. In 1958 he inspired Guineans to vote for immediate independence from France. At the time Guinea was the only territory to opt out of Charles de Gaulle's newly established French Community. The French reacted spitefully, withdrawing all aid, personnel, and equipment from the new nation, an event that influenced Guinea's postindependence path. The ability of Touré's Democratic Party of Guinea (PDG) to step into the administrative vacuum was the basis for the quick transformation into the continent's first one-party socialist state, a process that was further encouraged by the prompt assistance from the then–Soviet bloc.

Touré's rule was characterized by economic mismanagement and the widespread abuse of human rights. It is estimated that some 2 million people, about 1 out of every 4 Guineans, fled the country during his rule, while at least 2,900 individuals disappeared under detention.

By the late 1970s Touré, pressured by rising discontent and his own apparent realization of his country's poor economic performance, began to modify both his domestic and foreign policies. This shift led to better relations with Western countries but little improvement in the lives of his people. In 1982 Amnesty International launched a campaign to publicize the Touré regime's dismal record of political killings, detentions, and torture, but the world remained largely indifferent.

On April 3, 1984, a week after Touré's death, the army stepped in, claiming that it wished to end all vestiges of the late president's dictatorial regime. The bloodless coup was well received by Guineans. Hundreds of political prisoners were released and the once-powerful Democratic Party of Guinea, which during the Touré years had been reduced from a mass party into a hallow shell, was disbanded. A new government was formed, under the leadership of then–Colonel Conte, and a 10-point program for national recovery was set forth, including the restoration of human rights and the renovation of the economy.

Faced with an empty treasury, the new government committed itself to a severe Structural Adjustment Program. This has led to a dismantling of many of the socialist structures that had been established by the previous government. While international financiers have generally praised it, the government has had to weather periodic unrest and coup attempts. In spite of these challenges, it has remained committed to SAP.

Despite its status as one of the world's poorest countries, Guinea is blessed with mineral resources, which could lead to a more prosperous future. The country is rich in bauxite and has substantial reserves of iron and diamonds. New mining agreements, leading to a flow of foreign investment, have already led to a modest boom in bauxite and diamond exports. Small-scale gold mining is also being developed.

Guinea's greatest economic failing has been the poor performance of its agricultural sector. Unlike many of its neighbors, the country enjoys a favorable climate and soils. But, although some 80 percent of the population is engaged in subsistence farming, only 3 percent of the land is cultivated, and foodstuffs remain a major import. Blame for this situation largely falls on the Touré regime's legacy of an inefficient, state-controlled system of marketing and distribution. In 1987 the government initiated an ambitious plan of road rehabilitation, which, along with better produce prices, has begun to encourage farmers to produce more for the domestic market.

DEVELOPMENT

Recent economic growth in Guinea is reflected in the rising traffic in Conakry harbor, whose volume between 1983 and 1987 rose 415%. Plans are being made to improve the port's infrastructure.

FREEDOM

In 1991 Guineas approved a new Constitution, which includes recognition of freedom of speech, assembly, and association as well as human-rights guarantees. But a complementary culture of political tolerance has yet to take hold.

HEALTH/WELFARE

The life expectancy of Guineans, 41 years for men and 45 years for women, is among the lowest in the world, reflecting the actual stagnation of the nation's health service during the Touré years.

ACHIEVEMENTS

More than 80% of the programming broadcast by Guinea's television service is locally produced. This output has included more than 3,000 movies. A network of rural radio stations is currently being installed.

Guinea-Bissau (Republic of Guinea-Bissau)

GEOGRAPHY

Area in Square Kilometers (Miles):
36,125 (13,948) (about the size of
Indiana)
Capital (Population): Bissau (125,000)
Climate: tropical

PEOPLE

Population
Total: 1,024,000
Annual Growth Rate: 2.4%
Rural/Urban Population Ratio: n/a
Languages: official: Portuguese;
others spoken: Kriolo, Fula,
Mandinka, Manjara, Balante, others

Health
Life Expectancy at Birth: 45 years
(male); 48 years (female)
Infant Mortality Rate (Ratio):
125/1,000
Average Caloric Intake: 74% of FAO
minimum
Physicians Available (Ratio): 1/9,477

Religion(s)
65% traditional indigenous; 30%
Muslim; 5% Christian

Education
Adult Literacy Rate: 36%

COMMUNICATION
Telephones: 3,000
Newspapers: 1

AMILCAR CABRAL

Amilcar Cabral (1924–1973), born in Cape Verde and raised in Guinea-
Bissau, was an idealist who developed plans for his country's liberation
and an activist who worked to put these plans into action. He was a
friend of Agostinho Neto of Angola, a founding member of Angola's
current ruling party, MPLA, and he worked in Angola. Cabral worked
for an African system of government, a change in structures that would
mean "a reorganization of the country on new lines." He believed that a
revolution could not result from leadership alone; all must fight a
mental battle and know their goals before taking arms. Cabral's work
with peasants from 1952 to 1954, while carrying out an agricultural
census, helped him to understand and reach rural peoples who were to
be the crucial force in the development of Guinea-Bissau's independence from Portugal.

TRANSPORTATION
Highways—Kilometers (Miles): 5,058
(3,135)
Railroads—Kilometers (Miles): none
Usable Airports: 18

GOVERNMENT
Type: republic; overseen by
Revolutionary Council
Independence Date: September 24,
1973
Head of State: President (Major) João
Bernardo Vieira
Political Parties: African Party for the
Independence of Guinea-Bissau and
Cape Verde (PAIGC); Democratic
Social Front; Democratic Front; others
Suffrage: universal over 15

MILITARY
Number of Armed Forces: 7,200
*Military Expenditures (% of Central
Government Expenditures):* 3.2%
Current Hostilities: recent border
clashes with Senegal

ECONOMY
Currency ($ U.S. Equivalent): 4,995
pesos = $1
Per Capita Income/GDP: $160/$164
million
Inflation Rate: 25%
Natural Resources: bauxite; timber;
shrimp; fish
Agriculture: peanuts; rice; palm
kernels; groundnuts
Industry: agricultural processing; hides
and skins; beer; soft drinks

FOREIGN TRADE
Exports: $14.2 million
Imports: $68.9 million

GUINEA-BISSAU

Guinea-Bissau, a small country wedged between Senegal and Guinea on the west coast of Africa, has an unenviable claim to being perhaps the poorest country in the world. To many outsiders, the nation is better known for the liberation struggle waged by its people against Portuguese colonial rule between 1962 and 1974. Mobilized by the African Party for the Independence of Guinea-Bissau and Cape Verde (PAIGC), Guinea-Bissau played a major role in the overthrow of fascist rule within Portugal and the liberation of its other African colonies. The movement's effectiveness has led many to view its struggle as a model of anti-imperialist resistance.

COLONIALISM AND INDEPENDENCE

The origins of Portuguese rule in Guinea-Bissau go back to the late 1400s. For centuries the area was raided as a source of slaves, who were shipped to Portugal and its colonies of Cape Verde and Brazil. With the nineteenth-century abolition of slave-trading, the Portuguese began to impose forced labor within Guinea-Bissau itself. During the twentieth century the fascist government in Lisbon rationalized its repression by extending limited civil rights only to those educated Africans who were officially judged to have assimilated Portuguese culture—the *assimilados*. In Guinea-Bissau, only 0.3 percent of the local population were ever recognized as

assimilados. Many within this select group were migrants from Cape Verde who, in contrast to mainland Africans, automatically enjoyed the status.

In 1956 six assimilados, led by Amilcar Cabral, founded the PAIGC as a vehicle for the liberation of Cape Verde as well as Guinea-Bissau. From the beginning, many Cape Verdeans, such as Cabral, played a prominent role within the PAIGC. But the group's largest following and main center of activity was in Guinea-Bissau. In 1963 the PAIGC turned to armed resistance and began organizing itself as an alternative government. By the end of the decade the movement had gained a mass following and was in control of two-thirds of the countryside.

In its liberated areas, the PAIGC was

(FAO photo by F. Mattioli)

With the implementation of the 200-mile Exclusive Economic Zones (EEZs), the fishing industry of West African nations has increased in overall terms. Previously a large majority of the region's fish stocks were harvested by foreign vessels from the Soviet Union, Poland, Spain, Korea, and France; today the EEZ has effectively given countries like Guinea-Bissau a much-needed boost in food production.

Portuguese ships arrive; claimed as Portuguese Guinea; slave trading develops 1446	Portugal gains effective control over most of the region 1915	The African Party for the Independence of Guinea-Bissau and Cape Verde (PAIGC) is formed 1956	Liberation struggle in Guinea-Bissau under the leadership of the PAIGC and Amilcar Cabral 1963–1973	Cabral is assassinated; the PAIGC declares Guinea-Bissau independent 1973	Revolution in Portugal leads to Portugal's recognition of Guinea-Bissau's independence and the end of war 1974

1980s–1990s

João Vieira comes to power through a military coup

Guinea-Bissau refuses to accept the International Court decision awarding the potentially oil-rich ocean bed to Senegal

The country moves toward multipartyism

notably successful in establishing its own marketing, judicial, and educational as well as political institutions. Widespread participation throughout Guinea-Bissau in the election of a National Assembly, in 1973, encouraged a number of countries formally to recognize the PAIGC declaration of state sovereignty. This development also helped to convince leading Portuguese officers that the fight to maintain their African empire was futile. By then many of them had also begun to sympathize with their "enemy," in part through their clandestine exposure to the writings of Cabral and other revolutionaries. In 1974 the military seized power in Lisbon and moved quickly to recognize Guinea-Bissau's independence.

CHALLENGES OF INDEPENDENCE

Since 1974 the leaders of Guinea-Bissau have tried to confront the problems of independence while maintaining the idealism of their liberation struggle. Their nation's weak economy has limited their success. Guinea-Bissau has little in the way of mining or manufacturing, although explorations have revealed potentially exploitable reserves of oil, bauxite, and phosphates. Although more than 80 percent of the population are engaged in agriculture, urban populations depend on imported foodstuffs. This situation has been generally attributed to the poor infrastructure and a lack of incentives for farmers to grow surpluses. Only 8 percent of the small country is currently cultivated. Efforts to improve the rural economy during

the early years of independence were further marred by severe drought.

Under financial pressure, in 1987 the government adopted a Structural Adjustment Program. The peso was devalued, civil servants were dismissed, and various subsidies were reduced. The effects of these SAP reforms on urban workers were cushioned somewhat by external aid.

In 1988, in a desperate move, the government signed an agreement with the Intercontract Company, allowing the firm to use its territory for 5 years as a major dump site for toxic waste from Britain, Switzerland, and the United States. In return, the government was to earn up to $800 million, a figure 50 times greater than the annual value of the nation's exports. But the deal was revoked after it was exposed by members of the country's exiled opposition. It is believed that a major environmental catastrophe would have resulted had the deal gone through. The incident underscores the vulnerability of Guinea-Bissau's underdeveloped economy.

POLITICAL DEVELOPMENT

Following the assassination of Amilcar Cabral, in 1973, his brother, Luis Cabral, succeeded him as the leader of the PAICG, thereafter becoming Guinea-Bissau's first president. Before 1980 both Guinea-Bissau and Cape Verde were separately governed by a united PAIGC, which had as its ultimate goal the forging of a political union between the two territories. But in 1980 Luis Cabral was overthrown by the military, which accused him of governing through a "Cape Verdean clique." João

Vieira, a popular commander during the liberation war who had also served as prime minister, was appointed as the new head of state. As a result, relations between Cape Verde and Guinea-Bissau deteriorated, leading to a breakup in the political links between the two nations.

For 10 years the PAIGC under Vieira continued to rule Guinea-Bissau as a one-party state. The system's grass-roots democracy, which had been fostered in its liberated zones during the war, gave way to a centralization of power around Vieira and other members of his military dominated Council of State. Several coup attempts resulted in increased authoritarianism.

But, in 1990, the government reversed course. Vieira went so far as to denounce single-party rule as inherently undemocratic, elitist, and repressive. In April 1991 the country formally embraced multipartyism. The four major opposition movements came together in January 1992 as a Democratic Forum, which coordinated their joint efforts to unseat the PAIGC in elections scheduled for November and December.

DEVELOPMENT

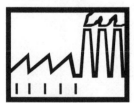

With help from the UN Development Program, the government has recently improved the tourist infrastructure of the 40-island Bijagos Archipelago. The increased flow of visitors has led to plans for an airline.

FREEDOM

Recent moves toward multiparty democracy have been accompanied by an opening up of public debate. Exiles have been allowed to return to take part in politics.

HEALTH/WELFARE

Despite genuine efforts on the part of the government and international aid agencies to improve the situation, Guinea-Bissau's health statistics remain appalling: an overall 46-year life expectancy, 12% infant mortality, and more than 90% of the population infected with malaria.

ACHIEVEMENTS

With Portuguese assistance, a new fiberoptic digital telephone system is being established, which will include Bissau's first satellite ground station.

Liberia (Republic of Liberia)

GEOGRAPHY

Area in Square Kilometers (Miles):
111,370 (43,000) (somewhat larger than Pennsylvania)
Capital (Population): Monrovia (425,000)
Climate: tropical

PEOPLE

Population
Total: 2,730,000
Annual Growth Rate: 3.4%
Rural/Urban Population Ratio: 54/46
Languages: official: English; others spoken: Kpelle, Bassa, Dan, Vai, Wee, Loma, Kru, Glebo, Mano, Gola, Mandinka

Health
Life Expectancy at Birth: 54 years (male); 59 years (female)
Infant Mortality Rate (Ratio): 124/1,000
Average Caloric Intake: 114% of FAO minimum
Physicians Available (Ratio): 1/11,185

Religion(s)
70% traditional indigenous; 20% Muslim; 10% Christian

Education
Adult Literacy Rate: 40%

COMMUNICATION
Telephones: 8,510
Newspapers: 4

TRANSPORTATION
Highways—Kilometers (Miles): 10,087 (6,254)
Railroads—Kilometers (Miles): 480 (298)
Usable Airports: 58

KRU MARINERS

For 400 years Kru-speaking peoples from the southeast of Liberia have worked on European ships as sailors, navigators, and stevedores. They have guided ships to shore, unloaded cargo, and provided food supplies to passing traders. Many have sold goods from their canoes on their return trips to the Liberian coast, while others have established Kru communities in port cities such as Freetown, Accra, and Calabar. Their trading activities, acquaintance with European culture, and mobility enabled them to resist Liberian settler control throughout the nineteenth century. In 1915 their revolt against the Liberian government ended when U.S. troops bombarded the Kru Coast.

GOVERNMENT

Type: republic
Independence Date: July 26, 1847
Head of State: Interim President Amos Sawyer
Political Parties: National Democratic Party of Liberia; Liberian Action Party; Liberian People's Party (banned); Liberian Unification Party; Unity Party; United People's Party
Suffrage: universal over 18

MILITARY

Number of Armed Forces: —
Military Expenditures (% of Central Government Expenditures): —
Current Hostilities: internal hostilities

ECONOMY

Currency ($ U.S. Equivalent): 1 Liberian dollar = $1
Per Capita Income/GDP: $400/$1.09 billion
Inflation Rate: 12%
Natural Resources: iron ore; rubber; timber; diamonds
Agriculture: rubber; rice; palm oil; cassava; coffee; cocoa; sugar
Industry: iron and diamond mining; rubber processing; food processing; lumber milling

FOREIGN TRADE

Exports: $505 million
Imports: $394 million

LIBERIA

Since December 1989 Liberia has been sinking ever deeper into a quagmire of self-destruction. A series of externally brokered peace agreements, backed up by a large multinational West African peacekeeping force, have so far failed to end the conflict. But amid the despair Liberians find hope in their collective determination to rebuild Africa's oldest republic.

AFRICAN-AMERICAN-AFRICANS

Among the African states, Liberia shares with Ethiopia the distinction of having avoided European rule. Between 1847 and 1980 Liberia was governed by an elite made up primarily of descendants of African Americans who had begun settling along its coastline 2 decades earlier. These Americo-Liberians make up only 3 percent of the population but for decades dominated politics through their control of the governing True Whig Party (TWP). Although the Republic's constitution was ostensibly democratic, the TWP rigged the electoral process.

Most Liberians belong to indigenous ethnolinguistic groups, such as the Kpelle, Bassa, Gio, Kru, Krahn, and Vai, who were conquered by the Americo-Liberians during the nineteenth and early twentieth centuries. Some from these subjugated communities accepted Americo-Liberian norms. Yet book-learning, Christianity, and an ability to speak English helped an indigenous person to advance within the state only if he or she accepted its social hierarchy by becoming a client of an Americo-Liberian patron. In a special category were the important interior "chiefs," who were able to maintain their local authority as long as they remained loyal to the republic.

During the twentieth century Liberia's economy was transformed by vast Firestone rubber plantations, iron-ore mining, and urbanization. President William Tubman (1944–1971) proclaimed a Unification Policy, to promote national integration, and an Open-Door Policy, to encourage outside investment. However, most of the profits that resulted from the modest external investment that did occur left the country, while the wealth that remained was concentrated in the hands of the TWP elite.

During the administration of Tubman's successor, William Tolbert (1971–1980), Liberians became more conscious of the inability of the TWP to address the inequities of the status quo. Educated youth from all ethnic backgrounds began to join

dissident associations rather than the regime's patronage system.

As economic conditions worsened, the top 4 percent of the population came to control 60 percent of the wealth. Rural stagnation drove many to the capital city of Monrovia (named after U.S. President James Monroe), where they suffered from high unemployment and inflation. The inevitable explosion occurred in 1979, when the government announced a 50 percent price increase for rice, the national staple. Police fired on demonstrators, killing and wounding hundreds. Rioting, which resulted in great property damage, led the government to appeal to neighboring Guinea for troops. It was clear that the TWP was losing its grip. Thus Sergeant Samuel Doe enjoyed widespread support when, in 1980, he led a successful coup.

DOE DOESN'T DO

Doe came to power as Liberia's first indigenous president, a symbolically important event that many believed would herald major substantive changes. Some institutions of the old order, such as the TWP and the Masonic Temple (looked upon as Liberia's secret government) were disbanded. The House of Representatives and Senate were suspended. Offices changed hands, but the old administrative system persisted. Many of those who came to power were members of Doe's own ethnic group, the Krahn, who had long been prominent in the lower ranks of the army.

Doe's People's Redemption Council (PRC) promised to return Liberia to civilian rule in 1986. A new Constitution was approved, which, like the old one, was based on that of the United States. The 4-year ban on politics was lifted in 1984, but the PRC prevented two parties from organizing and banned several opposition leaders.

Doe declared a narrow victory for himself in the October 1985 elections, but there was widespread evidence of ballot tampering. A month later, exiled General Thomas Quiwonkpa led an abortive coup attempt. During and after the uprising, thousands of people were killed, mostly civilians belonging to Quiwonkpa's Gio group who were slaughtered by loyalist (largely Krahn) troops. Doe was inaugurated, but opposition-party members refused to take their seats in the National Assembly. Some, fearing for their lives, went into exile.

During the late 1980s Doe became increasingly dictatorial. Many called on the U.S. government, in particular, to withhold aid until detainees were freed and new elections held. The U.S. Congress criticized the regime but authorized more than half a billion dollars in financial and military support. Meanwhile Liberia suffered from a shrinking economy and a growing foreign debt, which by 1987 had reached $1.6 billion. Doe's government was not entirely to blame for Liberia's financial condition. When it came to power, the Liberian Treasury was already empty, in

(United Nations photo by N. van Praag)

The chaos that has inflicted Libera in recent times has left the country destitute. Virtual political anarchy has destroyed the infrastructure, economy, cities, and culture of the land.

The Vai move onto the Liberian coast from the interior
1500s

The first African-American settlers arrive from the United States
1822

The first coup changes one Americo-Liberian government for another
1871

The League of Nations investigates forced labor charges
1931

President William Tubman comes to office
1944

William Tolbert becomes president
1972

The first riots in contemporary Liberian history occur when the price of rice is raised
1979

1980s–1990s

The assassination of Tolbert; a military coup brings Samuel Doe to power

Doe is elected president amid accusations of election fraud

Civil war leads to the execution of Doe, anarchy, and foreign intervention

large part due to the vast expenditure incurred by the previous administration in hosting the 1979 Organization of African Unity Conference. The rising cost of oil and decline in world prices for natural rubber, iron ore, and sugar further crippled the economy. Government corruption and instability under Doe made a bad situation worse.

DOE'S DOWNFALL

Liberia's descent into violent anarchy began on December 24, 1989, when a small group of insurgents, led by Charles Taylor, who had earlier fled the country amid corruption charges, began a campaign to overthrow Doe. As Taylor's National Patriotic Front of Liberia (NPFL) rebels gained ground, the war developed into an increasingly vicious interethnic struggle among groups who had been victimized by or associated with the regime. Thousands of civilians were thus massacred by ill-disciplined gunmen on both sides; hundreds of thousands began to flee for their lives. By June 1990, with the rump of Doe's forces besieged in Monrovia, a small but efficient breakaway armed faction of the NPFL, under the ruthless leadership of a former soldier named Prince Johnson, emerged as a deadly third force.

By August, with the United States unwilling to do more than evacuate foreign nationals from Monrovia (the troops of Doe, Johnson, and Taylor had begun kidnapping expatriates and violating diplomatic immunity), members of the Economic Community of West African States decided to establish a framework for peace by installing an interim

government, with the support of a regional peacekeeping force known as ECOMOG: the ECOWAS Monitoring Group. The predominantly Nigerian force, which also included contingents from Ghana, Guinea, Sierra Leone, The Gambia, and, later, Senegal, landed in Monrovia in late August. This coincided with the nomination, by a broad-based but NPFL-boycotted National Conference, of Dr. Amos Sawyer, a respected academic, as the head of the proposed interim administration.

Initial hopes that ECOMOG's presence would end the fighting proved to be naïve. On September 9, 1990, Johnson captured Doe by shooting his way into ECOMOG headquarters. The following day, Doe's gruesome torture and execution were videotaped by his captors. This "outrage for an outrage" did not end the suffering. Protected by a reinforced ECOMOG, Sawyer was able to establish his interim authority over most of Monrovia, but the rest of the country remained in the hands of the NPFL or of local thugs.

Repeated attempts to get Johnson and Taylor to cooperate with Sawyer in establishing an environment conducive to holding elections have so far proved fruitless. While most neighboring states have supported ECOMOG's mediation efforts, some have provided support (and, in the case of Burkina Faso, troops) to the NPFL, which has encouraged Taylor in his on-again, off-again approach toward national reconciliation.

Hopes were raised in October 1991, when an accord was signed in Côte d'Ivoire that seemed to commit all the internal and external parties to a definite

blueprint for national reconciliation. But progress has been slow. In the Liberian countryside there has been renewed fighting between the NPFL and Raleigh Seekie's United Liberation Movement of Liberia (ULIMO), a Sierra Leone-based group identified with former Doe supporters. For its part, the NPFL has been accused of invading Sierra Leone, in a destabilization process that contributed to the fall of that country's government in April 1992. In November 1992 full-scale fighting broke out between ECOMOG and the NFPL, for which the latter party blamed Nigerian interference. With Guinean as well as Sierra Leonean villages coming under attack and some Nigerians beginning to speak of "our Vietnam," Liberia's ongoing disintegration is an increasing threat to the entire region.

DEVELOPMENT

Liberia's economic and social infrastructure has been devastated by the war. People are surviving through informal-sector trading, which is controlled by those with guns.

FREEDOM

Many Liberians remain committed to the ideal of establishing a genuine democracy with freedom of association, belief, and speech. But under current conditions, there are no guarantors of human rights.

HEALTH/WELFARE

Outside aid and local self-help were mobilized against famine in 1990–1991. But the war continues to take a dreadful toll. Orphans have reportedly been used as human shields.

ACHIEVEMENTS

Through a shrewd policy of diplomacy, Liberia managed to maintain its independence when Britain and France conquered neighboring areas during the late nineteenth century. It espoused African causes during the colonial period; for instance, Liberia brought the case of Namibia to the World Court in the 1950s.

Mali (Republic of Mali)

GEOGRAPHY

Area in Square Kilometers (Miles): 1,240,142 (478,819) (about the size of Texas and California combined)
Capital (Population): Bamako (404,000)
Climate: tropical to arid

PEOPLE

Population

Total: 8,339,000
Annual Growth Rate: 2.4%
Rural/Urban Population Ratio: 81/19
Languages: official: French; others spoken: Bamanankan, Mandinka, Voltaic, Tamacheg (Tuareg), Dogon, Fulde, Songhai, Malinké

Health

Life Expectancy at Birth: 41 years (male); 44 years (female)
Infant Mortality Rate (Ratio): 173/1,000
Average Caloric Intake: 83% of FAO minimum
Physicians Available (Ratio): 1/12,652

Religion(s)

90% Muslim; 9% traditional indigenous; 1% Christian

Education

Adult Literacy Rate: 32%

COMMUNICATION

Telephones: 11,000
Newspapers: 2

JAMANA

Mali's new president, Dr. Alpha Konare, is the founder of Jamana, a highly successful cultural cooperative, which has sponsored forums, festivals, publications, and literacy programs since 1983. It has also established museum-documentation centers, craft workshops, a printing and publishing company, and Mali's first private radio station. Mali's rich cultural diversity, which Jamana has sought to promote, is exemplified by such aspects as the popular singing of epic praise poems, local Kora music, which has evolved popular and classical styles, sophisticated carvings, and often satirical puppet theaters. Although rooted in traditional esthetics, each of these arts reflects upon contemporary society: under the former dictatorship, the dynamism of their indigenous culture provided Malians with avenues of sociopolitical criticism and debate.

TRANSPORTATION

Highways—Kilometers (Miles): 15,700 (9,756)
Railroads—Kilometers (Miles): 642 (400)
Usable Airports: 29

GOVERNMENT

Type: republic
Independence Date: June 20, 1960
Head of State: President Alpha Konare
Political Parties: Democratic Union of Malian People
Suffrage: universal over 21

MILITARY

Number of Armed Forces: 6,400
Military Expenditures (% of Central Government Expenditures): 17%
Current Hostilities: none

ECONOMY

Currency ($ U.S. Equivalent): 256 CFA francs = $1
Per Capita Income/GDP: $250/$2.08 billion
Inflation Rate: n/a
Natural Resources: bauxite; iron ore; manganese; lithium; phosphate; kaolin; salt; limestone; gold
Agriculture: millet; sorghum; corn; rice; sugar; cotton; peanuts; livestock
Industry: food processing; textiles; cigarettes; fishing

FOREIGN TRADE

Exports: $285 million
Imports: $513 million

MALI

In 1992 Malians elected a new president and Legislature, in the country's first multiparty elections since independence in 1960. The new government was inaugurated a year after a coup ended the authoritarian regime of Moussa Traoré. Like his predecessor, the first president of Mali, Modibo Keita, Traoré had governed Mali as a single-party state. True to their word, the young officers who seized power in 1991 following bloody antigovernment riots, presided over a quick transition to civilian rule. The new president, Dr. Alpha Konare, is an activist scholar who, like many Malians, finds political inspiration in his country's rich heritage.

AN IMPERIAL PAST

The published epic of Sundiata Keita, the thirteenth-century founder of the great Mali empire, is recognized throughout the world as a masterpiece of classical African literature. In Mali itself, the story and deeds of the legendary hero-king can still be heard from the lips of the *griots,* or traditional bards, who sing at public gatherings and over the radio. Sundiata remains a source of national pride and unity.

Sundiata's state was one of three great West African empires whose centers lay in modern Mali. Between the fourth and thirteenth centuries, the area was the site of ancient Ghana, which prospered through its export of gold to Asia, Europe, and the rest of Africa (the modern state of Ghana, whose territory was never part of the earlier empire, adopted its name at independence as a symbol of Pan-African rather than local grandeur). The Malian empire was superseded by that of Songhai, which was conquered by the Moroccans at the end of the sixteenth-century. All these empires were in fact confederations. Although they encompassed vast areas united under a single supreme ruler, local communities generally enjoyed a great deal of autonomy.

From the 1890s until 1960 another form of imperial unity was imposed over Mali (then called the French Sudan) and the adjacent territories of French West Africa. The legacy of broader colonial and precolonial unity as well as its landlocked position have inspired Mali's postcolonial leaders to seek closer ties with neighboring countries.

Mali formed a brief confederation with Senegal during the transition period to independence. This initial union broke down after only a few months, but since then the two countries have cooperated in the Organization for the Development of

(United Nations photo by John Isaac)

Countries in the Sahel, a band of land on the southern edge of the Sahara, are still affected by a crisis of alarming proportions. In Mali, drought and famine, which have manifested themselves since the late 1960s, still continue. The smile on the face of this young girl in Bamako belies the hardship she must endure.

| The Mali empire extends over much of the upper regions of West Africa 1250–1400s | The Songhai empire controls the region late 1400s– late 1500s | The French establish control over Mali 1890 | Mali gains independence as part of the Mali Confederation; Senegal secedes from the confederation months later 1960 | A military coup brings Traoré and the Military Committee for National Liberation to power 1968 | The Democratic Union of the Malian People (UDPM) is the single ruling party; Traoré is the secretary general 1979 | School strikes and demonstrations; teachers and students are detained 1979–1980 |

1980s–1990s

| Pope John Paul II, while visiting Bamako, praises tolerance between Christians and Muslims | Representatives from Mali, Niger, and Algeria meet to examine the "serious security problem" caused by the movement of nomadic Tuareg communities across their borders | Mali's transitional government signs a peace accord with local Tuareg rebels |

the Senegal River and other regional groupings. The Senegalese port of Dakar, which is linked by rail to Mali's capital city of Bamako, remains the major outlet for Malian exports.

Mali has also sought to strengthen its ties with nearby Guinea. In 1983 the two countries signed an agreement to harmonize policies and structures. Sekou Touré, the late president of Guinea, then spoke of "the reconstitution on the basis of an egalitarian and democratic state, of the ancient Mali Empire" as a political entity that could eventually embrace all the states in the region. But this lofty goal remains a distant dream.

ENVIRONMENTAL CHALLENGES

In terms of its per capita gross national product, Mali is one of the poorest countries in the world. More than 85 percent of the people are employed in (mostly subsistence) agriculture, but during most years the government has had to rely on international aid to make up for local food deficits. Most of the country lies within either the expanding Sahara Desert or the semi-arid region known as the Sahel, which has become drier as a result of recurrent drought. Much of the best land lies along the Senegal and Niger rivers, which support most of the nation's agropastoral production. In earlier centuries the Niger was able to sustain great trading cities such as Timbuctu and Djenne, but today most of its bank does not support crops. Efforts to increase cultivation, through expanded ir-

rigation and various crop schemes, have so far been met with limited overall success.

While Mali's frequent inability to feed itself has been largely blamed on environmental constraints, namely locust infestation, drought, and desertification, the inefficient state-run marketing and distribution system has also had a negative impact. Low official produce prices have encouraged farmers either to engage in subsistence agriculture or to sell their crops on the black market. Thus, while some regions of the country remain dependent on international food donations, crops continue to be smuggled across Mali's borders. New policy commitments to liberalize agricultural trading, as part of an IMF-approved structural adjustment program, have yet to take hold, although a record cereal harvest was produced in 1989–1990.

In contrast to agriculture, Mali's mining sector has experienced promising growth. The nation exports modest amounts of gold, phosphates, marble, and uranium. Potentially exploitable deposits of bauxite, manganese, iron, tin, and diamonds exist. Small-scale manufacturing is concentrated in Bamako.

For decades Mali was officially committed to state socialism. Its first president, Keita, a descendant of Sundiata, established a command economy and one-party state during the 1960s. His attempt to go it alone outside the French-sponsored African Financial Community (CFA Franc Zone) proved to be a major failure. Under Traoré, socialist structures were modified

but not abandoned. Agreements with the IMF ended some government monopolies, and the country adopted the CFA franc as its currency. But the lack of a significant class of private entrepreneurs and the role of otherwise unprofitable public enterprises in providing employment discouraged radical privatization. The economic direction of the new government remains to be seen.

DEVELOPMENT

In 1989 the government received international financial backing for ongoing efforts to overhaul its energy infrastructure. A new oil-storage depot is to be built, and the country's hydroelectric capacity is to be expanded.

FREEDOM

The introduction of multipartyism has allowed for freedom of expression and association. Unrest among the Tuaregs has led to human-rights violation.

HEALTH/WELFARE

About a third of Mali's budget is devoted to education. A special literacy program in Mali teaches rural people how to read and write and helps them with the practical problems of daily life by using booklets that concern fertilizers, measles, and measuring fields.

ACHIEVEMENTS

For centuries the ancient Malian city of Timbuctu was a leading center of Islamic learning and culture. Chronicles published by its scholars of the Middle Ages still enrich local culture.

Mauritania (Islamic Republic of Mauritania)

GEOGRAPHY

Area in Square Kilometers (Miles):
1,030,700 (398,000) (about the size of
Texas and California combined)
Capital (Population): Nouakchott
(500,000)
Climate: arid to semiarid

PEOPLE

Population

Total: 1,996,000
Annual Growth Rate: 3.1%
Rural/Urban Population Ratio: 53/47
Languages: official: Arabic, French;
others: Hasanya, Bamanankan, Fulde,
Sarakole, Wolof, Berber languages

Health

Life Expectancy at Birth: 44 years
(male); 50 years (female)
Infant Mortality Rate (Ratio): 94/1,000
Average Caloric Intake: 94% of FAO
minimum
Physicians Available (Ratio): 1/19,563

Religion(s)

More than 99% Sunni Muslim

Education

Adult Literacy Rate: 34%

SLAVERY IN MAURITANIA

Mauritania has been one of the few regions in the world where the
widespread practice of slavery has continued. In 1980 slavery was
formally abolished, but there have been several reports of its persistence. A 1984 United Nations report, like the reports of past French
colonial administrators, noted that slavery had still to be eliminated in
isolated areas. However, the human-rights organization Africa Watch
has recently accused successive Mauritanian regimes of passing anti-
slavery legislation to appease world opinion while pursuing policies
that ensure the institution's survival. Africa Watch estimates that there
are at least 100,000 black slaves (5 percent of the nation's population)
serving Maurish masters in the country.

COMMUNICATION

Telephones: 5,200
Newspapers: 1

TRANSPORTATION

Highways—Kilometers (Miles): 8,900
(5,530)
Railroads—Kilometers (Miles): 650
(404)
Usable Airports: 29

GOVERNMENT

Type: military republic
Independence Date: November 28,
1960
Head of State: President Moauia Ould
Sidi Mohamed Taya
Political Parties: Republican Social
Democratic Party; Union of
Democratic Forces (opposition
grouping)
Suffrage: none

MILITARY

Number of Armed Forces: 11,750
*Military Expenditures (% of Central
Government Expenditures):* 81
Current Hostilities: internal conflicts

ECONOMY

Currency ($ U.S. Equivalent): 81
ouguiyas = $1
Per Capita Income/GDP: $500/$997
million
Inflation Rate: 8.2%
Natural Resources: iron ore; gypsum;
fish; copper
Agriculture: livestock; millet; corn;
wheat; dates; rice; peanuts
Industry: iron-ore mining; fish
processing

FOREIGN TRADE

Exports: $519 million
Imports: $567 million

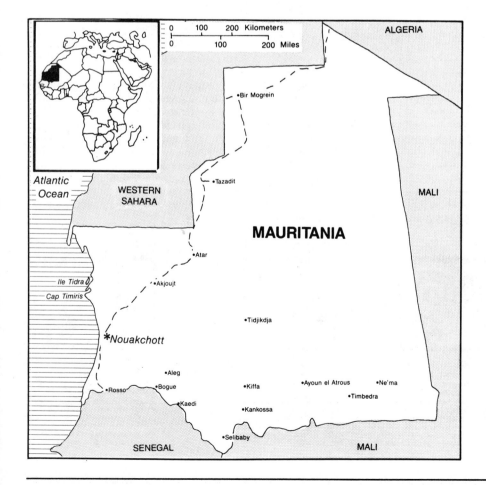

The Almoravids
spread Islam in
the Western
Sahara areas
through conquest
1035–1055

The Mauritanian
area becomes a
French colony
1920

Mauritania
becomes
independent
under President
Moktar Ould
Daddah
1960

A military coup
brings Khouma
Ould Haidalla and
the Military Com-
mittee for National
Recovery to power
1978

The Algiers Agree-
ment: Mauritania
makes peace with
Polisario and
abandons claims
to Western Sahara
1979

1980s–1990s

Slavery is
formally
abolished

Race riots touch
off population
exchanges
between
Mauritania and
Senegal

Multiparty
elections are
boycotted by the
opposition

MAURITANIA

In 1992, for the first time in decades, Mauritania held multiparty elections, electing incumbent President Ould Taya and his newly formed Republican Social Democratic Party (PRDS) with large majorities. But after the first round of voting the polls were boycotted by the leading opposition grouping, the Union of Democratic Forces (UFD), which alleged that voting fraud and continued repression had turned the exercise into a farce. As a result, Mauritania's move to multipartyism is unlikely to resolve the country's severe social and economic problems.

For decades Mauritania has grown progressively drier. Today three-quarters of the country is covered by sand. Less than 1 percent of the land is suitable for cultivation, 10 percent for grazing. To make matters worse, the surviving arable and pastoral areas have been plagued by grasshoppers and locusts.

In the face of natural disaster, people have moved. Since the mid-1960s the percentage of urban dwellers has swelled, from less than 10 percent to 53 percent, while the nomadic population during the same period has dropped, from more than 80 percent to about 20 percent. In Nouakchott, vast shantytowns now house nearly a quarter of the population. As the capital has grown, from a few thousand to a half-million in a single generation, its poverty—and that of the nation as a whole—has become more obvious. People seek new ways to make a living away from the land, but there are few jobs.

Mauritania's faltering economy has coincided with an increase in racial and ethnic tensions. Since independence the government has been dominated by the Maurs, or Moors, who speak Hassaniya Arabic. This community has historically been divided between the aristocrats and commoners, of Arab and Berber origin, and their black African slaves who have been assimilated into Maurish culture but remain socially segregated as "Haratine." Together the Maurs account for anywhere from 30 to 60 percent of the citizenry (the government has refused to release comprehensive data from the last two censuses).

The other half of Mauritania's population is composed of the "blacks," who are mostly Pulaar, Soninke, and Wolof speakers. Like the Maurs, all these groups are Muslim. Thus Mauritania's rulers have stressed Islam as a source of national unity. The country proclaimed itself an Islamic republic at independence, and since 1980 the Shari'a, the Islamic penal code, has been the law of the land.

Muslim brotherhood has not been able to overcome the divisions between the northern Maurs and southern blacks. One major source of friction has been official Arabization efforts, which are opposed by most southerners. In recent years the country's desertification has created new sources of tension. As their pastures turned to sand, many of the Maurish nomads who did not find refuge in the urban areas moved southward. There, with state support, they began in the 1980s to deprive southerners of their land.

Growing oppression of blacks has been met with resistance from the underground Front for the Liberation of Africans in Mauritania (FLAM). Black grievances were also linked to an unsuccessful coup attempt in 1987. In 1989 interethnic hostility exploded when a border dispute with Senegal led to race riots which left several hundred "Senegalese" dead in Nouckchott. In response, the "Moorish" trading community in Senegal became the target of reprisals. Mauritania claimed that 10,000 Maurs were killed, but other sources put the number at about 70. Following this bloodshed, more than a hundred thousand refugees were repatriated across both sides of the border. Mass deportations of "Mauritanians of Senegalese origin" have fueled charges that the Nouckchott regime is trying to eliminate its non-Maurish population.

Despite international mediation efforts, a state of belligerence persists between Senegal and Mauritania. Deported black Mauritanians have organized cross-border raids, often hoping to regain property. At the same time Mauritania's military regime has sent conflicting signals about its willingness to accommodate its black population and ease tensions with Senegal. President Taya's government has legalized opposition parties but has also stepped up its Arabization program, and it has been selectively arming Maur militias. The regular Mauritanian Army has also been greatly expanded with assistance from Iraq and Libya.

DEVELOPMENT

Mauritania's coastal waters are among the richest in the world. During the 1980s the local fishing industry grew at an average annual rate of more than 10%. Many now believe that the annual catch has reached the upper levels of its sustainable potential.

FREEDOM

Most freedoms are restricted, and there have been reports of the perpetuation of chattel slavery. Mauritania's prison at Oualata, where many black activists have been detained, is notorious for its particularly brutal conditions of incarceration.

HEALTH/WELFARE

There have been modest improvements in the areas of health and education since independence, but conditions remain poor. The 1990 *Human Development Report* gave Mauritania low marks regarding its commitment to human development.

ACHIEVEMENTS

There is a current project to restore ancient Mauritanian cities, such as Chinguette, which are located on traditional routes from North Africa to the Sudan. These centers of trade and Islamic learning were points of origin for the pilgrimage to Mecca and were well known in the Middle East.

Niger (Republic of Niger)

GEOGRAPHY

Area in Square Kilometers (Miles): 1,267,000 (489,191) (almost 3 times the size of California)
Capital (Population): Niamey (398,000)
Climate: arid to semiarid

PEOPLE

Population

Total: 8,154,000
Annual Growth Rate: 3.4%
Rural/Urban Population Ratio: 80/20
Languages: official: French; others spoken: Hausa, Zarma/Songhai, Kanuri, Fulde, Tamacheg (Tuareg), others

Health

Life Expectancy at Birth: 49 years (male); 53 years (female)
Infant Mortality Rate (Ratio): 129/1,000
Average Caloric Intake: 91% of FAO minimum
Physicians Available (Ratio): 1/38,500

Religion(s)

80% Muslim; 20% traditional indigenous and Christian

MATERNAL-LANGUAGE SCHOOLS

In Niger, more and more primary-school pupils are attending classes conducted in their maternal languages. These maternal-language schools, as they are called, have been developed over a number of years through careful planning and experimentation and are based on the idea that the mastery of basic concepts is most successfully achieved in one's first language. These schools also work to foster and reinforce values of the community through a curriculum that reflects the cultural heritage of the pupils. Niger's maternal-language schools are dedicated to providing students with strong foundations in reading, writing, and arithmetic as well as to encouraging individuals' strong sense of their own cultural identities.

Education

Adult Literacy Rate: 28%

COMMUNICATION

Telephones: 11,900
Newspapers: 1

TRANSPORTATION

Highways—Kilometers (Miles): 39,970 (24,781)
Railroads—Kilometers (Miles): none
Usable Airports: 29

GOVERNMENT

Type: republic, administered by the Supreme Military Council
Independence Date: August 3, 1960
Head of State: President (Brigadier General) Ali Saibou
Political Parties: National Movement for the Development of Society
Suffrage: universal over 18

MILITARY

Number of Armed Forces: 4,600
Military Expenditures (% of Central Government Expenditures): n/a
Current Hostilities: none

ECONOMY

Currency ($ U.S. Equivalent): 257 CFA francs = $1
Per Capita Income/GDP: $270/$2.2 billion
Inflation Rate: − 3.3%%
Natural Resources: uranium; coal; iron; tin; phosphates
Agriculture: millet; sorghum; peanuts; beans; cotton
Industry: mining; textiles; cement; agricultural products; construction

FOREIGN TRADE

Exports: $308 million
Imports: $386 million

NIGER

In recent years Niger's farmers have produced a modest surplus in cereals. Although boosted by a temporary return of adequate rains, the good harvests are primarily an outgrowth of determined efforts to promote local agricultural productivity. President Ali Saibou has said, "No Nigerien will die of hunger and thirst, even if it means devoting the entire budget to it." In fact, spending on agriculture accounted for one-third of Niger's 1990 budget, one of the highest levels in the world.

DROUGHT AND DESERTIFICATION

Farming is especially difficult in Niger. Less than 10 percent of the nation's vast territory is suitable for cultivation even during the best of times. Most of the cultivable land is along the banks of the Niger River. Unfortunately, much of the past 2 decades has been the worst of times. Nigeriens have been constantly challenged by recurrent drought and an ongoing process of desertification.

Drought had an especially catastrophic effect during the late 1970s. Most Nigeriens were reduced to dependency on foreign food aid, while about 60 percent of their livestock perished. Some believe that the ecological disaster that afflicted Africa's Sahel region, which includes southern Niger, during this period was of such severity as to disrupt the delicate long-term balance between desert and savanna. However, a growing number of others have concluded that the intensified desertification of recent years is primarily rooted in human, rather than natural, causes, which can be reversed. In particular, many attribute environmental degradation to the introduction of inappropriate forms of cultivation, overgrazing, deforestation, and new patterns of human settlement.

Ironically, much of the debate on people's negative impact on the Sahel environment has been focused on some of the agricultural development schemes that once were conceived as the region's salvation. In their attempts to boost local food production, international aid agencies have often promoted so-called green-revolution programs. These were designed to increase per acre yields, typically through the intensive planting of new, higher yielding, seeds and reliance on imported fertilizers and pesticides. Such projects often led to higher initial local outputs that proved unsustainable, largely due to expensive overhead. In addition, many experts promoting the new agricultural techniques failed to appreciate the value of traditional technologies and forms of social organiza-

(United Nations photo)

Drought and desertification have, for the last 2 decades, been amplified by inappropriate forms of cultivation, overgrazing, deforestation, and new patterns of human settlement. The attempted "improvements" to increase local food production have discouraged the traditional nomadic pattern of life, and, in consequence, have upset the delicate long-term balance between desert and savanna.

The Mali empire includes territories and peoples of current Niger areas **1200s–1400s**	Hausa states develop in the south of present-day Niger **1400s**	The area is influenced by the Fulani empire centered at Sokoto, now in Nigeria **1800s**	France consolidates rule over Niger **1906**	Niger becomes independent **1960**	A military coup brings Colonel Seyni Kountché and a Supreme Military Council to power **1974**

1980s–1990s

President Kountché dies and is replaced by Ali Saibou

A French DC-10 on a flight between Brazzaville and Paris is blown up by terrorists over Niger, killing 172; France implicates Libya

The Nigerien National Conference adopts multipartyism

tion in limiting desertification while allowing people to cope with drought. It is now appreciated that extensive patterns of cultivation long championed by Nigerien farmers allowed for soil conservation and reduced the risks associated with pests and poor climate.

The government's recent emphasis has been on helping Niger's farmers to help themselves through the extension of credit, better guaranteed minimum prices, and better communications. Vigorous efforts have been made in certain regions to halt the spread of desert sands by supporting village tree-planting campaigns. Given the local inevitability of drought, the government has also increased its commitment to the stockpiling of food in granaries. But, for social and political as much as economic reasons, government policy has continued to discourage the flexible, nomadic pattern of life that is characteristic of many Nigerien communities.

The Nigerien government's emphasis on agriculture has, in part, been motivated by the realization that the nation could not rely on its immense uranium deposits for future development. During the 1970s the opening of uranium mines resulted in the country becoming the world's fifth-largest producer. By the end of that decade uranium exports accounted for some 90 percent of Niger's foreign-exchange earnings. Depressed international demand throughout the 1980s, however, resulted in substantially reduced prices and output. Although uranium still accounts for 75 percent of foreign-exchange earnings, its revenue contribution in recent years is only about a third of what it was prior to the slump.

MILITARY RULE

For nearly half of its independent existence Niger was governed by a civilian administration, under President Hamani Diori. In 1974, during the height of drought, Lieutenant Colonel (later Major General) Seyni Kountché took power in a bloodless coup. Kountché ruled as the leader of a Supreme Military Council, which met behind closed doors. Ministerial portfolios, appointed by the president, were filled by civilians as well as military personnel. In 1987 Kountché died of natural causes and was succeeded by then–Colonel (now Brigadier General) Saibou.

A National Movement for the Development of Society (MNSD) was established in 1989 as the country's sole political party, after a constitutional referendum in which less than 4 percent of the electorate participated. But, as elsewhere in Africa, 1990 saw a groundswell of local support for a return to multipartyism. This prodemocracy agitation was spearheaded by the nation's labor confederation, which organized a widely observed 48-hour general strike. Having earlier rejected the strikers "as a handful of demagogues," in 1991, President Saibou agreed to the formation of a National Conference to prepare a new constitution. The conference ended its deliberations with the appointment of an interim government, headed by Amadou Cheffou, which, ruling alongside Saibou, is preparing the country for multiparty elections, now scheduled for January 1993. The transition may prove difficult. In March 1992 army mutineers briefly occupied the national radio station.

The government is also seeking a political settlement with Niger's Tuareg nomads. Relations between the Tuaregs and Saibou's administration grew worse in the aftermath of a 1990 Tuareg raid on an army post. Following this incident, government troops carried out reprisals on Tuareg communities, reportedly resulting in the massacre of hundreds of civilians. The government suggested that the Tuaregs were being incited by Libya. But others maintain that Niger's interethnic violence is rooted in the regime's favoritism toward members of the Zarma (or Djerma), one of five major ethnolinguistic groups within the country (the largest of which is the Hausa).

DEVELOPMENT

Village cooperatives, especially marketing cooperatives, predate independence and have grown in size and importance in recent years. They have successfully competed with well-to-do private traders for control of the grain market.

FREEDOM

The new interim government is pledged to assure freedom of speech and association in the time up to multiparty elections, in January 1993. Reports of human-rights abuses against Tuaregs have continued.

HEALTH/WELFARE

A national conference on educational reform in Zinder stimulated a program to use Nigerien languages in primary education and integrated the adult-literacy program into the rural-development efforts. The National Training Center for Literacy Agents is crucial to literacy efforts.

ACHIEVEMENTS

Niger has consistently demonstrated a strong commitment to the preservation and development of its national cultures through its media and educational institutions, the National Museum, and events such as the annual youth festival at Agades.

Nigeria (Federal Republic of Nigeria)

GEOGRAPHY

Area in Square Kilometers (Miles):
923,768 (356,669) (twice the size of
California)
Capital (Population): Lagos
(5,000,000 est.)
Climate: tropical to arid

PEOPLE

Population
Total: 88,500,000
Annual Growth Rate: 3.0%
Rural/Urban Population Ratio: 65/35
Languages: official: English; others
spoken: Hausa, Yoruba, Igbo, Efik,
Idoma, Ibibio, others (250 languages
are recognized by the Nigerian
government)

Health
Life Expectancy at Birth: 48 years
(male); 50 years (female)
Infant Mortality Rate (Ratio):
118/1,000 est.
Average Caloric Intake: 91% of FAO
minimum
Physicians Available (Ratio): 1/11,347

CULTURAL GIANTS

Nigeria is renowned for its arts. Contemporary giants include Wole
Solyinka, who received the Nobel Prize for Literature for plays such as
"The Trials of Brother Jero" and "The Road," novels such as *The
Interpreters,* and poems and nonfiction works. Two other literary giants
are Chinua Achebe, author of *Things Fall Apart, A Man of the People,*
and *Anthills of the Savannah,* and the feminist writer Buchi Emecheta,
whose works include *The Joy of Motherhood.* In music, the legendary
Fela Anikulado Kuti's "Afro-Beat" sound and critical lyrics have made
him a local hero and international megastar. Also prominent is "King"
Sunny Ade, who has brought Nigeria's distinctive Juju music to
international audiences.

Religion(s)
50% Muslim; 40% Christian; 10%
traditional indigenous

Education
Adult Literacy Rate: 51%

COMMUNICATION

Telephones: 708,390
Newspapers: 48

TRANSPORTATION

Highways—Kilometers (Miles):
107,990 (67,104)
Railroads—Kilometers (Miles): 3,505
(2,178)
Usable Airports: 68

GOVERNMENT

Type: federal republic; under control
of military government
Independence Date: October 1, 1960
Head of State: President Ibrahim
Babangida
Political Parties: Social Democratic
Party; National Republican
Convention
Suffrage: universal for adults at 21

MILITARY

Number of Armed Forces: 94,500
*Military Expenditures (% of Central
Government Expenditures):* 1%
Current Hostilities: occasional border
incidents over Lake Chad

ECONOMY

Currency ($ U.S. Equivalent): 10.49
naira = $1
Per Capita Income/GDP: $395/$35
billion
Inflation Rate: 16%
Natural Resources: oil; minerals;
timber
Agriculture: cotton; cocoa; rubber;
yams; cassava; sorghum; palm
kernels; millet; corn; rice; livestock
Industry: mining; crude oil; natural
gas; coal; tin; columbite; processing:
oil, palm, cotton, rubber, petroleum;
manufacturing: textiles, cement,
building materials, chemicals, beer
brewing

FOREIGN TRADE

Exports: $13.0 billion
Imports: $9.5 billion

NIGERIA

Since Nigeria's independence, in 1960, its citizens have been through an emotional and material rollercoaster ride. It has been a period marred by interethnic violence, economic downturns, and mostly military rule. But there have also been impressive levels of economic growth, cultural achievement, and human development. To some people, this great land of great extremes thus typifies both the hopes and frustrations of its continent.

With the elephant as a symbol, many Nigerians like to think of their country as the giant of Africa. In 1992 its status as Africa's most populous country was confirmed by the first seemingly successful census since 1963. With a population of 88.5 million, Nigeria still far outranks second-place Egypt's 52 million. But the country is far less crowded than had been suggested by commonly quoted precensus estimates of 120 million or more.

Nigeria's hard-working population is also responsible for Africa's second-largest economy as measured by gross domestic product, which stands at $35 billion, as compared to South Africa's GDP of $90 billion. But per capita income is still only $395 per year (about the same as per capita debt), which is about average for the globe's most impoverished continent but way down from Nigeria's estimated 1980 per capita income of $1,500. A decade ago it was common to equate Nigerian wealth with its status as Africa's leading oil producer, but oil earnings have since plummeted. Although hydrocarbons still account for about 90 percent of the country's export earnings and 75 percent of its government revenue, the sector's current contribution to total GDP is a more modest 20 percent.

NIGERIA'S ROOTS

For centuries the river Niger, which cuts across much of Nigeria, has facilitated long-distance communication among various communities of West Africa's forest and savanna regions. This fact helps to account for the rich variety of cultures that have emerged within the territory of Nigeria over the past millennium. Archaeologists and historians have revealed the rise and fall of many states whose cultural legacies continue to define the nation.

Precolonial Nigeria produced a wide range of craft goods, including leather, glass, and metalware. The cultivation of cotton and indigo supported the growth of a local textiles industry. During the mid-nineteenth century southern Nigeria prospered through palm-oil exports, which lubricated the wheels of Europe's industrial

revolution. Earlier much of the country was disrupted through its participation in the slave trade. Most African-Americans have Nigerian roots.

Today more than 250 languages are spoken in Nigeria. Pidgin, which combines an English-based vocabulary with local grammar, is widely used as a *lingua franca* in the cities and towns. Roughly two-thirds of Nigerians speak either Hausa, Yoruba, or Igbo as a home language. During and after the colonial era, the leaders of these three major ethnolinguistic groups clashed politically from their separate regional bases.

The British, who conquered Nigeria in the late nineteenth and early twentieth centuries, administered the country through a policy of divide and rule. In the predominantly Muslim, Hausa-speaking north, they co-opted the old ruling class, while virtually excluding Christian missionaries. But, in the south, the missionaries, along with their schools, were encouraged, and Christianity and education spread rapidly. Many Yoruba farmers of the southwest profited through their cultivation of cocoa. Although most remained as farmers, many of the Igbo of the southeast became prominent in nonagricultural pursuits, such as state employees, artisans, wage workers, and traders. As a result, the Igbo tended to migrate in relatively large numbers to other parts of the colony.

REGIONAL CONFLICTS

At independence, the Federal Republic of Nigeria was composed of three states: the Northern Region, dominated by Hausa speakers; the Western Region, of the Yoruba; and the predominantly Igbo Eastern Region. National politics quickly deteriorated into conflict between these three regions. At one time or another politicians in each of the areas threatened to secede from the federation. In 1966 this strained situation turned into a crisis following the overthrow of the first civilian government by the military.

In the coup's aftermath, the army itself was divided along ethnic lines; its ranks soon became embroiled in an increasingly violent power struggle. The unleashed tensions culminated in the massacre of up to 30,000 Igbos living in the north. In response, the Eastern Region declared its independence, as the Republic of Biafra. The ensuing civil war between the Biafran partisans and federal forces lasted for 3 years, claiming an estimated 2 million lives. During this time, much of the outside world's attention became focused on the conflict through visual images of the mass starvation that was occurring in rebel-controlled areas under federal block-

ade. Despite the extent of the war's tragedy, the collapse of Biafran resistance was followed by a largely successful process of national reconciliation. The military government of Yakubu Gowon (1966–1975) succeeded in diffusing ethnic politics, through a restructured federal system based on the creation of new states. The oil boom, which began soon after the conflict, helped the nation-building process by concentrating vast resources in the hands of the federal government in Lagos.

CIVILIAN POLITICS

Thirteen years of military rule ended in 1979. A new Constitution was implemented, which abandoned the British parliamentary model and instead adopted a modified version of the American balance-of-powers system. In order to encourage a national outlook, Nigerian presidential candidates needed to win a plurality that included at least one-fourth of the vote in two-thirds of the states.

Five political parties competed in the 1979 elections. Each had similar platforms, promising social welfare for the masses, support for Nigerian business, and a foreign policy based on nonalignment and anti-imperialism. Ideological differences tended to exist within the parties as much as among them, although the People's Redemption Party (PRP) of Aminu Kano became the political home for many socialists. The most successful party was the somewhat right-of-center National Party of Nigeria (NPN), whose candidate, Shehu Shagari, won the presidency.

New national elections took place in August and September 1983, in which Shagari received more than 12 million of 25.5 million votes. However, the reelected government did not survive long. On December 31, 1983, there was a military coup, led by Major General Muhammad Buhari. The 1979 Constitution was suspended, Shagari and others were arrested, and a federal military government was reestablished.

Although no referendum was ever taken on the matter, it is clear that many Nigerians welcomed the coup. Their initial response was a reflection of widespread disillusionment with the Second (civilian) Republic. The political picture had seemed very bright in the early 1980s. A commitment to national unity was well established. Although marred by incidents of political violence, two elections had successfully taken place. Due process of law, judicial independence, and press freedom—never entirely eliminated under previous military rulers—were extended and seemingly entrenched.

But the state was increasingly seen as an instrument of the privileged that offered little to the impoverished masses, with an electoral system that, while balancing the interests of the elite in different sections of the country, failed to empower ordinary citizens. A major reason for this failing was pervasive corruption. People lost confidence as certain officials and their cronies became overnight millionaires. Transparent abuses of power had also occurred under the previous military regime. Conspicuous kleptocracy (rule by thieves) had been tolerated during the oil-boom years of the 1970s, but it became the focus of popular anger as Nigeria's economy contracted during the 1980s.

OIL BOOM AND BUST

Nigeria, as a leading member of the Organization of Petroleum Exporting Countries, experienced a period of rapid social and economic change during the 1970s. The recovery of oil production after the Civil War and the subsequent hike in its prices led to a massive increase in government revenue. This allowed for the expansion of certain types of social services. Universal primary education was introduced, and the number of universities increased from 5 in 1970 to 21 in 1983. A few Nigerians became very wealthy, while a growing middle class was able to afford what previously had been luxuries. Rising public consumption of largely imported goods and runaway government spending fueled high rates of inflation, undermining local production in many nonpetroleum sectors of the economy.

Oil revenues had already begun to fall off when the NPN government embarked upon a dream list of new prestige projects, most notably the construction of a new federal capital at Abuja, in the center of the country. While such expenditures provided lucrative opportunities for many businesspersons and politicians, they did little to promote local production.

Agriculture, burdened by inflationary costs and low prices, entered a period of crisis, leaving the rapidly growing cities dependent on foreign food. Nonpetroleum exports that once were the mainstay of the economy either virtually disappeared or declined drastically.

While gross indicators appeared to report impressive industrial growth in Nigeria, most of the new industry depended heavily on foreign inputs and was geared toward direct consumption rather than the production of machines or spare parts. Selective import bans merely led to the growth of smuggling.

STRUCTURAL ADJUSTMENT

The golden years of the 1970s were also banner years for inappropriate expenditure, corruption, and waste. For a while, given the scale of incoming revenue, it looked as if these were manageable problems. But GDP fell drastically in the 1980s with the collapse of oil prices. The entire social and political system had owed its stability to the effective distribution of the oil wealth to many groups of Nigerians. As the economy worsened, populist resentment grew.

In 1980 an Islamic movement condemning corruption, wealth, and private property defied authorities in the northern metropolis of Kano. The army was called in, killing nearly 4,000. Similar riots subsequently occurred in the cities of Maiduguri, Yola, and Gombe. Attempts by the government to control organized labor by reorganizing the union movement into one centralized federation sparked unofficial strikes (including a general strike in 1981). In an attempt to placate the growing number of unemployed Nigerians, more than 1 million expatriate West Africans, mostly Ghanaians, were suddenly expelled, a domestically popular but futile gesture.

REFORM OR RETRIBUTION?

Major-General Buhari justified the military's return to power on the basis of the need to take drastic steps to rescue the economy, whose poor performance he blamed almost exclusively on official corruption. A "War Against Indiscipline" was declared, which initially resulted in the trial of a number of political leaders, some of whose economic crimes were indeed staggering. The discovery of large private caches of naira, the local currency, and foreign exchange fueled public outrage (and added modestly to the country's treasury). Tribunals sentenced former politicians to long jail terms. In its zeal, the government looked for more and more culprits, while jailing journalists and others who questioned aspects of its program. In 1985 Major General Ibrahim Babangida led a successful military coup, charging Buhari with human-rights abuses, autocracy, and economic mismanagement.

Babangida released political detainees. In a clever strategy, he also encouraged all Nigerians to participate in national forums on the benefits of an International Monetary Fund loan and Structural Adjustment Program. The government turned down the loan but used the consultations to legitimize the implementation of "homegrown" austerity measures consistent with IMF and World Bank prescriptions.

The 1986 budget signaled the beginning of SAP. The naira was devalued, budgets were restricted, and the privatization of many state-run industries was planned. Because salaries remained the same while prices rose, the cost of basic goods rose dramatically, with painful consequences for middle- and working-class Nigerians as well as the poor.

Although the international price of oil improved somewhat in the late 1980s, there was no immediate return to prosper-

(United Nations photo)

Nigeria experienced a tremendous influx of money when its oil industry took advantage of the 1970s' worldwide oil panics. The huge increase in cash resources led to the growth of a middle class and a flurry of expensive new projects. One such project is the Kainji Dam, shown above, which will supply a significant amount of energy to agriculture, industry, and the populace.

Ancient life flourishes 1100–1400	The beginning of Usuman dan Fodio's Islamic jihad (struggle) 1804	The first British protectorate is established at Lagos 1851	A protectorate is proclaimed over the north 1900	Nigeria becomes independent as a unified federal state 1960	Military seizure of power; proclamation of Biafra; civil war 1966–1970	An oil-price hike inaugurates the oil boom 1973	Elections restore civilian government 1979

1980s–1990s

Muhammed Buhari's military coup ends the Second Republic; later Buhari is toppled by Ibrahim Babangida

Wole Soyinka is awarded the Nobel Prize for Literature

Lean times; austerity measures provoke protests and strikes

ity. Continued budgetary excesses on the part of the government (which have heaped perks on its officer corps and created more state governments to soak up public coffers), coupled with instability, have undermined SAP sacrifices. In 1988 the government attempted a moderate reduction in local fuel subsidies. But when as a result some transport owners raised fares by 50 to 100 percent, students and workers protested, and bank staff and other workers went on strike. In Jos, police killed demonstrators. Domestic fuel prices have since remained among the lowest in the world, encouraging a massive smuggling of petroleum to neighboring states. This has recently led to the ironic situation of a severe local petroleum shortage.

The Babangida government faced additional internal challenges while seeking to project an image of stability to foreign investors. Coup attempts were foiled in 1985 and 1991, while chronic student unrest led to the repeated closure of university campuses. Religious riots between Christians and Muslims became endemic in many areas, leading to hundreds, if not thousands, of deaths.

Despite statements supporting press freedom, restrictions on the media resurfaced under Babangida. Dele Giwa, the prominent editor of *Newswatch* magazine, was killed by a parcel bomb in 1986. The remaining editors were arrested in 1986, and the magazine was banned for several months in 1987. In 1988 the government banned satellite monitoring of foreign broadcasts. A further press clampdown occurred in 1992.

Babangida has promised to return Nigeria to full civilian control, but many are skeptical and/or indifferent about his Transitional Program for the restoration of democracy. Local nonparty elections were held in 1987, and a (mostly elected) Constituent Assembly subsequently met and approved modifications to Nigeria's 1979 Constitution. Despite the trappings of electoral involvement, the Transitional Program has been tightly controlled. Many politicians have been banned as Babangida has tried to impose a two-party system on what traditionally has been a multiparty political culture. When none of 13 potential parties gained his approval, the general decided to create two new parties of his own, one "a little to the left" and another "a little to the right." Neither of these parties seriously challenged the excesses of the military nor the failures of SAP.

The rise of prodemocracy protests throughout Africa, including the dramatic capitulation of the military rulers in neighboring Benin, raised questions about Babangida's ability to impose his turnkey brand of democracy. After 20 years of military rule, few Nigerians see the army as their savior from the venal politicians.

Doubts about the military in general and Babangida's grasp on power in particular were raised in April 1990, when a group of dissident officers launched yet another coup attempt to "stop intrigues, domination, and internal colonization of the Nigerian state by the so-called chosen few." In radio broadcasts, the insurrectionists announced the expulsion of five northern states from the federal republic, thus raising the specter of a return to interethnic civil war. The uprising was crushed, but confidence in Babangida and his Transitional Program was badly shaken.

A series of national elections were, nonetheless, held in 1992 between the two officially sponsored parties. But public indifference and/or fear of intimidation, institutionalized by the replacement of the (ideally secret) ballot with a procedure of publicly queuing for one's candidate, compromised the results. Allegations of gross irregularities led to the voiding of first-round presidential primary elections. Serious antigovernment rioting in Lagos and other urban areas, a continued escalation of intercommunal violence, and a renewed government clampdown on dissent further marred the process.

Yet, despite Nigeria's current difficulties, there are grounds for optimism about the future. Recently there has been modest growth in the economy. After years of little accomplishment, hopes have been revived that the Economic Community of West African States will begin to play a greater role in promoting regional economic cooperation. Such a development should prove especially beneficial to Nigeria, whose size and infrastructure make it ECOWAS's natural leader. Furthermore, Nigeria's strong civil society bolsters the chances that a stable, democratic political culture will eventually take root, checking the economic and political abuses that have plagued the country.

DEVELOPMENT

Nigeria hopes to mobilize its human and natural resources to encourage labor-intensive production and self-sufficient agriculture. Recent bans on food imports such as rice and maize will increase local production, and restrictions on imported raw materials should encourage research and local input for industry.

FREEDOM

Although the Babangida government freed journalists and critics jailed by Buhari, student protests have been dealt with harshly, and journalists and trade-union officials have been arrested. Convicted criminals and drug dealers are executed.

HEALTH/WELFARE

Nigeria's infant mortality rate is now believed to be about 118 per 1,000. (Some estimate it to be as high as 150 per 1,000.) While social services grew rapidly during the 1970s, Nigeria's strained economy since then has led to cutbacks in health and education.

ACHIEVEMENTS

Nigeria has a long tradition of an outspoken and lively press, under both civilian and military governments. Private and state-sponsored newspapers abound in all the large cities and are eagerly read by Nigerian citizens. National and international magazines specializing in investigative journalism have recently expanded their readership.

Senegal (Republic of Senegal)

GEOGRAPHY

Area in Square Kilometers (Miles):
196,840 (76,000) (about the size of
South Dakota)
Capital (Population): Dakar
(1,380,000)
Climate: tropical

PEOPLE

Population
Total: 7,953,000
Annual Growth Rate: 3.1%
Rural/Urban Population Ratio: 62/38
Languages: official: French; others
spoken: Wolof, Fulde, Oyola,
Mandinka, Sarakole, Serer

Health
Life Expectancy at Birth: 54 years
(male); 56 years (female)
Infant Mortality Rate (Ratio): 86/1,000
Average Caloric Intake: 100% of FAO
minimum
Physicians Available (Ratio): 1/10,441

Religion(s)
92% Muslim; 6% traditional
indigenous; 2% Christian

Education
Adult Literacy Rate: 38%

GORÉE ISLAND

The tiny, rocky island of Gorée, opposite Dakar on the mainland, has a
tragic history. Beginning in the seventeenth century Gorée was occupied by European traders as an easily defensible slave entrepôt. For
more than 200 years the French, Dutch, and English used Gorée as a
collection and distribution center for the Atlantic slave trade. Slaves
from the Senegalese interior and many other parts of West Africa were
housed and examined in cramped slave quarters before walking the
narrow passageway to the sea and transport to the Americas. The
Senegalese government has preserved the site as a reminder of the slave
trade's horrors. Gorée attracts visitors from around the world, including
many African-Americans.

COMMUNICATION
Telephones: 40,200
Newspapers: 3

TRANSPORTATION
Highways—Kilometers (Miles): 14,700
(9,114)
Railroads—Kilometers (Miles): 1,034
(641)
Usable Airports: n/a

GOVERNMENT
Type: republic
Independence Date: April 4, 1960

Head of State: President Abdou Diouf
Political Parties: Socialist Party;
Democratic Party; African
Independence Party; Republican
Movement; National Democratic
Alliance; others
Suffrage: universal for adults (age 21)

MILITARY
Number of Armed Forces: 9,700
*Military Expenditures (% of Central
Government Expenditures):* 2.3%
Current Hostilities: none

ECONOMY
Currency ($ U.S. Equivalent): 257
CFA francs = $1
Per Capita Income/GDP: $615/$4.8
billion
Inflation Rate: 0.4%
Natural Resources: fish; phosphates
Agriculture: millet; sorghum; manioc;
rice; cotton; groundnuts
Industry: fishing; food processing;
light manufacturing

FOREIGN TRADE
Exports: $801 million
Imports: $1.0 billion

SENEGAL

While most African states have recently moved away from systems of authoritarian control, Senegal has struggled for decades to build a tolerant, multiparty system of government. This genuine, if imperfectly realized, commitment has not been easy. A heterogeneous mix of indigenous, Islamic, and European influences, Senegal's multiethnic society has maintained its balance in the face of economic adversity, regional separatism, external disputes, and sectarian pressures.

THE IMPACT OF ISLAM

The vast majority of Senegalese are Muslim. Islam was introduced into the region by the eleventh century A.D. and was spread through trade, evangelism, and the establishment of a series of theocratic Islamic states during the seventeenth, eighteenth, and nineteenth centuries.

Today most Muslims are associated with one or another of the Islamic Brotherhoods. The leaders of these Brotherhoods, who are usually referred to as *marabouts,* often act as rural spokespeople as well as the spiritual directors of their followers. Abdou Diouf, the current president of Senegal, has relied on the political support of prominent marabouts in his election campaigns. The Brotherhoods also play an important economic role: for example, the Mouride Brotherhood, who number about 700,000, cooperate in the growing of groundnuts, the nation's principal exported cash crop.

FRENCH INFLUENCE

During the seventeenth century French merchants established coastal bases to facilitate their trade in slaves and gum. As a result, the coastal communities have been influenced by French culture for generations. More territory in the interior gradually fell under French political control.

Although Wolof is used by many as a *lingua franca,* French continues to be the common language of the country, and the educational system maintains a French character. Many Senegalese migrate to France, usually to work as low-paid la-

(United Nations photo by Purcell/AB)

The potential of drought is an ongoing concern in the Sahel zone of Senegal. It is an ever-present factor in any agricultural program. The young herder above with his starving cattle is an all-too-familiar image.

The French occupy present-day St. Louis and, later, Gorée Island **1659**	The Jolof kingdom controls much of the region **1700s**	All Africans in 4 towns of the coast vote for a representative to the French Parliament **1848**	Interior areas are added to the French colonial territory **1889**	Senegal becomes independent as part of the Mali Confederation; shortly afterward, it breaks from the confederation **1960**	**1980s–1990s**

President Leopold Senghor retires and is replaced by Abdou Diouf

Senegalese political leaders unite in the face of threats from Mauritania

Senegal hosts the Islamic Conference Organization and African (Soccer) Cup of Nations

borers. The French maintain a military force near the capital, Dakar, and are major investors in the Senegalese economy. Senegal's judiciary and bureaucracy are also modeled after those of France.

POLITICS

Under Diouf, Senegal has strengthened its commitment to multipartyism. After succeeding the nation's scholarly first president, Leopold Senghor, Diouf liberalized the political process by allowing an increased number of opposition parties effectively to compete against his own ruling Socialist Party. He also restructured his administration in ways that were credited with making it less corrupt and more efficient. Some say that these moves have not gone far enough, but the reformist Diouf has had to struggle against reactionary elements within his own party.

In national elections in 1988, Diouf won 77 percent of the vote and the Socialists took 103 out of 120 seats. Although outside observers believed that the election had been plagued by fewer irregularities than in the past, opposition protests against alleged fraud touched off serious rioting in Dakar. As a result, the city was placed under a 3-month state of emergency. Diouf's principal opponent, Maitre Abdoulaye Wade of the Democratic Party, was among those arrested and tried for incitement. But subsequent meetings between Diouf and Wade resulted in an easing of tensions; and in April 1991 Wade shocked many by accepting the post of minister of state in Diouf's cabinet.

THE ECONOMY

Many believe that the *Sopi* (Wolof for "change") riots of 1988 were primarily motivated by popular frustration with Senegal's weak economy, especially among its youth (about half the population are under age 21), who face an uncertain future. Senegal's relatively large (38 percent) urban population has suffered from rising rates of unemployment and inflation, which have been aggravated by the country's attempt to implement an IMF-approved Structural Adjustment Program. In recent years the economy has grown modestly but has so far failed to attract the new investment needed to meet ambitious privatization goals. Among rural dwellers, drought and locusts have also made life difficult. Fluctuating world market prices and disease as well as drought have undermined groundnut exports.

Senegal has also been beset by difficulties in its relations with neighboring states. The Senegambia Confederation, which many hoped would lead to greater cooperation with The Gambia, was dissolved in September 1989. Relations with Guinea-Bissau are strained as a result of that nation's failure to recognize the result of international arbitration over disputed, potentially oil-rich waters. Senegalese further suspect that individuals in Bissau may be linked to separatist unrest in Senegal's southern province of Casamance. Senegalese peacekeeping troops have also been attacked in Liberia by the National Patriotic Front of Liberia. (A small contingent of Senegalese also participated in the Persian Gulf War against Iraq.)

But the major source of cross-border tension has been Mauritania. In 1989 long-standing border disputes between the two countries led to a massacre of Senegalese in Mauritania, setting off widespread revenge attacks against Mauritanians in Senegal. More than 200,000 Senegalese and Mauritanians were repatriated. The situation between the two countries has remained tense, in large part due to the persecution of Mauritania's "black" communities by its Arab-dominated military government. Many Mauritanians belonging to the persecuted groups have been pushed into Senegal, leading to calls for war, but in April 1992 the two countries agreed to restore diplomatic, air, and postal links.

DEVELOPMENT

The newly built Diama and Manantali dams will allow for the irrigation of many thousands of acres for domestic rice production. At the moment large amounts of rice are imported, mostly to feed the urban population.

FREEDOM

Senegal's reputation has continued to be tarnished by charges of vote rigging and the occasional harassment of opposition leaders and journalists, but the trend appears to favor the strengthening of multiparty democracy.

HEALTH/WELFARE

Like other Sahel countries, Senegal has a relatively high infant mortality rate and a low life expectancy rate. Health facilities are considered to be below average, even for a country of Senegal's modest income, but recent child-immunization campaigns have been fairly successful.

ACHIEVEMENTS

Dakar, sometimes described as "the Paris of West Africa," has long been a major cultural center for the region. Senegalese writers such as former President Leopold Senghor were founders of the Francophonic African tradition of Negritude. The University of Dakar is renamed after Cheikh Anta Diop, a world-renowned scholar.

Sierra Leone (Republic of Sierra Leone)

GEOGRAPHY

Area in Square Kilometers (Miles):
72,325 (27,925) (slightly smaller than
South Carolina)
Capital (Population): Freetown
(470,000)
Climate: tropical

PEOPLE

Population
Total: 4,275,000
Annual Growth Rate: 2.6%
Rural/Urban Population Ratio: 68/32
Languages: official: English; others
spoken: Krio, Temne, Mende, Vai,
Kru, Fulde, Mandinka, others

Health
Life Expectancy at Birth: 42 years
(male); 48 years (female)
Infant Mortality Rate (Ratio):
270/1,000
Average Caloric Intake: 85% of FAO
minimum
Physicians Available (Ratio): 1/18,609

Religion(s)
60% traditional indigenous; 30%

FOURAH BAY COLLEGE

Fourah Bay College, a significant educational institution for all of West
Africa, was founded in Sierra Leone in 1814 as a Christian school. By
1827 it was a training institution for teachers and missionaries, and in
1876 it was affiliated with the University of Durham in the United
Kingdom. As the only option for higher education for Africans on the
continent before 1918, during the colonial period Fourah Bay College
trained many early nationalists and coastal elites. These graduates
formed a network of Western-educated African leaders throughout West
Africa.

Religion(s)
60% traditional indigenous; 30%
Muslim; 10% Christian

Education
Adult Literacy Rate: 21%

COMMUNICATION
Telephones: 23,650
Newspapers: 1

TRANSPORTATION
Highways—Kilometers (Miles): 7,460
(4,635)
Railroads—Kilometers (Miles): 84
(54)
Usable Airports: 8

GOVERNMENT
Type: republic
Independence Date: April 27, 1961
Head of State: President (Captain)
Valentine Strasser
Political Parties: National Provisional
Ruling Council
Suffrage: universal at 18

MILITARY
Number of Armed Forces: 3,180
*Military Expenditures (% of Central
Government Expenditures):* 7.4%
Current Hostilities: none

ECONOMY
Currency ($ U.S. Equivalent): 430
leones = $1
Per Capita Income/GDP: $325/$1.4
billion
Inflation Rate: more than 100%
Natural Resources: diamonds; bauxite;
rutile; chromite; iron ore
Agriculture: coffee; cocoa; ginger;
rice; piassava
Industry: mining; beverages;
cigarettes; construction materials

FOREIGN TRADE
Exports: $130 million
Imports: $183 million

| Early inhabitants arrive from Africa's interior 1400–1750 | Settlement by people from the New World and recaptured slave ships 1787 | Sierra Leone is a Crown colony 1801 | Mende peoples unsuccessfully resist the British in the Hut Tax War 1898 | Independence 1961 | The new Constitution makes Sierra Leone a one-party state 1978 | 1980s–1990s |

| President Siaka Stevens steps down; Joseph Momoh, the sole candidate, is elected | Debt-servicing cost mounts; SAP is introduced | Liberian rebels destabilize Sierra Leone; Momoh is overthrown in a coup |

SIERRA LEONE

On April 30, 1992, Captain Valentine Strasser announced the overthrow of Sierra Leone's long-governing All People's Congress (APC). Most Sierra Leoneans welcomed the coup. The APC government of the deposed President Joseph Momoh and his predecessor Siaka Stevens had been renowned for its institutionalized corruption and incompetence. But its overthrow came at a time when popular pressure had been pushing the country toward a return to multiparty democracy. Whether this process will continue under the new, Strasser-led National Provisional Ruling Council (NPRC) remains to be seen.

THE KRIO

Sierra Leone is the product of a unique colonial history. Its capital city, Freetown, was founded by waves of black settlers who were brought there by the British. The first to arrive were the so-called Black Poor, a group of 400 sent from England in 1787. Shortly thereafter former slaves from Jamaica and Nova Scotia arrived. The latter group had gained their freedom by fighting with the British, against their American masters, in the U.S. War of Independence. About 40,000 Africans who were liberated by the British and others from slave ships captured along the West African coast were also settled in Freetown and the surrounding areas in the first half of the nineteenth century. The descendants of Sierra Leone's various black settlers blended African and British ways into a distinctive *Krio*, or Creole, culture. Be-

sides speaking English, they developed their own Krio language, which has become the nation's *lingua franca.*

Today the Krio make up only about 5 percent of Sierra Leone's multiethnic population. Indigenous groups—the Temne, Mende, Limba, Kru, and others—make up the majority. There is also a small but commercially influential Asian, mostly Lebanese, community.

THE APC REGIME

As more people were given the vote in the 1950s, the indigenous communities ended Krio domination in local politics. The first party to win broad national support was the Sierra Leone People's Party (SLPP), under Sir Milton Margai, which led the country to independence in 1961. During the 1967 national elections the SLPP was narrowly defeated by Stevens' APC. Between 1968 and 1985 Stevens presided over a steady erosion of Sierra Leone's economy and civil society.

In 1978 the APC, through a blatantly rigged referendum, elevated itself as the sole political party. Elections thereafter became meaningless. In 1985 the then–80-year-old Stevens stepped down in favor of his chosen successor, Major General Momoh, whose promotion to the presidency underscored the military's stake in the regime.

ECONOMIC DECLINE

The APC's increasingly authoritarian control coincided with the country's economic decline. Although rich in its human, as

well as natural, resources at independence, today Sierra Leone is one of the world's poorest countries. Revenues from diamonds, which formed the basis for prosperity during the 1950s, and gold have steadily fallen due to the depletion of old diggings and massive smuggling.

The two-thirds of Sierra Leone's labor force employed in agriculture have suffered the most from the nation's faltering economy. Poor producer prices, coupled with an international slump in demand for cocoa and robusta coffee, have cut into rural incomes. Momoh's promise to improve producer prices as part of a green-revolution program was largely unfulfilled. Like its minerals, much of the country's agricultural production has been smuggled abroad. In 1989 the cost of servicing Sierra Leone's foreign debt is estimated to have amounted to 130 percent of the total value of its exports. This grim figure led to the introduction of an IMF-supported Structural Adjustment Program, whose austerity measures have made life even more difficult for urban dwellers. Having aroused popular expectations of a better life, the new NPRC administration will face difficulties in continuing with SAP. It will also be challenged to restore security to Sierra Leone's eastern border region, where incursions by Liberian rebels in 1992 displaced some 400,000 people.

DEVELOPMENT

The recently relaunched Bumbuna hydroelectric project should reduce Sierra Leone's dependence on foreign oil, which has accounted for nearly a third of its imports. In response to threats of boycotting, the country's Lungi International Airport was upgraded. Hyperinflation and unemployment are taking a toll.

FREEDOM

In an effort to root out corruption, the NPRC government has detained senior APC members and high-ranking civil servants and has frozen their assets. Moves toward multipartyism have been suspended.

HEALTH/WELFARE

Life expectancy for both males and females is only in the forties, while the infant mortality rate, 270 per 1,000, is one of the highest in the world. In 1990 hundreds, possibly thousands, of Sierra Leone children were reported to have been exported to Lebanon on what amounted to slave contracts.

ACHIEVEMENTS

The Sande Society, a women's organization that trains Mende young women for adult responsibilities and regulates women's behavior, has contributed positively to life in Sierra Leone. Beautifully carved wooden helmet masks are worn by women leaders in the society's rituals. Ninety-five percent of Mende women of all classes and education join the society.

Togo (Republic of Togo)

GEOGRAPHY

Area in Square Kilometers (Miles):
56,600 (21,853) (slightly smaller than
West Virginia)
Capital (Population): Lomé (366,000)
Climate: tropical

PEOPLE

Population
Total: 3,811,000
Annual Growth Rate: 3.6%
Rural/Urban Population Ratio: 74/26
Languages: official: French; others
spoken: Ewe, Mina, Dagomba, Kabye,
others

Health
Life Expectancy at Birth: 54 years
(male); 58 years (female)
Infant Mortality Rate (Ratio):
110/1,000
Average Caloric Intake: 92% of FAO
minimum
Physicians Available (Ratio): 1/22,727

Religion(s)
70% traditional indigenous; 20%
Christian; 10% Muslim

Education
Adult Literacy Rate: 43%

"THE GUIDE"

For years Togo's President Gnassingbé Eyadéma has tried to make himself the focus of a cult of personality. His public pictures, sometimes enhanced with angle wings, have been omnipresent as state icons. Official publications, including a hagiographic comic book, have further extolled his supposedly heroic accomplishments as "The Guide," "accomplishments" that once included taking personal credit for the murder of his predecessor. A failed assassination attempt against himself was annually commemorated as "the Feast of Victory Over Forces of Evil." Until recently Eyadéma and his foreign backers justified his personal rule as a necessary burden to encourage national unity among Togo's more than 40 ethnic groups. But the great dictator has made sure that his fellow Kabye account for up to 90 percent of the military and security forces.

COMMUNICATION
Telephones: 12,000
Newspapers: 1

TRANSPORTATION
Highways—Kilometers (Miles): 6,462
(4,006)
Railroads—Kilometers (Miles): 515
(319)
Usable Airports: 9

GOVERNMENT
Type: republic; under military rule
Independence Date: April 27, 1960
Head of State: President (General)
Gnassingbé Eyadéma
Political Parties: Coalition of the
Togolese People
Suffrage: universal for adults

MILITARY
Number of Armed Forces: 5,910
*Military Expenditures (% of Central
Government Expenditures):* 3.7%
Current Hostilities: none

ECONOMY
Currency ($ U.S. Equivalent): 279
CFA francs = $1
Per Capita Income/GDP: $395/$1.5
billion
Inflation Rate: − 1.2%
Natural Resources: phosphates;
limestone
Agriculture: yams; manioc; millet;
sorghum; cocoa; coffee; rice
Industry: phosphates; textiles;
agricultural products; tourism

FOREIGN TRADE
Exports: $331 million
Imports: $344 million

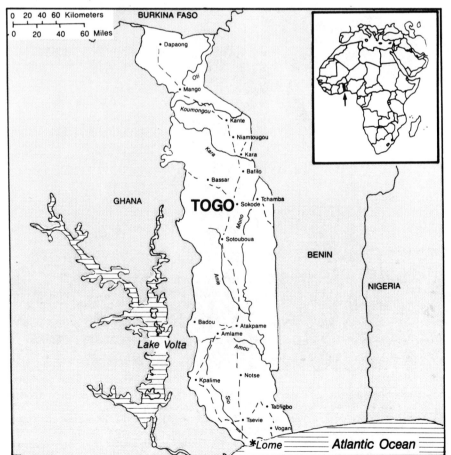

TOGO

In 1963 Togo's army set a sad regional precedent by assassinating the nation's first president, Sylvanus Olympio. After a subsequent period of instability, power was seized by Gnassingbé Eyadéma. In 1969 Eyadéma institutionalized his increasingly dictatorial regime as a one-party state. All Togolese have been required to belong to his Coalition of the Togolese People (RPT). But there are signs that the Eyadéma era may be coming to an end.

DEMOCRACY VS. DICTATORSHIP

In 1991, in the face of mass prodemocracy demonstrations in Lomé, Togo's capital city, Eyadéma acquiesced to opposition calls for a National Conference. Meeting in July–August 1991, the gathering turned into a public trial of the abuses of the ruling regime. Resisting the president's attempts to dissolve it, the Conference appointed Kokou Koffigoh as the head of an interim government, charged with preparing the country for multiparty elections. The RPT was to be disbanded, while the president himself was barred from standing in for reelection (in the last election Eyadéma claimed that he had received 99.7 percent of the vote).

But late in 1991 the reform process was set back when soldiers still loyal to Eyadéma launched a bloody attack on Koffigoh's residence. The French, whose troops have in the past intervened to keep Eyadéma in power, refused Koffigoh's plea for help. Instead, the coup attempt ended with a compromise. Koffigoh and Eyadema agreed to maintain their uneasy cohabitation while preparing for elections, which will include the RPT. Despite this seeming reconciliation, to many it appeared that Koffigoh was being held under duress. An upsurge in political violence during 1992, including the May shooting of Gilchrist Olympio, the son of Sylvanus and a leading anti-Eyadéma presidential candidate, led to the election's postponement. With the country polarized between the largely northern, Kabye-speaking supporters of Eyadéma, who control the army, and the opposition, there are fears on all sides about the potential for civil war.

STRUCTURAL ADJUSTMENT

Togo's political crisis has taken place against a backdrop of economic restructuring. In 1979 Togo adopted a economic-recovery strategy that many consider to have been a forerunner of other Structural Adjustment Programs introduced throughout most of the rest of Africa. Faced with

mounting debts as a result of falling export revenue, the government began to loosen the state's grip over the local economy.

Since 1982 a more rigorous IMF/World Bank-supported program of privatization and other market-oriented reforms has

(United Nations photo by Anthony Fisher)

Water is of extreme importance to the livelihood of Togo. In recent years cash crops such as cotton and coffee have increased in production at the sacrifice of cocoa, the traditional exportable crop. The positive world market for cotton has given Togo much-needed income. While food production in Togo is officially adequate, the situation is complicated by the drought-prone north and its need for support from the more productive southern areas. The water these children are drawing is not universally available.

Germany occupies Togo 1884	Togo is mandated to the United Kingdom and France by the League of Nations following Germany's defeat in World War I 1919	UN plebicites result in the independence of French Togo and incorporation of British Togo into Ghana 1956–1957	Independence is achieved 1960	Murder of President Sylvanus Olympio; a new civilian government is organized after the coup 1963	The coup of Colonel Etienne Eyadéma, now President Gnassingbé Eyadéma 1967	The Coalition of the Togolese People (RPT) becomes the only legal party in Togo 1969	1980s–1990s

A coup attempt leads to French military intervention

Prodemocracy demonstrations lead to interim government and the promise of multiparty elections

Interim leader Kokou Koffigoh is forced by the army to back down

been pursued. Given this chronology, Togo's economic prospects have become a focus of attention for those looking for lessons about the possible effects of SAP elsewhere. Both proponents and opponents of SAP have grounds for debate.

Supporters of Togo's SAP point out that, since 1985, the country has enjoyed an average growth in gross domestic product of 3.3 percent per annum, modestly above that for population growth. While this statistic is an improvement over the 1.7 percent rate recorded between 1973 and 1980, it is well below the 7.2 percent growth that prevailed from 1965 to 1972. During the late 1980s there was also a rise in private consumption, 7.6 percent per year, and a drop in inflation, from about 13 percent in 1980 to an estimated 2 percent in 1989. In 1992 a negative inflation rate (of −1.2 percent) was estimated.

The livelihoods of certain segments of the Togolese population have also materially improved during the past decade. Beneficiaries include some of the more than two-thirds of the work force employed in agriculture. Encouraged by increased official purchase prices, cash-crop farmers have expanded their outputs of cotton and coffee. This is especially true in the case of cotton production, which tripled between 1983 and 1989. Nearly half the nation's small farmers now grow the crop.

Balanced against the growth of cotton has been a decline in cocoa, which emerged as the country's principal cash crop under colonialism. Despite better producer prices during the mid-1980s, output fell as a result of past decisions not to plant

new trees. Given the continuing uncertainty of cocoa prices, this earlier shift may prove to have been opportune. The long-term prospects of coffee are also in doubt, due to a growing global preference for the arabica beans of Latin America over the robusta beans that thrive throughout much of West Africa. As a result, the government has had to reverse course since 1988, drastically reducing its prices for both coffee and cocoa, a move that it hopes will prove to be only temporary.

Eyadéma's regime has claimed great success in food production, but its critics have long countered official reports of food self-sufficiency by citing the importation of large quantities of rice, a decline in food production in the cotton-growing regions, and widespread childhood malnutrition. The country's food situation is complicated by an imbalance between the drought-prone northern areas and the more productive south. In 1992 humanitarian organizations warned that 250,000 Togolese, mostly northerners, could face famine unless emergency relief was provided.

There have been improvements in transport and telecommunications. The national highway system, largely built by the European Development Fund, has allowed the port of Lomé to develop as a transshipment center for exports from neighboring states as well as Togo's interior. At the same time there has been modest progress in cutting the budget deficit. But it is in precisely this area that the cost of Togo's adjustment is most apparent. Public expenditure in health and education declined by about 50 percent between 1982 and 1985. Whereas school enrollment rose from 40

percent to more than 70 percent during the 1970s, it has slipped back below 60 percent in recent years.

The ultimate justification for SAP has been a desire to attract overseas capital investment. In addition to sweeping privatization, a Free Trade Zone has been established. But overseas investment in Togo has always been modest. There have also been complaints that many foreign investors have simply bought former state industries on the cheap rather than starting up new enterprises. Furthermore, privatization and austerity measures are blamed for unemployment and wage cuts among urban workers. One-third of the state-divested enterprises have been liquidated.

Whatever the long-term merits of SAP, it is clear that it has so far resulted in neither a clear pattern of sustainable growth nor an improved standard of living for most Togolese. For the foreseeable future the health of Togo's economy will continue to be tied to export earnings derived from three commodities—phosphates, coffee, and cocoa—whose price fluctuations were responsible for the nation's past cycle of boom and bust.

DEVELOPMENT

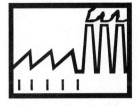

Much hope for the future of Togo is riding on the recently created Free Trade Zone at Lomé. Firms within the zone are promised a 10-year tax holiday if they export at least three-quarters of their output. The project is backed by the U.S. Overseas Private Investment Corporation.

FREEDOM

Human-rights progress in Togo has been set back by the army's intervention in the democratization process. In 1992 there was a serious rise in political killings and interethnic violence, leading to population displacements.

HEALTH/WELFARE

The nation's health service has declined as a result of austerity measures. Juvenile mortality is 15%. Self-induced abortion now causes 17% of the deaths among Togolese women of child-bearing age.

ACHIEVEMENTS

The name of Togo's capital, Lomé, is well known in international circles for its association with the Lomé Convention, a periodically renegotiated accord through which products from various African, Caribbean, and Pacific countries are given favorable access to European markets.

Central Africa

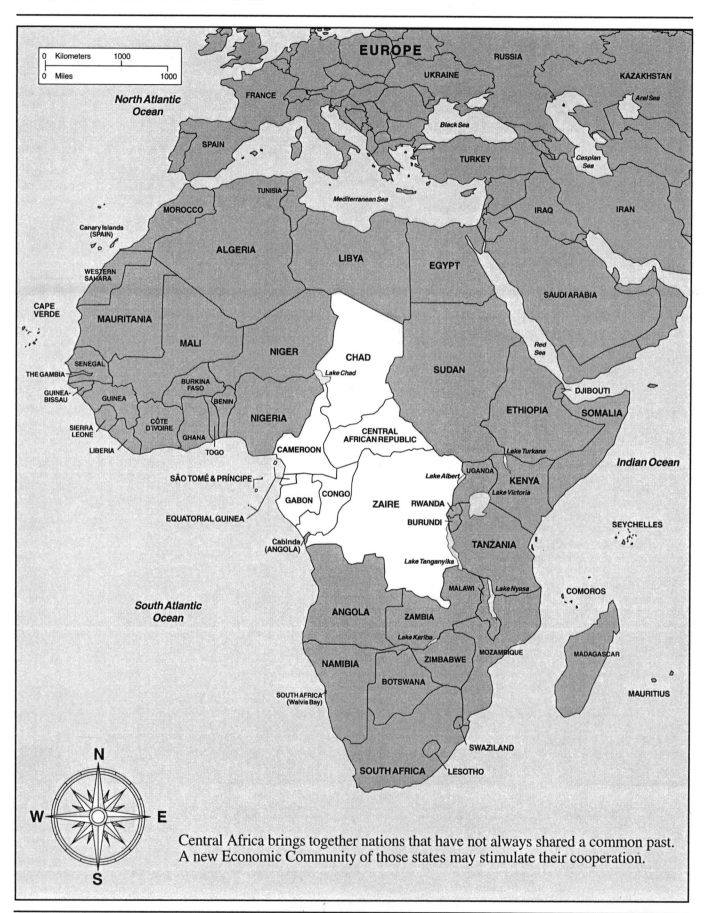

0	Kilometers	1000
0	Miles	1000

North Atlantic
Ocean

EUROPE

RUSSIA

UKRAINE

KAZAKHSTAN

FRANCE

Aral Sea

SPAIN

Black Sea

Caspian
Sea

TURKEY

TUNISIA

Mediterranean Sea

MOROCCO

IRAQ

IRAN

Canary Islands
(SPAIN)

ALGERIA

LIBYA

EGYPT

WESTERN
SAHARA

SAUDI ARABIA

CAPE
VERDE

MAURITANIA

Red
Sea

MALI

NIGER

CHAD

SUDAN

DJIBOUTI

SENEGAL

Lake Chad

THE GAMBIA

BURKINA
FASO

ETHIOPIA

SOMALIA

GUINEA-
BISSAU

GUINEA

BENIN

NIGERIA

CENTRAL
AFRICAN REPUBLIC

Lake Turkana

SIERRA
LEONE

CÔTE
D'IVOIRE

GHANA

CAMEROON

UGANDA

LIBERIA

TOGO

Lake Albert

KENYA

SÃO TOMÉ & PRÍNCIPE

CONGO

ZAIRE

RWANDA

Lake Victoria

Indian Ocean

GABON

BURUNDI

EQUATORIAL GUINEA

SEYCHELLES

Cabinda
(ANGOLA)

TANZANIA

Lake Tanganyika

MALAWI

Lake Nyasa

COMOROS

South Atlantic
Ocean

ANGOLA

ZAMBIA

Lake Kariba

MOZAMBIQUE

MADAGASCAR

NAMIBIA

ZIMBABWE

BOTSWANA

MAURITIUS

SOUTH AFRICA
(Walvis Bay)

SWAZILAND

SOUTH AFRICA

LESOTHO

N

W   E

S

Central Africa brings together nations that have not always shared a common past.
A new Economic Community of those states may stimulate their cooperation.

Central Africa: Possibilities for Cooperation

(United Nations photo)

In Africa, cooperative work groups often take on jobs that would be done by machinery in industrialized countries.

The Central African region, as defined in this book, brings together countries that have not shared a common past, nor do they necessarily seem destined for a common future. Cameroon, Chad, Central African Republic, the Congo, Equatorial Guinea, Gabon, São Tomé and Príncipe, and Zaire are not always grouped together as one region. Indeed, users of this volume who are familiar with the continent may also associate the label "Central Africa" with other states such as Angola and Zambia rather than with some of the states mentioned here. Geographically, Chad is more closely associated with the Sahelian nations of West Africa than with the heavily forested regions of Central Africa to its south. Similarly, southern Zaire has longstanding cultural and economic links with Angola and Zambia, which in this text are associated with the states of Southern Africa, largely because of their political involvements.

Yet, despite its seemingly arbitrary nature, the eight states

that are designated here as belonging to Central Africa have much in common. French is a predominant language in the states, except for Equatorial Guinea and São Tomé and Príncipe. All the states, except for São Tomé and Príncipe and Zaire, share a common currency. While Chad's current economic prospects appear to be exceptionally poor, the natural wealth found throughout the rest of Central Africa makes the region as a whole one of enormous potential. In the postcolonial era all the Central African governments have made some progress in better realizing their developmental possibilities through greater regional cooperation.

The countries of Central Africa incorporate a variety of peoples and cultures, resources, environments, systems of government, and national goals. Most of the modern nations overlay both societies that were village-based and localized and others that were once part of extensive state formations. Islam has had little influence in the region, outside of Chad and northern Cameroon. In most areas Christianity coexists with indigenous systems of belief.

Sophisticated wooden sculptures are one of the great cultural achievements associated with most Central African societies. To many people the carvings are only material manifestations of the spiritual potential of complex local cosmologies. However, the art forms are myriad and distinctive, and their diversity is as striking as the common features that they share.

At a surface level the postcolonial political orders of Central Africa have ranged from the conservative regimes in Gabon and Zaire to the Marxist-Leninist states of the Congo or São Tomé and Príncipe. More fundamentally, all the states have fallen under the rule of unelected autocracies, whose continued existence has been dependent on military force, sometimes external. But in recent years this authoritarian status quo has begun to collapse. In the Congo and São Tomé and Príncipe the introduction of multiparty democracy has resulted in the peaceful election of new governments. Opposition politics has also been legalized in the region's other states, though their old regimes are still tenuously holding on to power.

GEOGRAPHIC DISTINCTIVENESS

All the states of the Central African region, except Chad, encompass equatorial rain forests. Citizens who live in these regions must cope with a climate that is hot and moist, while facing the challenges of clearing and using the great equatorial forests. The problems of living in these heavily forested areas account, in part, for the relatively low, albeit growing, population densities of most of the states. The difficulty of establishing roads and railroads impedes communication and thus economic development. The peoples of the rain-forest areas tend to cluster along river banks and existing rail lines. In modern times, largely because of the extensive development of minerals, many inhabitants have

(Peace Corps photo)

The manufacture and sale of traditional crafts are important to many Central African economies. The Traditional Handicrafts Cooperative Society in Cameroon facilitates trade in these local items.

moved to the cities, accounting for a comparatively high urban population in all the states.

Central Africa's rivers have long been its lifelines. The watershed in Cameroon between the Niger and Zaire rivers provides a natural divide between the West and Central African regions. The Congo, or Zaire, River is the largest in the region, but the Oubangi, Chari, and Ogooue, as well as others, are also important for the communication and trading opportunities they offer. The rivers flow to the Atlantic Ocean, a fact that has encouraged the orientation of Central Africa's external trade toward Europe and the Americas.

Many of the countries of the region share similar sources of wealth. The rivers are capable of generating enormous amounts of hydroelectric power. The rain forests are also rich in lumber, which is a major export of every country, except Chad and São Tomé and Príncipe. Other forest products, such as rubber and palm oil, are widely marketed. Lumbering and clearing activities for agriculture have led to environmentalist concerns about the depletion of the rain forests. As a result, in recent years there have been some organized boycotts in Europe of the region's hardwood exports, although far more trees are felled to process plywood.

As one might expect, Central Africa as a whole is one of the areas least affected by the drought conditions that periodically plague much of Africa. However, serious drought is a well-known visitor in Chad, the Central African Republic, and the northern regions of Cameroon, where it contributes to local food shortages. Savanna lands are found to the north and the south (in southern Zaire) of the forests. Whereas rain forests have often inhibited travel, the savannas have long been transitional areas, great avenues of migration linking the regions of Africa, while providing agricultural and pastoral opportunities for their residents.

Besides the products of the forest, the Central African countries share other resources. Cameroon, the Congo, and Gabon derive considerable revenues from their petroleum reserves. Other important minerals include diamonds, copper, gold, manganese, and uranium. The processes involved in the exploitation of these commodities, as well as the demand for them in the world market, are issues of common concern among the producing nations. Many of the states also share an interest in exported cash crops such as coffee, cocoa, and cotton, whose international prices are subject to sharp fluctuations. The similarity of their environments and products provides an economic incentive for Central African cooperation.

THE LINKS TO FRANCE

Many of the different ethnic groups in Central Africa overlap national boundaries. Examples include the Fang,

(WFP photo by F. Mattioli)

Women in Chad winnow sesame seed. Cash crops such as sesame seed and cotton can encourage an economy, but they also can divert labor from food production.

who are found in Cameroon, Equatorial Guinea, and Gabon; the Bateke of the Congo and Gabon; and the Kongo, who are concentrated in Angola as well as in the Congo and Zaire. Such cross-border ethnic ties are less important as sources of regional unity than the European colonial systems that the countries inherited. While Equatorial Guinea was controlled by Spain, São Tomé and Príncipe by Portugal, and Zaire by Belgium, the predominant external power in the region remains France. The Central African Republic, Chad, the Congo, and Gabon were all once part of French Equatorial Africa. Most of Cameroon was also governed by the French, who were awarded the bulk of the former German colony of the Kamerun as a "trust territory" in the aftermath of World War I. French administration provided the five states with similar colonial experiences.

Early colonial development in the former French colonies and Zaire were affected by European concessions companies, institutions that were sold extensive rights (often 99-year leases granting political as well as economic powers) to exploit such local products as ivory and rubber. At the beginning of the twentieth century, some 41 companies controlled 70 percent of the territory of contemporary Central African Republic, the Congo, and Gabon. Mining operations as well as large plantations were established that often relied on forced labor. Individual production by Africans was also encouraged, again often through coercion rather than economic incentives. While the colonial companies encouraged production and trade, they did little to aid the growth of infrastructure or long-term development. Only in Zaire was industry promoted to any great extent.

In general, French colonial rule, along with that of the Belgians, Portuguese, and Spanish, and the activities of the companies, offered few opportunities for Africans to gain training and education. There was also little encouragement of local entrepreneurship. An important exception to this pattern was the policies pursued by Felix Eboue, a black man from French Guiana who served as a senior administrator in the Free French administration of French Equatorial Africa during the 1940s. Eboue increased opportunities for the urban elite in the Central African Republic, the Congo, and Gabon. He also played an important role in the Brazzaville Conference of 1944, which, recognizing the important role that the people of the French colonies had played in World War II, abolished forced labor and granted citizenship to all. Yet political progress toward self-government was uneven. Because of the lack of local manpower development, at independence there were too few people who were qualified to shoulder the bureaucratic and administrative tasks of the regimes that took power. People who could handle the economic institutions for the countries' benefit were equally scarce; and, in any case, the nations' economies remained for the most part securely in outside, largely French, hands.

The Spanish on the Equatorial Guinea island of Fernando Po and the Portuguese of São Tomé and Príncipe also profited from the exploitation of forced labor on their plantations. Political opportunities in these territories were even more limited than on the mainland. Neither country gained independence until fairly recently: Equatorial Guinea in 1968 and São Tomé and Príncipe in 1975.

In the years since independence most of the countries of Central Africa have been influenced, pressured, and supported by France and the other former colonial powers. French firms in the Central African Republic, the Congo, and Gabon continue to be predominant in the exploitation of local resources. Most of these companies are only slightly encumbered by the regulations of the independent states in which they operate, and all are geared toward European markets and needs. Financial institutions are generally branches of French institutions, and all the former French colonies as well as Equatorial Guinea are members of the Central African Franc Zone. French expatriates occupy senior positions in local civil-service establishments and in companies; many more of them are resident in the region today than was true 30 years ago. In addition, French troops are stationed in the Central African Republic, Chad, and Gabon, regimes that owe their very existence to past French military interventions. Besides being a major trading partner, France has contributed significantly to the budgets of its former possessions, especially the poorer states of Central African Republic and Chad.

Despite having been under Belgian rule, Zaire is an active member of the Francophonic bloc in Africa. In 1977 French troops put down a rebellion in southeastern Zaire. Zaire, in turn, has sent its troops to serve beside those of France in Chad and Togo. Since playing a role in the 1979 coup that brought the current regime to power, France has also had a predominant influence in Equatorial Guinea.

(World Bank/CIRC photo by Alain Prott)

Timber from rain forests is one of the major resources of Central Africa. Environmentalists are very concerned about ecological effects of the exploitation of this resource.

EFFORTS AT COOPERATION

Although many Africans in Central Africa recognize that closer links among their countries would be beneficial, there have been fewer initiatives toward political unity or economic integration in this region than in East, West, or Southern Africa. In the years before independence, Barthelemy Boganda, of what is now the Central African Republic, espoused and publicized the idea of a "United States of Latin Africa," which was to include contemporary Angola and Zaire as well as the territories of French Equatorial Africa, but he was frustrated by Paris as well as by local politicians. When France offered independence to its colonies in 1960, soon after Boganda's death, the possibility of forming a federation was discussed. But Gabon, which was wealthier than the other countries, declined to participate. The Central African Republic, Chad, and the Congo drafted an agreement that would have created a federal legislature and executive branch governing all three countries, but local jealousies defeated this plan.

(World Bank photo by Ivan Albert Andrews)

This palm oil processing mill was financed by the World Bank as part of a development project in Cameroon.

There have been some formal efforts at economic integration among the former French states. A Customs and Economic Union of the Central African States (UDEAC) was established in 1964, but its membership has been unstable. Chad and the Central African Republic withdrew to join Zaire in an alternate organization. (The Central African Republic later returned, bringing the number of members to six.) The East and Central African states together planned an economic community in 1967, but this did not materialize.

Only recently have there been new and hopeful signs of progress toward greater economic cooperation. Urged on by the UN Economic Commission on Africa, and with the stimulus of the 1980 Lagos Plan of Action, the Central African states met in 1982 to prepare for a new economic grouping. In 1983 all the Central African states, as well as Rwanda and Burundi in East Africa, signed a treaty establishing the Economic Community of Central African States (ECCA) to promote economic and industrial cooperation.

Some have criticized the ECCA as a duplicate of UDEAC, but its goals are broader than a customs union (though it does urge cooperation in that area). Members hoped that the union would stimulate industrial activity, increase markets, and reduce the dependence on France and other countries for trade and capital. But with dues often unpaid and meetings postponed, the ECCA has so far failed to meet its potential.

Central African states, while sharing a rich environment, have suffered more than other regions in Africa from the neglect and exploitation of their former colonial powers. They have not found common ways to develop mineral and forest resources and to deal with outside companies. Little implementation has resulted from former unions. As the Swahili proverb goes, "The toughness of the hoe is tested in the garden." Many hope that ECCA will lead to a pragmatic Central African market, thus fulfilling the need for a harmonization of trade and industrial policies and, perhaps, becoming a building block for greater continental as well as Central African unity.

Cameroon (United Republic of Cameroon)

GEOGRAPHY

Area in Square Kilometers (Miles):
475,400 (183,568) (somewhat larger
than California)
Capital (Population): Yaoundé
(852,000)
Climate: tropical to semiarid

PEOPLE

Population

Total: 11,390,000
Annual Growth Rate: 2.7%
Rural/Urban Population Ratio: 59/41
Languages: official: English, French;
others spoken: Fulde, Ewondo, Duala,
Bamilike, Bassa, Bali, others

Health

Life Expectancy at Birth: 49 years
(male); 53 years (female)
Infant Mortality Rate (Ratio):
118/1,000
Average Caloric Intake: 106% of FAO
minimum
Physicians Available (Ratio): 1/18,365

Religion(s)

51% traditional indigenous; 33%
Christian; 16% Muslim

Education

Adult Literacy Rate: 54%

THE KORUP FOREST

"Do not call the forest that shelters you a jungle" is an African proverb.
The primary rain forests in Cameroon and other parts of Central Africa
are the homes of plants and animals that have developed in this
environment over thousands of years and that serve humanity. Korup is
one Cameroon rain forest that is to be designated a national park. A
recent survey discovered more than 42,000 trees and climbers in Korup,
including 17 tree species never described before. An international
campaign has been launched to preserve such rain forests, under the
auspices of the World Wildlife Fund and the International Union for the
Conservation of Nature and Natural Resources. Korup is the subject of
a film that is being shown to raise funds for its preservation and that of
other rain forests.

COMMUNICATION

Telephones: 26,000
Newspapers: 1

TRANSPORTATION

Highways—Kilometers (Miles): 65,000
(40,300)
Railroads—Kilometers (Miles): 1,003
(622)
Usable Airports: 52

GOVERNMENT

Type: republic
Independence Date: January 1, 1960
Head of State: President Paul Biya
Political Parties: Cameroon People's
Democratic Movement; Movement for
the Defense of the Republic; Union
for Progress; Social Democratic Party;
Union of Cameroonian People; others
Suffrage: universal at 21

MILITARY

Number of Armed Forces: 7,700
*Military Expenditures (% of Central
Government Expenditures):* $219
million (1.7%)
Current Hostilities: none

ECONOMY

Currency ($ U.S. Equivalent): 279
CFA francs = $1
Per Capita Income/GDP: $1,040/$11.8
billion
Inflation Rate: 8.6%
Natural Resources: timber; oil;
bauxite; iron ore; rubber
Agriculture: coffee; cocoa; food crops;
cotton; bananas; peanuts; tobacco; tea
Industry: small manufacturing;
consumer goods; aluminum

FOREIGN TRADE

Exports: $2.1 billion
Imports: $2.1 billion

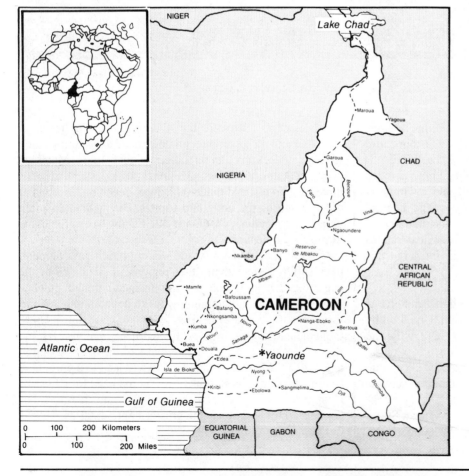

CAMEROON

On March 1, 1992, Cameroonians voted in their country's first nationwide multiparty elections in a quarter-century, ending the Cameroon People's Democratic Movement's (CPDM) monopoly of power. The results gave the CPDM a plurality of 88 out of 180 seats in the new National Assembly, allowing it to form a coalition government with the Movement for the Defense of the Republic (MDR), which won 6 seats. The Union for Progress and Democracy (UNDP) captured 68 seats, while the Union of the Cameroonian People (UPC) won 18.

But many reject the legitimacy of the new government. Most of the opposition parties—most notably including the Social Democratic Front (SDF), the Democratic Union (CDU), and a faction of the UPC—boycotted the polls, allowing the CPDM to win numerous constituencies by default. The situation was aggravated in October 1992, when the incumbent CPDM president, Paul Biya, was declared the victor in a snap election accompanied by opposition allegations of vote-rigging. As a result, after 2 years of political turmoil, stability has yet to return to Cameroon's population.

Cameroon's fractious politics is a reflection of its diversity. In geographical terms, the land is divided between the tropical forests in the south, the drier savanna of the north-central region, and the mountainous country along its western border, which forms a natural division between West and Central Africa. In terms of religion, the country has many Christians, Muslims, and followers of indigenous belief systems. More than a dozen major languages, with numerous dialects, are spoken. The languages of southern Cameroon are linguistically classified Bantu. The "Bantu line" that runs across the country, roughly following the course of the Sanaga River, forms a boundary between the Bantu languages of Central, East, and Southern Africa and the non-Bantu tongues of North and West Africa. Many scholars believe that the roots of the Bantu language tree are buried in Cameroonian soil. Cameroon is also unique among the continental African states in sharing two European languages, English and French, as its official mediums. This circumstance is a product of the country's unique colonial heritage.

Three European powers have ruled over Cameroon. The Germans were the first. From 1884 to 1916 they laid the foundation of much of the country's communications infrastructure and, primarily through the establishment of European-run plantations, export agriculture. During World War I the area was divided between the British and French, who subsequently ruled their respective zones as League of Nations (later UN) mandates. French "Cameroun" included the eastern four-fifths of the former German colony; while British "Cameroons" consisted of two narrow strips of territory, which were administered as part of its Nigerian territory.

During the 1950s Cameroonians in both the British and French zones began to agitate for unity and independence. At the core of their nationalist vision was the Kamerun Idea, a belief that the period of German rule had given rise to a pan-Cameroonian identity. The largest and most radical of the nationalist movements in the French zone was the Union of the Cameroonian People, which turned to armed struggle. Between 1955 and 1963, when most of the UPC guerrillas had been defeated, some 10,000 to 15,000 people were killed. Most of the victims belonged to the Bamileke and Bassa ethnic groups, of southwestern Cameroon, which continues to be the core area of UPC support. (Some books refer to the UPC uprising as

(United Nations photo by Shaw McCutcheon)

In recent years Cameroon has experienced political unrest as various factions have moved to establish a stable form of government. At the base of this political turmoil, however, is a need to raise the living standards of the population through an increase in agricultural production. These farmers with their cattle herds are the image of this essential agricultural element.

| The establishment of the German Kamerun Protectorate **1884** | The partition of Cameroon; separate British and French mandates are established under the League of Nations **1916** | The UPC is formed **1948** | The UPC is outlawed for launching revolts in the cities **1955** | The Independent Cameroon Republic is established with Ahmadou Ahidjo as the first president **1960** | The Cameroon Federal Republic reunites French Cameroon with British Cameroon after a UN-supervised referendum **1961** | The new Constitution creates a unitary state **1972** | **1980s–1990s** |

| Ahidjo resigns and is replaced by Paul Biya | Lake Nyos releases lethal volcanic gases, killing an estimated 2,000 people | Nationwide agitation for a restoration of multiparty democracy |

the Bamileke Rebellion.)

To counter the UPC revolt, the French adopted a dual policy of repression against the guerrillas' supporters and the devolution of political power to local non-UPC politicians. Most of these "moderate" leaders, who enjoyed core followings in both the heavily Christianized southeast and the Muslim north, coalesced as the Cameroonian Union, whose leader was Ahmadou Ahidjo, a northerner. In preindependence elections Ahidjo's party won just 51 out of the 100 seats. Ahidjo thus led a divided, war-torn state to independence in 1960.

THE QUEST FOR UNITY

In 1961 the southern section of British Cameroons voted to join Ahidjo's republic. The northern section opted to remain part of Nigeria. The principal party in the south was the Kamerun National Democratic Party, whose leader, John Foncha, became the vice president of the Cameroon republic, while Ahidjo served as president. The former British and French zones initially maintained their separate local parliaments, but the increasingly authoritarian Ahidjo pushed for a unified form of government. In 1966 all of Cameroon's legal political groups were dissolved into Ahidjo's new Cameroon National Union (CNU), creating a de facto one-party state. Trade unions and other mass organizations were also brought under CNU control. In 1972 Ahidjo proposed the abolition of the federation, and a constitution for a unified Cameroon. This was approved by a suspiciously lopsided vote of 3,217,058 to 158.

In 1982, Ahidjo, believing that his health was graver than was actually the case, suddenly resigned. His handpicked successor was Paul Biya. To the surprise of many, the heretofore self-effacing Biya quickly proved to be his own man. He brought young technocrats into the ministries and initially called for a more open and democratic society. But as he pressed forward, Biya came into increasing conflict with Ahidjo, who tried to reassert his authority as CNU chair. The ensuing power struggle took on overtones of an ethnic conflict between Biya's largely southern Christian supporters and Ahidjo's core following of northern Muslims. In 1983 Ahidjo lost and went into exile. The next year he was tried and convicted, in absentia, for allegedly plotting Biya's overthrow.

In April 1984, only 2 months after the conviction, Ahidjo's supporters in the Presidential Guard attempted to overthrow Biya. The revolt was put down, but up to 1,000 people were killed. In the coup's aftermath Biya combined repression with attempts to restructure the ruling apparatus. In 1985 the CNU was overhauled as the Cameroon People's Democratic Movement. However President Biya became increasingly reliant on the support of his own Beti group.

An upsurge of prodemocracy agitation began in 1990. In March the Social Democratic Front was formed in Bamenda, the main town of the Anglophonic west, over government objections. In May as many as 40,000 people from the vicinity of Ba-

menda, out of a total population of about 100,000, attended an SDF rally. Government troops opened fire on schoolchildren returning from the demonstration. This action led to a wave of unrest, which spread to the capital city of Yaoundé. The government media tried to portray the SDF as a subversive movement of "English speakers," but it attracted significant support in Francophonic areas. Dozens of additional opposition groups, including the UNDP (which is loyal to the now late Ahidjo's legacy) and the long-underground UPC, joined forces with the SDF in calling for a transition government, a new constitution, and multiparty elections.

Throughout much of 1991 Cameroon's already depressed economy was further crippled by opposition mass action, dubbed the Ghost Town campaign. A series of concessions by Biya culminated in a November agreement between Biya and most of the opposition (the SDF being among the holdouts) to formulate a new constitution and prepare for elections. In this context, the government's decision to hold early elections (on March 1) was rejected by most of its opponents, although some reluctantly participated. The CPDM's subsequent failure to gain a majority of the vote, despite the partial opposition boycott and the CPDM's control of the election process, has left the government weak but the opposition divided.

DEVELOPMENT

The Cameroon Development Corporation (CDC) coordinates more than half of the agricultural exports and, after the government, employs the most people. Cocoa and coffee comprise more than 50% of Cameroon's exports. Lower prices for these commodities have reduced the country's income.

FREEDOM

While Cameroon's human-rights record has improved since its return to multipartyism, political detentions and harassment continue. Amnesty International has drawn attention to the alleged starvation of detainees at the notorious Tchollire prison.

HEALTH/WELFARE

The literacy rate in Cameroon, 76%, is among the highest in Africa. There exist, however, great divergences in regional figures. In addition to public schools, the government devotes a large proportion of its budget to subsidizing private schools.

ACHIEVEMENTS

The strong showing by Cameroon's national soccer team, the Indomitable Lions, in the 1990 World Cup Competition is a source of pride for sports fans throughout Africa. Their success, along with the record numbers of medals won by African athletes in the 1988 and 1992 Olympics, is symbolic of the continent's coming of age in international sports competitions.

Central African Republic

GEOGRAPHY

Area in Square Kilometers (Miles): 622,436 (240,324) (slighty smaller than Texas)
Capital (Population): Bangui (597,000)
Climate: tropical to semiarid

PEOPLE

Population

Total: 2,952,000
Annual Growth Rate: 2.6%
Rural/Urban Population Ratio: 53/47
Languages: official: French; others spoken: Songo, Banda, Baya, Mangia, M'Baka

Health

Life Expectancy at Birth: 45 years (male); 49 years (female)
Infant Mortality Rate (Ratio): 138/1,000
Average Caloric Intake: 92% of FAO minimum
Physicians Available (Ratio): 1/25,690

Religion(s)

25% traditional indigenous; 25% Protestant; 25% Roman Catholic; 15% Muslim; 10% others

---

THE BREAKUP OF FRENCH EQUATORIAL AFRICA

In 1959, as the Central African Republic moved toward independence, Barthelemy Boganda, the leader of the territory's nationalist movement, did not share the sense of euphoria exhibited by many of his colleagues. To him, the French path to independence had become a trap. Where there once had been a united French Equatorial Africa (A.E.F.) there were now five separate states, each struggling toward its own nationhood. Boganda, as president of the Grand Council of the A.E.F., had led the struggle to transform the territory into a true Central African Republic. But in 1958 French President Charles de Gaulle overruled all objections in forcing the breakup of the A.E.F. Boganda believed that, thus balkanized, the Central African states would each be too weak to achieve true independence, but he still hoped that A.E.F. reunification might prove possible after independence.

Education

Adult Literacy Rate: 27%

COMMUNICATION

Telephones: 6,000
Newspapers: 1

TRANSPORTATION

Highways—Kilometers (Miles): 22,560 (13,987)
Railroads—Kilometers (Miles): none
Usable Airports: 49

GOVERNMENT

Type: republic; under military rule
Independence Date: August 13, 1960
Head of State: General André-Dieudonné Kolingba (chief of state)
Political Parties: C.A.R. Democratic Rally Party; opposition groups
Suffrage: suspended

MILITARY

Number of Armed Forces: 3,380
Military Expenditures (% of Central Government Expenditures): 1.8%
Current Hostilities: none

ECONOMY

Currency ($ U.S. Equivalent): 279 CFA francs = $1
Per Capita Income/GDP: $440/$1.29 billion
Inflation Rate: − 4.2%
Natural Resources: diamonds; uranium; timber
Agriculture: coffee; cotton; peanuts; food crops; livestock
Industry: timber; textiles; soap; cigarettes; processed food; diamond mining

FOREIGN TRADE

Exports: $148 million
Imports: $239 million

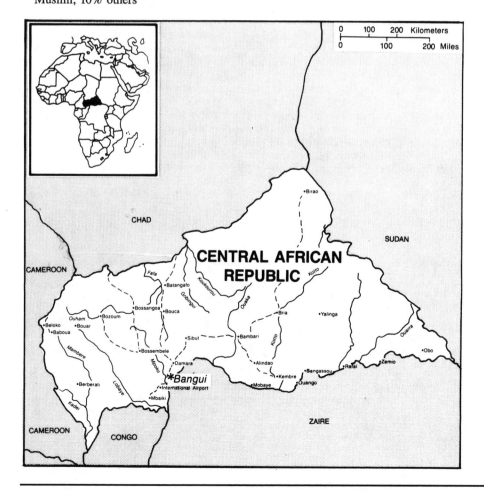

Separate French
administration of
the Oubangui-
Chàri colony is
established
1904

Gold and
diamonds are
discovered
1912–1913

Barthelemy
Boganda sets up
MESAN, which
gains wide
support
1949

Boganda dies;
David Dacko, his
successor,
becomes
president at the
time of
independence
1960

Jean-Bedel
Bokassa takes
power after the
first general
strike
1966

Bokassa
becomes
emperor
1976

Bokassa is
involved in the
massacre of
students; Dacko
returns as head
of state
1979

1980s–1990s

André Kolingba
takes power from
Dacko

Bokassa is tried
for murder,
embezzlement,
and other abuses

Kolingba
legalizes
opposition parties

CENTRAL AFRICAN REPUBLIC

Since the Central African Republic's independence from France, in 1960, the political, economic, and military presence of the French has nonetheless remained pervasive. At the same time the country's resources as well as French largesse have been dissipated. It is a history made sadder by the fact that the C.A.R. remains a land of considerable potential. With diamonds, timber, and a resilient peasantry, the country is better endowed than many of its neighbors. Although the country's population has traditionally been divided between the so-called river peoples and savanna peoples, most of the population as a whole are united by the Songo language. What the C.A.R. has lacked is a leadership firmly committed to national development rather than to internationally sanctioned waste.

France conquered the C.A.R. region in a series of brutal pacification campaigns. Even more destructive were the operations of the 39 French companies that gained concessions for the local exploitation of rubber and other raw materials. Many communities have never fully recovered from the havoc unleashed during the colonial era.

The independence movement was led by Barthelemy Boganda, a former priest who in 1949 founded the Popular Movement for the Social Evolution of Black Africa (MESAN). While Boganda was a pragmatist willing to use moderate means in his struggle, his vision was radical, for he hoped to unite French, Belgian, and Portuguese territories into an independent republic. His movement succeeded in gaining a local following among the peasantry as well as intellectuals. In 1958 Boganda led the territory to self-government, but he died in a mysterious plane crash just before independence.

Boganda's successors have failed to live up to his stature. At independence the country was led by David Dacko, a nephew of Boganda's, who succeeded to the leadership of MESAN but also cultivated the political support of local French settlers who had seen Boganda as an agitator. Dacko's MESAN became the vehicle of the wealthy elite.

A general strike in December of 1965 was followed by a military coup on New Year's Eve, which put Dacko's cousin, Army Commander Jean-Bedel Bokassa, in power. Dacko's overthrow was justified by the need to launch political and economic reforms. But more likely motives for the coup were French concern about Dacko's growing ties with the Chinese and Bokassa's own budding megalomania.

The country suffered greatly under Bokassa's eccentric rule. He was often portrayed, alongside Idi Amin of Uganda, as an archetype of African leadership at its worst. It was more the sensational nature—such as public torture and dismemberment of prisoners—rather than the scale of his brutality that captured headlines. In 1972 he made himself president-for-life. Unsatisfied with this position, in 1976 he went a step further and proclaimed himself emperor, in the image of his hero Napoleon Bonaparte. The $22 million spent on his coronation ceremony,

which attracted widespread coverage in the global media, was underwritten by the French government.

In 1979 reports surfaced that Bokassa himself had participated in the beating to death of school children who had protested his decree that they purchase new uniforms bearing his portrait.

The French government decided that its ally had become a liability. While Bokassa was away on a state visit to Libya, French paratroopers returned Dacko to power. In 1981 Dacko was once more toppled, in a coup that installed the nation's current leader, General André Kolingba. In 1985 Kolingba's provisional military regime was transformed into a one-party state. But in 1991, under a combination of local and French pressure, he agreed to the legalization of opposition parties, most of which have formed a united front to press for further reforms.

Unrest has increased as the government has sunk deeper into debt, despite financial intervention on the part of France, the World Bank, and the IMF. Landlocked C.A.R.'s poor economy has long been constrained by high transport costs. But a perhaps greater burden has been the smuggling of its diamonds and other resources, including poached ivory, by high government officials.

DEVELOPMENT

C.A.R.'s timber industry has suffered from corruption and environmentally destructive forms of exploitation. However, the nation has considerable forestry potential, with dozens of commercially viable and renewable species.

FREEDOM

Human rights continue to be restricted. There have been allegations of forced labor in the form of corvée and enforced cultivation. Political prisoners have included Thomas Kwazo, a journalist who in 1986 reported on an alleged meeting between Kolingba and Bokassa.

HEALTH/WELFARE

The literacy rate is very low in the Central African Republic. Teacher training is currently being emphasized, especially for primary-school teachers.

ACHIEVEMENTS

Despite recurrent drought, a poor infrastructure, and inefficient official marketing, the farmers of the Central African Republic have generally been able to meet most of the nation's basic food needs.

Chad (Republic of Chad)

GEOGRAPHY

Area in Square Kilometers (Miles):
1,284,634 (496,000) (four-fifths the
size of Alaska)
Capital (Population): N'Djamena
(595,000)
Climate: arid to semiarid

PEOPLE

Population

Total: 5,122,000
Annual Growth Rate: 2.1%
Rural/Urban Population Ratio: 70/30
Languages: official: French; others
spoken: Chadian Arabic, Fulde,
Hausa, Kotoko, Kanembou, Sara
Maba, others

Health

Life Expectancy at Birth: 39 years
(male); 41 years (female)
Infant Mortality Rate (Ratio):
134/1,000
Average Caloric Intake: 72% of FAO
minimum
Physicians Available (Ratio): 1/53,376

Religion(s)

44% Muslim; 33% Christian; 23%
traditional indigenous

Education

Adult Literacy Rate: 30%

COMMUNICATION

Telephones: 5,000
Newspapers: 4

TRANSPORTATION

Highways—Kilometers (Miles): 31,322
(19,420)
Railroads—Kilometers (Miles): none
Usable Airports: 54

THE KNIGHTS OF KANEM-BORNU

Between the ninth and nineteenth centuries A.D. much of modern Chad
prospered under the rulers of Kanem and Bornu. The sultans of these
two states, which were usually united, established great trading empires, linking the Mediterranean coast of North Africa with the Central
African interior. As was the case in medieval Europe and Japan, the
leading element in the sultans' armies was heavily armored cavalry.
Despite the local introduction of firearms by the sixteenth century, the
tradition of armored knighthood survived until the arrival of the French
colonialists. Kanem-Bornu armored costume is distinctive, being designed for the hot Sahelien climate.

GOVERNMENT

Type: republic
Independence Date: August 11, 1960
Head of State: President Indriss Deby
Political Parties: Patriotic Salvation
Movement
Suffrage: universal over 18

MILITARY

Number of Armed Forces: 22,900
(including paramilitary force)
*Military Expenditures (% of Central
Government Expenditures):* 4.3%
Current Hostilities: none

ECONOMY

Currency ($ U.S. Equivalent): 279
CFA francs = $1
Per Capita Income/GDP: $130/$973
million
Inflation Rate: − 4.9%
Natural Resources: petroleum;
uranium; natron; kaolin
Agriculture: subsistence crops; cotton;
cattle; fish; sugar
Industry: livestock products; beer;
bicycle and radio assembly; textiles;
cigarettes

FOREIGN TRADE

Exports: $174 million
Imports: $264 million

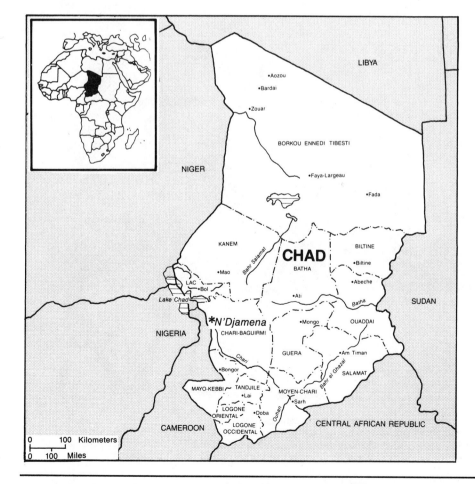

CHAD

During the 1980s Chad became the focus of outside media interest as a result of the internationalization of its long-running civil war. Although no longer much in the global spotlight, this so-called Lebanon of Africa continues to be divided by its numerous, often externally backed, armed factions. The current president, Colonel Idriss Deby, has promised to introduce multiparty democracy. But despite the support of French troops, his bankrupt regime is currently hard-pressed to maintain a semblance of law and order in the capital, N'Djamena. Elsewhere, Chad's impoverished masses, whose per capita income was last estimated at a mere $130 a year, remain vulnerable to famine as well as to the murderous intent of bandits, rebels, and warlords.

CIVIL WAR

Chad's conflicts are partially rooted in the country's ethnic and religious divisions. It has been common for outsiders to portray the struggle as being between Arab-oriented Muslim northerners and black Christian southerners, but Chad's regional and ethnic allegiances are much more complex. Geographically, the country is better divided into three zones: the northern Sahara, a middle Sahel region, and the southern savanna. Within each of these ecological areas live peoples who speak different languages and engage in a variety of economic activities. Wider ethnoregional and religious loyalties have emerged in the civil war, but such aggregates have tended to be fragile and their allegiances shifting.

At Chad's independence, in 1960, France turned over power to François Tombalbaye, a Sara-speaking Christian southerner. Tombalbaye ruled with a combination of repression, ethnic favoritism, and incompetence, which quickly alienated his regime from broad sectors of the population. A northern-based coalition of armed groups, the National Liberation Front, or Frolinat, launched an increasingly successful insurgency. The intervention of French troops on Tombalbaye's behalf failed to stem the rebellion. In 1975 the army, tired of the war and upset by the president's increasingly conspicuous brutality, overthrew Tombalbaye and established a military regime, headed by Felix Malloum.

Malloum's government was also unable to defeat Frolinat; so, in 1978, it agreed to share power with the largest of the Frolinat groups, the Armed Forces of the North (FAN), led by Hissène Habré. This agreement broke down in 1979, resulting in fighting in N'Djamena. FAN came out ahead, while Malloum's men withdrew to the south. The triumph of the "northerners" immediately led to further fighting among various factions, some allied to Habré, others loyal to his main rival within the Frolinat, Goukkouni Oueddie. Habré earlier had split from Oueddie, whom he accused of indifference toward Libya's unilateral annexation in 1976 of the Aouzou Strip, along Chad's northern frontier. At the time, Libya was the principal foreign backer of Frolinat.

(United Nations photo by John Isaac)

Thousands upon thousands of Chadians died during the civil war of the 1980s. Compounding the civil strife was severe drought, which caused a great deal of internal migration. Migrating families such as that shown above were the rule rather than the exception of this period. Rains and more peaceful conditions have since expanded agriculture, but the depopulation of many areas has hampered potentially significant additional agricultural advancements.

1980s–1990s

Habré seizes power and reunites the country in a U.S.-supported war against Libyans

Habré is overthrown by Indriss Deby; the United States evacuates a force of anti-Qadhafi Libyans

Deby promises to create a multiparty democracy, but conditions remain anarchic

In 1980, shortly after the last French forces withdrew from Chad, the Libyan army invaded the country, at the invitation of Oueddie. Oueddie was then proclaimed the leader in a Transitional Government of National Unity (GUNT), which was established in N'Djamena. Nigeria and other neighboring states, joined by France and the United States, pressed for the withdrawal of Libyan forces. This pressure grew in 1981, after Libyan leader Muammar al-Qadhafi announced the merger of Chad and Libya. Following a period of intense multinational negotiations, the Libyan military presence was reduced at Oueddie's request.

The removal of the Libyan forces from most of Chad was accompanied by revived fighting between GUNT and FAN, with the latter receiving substantial U.S. support, via Egypt and Sudan. A peacekeeping force assembled by the Organization of African Unity proved ineffectual. The collapse of GUNT in 1982 led to a second major Libyan invasion. The Libyan offensive was countered by the return of French forces, assisted by Zairian troops and by smaller contingents from several other Francophonic African countries. Between 1983 and 1987 the country was virtually partitioned along the 16th Parallel, with Habré's French-backed, FAN-led coalition in the south and the Libyan-backed remnants of GUNT in the north.

A political and military breakthrough occurred in 1987. Habré's efforts to unite the country led to a reconciliation with Malloum's followers and with elements within GUNT. Oueddie himself was apparently placed under house arrest in

Libya. Emboldened, Habré launched a major offensive north of the 16th Parallel that rolled back the better-equipped Libyan forces, who by now included a substantial number of Lebanese mercenaries. A factor in the Libyan defeat was U.S.-supplied Stinger missiles, which allowed Habré's forces to neutralize Libya's powerful air force (Habré's government lacked significant air power of its own). A ceasefire was declared after the Libyan's had been driven out of all of northern Chad with the exception of a portion of the disputed Aouzou Strip.

In 1988 Qadhafi announced that he would recognize the Habré government and pay compensation to Chad. The announcement was welcomed—with some skepticism—by Chadian and other African leaders, although no mention was made of the conflicting claims to the Aouzou Strip.

The long-running struggle for Chad took another turn in November 1990, with the sudden collapse of Habré's regime in the face of a three-week offensive by guerrillas loyal to his former army commander, Indriss Deby. Despite substantial Libyan (and Sudanese) backing for his seizure of power, Deby has the support of France, Nigeria, and the United States (Habré had supported Iraq's annexation of Kuwait). A 1,200-man French force began assisting Deby against rebels loyal to Habré.

A BETTER FUTURE?

The long, drawn-out conflict in Chad has led to immense suffering. Up to a half a million people—the equivalent of 10 per-

cent of the total population—have been killed in the fighting. Even if peace could be restored, the overall prospects for national development are bleak. The country has potential mineral wealth, but its geographic isolation as well as current world prices are disincentives to investors. Local food self-sufficiency should be obtainable despite the possibility of recurrent drought, but geography limits the potential of export crops. Chad thus appears to be an extreme case of the more general African need for a radical transformation of prevailing regional and global economic interrelationships. Had outside powers devoted half the resources to Chad's development over the past decades as they have provided to its civil conflicts, perhaps the country's future would appear brighter.

DEVELOPMENT

Chad has potential petroleum and mineral wealth that can help the economy if stable central government can be created. Deposits of chromium, tungsten, titanium, gold, uranium, and tin as well as oil are known to exist.

FREEDOM

The only law in Chad is that of the gun. Murderous criminal gangs, recently dubbed "Inkatha Zoulou" (after the South African movement), engage in widespread pillage. The vice president of a newly formed Human Rights League was assassinated in March 1992.

HEALTH/WELFARE

In 1992 there were reports of catastrophic famine in the countryside. Limited human services were provided by external aid agencies.

ACHIEVEMENTS

In precolonial times the town of Kanem was a leading regional center of commerce and culture. Since independence the major achievement has been the resiliency of its people under the most trying of circumstances.

The Congo (People's Republic of the Congo)

GEOGRAPHY

Area in Square Kilometers (Miles):
349,650 (132,000) (slightly smaller than Montana)
Capital (Population): Brazzaville (760,000)
Climate: tropical

PEOPLE

Population

Total: 2,309,000
Annual Growth Rate: 3%
Rural/Urban Population Ratio: 59/41
Languages: official: French; others spoken: Lingala, Kikongo, Teke, Sangha, M'Bochi, others

Health

Life Expectancy at Birth: 52 years (male); 56 years (female)
Infant Mortality Rate (Ratio): 108/1,000
Average Caloric Intake: 99% of FAO minimum
Physicians Available (Ratio): 1/8,065

Religion(s)

50% Christian; 48% traditional indigenous; 2% Muslim

Education

Adult Literacy Rate: 57%

RELIGIOUS LIFE

Many different religions have gained followings among peoples of the Congo in recent times. There is even a Tenrikyo Shinto center from Japan in the country. Many people claim affiliation with Christian faiths, and one-third are Roman Catholic. Swedish evangelical missionaries came to the Congo in the early twentieth century, and the Salvation Army and Jehovah's Witnesses gained followers in the pre-independence period. Many new religious movements developed after World War I, often centered around figures who were considered messiahs, such as Simon Kimbangu, who founded a Christian church that is now a member of the World Council of Churches, and André Matsoua, an early nationalist. Until the 1950s the only secondary schools in the country were the two seminaries preparing priests for the Roman Catholic Church.

COMMUNICATION

Telephones: 18,100
Newspapers: 3

TRANSPORTATION

Highways—Kilometers (Miles): 12,000 (7,440)
Railroads—Kilometers (Miles): 797 (494)
Usable Airports: 45

GOVERNMENT

Type: people's republic
Independence Date: August 15, 1960
Head of State: President Pascal Lissouba
Political Parties: Union of Congolese Socialist Youth; Congolese Trade Union Congress; Revolutionary Union of Congolese Women; General Union of Congolese Pupils and Students
Suffrage: universal over 18

MILITARY

Number of Armed Forces: 12,000
Military Expenditures (% of Central Government Expenditures): 4.6%
Current Hostilities: none

ECONOMY

Currency ($ U.S. Equivalent): 279 CFA francs = $1
Per Capita Income/GDP: $1,050/$2.4 billion
Inflation Rate: 4.6%
Natural Resources: wood; potash; petroleum; natural gas
Agriculture: cocoa; coffee; tobacco; palm kernels; sugarcane; rice; peanuts
Industry: processed agricultural and forestry goods; cement; textiles

FOREIGN TRADE

Exports: $751 million
Imports: $564 million

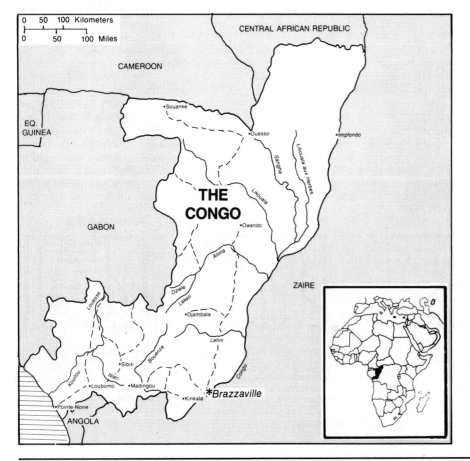

A TIME OF TRANSITION

The Congo, like many of its neighbors, has recently been undergoing a difficult political transition toward multiparty democracy. For more than 2 decades the country had been ruled as a self-proclaimed Marxist-Leninist single-party state. But in 1990 a conference of the ruling Congolese Workers Party (PCT) agreed to abandon both its ideology and monopoly of power. In 1991 the proceedings of the 4-month-long National Conference paved the way for a new constitutional order. An interim government, headed by Andre Milongo, was appointed pending elections, while the former regime's strongman, President Denis Sassou-Nguesso, was stripped of all but ceremonial authority. In the face of coup attempts by elements of the old order and a deteriorating economy, legislative and executive elections were finally held in 1992, resulting in a new multiparty government with Pascal Lissouba as the new President. While its return to a liberal democratic politics is fragile and its economy remains depressed, Congolese can look to the future with optimism.

THE CONGO

The People's Republic of the Congo takes its name from the river that forms its southeastern border, with Zaire. Because Zaire prior to 1971 (and perhaps again in the near future) also called itself the Congo, the two countries are sometimes confused. Close historical and ethnic ties do in fact exist between the nations. The BaKongo are the largest ethnolinguistic group in the Congo and western Zaire as well as in northern Angola. During the fifteenth and sixteenth centuries this group was united under a powerful Kingdom of the Kongo, which ruled over much of Central Africa while establishing commercial and diplomatic ties with Europe. But the kingdom had virtually disappeared by the late nineteenth century when the territory along the northwest bank of the Congo River, the modern republic, was annexed by France, while the southeast bank, Zaire, was placed under the rule of King Leopold of Belgium.

Despite the establishment of this political division, cultural ties between the Congo and Zaire, the former French and Belgium Congos, remain strong. Brazzaville, the Congolese capital, sits across the river from the Zairian capital of Kinshasha. The metropolitan region formed by these two centers has, through such figures as the late Congolese artist Franco, given rise to *soukous,* a musical style that is now popular in such places as Tokyo and Paris as well as throughout much of Africa.

(United Nations photo by Sean Sprague)

Since the Congo achieved its independence in 1960, it has made enormous educational strides. Almost all children in the country now attend school, which has had a tremendous effect on helping to realize the potential of the country's natural resources.

Middle Congo becomes part of French Equatorial Africa 1910	Conference establishes French Union; Felix Eboue establishes positive policies for African advancement 1944	Independence is achieved, with Abbe Fulbert Youlou as the first president 1960	A general strike brings the army and a more radical government (National Revolutionary Movement) to power 1963	A new military government under Marien Ngouabi takes over; Congolese Workers' Party is formed 1968–1969	Ngouabi is assassinated; Colonel Yhombi-Opango rules 1977	Denis Sassou-Nguesso becomes president 1979

1980s–1990s

The arrest of 20 army officers, all belonging to the Kouyou ethnic group, leads to a rebellion in the north, which is crushed after several weeks of fighting

The ruling PCT abandons Marxism and its monopoly of power

Andre Milongo's interim government survives a military uprising

ECONOMIC DEVELOPMENT

Brazzaville, which today houses more than one-quarter of the Congo's population, was established during the colonial era as the administrative headquarters of French Equatorial Africa, a vast territory that included the modern states of Chad, Central African Republic, Gabon, and the Congo. As a result, the city expanded, and the area around it developed as an imperial crossroads. The Congolese paid a heavy price for this growth. Thousands died while working under brutal conditions to build the Congo-Ocean Railroad, which linked Brazzaville with Pointe-Noire on the coast. Many more suffered as forced laborers for foreign concessionaires during the early decades of the twentieth century.

While the economies of many African states stagnated or declined during the late 1970s and '80s, the Congo generally experienced growth, a result of its oil wealth. Hydrocarbons currently account for 90 percent of the total value of the nation's exports. But the danger of this dependence has been apparent since 1986, when falling oil prices led to a sharp decline in gross domestic product. An even greater threat to the nation's economic health is its mounting debt. As a result of heavy borrowing during the oil-boom years, by 1989 the total debt was estimated to be 50 percent greater than the value of the country's annual economic output. The annual cost of servicing the debt is almost equal to domestic expenditure.

The debt led to International Monetary Fund pressure on the Congo's rulers to introduce austerity measures as part of a Structural Adjustment Program (SAP). The PCT regime and its interim successor were willing to move away from the country's emphasis on central planning toward a greater reliance on market economics. But after an initial round of severe budgetary cutbacks, both administrations found it difficult to reduce their spending further on such things as food subsidies and state-sector employment.

With more than half of the Congolese now urbanized, there has been deep concern about the social and political consequences of introducing harsher austerity measures. Many urbanites are already either unemployed or underemployed; even those with steady formal-sector jobs have already been squeezed by wages that fail to keep up with the inflation rate. The country's powerful trade unions, which are hostile to SAP, have been in the forefront of the democratization process.

Although most Congolese appear to be facing tough times in the immediate future, the economy's long-term prospects remain hopeful. Besides oil, the country is endowed with a wide variety of mineral reserves: iron, zinc, gold, potash, copper, lead, bauxite, and phosphates. Timber has long been a major industry. The Congolese forests, along with those of neighboring Gabon, are the world's main source of okoume logs, which are a preferred material for manufacturing plywood. And after years of neglect, the agricultural sector is growing. The goal of a return to food self-sufficiency appears achievable. Despite their currently low commodity prices, cocoa, coffee, tobacco, and sugar are major cash crops, while palm-oil estates are being rehabilitated.

The small but well-established Congolese manufacturing sector also has much potential. The Congo's urbanized population is relatively skilled, thanks to the enormous educational strides that have been made since independence. Almost all children now attend school. The infrastructure serving Brazzaville and Pointe-Noire, coupled with the government's new emphasis on private-sector growth, should prove attractive to outside investors as well as local entrepreneurs.

DEVELOPMENT

The Congo's Niari Valley has become the nation's leading agricultural area, due to its rich alluvial soils. The government has been encouraging food-processing plants to locate in the region.

FREEDOM

Until 1990 opposition groups, along with Jehovah's Witnesses and certain other religious sects, were vigorously suppressed. The new Constitution provides for basic freedoms of association, belief, and speech.

HEALTH/WELFARE

Almost all Congolese between ages 6 and 16 currently attend school. Adult-literacy programs have also proved successful, giving the country one of the highest literacy rates in Africa. However, 30% of Congolese children under age 5 are reported to suffer from chronic malnutrition.

ACHIEVEMENTS

There are a number of Congolese poets and novelists who combine their creative efforts with teaching and public service. Tchicaya U'Tam'si, who died in 1988, wrote poetry and novels and worked for many years for UNESCO in Geneva, Switzerland.

Equatorial Guinea (Republic of Equatorial Guinea)

GEOGRAPHY

Area in Square Kilometers (Miles):
28,023 (10,820) (about the size of
Maryland)
Capital (Population): Malabo (38,000)
Climate: equatorial

PEOPLE

Population
Total: 379,000
Annual Growth Rate: 2.6%
Rural/Urban Population Ratio: n/a
Languages: official: Spanish; others
spoken: Fang, Benge, Combe, Bujeba,
Balengue, Fernandino, Bubi

Health
Life Expectancy at Birth: 49 years
(male); 53 years (female)
Infant Mortality Rate (Ratio):
116/1,000
Average Caloric Intake: n/a
Physicians Available (Ratio): 1/76,800

Religion(s)
60% Catholic; 40% Protestant or
traditional indigenous

Education
Adult Literacy Rate: 50%

COMMUNICATION
Telephones: 2,000
Newspapers: 2

AID ATROCITIES

Since 1979 Obiang Nguema and his relatives have maintained their grip
over Equatorial Guinea by taking advantage of competition between
France and Spain for neocolonial influence. Foreign aid accounts for 70
percent of the economy. Spain and France are the principal donors.

The former Spanish colony has recently associated itself with its
Francophonic neighbors and with France by joining the Central African
Franc Zone. The use of the French language within governing circles is
increasing, especially among the French-trained security forces. But
Madrid recently financed a Spanish television service, and Spain
remains the major trading partner. Equatorial Guinea has also sought
closer relations with the United States, via the Hispanic states of Latin
America, by becoming the only African state with observer status in the
Organization of American States. U.S. assistance is increasing, in line
with growing U.S. corporate involvement in local oil and gas.

TRANSPORTATION
Highways—Kilometers (Miles): 1,240
(769)
Railroads—Kilometers (Miles): none
Usable Airports: 3

GOVERNMENT
Type: unitary republic; governed by
Supreme Military Council
Independence Date: October 12, 1968
Head of State: Brigadier General
Teodoro Obiang Ngeuma Mbasogo
Political Parties: Democratic Party of
Equatorial Guinea; opposition United
Front
Suffrage: universal for adults

MILITARY
Number of Armed Forces: 3,100
*Military Expenditures (% of Central
Government Expenditures):* 11%
Current Hostilities: none

ECONOMY
Currency ($ U.S. Equivalent): 279
CFA francs = $1
Per Capita Income/GDP: $411/$155
million
Inflation Rate: 5.9%
Natural Resources: wood
Agriculture: cocoa; coffee; timber;
rice; yams; bananas
Industry: fishing; sawmilling; palm-oil
processing

FOREIGN TRADE
Exports: $41 million
Imports: $57 million

| Europeans explore modern Equatorial Guinea **1500s** | The Dutch establish slave-trading stations **1641** | Spain claims the area of Equatorial Guinea; de facto control is not completed until 1926 **1778** | The League of Nations investigates charges of slavery on Fernando Po **1930** | The murder of nationalist leader Acacio Mane leads to the founding of political parties **1958** | Local autonomy is granted **1963** | Independence; Macias Nguema begins his reign **1968** | A coup ends the dictatorial regime of Macias Nguema; Obiang Nguema becomes the new ruler **1979** | **1980s–1990s** |

| Equatorial Guinea joins the Central African Franc Zone | The South African presence on Fernando Po (now Bioko) leads to military tensions with Nigeria | A shift to multipartyism is accompanied by wave of political detentions |

EQUATORIAL GUINEA

With the possible exception of Cambodia during the time of Pol Pot's Khmer Rouge, no country in modern times has been more misruled than Equatorial Guinea. Having been traumatized during its first decade by the sadistic Macias Nguema (1968–1979), the country continues to decay under his nephew and former security chief, Obiang Nguema. In 1992 Obiang officially transformed his regime into a multiparty democracy. Most independent observers view this gesture as a thinly disguised sham for the consumption of the Western governments that finance his brutally corrupt dictatorship. Nevertheless, an opposition United Front is attempting to take advantage of the political opening.

Equatorial Guinea's current suffering contrasts with the mood of optimism that characterized the country when it gained its independence from Spain, in 1968. Confidence was then buoyed by a strong and growing gross domestic product, potential mineral riches, and exceptionally good soil. The major responsibility for subsequent decline lies with the excesses of the two Nguemas and their close accomplices, most of whom have been drawn from among Nguemas' own Esangui clan. But the uneven pattern of colonial development between the nation's diverse regions contributed to its internal weakness at independence.

The republic is comprised of two small islands, Fernando Po (now officially known as Bioko) and Annobon, and the relatively larger and more populous coastal enclave of Rio Muni. Before the two islands and the enclave were united, during the nineteenth century, as Spain's only colony in sub-Saharan Africa, all three areas were victimized by their intense involvement in the slave trade.

Spain's major colonial concern was the prosperity of the large cocoa and coffee plantations that were established on the islands, particularly on Fernando Po. Because of local resistance from the local Bubi, labor for these estates was imported from elsewhere in West Africa. Coercive recruitment and poor working conditions led to frequent charges of slavery.

Despite early evidence of its potential riches, Rio Muni was largely neglected by the Spanish, who did not occupy its interior until 1926. During the 1930s and 1940s much of the enclave was under the political control of the Elar-ayong, a nationalist movement that sought to unite the Fang, Rio Muni's principal ethnic group, against both the Spanish and the French rulers in neighboring Cameroon and Gabon. The territory has remained one of the world's least developed areas.

In 1968 then–fascist-ruled Spain entrusted local power to Macias Nguema, who had risen through the ranks of the security service. Under his increasingly deranged misrule, virtually all public and private enterprise collapsed; indeed, between 1974 and 1979 the country had no budget. One-third of the nation's population went into exile; tens of thousands of others were either murdered or allowed to die of disease and starvation. Many of the survivors were put to forced labor, and the rest were left to subsist off the land. Killings were carried out by boys conscripted between the ages of 7 and 14.

Although no community was left unscarred by Macias's tyranny, the greatest disruption occurred on the islands. By 1976 the entire resident-alien population had left, along with most surviving members of the educated class. On Annobon, the government blocked all international efforts to stem a severe cholera epidemic in 1973. The near total depopulation of the island was completed in 1976, when all able-bodied men on Annobon, along with another 20,000 from Rio Muni, were drafted for forced labor on Fernando Po.

"SAME DOG, DIFFERENT COLLAR"

If Equatorial Guinea's first decade of independence was hell, the years since have been purgatory. Under Obiang and the still entrenched Esangui, no sector of the economy is free of corruption. Uncontrolled—and in theory illegal—logging is destroying Rio Muni's environment, while in Malabo the police routinely engage in theft. Despite the country's rich soil and regular rainfall, food is imported and malnutrition commonplace.

At least one-fifth of the Equato-Guinean population continue to live in exile, mostly in Cameroon and Gabon. This community has fostered a number of opposition groups. The government relies financially on French and Spanish aid. But Madrid's commitment has been strained by criticism from the Spanish press, which has been virtually alone in publicizing Equatorial Guinea's continued suffering.

DEVELOPMENT

The exploitation of oil and gas by U.S., French, and Spanish companies should soon greatly increase government revenue. The U.S. company Walter International has finished work on a new gas-separation plant.

FREEDOM

People continue to be detained, tortured, and disappear for such crimes as "Disrespect to the President." The local media are government-controlled, and there are few foreign periodicals. Possession of the clandestine antigovernment paper *The Truth* is a serious offense.

HEALTH

At independence, Equatorial Guinea had one of the best doctor-to-population ratios in Africa, but Macias's rule left it with the lowest. Health care is gradually reviving, with major assistance coming from public and private Spanish sources. China and Cuba have also contributed skilled personnel.

ACHIEVEMENTS

At independence, 90% of all children attended school, but the schools were closed under Macias. Since 1979 primary education has revived and now incorporates most children. Major assistance currently comes from the World Bank and from Spanish missionaries.

Gabon (Gabonese Republic)

GEOGRAPHY

Area in Square Kilometers (Miles):
264,180 (102,317) (about the size of
Colorado)
Capital (Population): Libreville
(350,000)
Climate: tropical

PEOPLE

Population
Total: 1,080,000
Annual Growth Rate: 1.4%
Rural/Urban Population Ratio: 54/46
Languages: official: French; others
spoken: Fang, Eshira, Bopounou,
Bateke, Okande, others

Health
Life Expectancy at Birth: 51 years
(male); 56 years (female)
Infant Mortality Rate (Ratio):
104/1,000
Average Caloric Intake: 102% of FAO
minimum
Physicians Available (Ratio): 1/4,031

Religion(s)
55%–75% Christian; less than 1%
Muslim; remainder traditional
indigenous

Education
Adult Literacy Rate: 61%

COMMUNICATION
Telephones: 13,800
Newspapers: 2

ALBERT SCHWEITZER AT LAMBARENE

Lambarene, a town of about 7,000 residents on the Ogooue River in
Gabon's interior, is the site of the mission hospital that Albert Schweitzer built and in which he practiced medicine. Schweitzer, born in
Alsace-Lorraine, then a part of Germany, was a philosopher, theologian,
organist, and specialist on Bach as well as a medical missionary. At age
38 he came to Lambarene, where he lived and worked for 52 years. The
hospital that he built was like an African village, consisting of many
simple dwellings. It accommodated many patients and their relatives
and operated without all of the necessities of hospitals in Europe. In
later times innovative changes were not always accepted by the
authoritarian Schweitzer or his staff. The work at Lambarene saved
lives and cured thousands. Schweitzer was awarded the Nobel Peace
Prize for his efforts for "the Brotherhood of Nations." Yet he shared the
distorted images of Africans so deeply ingrained among Westerners,
and he did not believe that Africans could advance in Western ways.

TRANSPORTATION
Highways—Kilometers (Miles): 7,500
(4,650)
Railroads—Kilometers (Miles): 649
(402)
Usable Airports: 61

GOVERNMENT
Type: republic; one-party presidential
regime
Independence Date: August 17, 1960
Head of State: President Omar Bongo
Political Parties: Gabonese
Democratic Party; Gabonese Party for
Progress; others
Suffrage: universal over 18

MILITARY
Number of Armed Forces: 6,750
*Military Expenditures (% of Central
Government Expenditures):* 3.2%
Current Hostilities: none

ECONOMY
Currency ($ U.S. Equivalent): 279
CFA francs = $1
Per Capita Income/GDP: $3,090/$3.3
billion
Inflation Rate: 3%
Natural Resources: timber; petroleum;
iron ore; manganese; uranium; gold;
zinc
Agriculture: cocoa; coffee; palm oil
Industry: petroleum; lumber; minerals

FOREIGN TRADE
Exports: $1.1 billion
Imports: $780 million

Libreville is
founded by the
French as a
settlement for
freed slaves
1849

Gabon becomes
a colony within
French Equatorial
Africa
1910

The Free French
in Brazzaville
seize Gabon
from the pro-
Vichy
government
1940

Independence is
gained; Leon
M'ba becomes
president
1960

Bongo becomes
Gabon's second
president after
M'ba's death
1967

The Gabonese
Democratic Party
(PDG) becomes
the only party of
the state
1968

1980s–1990s

Bongo agrees to
multiparty
elections but
seeks to put
limits on the
opposition

Riots in Port-
Gentil lead to
French military
intervention

The PDG
narrowly wins the
multiparty
election, amid
charges of fraud

GABON

Since independence Gabon has achieved one of the highest per capita GDPs in Africa. Exploitation of the country's natural riches, especially its oil, has given the average Gabonese an annual income of more than $3,000. Unfortunately, there is a wide gap between such statistical wealth and the real poverty that still shapes the lives of most Gabonese.

At the top of the local governing elite is President Omar Bongo, whose main palace, built at a reported cost of $300 million, symbolizes his penchant for grandeur. Shortly after taking office, in 1967, Bongo institutionalized his personal rule as the head of a one-party state. Until recently his Democratic Party of Gabon (PDG) held a legal monopoly of power. But although the PDG's constitution restricted the presidency to the "Founder President," it has been Gabon's former colonial master, France, not the ruling party's by-laws, that has upheld the Bongo regime.

The French colonial presence in Gabon dates back to 1843. Between 1898 and 1930 many Gabonese were subject to long periods of forced labor, cutting timber for French concessions companies. World War II coincided with a period of political liberalization in the territory under the Free French government of Felix Emboue, a black man born in French Guiana. Educated Gabonese were promoted for the first time to important positions in the local administration. During the 1950s two major political parties emerged to compete in local politics: the Social Democratic Union of Gabon (UDSG), led by Jean-Hilaire Aubame, and the Gabonese Democratic Bloc (BDG) of Indjenjet Gondjout and Leon Mba.

In the 1957 elections, the USDG received 60 percent of the popular vote but gained only 19 seats in the 40-seat Assembly. Mba, who had the support of French logging interests, was elected leader by 21 BDG and independent deputies. As a result, it was Mba who was at the helm when Gabon gained its independence, in 1960. This birth coincided with Mba's declaration giving himself emergency powers, provoking a period of prolonged constitutional crisis.

In January 1964 Mba dissolved the Assembly over its members' continued refusal to accept a one-party state under his leadership. In February the president himself was forced to resign by a group of army officers. Power was transferred to a civilian Provisional Government, headed by Aubame, which also included BDG politicians such as Grondjout and several prominent, unaffiliated citizens. However, no sooner had the Provisional Government been installed than Gabon was invaded by French troops. Local military units were massacred in the surprise attack, which returned Mba to office. Upon his death Mba was succeeded by his hand-picked successor, Bongo.

It has been suggested that France's 1964 invasion was primarily motivated by a desire to maintain absolute control over Gabon's uranium deposits, which were vital to France's nuclear-weapons program. Many Gabonese have believed that their country has remained a de facto French possession. France has maintained its military presence, and the Gabonese Army is outgunned by the Presidential Guard, mainly officered by Moroccan and French mercenaries. The 20,000 French residents occupy management positions in the civil service and business. France dominates Gabon's resource-rich economy. Typically, France is the source of half of Gabon's imports and the destination of half its exports.

Gabon's status quo has been challenged by its increasingly urbanized population. Although Bongo was able to co-opt or exile many of the figures who had once opposed Mba, a new generation of opposition has emerged both at home and in exile. The leading opposition group during the past decade has been the underground Movement for National Recovery (MORENA). In 1989 Bongo began talks with some elements within MORENA, which led to a division within its ranks. But the breakup of MORENA failed to stem the emergence of new groups calling for a return to multiparty democracy.

An outbreak of demonstrations and strikes at the beginning of 1990 led to the legalization of opposition parties. But the murder of a prominent opposition leader in May of that year sparked further unrest, leading to serious rioting at Port-Gentil, Gabon's second city. In response, France sent troops into the area to protect its expatriates and corporate property. Despite this intervention, Paris is said to have warned Bongo of its unwillingness to continue to prop up his regime in the absence of democratic reform.

DEVELOPMENT

The Trans-Gabonais Railway is one of the largest construction projects in Africa. Work began in 1974 and, after some delays, most of the line is now complete. The railway has opened up much of Gabon's interior to commercial development.

FREEDOM

Since 1967 Bongo has maintained power through a combination of repression and the deft use of patronage. The current transition to a multiparty process has led to an improvement in human rights.

HEALTH/WELFARE

The government claims to have instituted universal, compulsory education for Gabonese up to age 16. Independent observers doubt the government's claim but concur that major progress has been made, with recent estimates of 70% attendance within the age group. Health services have also expanded greatly.

ACHIEVEMENTS

Gabon will soon have a second private television station, funded by a French cable station. Profits will be used to fund African films that will be shown on other African stations. Gabon's first private station is funded by Swiss and Gabonese capital.

São Tomé and Príncipe
(Democratic Republic of São Tomé and Príncipe)

GEOGRAPHY

Area in Square Kilometers (Miles):
1,001 (387) (slightly larger than New York City)
Capital (Population): São Tomé (40,000)
Climate: tropical

PEOPLE

Population
Total: 128,500
Annual Growth Rate: 3%
Rural/Urban Population Ratio: n/a
Languages: official: Portuguese; other spoken: Fang; Kriolu

Health
Life Expectancy at Birth: 64 years (male); 68 years (female)
Infant Mortality Rate (Ratio): 60/1,000
Average Caloric Intake: 78% of FAO minimum
Physicians Available (Ratio): 1/2,354

Religion(s)
80% Christian; 20% traditional indigenous

Education
Adult Literacy Rate: 57%

COMMUNICATION
Telephones: 2,200
Newspapers: 2 weeklies

TRANSPORTATION
Highways—Kilometers (Miles): 300 (186)

THE PEOPLE OF THE ISLANDS

The current inhabitants of São Tomé and Príncipe mostly are of mixed African and European descent. During the colonial period the society was stratified along racial lines. At the top were the Europeans—mostly Portuguese. Just below them were the *mesticos* or *filhos da terra*, the mixed-blood descendants of slaves. Descendants of slaves who arrived later were known as *forros*. Contract workers were labeled as *servicais*, while their children became known as *tongas*. Still another category was the *angolares*, who reportedly were the descendants of ship-wrecked slaves. All of these colonial categories were used to divide and rule the local population; the distinctions have begun to diminish as an important sociological factor on the islands.

Railroads—Kilometers (Miles): none
Usable Airports: 2

GOVERNMENT
Type: republic
Independence Date: July 12, 1975
Head of State: President Miguel Trovoada
Political Parties: Party for Democratic Convergence-Group of Reflection; Movement for the Liberation of São Tomé and Príncipe; Christian Democratic Front; Democratic Opposition Coalition; others
Suffrage: universal over 18

MILITARY
Number of Armed Forces: n/a
Military Expenditures (% of Central Government Expenditures): 1.6%
Current Hostilities: none

ECONOMY
Currency ($ U.S. Equivalent): 240 dobras = $1
Per Capita Income/GDP: $380/$48.8 million
Inflation Rate: 39%
Natural Resources: fish
Agriculture: cacao; coconut palms; coffee; bananas; palm kernels
Industry: beer; soft drinks; palm oil; copra; tourism; manufacturing; construction

FOREIGN TRADE
Exports: $5.9 million
Imports: $26.8 million

The Portuguese settle São Tomé and Príncipe
1500s

Slavery is abolished, but forced labor continues
1876

The Portuguese massacre hundreds of islanders
1953

Factions within the liberation movement unite to form the MLSTP in Gabon
1972

Independence
1975

Manuel Pinto da Costa deposes and exiles Miguel Trovoada, the premier and former number-two man in the MLSTP
1979

1980s–1990s

New policy of economic and political liberalization

An attempted invasion by a 42-man force of South African-backed, anti-MLSTP-PSD mercenaries is foiled

Multiparty elections lead to the defeat of the MLSTP-PSD and the election to the presidency of Trovoada

SÃO TOMÉ AND PRÍNCIPE

In January 1991 the small island nation of São Tomé and Príncipe held its first multiparty elections, resulting in the defeat of the former ruling party, the Liberation Movement of São Tomé and Príncipe-Social Democratic Party (MLSTP-PSD), by a newly formed Party of Democratic Convergence-Group of Reflection (PDC-GR). A month later the PDC-GR leader, Miguel Trovoada, was unopposed in his election as president. The new political climate has been accompanied by a modest improvement in the impoverished nation's economic prospects.

São Tomé and Príncipe gained its independence in 1975, after a half-millennium of Portuguese rule. During the colonial era economic life centered around the interests of a few thousand Portuguese settlers, particularly a handful of large-plantation owners who controlled more than 80 percent of the land. After independence most of the Portuguese fled, taking their skills and capital and leaving the economy in disarray. But production on the plantations has since been revived.

The Portuguese began the first permanent settlement of São Tomé and Príncipe in the late fifteenth century. Through the intensive use of slave labor, the islands developed rapidly as one of the world's leading exporters of sugar. Only a small fraction of the profits from this boom were consumed locally, and high mortality rates, caused by brutal working conditions, led to an almost insatiable demand for more slaves. After the mid-sixteenth century, profits from sugar declined, due to competition from Brazil and the Caribbean. A period of prolonged depression set in.

In the early nineteenth century a second economic boom swept the islands, when they became leading exporters of coffee, and, more importantly, cocoa. São Tomé and Príncipe's position in the world market has since declined, yet these two cash crops, along with copra, have continued to be economic mainstays. Although slavery was officially abolished during the nineteenth century, forced labor was maintained by the Portuguese into modern times. Involuntary contract workers, known as *servicais,* were imported to labor on the islands' plantations, which had notoriously high mortality rates. Sporadic labor unrest and occasional incidents of international outrage led to some improvement in working conditions, but fundamental reforms came about only after independence. A historical turning point for the islands was the Batepa Massacre in 1953, when several hundred African laborers were killed following local resistance to labor conditions.

POLITICS AND THE ECONOMY

Between 1975 and 1991 São Tomé and Príncipe was ruled by the MLSTP-PSD, which had emerged in exile as the island's leading anticolonial movement, as a one-party state initially committed to Marxist-Leninism. But, in 1990, a new policy of *abertura,* or political and economic "opening," resulted in the legalization of opposition parties and the introduction of direct elections with secret balloting. Press restrictions were also lifted, and the nation's security police were purged. The democratization process was welcomed by previously exiled opposition groups, most of which united as the DCP-GR. The changed political climate has also been reflected in the establishment of an independent labor movement. Strikes were previously forbidden.

The move toward multiparty politics was accompanied by an evolution to a market economy by the former socialist government. Since 1985 a Free Trade Zone has been established, state farms have been privatized, and private capital has been attracted to build up a tourist industry, most notably on the island of Bom-Bom. These moves have been accompanied by a major expansion of Western loans and assistance to the islands, an inflow of capital that now accounts for nearly half of the GDP.

Besides tourism, the government has focused its development efforts on fishing. In 1978, a 200-mile maritime zone was declared over the tuna-rich waters around the islands. The state-owned fishing company, Empesca, is upgrading the local fleet, which still consists mostly of canoes using old-fashioned nets. The influx of aid and investment has resulted in several years of sustained economic growth.

DEVELOPMENT

Local food production has been significantly boosted by a French-funded scheme. Japan is assisting in fishery development. There is some concern that tourist fishermen may adversely affect the local industry.

FREEDOM

Prior to 1987 human rights were circumscribed in São Tomé and Príncipe. Gradual liberalization has now given way to a commitment to pluralism.

HEALTH/WELFARE

The government since independence has had enormous progress in expanding health care and education. The Sãotoméan infant mortality rate, 60 per 1,000, is now among the lowest in Africa and average life expectancy, 66 years overall, is among the highest. Sixty-three percent of the population between 6 and 19 years of age are now in school.

ACHIEVEMENTS

São Tomé and Príncipe shares in a rich Luso-African artistic tradition. The country is particularly renowned for poets such as Jose de Almeida and Francisco Tenriero, who were among the first to express in the Portuguese language the experiences and pride of Africans.

Zaire (Republic of Zaire)

GEOGRAPHY
Area in Square Kilometers (Miles):
2,300,000 (905,063) (one-quarter the size of the United States)
Capital (Population): Kinshasa (3,000,000)
Climate: equatorial

PEOPLE

Population
Total: 37,800,000
Annual Growth Rate: 3.3%
Rural/Urban Population Ratio: 60/40
Languages: official: French; others spoken: Kiswahili, Lingala, Azande, Luba, Chokwe, Songo, Kongo, Kuba, Lunda, Bemba, Alur, many others

Health
Life Expectancy at Birth: 52 years (male); 56 years (female)
Infant Mortality Rate (Ratio): 99/1,000
Average Caloric Intake: 94% of FAO minimum
Physicians Available (Ratio): 1/18,294

Religion(s)
70% Christian; 20% traditional indigenous; 10% Muslim

Education
Adult Literacy Rate: 72%

A SCENE FROM LEOPOLD'S GENOCIDES

The following passage is an excerpt from E. D. Morel's *Red Rubber* (p. 97).

Look inside the hostage house, staggering back as you enter from odours which belch forth in poisonous fumes. As your eyes get accustomed to the half-light, they will not rest on those skeleton-like forms—bones held together by black skin—but upon the faces. The faces turn upward in mute appeal for pity; the hollow cheeks, the misery and terror in their eyes, the drawn parched lips emitting inarticulate sounds. A woman, her pendulous, pear shaped breasts hanging like withered parchment against her sides, where ribs seem bursting from its covering, holds in her emaciated arms a small object more pink than black. You stoop to touch it—a new born babe, twenty-four hours hold, assuredly not more. It is dead but the mother clasps it still. She herself is almost past speech, and will soon join her babe in the great Unknown. The horror of it the unspeakable horror of it.

COMMUNICATION
Telephones: 31,200
Newspapers: 4

TRANSPORTATION
Highways—Kilometers (Miles):
146,500 (90,830)
Railroads—Kilometers (Miles): 5,254 (3,257)
Usable Airports: 255

GOVERNMENT
Type: republic; strong presidential authority
Independence Date: June 30, 1960
Head of State: President Marshal Mobutu Sese Seko
Political Parties: Popular Movement of the Revolutionary Party; Democratic Social Christian Party; Union for Democracy and Social Progress; Sacred Union (opposition affiliation)
Suffrage: universal over 18

MILITARY
Number of Armed Forces: 31,700
Military Expenditures (% of Central Government Expenditures): n/a
Current Hostilities: low-intensity insurgency

ECONOMY
Currency ($ U.S. Equivalent): 112, 314 Zaires = $1
Per Capita Income/GDP: $180/$6.8 billion
Inflation Rate: more than 1,000%
Natural Resources: copper; cobalt; zinc; diamonds; manganese; tin; gold; rare metals; bauxite; iron; coal; hydroelectric potential; timber
Agriculture: coffee; palm oil; rubber; tea; cotton; cocoa; manioc; bananas; plantains; corn; rice; sugar
Industry: mineral mining; consumer products; food processing; cement

FOREIGN TRADE
Exports: $2.2 billion
Imports: $2.1 billion

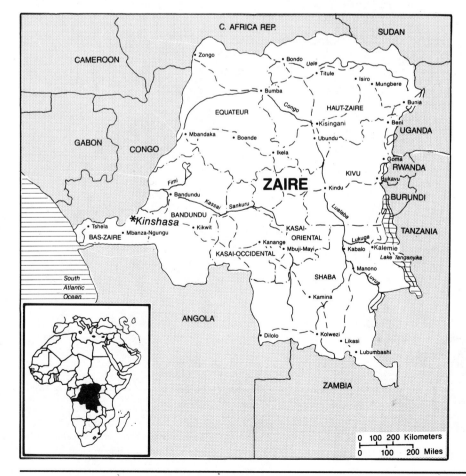

ZAIRE

Since 1990 Zaire has been paralyzed by a power struggle between its long-reigning dictator, Mobutu Seso Seko, and the fractious politicians who wish to replace him. In the process, the country's already decayed social and economic infrastructure has begun to disintegrate. All sides in the current political conflict claim to favor a transition to multiparty democracy, but the chances for the peaceful emergence of a stable constitutional order in the immediate future are waning. Zaire is a vast country of potentially great wealth; developments there will continue to affect the fates of other nations as well as its own citizenry.

"Together, my brothers, we are going to start a new struggle which will lead our country to peace, prosperity and greatness . . . [W]e are going to make the Congo the hub of all Africa." So spoke Prime Minister Patrice Lumumba on June 30, 1960, the day when Zaire, then the Democratic Republic of the Congo, gained independence.

Geographically, Zaire is the hub of Africa. Located at Africa's center, it encompasses the entire Congo, or Zaire, River Basin, whose waters are the potential source of 13 percent of the world's hydro-electric power. This immense area, about one-quarter the size of the United States, encompasses a variety of land forms with good agricultural possibilities. It contains a wide range of natural resources, some of which have been intensively exploited for decades.

Zaire links Africa from west to east. The country faces the Atlantic, with a very narrow coastline. Eastern Zaire, however, has been influenced by forces from the East African coast. In the mid-nineteenth century Swahili, Arab, and Nyamwezi traders from Tanzania established their hegemony over much of southeastern Zaire, pillaging the countryside for ivory and slaves. While the slave trade has left bitter memories, the Swahili language has spread to become a *lingua franca* throughout the eastern third of the country.

Zaire's 38 million people belong to about 250 different ethnic groups, speak nearly 700 languages and dialects, and have varied life-styles. Boundaries established in the late nineteenth century hemmed in portions of the Azande, Konga, Chokwe, and Songye peoples within present-day Zaire, yet they maintain contact with their kin in other countries.

Many important precolonial states were centered in Zaire, including the Luba, Kuba, and Lunda kingdoms—the latter of which, in earlier centuries, exploited the salt and copper of southeast Zaire. The kingdom of Kongo, located at the mouth of the Congo River, flourished during the fifteenth and sixteenth centuries, establishing important diplomatic and commercial relations with Portugal. The elaborate political systems of these kingdoms are an important heritage for Zaire.

LEOPOLD'S GENOCIDE

The European impact, like the Swahili and Arab influences from the east, had deeply destructive results. The Congo Basin was explored and exploited by private individuals before it came under Belgian domination. King Leopold of Belgium, as a private citizen, sponsored H. M. Stanley's expeditions to explore the basin. In 1879 Leopold used Stanley's "treaties" as a justification for setting up the "Congo Independent State" over the whole region. This state was actually a private proprietary colony. To turn a profit on his vast enterprise, Leopold acted under the assumption that the people and resources in the territory were his personal property. His commercial agents and various concessionaires, to whom he leased portions of his colony, began brutally to coerce the local African population into providing

(United Nations photo by Caracciolo/Banoun)

Zaire is the hub of Africa. On the west, the Congo (or Zaire) River Basin empties into the South Atlantic, where a small fishing industry survives.

ivory, wild rubber, and other commodities. The armed militias sent out to collect quotas of rubber and other goods committed numerous atrocities, including destroying whole villages.

No one knows for sure how many Africans perished in the Congo Independent State as a result of the brutalities of Leopold's agents. Some critics estimate that the territory's population was reduced by 10 million people over a period of 20 years. Many were starved to death as forced laborers. Others were massacred in order to induce survivors to produce more rubber. Women and children suffocated in "hostage houses" while their men did their masters' bidding. Thousands fled to neighboring territories.

For years the Congo regime was able to keep information of its crimes from leaking overseas, but eventually tales from missionaries and others did emerge. Accounts such as E. D. Morel's *Red Rubber* and Mark Twain's caustic *King Leopold's Soliloquy,* as well as gruesome pictures of men, women, and children whose hands had been severed by troops (who were expected to produce the hands for their officers as evidence of their diligence), stirred public opinion. Joseph Conrad's fictionalized account of his experiences, *The Heart of Darkness,* became a popular literary classic. Eventually even the European imperialists, during an era when their racial arrogance was at its height, could no longer stomach Leopold, called by some

"the king with ten million murders on his soul."

During the years of Belgian rule, 1908–1960, foreign domination was less genocidal, but nevertheless a tradition of abuse had been established. The colonial authorities still used armed forces for "pacification" campaigns, tax collection, and labor recruitment. Local collaborators were turned into chiefs and given arbitrary powers that they would not have had under indigenous political systems. Concessionary companies continued to use force to recruit labor for their plantations and mines. The two firms that gained the most were Lever Brothers and the Union Minière, which exploited the minerals of Shaba Province. The colonial regime encouraged the work of Catholic missionaries. Health facilities as well as a paternalistic system of education were developed. A strong elementary-school system was part of the colonial program, but the Belgians never instituted a major secondary-school system, and there was no institution of higher learning. By independence only 16 Congolese had been able to earn university degrees, all but 2 in non-Belgian institutions. A small group of high-school-educated Congolese, known as *évolués* ("evolved ones"), served the needs of an administration that never intended nor planned for Zaire's independence.

During the 1950s the Congolese, especially townspeople, were affected by the independence movements emerging through-

out Africa. The Belgians began to recognize the need to prepare for a different future. Small initiatives were allowed; in 1955 nationalist associations were first permitted and a 30-year timetable for independence was proposed, sparking heated debate. Some évolués agreed with the Belgians' proposal. Others, including the members of the Alliance of the BaKongo (ABAKO), an ethnic association in Kinshasa, and the National Congolese Movement (MNC), led by Lumumba, rejected it.

A serious clash at an ABAKO demonstration in 1959 resulted in about 50 deaths. In the face of mounting unrest, further encouraged by the imminent independence of the French Congo (the Republic of the Congo), the Belgians conceded a rapid transition to independence. A constitutional conference in January 1960 established a federal-government system for the future independent state. But there was no real preparation for such a drastic political change. Belgian civil servants expected that they would stay on to work with each new Congolese government minister or administrator; they were to be disappointed.

THE CONGO CRISIS

The Democratic Republic of the Congo became independent on June 30, 1960, under the leadership of President Joseph Kasavubu and Prime Minister Patrice Lumumba. Within a week, an army mutiny

(United Nations photo by Milton Grant)

The eastern area of Zaire faces many of the same forces as East Africa; while the land supports agriculture, drought is a constant threat.

had stimulated widespread disorder. The scars of the Congo's uniquely bitter colonial experience showed. Unlike in Africa's other postcolonial states, in the Congo, hatred of the white former masters turned to violence, resulting in the hurried flight of the majority of its large European community. Ethnic and regional bloodshed took a much greater toll among the African population. The wealthy Katanga Province (now Shaba) and South Kasai seceded.

Lumumba called upon the United Nations for assistance, and troops came from a variety of countries to serve in the UN force. Later, as a result of a dispute between President Kasavubu and himself, Lumumba sought Soviet aid. The Congo could have become a cold-war battlefield, but the army, under Lumumba's former confidant, Joseph Desiré Mobutu, intervened, and Lumumba was arrested and turned over to the Katanga rebels, later to be assassinated. Western interests and, in particular, the U.S. Central Intelligence Agency played a substantial if not fully revealed role in the downfall of the idealistic Lumumba and the rise of his cynical successor, Mobutu. Rebellions by Lumumbists in the northeast and Katanga secessionists, supported by foreign mercenaries, continued through 1967.

MOBUTUISM

Mobutu seized full power in 1965, ousting Kasavubu in a military coup. With ruthless energy, he eliminated the rival political factions within the central government and crushed the regional rebellions. Mobutu banned party politics. In 1971 he established the Second Republic as a one-party state in which all power was centralized around "the Founding President." Every citizen, at birth, was legally expected to be a disciplined member of Mobutu's Popular Revolutionary Movement (MPR). With the exception of some religious organizations, virtually all social institutions were to function as MPR organs. The official ideology of the MPR republic became "Mobutuism," the words, deeds, and decrees of "the Guide" Mobutu. All citizens were required to sing his praises daily at the workplace, at schools, and at social gatherings. In hymns and prayers, the name Mobutu was often substituted for that of Jesus. A principal slogan of Mobutuism was "authenticity." Supposedly this meant a rejection of European values and norms for African ones. But it was Mobutu alone who defined what was authentic. He added to his own name the title "Sese Seko," or "the all powerful," while declaring all European personal names illegal. He also established a national dress

code in which ties were outlawed and men were expected to wear his abacost suit, while women were obliged to wear the paigne, or wrapper. The name of the country was changed from the Congo to Zaire, a name derived from sixteenth-century Portuguese mispronunciation of the (Ki)Kongo word for "river."

Outside of Zaire, some took Mobutu's protestations of authenticity at face value, while a few other African dictators, such as Togo's Gnassingbé Eyadéma, emulated aspects of his fascist methodology. But the majority of Zairians grew to loathe his cultural revolution. Zaire is perhaps the only place in the world where the necktie is a symbol of resistance. On a more substantial level, authenticity was briefly accompanied by a program of nationalization. Union Minière and other corporations were placed under government control. In 1973–1974 plantations, commercial institutions, and other businesses were also taken over, in a "radicalizing of the Zairian Revolution."

But the expropriated businesses simply enriched a small elite. In many cases, Mobutu gave them away to his cronies, who often simply sold off the assets. Consequently, the economy suffered. Industries and businesses were mismanaged or ravaged. Some individuals became extraordinarily wealthy, while the population as a whole became progressively poorer with each passing year. Mobutu allegedly has become the wealthiest person in Africa, with a fortune estimated in excess of $5 billion (about equal to Zaire's national debt), most of which is invested or spent outside of Africa. He and his relatives own mansions all over the world.

Until recently no opposition to Mobutu has been allowed. Those critical of the regime faced imprisonment, torture, or death. The Roman Catholic Church and the Kimbanguist Church of Jesus Christ Upon This Earth were the only institutions able to speak out. Strikes were not allowed. In 1977 and 1978 new revolts in the Shaba Province were crushed by U.S.-backed Moroccan, French, and Belgian military interventions, but small-scale rural insurrections continued.

ECONOMIC DISASTER

Zaire's economic potential was developed by and for the Belgians, but by 1960 that development had gone further than in most other African colonial territories. Zaire started with a good economic base, but the chaos of the early 1960s brought development to a standstill, and the Mobutu years have been marked by regression. Development projects have been initiated, but

often without careful planning. World economic conditions, including falling copper and cobalt prices, have contributed to Zaire's difficulties.

But the main obstacle to any sort of economic progress is the rampant corruption of Mobutu and those around him. The governing system in Zaire has been characterized as a kleptocracy, or rule by thieves. An organized system of graft transfers wealth from ordinary citizens to officials and other elites. With Mobutu stealing billions and those closest to him stealing millions, the entire society operates on an invisible tax system whereby citizens must, for example, bribe nurses for medical care, bureaucrats for documents, principals for school admission, and police to stay out of jail. For most civil servants, who are paid little or nothing, accepting bribes is a necessary activity. This fundamental fact also applies to most soldiers, who thus survive by living off the civilian population. Recently the U.S. military learned this lesson first-hand when it conducted joint military exercises with Zairian paratroopers. When a number of American troops' parachutes got caught in trees, the soldiers were robbed of their possessions by Zairian troops who then deserted into the forest.

Ordinary people suffer. By 1990 real wages of urban workers in Zaire were only 2 percent of what they were in 1960. Rural incomes had also deteriorated. The official 1990 price paid to coffee farmers, for example, was only one-fifth of what it was in 1954 under the exploitive Belgian regime. The situation has worsened in the 1990s, due to escalating hyperinflation, which by July 1992 was in excess of 1,000 percent.

Much of the state's coffee and other cash crops have long been smuggled, more often than not through the connivance of senior government officials. Thus, although Zaire's agriculture has great economic potential, the returns from this sector continue to shrink. Despite its immense size and plentiful rainfall, Zaire must import about 60 percent of its food requirements. Rural people move to the city or, for lack of employment, move back to the country and take up subsistence agriculture, rather than cash-crop farming, in order to ensure their own survival. The deterioration of roads and bridges has led to the decline of all trade.

In 1983 the government adopted International Monetary Fund austerity measures, but this has only cut public expenditures. It has had no effect on the endemic corruption, nor has it increased taxes on the rich. Today more than 30

Leopold sets up the Congo Independent State as his private kingdom **1879**	Congo becomes a Belgian colony **1906**	Congo gains independence; civil war begins; a UN force is involved; Patrice Lumumba is murdered **1960**	Mobutu takes command in a bloodless coup **1965**	The name of the state is changed to Zaire **1971**	1980s–1990s

Mobutu proclaims a multiparty Third Republic; students are massacred at Lumumbashi	Tens of thousands of foreigners flee Zaire as central authority crumbles	The National Conference unanimously agrees to restore the name and flag of the Democratic Republic of the Congo

percent of Zaire's budget goes for debt servicing.

U.S. SUPPORT FOR MOBUTU

Mobutu's regime has been able to sidestep its financial crises and maintain power through the support of foreign powers, especially Belgium, France, Germany, and the United States. A U.S. intelligence report prepared in the mid-1950s concluded that the then-Belgian Congo was indeed the hub of Africa and thus vital to America's strategic interests. U.S. policy has thus been first to promote and then to perpetuate Mobutu as a pro-Western source of stability in the region. Mobutu himself has skillfully cultivated this image.

Mobutu has collaborated with the United States in opposing the Marxist-oriented Popular Movement for the Liberation of Angola. By so doing, he has not only set himself up as an important cold-war ally but has also been able to pursue regional objectives of his own. The National Front for the Liberation of Angola, long championed by the CIA as a counterforce to the MPLA, is led by an in-law of Mobutu, Holden Roberto. Mobutu has also long coveted Angola's oil-rich enclave of Cabinda and has thus sought CIA and South African assistance for the "independence" movement there. In recent years millions of U.S. dollars have been spent upgrading the airstrip at Kamina in Shaba Province, which has been used by the CIA to supply the guerrillas of the National Union for the Total Independence of Angola, another faction opposed to the MPLA government. In 1989 Mobutu attempted to set himself up as a mediator between the government and the UNITA rebels, but even the latter have grown to distrust him.

The United States has long known of Mobutu's human-rights violations and of the oppression and corruption that characterize his regime. High-level defectors as well as victims have publicized its abuses. Since 1987 Mobutu has responded with heavily financed public-relations efforts aimed at lobbying U.S. legislators. U.S. support for Mobutu has continued, but the recent collapse of much of his authority has led Washington belatedly to search for alternatives.

Mobutu has also allied himself with other conservative forces in Africa and the Middle East. Moroccan troops came to his aid during the revolts in Shaba Province in 1977 and 1978. For his part, Mobutu has been a leading African supporter of Morocco's stand with regard to the Western Sahara dispute. Zaire has been an active member of the Francophonic African bloc. In 1983 Mobutu dispatched 2,000 Zairian troops to Chad in support of the government of Hissène Habré, then under attack from Libya, while in 1986 his men again joined French forces in propping up the Eyadéma regime in Togo. He has also maintained and strengthened his ties with South Africa; today Zaire imports almost half its food from that state. In 1982 Zaire renewed the diplomatic ties with Israel that had been broken after the Arab-Israeli War of 1973. Israelis have since joined French and Belgians as senior advisers and trainers working within the Zairian Army. During 1990 the outbreak of violent unrest in Kinshasha once more led to the intervention of French and Belgium troops.

Despite Mobutu's cultivation of foreign assistance to prop up his dictatorship, internal opposition has been growing. In 1990 he tried to head off his critics both at home and abroad by promising to set up a new Third Republic, based on multiparty democracy. Despite this step, repression in Zaire has intensified. Mobutu initially hoped to window-dress his authoritarianism by having two new parties, dedicated to shades of Mobutuism, join the MPR in a rubber-stamp assembly. But this was rejected by the opposition, who have now fractured into dozens of parties, many of which have affiliated as the Sacred Union. Amid growing disorder, with units of the army acting increasingly on their own behalf, a National Conference was convened in September 1991 to draft a new constitution. Despite being suspended more than once by Mobutu, the Conference has continued to meet. Its attempts to reach a consensus on an interim government have so far been frustrated, while Mobutu himself has abandoned the presidential palace for the security of his well-guarded, mobile, yacht. As the center collapses, disorder is growing across the land.

DEVELOPMENT

Western aid and development assistance were drastically reduced in 1992. An agreement was signed with Egypt for the long-term development of Zaire's hydroelectric power.

FREEDOM

Zaire has shown little respect for human rights. One Amnesty International report concluded that all political prisoners are tortured. Death squads are active.

HEALTH/WELFARE

In 1978 more than 5 million students were registered for primary schools and 35,000 for college. However, the level of education is declining. Many teachers were laid off in the 1980s, though nonexistent "ghost teachers" remained on the payroll. The few innovative educational programs are outside the state system.

ACHIEVEMENTS

Kinshasha has been called the dance-music capital of Africa. The most popular sound is souskous, or "Congo rumba." The grand old man of the style, Rochereau Tabu Ley, is still going strong, while other artists, like Papa Wemba, Pablo Lubidika, and Sandoka, have joined him in spreading its rhythms internationally.

East Africa

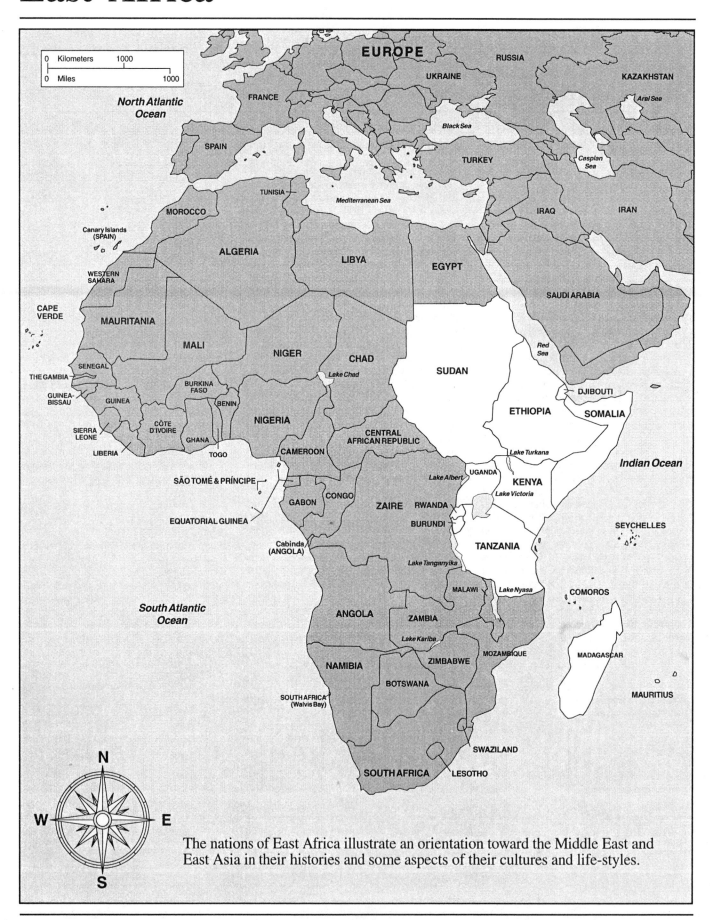

The nations of East Africa illustrate an orientation toward the Middle East and East Asia in their histories and some aspects of their cultures and life-styles.

94

East Africa: A Mixed Inheritance

The vast East African region, ranging from the Sudan in the north to Tanzania and the Indian Ocean islands in the south, is an area of great diversity. Although the islands are the homes of distinctive civilizations with ties to Asia, their interactions with the African mainland give their inclusion here validity. Ecological features, such as the Great Rift Valley, the prevalence of cattle-herding life-styles, and longstanding participation in the Indian Ocean trading networks are some of the region's unifying aspects.

CATTLE-HERDING SOCIETIES

A long-horned cow would be an appropriate symbol for East Africa. Most of the region's rural inhabitants, who make up the majority of people from the Horn, to Lake Malawi, to Madagascar, value cattle for their social as well as economic importance. The Nuer of the Sudan, the Somali near the Red Sea (who, like many other peoples of the Horn, herd camels as well as cattle, goats, and sheep), and the Maasai of Tanzania and Kenya are among the pastoral peoples whose herds are their livelihoods. Farming communities such as the Kikuyu of Kenya, the Baganda of Uganda, and the Malagasey of Madagascar also prize cattle.

Much of the East African landmass is well suited for

(World Bank photo by Kay Muldoon)

Lively and extensive trade and migration patterns have characterized East Africa throughout much of its history.

herding. Whereas the rain forests of West and Central Africa are generally infested with tsetse flies, whose bite is fatal to livestock, most of East Africa is made up of belts of tropical and temperate savanna, which are ideal for grazing. Thus pastoralism has long been predominant in the savanna zones of West and Southern, as well as East, Africa. Tropical rain forests are almost nonexistent in East Africa, being found only on the east coast of Madagascar and scattered along the mainland's coast. Much of the East African interior is dominated by the Great Rift Valley, which stretches from the Red Sea as far south as Malawi. This geological formation is characterized by mountains as well as valleys, and it features the region's great lakes, such as Lake Albert, Lake Tanganyika, and Lake Malawi.

People have been moving into and through the East African region since the existence of humankind; indeed most of the earliest human fossils have been unearthed in this region. Today almost all the mainland inhabitants speak languages that belong to either the Bantu or Nilotic linguistic families. There has been much historical speculation about the past migration of these peoples, but current archaeology indicates that both linguistic groups have probably been established in the area for a long time, although oral traditions and other forms of historical evidence indicate locally important shifts in settlement patterns into the contemporary period. Iron working and, in at least a few cases, small-scale steel production have long been a part of the regional economy. Long-distance trade and the production of various crafts have also existed since ancient times. The inhabitants of the region have had to confront insufficient and unreliable rainfall. Drought and famine in the Horn and in areas of Kenya and Tanzania have in recent years caused suffering, changed life-styles, and dislocated many people.

ISLAMIC INFLUENCE

Many of the areas of East Africa have been influenced, since at least as far back as Roman times and perhaps much further, by the Middle East and other parts of Asia. Over the past thousand years most parts of East Africa, including the Christian highlands of Ethiopia and the inland interlake states such as Buganda, Burundi, and Rwanda, became familiar to the Muslim Arab traders of the Swahili and Red Sea coasts and the Sudanese interior. Somalia, Djibouti, and the Sudan, which border the Red Sea and are close to the Arabian Peninsula, have been the most influenced by Arab Islamic culture. Mogadishu, the capital of Somalia, began as an Islamic trading post in the tenth century. The Islamic faith, its various sects or brotherhoods, the Koran, and the Shari'a (the Islamic legal code) are predominant throughout the Horn, except in the Ethiopian interior and southern Sudan. In recent years many Somali, Sudanese, and others have migrated to the oil-rich states of Arabia to work.

Farther south, in the communities and cultures on the perimeters of the east coast, Arabs and local Bantu-speaking Africans combined, from as early as the ninth century but especially during the 1200s to 1400s, to form the culture and the language that we now call Swahili. In the first half of the nineteenth century the sultan of Oman, Seyyid Said, transferred his capital to Zanzibar, in recognition of the outpost's economic importance. Motivated by the rapid expansion of trade in ivory and slaves, many Arab-Swahili traders began to establish themselves and build settlements as far inland as the forests of eastern Zaire. As a result, some of the noncoastal peoples also adopted Islam, while Swahili developed into a regional *lingua franca.*

The whole region from the Horn to Tanzania continued to be affected by the slave trade through much of the nineteenth century. Slaves were sent north from Uganda and southern Sudan, to Egypt and the Middle East, and from Ethiopia across the Red Sea. Others were taken to the coast by Arab, Swahili, or African traders, either to work on the plantations in Zanzibar or to be transported to the Persian Gulf and the Indian Ocean islands.

In the late nineteenth and early twentieth centuries, South Asian laborers from what was then British India were brought in by the British to build the East African railroad. South Asian traders already resided in Zanzibar; others now came and settled in Kenya and Tanzania, becoming shopkeepers and bankers in inland centers such as Kampala and Nairobi as well as on the coast in Mombasa and Dar es Salaam or in smaller stops along the railroad. South Asian laborers were also sent in large numbers to work on the sugar plantations of Mauritius; their descendants there now make up about two-thirds of that island's population.

The subregions of East Africa include the following: the countries of the Horn, East Africa proper, and the islands. The Horn includes Djibouti, Ethiopia, Somalia, and Sudan, which are associated here with one another not so much because of a common heritage, or on account of any compatibility of their governments (for, indeed, they are often hostile to one another), but because of the movements of peoples across borders in recent times. East Africa proper is comprised of Kenya, Tanzania, and Uganda, which do have underlying cultural ties and a history of economic relations, in which Rwanda and Burundi have also shared. The Indian Ocean islands include the Comoros, Madagascar, Mauritius, and the Seychelles, which, notwithstanding the expanses of ocean that separate them, have certain cultural aspects and current interests in common.

THE HORN

Ethiopia traditionally has had a distinct, semi-isolated history that has separated the nation from its neighbors. This early Christian civilization, which was periodically united by a strong dynasty but at other times was disunited, was centered in the highlands of the interior, surrounded by often hostile lowland peoples. Before the nineteenth century it was in infrequent contact with other Christian societies. During 1800s, however, a series of strong rulers reunified the highlands and went on to conquer surrounding peoples such as the Afar, Oromo, and Somali. In the process, the state (with the exception of Eritrea, which was incorporated after World War II) expanded to its current boundaries. While the empire's expansion helped it to preserve its independence during Africa's colonial partition, today sectarian and ethnic divisions, a legacy of the imperial state-building process, threaten to tear the polity apart.

Ethiopia and the other contemporary nations of the Horn have been influenced by outside powers, whose interests in the region have been primarily rooted in its strategic location. In the nineteenth century both Britain and France became interested in the Horn, because the Red Sea was the link between their countries and the markets of Asia. This was especially true after the completion of the Suez Canal in 1869. Both of the imperial powers occupied ports on the Red Sea at the time. They then began to compete over the upper Nile in modern Sudan. In the 1890s French forces, led by Captain Jean Baptiste Marchand, literally raced from the present-day area of the Congo to reach the center of the Sudan before the arrival of a larger British expeditionary

(United Nations photo by Ray Witlin)

In the drought-affected areas of East Africa, people must devote considerable time and energy to the search for water.

force, which had invaded the region from Egypt. Ultimately the British were able to consolidate their control over the entire Sudan.

Italian ambitions in the Horn were initially encouraged by the British, in order to counter the French. Italy's defeat by the Ethiopians at the Battle of Adowa in 1896 did not deter its efforts to dominate the coastal areas of Eritrea and southeastern Somalia. Later Italy, under Benito Mussolini, briefly (1936–1942) occupied Ethiopia itself.

During the cold war, great-power competition for control of the Red Sea and the Gulf of Aden, which are strategically located near the oil fields of the Middle East as well as along the course of Suez shipping, continued between the United States and the Soviet Union. Local events sometimes led to shifts in alignments. Before 1977, for instance, the United States was closely allied with Ethiopia and the Soviet Union with Somalia. However, in 1977–1978 Ethiopia, having come under a self-proclaimed Marxist-Leninist government, allied itself with the Soviet Union, receiving in return the support of Cuban troops and billions of dollars' worth of socialist-bloc military aid, on loan, for use in its battles against Eritrean and Somali rebels. The latter group, living in Ethiopia's Ogaden region, were seeking to become part of a greater Somalia. In this irredentist adventure they had the direct support of invading Somalia troops. Although the United States refused to counter the Soviets by in turn backing the irredentists, it subsequently established relations with the Somali government at a level that allowed it virtually to take over the former Soviet military facility at Berbera.

Discord and Drought

The countries of the Horn, unlike the East African states farther south or the island states, are alienated from one another, and there are no prospects for a regional community among them in the foreseeable future. Although the end of the cold war has greatly reduced superpower competition, local animosities continue to wreak havoc in the region. Today the Horn is bound together and torn apart by its millions of refugees, who continue to flee civil wars in all four of the horn's states. Over the past 2 decades Ethiopia, Somalia, and the Sudan have suffered under vicious authoritarian regimes, which engaged in genocide against dissident segments of their populations. Although the old regimes have recently been overthrown in Ethiopia and Somalia, peace has yet to come to either society. Djibouti, long a regional enclave of tranquillity, is now also being undermined by political violence. The horrible effects of these wars have been magnified by recurrent droughts. Hundreds of thousands of people have starved to death in the past decade, while many more have only survived because of international aid efforts.

Ethiopians leave their homes for Djibouti, Somalia, and the Sudan for relief from war and famine. Sudanese and Somali flee to Ethiopia for the same reasons. Today every

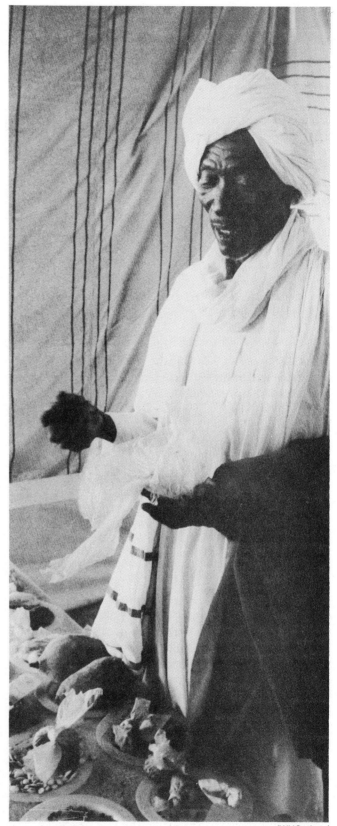

(WHO photo)

East African peoples, especially along the coast, blend heritages from Asia, the Middle East, and Africa.

EAST AFRICA

The peoples of Kenya, Tanzania, and Uganda as well as Burundi and Rwanda have underlying connections rooted in the past. The kingdoms of the Lakes region of Uganda, Rwanda, and Burundi, though they have been politically superseded in the postcolonial era, have left their legacies. For example, myths about a heroic dynasty of rulers, the Chwezi, who ruled over an early Ugandan-based kingdom, are widespread. Archaeological evidence attests to the actual existence of the Chwezi, probably in the sixteenth century. Peoples in western Kenya and Tanzania, who have lived under less centralized systems of governance but nonetheless have rituals similar to those of the Ugandan kingdoms, also share the traditions of the Chwezi dynasty, which have become associated with a spirit cult.

The precolonial kingdoms of Rwanda and Burundi, both of which came under German and, later, Belgian control during the colonial era, were socially divided between a ruling warrior class, the Tutsi, and a much larger peasant class, the Hutu. Although both states are now independent republics, their societies remain bitterly divided along these ethnoclass lines. In Rwanda, the feudal hegemony of the Tutsi was overthrown, but it has been maintained in Burundi through a repressive police state, which in 1972 and 1988 resorted to the mass murder of Hutu. Both countries also share the burden of being predominantly agricultural countries with little land to support their large populations.

Kenya and Uganda were taken over by the British in the late nineteenth century, while Tanzania, originally conquered by Germany, became a British colony after World War I. In Kenya, the British encouraged the growth of a settler community. Although never much more than 1 percent of the colony's resident population, the settlers were given the best agricultural lands in the rich highlands region around Nairobi and, throughout most of the colonial era, were allowed to exert their political and economic hegemony over the local Africans. The settler populations in Tanzania and Uganda were smaller and less powerful. While the settler presence in Kenya led to land alienation and consequent immiseration for many Africans, it also fostered a fair amount of colonial investment in infrastructure. As a result, Kenya had a relatively sophisticated economy at the time of its independence, a fact that was to complicate proposals for its economic integration with Tanzania and Uganda.

During the 1950s the British established the East African Common Services Organization to promote greater economic cooperation among its Kenyan, Tanganyikan (Tanzanian), and Ugandan territories. By the early 1960s the links among the states were so close that President Julius Nyerere of Tanzania proposed that his country delay its independence until Kenya also gained its freedom, in hopes that the two countries would then join together. This did not occur.

(United Nations photo by Y. Müller)
Of the millions of refugees displaced by civil wars in Ethiopia, Somalia, and the Sudan, fully 60 percent are children.

country harbors not only refugees but also dissidents from neighboring lands and has a citizenry related to those who live in adjoining countries. Peoples such as the Afar minority in Djibouti often seek support from their kin in Ethiopia. Many Somali guerrilla groups have used Ethiopia as a base, while Somali factions have continued to give aid and comfort to Ethiopia's rebellious Ogaden population. Ethiopian factions allegedly continue to assist southern rebels against the government of the Sudan, which had long supported the Tigray and Eritrean rebel movements of northern Ethiopia.

At times the states of the region have reached agreements among themselves to curb their interference in one another's affairs. But they have made almost no progress in the more fundamental task of establishing internal peace, thus assuring that the region's violent downward spiral continues.

In 1967 the Common Services Organization was transformed by its three, now-independent, members into a full-fledged common market, known as the East African Community (EAC). The EAC collectively managed the railway system, development of harbors, and international air, postal, and telecommunication facilities. It also maintained a common currency, development bank, and other economic, cultural, and scientific services. Peoples moved freely across the borders of the three EAC states. However, the EAC soon began to unravel, as conflicts over its operations grew. It finally collapsed in 1977. The countries disputed the benefits of the association, which seemed to have been garnered primarily by Kenya. The ideologies and personalities of its leaders at the time—Nyerere, Jomo Kenyatta of Kenya, and Idi Amin of Uganda—differed greatly. Relations between Kenya and Tanzania deteriorated to the point that the border between them was closed for several years.

In 1983 Kenya, Tanzania, and Uganda agreed on the division of the assets of the old Community; Kenya experienced the largest losses. Tanzania and Kenya opened their borders and began rebuilding their relationship. The economic strains that all three countries face in their dealings with the world economy make clear the value of the defunct EAC. But political factors continue to complicate the quest for greater regional cooperation. Kenyatta was succeeded by his vice president, Daniel arap Moi, whose regime over the past decade has become increasingly repressive in the face of mounting opposition. Uganda still suffers from years of warfare and instability, the legacies of the brutal regimes of Amin and Milton Obote, whose second administration was overthrown in a 1985 coup. Uganda's current president, Yoweri Museveni, maintains an uneasy control over a country still plagued by violence. Although the governments of Kenya, Rwanda, the Sudan, Tanzania, and Zaire pledged in 1986 to prevent exiles from using asylum to destabilize their homelands, tensions in the region continue. Relations between Uganda and Kenya have been strained over allegations that each has harbored the other's dissidents. However, the two governments agreed to ease tensions after trade and transport disputes led to border clashes in 1987–1988.

A number of joint projects may contribute to the rebirth of some form of East African community. A Preferential Trade Area of 19 East and Southern African nations was established in 1981. Burundi, Rwanda, Tanzania, and Uganda are sharing in the construction of a hydroelectric project on the Kagera River. Uganda has established cooperative military links with both Kenya and Tanzania. The governments of Burundi, Rwanda, Tanzania, and Zaire have met to discuss security, trade, and cultural exchange in the region. Rwanda and Burundi are members of the Economic Community of Central African States, but their economic ties with East African states have led the UN Economic Commission on Africa, as well as other multinational organizations, to include them in the East African regional groupings.

There has been much talk of improving relations. "Think East Africa," *The Standard* of Kenya wrote, commenting on the cultural links that existed in the area before colonialism. Salim Salim, a Tanzanian statesman, noted, "You can choose a friend, but you cannot choose a brother. . . . In this case Kenyans and Ugandans are our brothers."

THE ISLANDS

The Comoros, Madagascar, Mauritius, and the Seychelles each has its own special characteristics. Nonetheless, they share some common traits. All four island nations have been strongly influenced historically by contacts with Asia as well as with mainland Africa and Europe. Madagascar and the Comoros have populations that originated in Indonesia and the Middle East as well as in Africa; the Malagasey language is related to Indonesian Malay. The citizens of Mauritius and the Seychelles are of European as well as African and Asian origin.

All four island groups have also been influenced by France. Mauritius and the Seychelles were not permanently inhabited until the 1770s, when French settlers arrived with their African slaves. The British subsequently took control of these two island groups and, during the 1830s, abolished slavery. Thereafter the British encouraged migration from South Asia and, to a lesser extent, from China to make up for labor shortages on the islands' plantations. Local French-based creoles remain the major languages on the islands.

In 1978 all the islands, along with opposition groups from the French possession of Réunion, formed the Indian Ocean Commission. Originally a body with a socialist orientation, the commission campaigned for the independence of Réunion and the return of the island of Diego Garcia by Britain to Mauritius, as well as the dismantling of the U.S. naval base located there. By the end of the 1980s, however, the export-oriented growth of Mauritius and the continuing prosperity of the Seychelles' tourist-based economy were helping to push all four nations toward a greater emphasis on market economics in their multilateral, as well as internal, policy initiatives. Madagascar and the Comoros have recently offered investment incentives for Mauritius-based private firms. Mauritians have also played prominent roles in the development of tourism in the Comoros.

In addition to their growing economic ties, the Comoros and Mauritius, and to a somewhat lesser extent Madagascar and the Seychelles, have developed economic ties with South Africa, despite their opposition to its racist policies. Should South Africa succeed in dismantling apartheid, its links with the islands would undoubtedly grow and become less ambiguous.

Burundi (Republic of Burundi)

GEOGRAPHY

Area in Square Kilometers (Miles): 27,834 (10,759) (about the size of Maryland)
Capital (Population): Bujumbura (272,000)
Climate: tropical to temperate

PEOPLE

Population
Total: 5,931,000
Annual Growth Rate: 3.2%
Rural/Urban Population Ratio: 94/6
Languages: official: Kirundi, French; others spoken: Kiswahili, others

Health
Life Expectancy at Birth: 50 years (male); 54 years (female)
Infant Mortality Rate (Ratio): 109/1,000
Average Caloric Intake: 99% of FAO minimum
Physicians Available (Ratio): 1/31,713

Religion(s)
67% Christian; 32% traditional indigenous; 1% Muslim

THE BUTLER-OBIOZOR REPORT

"The Burundian Affair," a report drafted by William Butler and George Obiozor and issued in 1972 by the International Commission of Jurists and the International League of the Rights of Man, was an early indictment of the role of the Burundi government in its ongoing atrocities against the Hutu population. It concluded that the government was guilty of genocidal acts, defining genocide as "a denial of the right of existence of entire human groups" and/or the "systematic killing of people based on their race or ethnic origin, creed or color." The report served as the major evidence for introducing the situation in Burundi as a case for consideration by the UN Commission on Human Rights. However, the Commission dropped the case in 1975, without having undertaken any action.

Education
Adult Literacy Rate: 50%

COMMUNICATION
Telephones: 8,000
Newspapers: 1 daily

TRANSPORTATION
Highways—Kilometers (Miles): 5,900 (3,658)

Railroads—Kilometers (Miles): none
Usable Airports: 7

GOVERNMENT
Type: republic
Independence Date: July 1, 1962
Head of State: President (Major) Pierre Buyoya
Political Parties: National Party of Unity and Progress
Suffrage: universal over 19

MILITARY
Number of Armed Forces: 7,200
Military Expenditures (% of Central Government Expenditures): 3.1%
Current Hostilities: none

ECONOMY
Currency ($ U.S. Equivalent): 197.8 Burundi francs = $1
Per Capita Income/GDP: $200/$1.1 billion
Inflation Rate: 11.7%
Natural Resources: nickel; uranium; cobalt; copper; platinum
Agriculture: coffee; tea; cotton; food crops
Industry: light consumer goods; beer brewing

FOREIGN TRADE
Exports: $81 million
Imports: $197 million

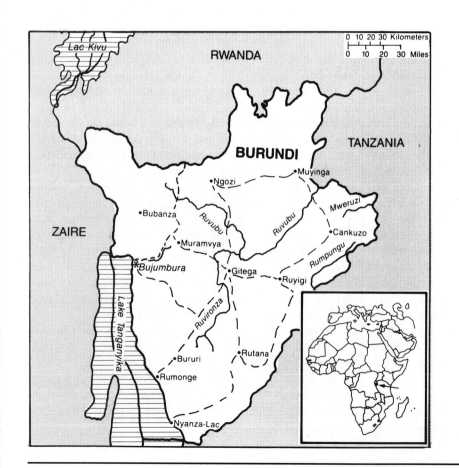

BURUNDI

Burundi is a small, beautiful, and crowded country whose people are deeply divided. In the recent past those in power have resorted to mass murder to maintain a system of domination based on ethnicity and class. In 1972 and again in 1988, tens of thousands of people perished in the killing fields of Burundi. The general response of the outside world, both official and nonofficial, was opportunistic support for the oppressor and near total indifference to the plight of the oppressed.

A DIVIDED SOCIETY

Burundi's population is ethnosocially divided into three distinctive groups. At the bottom of the social hierarchy are the Twa, commonly stereotyped as "pygmies." Believed to be the earliest inhabitants of the country, the Twa today account for only about 1 percent of the population. The largest group, constituting 83 percent of the population, are the Hutu, who largely subsist as peasant farmers. The dominant group are the Tutsi, who comprise some 15 percent of the population. Among the Tutsi, who are subdivided into clans, status has long been associated with cattle-keeping. Leading Tutsi continue to form an aristocratic ruling class over the whole of Burundi society. Until 1966 the leader of Burundi's Tutsi aristocracy was the Mwami, or king.

The history of the Burundi kingdom goes back at least as far as the sixteenth century. By the late nineteenth century, when the kingdom was incorporated into German East Africa, the Tutsi had subordinated the Hutu, who became clients of local Tutsi aristocrats, herding their cattle and rendering other services. The Germans and subsequently the Belgians, who assumed paramount authority over the kingdom after World War I, were content to rule through Burundi's established social hierarchy. But many Hutu as well as Tutsi were educated by Christian missionaries.

NATIONALIST MOVEMENT

In the late 1950s the Tutsi Prince Louis Rwagazore tried to accommodate Hutu as well as Tutsi aspirations by establishing a nationalist reform movement known as the Union for National Progress (UPRONA). Rwagazore was assassinated before independence, but UPRONA led the country to independence in 1962, with King Mwambutsa IV retaining considerable power as head of state. The Tutsi elite remained dominant, but the UPRONA cabinets contained representation from the two major groups. This attempt to balance the interests of the Tutsi and Hutu broke down in 1965, when Hutu politicians within both UPRONA and the rival People's Party won 80 percent of the vote and the majority of the seats in both houses of the bicameral Legislature. In response, the king abolished the Legislature before it could convene. A group of Hutu army officers then attempted to overthrow the government. Mwambutsa fled the country, but the revolt was crushed in a countercoup by Tutsi officers, led by Michel Micombero.

In the aftermath of the uprising Micombero took power amidst a campaign of reprisals in which some 5,000 Hutu are estimated to have been killed. He deposed Mwambutsa's son, Ntare V, from kingship and set up a "Government of Public Safety,"

(United Nations photo by Derek Lovejoy)

Burundi remains one of the poorest countries in the world, and any money saved in energy needs is an essential goal. By using solar energy to preserve the fish caught in Lake Tanganyika, these fish-drying nets are an important element in assuring an inexpensive food product.

| Mwami Ntare Rugaamba expands the boundaries of the Nkoma kingdom **1795** | The area is mandated to Belgium by the League of Nations after the Germans lose World War I **1919** | Prince Louis Rwagasore leads a nationalist movement and founds Uprona **1958–1961** | Rwagasore is assassinated; independence is achieved **1961** | A failed coup results in purges of Hutu in the government and army; Michel Micombero seizes power **1965–1966** | Government forces massacre 200,000 Hutu **1972** | Jean-Baptiste Bagaza comes to power in a military coup **1976** | **1980s–1990s** |

Bagaza is overthrown in a military coup led by Pierre Buyoyo

Ethnic violence leaves 5,000 to 25,000 dead, mostly Hutu

Buyoyo proposes a restricted form of multiparty democracy

which set about purging Hutu members from the government and the army. Political struggle involved interclan competition among the Tutsi as well as the maintenance of their hegemony over the Hutu.

CHALLENGES TO THE GOVERNMENT

Under Micombero, Burundi continued to be marred by interethnic violence, occasional coup attempts, and promonarchist agitation. A major purge of influential Hutu was carried out in 1969. In 1972 Ntare V was lured to Uganda by Idi Amin, who turned him over to Micombero. Ntare was placed under arrest upon his arrival and was subsequently murdered by his guards.

A declaration of martial law then set off an explosion of violence. In response to an alleged uprising involving the deaths of up to 2,000 Tutsi, government supporters began to massacre large numbers of Hutu. Educated Hutu were especially targeted in a 2-month campaign of selective genocide, which is generally estimated to have claimed some 200,000 victims (estimates range from 80,000 to 500,000 deaths for the entire period, with additional atrocities being reported through 1973). More than 100,000 Hutu fled to Uganda, Rwanda, Zaire, and Tanzania; most still reside in those countries. Among the governments of the world, only Tanzania and Rwanda showed any deep concern for the course of events. China, France, and Libya used the crisis to upgrade significantly their military aid to the Burundi regime.

In 1974 Micombero formally transformed Burundi into a single-party state

under UPRONA. Although Micombero was replaced 2 years later, in a military coup by Colonel Jean-Baptiste Bagaza, power remained effectively in the hands of members of the Tutsi elite who controlled UPRONA, the civil service, and the army. In 1985 Bagaza widened existing state persecution of Seventh Day Adventists and Jehovah's Witnesses to include the Catholic Church, to which two-thirds of Burundi's population belong, suspecting it of fostering seditious—that is, pro-Hutu—sympathies. (The overthrow of Bagaza by Pierre Buyoyo, in a 1987 military coup, led to a lifting of the anti-Catholic campaign.)

Ethnic violence erupted again in 1988. Apparently some Tutsi were killed by Hutu in northern Burundi, in response to rumors of another massacre of Hutu. In retaliation, the army massacred between 5,000 and 25,000 Hutu. Another 60,000 Hutu took temporary refuge in Rwanda, while more than 100,000 were left homeless. In 1991 the revolutionary Party for the Liberation of the Hutu People, or Palipehutu, launched its own attacks on Tutsi soldiers and civilians, leading to further killing on all sides.

LAND ISSUES

Burundi remains one of the poorest countries in the world, despite its rich volcanic soils and generous international development assistance (it has consistently been one of the highest per capita aid recipients on the continent). In addition to the dislocations caused by cycles of interethnic violence, the nation's development prospects are seriously compromised by geo-

graphic isolation and population pressure on the land. About 25 percent of Burundi is under cultivation, generally by individual farmers trying to subsist on plots of usually no more than 3 acres. Another 60 percent of the country is devoted to pasture for mostly Tutsi livestock. Hutu farmers continue to be tied by patron–client relationship to Tutsi overlords. In recent years the government has tied its rural development efforts to an unpopular villagization scheme.

The land issue has complicated President Buyoyo's attempts to reach some kind of accommodation with Hutu aspirations. He has cautiously increased Hutu participation in his government. (The current cabinet boasts a Hutu majority, but ultimate power remains in the hands of the all-Tutsi Military Committee of National Salvation.) After initially rejecting the idea, Buyoyo agreed to the restoration of multiparty politics in 1991. A new Constitution was approved in March 1992, which will allow competition between approved, ethnically balanced, parties in 1993 elections. With some Tutsi hard-liners as well as prominent Hutu rejecting this initiative, the chances of Buyoyo achieving a genuine national reconciliation are uncertain.

DEVELOPMENT

Burundi's sources of wealth are limited. There is no active development of mineral resources, although sources of nickel have been located and may be mined soon. There is little industry, and the coffee crop, which contributes 75% to 90% of export earnings, has declined.

FREEDOM

Burundi remains a repressive military regime dominated by Tutsi. Recent reforms have, however, allowed for a greater degree of internal openness than in the past.

HEALTH/WELFARE

Much of the educational system has been in private hands, especially the Roman Catholic Church. Burundi lost many educated and trained personnel because of the Hutu massacres in the 1970s and '80s.

ACHIEVEMENTS

Burundi's plans for future economic development show consideration of regional possibilities. Sugar, cheese, cooking oil, and soft-drink and beer factories are expected to benefit from demand throughout the area. Transportation will be improved through regional cooperation with East African rail networks.

Comoros (Comoros Federal Islamic Republic)

GEOGRAPHY

Area in Square Kilometers (Miles): 2,171 (838) (about the size of Delaware)
Capital (Population): Moroni (28,000)
Climate: tropical; marine

PEOPLE

Population
Total: 477,000
Annual Growth Rate: 3.5%
Rural/Urban Population Ratio: n/a
Languages: official: Shaafi-Islam; others spoken: Swahili, French, Arabic

Health
Life Expectancy at Birth: 54 years (male); 59 years (female)
Infant Mortality Rate (Ratio): 87/1,000
Average Caloric Intake: 102% of FAO minimum
Physicians Available (Ratio): 1/23,009

Religion(s)
86% Sunni Muslim; 14% Roman Catholic

Education
Adult Literacy Rate: 48%

COMMUNICATION
Telephones: 1,800
Newspapers: n/a

MAYOTTE ISLAND

In 1974, when the other Comoran islands voted overwhelmingly for independence, Mayotte opted to remain French, by a two-to-one margin. Since then the French have continued to administer the island, with the support of the local population—more than 95 percent of whom have, in recent years, voted in favor of becoming an overseas department of France. Unlike the other islands, Mayotte is predominantly Christian. Historically, it has been greatly influenced by Malagasy and French culture. Comoran claims to the island are supported by the Organization of African Unity, and in the United Nations only France voted against a resolution calling for its inclusion in the Comoros. Despite the location of its naval base on the island, France may be eager to withdraw from Mayotte, but is reluctant to do so against the wishes of Mayotte and domestic opinion.

TRANSPORTATION
Highways—Kilometers (Miles): 750 (465)
Railroads—Kilometers (Miles): none
Usable Airports: 4

GOVERNMENT
Type: Islamic republic
Independence Date: July 6, 1975
Head of State: President Said Mohamed Djohar
Political Parties: Comoran Union for Progress; National Union for Democracy
Suffrage: universal at 18

MILITARY
Number of Armed Forces: 900
Military Expenditures (% of Central Government Expenditures): 3%
Current Hostilities: none

ECONOMY
Currency ($ U.S. Equivalent): 279 Comoran francs = $1
Per Capita Income/GDP: $530/$252 million
Inflation Rate: 2.9%
Natural Resources: agricultural land
Agriculture: perfume essences; copra; coconuts; cloves; vanilla; cinnamon; yams; rice
Industry: perfume distillation; tourism

FOREIGN TRADE
Exports: $16 million
Imports: $41 million

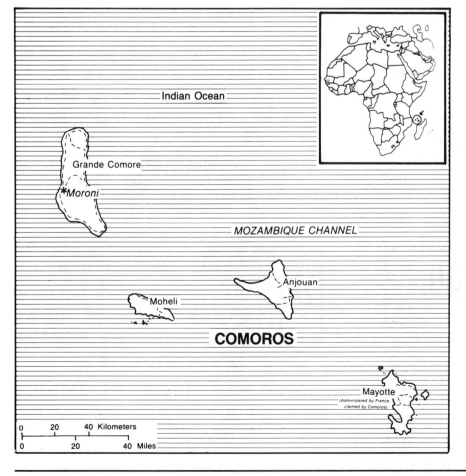

Various groups
settle in the
islands, which
become part of a
Swahili trading
network
1500s

French rule over
Mayotte is
established
1843

A French
protectorate over
the remaining
Comoro islands
is proclaimed
1886

The islands are
ruled as part of
the French
colony of
Madagascar
1914–1946

Independence is
followed by a
mercenary coup,
which installs Ali
Soilih
1975

Ali Soilih is
overthrown by
mercenaries;
Ahmed Abdullah
is restored
1978

1980s–1990s

Abdullah
proclaims a one-
party state; real
power remains in
the hands of
mercenary leader
Bob Denard

Comoros is
linked to the
South African
supply of
Renamo rebels
in Mozambique

The
assassination of
Abdullah leads to
the removal of
Denard and to
multiparty
elections

COMOROS

At the time of its unilateral declaration of independence from France, in 1975, the Comoros was listed by the United Nations as one of the world's least developed nations. The succeeding years have not been especially kind to the Comorans; their lives have been made even more difficult by natural disaster, eccentric and authoritarian leadership, and external intervention. However, the recent restoration of a multiparty democratic process on the islands has raised hopes for a better future.

HISTORY AND POLITICS

The Comoros archipelago was populated by a number of Indian Ocean peoples, who—by the time of the arrival of the first Europeans during the early sixteenth century—had combined to form the predominantly Muslim, Swahili-speaking society found on the islands today. In 1886 the French, who had already colonized the neighboring island of Mayotte, proclaimed a protectorate over the three main islands that currently constitute the Comoros Federal Islamic Republic. Throughout the colonial period the Comoros were especially valued by the French, for strategic reasons. A local elite of large landholders prospered from the production of cash crops, particularly vanilla, ylang-ylang, and cloves. Life for most Comorans, however, remained one of extreme poverty.

A month after independence the first Comoran government, led by Ahmed Abdullah Abderemane, was overthrown by mercenaries who installed Ali Soilih in power. The new leader promised a socialist transformation of the nation and began to implement land reform. But Soilih rapidly lost support both at home and abroad: under his leadership, gangs of undisciplined youths terrorized society, while the basic institutions and services of government all but disappeared. In 1977 the situation was made even worse by a major volcanic eruption, which left 20,000 people homeless, and by the arrival of 16,000 Comoran refugees following massacres in neighboring Madagascar.

In 1978 another band of mercenaries—this time led by the notorious Bob Denard, whose previous exploits in Zaire, Togo, and elsewhere had made his name infamous throughout Africa—overthrew Soilih and restored Abdullah to power. Denard, however, remained the true power behind the throne.

The Denard–Abdullah government enjoyed close ties with influential right-wing elements in France and South Africa. Connections with Pretoria were manifested through the use of the Comoros as a major conduit for South African supplies to the Renamo rebels in Mozambique. Economic ties with South Africa, especially in tourism and sanctions busting, also grew. Besides France, the government also established good relations with Saudi Arabia, Kuwait, and other conservative Arab governments, while attracting significant additional aid from the international donor agencies.

In 1982 the country legally became a one-party state. Attempted coups in 1985 and 1987 aggravated political tensions. Many Comorans particularly resented the overbearing influence of Denard and his men. By November 1989 this group included President Abdullah himself. With the personal backing of President François Mitterand of France and the newly installed President F. W. de Klerk of South Africa, Abdullah moved to replace Denard's mercenaries with a French-approved security unit. But before this move could be implemented, Abdullah was murdered following a meeting with Denard.

The head of the Supreme Court, Said Mohamed Djohar, was appointed as interim president in the wake of the assassination. After a period of some confusion, during which popular protests against Denard swelled, Djohar quietly sought French intervention to oust the mercenaries. With both Paris and Pretoria united against him, Denard agreed to relinquish power, in exchange for safe passage to South Africa.

The removal of Denard and temporary stationing of a French peacekeeping force was accompanied by the lifting of political restrictions in preparation for presidential elections. In March 1990 a runoff resulted in a 55 percent electoral mandate for Djohar. In 1992 a National Conference was convened amidst calls for a greater degree of federal autonomy for the islands of Anjouan and Moheli.

DEVELOPMENT

One of the major projects undertaken since independence has been the ongoing expansion of the port at Mutsamundu, which will allow large ships to visit the islands. Vessels of up to 25,000 tons can now dock at the harbor.

FREEDOM

Freedom was abridged after independence under both Ahmed Abdullah and Ali Soilih. The government elected in 1990 has ended abuses.

HEALTH/WELFARE

Health statistics improved during the 1980s. A recent World Health Organization survey estimated that 10% of children ages 3 to 6 years are seriously malnourished and another 37% are moderately malnourished.

ACHIEVEMENTS

Since ancient times the Comoros has been famous for its high-quality ylang-ylang essence, which is used in the manufacture of the finest of perfumes.

Djibouti (Republic of Djibouti)

GEOGRAPHY

Area in Square Kilometers (Miles):
23,200 (8,960) (about the size of New Hampshire)
Capital (Population): Djibouti (412,000) (est.)
Climate: arid to semiarid

PEOPLE

Population

Total: 550,000 (est.)
Annual Growth Rate: 2.6%
Rural/Urban Population Ratio: 25/75
Languages: official: French, Arabic; others spoken: Somali, Saho-Afar

Health

Life Expectancy at Birth: 46 years (male); 50 years (female)
Infant Mortality Rate (Ratio): 117/1,000
Average Caloric Intake: n/a
Physicians Available (Ratio): 1/3,790

Religion(s)

94% Muslim; 4% Christian

Education

Adult Literacy Rate: 48%

DJIBOUTI POLITICS

Local politics in Djibouti has been dominated since independence by the aging President Hassan Gouled Aptidon. No clear-cut successor currently exists. Since the creation of a one-party state, a number of underground movements have emerged in opposition to the continued domination of the president's Popular Rally for Progress. One group that surfaced in 1989, the Movement for Unity and Democracy, poses a potential threat through its alleged association with the Somali National Movement, which is currently waging an armed struggle in northern Somalia against that country's government. In 1990 two other dissident movements, one Afar-oriented and the other Issa-oriented, combined forces as the Union of Movements for Democracy. Another important nonparty political force is the Ugaz, or sultan, of the Issa Somali, who is based in the Ethiopian town of Dire Diwa. It is said that the Ugaz and his council confirmed Gouled Aptidon as the political leader of Djibouti's Issa in 1975. Other Afar and Somali clan heads, living on both sides of the border, are also influential.

COMMUNICATION

Telephones: 7,300
Newspapers: 3 weeklies

TRANSPORTATION

Highways—Kilometers (Miles): 2,906 (1,801)

Railroads—Kilometers (Miles): 97 (60)
Usable Airports: 10

GOVERNMENT

Type: republic
Independence Date: June 27, 1977
Head of State: President Hassan Gouled Aptidon
Political Parties: People's Progress Assembly
Suffrage: universal for adults

MILITARY

Number of Armed Forces: 2,770
Military Expenditures (% of Central Government Expenditures): n/a
Current Hostilities: none

ECONOMY

Currency ($ U.S. Equivalent): 177.1 Djibouti francs = $1
Per Capita Income/GDP: $1,030/$357 million
Inflation Rate: 3.7%
Natural Resources: none
Agriculture: goats; sheep; camels; cattle; coffee
Industry: port and maritime support; construction

FOREIGN TRADE

Exports: $190 million
Imports: $311 million

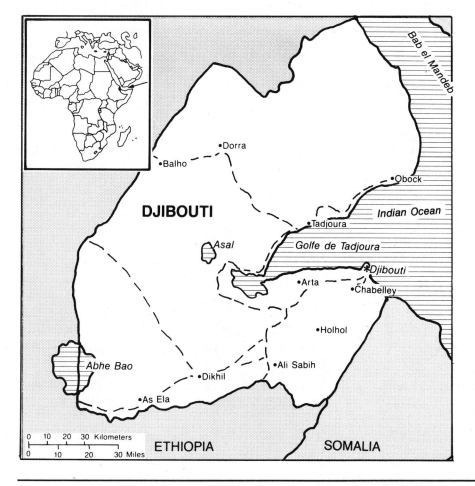

France buys the
port of Obock
1862

France acquires
the port of
Djibouti
1888

The Addis
Ababa-Djibouti
Railroad is
completed
1917

Djibouti votes to
remain part of
Overseas France
1958

Independence;
the Ogaden War
1977

1980s–1990s

The underground
Union of
Movements for
Democracy is
formed as an
interethnic
antigovernment
coalition

Djibouti's ties to
Iraq lead to
tensions with
France and
conservative
Arab donors
during the
Persian Gulf War

Famine and
warfare in
Somalia and
Ethiopia lead to a
massive flow of
refugees to
Djibouti

DJIBOUTI

Djibouti, long a small zone of peace in the troubled Horn of Africa, recently has appeared to be drifting toward full-scale civil war. Growing opposition to long-serving President Hassan Gouled Aptidon's mildly authoritarian regime has increasingly manifested itself as an ethnic power struggle between Afar- and Somali-speaking groups, with Afar rebels holding northern areas of the country. This conflict has overshadowed cautious government consideration of constitutional reform away from the current single-party state.

Since achieving its independence from France, in 1977, Djibouti has had to strike a cautious balance between the competing interests of its larger neighbors, Ethiopia and Somalia. Most of the nation's population are divided between Afar and Somali speakers. In the past Somalia has claimed ownership of the territory, based on the numerical preponderance of Djibouti's Somali population, variously estimated at 50 to 70 percent. However, local Somali as well as Afars also have strong ties to communities in Ethiopia. Furthermore, Djibouti's location at the crossroads of Africa and Eurasia has made it a focus of continuing strategic concern to nonregional powers, particularly France, which maintains a large military presence in the country.

Modern Djibouti's colonial genesis is a product of mid-nineteenth-century European rivalry over control of the Red Sea. In 1862 France occupied the town of Obock, across the harbor from Djibouti city. This move was taken in anticipation of the 1869 opening of the Suez Canal, which transformed the Red Sea into the major shipping route between Asia, East Africa, and Europe. In 1888 Paris, having acquired

Djibouti city and its hinterland, proclaimed its authority over French Somaliland, the modern territory of Djibouti.

The independence of France's other mainland African colonies by 1960, along with the formation in that year of the Somali Democratic Republic, led to local agitation for an end to French rule. To counter the effects of Somali nationalism, the French began to favor the Afar minority in local politics and employment. Charles de Gaulle's 1966 visit was accompanied by large, mainly Somali, proindependence demonstrations. As a result, a referendum on the question of independence was held. Colonial control of voter registration assured a predominantly Afar electorate who, motivated by fears of Somali domination, opted for continued French rule. French Somaliland was then transformed into the self-governing Territory of Afars and Issas. The name reflected a continuing colonial policy of divide and rule; members of the Issas clan constituted just over half of the area's Somali speakers.

By the 1970s neither Ethiopia nor France was opposed to Djibouti's independence but, for their own strategic reasons, both backed the Afar community in its desire for assurances that the territory would not be incorporated into Somalia. An ethnic power-sharing arrangement was established that in effect acknowledged local Somali preponderance. The empowerment of local Somali, in particular the Issa, was accompanied by diminished pan-Somali sentiment. On June 27, 1977, the Republic of Djibouti became independent. French troops remained in the country, supposedly as a guarantee of its sovereignty. Internally, political power was divided by means of ethnically balanced cabinets, with the prime minister always being an Afar. The presi-

dency has remained in the hands of Aptidon, an Issa-Somali.

War broke out between Ethiopia and Somalia a few months after Djibouti's independence. Djibouti remained neutral, but ethnic tensions mounted with the arrival of Somali refugees. In 1981 the Afar-dominated Djiboutian Popular Movement was outlawed. The Issa-dominated Popular Rally for Progress (RPP) then became the country's sole legal party.

Refugees have poured into Djibouti for years now, fleeing the continuing conflicts and famines in both Ethiopia and Somalia. The influx has swelled the country's population by about one-third to an estimated 550,000. This increase has deepened Djibouti's dependence on external food aid (the country has never been able to feed itself in modern times): at least 95 percent of current food requirements are imported.

Traffic in the port of Djibouti has been increasing, in large part due to its status as a safe haven from regional conflicts. With financial assistance from Arab donors, a phased project to rehabilitate and upgrade maritime facilities is being implemented. Another promising project has been the development of the Assal Geothermal Field, which has the potential of making the country an exporter of electricity. Massive unemployment among Djibouti's largely urbanized population, however, remains a critical problem.

DEVELOPMENT

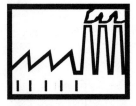

Recent discoveries of gas reserves
could result in a surplus for export.
A number of small-scale irrigation
schemes have been established.
There is also a growing, though
still quite small, fishing industry.

FREEDOM

Freedom of speech, association,
and other rights are restricted by
Djibouti's single-party system.
However, the government has not
been associated with acts of
arbitrary repression or gross
violations of human rights.

HEALTH/WELFARE

Progress has been made in
reducing infant mortality, but health
services are strained. School
enrollment has expanded by nearly
one-third since 1987.

ACHIEVEMENTS

Besides feeding its own refugees,
the government of Djibouti has
played a major role in assisting
international efforts to relieve the
recurrent famines in Ethiopia,
Somalia, and Sudan.

Ethiopia (People's Democratic Republic of Ethiopia)

GEOGRAPHY

Area in Square Kilometers (Miles):
1,221,900 (471,800) (about four-fifths
the size of Alaska)
Capital (Population): Addis Ababa
(1,412,000)
Climate: temperate in highlands; arid
to semiarid in lowlands

PEOPLE

Population

Total: 53,100,000
Annual Growth Rate: 3.1%
Rural/Urban Population Ratio: 87/13
Languages: official: Amharic; others
spoken: Tigrinya, Oromo, Somali,
Arabic, Italian, English, others

Health

Life Expectancy at Birth: 50 years
(male); 53 years (female)
Infant Mortality Rate (Ratio):
114/1,000
Average Caloric Intake: 78% of FAO
minimum in areas not severely
affected by drought
Physicians Available (Ratio): 1/95,856

Religion(s)

40%–45% Muslim; 35%–40%
Ethiopian Orthodox Christian;
15%–25% traditional indigenous and
others

Education

Adult Literacy Rate: 62%

KING LABILA

During the twelfth and thirteenth centuries the Ethiopian state, having
declined since the days of the Axumites, was revived under the Zagwe
dynasty. The best known of the Zagwe rulers is Labila, who is remembered for his architectural legacy. At his capital of Roha, he built
an impressive palace which survives to this day. More famous, however, are the churches which he had carved out of solid rock, supposedly to fulfill a heavenly injunction which he received in his sleep.
The churches survive as centers of worship, attracting pilgrims from
throughout Coptic Ethiopia.

COMMUNICATION

Telephones: 162,000
Newspapers: 3

TRANSPORTATION

Highways—Kilometers (Miles): 44,300
(27,466)
Railroads—Kilometers (Miles): 988
(612)
Usable Airports: 111

GOVERNMENT

Type: provisional military government
Independence Date: none
Head of State: Interim President
Meles Zenawi
Political Parties: Workers' Party of
Ethiopia; dozens of opposition groups
Suffrage: universal over 18

MILITARY

Number of Armed Forces: 131,500
*Military Expenditures (% of Central
Government Expenditures):* 8.5%
Current Hostilities: border disputes
with Somalia

ECONOMY

Currency ($ U.S. Equivalent): 2.05
birrs = $1
Per Capita Income/GDP: $130/$6.9
billion
Inflation Rate: 8%
Natural Resources: potash; salt; gold;
copper; platinum
Agriculture: cereals; coffee; pulses; oil
seeds; livestock
Industry: processed food; textiles;
cement; building materials;
hydroelectric power

FOREIGN TRADE

Exports: $429 million
Imports: $1.1 billion

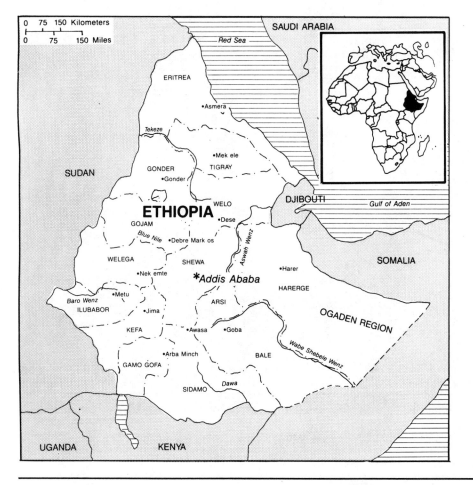

ETHIOPIA (including ERITREA)

In May 1991 Ethiopia was liberated from 17 years of repressive rule under its once revolutionary Provisional Military Administrative Council, popularly known as the *Dergue* (Amharic for "Committee"). The Dergue's overthrow was the culmination of decades of armed resistance by a variety of groups, some of which coalesced in the later stages of the conflict as the Ethiopian People's Revolutionary Democratic Front (EPRDF). Today the EPRDF is the predominant armed faction in a new caretaker government, but its hold is challenged by both armed and unarmed opposition movements. Time will tell whether Ethiopia's second revolution since 1974 will succeed where its first one failed. Over the past 2 decades political instability helped to reduce Ethiopia from a developing breadbasket to a famine-ridden basket case. Growing interethnic conflict among the increasingly desperate population, many of whom have long had better access to arms and ammunition than to food and medicine, could lead to the state's ultimate disintegration. Such is the contemporary crisis that afflicts one of humankind's most ancient civilizations.

Local history is established from the time of the Axum empire, which prospered from the first century. During the fourth century the Axumite court adopted the Coptic Christian faith, which has remained central to the culture of Ethiopia's highland region. The church still uses the Geez, the ancient Axumite tongue from which the modern Ethiopian languages of Amharic and Tigrinya are derived, in its services.

From the eighth century much of the area surrounding the highlands fell under Muslim control, all but cutting off the Copts from their European coreligionists. Today most Muslim Ethiopians live in the lowlands. For many centuries Ethiopia's history was characterized by struggles among the groups inhabiting these two regions and religions. At times a powerful ruler would succeed in making himself truly "King of Kings," by uniting the Christian highlands and expanding into the lowlands. At other times the mountains would be divided into weak polities, which were vulnerable to the raids of both Muslim and non-Muslim lowlanders.

Modern Ethiopian history began in the nineteenth century, when the highlands became politically reunited by a series of kings, culminating in Menilik II, who built up power by importing European armaments. Once the Coptic core of his kingdom was intact, Menilik began to spread his authority across the lowlands, thus uniting most of contemporary Ethiopia. In 1889 and 1896 Menilik also defeated invading Italian armies, thus preserving his empire's independence during the European partition of Africa.

From 1916 to 1974 Ethiopia was ruled by Ras Tafari (from which is derived the term Rasta, or Rastafarian), who, in 1930, was crowned Emperor Haile Selassie. The late Selassie remains a controversial figure. For many decades he was seen both at home and abroad as a reformer who was modernizing his state. In 1936, after his kingdom had been occupied by Benito Mussolini, he made a memorable speech before the League of Nations, warning the world of the price it would inevitably pay for appeasing fascist aggression. At the time many African-Americans and Africans outside of Ethiopia saw Selassie as a great hero in the struggle of black peoples everywhere for dignity and empowerment. Selassie returned to his thrown in 1941 and thereafter served as an elder statesman to the African nationalists of the 1950s and 1960s. However, by the latter decade his own domestic authority was being increasingly questioned.

In his later years Selassie could not, or would not, move against the forces that were undermining his empire. Despite its trappings of progress, the Ethiopian state remained quasi-feudal in character. Much of the best lands were controlled by the nobility and church, whose leading members lived privileged lives at the expense of the peasantry. Many educated people grew disenchanted with what they perceived as a reactionary monarchy and social order. Urban workers resented being paid low wages by often foreign owners. Within the junior ranks of the army and civil service, there was also great dissatisfaction with the way in which their superiors were able to siphon off state revenues for personal enrichment. But the empire's greatest weakness was its inability to accommodate the aspirations of the various ethnic, regional, and sectarian groupings living within its borders.

Ethiopia is a multiethnic state. Since the time of Menilik the dominant group has been the Coptic Amhara speakers, whose preeminence has been resented by their Tigrinya coreligionists as well as by predominantly non-Coptic groups such as the

(United Nations photo by Muldoon)

From 1916 to 1974 Ethiopia was ruled by Haile SeLassie, also known as Ras Tafari (from which today's term Rastafarian is derived). He is pictured above, on the left, shaking hands with the infamous Idi Amin, past president of Uganda.

Afars, Gurages, Oromo, and Somali. In recent years movements fighting for ethno-regional autonomy have emerged among the Tigrinya of Tigray, the Oromo, and, to a lesser extent, the Afars, while many Somali in Ethiopia's Ogaden region have long struggled for union with neighboring Somalia. Somali irredentism led to open warfare between the two principal Horn of Africa states in 1963–1964 and again in 1977–1978.

The northern coastal province of Eritrea has been a special case. From the late nineteenth century until World War II, it was an Italian colony. After the war it was federated with Selassie's empire. After a questionable 1962 referendum, Eritrea's autonomy was abrogated and the territory was annexed as an integral part of Ethiopia. Thereafter a local independence movement, largely united as the Eritrean People's Liberation Front (EPLF), has waged an armed struggle. Eritrea is itself a multi-ethnic and bisectarian area, with the greatest support for the EPLF coming from local Tigrinya, while the central government has maintained some support among the southern Afars.

REVOLUTION AND REPRESSION

In 1974 Haile Selassie was overthrown by the military, after months of mounting unrest throughout the country. A major factor in triggering the coup was the government's inaction in 1972–1974, when famine swept across the northern provinces, claiming 200,000 lives. Some accused the Amhara government of using the famine as a way of weakening the predominantly Tigrinya areas of the empire. Others simply saw the tragedy as proof of the venal incompetence of Selassie's administration.

The overthrow of the old order was welcomed by most Ethiopians. Unfortunately, what began as a promising revolutionary transformation quickly degenerated into a repressive dictatorship, which pushed the nation into chronic instability and distress. By the end of 1974, after the first in a series of bloody purges within its ranks, the Dergue had embraced Marxism as its guiding philosophy. Revolutionary measures followed. Companies and lands were nationalized. Students were sent into the countryside to assist in land reforms and to teach literacy. Peasants and workers were organized into cooperative associations, called *kebeles*. Initial steps were also taken to end Amhara hegemony within the state.

Progressive aspects of the Ethiopian revolution were offset by the murderous nature of the regime. Power struggles within the Dergue, as well as its deter-

mination to eliminate all alternatives to its authority, contributed to periods of "red terror," during which thousands of supporters of the revolution as well as those associated with the old regime were killed. By 1977 the Dergue itself had been transformed from a collective decision-making body to a small clique loyal to Colonel Mengistu Haile Mariam, who became a presidential dictator.

For years Mengistu sought to legitimize his rule through a commitment to Marxist-Leninism. He formally presided over a Commission for Organizing the Party of the Working People of Ethiopia, which, in 1984, announced the formation of a single-party state, led by the new Workers' Party. But real power remained in the hands of Mengistu's Dergue.

CIVIL WAR

From 1974 to 1991 Ethiopia suffered through civil war. In the face of oppressive central authority, ethnic-based resistance movements became increasingly effective in their struggles throughout much of the country. In the late 1970s the Mengistu regime began to receive massive military aid from the Soviet bloc in its campaigns against the Eritreans and Somali. Some 17,000 Cuban troops and thousands of other military personnel from the Warsaw Pact countries allowed the government temporarily to gain the upper hand in the fighting. For its own part, the Ethiopian Army grew to more 300,000 men under arms at any given time, the largest military force on the continent. Throughout the

(United Nations photo by John Isaac)

Ethiopia was in a civil war from 1974 to 1991. This continuous fighting displaced millions of people. The problem of this forced migration was compounded by drought and starvation. The drought victims, pictured above, gathered at one of the many relief camps.

Emperor
Tewodros begins
the conquest and
development of
modern Ethiopia
1855

Ethiopia defeats
Italian invaders
at the Battle of
Adowa
1896

Fascist Italy
invades Ethiopia
and rules until
1941
1936

The Eritrean
liberation struggle
begins
1961

Famines in
Tigray and Welo
provinces result
in up to 200,000
deaths
1972–1973

Emperor Haile
Selassie is
overthrown; the
PMAC is
established
1974

Diplomatic
realignment and
a new arms
agreement with
the Soviet Union
1977

1980s–1990s

Massive famine,
resulting from
drought and
warfare

Tigray and
Eritrean struggles
intensify; many
are killed; cities
are captured and
recaptured

The Mengistu
regime is
overthrown by
ERPDF rebels

1980s military expenditure claimed more than half of the national budget.

Despite the massive domestic and international commitment on the side of the Mengistu regime, the rebels gradually gained the upper hand. Before 1991 almost all of northern Eritrea, except its besieged capital city of Asmara, had fallen to the EPLF, which has built up its own powerful arsenal, largely from captured government equipment. Local rebels had also liberated the province of Tigray and, as part of the EPRDF coalition, pushed south toward the capital city of Addis Ababa. In the south, independent Oromo and Somali rebels challenged government authority. There was also resistance to Mengistu from within the ranks of the national army. A major rebellion against his authority in 1989 was crushed, devastating military moral in the process. The regime was further undermined by the withdrawal of remaining Cuban and former Socialist bloc support.

Ethiopians have paid a terrible price for their nation's conflicts. Tens of thousands have been killed in combat, while many more have died from the side effects of war. In 1984–1985 the conscience of much of the world was moved by the images of mass starvation in the northern war zone. At the time the global media and concerned groups like Band Aid paid relatively little attention to the nonenvironmental factors that contributed to the crisis. Up to 1 million lives were lost before adequate relief supplies reached the famine areas. Although drought and other environmental factors, such as soil erosion, contributed to the catastrophe, the fact that people continued to starve despite the availability of

international relief can only be attributed to the use of food as a weapon of war.

There were other political constraints on local crop production. Having seized the lands of the old ruling class, the Mengistu regime, in accordance with its Marxist-Leninist precepts, invested most of its agricultural inputs in large state farms, whose productivity was abysmal. Peasant production also fell in nondrought areas, due to insecure tenure, poor producer prices, lack of credit, and an absence of consumer goods. Ethiopia's rural areas were further disrupted by the government's heavy-handed villagization and relocation schemes. In 1984–1985 thousands died when the government moved some 600,000 northerners to what were supposedly more fertile regions in the southwest. Many considered the scheme to be part of the central government's war effort against local communities resistant to its authority. By the same token, villagization has long been associated with counterinsurgency efforts; concentrated settlements allow occupying armies to exert greater control over potentially hostile populations.

UNCERTAIN PROSPECTS

Unfortunately, the 1991 collapse of the Dergue has not ended the long suffering of the Ethiopian people. Meles Zenawi, head of the EPRDF caretaker administration, has promised to bring about national reconciliation by transforming Ethiopia into a democratic, multiethnic federation. But while some critics see this as a recipe for the breakup of the state, others fear that the EPRDF, especially former Stalinists within

the Tigray People's Liberation Front (TPLF), which has been its predominant element, will try to create its own monopoly of power. In 1992 there were outbreaks of fighting between the EPRDF and the forces of its former rebel partner the Oromo Liberation Front (OLF), which claims to represent Ethiopia's largest ethnic group. The OLF was prominent among those who boycotted the June 1992 elections, which were further marred by allegations of widespread vote-rigging and intimidation on behalf of the EPRDF. The EPRDF claimed an overwhelming electoral mandate, but its hold over the country is being increasingly contested by the OLF and others.

The status of Eritrea is another source of continuing controversy. Since the fall of Mengistu the entire territory has come under the effective control of the EPLF, which is governing it as an independent entity. A formal referendum on the question of full independence is promised for 1993. Few doubt that the Eritreans, themselves, are overwhelmingly in favor of becoming a separate nation. For its part, the EPRDF government lacks the desire, much less the means, to block Eritrea's succession. But many Ethiopians remain bitterly opposed to the development, while, even if the peaceful divorce of Eritrea goes ahead, its future relationship with Ethiopia will remain a source of contention.

DEVELOPMENT

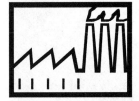

There has been some progress in the country's industrial sector over the past decade, after sharp decline during the 1970s. Soviet bloc investment resulted in the establishment of new enterprises in such areas as cement, textiles, and farm machinery.

FREEDOM

The new ERPDF has promised to respect the human rights and democratic desires of Ethiopians, but its critics accuse it of harboring authoritarian tendencies. For the moment at least, basic freedoms are compromised by armed clashes between pro- and antigovernment forces, coupled with escalating banditry in many areas.

HEALTH/WELFARE

Progress in spreading literacy during the 1970s has been undermined by the dislocations of the 1980s. By 1991 Ethiopia had some 500 government soldiers for every teacher.

ACHIEVEMENTS

With a history spanning 2 millennia, the cultural achievements of Ethiopia are vast. Addis Ababa is the headquarters of the Organization of African Unity. Ethiopia's Kefe Province is the home of the coffee plant, from whence it takes its name.

Kenya (Republic of Kenya)

GEOGRAPHY

Area in Square Kilometers (Miles):
582,488 (224,900) (slightly smaller than Texas)
Capital (Population): Nairobi (959,000)
Climate: tropical to arid

PEOPLE

Population
Total: 25,242,000
Annual Growth Rate: 3.6%
Rural/Urban Population Ratio: 76/24
Languages: official: English, Kiswahili; others spoken: Kikuyu Luo, Kamba, Kipsigi, Maasai, Luhya, Gusii, Nandi, Somali, others

Health
Life Expectancy at Birth: 60 years (male); 64 years (female)
Infant Mortality Rate (Ratio): 69/1,000
Average Caloric Intake: 88% of FAO minimum
Physicians Available (Ratio): 1/7,728

Religion(s)
38% Protestant; 28% traditional indigenous; 28% Catholic; 6% Muslim

Education
Adult Literacy Rate: 69%

COMMUNICATION
Telephones: 260,000
Newspapers: 4

CULTURE AND POLITICS

In the past as well as today, cultural activities in Kenya have been closely connected to politics, encouraging nationalism and revealing inequities. Events occurring at the Kamriitha Community Educational and Cultural Center illustrate this statement. The center was built by community efforts in Kamriithu, a Kenyan town of 10,000 people. The villagers developed a program at the center and operated it. The literacy committee organized a literacy study course, and the community organized dramas that illustrated the people's experiences and ideas. Ngugi wa Thiong'o was commissioned to write the first play—about the townspeople's own lives—and they discussed and criticized it as well as performed it in a theater that the town had built. The production was highly successful, but was banned, because the authorities felt it encouraged class conflict. Its potential for organizing peasants was a threat to the government. Ngugi was detained (he is now in exile). Later the center was closed and the theater destroyed.

TRANSPORTATION
Highways—Kilometers (Miles): 64,590 (40,046)
Railroads—Kilometers (Miles): 2,040 (1,265)
Usable Airports: 213

GOVERNMENT
Type: republic; one-party state
Independence Date: December 12, 1963
Head of State: President Daniel arap Moi
Political Parties: Kenya African National Union
Suffrage: universal over 18

MILITARY
Number of Armed Forces: 23,600
Military Expenditures (% of Central Government Expenditures): 1%
Current Hostilities: border conflict with Uganda

ECONOMY
Currency ($ U.S. Equivalent): 29.37 Kenya shillings = $1
Per Capita Income/GDP: $380/$9.6 billion
Inflation Rate: 11%
Natural Resources: wildlife; land; soda ash; wattle
Agriculture: corn; wheat; rice; sugarcane; coffee; tea; sisal; pyrethrum; livestock
Industry: petroleum products; cement; beer; automobile assembly; food processing; tourism

FOREIGN TRADE
Exports: $1.1 billion
Imports: $2.4 billion

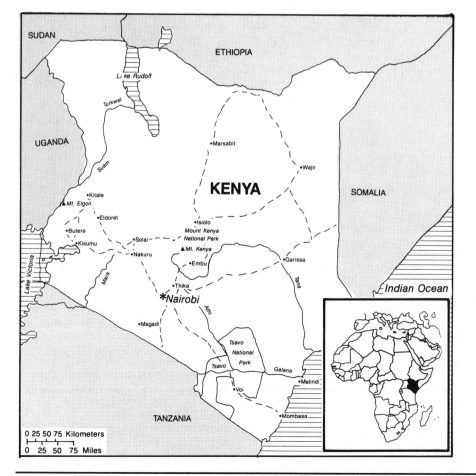

KENYA

Years of economic growth have helped to make Kenya the commercial center of East Africa. As changes in the global economy encourage greater transnational integration, some observers expect that this geographically diverse country will prosper while playing an increasingly critical role in the future development of its region. But, despite 3 decades of postindependence progress, most Kenyans remain the impoverished citizens of a state struggling to develop as a nation.

HISTORY

In the precolonial past, Kenyan communities belonged to relatively small-scale, but economically interlinked, societies. Predominantly pastoral groups, such as the Maasai and Turkana, exchanged cattle for the crops of the Kalinjin, Kamba, Kikuyu, Luo, and others. Swahili city-states developed on the coast. During the nineteenth century, caravans of Arab as well as Swahili traders stimulated economic and political changes. However, the outsiders who had the greatest modern impact on the Kenyan interior were the European settlers, who began to arrive in the first decade of the twentieth century.

By the 1930s much of the temperate hill country around Nairobi, Kenya's capital city, had become the "White Highlands." More than 6 million acres of land—Maasai pasture and Kikuyu and Kamba farms—were stolen. African communities were often removed to increasingly overcrowded reserves. Laborers, mostly Kikuyu migrants from the reserves, worked for the new European owners, sometimes on lands that they had once farmed for themselves.

By the 1950s African grievances had been heightened by increased European settlement and the growing removal of African "squatters" from their estates. There were also growing class and ideological differences among Africans, which led to tensions between educated Christians with middle-class aspirations and displaced members of the rural underclass. Many members of the latter group, in particular, began to mobilize themselves in largely Kikuyu oathing societies, which coalesced into the Mau Mau movement.

Armed resistance by Mau Mau guerrillas began in 1951, with isolated attacks on white settlers. In response, the British proclaimed a state of emergency, which lasted for 10 years. Without any outside support, the Mau Mau held out for years by making effective use of the highland forests as sanctuaries. Nonetheless, by 1955 the uprising had largely been crushed.

Although the name Mau Mau became for many outsiders synonymous with antiwhite terrorism, only 32 European civilians actually lost their lives during the rebellion. By contrast, at least 13,000 Kikuyu were killed. Another 80,000 Africans were detained by the colonial authorities, and more than 1 million persons were resettled in controlled villages. While the Mau Mau were overwhelmed by often ruthless counterinsurgency measures, they achieved an important victory: the British realized that the preservation of Kenya as a white-settler-dominated colony was militarily and politically untenable.

In the aftermath of the emergency the person who emerged as the charismatic leader of Kenya's nationalist movement was Jomo Kenyatta, who had been detained and accused by the British—without any evidence—of leading the resistance movement. At independence, in 1963, he became the president, remaining in office until his death in 1978.

To many, the situation in Kenya under Kenyatta looked promising. His government encouraged racial harmony, and the slogan *Harambee* (Swahili for "Pull together") became a call for people of all ethnic groups and races to work together for development. Land reforms provided plots to 1.5 million farmers. A policy of Africanization created business opportunities for local entrepreneurs, and industry grew. Although the ruling Kenya African National Union (KANU) was supposedly guided by a policy of "African Socialism," the nation was seen by many as a showcase of capitalist development.

POLITICAL DEVELOPMENT

Kenyatta's Kenya quickly became a de facto one-party state. The principal opposition party, the Kenyan People's Union (KPU), was suppressed and its leadership harassed and jailed. KANU became the focus of political competition, and voters were allowed to remove sitting MPs, including cabinet ministers. But politics was marred by intimidation and violence, including the assassinations of prominent critics within government, most notably Economic Development Minister Tom Mboya, in 1969, and Foreign Affairs Minister J. M. Kariuki, in 1975. Constraints on freedom of association were justified in the interest of preventing ethnic conflict—much of the KPU support came from the Luo group. However, ethnicity has always been important in shaping intraparty struggles within KANU itself.

Under Daniel arap Moi, Kenyatta's successor, the political climate grew steadily more repressive. In 1982 his government was badly shaken by a failed coup attempt, in which about 250 persons died and approximately 1,500 others were detained. The old Air Force was disbanded and the university, whose students came out in support of the coup-makers, was temporarily closed.

In the aftermath of the coup all parties other than KANU were formally outlawed. Moi followed this step up by declaring, in 1986, that KANU was above the government, the Parliament, and the judiciary. Press restrictions, detentions, and blatant acts of intimidation became common. Those MPs brave enough to be critical of Moi's imperial presidency were removed from KANU and thus Parliament. Political tensions were blamed on the local agents of an ever-growing list of outside forces, including Christian missionaries and Muslim fundamentalists, foreign academics and the news media, and Libyan and U.S. meddlers.

A number of underground opposition groups emerged during the mid-1980s, most notably the socialist-oriented Mwakenya movement, whose ranks include such prominent exiles as the writer Ngugi wa Thiong'o. In 1987 many of these groups came together to form the United Movement for Democracy, or UMOJA (Swahili for "unity"). But in the immediate aftermath of the 1989 KANU elections, which in many areas were blatantly rigged, Moi's grip on power appeared strong.

But the early months of 1990 witnessed an upsurge in antigovernment unrest. In February the suspicious murder of Foreign Minister Robert Ouko touched off rioting in Nairobi and his home city of Kisumu. Another riot occurred when squatters were forcibly evicted from the Nairobi shantytown of Muoroto. Growing calls for the restoration of multiparty democracy fueled a cycle of unrest and repression. The detention in July of two ex-cabinet ministers, Kenneth Matiba and Charles Rubia, for their part in the democracy agitation sparked nationwide rioting, which left at least 28 people dead and 1,000 arrested. Opposition movements, most notably the Forum for the Restoration of Democracy (FORD), began to emerge in defiance of the government's ban on their activities. Moi became increasingly isolated as a number of his ministers deserted him.

Under mounting external pressure from Western donor countries, which in the aftermath of the cold war became increasingly willing to link their foreign aid and loans to "good governance," as well as from his internal opponents, Moi, in December 1991, finally agreed to the legalization of opposition parties. Unfortunately, this move has failed to diffuse Kenya's

The British East
African
Protectorate is
proclaimed
1895

British colonists
begin to settle in
the Highlands
area
1900–1910

Mau Mau, a
predominately
Kikuyu
movement,
resists colonial
rule
1952

Kenya gains
independence
under the
leadership of
Jomo Kenyatta
1963

Tom Mboya, a
leading trade
unionist and
government
minister, is
assassinated
1969

Daniel arap Moi
becomes
president upon
the death of
Kenyatta
1978

1980s–1990s

A coup attempt
by members of
the Kenyan Air
Force is crushed;
political
repression grows

Prodemocracy
agitation leads to
a return of
multiparty politics

An upsurge in
interethnic
violence in the
Rift Valley
threatens
democratic
transition

increasingly violent political, social, and ethnic tensions.

Continued police harassment of the opposition has triggered renewed rioting throughout the country. There has also been a rise in interethnic clashes in both the rural and urban areas, which many, even within KANU, attribute to government incitement. In the Rift Valley, armed members of Moi's own Kalinjin grouping have attacked other groups for supposedly settling on their land. Hundreds have been killed and thousands injured and displaced in the worst violence since the Mau Mau era. There are signs of a growing splintering of the opposition as well as the government along ethnic lines. Whether the promised, but as yet unscheduled, multiparty elections will diffuse or deepen the current crisis is unclear. Some fear a coup by the security establishment, whose upper echelons are predominantly Kalinjin.

Kenyan politics reflects class as well as ethnic divisions. The top 10 percent of the population own an estimated 40 percent of the wealth, while the bottom 30 percent own only 10 percent. Past economic growth has failed to alleviate poverty. While Kenya's relatively large middle class has grown resentful of increased repression and the evident corruption at the very top, it is also fearful about perceived anarchy from below.

ECONOMIC DEVELOPMENT

Although its rate of growth declined during much of the 1980s, the Kenyan economy has, until the current crisis, consistently expanded since independence. Kenya is the most industrialized country of East Africa. Manufacturing, which accounts for 13 percent of the gross domestic product, is concentrated in import substitution and the processing of domestic products. Foreign capital has played an important role in industrial development, but the largest share of investment has come from the government and the local private sector. Policymakers see a need to move toward more export-oriented industries, but global competition and the economic balkanization of the potential East African market are major constraints.

The bulk of Kenya's foreign-exchange earnings has come from agriculture. A wide variety of cash crops are exported, including coffee, cotton, horticulture, pyrethrum, sisal, sugar, tobacco, and tea. This diversity has buffered the nation's economy to some degree from the uncertainties associated with single-commodity dependence. While large plantations, now often owned by wealthy Kenyans, have survived from the colonial era, much of the commercial production is carried out by small landholders.

Tourism has accounted for about 20 percent of Kenya's foreign-exchange earnings, but its immediate prospects are not good. The sector has suffered from a combination of increased competition from other African destinations, widely publicized attacks on visitors, the current political unrest, fears about AIDS, and a declining wildlife population.

Another major challenge to Kenya's well-being has been its rapidly expanding population. Although there are some hopeful signs that women are beginning to plan for fewer children than in the past, the nation has been plagued with one of the highest population growth rates in the world, 3.6 percent per annum. More than half of all Kenyans are under age 15. Only about 20 percent of the countryside is arable. As a consequence, pressure on these lands is enormous (and aggravated by the continued existence of large estates). It will be difficult to create nonagricultural employment for the burgeoning rural-turned-urban work force, even in the context of democratic stability and renewed economic growth.

DEVELOPMENT

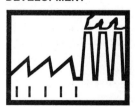

To counteract stagnating tourist revenues, the Kenyan government has placed itself at the forefront of the movement to ban ivory trading. Besides reducing the elephant population, poachers in Kenya have threatened tourist traffic by creating lawless conditions in their areas of operation.

FREEDOM

The restoration of multiparty democracy has allowed for more open debate. The news media has become increasingly diverse and critical in its outlook. But government harassment of the opposition continues amidst growing political violence.

HEALTH/WELFARE

Kenya's social infrastructure has recently been burdened by the influx of some 300,000 refugees from the neighboring, strife-torn states of Ethiopia, Somalia, and the Sudan. In addition to mounting relief efforts to feed and settle the new arrivals, the government has had to combat growing lawlessness in its border regions as some armed foreigners turn to banditry.

ACHIEVEMENTS

Kenya annually devotes about half of its government expenditures to education. Most Kenyan students can now expect 12 years of schooling. Tertiary education is also expanding.

Madagascar (Democratic Republic of Madagascar)

GEOGRAPHY

Area in Square Kilometers (Miles):
587,041 (226,658) (slightly smaller than Texas)
Capital (Population): Antananarivo (802,000)
Climate: tropical and moderate

PEOPLE

Population
Total: 12,185,000
Annual Growth Rate: 3.2%
Rural/Urban Population Ratio: 75/25
Languages: official: Malagasy; others spoken: French, others

Health
Life Expectancy at Birth: 51 years (male); 54 years (female)
Infant Mortality Rate (Ratio): 95/1,000
Average Caloric Intake: 111% of FAO minimum
Physicians Available (Ratio): 1/9,780

Religion(s)
52% traditional indigenous; 41% Christian; 7% Muslim

Education
Adult Literacy Rate: 80%

MALAGASY POETS

What invisible rat
comes from the walls of night
gnaws at the milky cake of the moon?

Thus begins one of the poems of Jean-Joseph Rabearivelo (1901–1937), one of Madagascar's greatest twentieth-century poets. Like the poets who followed him, such as Jean Jacques Rebemananjara and Jacques Flavien Ranaivo, Rabearivelo wrote in French and was deeply affected by French poets, literature, and culture. Yet all of these poets were attached to local Malagasy forms and rhythms and were inspired by the *hainteny* form, which was so characteristic of the popular songs of the island. Several of the poems of Rabearivelo and Ranaivo are reprinted in *A Book of African Verse*, edited by J. Reed and C. Wake (London, 1964).

COMMUNICATION
Telephones: 38,200
Newspapers: 7

TRANSPORTATION
Highways—Kilometers (Miles): 40,000 (24,800)
Railroads—Kilometers (Miles): 1,020 (632)
Usable Airports: 115

GOVERNMENT
Type: republic; authority held by Supreme Revolutionary Council
Independence Date: June 26, 1960
Head of State: the interim government is headed by Albert Zafy
Political Parties: Advance Guard of Malagasy Revolution; Congress Party for Malagasy Independence; Movement for National Unity; Malagasy Christian Democratic Union; Militants for the Establishment of a Proletarian Regime; National Movement for Independence of Madagascar; others
Suffrage: universal over 18

MILITARY
Number of Armed Forces: 20,800
Military Expenditures (% of Central Government Expenditures): 2.2%
Current Hostilities: none

ECONOMY
Currency ($ U.S. Equivalent): 1,785 Malagasy francs = $1
Per Capita Income/GDP: $200/$2.4 billion
Inflation Rate: 12%
Natural Resources: graphite; chrome; coal; bauxite; ilmenite; tar sands; semiprecious stones; timber; mica; nickel
Agriculture: rice; livestock; coffee; vanilla; sugar; cloves; cotton; sisal; peanuts; tobacco
Industry: food processing; textiles; mining; paper; petroleum refining; automobile assembly; construction; cement; farming

FOREIGN TRADE
Exports: $290 million
Imports: $436 million

MADAGASCAR

Madagascar has been called "the smallest continent"; indeed, many geologists believe that it once formed the core of a larger landmass, whose other principal remnants are the Indian subcontinent and Australia. The world's fourth-largest island remains a world unto itself in other ways. Botanists and zoologists know it as the home of flora and fauna not found elsewhere. The island's culture is also distinctive. The Malagasy language, which with dialectical variations is spoken throughout the island, is related to the Malay tongues of Indonesia. But despite their geographic separation and Asiatic roots, the Malagasy are conscious of their African identity.

While the early history of Madagascar is the subject of much scholarly debate, it is clear that by the year A.D. 500 the island was being settled by Malay-speaking peoples who may have migrated via the East African coast rather than directly from Indonesia. The cultural imprint of Southeast Asia is also evident in such things as local architecture, music, cosmology, and agricultural practices. African influences

are equally apparent. During the precolonial period the peoples of Madagascar were in communication with communities on the mainland. Waves of migration across the Mozambique channel contributed to the island's modern ethnic diversity.

During the early nineteenth century most of Madagascar was united by the rulers of Merina. In seeking to build up their realm and preserve the island's independence, the Merina kings and queens welcomed European, mostly English, missionaries, who helped introduce new ideas and technologies. As a result, many Malagasy, including the royalty, adopted Christianity. The kingdom had established diplomatic relations with the United States and various European powers and was thus a recognized member of the international community. Foreign businesspeople were attracted to invest in the island's growing economy, while the rapid spread of schools and medical services, increasingly staffed by Malagasy, brought profound changes to the society.

The Merina court hoped that their "Christian civilization" and modernizing army would deter European aggression.

But the French were determined to rule the island. An 1884–1885 Franco-Malagasy War ended in a stalemate, but an 1895 French invasion led to the kingdom's destruction. It was not an easy conquest. The Malagasy army, with its artillery and modern fortifications, held out for many months, but eventually it was outgunned by the invaders. French sovereignty was proclaimed in 1896, but "pacification" campaigns continued for another decade.

French rule reduced what had been a prospering state into a colonial backwater. The pace of development slowed as the local economy was restructured to serve the interests of French settlers, whose numbers had swelled to 60,000 by the time of World War II. Probably the most important French contribution to Madagascar was the encouragement their misrule gave to the growth of local nationalism. By the 1940s a strong sense of Malagasy identity had been forged through common hatred of the colonialists.

The local overthrow of Vichy power by the British in 1943 created an opening for Malagasy nationalists to organize themselves into mass parties, the most prominent

United Nations photo

Madagascar has a unique ethnic diversity, influenced by migrations from the African mainland and from Southeast Asia. The varied cultural makeup of the population can be seen on the faces of these school children.

Merina rulers gain sovereignty over other peoples of the island **1828**	The French complete the conquest of the island **1904**	A revolt is suppressed by the French, with great loss of life **1947–1948**	Independence from France; Philibert Tsiranana becomes the first president **1960**	A coup leads to the fall of the First Malagasy Republic **1972**	Didier Ratsiraka becomes president by military appointment **1975**

1980s–1990s

Dissidents organized as Kung Fu societies engage in violent clashes with AREMA supporters	Elections in 1989–1990 strengthen multiparty democracy; a short-lived coup attempt takes place	A mass-action campaign by opponents of Ratsiraka leads to the appointment of an interim government

of which was the Malagasy Movement for Democratic Renewal (MRDM). In 1946 the MRDM elected two overseas deputies to the French National Assembly, on the basis of its call for immediate independence. Paris responded by instructing its administrators to "fight the MRDM by every means." Arrests led to resistance. In March 1947 a general insurrection began. Peasant rebels, using whatever weapons they could find, liberated large areas from French control. French troops countered by destroying crops and blockading rebel areas, in an effort to starve the insurrectionists into surrendering. Thousands of Malagasy were massacred. By the end of the year the rebellion had been largely crushed, although a state of siege was maintained until 1956. No one knows for sure how many Malagasy lost their lives in the uprising, but contemporary estimates indicate about 90,000.

INDEPENDENCE AND REVOLUTION

Madagascar gained its independence in 1960. However, many viewed the new government, led by Philibert Tsiranana of the Social Democratic Party (PSD), as a vehicle for continuing French influence; memories of 1947 were still strong. Lack of economic and social reform led to a peasant uprising in 1971. This Maoist-inspired rebellion was suppressed, but the government was left weakened. In 1972 new unrest, this time spearheaded by students and workers in the towns, led to Tsiranana's overthrow by the military. After a period of confusion, radical forces

consolidated power around Lieutenant Commander Didier Ratsiraka, who assumed the presidency in 1975.

Under Ratsiraka, a new Constitution was adopted that allowed for a controlled process of multiparty competition in which all parties were grouped within the National Front. Within this framework, the largest party was Ratsiraka's Vanguard of the Malagasy Revolution (AREMA). Initially, all parties were expected to support the president's Charter of the Malagasy Revolution, which called for a Marxist-oriented socialist transformation. In accordance with the Charter, foreign-owned banks and financial institutions were nationalized. A series of state enterprises was also established to promote industrial development, but few proved viable.

Although 80 percent of the Malagasy were employed in agriculture, rural investment was modest. The government attempted to work through *fokonolas,* indigenous village management bodies. State farms and collectives were also established on land expropriated from French settlers. While these efforts led to some improvements, such as increased mechanization, state marketing monopolies and planning constraints contributed to shortfalls. Efforts to keep consumer prices low were blamed for a drop in rice production, the Malagasy staple, while cash-crop production, primarily coffee, vanilla, and cloves, suffered from falling world prices.

Since 1980 Madagascar has experienced great economic difficulties. Food shortages in the towns have led to rioting, while frustrated peasants have abandoned their fields. Although some critics have blamed

the government for not going far enough in promoting socialist change, it has increasingly abandoned its revolutionary ideology for market economics.

By 1990 there were signs of sustained economic growth, but this has since been thrown into jeopardy by political instability. In 1985, having abandoned attempts to make the National Front into a vehicle for a single-party state, Ratsiraka began to preside over a gradual loosening of his once-authoritarian control. In February 1990 most remaining restrictions on freedom of association were lifted. But by 1991 Ratsiraka's opponents, which now included a revived PSD, had become militant in their demands for his immediate removal and the establishment of a new Constitution. After 6 months of crippling strikes and mass action in the capital, Antananarivo, in November 1991 the president formally ceded many of his powers to a transitional government, headed by Albert Zafy. But hopes for rapid progress toward a new political order and elections have since been frustrated by political paralysis. With no administration fully in charge, there has been further economic decline.

DEVELOPMENT

In 1989 Export Processing Zones were established in order to attract foreign investment through tax and currency incentives. The government especially hopes to attract business from neighboring Mauritius, whose success with such zones has led to labor shortages and a shift toward more value-added production.

FREEDOM

Most legal restrictions on politics have been lifted. But a new, liberal constitutional order has not yet consolidated itself. The current erosion of central authority has been accompanied by an increase in political violence.

HEALTH/WELFARE

Primary-school enrollment is now universal. Thirty-six percent of the appropriate age group attend secondary school, while 5% ages 20–24 are in tertiary institutions. Malaria remains a major health challenge.

ACHIEVEMENTS

A new wildlife preserve will allow the unique animals of Madagascar to survive and develop. Sixty-six species of land animals are found nowhere else on earth, including the aye-aye, a nocturnal lemur which has bat ears, beaver teeth, and an elongated clawed finger, all of which serve the aye-aye in finding food.

Mauritius (Republic of Mauritius)

GEOGRAPHY

Area in Square Kilometers (Miles):
1,865 (720) (about the size of Rhode Island)
Capital (Population): Port Louis (155,000)
Climate: subtropical; marine

PEOPLE

Population
Total: 1,081,000
Annual Growth Rate: 0.8%
Rural/Urban Population Ratio: 59/41
Languages: official: English and French; others spoken: Creole, Hindi, Urdu

Health
Life Expectancy at Birth: 66 years (male); 74 years (female)
Infant Mortality Rate (Ratio): 20/1,000
Average Caloric Intake: 122% of FAO minimum
Physicians Available (Ratio): 1/1,900

Religion(s)
51% Hindu; 30% Christian; 16% Muslim; 3% others

DIEGO GARCIA

On the eve of the nation's independence, secret negotiations between British and Mauritian representatives resulted in Mauritius's sale of the island of Diego Garcia and neighboring atolls to the British, for the small sum of $7 million. The inhabitants of Diego Garcia were completely ignored; moreover, they were subsequently moved to Mauritius in order to make room for a U.S. military base (which increased the militarization of the Indian Ocean). The people of Mauritius, through their government, have demanded the island's return. Britain and the United States have offered more money to former inhabitants of the island and have agreed to their eventual return in an unspecified, but distant, future. The first National Congress of the ruling Militant Socialist Movement in 1986 called for the restoration of Mauritian sovereignty over Diego Garcia, "currently occupied by the American Army." Mauritian claims enjoy widespread support from the international community, but the issue remains unresolved.

Education
Adult Literacy Rate: 61%

COMMUNICATION
Telephones: 48,460
Newspapers: 7

TRANSPORTATION

Highways—Kilometers (Miles): 1,801 (1,116)
Railroads—Kilometers (Miles): none
Usable Airports: 4

GOVERNMENT

Type: parliamentary democracy
Independence Date: March 12, 1968
Head of State: Prime Minister Aneerood Jugnauth; President Veerasamy Ringadoo
Political Parties: Mauritian Labor Party; Mauritian Militant Movement; Militant Socialist Movement; Mauritian Labor Party; others
Suffrage: universal over 18

MILITARY

Number of Armed Forces: 6,580
Military Expenditures (% of Central Government Expenditures): 0.2%
Current Hostilities: none

ECONOMY

Currency ($ U.S. Equivalent): 15.77 rupees = $1
Per Capita Income/GDP: $2,600/$2.8 billion
Inflation Rate: 12.7%
Natural Resources: agricultural land
Agriculture: sugar; tea; tobacco
Industry: sugar production; consumer goods; labor-intensive goods for export; tourism

FOREIGN TRADE

Exports: $993 million
Imports: $1.2 billion

The Dutch claim, but abandon Mauritius
1600s

French settlers and slaves arrive
1722

The Treaty of Paris formally cedes Mauritius to the British
1814

Slavery is abolished; South Asians arrive
1835

Rioting on sugar estates shakes the political control of the Franco-Mauritian elite
1937

An expanded franchise allows greater democracy
1948

Independence
1968

Labor unrest leads to the detention of MMM leaders
1971

A cyclone destroys homes as well as much of the sugar crop
1979

1980s–1990s

Sir Aneerood Jugnauth replaces Sir Seewoosagur Ramgoolam as prime minister

Labor shortages encourage Mauritius to sign trade and investment agreements with Madagascar

France reaffirms European Community ties; Mauritius becomes a republic

MAURITIUS

Although it was not permanently settled until 1722, today Mauritius is the home of more than a million people of South Asian, Euro-African, Chinese, and other origins. Out of this human diversity has emerged a society that in recent decades has become a model of democratic stability and economic growth as well as ethnic, racial, and sectarian tolerance.

Mauritius was first settled by the French, some of whom achieved great wealth by setting up sugar plantations. From the beginning the plantations prospered through their exploitation of slave labor imported from the African mainland. Over time the European and African communities merged into a common Creole culture; that membership currently accounts for one-quarter of the Mauritian population. A small number also claim pure French descent. For decades members of this latter group have formed an economic and social elite. More than half the sugar acreage remains the property of 21 large Franco-Mauritian plantations, while the rest is divided among nearly 28,000 small landholdings. French cultural influence remains strong. Most of the newspapers on the island are in French, which shares official-language status with English. Most Mauritians also speak a local, French-influenced, Creole language. Most Creoles are Roman Catholics.

In 1810 Mauritius was occupied by the British, who ruled the island until 1968. (After years of debate, in 1991 the country cut its ties with Britain to become a republic.) When the British abolished slavery, in 1835, the plantation owners turned to large-scale use of indentured labor from what was then British India. Today nearly two-thirds of the population are of South Asian descent and have maintained their home languages. Most are Hindu, but a substantial minority are Muslim. Other faiths, such as Buddhism, are also represented.

Although the majority of Mauritians gained suffrage after World War II, the island has maintained an uninterrupted record of parliamentary rule since 1886. Ethnic divisions have long been important in shaping political allegiances. But ethnic constituency-building has not led, in recent years, to communal polarization. Other factors—such as class, ideology, and opportunism—have also been been influential. All postindependence governments have been multiethnic coalitions.

Prime Minister Sir Aneerood Jugnauth has been in power since 1982, at the head of constantly shifting coalitions. Although most major parties have embraced various shades of socialism, Mauritius's economic success in recent years has created a strong consensus in favor of market economics.

Until the 1970s the Mauritian economy was almost entirely dependent on sugar. While 45 percent of the island's total landmass continues to be planted with the crop, sugar now ranks below textiles and tourism in its contribution to export earnings and gross domestic product. The transformation of Mauritius over the past 2 decades from monocrop dependency into a fledgling industrial state with a strong service sector has made it one of the major economic success stories of the developing world. Mauritian growth has been built on a foundation of export-oriented manufacturing. At the core of the Mauritian take-off is its island-wide Export Processing Zone (EPZ), which has attracted industrial investment through a combination of low wages, tax breaks, and other financial incentives. Although most of the EPZ output has been in the field of cheap textiles, the economy has begun to diversify into more capital- and skill-intensive production. In 1989 Mauritius also entered the international financial-services market by launching Africa's first offshore banking center.

The success of the Mauritian economy is relative. Mauritius is still considered a middle-income country. In reality there are, as with most developing societies, great disparities in the distribution of wealth. Nonetheless, quality-of-life indicators confirm a rising standard of living for the population as a whole. While great progress has been made toward eliminating poverty and disease, concern has also grown about the environmental capacity of the small, crowded country to sustain its current rate of development. There is also a general recognition that Mauritian prosperity is, and will for the foreseeable future remain, extremely vulnerable to global market forces.

DEVELOPMENT

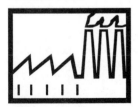

The success of the Mauritian EPZ along with the export-led growth of various Asian economies has encouraged a growing number of other African countries, such as Botswana, Cape Verde, and Madagascar, to launch their own export zones.

FREEDOM

Political pluralism and human rights are respected on Mauritius. The nation has more than 30 political parties, of which about a half-dozen are important at any given time. The Mauritian labor movement is one of the strongest in Africa.

HEALTH/WELFARE

Medical and most educational expenses are free. Food prices are heavily subsidized. Rising government deficits, however, threaten future social spending. Mauritius has a high life expectancy rate and a low infant mortality rate.

ACHIEVEMENTS

Perhaps Mauritius's most important modern achievement has been its successful efforts to reduce its birthrate. This has been brought about by government-backed family planning as well as by increased economic opportunities for women.

Rwanda (Republic of Rwanda)

GEOGRAPHY

Area in Square Kilometers (Miles): 26,338 (10,169) (about the size of Maryland)
Capital (Population): Kigali (300,000)
Climate: temperate

PEOPLE

Population
Total: 7,900,000
Annual Growth Rate: 3.8%
Rural/Urban Population Ratio: 92/8
Languages: official: Kinyarwanda; others spoken: French, Kiswahili

Health
Life Expectancy at Birth: 51 years (male); 54 years (female)
Infant Mortality Rate (Ratio): 110/1,000
Average Caloric Intake: 94% of FAO minimum
Physicians Available (Ratio): 1/33,090

Religion(s)
65% Roman Catholic; 25% traditional indigenous; 9% Protestant; 1% Muslim

Education
Adult Literacy Rate: 50%

RWANDA'S HISTORIANS

A number of specialists were attached to the ruling dynasty of the traditional kingdom of Rwanda, including several categories of official historians. Each group was responsible for preserving particular materials. Some were genealogists who told the lists of kings and queens; some told *ibisigo,* dynastic poems that glorified the rulers; and others preserved secrets of the dynasty. This traditional knowledge was passed down orally, since the language was not written. Particular families were responsible for passing this knowledge from one generation to another, it was memorized exactly. Such historical information is different from the written sources upon which Western historians have relied, but it is valid data that can be used in the reconstruction of Rwanda's past.

COMMUNICATION

Telephones: 6,600
Newspapers: 1

TRANSPORTATION

Highways—Kilometers (Miles): 4,885 (3,069)
Railroads—Kilometers (Miles): none
Usable Airports: 8

GOVERNMENT

Type: republic
Independence Date: July 1, 1962

Head of State: President (Major General) Juvenal Habyarimana
Political Parties: National Revolutionary Movement for Development; Liberal Party; Social Democratic Party; Democratic Republic Movement; Rwanda Patriotic Front; others
Suffrage: universal for adults

MILITARY

Number of Armed Forces: 5,200
Military Expenditures (% of Central Government Expenditures): 1.6%
Current Hostilities: civil war

ECONOMY

Currency ($ U.S. Equivalent): 125 Rwanda francs = $1
Per Capita Income/GDP: $310/$2.4 billion
Inflation Rate: 1%
Natural Resources: tungsten; tin; cassiterite
Agriculture: coffee; tea; pyrethrum; beans; potatoes
Industry: food processing; mining; light consumer goods

FOREIGN TRADE

Exports: $117 million
Imports: $293 million

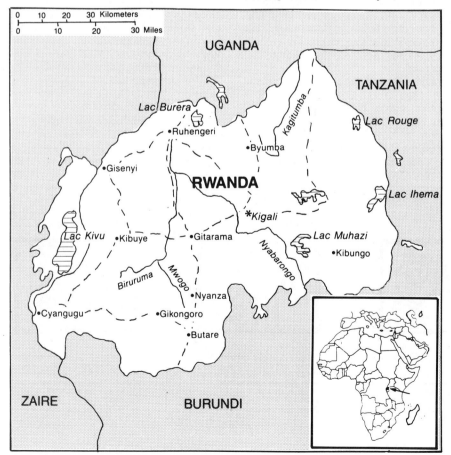

| Mwami Kigeri Rwabugiri expands and consolidates the kingdom 1860–1895 | Belgium rules Rwanda as a mandate of the League of Nations 1916 | The Hutu rebellion 1959 | Rwanda becomes independent; Gregoire Kayibana is president 1962 | Juvenal Habyarimana seizes power 1973 | The National Revolutionary Movement for Development is formed 1975 | A new Constitution is approved in a nationwide referendum; Habyarimana is reelected president 1978 | 1980s–1990s |

| Habyarimana agrees to a gradual transition to multipartyism | FPR rebels invade from Uganda; massacres of Tutsi by government forces are reported | French military "advisers" assist the government; the rebels agree to a ceasefire |

RWANDA

Since October 1990 Rwanda has been ravaged by civil war, following an invasion by Uganda-based exiles of the Rwanda Patriotic Front (FPR). Despite considerable military support from France, the authoritarian National Revolutionary Movement for Development (MRND) regime of President Juvenal Habyarimana has been unable to defeat the rebels. In 1992, amid other signs of discontent, Habyarimana formed a new multiparty government and began negotiations with the rebels in the hope of finding a political solution to the ongoing crisis. But the divisions within Rwandan society are deeply rooted, making any path to national reconciliation difficult.

In the beginning, according to an epic poem, the godlike ruler Kigwa fashioned a test to choose his successor. He gave each of his sons a bowl of milk to guard during the night. His son Gatwa drank the milk. Yahutu slept and spilled the milk. Only Gatutsi guarded it well. The myth justifies the old Rwandan social order, in which the Twa, commonly stereotyped as "pygmies" (1 percent of the population), were the outcasts, the Hutu (89 percent) servants, the Tutsi (10 percent) the aristocrats. Historically, Hutu serfs herded cattle and performed various other services for their Tutsi "protectors." At the top of the hierarchy was the Mwami, or king. Rwanda's feudal system survived into the colonial era. German and, later, Belgian administrators opted to rule through the existing order.

In the late 1950s, under United Nations pressure, Belgium began to devolve political power to Rwandans. The death of the Mwami in 1959 sparked bloody Hutu uprisings against the Tutsi aristocracy. Against this violent backdrop, preindependence elections were held in 1961, which resulted in a victory for the Hutu Emancipation Movement, better known as Parmehutu. Thus, at independence, in 1962, Rwanda's traditionally Tutsi-dominated society was suddenly under a Hutu-dominated government.

In 1963–1964 continued interethnic competition for power exploded into more violence, which resulted in the flight of tens of thousands, if not hundreds of thousands, of ethnic Tutsi to neighboring Burundi, Tanzania, and Uganda. Along with their descendants, this refugee population today numbers between 200,000 and 1 million. Successive Rwandan governments have barred their return, by questioning their citizenship, while also citing extreme land pressure (Rwanda is Africa's most densely populated country) as a barrier to their reabsorption. But the implied hope that the refugees would integrate into their host societies has failed to materialize. The current FPR rebels are mostly Tutsi exiles. They demand the repatriation of all Rwandan Tutsi.

Major General Juvenal Habyarimana, a Hutu from the north, seized power in a military coup in 1973. Two years later he institutionalized his still-army-dominated regime as a one-party state under the MRND, in the name of overcoming ethnic divisions. Yet hostility between the Hutu and Tutsi remained. A system of ethnic quotas was introduced that formally limited the remaining Tutsi minority to a maximum of 14 percent of the positions in schools and at the workplace. In reality, the Tutsi have often been allocated less.

In recent years there has been growing evidence that many Hutu as well as Tutsi have grown impatient with their government's corrupt authoritarianism. The international collapse of coffee prices, Rwanda's major export earner, since 1987 has led to an economic decline, fueling popular discontent. Even before the armed challenge of the FPR, the MRND had agreed to give up its monopoly of power, although this pledge was compromised by continued repression. Prominent among the new parties that have emerged are the Democratic Republic Movement (MDR), the Social Democrats (PSD), and the Liberals (PL). The PL has so far had the greatest success in attracting both Hutu and Tutsi support, while the MDR has been associated with southern regional resentment at the MRDN's supposed northern bias. A political breakthrough occurred in March 1992 with the formation of a transitional coalition government, headed by the MDR's Dismas Nsengiyaremye. Habyarimana remained as president.

DEVELOPMENT

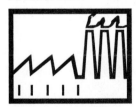

Hydroelectric stations meet much of the country's energy needs. Plans are being made to exploit methane gas reserves under Lake Kivu.

FREEDOM

The recent creation of a multiparty coalition government should assure continued liberalization in Rwanda. Independent periodicals and unions, as well as parties, are emerging. The security forces and MRDN militias have been accused of serious abuses.

HEALTH/WELFARE

The government recognizes that the high rate of population growth can eat up economic gains as well as increasing already severe pressures on land. A national population office was created, and resources committed to family planning were increased. Some question the reservation of large game reserves for European hunters when farmland is scarce.

ACHIEVEMENTS

Abbé Alexis Kagame, a Rwandan Roman Catholic churchman and scholar, has written studies of traditional Rwanda poetry and has written poetry about many of the traditions and rituals. Some of his works have been composed in Kinyarwanda, the official language of Rwanda, and translated into French. He has gained an international reputation among scholars.

Seychelles (Republic of the Seychelles)

GEOGRAPHY

Area in Square Kilometers (Miles): 435 (175) (about twice the size of Washington, D.C.)
Capital (Population): Port Victoria (23,000)
Climate: subtropical; marine

PEOPLE

Population
Total: 69,000
Annual Growth Rate: 0.9%
Rural/Urban Population Ratio: 50/50
Languages: official: English, French; other spoken: Creole

Health
Life Expectancy at Birth: 65 years (male); 75 years (female)
Infant Mortality Rate (Ratio): 15/1,000
Average Caloric Intake: n/a
Physicians Available (Ratio): 1/1,847

Religion(s)
98% Christian; 2% other

Education
Adult Literacy Rate: 58%

COCO DE MER

To botanists around the world, the Seychelles has long been famous as the home of the exotic coco de mer palm. The fruit of this tree, the *coco de mer,* or "sea coconut," is both the largest and heaviest of all seeds, taking 7 years to mature and weighing between 30 to 40 pounds. For centuries these nuts, which were carried by Indian Ocean currents to distant shores, were worth more than their weight in gold. Their sensual shape, like that of a female pelvis, made them highly valued as an aphrodisiac; indeed, ancient legend held that the coco de mer was the forbidden fruit of the biblical Garden óf Eden. The source of the nuts remained a mystery until 1768, when a Frenchman discovered the palms.

COMMUNICATION

Telephones: 13,000
Newspapers: 1

TRANSPORTATION

Highways—Kilometers (Miles): 259 (160)
Railroads—Kilometers (Miles): none
Usable Airports: 14

GOVERNMENT

Type: republic
Independence Date: June 29, 1976
Head of State: President France Albert René
Political Parties: Seychelles People's Progressive Front; Democratic Party; others
Suffrage: universal at 17

MILITARY

Number of Armed Forces: 1,300
Military Expenditures (% of Central Government Expenditures): 6.0%
Current Hostilities: none

ECONOMY

Currency ($ U.S. Equivalent): 5.20 rupees = $1
Per Capita Income/GDP: $4,500/$255 million
Inflation Rate: 1.5%
Natural Resources: agricultural land; fish
Agriculture: vanilla; coconuts; cinnamon
Industry: tourism; copra and vanilla processing; coconut oil; construction

FOREIGN TRADE

Exports: $31 million
Imports: $164 million

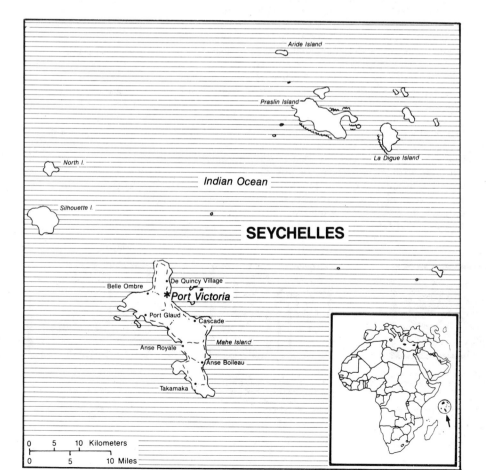

| French settlement begins 1771 | British rule is established 1814 | The British end slavery 1830 | Seychelles is detached from Mauritius by the British and made a Crown colony 1903 | Legislative Council with qualified suffrage is introduced 1948 | Universal suffrage 1967 | Independence 1976 | Coup of Albert René against James Mancham 1977 | 1980s–1990s |

A mercenary coup attempt fails

A 1988 Amnesty International report alleges government fabrication of drug-possession cases for political reasons

René agrees to a multiparty system

THE SEYCHELLES

The Republic of the Seychelles consists of a number of widely scattered archipelagos off the coast of East Africa. The country has made enormous economic and social progress but has been politically polarized under the leadership of first James Mancham and then Albert René. The holding of multiparty elections in July 1992, after 15 years of single-party rule under René, has raised the prospect of reconciliation between the partisans of these two longtime rivals.

The roots of the Seychelles' modern political economy go back to 1963, when Mancham's Democratic Party and René's People's United Party were established. The former originally favored private enterprise and the retention of the British imperial connection, while the latter advocated an independent socialist state. Electoral victories in 1970 and 1974 allowed Mancham to pursue his dream of turning the Seychelles into a tourist paradise and a financial and trading center, by aggressively seeking outside investment. Tourism began to flourish following the opening of an international airport on the main island of Mahe in 1971, fueling an economic boom. Between 1970 and 1980 per capita income rose from nearly $150 to $1,700 (today it is about $4,500).

In 1974 Mancham, in an about-face, joined René in advocating the islands' independence. The Democratic Party, despite its modest electoral and overwhelming parliamentary majority, set up a coalition government with the People's United Party. On June 29, 1976, the Sey-

chelles became independent, with Mancham as president and René as prime minister.

On June 5, 1977, with Mancham out of the country, René's supporters, with Tanzanian assistance, staged a successful coup in which several people were killed. Thereafter René assumed the presidency and suspended the Constitution. A period of rule by decree gave way in 1979, without the benefit of referendum, to a new constitutional framework in which the People's Progressive Front, successor to the People's United Party, was recognized as the nation's sole political voice.

The first years of one-party government were characterized by continued economic growth, which allowed for an impressive expansion of social-welfare programs. Despite the government's efforts to diversify the economy through private investment as well as state intervention, tourism has continued to be the predominant sector.

Political power since the coup has remained largely concentrated in the hands of René. The early years of his regime were marked by unrest. In 1978 the first in a series of unsuccessful countercoups was followed, several months later, by violent protests against the government's attempts to impose a compulsory National Youth Service, which would have removed the nation's 16- and 17-year-olds from their families in order to foster their sociopolitical indoctrination in accordance with the René government's socialist ideals. Another major incident occurred in November 1981, when a group of international mercenaries, who had the backing of authorities in Kenya and South Africa as well as exiled Seychellois, were forced to

flee in a hijacked jet after an airport shootout with local security forces. Following this attempt, Tanzanian troops were sent to the islands. A year later the Tanzanians were instrumental in crushing a mutiny of Seychellois soldiers, which resulted in a number of deaths and the detention of one-fifth of the local army. Since then a number of other alleged plots have been uncovered.

Despite its success in creating a model welfare state, which undoubtedly strengthened its popular acceptance, for years René continued to govern in a repressive manner. Internal opposition was not tolerated and exiled activists were largely neutralized. About one-fifth of the islands' population now live overseas, although not all left for political reasons.

In December 1991 René gave in to rising internal and external pressure for a return to multiparty democracy. In July 1992 his party won 58 percent of the vote for a commission to rewrite the Constitution. But, in an indication that the struggle for power is not yet over, in November 1992 the voters heeded Mancham's call by rejecting the revised constitution proposed by the pro-René commission.

DEVELOPMENT

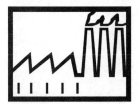

The Seychelles has declared an Exclusive Economic Zone of 200 miles around all of its islands in order to promote the local fishing industry. Most of the zone's catch is harvested by foreign boats, which are supposed to pay licensing fees to the Seychelles government. Canned tuna is now the island's leading export earner.

FREEDOM

Since the opening to multipartyism, there has been greater political freedom in the Seychelles. The opposition nonetheless continues to complain of police harassment and the government's control over the broadcast media.

HEALTH/WELFARE

A national health program has been established; private practice has been abolished. Free-lunch programs have raised nutritional levels among the young. Education is also free up to age 14.

ACHIEVEMENTS

Under its current government, Seychelles has become a world leader in wildlife preservation. An important aspect of the nation's conservation efforts has been the designation of one island as an international wildlife refuge.

Somalia* (Somali Democratic Republic)

GEOGRAPHY

Area in Square Kilometers (Miles): 638,000 (246,331) (slightly smaller than Texas)
Capital (Population): Mogadishu (1,000,000 est.)
Climate: arid to semiarid

PEOPLE

Population

Total: 6,709,000
Annual Growth Rate: 3.3%
Rural/Urban Population Ratio: 64/36
Languages: official: Somali; other spoken: Arabic, Oromo, Italian, English, others

Health

Life Expectancy at Birth: 56 years (male); 56 years (female)
Infant Mortality Rate (Ratio): 116/1,000
Average Caloric Intake: 100% of FAO minimum
Physicians Available (Ratio): 1/19,950

Religion(s)

99% Sunni Muslim; 1% other

Education

Adult Literacy Rate: 12%

COMMUNICATION

Telephones: 6,000
Newspapers: 2

TRANSPORTATION

Highways—Kilometers (Miles): 15,215 (9,433)
Railroads—Kilometers (Miles): —

REFUGEES IN AND OUT OF SOMALIA

Before the current crisis, life in Somalia had been disrupted by large influxes of refugees. Drought in 1974–1975 led to the relocation of some 150,000 nomadic people into the arable regions of the country. War in the Ogaden region during the late 1970s led to a further migration of at least 700,000 Ethiopian Somali. Although some returned to Ethiopia, drought and warfare there have led to new influxes since 1986. Today there are still perhaps 1 million Ogadeni refugees in Somalia, who have formed their own armed factions to fight on both sides of the border. Warfare within Somalia has also led to a reverse flow of some 1 million Somali into Ethiopia and Kenya. Even before the current famine the refugee situation has been responsible for the injection of outside relief aid, which in 1990 constituted up to one-third of the national budget.

Usable Airports: 46

GOVERNMENT

Type: republic; under military regime
Independence Date: July 1, 1960
Head of State: President Ali Mahdi Mohamed
Political Parties: Somali United Congress
Suffrage: universal at 18

MILITARY

Number of Armed Forces: —
Military Expenditures (% of Central Government Expenditures): n/a
Current Hostilities: border disputes with Ethiopia; conflicts with Ethiopian-backed Somali rebels

ECONOMY

Currency ($ U.S. Equivalent): 2,618 Somali shillings = $1
Per Capita Income/GDP: $210/$1.4 billion
Inflation Rate: 82%
Natural Resources: uranium; timber; fish
Agriculture: livestock; bananas; sugarcane; cotton; cereals
Industry: sugar refining; tuna and beef canning; textiles; iron-rod plants; petroleum refining

FOREIGN TRADE

Exports: $58 million
Imports: $354 million

*Note: The breakdown of government in Somalia has made the accurate gathering of statistics impossible. The figures listed on this page are only estimates.

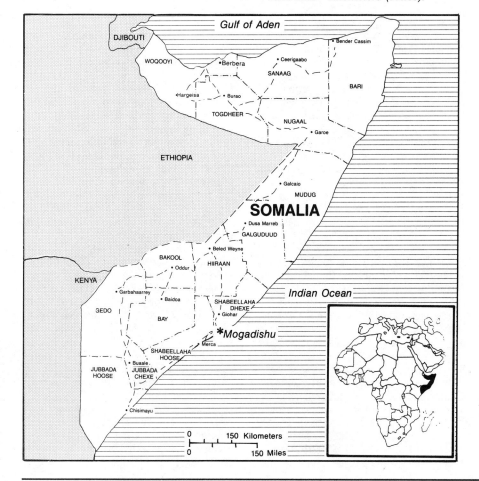

SOMALIA

Since the overthrow of the dictatorial regime of Mohammed Siad Barre, in January 1991, Somalia has been without an effective central government. As a result, its formal economy collapsed as the entire country became divided by dozens of armed factions obedient only to the law of the gun and their warlords' self-interest. The outbreak of drought in 1991 added to the catastrophe. Failed crops and dying livestock resulted in countrywide famine, but international food relief efforts were unable to deliver sufficient quantities of food to those most in need, due to the prevailing state of lawlessness. Desperately awaited relief supplies were often stolen by armed men before they could reach those in need. The International Red Cross estimated that, by mid-1992, of southern Somalia's 4.5 million people, 1.5 million were in immediate danger of starvation, while another 500,000 or so had fled the country. More than 300,000 children under age 5 were reported to have perished. There is also evidence of similar levels of suffering in northern Somalia.

Yet a massive, and unique, U.S.-led United Nations peacemaking intervention, begun in December 1992, had already shown positive results by the end of January 1993. The intervention's primary goal—delivery of food relief to famine areas—appeared to have been achieved, with minimal casualties. Operation Restore Hope, as it was named, consisting of approximately 22,000 U.S. troops and 7,000 troops from other countries, was met with general enthusiasm by the Somali population and a measure of cooperation from key warlords. However, the longer-term objectives of the operation have not yet been defined, and the problems underlying the havoc in Somalia have not been resolved.

SOMALI SOCIETY

The Somali have for centuries lived with the threat of famine, as Somalia is arid even in good years. Traditionally, most Somali were nomadic pastoralists, but in recent years this way of life has declined dramatically. Prior to the current crisis, about half of the population were still almost entirely reliant on livestock. Somali herds have been quite large: in the early 1980s, more than 1 million animals, mostly goats and sheep, were exported annually. Large numbers of cattle and camels have also been kept. But hundreds of thousands of animals were lost due to lack of rain during the mid-1980s, while since 1983 reports of rinderpest led to a sharp drop in

(United Nations)

The sovereign state of Somalia was formed on July 1, 1960 when the former British colony of Somaliland and the UN Trust Territory of Somaliland under Italian Administration were merged. This parade in Mogadishu exemplified the pride and optimism of the beginning of a new country; the chaos of subsequent years was to dampen this new sense of freedom.

exports, due to the closing of the once-lucrative Saudi Arabian market to East African animals. Besides leading to a drop in incomes, this ban aggravated the already-serious problem of overgrazing.

A quarter of the Somali population have long combined livestock-keeping with agriculture. Cultivation is possible in the area between the Juba and Shebelle rivers and in portions of the north. Although up to 15 percent of the country is potentially arable, only about 1 percent of the land has been put to plow in any given time. Bananas, cotton, and frankincense have been major cash crops, while maize and sorghum are subsistence crops. Like Somali pastoralists, Somali farmers walk a thin line between abundance and scarcity, for locusts as well as drought are common visitors.

The delicate nature of Somali agriculture helps to explain recent urbanization. By 1990, 1 out of 4 Somali lived in the large towns and cities. The principal center is the capital, Mogadishu, which, despite being divided by war, still houses more than 1 million people. Unfortunately, as Somali have migrated in from the countryside, they have found little employment. Even before the current collapse, the country's manufacturing and service sectors were small. By 1990, more than 100,000 Somali had become migrant workers in the Arab Gulf states. But, in 1990–1991, many were repatriated as a result of the conflict

over Kuwait.

Until recently many outsiders assumed that Somalia possessed a greater degree of national coherence than most other African states. Somali do share a common language and a sense of cultural identity. Islam is also a binding feature. However, competing clan and subclan allegiances have long played a divisive political role in the society. Membership in all the current armed factions is congruent with blood loyalties. Traditionally, the clans were governed by experienced, wise men. But the authority of these elders has now largely given way to the power of younger men with a surplus of guns and a surfeit of education and moral decency.

Past appeals to greater Somali nationalism have also been a source of conflict by encouraging irredentist sentiments against Somalia's neighbors. During the colonial era, contemporary Somalia was divided. For about 75 years, the northern region was governed by the British, while the southern portion was subject to Italian rule. The 2 colonial legacies have complicated efforts at nation-building. Many northerners feel that their region has been neglected and would benefit from greater political autonomy or independence. This belief has been intensified by recent warfare.

Somalia became independent on July 1, 1960, when the new national flag, a white,

| The British take control of northern regions of present-day Somalia **1886–1887** | Italy establishes a protectorate in the eastern areas of present-day Somalia **1889** | | The Somalia Youth League is founded; it becomes a nationalist party **1943** |

5-pointed star on a blue field, was raised in the former British and Italian territories. The star symbolized the 5 supposed branches of the Somali nation—that is, the now-united peoples of British and Italian Somalilands and the Somali still living in French Somaliland (modern Djibouti), Ethiopia, and Kenya.

THE RISE AND FALL OF SIAD BARRE

Siad Barre came to power in 1969, through a coup promising radical change. As chairperson of the military's Supreme Revolutionary Council, Barre combined Somali nationalism and Islam with a commitment to "scientific socialism." Some genuine efforts were made to restructure society through the development of new local councils and worker management committees. New civil and labor codes were written. The Somali Revolutionary Socialist Party was developed as the sole legal political party.

Initially the new order seemed to be making progress. The Somali language was alphabetized in a modified form of Roman script, which allowed the government to launch mass-literacy campaigns. A number of rural development projects were also implemented. In particular, roads were built, breaking down isolation among regions. The theme was "Tribalism divides, socialism unites." Tribalism in this case stood for the clan divisions.

The promise of Barre's early years in office gradually faded. Little was done to follow through the developments of the early 1970s, as Barre increasingly bypassed the participatory institutions he had helped to create. His government became one of personal rule; he took on emergency powers, relieved members of the governing council of their duties, surrounded himself with members of his own Marehan branch of the Darod clan, and isolated himself from the public. Barre also isolated Somalia from the rest of Africa, by pursuing irredentism, policies that would unite the other points of the Somali star under his rule. To accomplish this task, he began to encourage local guerrilla movements among the ethnic Somali living in Kenya and Ethiopia. Bad relations between Somalia and Kenya were eased in 1982, but tensions over the Ogaden region of Ethiopia remained.

In 1977 Barre sent his forces into the Ogaden region to assist the local rebels of the Western Somali Liberation Front. The invaders achieved initial military success against the Ethiopians, whose forces had been weakened by revolutionary strife and battles with Eritrean rebels. However, the intervention of some 17,000 Cuban troops

(UN photo by Rice)

Approximately half the Somali are nomadic pastoralists. The perennial problems of drought and disease have made such an existence difficult indeed.

Somalia is
formed through a
merger of former
British and Italian
colonies under
UN Trusteeship
1960

Siad Barre
comes to power
through an army
coup; the
Supreme
Revolutionary
Council is
established
1969

The Ogaden war
in Ethiopia
results in
Somalia's defeat
1977–1978

1980s–1990s

and other Soviet-bloc personnel on the side of the Ethiopians quickly turned the tide of battle. At the same time, the Somali incursion was roundly condemned by all members of the Organization of African Unity. Ground and air attacks across the borders of Ethiopia and Somalia continued into the 1980s.

The intervention of the Soviet bloc on the side of the Ethiopians was a bitter disappointment to Barre, who had enjoyed Russian support for his military buildup. In exchange, he had allowed the Soviets to establish a secret base at the strategic northern port of Berbera. However, in 1977 the Soviets decided to shift their allegiances decisively to the then-newly established revolutionary government in Ethiopia. Barre in turn tried to attract U.S. support with offers of basing rights at Berbera, but the Carter administration was unwilling to jeopardize its interests in either Ethiopia or Kenya by backing Barre's irredentist adventure. American-Somali relations became closer during the Reagan administration, which signed a 10-year pact giving U.S. forces access to air and naval facilities at Berbera, for which the United States increased its aid to Somalia, including limited arms supplies.

In 1988 Barre met with Ethiopian leader Mengistu Mariam. Together they pledged to respect their mutual border. This understanding came about in the context of growing internal resistance to both regimes. By 1990 several armed resistance movements, most notably the Somali Salvation Democratic Front (SSDF), the Somali Democratic

Alliance (SDA), the Somali Democratic Movement (SDM), the Somali National Movement (SNM), the Somali Patriotic Movement (SPM), and the (loosely) United Somali Congress (USC), were enjoying growing success against government forces.

Growing resistance was accompanied by massive atrocities on the part of government forces. Human-rights concerns were cited by the U.S. and other governments in ending their assistance to Somalia. In March 1990 Barre called for national dialogue and spoke of a possible end to one-party rule. But continuing atrocities, including the killing of more than 100 protesters at the national stadium, fueled further armed resistance.

In January 1991 Barre fled Mogadishu, which was seized by USC forces. The USC set up an interim administration, but its authority was not recognized by other groups. By the end of the year, the USC itself had split into two warring factions. Other factions, including forces still loyal to the now-exiled Barre, have also continued to fight one another. In the north the SNM declared its zone's sovereign independence as "Somaliland," but it has had to battle against the SDA and other local groups.

As Somalia's suffering grew and became publicized in the Western media, many observers suggested the need for the United Nations to intervene to restore order. But it wasn't until late in 1992 that the world body went beyond its ineffectual attempts to police the delivery of relief supplies. Although subsequent interven-

SNM rebels
escalate their
campaign in the
north;
government
forces respond
with genocidal
attacks on the
local Issaq
population

Barre pledges
political
liberalization;
government
death squads
remain active

The fall of Barre
leaves Somalia
without an
effective central
government;
unilateral UN
intervention
begins

tion created some tensions, it has also raised hopes of achieving food relief, providing medical care, and promoting a return to economic self-sufficiency, through such means as helping to revive the agricultural sector. But how to define and then meet Operation Restore Hope's long-term goals in such a fractured society is an elusive quest. It remains to be seen if the Somali themselves, with some measure of assistance from the international community, can find the path to economic and political reconstruction.

DEVELOPMENT

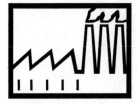

Somalia has the longest coastline in Africa. In the mid-1970s the government pressed some formerly nomadic communities into adopting fishing. After initial resistance, the program has led to growing catches in recent years.

FREEDOM

Plagued by hunger and the internal violence, and with the continuing threat of governance by the anarchic greed of the warlords, the living have no true freedom in Somalia.

HEALTH/WELFARE

Somalia's small 1990 health service has almost completely disappeared, leaving the country reliant on a handful of international health teams. By 1986 education's share of the national budget had fallen to 2%. Somalia had 525 troops per teacher, the highest such ratio in Africa.

ACHIEVEMENTS

Somalia has been described as "a nation of poets." Many scholars attribute the strength of the Somali poetic tradition not only to the nomadic way of life, which encourages oral arts, but to the local role of poetry as a social and political medium.

The Sudan (Democratic Republic of the Sudan)

GEOGRAPHY

Area in Square Kilometers (Miles):
2,504,530 (967,500) (about one-fourth
the size of the United States)
Capital (Population): Khartoum
(476,000)
Climate: desert in north to tropical in
south

PEOPLE

Population
Total: 27,220,000
Annual Growth Rate: 3.0%
Rural/Urban Population Ratio: 78/22
Languages: official: Arabic; others
spoken: Nuer, Dinka, Shilluki,
Masalatis, Fur, Nubian, English,
others

Health
Life Expectancy at Birth: 52 years
(male); 54 years (female)
Infant Mortality Rate (Ratio): 85/1,000
Average Caloric Intake: 99% of FAO
minimum
Physicians Available (Ratio): 1/11,513

Religion(s)
70% Sunni Muslim in north; 25%
traditional indigenous; 5% Christian

Education
Adult Literacy Rate: 27%

THE OPPRESSION OF WOMEN IN SUDAN

Since coming to power in 1989 the Sudanese government has instituted
a sweeping policy aimed at radically redefining the role of women in
society. Traditionally, both Muslim and non-Muslim women in Sudan
have enjoyed such basic freedoms as access to higher education,
professional employment, the right to engage in trade, and freedom of
movement. All these freedoms are currently being curtailed in the name
of Islamic propriety. Women are being systematically removed from the
Sudanese civil service and from many fields of tertiary education. It has
been suggested that, in the future, women will be free to be nurses and
primary-school teachers. Women are now no longer free to travel
without a male escort. Thousands of women, mostly non-Muslim, are
the principal victims of enslavement by local militias.

COMMUNICATION
Telephones: 73,400
Newspapers: 2

TRANSPORTATION
Highways—Kilometers (Miles): 20,000
(12,400)
Railroads—Kilometers (Miles): 5,500
(3,410)
Usable Airports: 66

GOVERNMENT
Type: (military) republic
Independence Date: January 1, 1956
Head of State: Prime Minister Umar
Hasan Ahmad al-Bashir
Political Parties: banned
Suffrage: universal for adults

MILITARY
Number of Armed Forces: 71,750
*Military Expenditures (% of Central
Government Expenditures):* 7.2%
Current Hostilities: civil war

ECONOMY
Currency ($ U.S. Equivalent): 90
Sudanese pounds = $1
Per Capita Income/GDP: $330/$8.5
billion
Inflation Rate: 60%
Natural Resources: oil; iron ore;
copper; chrome; other industrial
metals
Agriculture: cotton; peanuts; sesame;
gum arabic; sorghum; wheat
Industry: textiles; cement; cotton
ginning; edible oils; distilling;
pharmaceuticals

FOREIGN TRADE
Exports: $465 million
Imports: $1.0 billion

THE SUDAN

The Sudan is Africa's largest country. Its size as well as its ethnic and religious diversity have frustrated the efforts of successive postindependence governments to build a lasting sense of national unity. Since the takeover of the state in 1989 by a repressive military clique allied to the fundamentalist National Islamic Front (NIF), the polarization of Sudanese society has deepened to an unprecedented extent. At the moment there is little hope for unity and reconciliation in this vast, suffering land of enormous potential.

HISTORY

The Sudan, like its northern neighbor Egypt, is a gift of the Nile. The river and its various branches snake across the country, providing water to most of the 80 percent of the Sudanese who survive by farming. From ancient times the upper Nile region of northern Sudan has been the site of a series of civilizations, whose histories are closely intertwined with those of Egypt. There has been constant human interaction between the two zones. Some groups, such as the Nubians, expanded northward into the Egyptian lower Nile.

The last ruler to unite the Nile Valley politically was the nineteenth-century Turko-Egyptian ruler Muhammad Ali. After absorbing the by then predominantly Arabized Muslim, northern Sudan into his Egyptian state, Ali gradually expanded his authority to the south and west over non-Arabic and, in many cases, non-Muslim groups. This process, which was largely motivated by a desire for slave labor, for the first time united the diverse regions that today make up the Sudan. In the 1880s much of the Sudan fell under the theocratic rule of the Mahdists, a local anti-Egyptian Islamic movement. The Mahdists were defeated by an Anglo-Egyptian force in 1898. Thereafter the British dominated the Sudan until its independence, in 1956.

INTERNAL PROBLEMS

Since independence Sudanese society has remained divided. In the north there has been strong Pan-Arab sentiment, but 60 percent of the Sudanese, concentrated in the south and west, are non-Arab. Forty percent of the Sudanese, especially in the south, are also non-Muslim. Despite this fact, many, although by no means all, Sudanese Muslims have favored the creation of an Islamic state. Ideological divisions among various socialist- and nonsocialist-oriented factions have also been important. The Sudan has long had a strong Communist party, drawing on the support of organized labor, and an influential middle class.

The division between northern and southern Sudan has been especially deep. A mutiny by southern soldiers prior to independence escalated into a 17-year rebellion by southerners against what they perceived to be the hegemony of Muslim Arabs. Some 500,000 southerners perished before the Anya Nya rebels and the government reached a compromise settlement, recognizing southern autonomy in 1972.

In the north, the first 14 years of independence saw the rule of 7 different civilian coalitions as well as 6 years of military rule. Despite this chronic instability, a tradition of liberal tolerance among political factions was generally maintained.

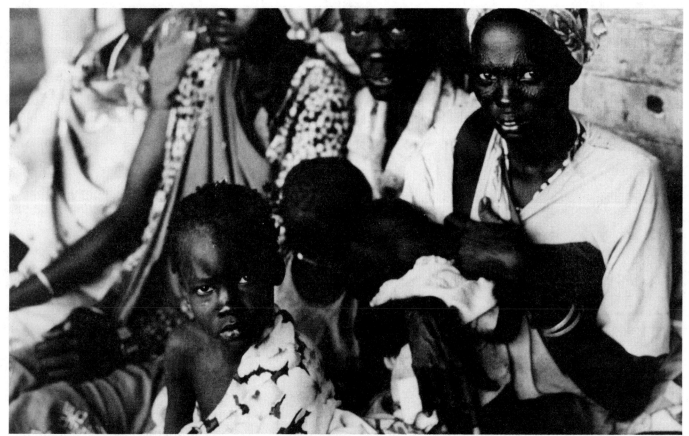

(United Nations photo by Milton Grant)

Some 30 percent of the Sudanese population have been displaced by warfare and drought. The effect on the people has been devastating, and even the best efforts of the international community have met with limited success.

		The Anglo-Egyptian Condominium begins **1899**		Independence **1956**	Jaafar Nimeiri comes to power **1969**	Hostilities end in southern Sudan **1972**	
Egypt invades northern Sudan **1820**	The Mahdist Revolt begins **1881**						1980s–1990s

Islamic law replaces the former penal code; renewed civil war in the south

Nimeiri is overthrown in a popular coup; an elected government is installed

A military coup installs a hard-line Islamic fundamentalist regime

Government became increasingly authoritarian during the administration of Jaafar Nimeiri, who came to power in a 1969 military coup.

Nimeiri quickly moved to consolidate his power by eliminating challenges to his government from the Islamic right and the Communist left. His greatest success was ending the Anya Nya revolt, but his subsequent tampering with the provisions of the peace agreement led to renewed resistance. In 1983 Nimeiri decided to impose Islamic law throughout Sudanese society. This led to the growth of the Sudanese People's Liberation Army (SPLA), which quickly seized control of much of the southern Sudanese countryside. Opposition to Nimeiri had also been growing in the north, as more people became alienated by the regime's increasingly heavy-handed ways and inability to manage the declining economy. Finally, in 1985, he was toppled in a coup.

The holding of multiparty elections in 1986 seemed to presage a restoration of the Sudan's tradition of pluralism. With the SPLA preventing voting in much of the south, the two largest parties were the northern-based Umma and Democratic Union (DUP). The third-largest vote-getter was the NIF, with 8 other parties plus a number of independents gaining parliamentary seats. The major challenge facing the new coalition government, led by Umma, was reconciliation with the SPLA. Because the SPLA, unlike the earlier Anya Nya, was committed to national unity, the task did not appear insurmountable. However, arguments within the government over meeting key SPLA demands, such as the repeal of Islamic law, caused the war to

drag on. A hard-line faction within Umma and the NIF sought to resist a return to secularism. In March 1989 a new government, made up of Umma and DUP, committed itself to accommodating the SPLA. However, a month later, on the day that the cabinet was to ratify an agreement with the rebels, there was a coup by pro-NIF officers.

Besides leading to a breakdown in all efforts to end the SPLA rebellion, the NIF/military regime has been responsible for establishing the most intolerant, repressive government in the Sudan's modern history. Extrajudicial executions have become common. Instances of pillaging and enslavement of non-Muslim communities by government-linked militias have increased. NIF-affiliated security groups have become a law unto themselves, striking out at their perceived enemies and intimidating Muslims and non-Muslims alike to conform to their fundamentalist norms. Supposedly Islamic norms are also being invoked to justify a radical campaign to undermine the status of women.

In 1990 most of the now-banned political parties, including Umma, DUP, and the Communists, aligned themselves with the SPLA as the National Democratic Alliance. But the northern-based parties have so far proved ineffectual. In September 1991 the SPLA split into a "Nasir" faction, favoring southern independence, and a "Torit" faction, committed to a secular federation. This division facilitated significant but costly advances by government forces in early 1992, but the Khartoum regime's continued unwillingness to compromise has led to a partial reconciliation within the SPLA on a platform of southern

"self-determination." The military situation remains a stalemate, with accusations of atrocities on all sides, including a growing number of regional militias with shifting loyalties.

ECONOMIC PROSPECTS

Although it has great potential, political conflict has left the Sudan one of the poorest nations in the world. The country's underutilized water resources have led to talk of creating "the breadbasket of the Arab world," while untapped oil reserves in the south could transform the country from an energy importer to an exporter. However, warfare and lack of financing are blocking needed infrastructural improvements. The Sudan's unwillingness to pay its foreign debt has led to calls for its expulsion from the International Monetary Fund.

By 1988 nearly 7 million Sudanese (out of a total population of 23 million) had been displaced—more than 4 million by warfare, with drought and desertification contributing to the remainder. For years the Sudan has been a major recipient of international emergency food aid, but warfare, corruption, and genocidal indifference have often blocked aid from reaching the needy. In 1992 an estimated 5 million Sudanese were threatened by famine.

DEVELOPMENT

Many ambitious development plans have been launched since independence, but progress has been limited by political instability. The periodic introduction and redefinition of "Islamic" financial procedures have complicated long-term planning.

FREEDOM

The current regime rules through massive repression. In August 1992 Africa Watch accused it of practicing genocide against the Nuba people. Elsewhere, tales of massacres, forced relocations, enslavement, torture, and starvation are commonplace.

HEALTH/WELFARE

Civil strife and declining government expenditures have resulted in rising rates of infant mortality. Warfare has also prevented famine relief from reaching needy populations, resulting in instances of mass starvation.

ACHIEVEMENTS

Although his music is banned in his own country, Mohammed Wardi is probably the Sudan's most popular musician. Now living in exile, he has been imprisoned and tortured for his songs against injustice, which also appeal to a large international audience, especially in North Africa and the Middle East.

Tanzania (United Republic of Tanzania)

GEOGRAPHY

Area in Square Kilometers (Miles):
939,652 (363,950) (more than twice the size of California)
Capital (Population): Dar es Salaam (1,360,000); Dodoma (new national capital) (1,238,000)
Climate: tropical; arid; temperate

PEOPLE

Population
Total: 26,870,000
Annual Growth Rate: 3.4%
Rural/Urban Population Ratio: 67/33
Languages: official: Kiswahili; others spoken: Chagga, Gogo, Ha, Haya, Luo, Maasai, Hindu, Arabic, English, others

Health
Life Expectancy at Birth: 50 years (male); 55 years (female)
Infant Mortality Rate (Ratio): 105/1,000
Average Caloric Intake: 87% of FAO minimum
Physicians Available (Ratio): 1/24,970

Religion(s)
34% traditional indigenous; 33% Muslim; 33% Christian; Zanzibar is all Muslim

Education
Adult Literacy Rate: 46%

COMMUNICATION
Telephones: 103,800
Newspapers: 5

THE SWAHILI COAST

A trading coastal culture, African-based with Arabian influence, developed over hundreds of years on the East African coast. For 2,000 years merchants from the Mediterranean and the Middle East traded along the coast of East Africa. The mingling of Bantu-speaking peoples with Arab culture eventually created the Swahili, an Afro-Arab people with their own African-based language. Based in cities on islands and along the coast, they traded with Arabia, Persia, India, and China, and eventually with the interior of what are now known as Kenya and Tanzania. Converted to Islam and also Arabic-speaking, these cosmopolitan peoples traded interior produce for porcelain, spices, and textiles from all over the world and created an impressive written and oral literature. They still play an important role in the political and commercial life of Tanzania.

TRANSPORTATION
Highways—Kilometers (Miles): 81,900 (50,778)
Railroads—Kilometers (Miles): 3,569 (2,212)
Usable Airports: 93

GOVERNMENT
Type: republic
Independence Date: December 9, 1961
Head of State: President Ali Hassan Mwinyi
Political Parties: Chama Cha Mapinduzi (Revolutionary Party)
Suffrage: universal over 18

MILITARY
Number of Armed Forces: 46,800
Military Expenditures (% of Central Government Expenditures): 3.9%
Current Hostilities: none

ECONOMY
Currency ($ U.S. Equivalent): 236 Tanzanian shillings = $1
Per Capita Income/GDP: $240/$6.4 billion
Inflation Rate: 31%
Natural Resources: hydroelectric potential; unexploited iron and coal; gemstones; gold; natural gas
Agriculture: cotton; coffee; sisal; tea; tobacco; wheat; cashews; livestock; cloves
Industry: agricultural processing; diamond mining; oil refining; shoes; cement; textiles; wood products

FOREIGN TRADE
Exports: $380 million
Imports: $1.2 billion

TANZANIA

After a period of harsh German rule followed by paternalistic British trusteeship, the Tanzanian mainland gained its independence, as Tanganyika, in 1961. In 1964 it merged with the small island state of Zanzibar, which had been a British protectorate, to form the new United Republic of Tanzania. Political activity in Tanzania has been restricted to the ruling Revolutionary or Chama Cha Mapinduzi (CCM) Party, which joined the former Tanganyika African National Union with its Zanzibar partner, the Afro-Shirazi Party. But in February 1992 the CCM agreed to compete with other "national parties," provided that they do not "divide the people along tribal, religious or racial lines."

By 1967 the CCM's predecessors had already eliminated legal opposition, when they proclaimed their commitment to the Arusha Declaration, a blueprint for "African Socialism." At the time Tanzania was one of the least developed countries in the world. It has remained so. Beyond this fact there is much controversy over the degree to which the goals of the Declaration have been achieved. To some critics, the Arusha experiment has been responsible for reducing a potentially well-off country to ruin. Supporters often counter that it has led to a stable society in which major strides have been made toward greater democracy, equality, and human development. Both sides exaggerate.

THE ECONOMY

Like many African states, Tanzania has a primarily agrarian economy that is constrained by a less than optimal environment. Although some 90 percent of the population are employed in agriculture, only 8 percent of the land is under cultivation. Rainfall for most of the country is low and erratic, while soil erosion and deforestation are critical problems in many areas. But geography and environmental problems are only one facet of Tanzania's low agricultural productivity. There has also been instability in world market demand for the nation's principal cash crops: coffee, cotton, cloves, sisal, and tobacco. And the cost of imported fuel, fertilizers, and other inputs has risen at the same time.

Government policies have also led to underdevelopment. Perhaps the greatest policy disaster was the program of villagization. Tanzania hoped to relocate its rural and unemployed urban populations into *ujaama* (Swahili for "familyhood") villages, which were to become the basis for agrarian progress. During the early 1970s coercive measures were adopted to force the pace of resettlement. Agricultural production is estimated to have fallen as much as 50 percent during the initial period of ujaama dislocation, transforming the nation from a grain exporter to a grain importer.

Another policy constraint was the exceedingly low official produce prices paid by the government to farmers. Many peasants withdrew from the market, while others turned to black-market sales. Since 1985 the official market has been liberalized and prices have risen. This has been accompanied by a modest rise in produc-

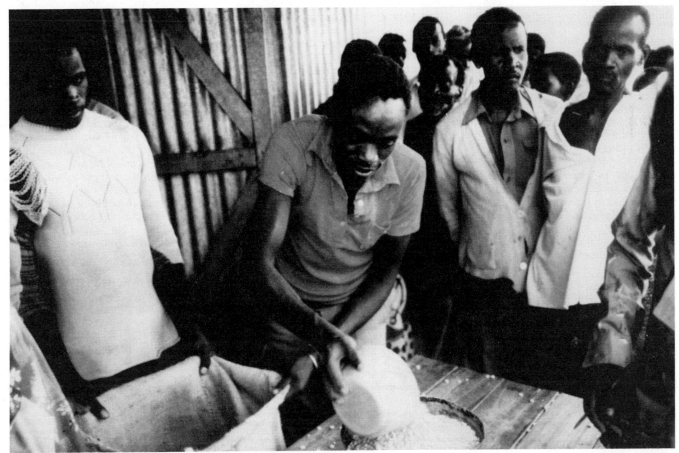

(UN photo by Ray Witlin)

The economy of Tanzania is primarily agrarian; however, rainfall for most of the country is sporadic. This, coupled with wide swings in world-market demand for its cash crops, has led to economic pressures affecting food crops. These men in the village of Lumeji are receiving seed grains needed to develop Tanzania's food production.

The sultan of
Oman transfers
the capital to
Zanzibar as Arab
commercial
activity increases
1820

Germany
declares a
protectorate over
the area
1885

The Maji Maji
rebellion unites
many ethnic
groups against
German rule
1905–1906

Tanganyika
becomes a
League of
Nations mandate
under the United
Kingdom
1919

Tanganyika
becomes
independent;
Julius Nyerere is
the leader
1961

Tanzania is
formed of
Tanganyika and
Zanzibar
1964

The Arusha
Declaration
establishes a
Tanzanian
socialist program
for development
1967

A Tanzanian
invasion force
enters Uganda
1979

1980s–1990s

Nyerere retires;
Ali Hassan
Mwinyi succeeds
as president

Tanzania accepts
IMF conditions
and loans

Tensions within
the CCM over
unrest in
Zanzibar

tion, yet the lack of consumer goods in the rural areas is widely seen as a disincentive to greater progress.

All sectors of the Tanzanian economy have suffered from deteriorating infrastructure. Here again there are both external and internal causes. Balanced against rising imported energy and equipment costs have been inefficiencies caused by poor planning, barriers to capital investment, and a relative neglect of communications and transport. Even when crops or goods are available, they often cannot reach their destination. Tanzania's few bituminized roads have long been in a chronic state of disrepair, and there have been frequent shutdowns of its railways. In particular, much of the southern third of the country is isolated from access to even inferior transport services.

Between 1980 and 1987 manufacturing declined from 10 to 4 percent of gross domestic product, with most sectors operating at less than half of their capacity. Inefficiencies also grew in the nation's mining sector. Diamonds, gold, iron, coal, and other minerals are currently exploited, but production has been generally falling and now accounts for less than 1 percent of GDP. Lack of capital investment has led to a deterioration of existing operations and an inability to open up new deposits.

As with agriculture, the Tanzanian government has in recent years increasingly abandoned socialism in favor of market economics, in its efforts to rehabilitate and expand the industrial and service sectors of the economy. A number of state enterprises are being privatized, and better opportunities are being offered to outside

investors. Tourism is being promoted, after decades of neglect.

SOCIAL AND POLITICAL DEVELOPMENT

Although the statistical evidence is inadequate, it is nonetheless clear that Tanzania has made real progress in extending health, education, and other social services to its population since independence. But past claims of achieving universal primary literacy are seemingly contradicted by the 1986 primary-school enrollment figure of 69 percent (just above the African average of 66 percent). Fewer than 1 percent of the population receive tertiary education.

Some 1,700 health centers and dispensaries have been built since 1961, but they have long been plagued by shortages of medicines, equipment, and even basic supplies such as bandages and syringes. Although the country has a national health service, patients often end up paying for material costs.

Much of the progress that has been made in human services is a function of outside donations. Despite the Arusha Declaration's emphasis on self-reliance, for decades Tanzania has been either at or near the top of the list of African countries in its per capita receipt of international aid. By 1987, aid, primarily from Western countries, accounted for more than one-third of the gross national product.

Even before the recent opening to multipartyism, Tanzania's politics was in a state of transition. Political life has been dominated since the 1950s by Julius Nyerere, who was the driving personality behind

the Arusha experiment. However, in 1985 he gave up the presidency in favor of Ali Hassan Mwinyi and, in 1990, Nyerere resigned as chairman of the CCM. While Nyerere remains influential, Mwinyi has consolidated his leadership in favor of those within the CCM who seek greater political and economic liberalization.

The move to multiparty politics is complicated by the omnipresent CCM. Outside of religion, the party has sought to control all organized social activity. A network of community and workplace cells has assured that all Tanzanians have at least one party official responsible for monitoring their affairs. Media are monopolized by the state.

So far no opposition parties have been recognized, but several movements—notably the National Committee for Constitutional Reform, the Union of Multiparty Democracy, the Civic Movement and the Democratic Party—have been internally active in the face of bans on political gatherings and police harassment. A genuine fear is that the new parties will polarize Tanzanian society. Although the nation has been relatively free of open ethnic conflict, sectarian tensions exist between Christians and Muslims, and in recent years there has been a revival of long-suppressed Zanzabari separatist feeling.

DEVELOPMENT

In April 1990 the World Bank approved a $200 million loan to assist Tanzania in the radical restructuring of its agricultural marketing system. Unprofitable state farms are to be sold off, the cereal marketing board is to be abolished, and the role of cash-crop marketing boards will be reduced.

FREEDOM

Despite the promise of multiparty democracy, the persecution of dissidents persists in Tanzania, while freedom of association, assembly, and speech continues to be denied. In July 1992 the leader of the outlawed Democratic Party, Reverend Christopher Mtikila, was jailed for 9 months for calling the president a "thief" at an "illegal public meeting."

HEALTH/WELFARE

The Tanzanian Development Plan calls for the government to give priority to health and education in its expenditures. This reflects a recognition that early progress in these areas has been undermined to some extent in recent years. Malnutrition remains a critical problem.

ACHIEVEMENTS

The government has had enormous success in its program of promoting the use of Swahili as the national language throughout society. Mass literacy in Swahili has facilitated the rise of a national culture, helping to make Tanzania one of the more cohesive African states.

Uganda (Republic of Uganda)

GEOGRAPHY

Area in Square Kilometers (Miles):
235,885 (91,076) (slightly smaller than
Oregon)
Capital (Population): Kampala
(650,000)
Climate: tropical to semiarid

PEOPLE

Population
Total: 18,700,000
Annual Growth Rate: 3.7%
Rural/Urban Population Ratio: 90/10
Languages: official: English; others
spoken: Kiswahili, Luganda, Iteso,
Soga, Acholi, Lugbara, Nyakole
Nyoro, others

Health
Life Expectancy at Birth: 50 years
(male); 52 years (female)
Infant Mortality Rate (Ratio): 94/1,000
Average Caloric Intake: 83% of FAO
minimum
Physicians Available (Ratio): 1/27,420

Religion(s)
66% Christian; 18% traditional
indigenous; 16% Muslim

Education
Adult Literacy Rate: 48%

COMMUNICATION
Telephones: 61,600
Newspapers: 5

TROUBLED WATER

Lake Victoria, which borders southeastern Uganda, is the world's
second-biggest body of freshwater. Millions of Ugandans survive by
consuming its fish. But now environmental change is threatening their
future. Rapidly rising levels of algae in the lake's lower depths are
reducing oxygen levels in the water, killing off fish stocks. Most
researchers now believe that the principal factor behind this shift was
the introduction 30 years ago of the Nile perch by local fishery officials.
The motive for introducing this new species was its size (up to 200
pounds) and the quality of its meat. Since the early 1980s the Nile perch
has significantly boosted the value of local catches. But it has also
greatly reduced the number of local haplochromines, some 400 species
of small fish that have kept algae levels down. Now there are fears that
fishing in Lake Victoria could soon collapse as more of its biomass dies
of asphyxiation, destroying its natural food chain.

TRANSPORTATION
Highways—Kilometers (Miles): 26,200
(16,244)
Railroads—Kilometers (Miles): 1,286
(797)
Usable Airports: 28

GOVERNMENT
Type: republic; under control of the
National Resistance Council
Independence Date: October 9, 1962
Head of State: President Yoweri
Kaguta Museveni
Political Parties: National Resistance
Movement (only party allowed public
political activities); Nationalist Liberal
Party; Democratic Party; Conservative
Party; Uganda People's Congress
Suffrage: universal over 18

MILITARY
Number of Armed Forces: 70,000
*Military Expenditures (% of Central
Government Expenditures):* 1.5%
Current Hostilities: none

ECONOMY
Currency ($ U.S. Equivalent): 370
Uganda shillings = $1
Per Capita Income/GDP: $290/$5.4
billion
Inflation Rate: 30%
Natural Resources: copper; other
minerals
Agriculture: coffee; tea; cotton
Industry: processed agricultural goods;
copper; cement; shoes; fertilizer; steel;
beverages

FOREIGN TRADE
Exports: $273 million
Imports: $652 million

Establishment of the oldest Ugandan kingdom, Bunyoro, followed by the formation of Baganda and other kingdoms **1500**	Kabaka Metesa I of Baganda welcomes British explorer H. M. Stanley **1870s**	A British protectorate over Uganda is proclaimed **1893**	An agreement gives Baganda special status in the British protectorate **1900**

UGANDA

After a decade and a half of repressive rule accompanied by massive interethnic violence, Uganda is still struggling for peace and reconciliation. A land rich in natural and human resources, Uganda suffered dreadfully during the despotic regimes of Milton Obote (1962–1971, 1980–1985) and Idi Amin (1971–1979). Under these two dictators, hundreds of thousands of Ugandans were murdered by the state.

The country had reached a state of general social and economic collapse by 1986, when the forces of the National Resistance Movement (NRM) established the current administration, which is led by Yoweri Museveni. This government has made considerable progress in restoring a sense of normalcy throughout most of the country, but it faces overwhelming challenges in its attempts to rebuild the nation. In 1992 a commission was formed to look into the possibility of returning the country to multiparty democracy.

HISTORIC GEOGRAPHY

The breakdown of Uganda is an extreme example of the disruptive role of ethnic and sectarian competition, which was fostered by policies of both its colonial and postcolonial governments. Uganda consists of two major zones: the plains of the northeast and the southern highlands. It has been said that you can drop anything into the rich volcanic soils of the well-watered south and it will grow. Until the 1960s the area was divided into four kingdoms—Buganda, Bunyoro, Ankole, and Toro—whose peoples speak related Bantu languages. The histories of these states stretch back to the fifteenth century. European visitors of the nineteenth century were impressed by their sophisticated social orders, which the Europeans equated with the feudal monarchies of medieval Europe. When the British took over, they integrated the ruling class of the southern highlands into a system of "indirect rule." By then missionaries had already succeeded in converting many southerners to Christianity; indeed, civil war among Protestants, Catholics, and Muslims within Buganda had been the British pretext for establishing their overrule.

The Acholi, Langi, Karamojang, Teso, Madi, and Kakwa peoples, who are predominant in the northeast, lack the politi-

(UN photo by T. Chen)

Uganda is a land rich in natural and human resources with tremendous potential for economic growth and improved quality of life. A major problem has been overcoming the abuses of Uganda's despotic regimes of the 1960s, 1970s, and 1980s. Idi Amin, above, was dictator from 1971 to 1979. Under his repressive rule, hundreds of thousands of Ugandans were murdered by the state.

cal heritage of hierarchical state-building found in the south. These groups are also linguistically separate, speaking either Nilotic or Nilo-Hametic languages. The two regions were united by the British as the Uganda Protectorate during the 1890s (the name "Uganda," which is a corruption of "Buganda," has since become the accepted term for the larger entity). But the zones developed separately under colonial rule.

Cash-crop farming, especially of cotton,

by local peasants spurred an economic boom in the south. The Bugandan ruling class benefited in particular. Growing levels of education and wealth led to the European stereotype of the "progressive" Bugandans as "the Japanese of Africa." A growing class of Asian entrepreneurs also played an important role in the local economy, although its prosperity, as well as that of the Bugandan elite, suffered from subordination to resident British interests.

The south's growing economy stood in

| Kabaka of Baganda is exiled to the United Kingdom by the British for espousing Bagandan independence **1953** | Uganda becomes independent **1962** | Milton Obote introduces a new unitary Constitution and forces Bagandan compliance **1966** | Idi Amin seizes power **1971** | Amin invades Tanzania **1978** | Tanzania invades Uganda and overturns Amin's government **1979** | **1980s–1990s** |

| The rise and fall of the second Obote regime leaves 300,000 dead | The NRM takes power under Yoweri Museveni | Recovery produces slow gains; unrest continues in the northeast |

sharp contrast to the relative neglect of the northeast. Forced to earn money to pay taxes, many northeasterners became migrant workers in the south. They were also recruited, almost exclusively, to serve in the colonial security forces.

As independence approached, many Bugandans feared that their interests would be compromised by other groups. Under the leadership of their king, Mutesa II, they sought to uphold their separate status. Other groups feared that Bugandan wealth and educational levels could lead to their dominance. A compromise federal structure was agreed to for the new state. At independence the southern kingdoms retained their autonomous status within the United Kingdom of Uganda. The first government was made up of Mutesa's royalist party and the United People's Congress (UPC), a largely non-Bugandan coalition, led by Milton Obote, a Langi. Mutesa was elected as president and Obote as prime minister.

THE REIGN OF TERROR

In 1966 the delicate balance of ethnic interests was upset when Obote used the army—still dominated by fellow northeasterners—to overthrow Mutesa and the Constitution. In the name of abolishing "tribalism," Obote established a one-party state and ruled in an increasingly dictatorial fashion. However, in 1971 he was overthrown by his army chief, Idi Amin. Amin began his regime with widespread public support but alienated himself by favoring fellow Muslims and Kakwa. He

expelled the 40,000-member Asian community and distributed their property to his cronies. The Langi, suspected of being pro-Obote, were also early targets of his persecution, but his attacks soon spread to other members of Uganda's Christian community, at the time about 80 percent of the total population. Educated people in particular were purged. The number of Ugandans murdered by Amin's death squads is unknown; the most commonly cited figure is 300,000, but estimates range from 50,000 to 1 million. Many others went into exile.

A Ugandan military incursion into Tanzania led to war between the two countries in 1979. Many Ugandans joined with the Tanzanians in defeating Amin's army and its Libyan allies. Unfortunately, the overthrow of Amin, who fled into exile, did not lead to better times. In 1980 Obote was returned to power through a fraudulent vote count.

The second Obote administration was characterized by a continuation of the violence of the Amin years. An estimated 300,000 people, mostly southerners, were massacred by Obote's security forces; an equal number fled the country. Much of the killing occurred in the Bugandan area known as the Luwero triangle, which was completely depopulated; today its fields are still full of skeletons. As the killings escalated, so did the resistance of Museveni's NRM guerrillas, who had taken to the bush in the aftermath of the failed election. In 1985 a split between Ancholi and Langi officers led to Obote's overthrow and yet another pattern of interethnic recrimination. Finally, in 1986, the NRM gained the upper hand.

THE STRUGGLE CONTINUES

Museveni's NRM administration has faced enormous challenges in trying to bring about national reconstruction. The task has been complicated by continued warfare in the northeast by armed factions representing elements of the former regimes, independent Karamojong communities, and followers of prophetic religious movements. In 1987 an uprising of the Holy Spirit rebels of Alice Lakwena was crushed, at the cost of some 15,000 lives.

Currently there is cause for both hope and despair in Uganda. A sense of civil society has been returning to much of the country. Since 1990 the level of insurgency has been low. With peace has come economic growth, which has made up for some of the past decline. But a stable political order has yet to emerge. Museveni has spoken of a "no party government," while so far resisting growing agitation for a restoration of multiparty democracy. Uganda also faces an acute AIDS epidemic. In 1989 the government released a study showing 800,000 Ugandans as being HIV-positive.

DEVELOPMENT

At least 35% of public spending goes toward supporting one of Africa's biggest militaries. This legacy of past conflicts hinders development.

FREEDOM

The human-rights situation has improved greatly under Uganda's NRM government, but detentions without trial, massacres of civilians, and other abuses have been carried out by the government as well as its opponents. Freedom of speech and association are curtailed.

HEALTH/WELFARE

Uganda's traditionally strong school system was not completely destroyed under Amin and Obote. In 1986 some 70% of primary-school children attended classes. The killing and exiling of teachers have resulted in a serious drop of standards at all levels of the education system, but progress is under way.

ACHIEVEMENTS

The Ugandan government was one of the first countries in Africa (and the world) to acknowledge the seriousness of the AIDS epidemic within its borders. It has instituted public-information campaigns and welcomed outside support. In urban areas, the seropositive rate is 25%.

Southern Africa

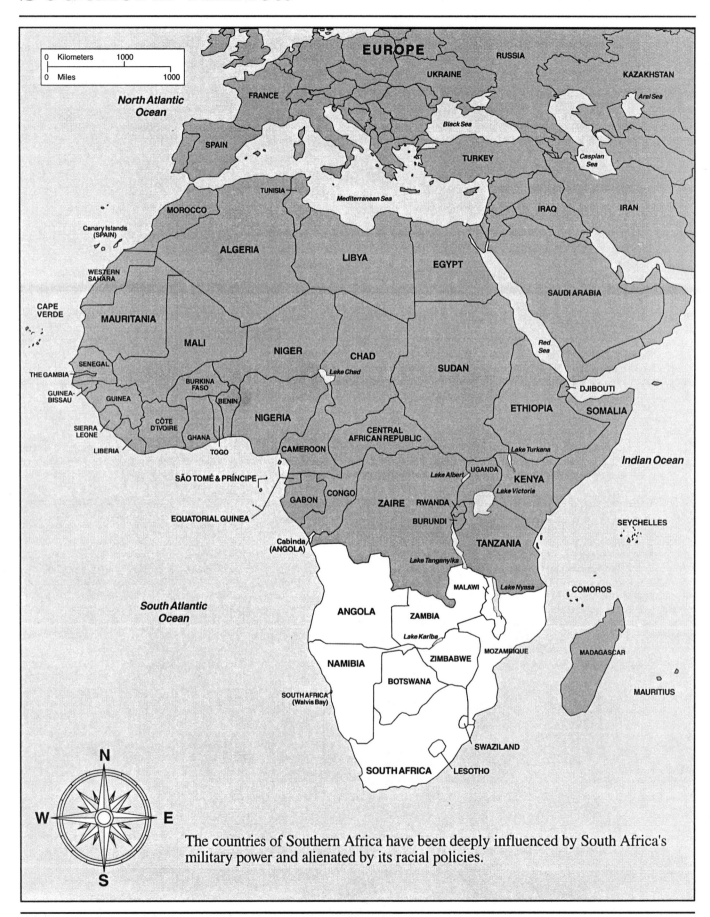

The countries of Southern Africa have been deeply influenced by South Africa's military power and alienated by its racial policies.

Southern Africa: The Struggle for Self-Determination

Southern Africa, which includes the nations of Angola, Botswana, Lesotho, Malawi, Mozambique, Namibia, South Africa, Swaziland, Zambia, and Zimbabwe, is a diverse region made up of savannas and forest, snow-topped mountains and desert, areas of temperate Mediterranean and torrid tropical climate. Southern African identity is, however, as much defined by the region's peoples and their past and present interactions as by its geographic features. An appreciation of local history is crucial to understanding the forces that both divide and unite the region today.

EUROPEAN MIGRATION AND DOMINANCE

A dominant theme in the modern history of Southern Africa has been the evolving struggle of the region's indigenous black African majority to free itself of the racial hegemony of white settlers from Europe and their descendants. By the eighth century, but probably earlier, the southernmost regions of the continent were populated by a variety of black African ethnic groups who spoke languages belonging to the Bantu as well as the Khoisan linguistic classifications. Members of these two groupings practiced both agriculture and pastoralism; archaeological evidence indicates that live-stock-keeping predates the time of Christ. Some, such as the Kongo of northern Angola and the Shona peoples of the Zimbabwean plateaux had, by the fifteenth century, organized strong states, while others, like most Nguni speakers,

prior to the early nineteenth century, lived in smaller communities. Throughout the region trade networks existed, linking various local peoples not only to one another but also to the markets of the Indian Ocean and beyond. In the grounds of the Great Zimbabwe, a stone-walled settlement that flourished in the fifteenth century, porcelains from China have been unearthed.

In the sixteenth century small numbers of Portuguese began settling along the coasts of Angola and Mozambique. A century later, in 1652, the Dutch established a settlement at Africa's southernmost tip, the Cape of Good Hope. While the Portuguese flag generally remained confined to coastal enclaves until the late nineteenth century, throughout the eighteenth century the Dutch colony expanded steadily into the interior, seizing the land of local Khoisan communities. Unlike the colonial footholds of the Portuguese and other Europeans on the continent, which prior to the nineteenth century were mostly centers for the export of slaves, the Dutch Cape Colony imported slaves from Asia as well as from elsewhere in Africa. Although not legally enslaved, conquered Khoisan were also reduced to servitude. In the process a new society evolved at the Cape that, much like the antebellum American South, was racially divided between free white settlers and subordinated peoples of mixed African and Afro-Asian descent.

During the Napoleonic wars Britain took over the Cape Colony. Shortly thereafter, in 1820, significant numbers of

(United Nations photo by Ray Witlin)

Countries throughout Southern Africa are developing projects to employ laborers who might otherwise migrate to urban centers in South Africa—a pattern established in colonial times. These workers are building a highway in Lesotho.

English-speaking colonists began arriving in the region. The arrival of the British coincided with a period of political realignment throughout much of Southern Africa, which is commonly referred to as the Mfecane. Until recently the historical literature has generally attributed this upheaval to dislocations caused by the rise of the Zulu state, under the great warrior prince Shaka. However, more recent scholarship has focused on the disruptive effects of increased traffic in contraband slaves from the interior to the Cape and the Portuguese stations of Mozambique, following the international ban on slave-trading.

During the 1830s the British abolished slavery throughout their empire and extended limited civil rights to nonwhites at the Cape. In response, a large number of white Dutch-descended Boers, or Afrikaners, moved into the interior, where they founded two republics, which were free of British control. This migration, known as the Great Trek, did not lead the white settlers into an empty land. Many African groups lost their farms and pastures to the superior fire-power of the early Afrikaners, who often coerced local communities into supplying corvee labor for their farms and public works. But a few African polities, like Lesotho and the western Botswana kingdoms, were able to preserve their independence by acquiring their own firearms.

During the second half of the nineteenth century white migration and dominance spread throughout the rest of Southern Africa. The discovery of diamonds and gold in northeastern South Africa encouraged white exploration and subsequent occupation farther north. During the 1890s Cecil Rhodes's British South Africa Company occupied modern Zambia and Zimbabwe, which then became known as the Rhodesias. British traders, missionaries, and settlers also invaded the area now known as Malawi. Meanwhile the Germans seized Namibia, while the Portuguese began to expand inland from their coastal enclaves. Thus by 1900 the entire region had fallen under white colonial control.

(United Nations photo by J. P. Laffont)

Angolan youths celebrated when the nation became independent in 1974.

With the exception of Lesotho and Botswana, which were occupied as British "protectorates," all the European colonies in Southern Africa had significant populations of white settlers, who in each case played a predominant political and economic role in their respective territories. Throughout the region this white supremacy was fostered and maintained through racially discriminatory policies of land alienation, labor regulation, and the denial of full civil rights to nonwhites. In South Africa, where the largest and longest-settled white population resided, the Afrikaners and English-speaking settlers were granted full self-government in 1910, with a constitution that left that country's black majority virtually powerless.

BLACK NATIONALISM AND SOUTH AFRICAN DESTABILIZATION

After World War II new movements advocating black self-determination gradually gained ascendancy throughout the region. However, the progress of these struggles for majority rule and independence was gradual. By 1968 the countries of Botswana, Lesotho, Malawi, Swaziland, and Zambia had gained their independence. The area was then polarized between liberated and nonliberated nations. In 1974 a military uprising in Portugal brought statehood to Angola and Mozambique, after long armed struggles by liberation forces within the two territories. Wars of liberation also led to the overthrow of white-settler rule in Zimbabwe, in 1980, and the independence of Namibia, in 1990.

Today South Africa stands alone on the continent as an area of continued white-minority rule. This fact has continued to have serious implications for the entire Southern African region as well as for the oppressed masses inside of South Africa itself. Since the late nineteenth century South Africa has developed into the region's dominant economic and military power. Most of the subcontinent's roads and rails run through South Africa. For generations South Africa has also recruited expatriate as well as local black African workers for its industries and mines. Today the country is the most economically developed country on the continent, with manufactured goods and agricultural surpluses that are in high demand elsewhere. Thus, in addition to the dependent economies of its own region, countries farther to the north trade with South Africa and use its infrastructure. Altogether some 46 countries in Africa import South African goods and crops.

To reduce their economic dependency on South Africa, while cooperating on mutually beneficial development projects, all the black-ruled countries of Southern Africa, plus the East African nation of Tanzania, joined together to form the Southern African Development Coordination Conference (SADCC). Founded in 1980, this organization is working to exploit the vast potential of its member countries, which have a large share of the continent's resources as well

as a combined population of 65 million. Each SADCC government has assumed responsibility for research and planning in a specific developmental area: that is, Angola for energy, Mozambique for transport and communication, Tanzania for industry, and so on. Over the past decade SADCC has succeeded in attracting considerable outside aid for building and rehabilitating its member states' infrastructure. The organization's greatest success so far has been the Beira corridor project, which has enabled said Mozambican port to serve once more as a major regional transit point. Other successes include total telecommunications independence of South Africa, new regional power grids, and the upgrading of Tanzanian roads to carry Malawian goods to the port of Dar es Salaam. In 1992 the SADCC states pledged themselves to embark upon more ambitious programs of full economic integration, in the process formally changing their organization's name to the Southern African Development Community (SADC).

Until recently the violent destabilizing policies of the South African military complicated efforts toward building greater regional cooperation. The independent, black-ruled states, especially the so-called Frontline States (Angola, Botswana, Mozambique, Tanzania, Zambia, and Zimbabwe), have been hostile to South Africa's racial policies and, to varying degrees, have long provided havens for those oppressed by them. South Africa has responded by striking out against its exiled opponents through overt and covert military operations, while encouraging insurgent movements among some of its neighbors, most notably in Angola and Mozambique.

In Angola, South Africa, along with the United States, backed the rebel movement Unita, while in Mozambique it has continued to assist Renamo. Both of these movements have resorted to the sabotaging of railways and roads in their operational areas, a tactic that has greatly increased the dependence on South African communications of the landlocked states of Botswana, Malawi, Zambia, and Zimbabwe. During the 1980s the overall monetary cost to the Frontline States of the destabilization campaign by South Africa and its proxies' forces has been estimated at $60 billion (the same countries' combined annual GNP was only about $25 billion in 1989). The human costs have been even greater. Hundreds of thousands of people have been killed and at least equal numbers maimed, while more than a million in Mozambique alone have become refugees.

In the context of its region, South Africa has been a military superpower. Despite the imposition of a mandatory UN arms embargo on it in 1977, the country's military establishment has been able to secure both the arms and sophisticated technology needed to develop its own military/industrial complex. South Africa today is nearly self-sufficient in basic munitions, with a vast and advanced arsenal of weapons and a possible nuclear-arms capacity. Whereas in 1978 it imported 75 percent of its weapons, today the figure is only about 5 percent. The embargo, however, has been effective. While South African industry produces many sophisticated weapons systems, some of which have been quietly sold abroad, it has faced increasing difficulties in maintaining its regional superiority in such high-technology components as fighter aircraft. By 1989 the increasing edge of Angolan pilots and air defense systems was a significant factor in South Africa's decision to disengage from that country's civil war. The economic costs of South African militarization have also been steep. In addition to draining some 20 percent of its total budget outlays, the destabilization campaign has contributed to increased international economic sanctions, which since 1985 have cost the South African economy at least $20 billion.

South Africa sought to justify its acts of aggression by claiming that it was simply engaged in counterinsurgency operations against guerrillas of the African National Congress (ANC) and Pan Africanist Congress (PAC), which have been struggling for the regime's overthrow. But, in fact, the various Frontline States throughout the 1980s took a cautious attitude toward the activities of South African political refugees, generally forbidding them from launching armed attacks from across their borders. In 1984 both Angola and Mozambique formally signed agreements of mutual noninterference with South Africa. Within a year of these agreements, however, it was South Africa that had repeatedly and blatantly violated their accords.

Over the past decade drought, along with continued warfare, has resulted in recurrent food shortages in much of Southern Africa, especially in Angola and Mozambique. The early 1980s drought in Southern Africa neither lasted as long nor was as widely publicized as those of West Africa or the Horn, yet it was no less destructive. Although some countries, such as Botswana, Mozambique, and Zimbabwe, as well as areas of South Africa, suffered more from nature than others, the main features of the crisis were the same: water reserves were depleted; cattle and game died; and crop production declined, often by 50 percent or more.

Maize and cereal production suffered everywhere. South Africa and Zimbabwe, usually grain exporters, had to import food. The countries of Angola, Botswana, and Lesotho each had more than half a million people who were affected by the shortfalls; some 2 million were malnourished in Mozambique. But in 1988 the rains returned to the region, raising cereal production by 40 percent. Zimbabwe was able not only to export but also to provide food aid to other African countries. However, South African destabilization has contributed to continuing food scarcities in many parts of Angola and Mozambique, despite improved rainfall. During the late 1980s there were 4.5 million people still at

(United Nations photo by Jerry Frank)

South Africa's economic and military dominance overshadows the region's planning. Pictured above is the South African city of Cape Town, the chief port and legislative capital of the country.

risk of starvation in Mozambique and another 3 million in Angola, while Malawi also faced food shortages, partially due to the presence of nearly a million refugees who have fled the warfare in Mozambique. In 1991–1992 the entire region once more was pushed toward catastrophe, with the onset of the worst single drought year in at least a century.

HOPES FOR PEACE

Recent events have given rise to hopes for peace in Southern Africa. In 1988 Angola, Cuba, and South Africa reached an agreement, with U.S. and Soviet support, that has led to South Africa's withdrawal from Namibia and the removal of Cuban troops from Angola, where they had been supporting government forces. In 1990 Namibia gained its independence under the elected leadership of SWAPO, the liberation movement that had fought against local South African occupation for more than a quarter of a century. After an on-again, off-again start, in 1991 direct negotiations between the Angolan government and Unita rebels led to a UN-supervised peace process based on multiparty elections, which may lead to lasting reconciliation through the establishment of a multiparty government of national unity. In 1992 the government of Mozambique signed a similar agreement with Renamo.

Perhaps the most significant opening has been in South Africa itself. The 1990 release of prominent political prisoners, including Nelson Mandela, the unbanning of the ANC and PAC, and the lifting of internal state-of-emergency restrictions have raised hopes for a negotiated end to white-minority rule. Direct talks between the government and the ANC are ongoing and have so far led the latter organization to suspend its armed struggle. This development has caused further hope throughout the rest of Southern Africa that the era of regional destabilization, along with white rule in South Africa itself, may be coming to a close. However, major obstacles remain to the realization of peace agreements in Angola and Mozambique as well as South Africa.

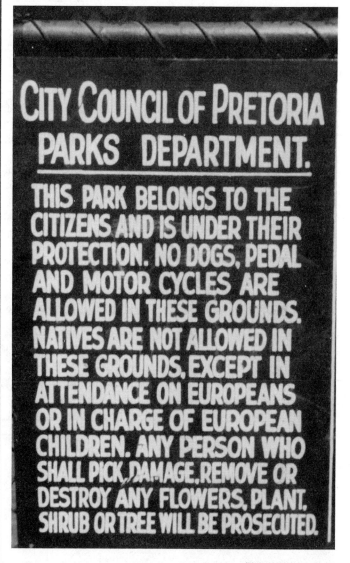

(United Nations photo)

This sign in a park in Pretoria, South Africa, is a reflection of the restrictions of apartheid, the South African government's policy of racial discrimination.

Angola (Republic of Angola)

GEOGRAPHY

Area in Square Kilometers (Miles):
1,246,699 (481,351) (larger than Texas
and California combined)
Capital (Population): Luanda
(1,100,000)
Climate: tropical and subtropical

PEOPLE

Population

Total: 8,668,000
Annual Growth Rate: 2.7%
Rural/Urban Population Ratio: 72/28
Languages: official: Portuguese;
others spoken: Ovimbundu,
Kimbundu, Bakongo

Health

Life Expectancy at Birth: 42 years
(male); 46 years (female)
Infant Mortality Rate (Ratio):
151/1,000
Average Caloric Intake: 83% of FAO
minimum
Physicians Available (Ratio): 1/17,750

Religion(s)

47% traditional indigenous; 38%
Roman Catholic; 15% Protestant

Education

Adult Literacy Rate: 42%

COMMUNICATION

Telephones: 40,300
Newspapers: 1

CABINDA

The tiny enclave of Cabinda, separated from the rest of Angola by a 25-mile strip of Zairian territory, is home to about 85,000 people. It is also the location of most of Angola's current petroleum output, which accounts for 86 percent of the nation's export earnings. Most of the oil is pumped from offshore fields by the Gulf Oil Corporation, whose royalty payments are the Angolan government's leading source of income. Ironically, during the war, this American company's installations were guarded by Cuban troops against attacks from UNITA rebels, who were backed by the U.S. CIA. Peace within the enclave continues to be threatened by various factions of the Front for the Liberation of the Cabinda State (FLEC), a local secessionist movement that in the past was sponsored by Zaire.

TRANSPORTATION

Highways—Kilometers (Miles): 73,828
(45,877)
Railroads—Kilometers (Miles): 3,189
(1,982)
Usable Airports: 183

GOVERNMENT

Type: people's republic
Independence Date: November 11,
1975
Head of State: President José
Edouardo dos Santos
Political Parties: Popular Movement
for the Liberation of Angola; National
Front for the Liberation of Angola;
National Union for the Total
Independence of Angola; others
Suffrage: universal at 18

MILITARY

Number of Armed Forces: 96,000
*Military Expenditures (% of Central
Government Expenditures):* n/a
Current Hostilities: none

ECONOMY

Currency ($ U.S. Equivalent): 183
kwanzas = $1 (fixed rate)
Per Capita Income/GDP: $925/$8.01
billion
Inflation Rate: 23%
Natural Resources: oil; diamonds;
manganese; gold; uranium
Agriculture: coffee; sisal; corn; cotton;
sugar; manioc; tobacco; bananas;
plantains
Industry: oil; diamond mining;
fish processing; brewing; tobacco;
sugar processing; textiles; cement;
food processing; construction

FOREIGN TRADE

Exports: $3.8 billion
Imports: $1.5 billion

ANGOLA

The successful holding of multiparty elections in September 1992 briefly raised expectations of a new beginning for Angola. While the incumbent President José Edouardo dos Santos and his ruling Popular Movement for the Liberation of Angola (MPLA) topped the poll, other parties, most notably the MPLA's long-time armed rivals, the National Union for the Total Independence of Angola (UNITA) and the smaller National Front for the Liberation of Angola (FNLA), secured considerable votes. Many hoped that a government of national unity would emerge, allowing Angolans finally to enjoy the fruits of their independence. But the rejection of the electoral outcome by UNITA now threatens to plunge the country into renewed civil war.

Angola is potentially one of the richest countries in Africa, but 16 years of civil war, mostly fought between the MPLA and UNITA, reduced this nation of less than 9 million people to near ruin. From 1975, the year of its independence from Portugal, to 1991, approximately a half-million Angolans perished due to the direct and indirect effects of the conflict. Up to 1 million others fled the country, while another 1 million or so were internally displaced. According to a report by the human-rights organization Africa Watch, tens of thousands of Angolans have lost their limbs "because of the indiscriminate use of landmines by both sides of the conflict." Angola's relatively small and impoverished population could not have perpetuated such carnage were it not for the long history of external interference in the nation's internal affairs. The United States, along with the former Soviet Union, South Africa, Cuba, Zaire, and many others, helped to create and sustain this tragedy.

THE COLONIAL LEGACY

The roots of Angola's long suffering lie in the area's colonial underdevelopment. The Portuguese first made contact with the peoples of the region in 1483. They initially established peaceful trading contact with the powerful Kongo kingdom and other coastal peoples, some of whom were converted to Catholicism by Jesuit missionaries. But from the sixteenth to the mid-nineteenth centuries, the outsiders primarily saw the area as a source of slaves. Angola has been called "the mother of Brazil" because up to 4 million Angolans were carried away from its shores to that country, chained in the holds of slave ships. With the possible exception of Nigeria, no African territory lost more of its people to the trans-Atlantic slave trade.

Following the nineteenth-century suppression of the slave trade, the Portuguese introduced internal systems of exploitation that very often amounted to slavery in all but name. Large numbers of Angolans were pressed into working on coffee plantations owned by a growing community of white settlers, while others were forced to labor in other sectors, such as diamond mines or public-works projects.

Although the Portuguese claimed that they encouraged Angolans to learn Portuguese and practice Catholicism, thus becoming "assimilated" into the world of the colonizers, they actually made little effort to provide education. No more than 2 percent of the population ever achieved the legal status of *assimilado*. The assimilados, many of whom were of mixed race, were concentrated in the coastal towns. Of the few interior Angolans who became literate, a large proportion were the products of Protestant, non-Portuguese, mission schools. Because each mission tended to operate in a particular region and teach, usually in the local language, from its own syllabi, an unfortunate by-product of these schools was the reinforcement (the creation, some would argue) of ethnic rivalries among the territory's educated elite.

During the late colonial period the FNLA, MPLA, and UNITA emerged as the three major liberation movements challenging Portuguese rule. Although all three sought a national following, by 1975 each had built up an ethnoregional core of support. The FNLA grew out of a movement whose original focus was limited to the northern Kongo-speaking population, while UNITA's principal stronghold has been the largely Ovimbundu-speaking south-central plateaux. The MPLA has its strongest following among assimilados and Kimbundu speakers, who are predominant in Luanda, the capital, and the interior to the west of the city.

From the beginning all three movements cultivated separate sources of external support. The MPLA, which had incorporated local members of the Portuguese Communist Party, enjoyed Soviet-bloc backing, while for a number of years UNITA received most of its arms from the Chinese (via Zambia) and thus adopted an appropriately Maoist posture. Despite its ties to Portugal, through the North Atlantic Treaty Organization, the United States occasionally provided covert support to the FNLA, which also had consistent backing from Zaire.

The armed struggle against the Portuguese began in 1961, with a massive FNLA-inspired uprising in the north and MPLA-led unrest in Luanda. To counter the northern rebellion, the Portuguese resorted to the saturation bombing of villages, which during the first year of fighting left an estimated 50,000 dead (about half of the total number killed throughout the anticolonial struggle). The liberation forces were as much hampered by their own disunity as by the brutality of Portugal's counterinsurgency tactics. Undisciplined rebels associated with the FNLA, for ex-

(United Nations photo by J. P. Laffont)
The war for independence from Portugal led to the creation of a one-party state.

| The Kongo state develops 1400 | The Kongo state is contacted by the Portuguese 1483 | Queen Nzinga defends the Mbundu kingdom against the Portuguese 1640 | The MPLA is founded in Luanda 1956 | The national war of liberation begins 1961 | Angolan independence from Portugal 1975 | South African-initiated air and ground incursions into Angola 1976 | President Agostinho Neto dies; José dos Santos becomes president 1979 | 1980s–1990s |

Jonas Savimbi visits the United States; U.S. "material and moral" support for UNITA resumes

Savimbi and dos Santos shake hands in Zaire, opening the door to direct peace negotiations; but the war continues

Efforts for national reconciliation; multiparty elections

ample, were known to massacre not only Portuguese plantation owners but many of their southern workers as well. Such incidents contributed to UNITA's split from the FNLA in 1966. There is also evidence of UNITA forces cooperating with the Portuguese in attacks on the MPLA. Besides competition with its two rivals, the MPLA also encountered some difficulty in keeping its urban and rural factions united.

CIVIL WAR

The overthrow of Portugal's fascist government in 1974 led to Angola's rapid decolonization. Attempts to create a transitional government of national unity between the three major nationalist movements failed. The MPLA succeeded in seizing Luanda, which led to a loose alliance between the FNLA and UNITA. As fighting between the groups escalated, so did the involvement of their foreign backers. Meanwhile, most of Angola's 300,000 or more white settlers fled the country, triggering the collapse of much of the local economy. With the notable exception of Angola's offshore oil industry, most economic sectors have since failed to recover their preindependence output as a result of the war.

While the chronology of outside intervention in the Angolan conflict is a matter of dispute, it is nonetheless clear that, by October 1975, up to 2,000 South African troops were assisting the FNLA-UNITA forces in the south. In response, Cuba dispatched a force of 18,000 to 20,000 to assist the MPLA, which had earlier gained control of Luanda. These events proved decisive during the war's first phase. On

the one hand, collaboration with South Africa led to the withdrawal of Chinese and much of the African support for the FNLA-UNITA cause. It also contributed to the U.S. Congress's passage of the Clarke Amendment, which abruptly terminated the United States' direct involvement. On the other hand, the arrival of the Cubans allowed the MPLA quickly to gain the upper hand on the battlefield. Not wishing to fight a conventional war against the Cubans by themselves, the South Africans withdrew their conventional forces in March 1976.

By 1977 the MPLA's "People's Republic" had established itself in all of Angola's provinces and was recognized by the United Nations and most of its membership as the nation's sole legitimate government, the United States numbering among the few that continued to withhold recognition. However, the MPLA's apparent victory did not bring an end to the hostilities. Although the remaining pockets of FNLA resistance were overcome following an Angola-Zaire rapprochement in 1978, UNITA maintained its largely guerrilla struggle. Until 1989 UNITA's major supporter was South Africa, whose destabilization of the Luanda government was motivated by its desire to keep the Benguela railway closed (thus diverting traffic to its own system) and harass Angolan-based SWAPO forces. Besides supplying UNITA with logistical support, the South Africans repeatedly invaded southern Angola and on occasion infiltrated sabotage units into other areas of the country. South African aggression in turn justified Cuba's maintenance, by 1988, of some 50,000 troops in support of the govern-

ment. In 1986 the U.S. Congress approved the resumption of "covert" U.S. material assistance to UNITA via Zaire.

An escalation of the fighting in 1987 and 1988 was accompanied by a revival of negotiations for a peace settlement among representatives of the Angolan government, Cuba, South Africa, and the United States. In 1988 South African forces were checked in a battle at the Angolan town of Cuito Cuanavale. South Africa agreed to withdraw from Namibia and end its involvement in the Angolan conflict. It was further agreed that Cuba would complete a phased withdrawal of its forces from the region by mid-1991.

The scaling back of external support, in the context of a relaxation of cold war tensions around the world, provided a basis for further contacts between the warring parties themselves. After off-and-on progress, an agreement was finally initialed in April 1991 between the MPLA president, dos Santos, and the UNITA leader, Savimbi, which led to the establishment of a UN-supervised ceasefire and a national reconciliation process. This process culminated in the September 1992 elections. Although UNITA's rejection of MPLA's electoral victory has led to renewed bloodshed, diplomatic efforts are trying to salvage the reconciliation process.

DEVELOPMENT

More than four-fifths of Angola's export revenues currently come from oil. There are important diamond and iron mines, but their output suffered due to the war, which also prevented the exploitation of the country's considerable reserves of other minerals. Angola has enormous agricultural potential, but currently only about 2% of its arable land is under cultivation.

FREEDOM

Despite new constitutional guarantees, pessimists note that neither UNITA nor MPLA have demonstrated a strong commitment to democracy and human rights in the past. Within UNITA, Jonas Savimbi's word has been law; he has been known to have critics within his movement burned as "witches." Many MPLA cadres who fought against the Portuguese were purged in 1977, in the aftermath of an alleged coup attempt.

HEALTH/WELFARE

According to a 1987 UNICEF report, the war caused a serious deterioration of Angola's health service, resulting in lower life expectancy, 43 years overall, and an infant mortality rate that was the highest in the world—200 per 1,000. This rate is now estimated at 151 per 1,000.

ACHIEVEMENTS

Between 1975 and 1980 the Angolan government claimed that it had tripled the nation's primary-school enrollment, to 76%. However, by 1984 the official figure had fallen back to 44% as a result of the war.

Botswana

GEOGRAPHY

Area in Square Kilometers (Miles):
600,372 (231,804) (about the size of Texas)
Capital (Population): Gaborone (139,000)
Climate: arid to semiarid

PEOPLE

Population

Total: 1,258,000
Annual Growth Rate: 2.7%
Rural/Urban Population Ratio: 72/28
Languages: official: (Se)Tswana, English; others spoken: Khiosan, Kalanga, Herero

Health

Life Expectancy at Birth: 59 years (male); 65 years (female)
Infant Mortality Rate (Ratio): 43/1,000
Average Caloric Intake: 90% of FAO minimum
Physicians Available (Ratio): 1/6,900

Religion(s)

50% traditional indigenous; 50% Christian

Education

Adult Literacy Rate: 23%

THE KGOTLA

By tradition, all political and judicial decision-making within a Tswana community has to be aired in an open public forum known as the *kgotla*. This institution, somewhat analogous to the New England town meeting, has long served as a foundation of Tswana democratic ideals, as expressed in this common axiom: "A chief is a chief by the people." Politicians running for office in Botswana today know that they must visit and speak at kgotlas in their areas. In Botswana's cities, "freedom squares" provide an urban counterpart to the traditional kgotla. At the freedom squares, party candidates speak out on issues to crowds of onlookers. This heritage of debate and democracy may, in part, explain the strength and success of Botswana as a functioning parliamentary democracy.

COMMUNICATION

Telephones: 17,900
Newspapers: 5

TRANSPORTATION

Highways—Kilometers (Miles): 11,514 (11,098)
Railroads—Kilometers (Miles): 712 (441)
Usable Airports: 87

GOVERNMENT

Type: parliamentary republic

Independence Date: September 30, 1966
Head of State: President Quett K. J. Masire
Political Parties: Botswana Democratic Party; Botswana National Front; Botswana People's Party; Botswana Independence Party
Suffrage: universal over 21

MILITARY

Number of Armed Forces: 4,500
Military Expenditures (% of Central Government Expenditures): 8.2%
Current Hostilities: none

ECONOMY

Currency ($ U.S. Equivalent): 2.14 pulas = $1
Per Capita Income/GDP: $2,500/$3.14 billion
Inflation Rate: 25%
Natural Resources: diamonds; copper; nickel; salt; soda ash; potash; coal
Agriculture: livestock; sorghum; corn; millet; cowpeas; beans
Industry: diamonds; copper; nickel; salt; soda ash; potash; frozen beef; tourism

FOREIGN TRADE

Exports: $1.8 billion
Imports: $1.7 billion

BOTSWANA

Botswana has been the Cinderella story of postcolonial Africa. In 1966 the country emerged from 80 years of British colonialism as one of the 10 poorest countries in the world, with an annual per capita income of $69. Yet over the past quarter-century the nation's economy has grown at an average annual rate of 11 percent, one of the world's highest. Infrastructure has been created and social services expanded. Whereas at independence the country had no paved roads, major settlements have become increasingly interlinked by ribbons of asphalt and tarmac. A vibrant city has emerged at Gaborone, the nation's capital. New schools, hospitals, and businesses dot the landscape. Such growth has translated into improved standards of living for most Botswana citizens. However, the gap between the small but growing middle class (and the few truly wealthy) and the majority who remain poor is also widening, resulting in social tension.

Botswana's economic success has come in the context of its unbroken postindependence commitment to political pluralism, respect for human rights, and racial and ethnic tolerance. Freedom of speech and association have been upheld. Yet the country's internal strengths remain vulnerable to the external uncertainties of international markets, weather, and the policies of its neighbors, especially South Africa.

HISTORY

Most of Botswana's people share (Se)Tswana as their mother tongue, a language that is also commonly spoken in much of South Africa. There also exist a number of sizable minority communities—Kalanga, Herero, Khalagari, Khiosan groups, and others—but contemporary ethnic conflict is relatively modest. During the nineteenth century most of Botswana was incorporated into 5 Tswana states, each centering around a large settlement of 10,000 people or more. These states, which incorporated non-Tswana communities, survived through agropastoralism, hunting, and their control of trade routes linking Southern and Central Africa. Lucrative dealing in ivory and ostrich feathers allowed local rulers to build up their arsenals and thus deter the aggressive designs of South African whites. However, European missionaries and traders were welcomed, leading to a growth of Christian education and the consumption of industrial goods.

A radical transformation took place after the imposition of British overrule in 1885. Colonial taxes and economic decline stimulated the growth of migrant labor to the mines and industries of South Africa. (In some regions, migrant earnings remain the major source of income.) Although colonial rule brought much hardship and little benefit, the twentieth-century relationship between the peoples of Botswana and the British was complicated by local fears of being incorporated into South Africa. For many decades leading nationalists championed continued rule from London as a shield against their powerful, racially oppressive neighbor.

ECONOMIC DEVELOPMENT

Economic growth since independence has been largely fueled by the rapid expansion of mining activity. Botswana has become one of the world's leading producers of diamonds, which typically account for 80 percent of its export earnings. Local production is managed by Debswana Corporation, an even partnership between the Botswana government and DeBeers, a South African-based global corporation;

(United Nations photo by E. Darroch)

Botswana, like many other African nations, is susceptible to periodic drought. The country, however, has a good supply of underground water and the governmental competence to utilize this resource. In this photograph, antelopes drink from a hole dug to allow water seepage.

| Emergence of the Tswana trading center at Toutswemogala **700** | Kololo and Ndebele invaders devastate the countryside **1820s** | Tswana begin to acquire guns through trade in ivory and other game products **1830s** | Batswana defeat Boer invaders **1852–1853** | The British establish colonial rule over Botswana **1885** | Botswana regains its independence **1966** | **1980s–1990s** |

| Seretse Khama, the nation's first president, dies in office and is succeeded by Quett Masire | Elections in 1984 and 1989 result in landslide victories for the Democratic Party; the National Front is major opposition party | South African raids kill Botswana citizens and South African exiles; new security laws are passed |

Debeers' Central Selling Organization has a near monopoly on diamond sales worldwide. The Botswana government has a good record of maximizing the local benefits of Debswana's production.

The nickel/copper/cobalt mining complex at Selibi-Pikwe is the largest non-government employer in Botswana. Falling metal prices and high development costs have reduced the mine's profitability, but high operating efficiency has assured its survival.

Given that mining can only make a modest contribution to local employment and the potential vulnerability of the diamond market, Botswana is seeking to expand its currently small manufacturing and service sectors. Meat processing is currently the largest industrial activity outside minerals, but efforts are under way to attract overseas investment in both private and parastatal production. Botswana already has a liberal foreign-exchange policy and has established an Export Processing Zone at Selibi-Pikwe. Small-scale production is encouraged through government subsidies.

Tourism is of growing importance. Northern Botswana is particularly noted for its bountiful wildlife and stunning scenery. The region includes the Okavango Delta, a vast and uniquely beautiful swamp area, and the Chobe National Park, home of the world's largest elephant herds.

AGRICULTURE

Agriculture is still the leading economic activity for most Botswana citizens. The standard Tswana greeting, *Pula,* ("Rain") reflects the significance attached to water

in a society prone to its periodic scarcity. Botswana suffered severe droughts between 1980–1987 and again in 1991–1992, which—despite the availability of underground water supplies—had a devastating effect on both crops and livestock. Up to a million cattle are believed to have perished. Small-scale agropastoralists, who make up the largest segment of the population, have been particularly hard hit. However, government relief measures have prevented famine. The government also provides generous subsidies to farmers, but environmental constraints hamper efforts to achieve food self-sufficiency even in nondrought years.

Commercial agriculture is dominated by livestock. The Lobatse abbatoir, opened in 1954, stimulated the growth of the cattle industry. Despite periodic challenges from disease and drought, beef exports have become relatively stable. Much of the output of the Botswana Meat Commission has preferential access to the European Community. There is some concern about the potential for future reductions in the European quota. Because most of Botswana's herds are grazed in communal lands, questions about the allocation of pasture are a source of local debate. There is also a growing, but largely misinformed, international concern that wildlife are being threatened by overgrazing livestock.

SOUTH AFRICA

South Africa is a lingering problem. Since the nineteenth century Botswana has sheltered refugees from racist oppression elsewhere in the region. This has led to

periodic acts of aggression against the country, especially during the 1980s, when Botswana became the repeated victim of overt military raids and covert terrorist operations. The reform process within South Africa has led to an easing of tensions; in 1992 the two countries established formal diplomatic ties for the first time. Botswana has, nonetheless, continued to increase its military spending in recent years, stirring public controversy.

Gaborone is the headquarters of the Southern African Development Community, which was originally conceived to reduce the economic dependence of its 10 member nations on the apartheid state. SADC now plans to transform itself into a common market that could eventually include a democratic South Africa. Despite their political differences, Botswana has maintained a customs union with South Africa that dates back to the colonial era.

DEVELOPMENT

Primary education has become nearly universal since independence. In 1991 more than 70% of those leaving primary school gained access to secondary education. A university, several other tertiary institutions, and 70 vocational centers have also been established.

FREEDOM

Democratic pluralism has been strengthened by the growth of a strong civil society and an independent press. Concern has been voiced about social and economic discrimination against Khiosan-speaking communities living in remote areas of the Kalahari, who are known to many outsiders as "Bushmen."

HEALTH/WELFARE

The national health service provides medical, dental, and optical care for all Botswana residents. More than 90% of the population live within 10 miles of a health-care facility. Efforts are now being made to upgrade facilities and staff. Malnutrition remains a major concern, automobile fatalities a growing one.

ACHIEVEMENTS

The UN's 1990 Human Development Report singles out Botswana among the nations of Africa for significantly improving the living conditions of its people. In 1989 President Masire was awarded the Hunger Project's leadership prize, based on Botswana's record of improving rural nutritional levels during the 1980s despite 7 years of severe drought.

Lesotho (Kingdom of Lesotho)

GEOGRAPHY

Area in Square Kilometers (Miles):
30,344 (11,716) (about the size of
Maryland)
Capital (Population): Maseru
(109,000)
Climate: temperate

PEOPLE

Population

Total: 1,800,000
Annual Growth Rate: 2.6%
Rural/Urban Population Ratio: 80/20
Languages: official: English and
Sesotho; others spoken: Xhosa, Zulu

Health

Life Expectancy at Birth: 59 years
(male); 63 years (female)
Infant Mortality Rate (Ratio): 78/1,000
Average Caloric Intake: 107% of FAO
minimum
Physicians Available (Ratio): 1/12,280

Religion(s)

80% Christian; 20% traditional
indigenous

THE SESOTHO LANGUAGE

Since the mid-nineteenth century Sesotho has been a leading literary language in Africa. Basotho writers have produced a wealth of prose, poetry, and nonfiction in their vernacular. The *Leselinyane La Lesotho*, first published in 1863, is sub-Saharan Africa's oldest continuous vernacular newspaper. Thomas Mofolo's play *Chaka* and Paulas Mopeli's novel *Blanket Boy* are among the many works that have been translated for international audiences. Sesotho also continues to be a major medium in music, journalism, and broadcasting. The South African government has promoted a separate Sesotho alphabet for use among Sotho peoples living in South Africa; this has created one more barrier for South Africans who have tried to encourage reconvergence among various regional dialects.

Education

Adult Literacy Rate: 59%

COMMUNICATION

Telephones: 5,920
Newspapers: 3

TRANSPORTATION

Highways—Kilometers (Miles): 5,167
(3,203)

Railroads—Kilometers (Miles): 1.6
(0.99)
Usable Airports: 28

GOVERNMENT

Type: constitutional monarchy
Independence Date: October 4, 1966
Head of State: King Letsie III
Political Parties: Basotho National
Party; Basutoland Congress Party;
National Independence Party; others
Suffrage: universal over 21

MILITARY

Number of Armed Forces: 2,000
*Military Expenditures (% of Central
Government Expenditures):* 8.6%
Current Hostilities: none

ECONOMY

Currency ($ U.S. Equivalent): 2.85
malotis = $1
Per Capita Income/GDP: $240/$432
million
Inflation Rate: 15%
Natural Resources: diamonds; water;
agricultural and grazing land
Agriculture: mohair; corn; wheat;
sorghum; peas; beans; potatoes;
asparagus; sheep; cattle
Industry: carpets; woolen apparel;
candle making; pottery; jewelry;
tapestries; tourism; mining

FOREIGN TRADE

Exports: $66 million
Imports: $499 million

Lesotho emerges as a leading state in Southern Africa
1820s

Afrikaners annex half of Lesotho
1866

The Sotho successfully fight to preserve local autonomy under the British
1870–1881

Independence is restored
1966

The elections and Constitution are declared void by Leabua Jonathan
1970

An uprising against the government fails
1974

The Lesotho Liberation Army begins a sabotage campaign
1979

1980s–1990s

South African destabilization leads to the overthrow of Jonathan by the military

Pope John Paul II's visit is accompanied by the hijacking of a bus carrying pilgrims; the hijackers are killed by South African commandos

Multiparty elections are promised amid political infighting within the ruling Military Council

LESOTHO

Lesotho is one of the most ethnically homogeneous nations in Africa. Almost all its citizens are Sotho. The country's emergence and survival were largely the product of the diplomatic and military prowess of its nineteenth-century rulers, especially its great founder, King Moshoeshoe I. During the 1860s warfare with South African whites led to the loss of land and people as well as an acceptance of British overrule. For nearly a century the British preserved the country but also taxed the inhabitants and generally neglected their interests. Consequently, Lesotho remains dependent on its neighbor, South Africa. However, despite South African attempts to incorporate the country politically as well as economically, Lesotho's independence was restored by the British in 1966.

Lesotho's politicians were bitterly divided at independence. The conservative National Party (BNP) had won an upset victory in preindependence elections, with strong backing from the South African government and the local Roman Catholic Church, Lesotho's largest Christian denomination. The opposition, which walked out of the independence talks, was polarized between a pro-royalist faction, the Marema-Tlou Freedom Party (whose regional sympathies largely lay with the African National Congress of South Africa), and the Congress Party (which was allied to the rival Pan-Africanist Congress).

Soon after independence the BNP prime minister, Leabua Jonathan, placed the king, Moshoeshoe II, under house arrest and later temporarily exiled him. The BCP won the 1970 elections, but Jonathan, possibly at the behest of South Africa, declared a state of emergency and nullified the results. Jonathan's subsequent attempt to establish a one-party state culminated in 1974 in an alleged coup attempt, which served as a pretext for violent reprisals against supporters of the opposition.

During the early 1980s armed resistance to Jonathan's dictatorship was carried out by the Lesotho Liberation Army (LLA), an armed faction of the BCP. The Lesotho government maintained that the LLA was aided and abetted by South Africa as part of that country's regional destabilization efforts. In fact, by 1983 both the South African government and the Catholic hierarchy were becoming nervous about Jonathan's establishment of diplomatic ties with various Communist-ruled countries and the growing sympathy within the BNP, in particular its increasingly radical youth wing, for the ANC. South African military raids and terrorist attacks targeting antiapartheid refugees in Lesotho became increasingly common. Finally, a South African blockade of Lesotho in 1986 directly led to Jonathan's ouster by his military.

Jonathan's rule had been the source of great resentment and his overthrow was generally welcomed. But there was widespread skepticism about the new regime. Lesotho's ruling Military Council, initially led by Major General Justinus Lekhanya, has been closely linked to South Africa. The Catholic Church has put pressure on the government to return, to civilian rule, and some military leaders want to return to the barracks. In 1990 Lekhanya had Moshoeshoe II exiled (for the second time), after he refused to agree to the dismissals of several senior officers. In 1991 Lekhanya was himself toppled by the army. The new leader, General Elias Rameama, promised to hold multiparty elections in late 1992. In July 1992 the king was allowed to return, to a hero's welcome. But in the run-up to elections, both the position of the king and the country's constitutional status remain uncertain.

Lesotho is economically integrated with South Africa, which accounts for 90 percent of the nation's exports and 97 percent of its imports. South African companies control Lesotho's small tourist and diamond industries. The Lesotho National Development Corporation actively seeks to attract further South African investment. The Highland Water Scheme, the biggest local development project ever launched, will provide hydroelectric power to South African industry. Besides being in a customs union with South Africa, Lesotho's currency, the maloti, is tied to the South African rand (which is also legal tender in Lesotho).

Many have long dismissed Lesotho as a South African homeland with international recognition. However, most Sotho are proud of their nation's heritage, although there is also a widespread belief that it will never be truly independent until apartheid is abolished. Whether Lesotho would politically unite with a postapartheid South Africa is uncertain.

DEVELOPMENT

Despite an infusion of international aid, Lesotho's economic dependence on South Africa has not decreased since independence; indeed, it has been calculated that the majority of outside funds expended on various projects aimed at increasing local self-sufficiency have actually ended up paying for South African services.

FREEDOM

Since the suspension of the Constitution in 1970, there has been widespread abuse of human rights. Many incidents of repression have involved the nation's security forces, which have long had close ties to their South African counterparts. After the 1986 military coup, a general amnesty for political prisoners was granted. Some exiles have returned, but abuses continue.

HEALTH/WELFARE

With many young men working in the mines of South Africa, much of the resident population relies on subsistence agriculture. Despite efforts to boost production, malnutrition, aggravated by drought, is a serious problem.

ACHIEVEMENTS

Lesotho has long been known for the high quality of its schools, which for more than a century and a half have trained many of the leading citizens of Southern Africa. The national university at Roma was established in 1945 and for a while served as the main campus of the University of Botswana, Lesotho, and Swaziland, until it resumed its autonomous status in 1976.

Malawi (Republic of Malawi)

GEOGRAPHY

Area in Square Kilometers (Miles):
118,484 (45,747) (about the size of
Pennsylvania)
Capital (Population): Lilongwe
(234,000)
Climate: subtropical

PEOPLE

Population
Total: 9,438,000
Annual Growth Rate: 1.8%
Rural/Urban Population Ratio: 88/12
Languages: official: Chichewa,
English; others spoken: Nyanja, Yao,
Sena, Tumbuka, others

Health
Life Expectancy at Birth: 48 years
(male); 51 years (female)
Infant Mortality Rate (Ratio):
136/1,000
Average Caloric Intake: 97% of FAO
minimum
Physicians Available (Ratio): 1/11,340

Religion(s)
75% Christian; 20% Muslim; 5%
traditional indigenous

Education
Adult Literacy Rate: 22%

JOHN CHILEMBWE

In 1915 John Chilembwe of Nyasaland (now Malawi) struck a blow against British colonialism and died in the attempt. Chilembwe was a Christian minister who had studied in South Africa as well as in the United States. He had returned home to establish the Providence Industrial Mission and to build a great church. His feelings against the British settlers developed from the injustices he had seen: European takeover of lands for plantations, poor working conditions for laborers, increased taxation, and, especially, the recruitment of Africans to fight and die in World War I. He rallied a few followers and planned an uprising, which led to the deaths of three settlers and the imprisonment or deaths of the Africans involved or suspected of involvement. Chilembwe appears to have planned his martyrdom. This uprising was the first effort in Southern Africa to resist colonialism and yet maintain many of the aspects of society that had developed from its influence.

COMMUNICATION
Telephones: 36,800
Newspapers: 4

TRANSPORTATION
Highways—Kilometers (Miles): 13,135
(8,143)
Railroads—Kilometers (Miles): 789
(489)
Usable Airports: 46

GOVERNMENT
Type: republic; one-party state
Independence Date: July 6, 1964
Head of State: President-for-Life
H. Kamuzu Banda
Political Parties: Malawi Congress
Party; Alliance for Democracy and
other opposition groups
Suffrage: universal over 21

MILITARY
Number of Armed Forces: 7,250
*Military Expenditures (% of Central
Government Expenditures):* 1.6%
Current Hostilities: none

ECONOMY
Currency ($ U.S. Equivalent): 2.75
kwachas = $1
Per Capita Income/GDP: $180/$1.7
billion
Inflation Rate: 12%
Natural Resources: limestone;
uranium potential
Agriculture: tobacco; tea; sugar; corn;
peanuts
Industry: food; beverages; tobacco;
textiles; footwear

FOREIGN TRADE
Exports: $390 million
Imports: $560 million

	Explorer David Livingstone arrives along Lake Malawi; missionaries follow **1859**	The British protectorate of Nyasaland (present-day Malawi) is declared **1891**	Reverend John Chilembwe and followers rise against settlers and are suppressed **1915**	The Nyasaland African Congress, the first nationalist movement, is formed **1944**	Independence, under the leadership of Hastings Banda **1964**	Diplomatic ties are established with South Africa **1967**	"Ngwazi" Hastings Kamuzu Banda becomes president-for-life **1971**	
Malawi trading kingdoms develop **1500s**								**1980s–1990s**

Support for Renamo declines; an influx of Mozambique refugees is accompanied by drought and food shortages

Banda's dictatorship is destabilized by prodemocracy agitation; police fire on protesters

Most foreign donors cut off all but emergency aid to Malawi, citing its human-rights abuses

MALAWI

For years observers have speculated about change in Malawi after the eventual death of its aging (born in 1898) "Life President" Dr. Kamuzu Banda. Since the early months of independence, in 1964, when he purged his cabinet and ruling Malawi Congress Party of most of the young politicians who had promoted him to leadership in the nationalist struggle, Banda has eliminated potential alternatives to his highly personalized dictatorship. Generations of Malawians, including those living abroad, have grown up with the knowledge that voicing unkind words about the self-proclaimed *Ngwazi* ("Great Lion") could prove fatal. Only senior army officers, Banda's long-time "official state hostess" Tamanda Kadzamira, and her uncle John Tembo (the powerful minister of state) have survived Banda's jealous exercise of power. But in 1992 Banda's grip began to weaken. Unprecedented antigovernment unrest has given rise to an internal opposition, spearheaded by churchmen, underground trade unionists, and new political movements, many of which came together in September 1992 as the Alliance for Democracy. After years of frustration exile organizations have also stepped up their activities.

While the ruthless efficiency of its security apparatus contributed to past perceptions of Malawi's stability, Banda has not survived by mere repression. A few have greatly benefited from the regime. Until 1979 the country enjoyed an economic growth rate averaging 6 percent per annum. Almost all this growth came from increased agricultural production. As was the case during the colonial period, the postindependence government favored large estates specializing in exported cash crops. While in the past the estates were almost exclusively the preserve of a few hundred white settlers, today many are controlled by either the state or local individuals, with Banda himself being the largest landholder.

During the 1970s the prosperity of the estates helped to fuel a boom in industries involved in agricultural processing. Malawi's limited economic success prior to the 1980s came at the expense of the vast majority of its citizens, who survive as small holders growing food crops. By 1985, 86 percent of rural households farmed on less than 5 acres. Overcrowding has contributed to serious soil depletion, while marginalizing most farmers to the point where they can have little hope of generating a significant surplus. In addition to land shortage, peasant production has suffered from low official produce prices and lack of other inputs. The northern half of the country, which has almost no estate production, has been relatively neglected in terms of government expenditure on transport and other forms of infrastructure. Many Malawian peasants have for generations turned to migrant labor as a means of coping with their poverty, but in recent years there have been far fewer opportunities for them in South Africa and Zimbabwe.

Under pressure from the World Bank, the Malawian government has since 1981 modestly increased its incentives to the small holders. Yet these reforms would have been insufficient to overcome the continuing impoverishment of rural households under even the best circumstances. In fact, Malawi's entire economy has for the past decade been in a state of crisis due to the effect of warfare in neighboring Mozambique. The activities of Renamo rebels across the border have largely deprived landlocked Malawi of access to the Mozambican ports of Beira and Nacala. Prior to 1982 these two harbors handled 95 percent of Malawi's exports. Since then most Malawian goods have had to be transported by truck and rail over much longer distances to South African ports (via Botswana, Zambia, and Zimbabwe). In addition to the loss of its transport routes, Malawi has also been burdened by the influx of about 1 million Mozambican refugees. In 1992 these difficulties were further aggravated by severe drought. Renamo's destabilization has contributed to growing cooperation among Malawi and neighboring Frontline States. While internal reform and an end to the civil war in Mozambique would be beneficial to Malawi, the nation's long-term prospects for development also depend on its relations with neighboring states.

DEVELOPMENT

After decades of relative neglect, educational opportunities have increased in recent years; today two-thirds of Malawian children receive some schooling. However, secondary education is limited to a small elite. Adult literacy is only 22%. The Malawian economy has been severely affected by the civil war in neighboring Mozambique.

FREEDOM

Banda has instilled a climate of fear in Malawi, which allows for little freedom. But of late the Catholic and mainstream Protestant Churches as well as a growing number of internal and externally based opposition groups have been challenging his authority.

HEALTH/WELFARE

Malawi's health service is considered expectionally poor even for an impoverished country. The country has one of the highest child mortality rates in the world, while more than half its children under age 5 are stunted by malnutrition.

ACHIEVEMENTS

Although it is the poorest, most overcrowded country in the region, Malawi's response to the influx of Mozambican refugees has been described by the U.S. Committee for Refugees as "no less than heroic." Unlike some of its better-endowed neighbors who have faced far smaller influxes, the Malawi government has so far resisted pressures for the forced repatriation of the refugees.

Mozambique (People's Republic of Mozambique)

GEOGRAPHY

Area in Square Kilometers (Miles):
786,762 (303,769) (about twice the
size of California)
Capital (Population): Maputo
(1,098,000)
Climate: tropical to subtropical

PEOPLE

Population
Total: 15,113,000
Annual Growth Rate: 4.6%
Rural/Urban Population Ratio: 91/9
Languages: official: Portuguese;
others spoken: Yao, Tubbuka,
Batonga, Makua

Health
Life Expectancy at Birth: 46 years
(male); 49 years (female)
Infant Mortality Rate (Ratio):
134/1,000
Average Caloric Intake: 78% of FAO
minimum
Physicians Available (Ratio): 1/52,206

Religion(s)
60% traditional indigenous; 30%
Christian; 10% Muslim and others

MOZAMBICAN WOMEN: PROGRESS AND PERIL

Women have played an important role as both fighters and support
personal during Frelimo's struggle against the Portuguese. Since independence they have become increasingly prominent in once male-
dominated social areas. One-sixth of the membership of the 1983
Frelimo Congress consisted of women. In general, the party and, more
particularly, its affiliate the Organization of Mozambican Women have
actively sought to end gender discrimination. Education and job opportunities have been opened up for working women, who are guaranteed 2
months of maternity leave. A Family Law has given women protection
in areas of divorce, desertion, and child custody, and rules against
sexual harassment have been vigorously enforced. Unfortunately for
most Mozambican women, such progress has been overshadowed by
the struggle for survival in the war-torn, drought-plagued countryside.
In Renamo-held areas, women, along with their children, are commonly
enslaved and raped. Some escaped children have testified that they were
forced to kill their own mothers when they became too weak.

Education
Adult Literacy Rate: 33%

COMMUNICATION
Telephones: 57,400
Newspapers: 2

TRANSPORTATION
Highways—Kilometers (Miles): 26,498
(16,465)
Railroads—Kilometers (Miles): 3,288
(2,038)
Usable Airports: n/a

GOVERNMENT
Type: republic
Independence Date: June 25, 1975
Head of State: President Joaquim
Chissano
Political Parties: Mozambique
Liberation Front (Frelimo); new
parties recently emerging
Suffrage: universal at 18

MILITARY
Number of Armed Forces: 51,000
*Military Expenditures (% of Central
Government Expenditures):* 8.4%
Current Hostilities: rebel attacks;
attacks by South Africa

ECONOMY
Currency ($ U.S. Equivalent): 1,934
meticais = $1
Per Capita Income/GDP: $110/$1.6
billion
Inflation Rate: 23%
Natural Resources: coal; iron ore;
tantalite; flourite; timber
Agriculture: cotton; tobacco; cashews;
sugar; tea; copra; sisal; subsistence
crops
Industry: processed foods; textiles;
beverages; refined oil; chemicals;
tobacco; cement; glass

FOREIGN TRADE
Exports: $90 million
Imports: $764 million

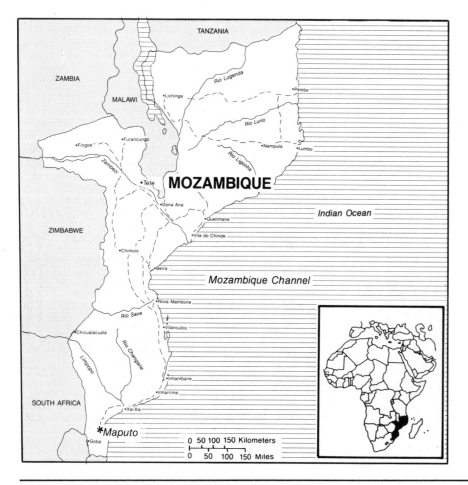

MOZAMBIQUE

For almost three decades Mozambique has been bled by war. Between 1964 and 1974, Frelimo—the Mozambique Liberation Front—struggled against Portuguese colonial rule. At the cost of some 30,000 lives, Mozambique, in June 1975, gained its independence under Frelimo's leadership. Although the new nation was one of the least developed countries in the world, many were optimistic that the lessons learned in the struggle could be applied to the task of building a dynamic new society based on Marxist-Leninist principles.

Unfortunately, hopes for any sort of postindependence progress were quickly sabotaged by the Mozambique National Resistance (MNR, or Renamo), which was originally established as a counterrevolutionary fifth column by the Rhodesian Central Intelligence Organization (refer to the country report on Zimbabwe). As of this date, more than 1 million people have died due to the rebellion, a large proportion murdered in cold blood by Renamo. It is further estimated that, out of a total population of 15 million, some 5 million people have been internally displaced, while about 2 million others have fled to neighboring states. No African nation has paid a higher price in its resistance against white supremacy.

Although some parts of Mozambique were occupied by the Portuguese for more than 400 years, most of the country came under colonial control only in the early twentieth century. The territory was developed as a dependency of neighboring colonial economies rather than that of Portugal itself. Mozambican ports were linked by rail to South Africa and the interior colonies of British Central Africa—that is, modern Malawi, Zambia, and Zimbabwe. In the southern provinces, most men, and many women, spent time as migrant laborers in South Africa. The majority of the males worked in the gold mines.

Most of northern Mozambique was granted to three predominantly British concessions companies, whose abusive policies led many to flee the colony. For decades the colonial state and many local enterprises also relied on forced labor. After World War II new demands were put on Mozambicans by a growing influx of Portuguese settlers, whose numbers swelled during the 1960s, from 90,000 to more than 200,000. Meanwhile, even by the dismal standards of European colonialism in Africa, there continued to be a notable lack of concern for human development. At independence 93 percent of the African population were illiterate. Furthermore, most of those who had acquired literacy or other skills had done so despite the Portuguese presence.

Although a welcome event in itself, the sudden nature of the Portuguese empire's collapse contributed to the destabilization of postindependence Mozambique. Because Frelimo had succeeded in establishing itself as a unified nationalist front, Mozambique was spared an immediate descent into civil conflict, such as that which engulfed Angola, Portugal's other major African possession. However, the economy was already bankrupt due to the Portuguese policy of running Mozambique on a nonconvertible local currency. The rapid transition to independence com-

(United Nations photo by Paul Heath Hoeffel)

Mozambique has been at war for nearly 3 decades. The resulting drain on natural resources, the displacement of approximately one-fifth of the population, and the persistent drought have led to the necessity of importing food to stave off famine.

Portuguese explorers land in Mozambique 1497	Mozambican laborers begin migrating to South African mines 1800–1890	The Northern Nguni of Shosagaane invade southern Mozambique, establishing the Gaza kingdom 1820s	Mozambican laborers begin migrating to South African mines 1870s	The Frelimo liberation movement officially launched 1962	Frelimo's leader, Eduardo Mondlane, is killed by a parcel bomb 1969	The liberation struggle is successful when the Portuguese revolution brings independence 1975

1980s–1990s

A South African commando unit attacks Maputo; increased Renamo attacks on civilian and military targets

President Samora Machel is killed in a mysterious airplane crash; Joaquim Chissano becomes president

Mozambique increases diplomatic efforts for peace in the region

pounded this problem by encouraging the sudden exodus of almost all the Portuguese settlers.

Perhaps even more costly to Mozambique in the long-term was the polarization between Frelimo and African supporters of the former regime, who included about 100,000 who had been active in its security forces. The rapid Portuguese withdrawal was not conducive to the difficult task of reconciliation. While the "compromised ones" were not subjected by Frelimo to bloody reprisals, their rights were circumscribed, and many were sent, along with prostitutes and other "antisocial" elements, to "reeducation camps." While the historically pro-Portuguese stance of the local Catholic hierarchy would have complicated its relations with the new state under any circumstance, Frelimo's Marxist rejection of religion initially alienated it from broader numbers of believers.

A TROUBLED INDEPENDENCE

Frelimo assumed power without the benefit or burden of a strong sense of administrative continuity. While it had begun to create alternative social structures in its "liberated zones" during the anticolonial struggle, these areas had only encompassed a small percentage of Mozambique's population and infrastructure. But Frelimo was initially able to fill the vacuum and launch aggressive development efforts. Health care and education were expanded, worker committees successfully ran many of the enterprises abandoned by the settlers, and communal villages coordinated rural development. However, efforts

to promote agricultural collectivization as the foundation of a command economy generally led to peasant resistance and economic failure. Frelimo's until-recent ability to adapt and implement many of its programs under trying conditions was largely due to its disciplined mass base (the party's 1990 membership stood at about 200,000).

No sooner had Mozambique begun to stabilize itself from the immediate dislocations of its decolonization process than it became embroiled in the Rhodesian conflict. Mozambique was the only neighboring state to impose fully the "mandatory" United Nations economic sanctions against Rhodesia. Between 1976 and 1980 this decision led to the direct loss of half a billion dollars in rail and port revenues. Furthermore, Frelimo's decision to provide bases for the fighters of the Patriotic Front led to a state of undeclared war with Rhodesia as well as its Renamo proxies.

Unfortunately, the fall of Rhodesia did not bring an end to externally sponsored destabilization. Renamo enjoyed the support of South Africa. By continuing Renamo's campaign of destabilization, the Pretoria regime gained leverage over its hostile neighbors, for the continued closure of Mozambique's ports meant that most of their traffic had to pass through South Africa. In 1984 Mozambique signed a nonaggression pact with South Africa, which should have put an end to the latter's support of Renamo. However, captured documents and other evidence indicate that official South African support for Renamo continued at least until 1989, while South African supplies are still

reaching the rebels under mysterious circumstances. In response, Zimbabwe, and to a lesser extent Malawi and Tanzania, have contributed troops to assist in the defense of Mozambique.

In its 1989 Congress, Frelimo formally abandoned its commitment to the primacy of Marxist-Leninist ideology and opened the door to further political and economic reforms. Multipartyism was formally embraced in 1991. The government, with the Catholic Church and a growing list of international mediators, has also opened direct, but so far inconclusive, talks with Renamo. In July 1992 Renamo's leader, Alfonso Dlakama, agreed in principle to implement a ceasefire, but the killing continues.

One factor that may push the party to peace before it pushes the country to complete collapse is the outbreak of severe drought. According to the UN, by 1992, 3 million Mozambicans were suffering from famine. Both government and Renamo forces are reportedly stealing food to survive. Widespread corruption and lawlessness, fueled by the war, have prevented much, if not most, international food aid from reaching the drought's victims.

DEVELOPMENT

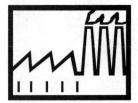

To maintain minimum services and to recover from wartime destruction, Mozambique relies on the commitment of its citizens and international assistance. Western churches have sent relief supplies, food aid, and vehicles; Britain is training a small number of Mozambican soldiers, and the United States has sent humanitarian aid.

FREEDOM

Mozambique has established campaigns against abuses by the security forces and against corruption, as a response to popular complaints. President Chissano offered an amnesty to Renamo rebels in 1987. Ongoing constitutional changes have liberalized the political climate, but such reforms will have little positive effect until there is an end to the fighting.

HEALTH/WELFARE

An immunization campaign that vaccinated 95% of Mozambicans against measles, tuberculosis, tetanus, and small pox has begun to have positive results. But civil strife, widespread Renamo attacks on health units, and food shortages have drastically curtailed health care goals and have led to Mozambique having the highest infant mortality rate in the world.

ACHIEVEMENTS

Between 1975 and 1980 Mozambique's illiteracy rate declined from 93% to 72% while classroom attendance more than doubled. However, progress slowed during the 1980s, due to Renamo attacks, which by 1988 had destroyed more than 2,600 schools. The rate of illiteracy is 67%.

Namibia

GEOGRAPHY

Area in Square Kilometers (Miles):
824,292 (318,261) (twice the size of California)
Capital (Population): Windhoek (114,500)
Climate: arid; semiarid

PEOPLE

Population
Total: 1,520,500
Annual Growth Rate: 3.6%
Rural/Urban Population Ratio: 72/28
Languages: official: English; others spoken: Ouambo, Kavango, Nama/Damara, Herero, Khoisan, German, Afrikaans

Health
Life Expectancy at Birth: 58 years (male); 63 years (female)
Infant Mortality Rate (Ratio): 69/1,000
Average Caloric Intake: n/a
Physicians Available (Ratio): 1/4,736

Religion(s)
70% Christian; 30% traditional indigenous

Education
Adult Literacy Rate: 99% whites; 16% nonwhites

COMMUNICATION
Telephones: 62,800
Newspapers: 11

WALVIS BAY

To many, Namibia's independence remains incomplete, due to the continuing South African occupation of the country's main port, Walvis Bay, as well as a number of strategic islands just off the coast. Most of the population at Walvis Bay are recognized as Namibian citizens and thus denied even a minimal say in the enclave's affairs—voting in the municipality is limited to "South African" citizens who earn an upper-middle-class salary. South Africa traces its claim to Walvis Bay to its 1878 annexation to the Cape Colony, but most of the international community, through such organizations as the United Nations, has backed Namibia's claims to the territory. Bilateral talks between Namibia and South Africa, which in 1991 seemed likely to lead to an interim joint administration, have become deadlocked. A growing number of the territory's white residents have joined their black counterparts in calling for a speedy integration into Namibia.

TRANSPORTATION
Highways—Kilometers (Miles): 54,500 (33,866)
Railroads—Kilometers (Miles): 2,340 (1,454)
Usable Airports: 123

GOVERNMENT
Type: democratic
Independence Date: March 21, 1990
Head of State: President Sam Nujoma
Political Parties: Action Christian National Party; National Patriotic Front; Federal Convention of Namibia; Democratic Turnhalle Alliance; South-West Africa People's Organization; United Democratic Party
Suffrage: universal at 18

MILITARY
Number of Armed Forces: 10,000
Military Expenditures (% of Central Government Expenditures): 4.9%
Current Hostilities: none

ECONOMY
Currency ($ U.S. Equivalent): 3.68 South African rands = $1
Per Capita Income/GDP: $1,240/$1.8 billion
Inflation Rate: 15%
Natural Resources: diamonds; copper; lead; zinc; uranium; silver; cadmium; lithium; coal; possible oil reserves; fish
Agriculture: corn; millet; sorghum; livestock
Industry: meat canning; dairy products; leather tanning; textiles; clothing; mineral concentrates

FOREIGN TRADE
Exports: $1.02 million
Imports: $864 million

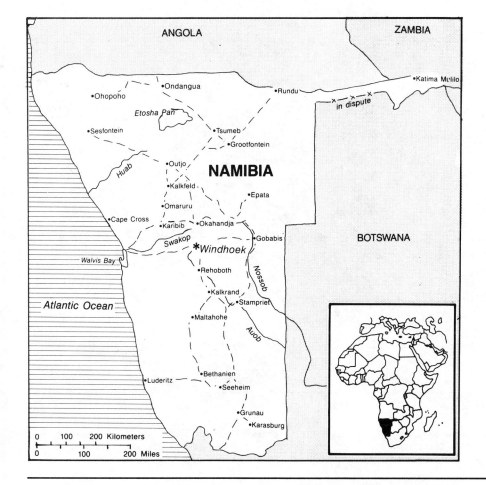

NAMIBIA

Namibia, Africa's newest country, became independent in March 1990. Its transition from the continent's last colony to a developing nation-state marked the end of a century of often brutal colonization, first by Germany and later South Africa. The German colonial period (1884–1917) was marked by the annihilation of more than 60 percent of the African population in the southern two-thirds of the country during the uprising of 1904–1907. The South African period (1917–1990) saw the imposition of apartheid as well as a bitter 26-year war for independence between the South African Army (SADF) and the South West Africa Peoples Organization (SWAPO). During this war countless civilians, especially in the northern areas of the country, were harassed, detained, and abused by South African-created death squads, such as the Koevoet (the Afrikaans word for "crowbar").

Namibia's final liberation was the result of South African military misadventures and U.S.—Soviet cooperation in reducing tensions in the region. In 1987, as it had done many times before, South Africa invaded Angola to assist Jonas Savimbi's UNITA movement. Their objective was Cuito Cuanavale, a small town in southeastern Angola where the Luanda government had set up an air-defense installation to keep South African aircraft from supplying UNITA troops. The SADF met with fierce resistance from the Angolan Army and eventually committed thousands of its own troops to the battle. In addition, black Namibian soldiers were recruited and given UNITA uniforms to fight on the side of the SADF. Many of these proxy UNITA troops later mutinied because of the poor treatment at the hands of white South African soldiers.

South Africa failed to capture Cuito Cuanavale, and its forces were eventually surrounded. Faced with military disaster, the Pretoria government bowed to decades of international pressure and agreed to withdraw from its illegal occupation of Namibia. In return, Angola and its ally Cuba agreed to send home troops sent by Havana in 1974 after South Africa invaded Angola for the first time. Key brokers of the ceasefire, negotiations, and implementation of this agreement were the United States and the Soviet Union. This was the first instance of their post-cold war cooperation.

A plebiscite was held in Namibia during early November 1989. Under United Nations supervision, more than 97 percent of eligible voters cast their ballots—a remarkable achievement given the vast distances many had to travel to reach polling stations. SWAPO emerged as the clear victor, achieving 60 percent of the votes cast, with the rest divided among a range of political parties, ranging from avowed white supremacists to ardent socialists.

CHALLENGES AND PROSPECTS

Namibia is a sparsely populated land. More than half its 1.5 million residents live in the northern region known as Ovamboland. Rich in minerals, Namibia is a major pro-

(United Nations photo by J. Isaac)

The importance of developing agricultural production in those parts of the country where it is possible is key to the economic future of Namibia. The sanctions that applied before independence have been lifted, and Namibia is now free to enter the potentially profitable markets in Europe and North America. This worker, pictured in a cornfield near Grootfontein, is part of this essential agricultural economy.

| Germany is given rights to colonize Namibia at the Conference of Berlin **1884–1885** | Herero, Nama, and Damara rebellions against German rule **1904–1907** | South Africa assumes League of Nations mandate **1920** | The UN General Assembly revokes the South African mandate; SWAPO begins war for independence **1966** | Bantustans, or "homelands," are created by South Africa **1968** | A massive strike paralyzes the economy **1971** | The Western Five contact group is formed to negotiate for South African withdrawal from Namibia **1977** | An internal government is formed by South Africa **1978** | **1980s–1990s** |

Defeat at Cuito Cuanavale leads to a South African agreement to withdraw from Namibia

SWAPO wins UN-supervised elections; a new Constitution is approved

World leaders gather to witness Namibia's independence

ducer of diamonds, uranium, copper, silver, tin, and lithium. A large gold mine recently began production. The end of hostilities has opened up northern parts of the country to further mineral explorations.

Much of Namibia is arid. Until now pastoral farming has been the primary agricultural activity, with beef, mutton, and goat meat the main products. Independence brought an end to international sanctions applied when South Africa ruled the country, giving Namibian agricultural goods access to the world market. Although some new investment has been attracted to the relatively well-watered but historically neglected northern border regions, currently most of Namibia's rural majority, including many relatively well-educated former exiles, are barely able to eke out a living even in nondrought years.

Despite the economic promise, the fledgling government of Namibia faces severe economic problems. It inherits an economy structurally perverted by apartheid to favor the tiny white minority. With a glaring division between fabulously wealthy whites and the oppressively poor black majority, the government is faced with the daunting problem of promoting economic development while at the same time encouraging the redistribution of wealth. Apartheid ensured that managerial positions were filled by whites, leaving a dearth of qualified and experienced nonwhite executives in the country. This past pattern of discrimination has contributed to high levels of black unemployment. According to government figures, only half the economically active population

had jobs in 1992. The hardest hit have been the youth and those living in the north. The demobilization of 53,000 former SWAPO and South African combatants and the return of 44,000 exiles have aggravated this problem. A few former soldiers—notably the Botsotsos, made up of former Koevet members—have turned to organized crime. Having already inherited a civil service bloated by too many white sinicures, the SWAPO administration has resisted the temptation of trying to hire its way out of the problem.

Another major problem lies in Namibia's total dependence on South African infrastructure. South Africa used Namibia as a classic colony, treating it as a captive market for South African goods while extracting as much of its resources as possible. As a result, all rail and most road links between Namibia and the rest of the world run through South Africa. Pretoria also maintains its occupation of Walvis Bay, Namibia's only port. In the past the South African government has used its control of the region's transportation system to sabotage economic development in countries such as Botswana, Zambia, Zimbabwe, Mozambique, and Swaziland. The possibility of Namibia falling prey to this tactic in the future is quite real.

The government of President Sam Nujoma has taken a hard look at these and other economic problems, and embarked on a program to solve them. SWAPO surprised everyone during the election campaign by modifying its previously strident socialist rhetoric and calling for a market-oriented economy. Since taking power it has joined the International Mon-

etary Fund and proposed a code for foreign investors that includes protection against undue nationalizations. A conservative, white businessperson, Dr. Otto Herrigel, was named minister of finance, in a move that calmed the business community.

At present the government is actively seeking both foreign investment and foreign aid from Western countries. Scandinavia and countries from the European Community have shown modest interest. France and Germany in particular have led the way. SWAPO appears to be well on its way to making the transition from revolutionary organization to a pragmatic ruling party within a vibrant democratic society. Its new attitude is best summed up in a quote by Hage Geingob, a prominent SWAPO official and now president of the National Assembly: "To distribute wealth," he said in an interview, "you must first create it."

DEVELOPMENT	**FREEDOM**	**HEALTH/WELFARE**	**ACHIEVEMENTS**

The new government has instituted English as the medium of instruction in all schools. Before independence English was discouraged for African school children, as a means of controlling their access to skills necessary to compete in the modern world. This effort requires new curricula and textbooks for the entire country.	The Namibian Constitution is considered a model of democratic government. Universal suffrage and a strong emphasis on human rights are prominent throughout the document. Freedom of the press, freedom of speech, an independent judiciary, and provisions against discrimination in any form are constitutional guarantees.	The social-service delivery system of Namibia must be rebuilt to eliminate the structural inequities of apartheid. Health care for the black majority, especially those in remote rural areas, will require significant improvements. Public health programs for blacks, nonexistent prior to independence, must be created.	The government led by President Nujoma has received high praise for its efforts at racial and political reconciliation after a bitter 26-year war for independence. Nujoma led these efforts and has astonished a number of observers with his political and consensus-building skills.

South Africa (Republic of South Africa)

GEOGRAPHY

Area in Square Kilometers (Miles):
1,222,480 (437,872) (about twice the size of Texas)
Capital (Population): Pretoria (administrative) (822,900); Cape Town (legislative) (1,911,500); Bloemfontein (judicial) (232,900)
Climate: temperate; semiarid; arid

PEOPLE

Population

Total: 41,688,000 (includes the 10 so-called homelands, which are not recognized by the United States)
Annual Growth Rate: 2.6%
Rural/Urban Population Ratio: 45/55
Languages: official: Afrikaans, English; others spoken: Xhosa, Zulu, Sesotho, Tswana, other Bantu languages

Health

Life Expectancy at Birth: 62 years (male); 67 years (female)*
Infant Mortality Rate (Ratio): 50/1,000*
Average Caloric Intake: 116% of FAO minimum*
Physicians Available (Ratio): 1/1,757*

Religion(s)

81% Christian; 19% Hindu and Muslim

Education

Adult Literacy Rate: 76%

COMMUNICATION

Telephones: 4,500,000
Newspapers: 39

TRANSPORTATION

Highways—Kilometers (Miles): 188,309 (116,751)
Railroads—Kilometers (Miles): 20,638 (12,796)
Usable Airports: 732

GOVERNMENT

Type: republic
Independence Date: May 31, 1910

Head of State: President Frederick W. de Klerk
Political Parties: National Party; Progressive Federal Party; New Republic Party; Conservative Party; Labour Party; Afrikaans Weerstand Beweging; Cape Democrats
Suffrage: universal at 18, but voting rights are racially based

MILITARY

Number of Armed Forces: 92,500 standing; 135,000 ready reserves; 140,000 paramilitary commando volunteers; 61,000 police
Military Expenditures (% of Central Government Expenditures): 3%
Current Hostilities: civil unrest

ECONOMY

Currency ($ U.S. Equivalent): 2.78 rands = $1
Per Capita Income/GDP: $2,600/$104 billion
Inflation Rate: 15.7%
Natural Resources: gold; diamonds; mineral ores; uranium; fish
Agriculture: corn; wool; wheat; sugarcane; tobacco; citrus fruits; dairy products
Industry: mining; automobile assembly; metal working; machinery; textiles; iron and steel; chemicals; fertilizer; fishing

FOREIGN TRADE

Exports: $24.0 billion
Imports: $18.8 billion

*Figures for blacks and whites, when separated, vary greatly.

THE AFRICAN NATIONAL CONGRESS

The African National Congress (ANC) was founded in 1912, in response to the taking of land from Africans and the introduction of "pass laws" controlling their employment and movement. For 50 years members carried on peaceful resistance to apartheid by organizing protest marches, supporting workers' demands and strike actions, and creating independent schools and services. ANC goals are expressed in the Freedom Charter, which states that "South Africa belongs to all who live in it, black and white . . ." and calls for "one man, one vote" and the abolition of the color bar. These beliefs caused the arrest of thousands and the trial of ANC leaders for treason. When the ANC was banned and Nelson Mandela, Walter Sisulu, and others were sentenced to life imprisonment, the ANC went underground in the 1960s, planning sabotage against military and political targets and organizing resistance. The ANC and Nelson Mandela, who since his release in 1990 has acted as the movement's de facto leader, gained supporters and stature as internal resistance against the apartheid state grew during the 1980s. Since coming to office President F. W. de Klerk has implicitly recognized the fact that the ANC is now the leading voice of his country's nonwhite majority.

SOUTH AFRICA

The coming decade may prove to be a turning point in the long, tragic history of racism in South Africa. For nearly 3½ centuries, the territory's white minority has expanded and entrenched its racial hegemony over the nonwhite majority. Since 1948 white supremacy has been consolidated into a governing system known as *apartheid* ("separatehood"). South Africa's rulers now claim that they are no longer committed to upholding apartheid. Political restrictions inside the country were significantly relaxed in 1990, through the unbanning of antiapartheid resistance organizations, most notably the African National Congress (ANC), the Pan Africanist Congress (PAC), and the South African Communist Party (SACP). Today there is hope that ongoing talks between the government, the ANC, and other parties will contribute to the emergence of a new, nonracial South Africa. But there are major obstacles to such an outcome.

South Africa remains a deeply divided country. In general, the ruling whites enjoy relatively affluent, comfortable lives, while the nonwhites survive in a state of impoverished deprivation. The boundary between these two worlds remains deep.

Nonwhites are still denied full citizenship rights today, whereas under the pre-1990 apartheid system they were legally divided as members of three officially subordinate race classifications: *Bantu* (black African), *Coloureds* (a person of mixed race), or *Asian.* (Note: Many members of these groups prefer the common label of "Black," which the government now commonly uses in place of Bantu as an exclusive term for black Africans, hereafter referred to in this text as *blacks.*)

THE ROOTS OF APARTHEID

White supremacy in South Africa began with the Dutch settlement at Cape Town in 1652. For a century and a half the domestic economy of the Dutch Cape Colony, which gradually expanded to include the southern third of modern South Africa, rested on a foundation of slavery and servitude. Much like the American South before the Civil War, Cape Colonial society was racially divided between free white settlers and nonwhite slaves and servants. Most of the slaves were Africans imported from outside the local region, although a minority were taken from Asia. The local blacks, who spoke various Khoisan languages, were not enslaved.

However, they were robbed by the Europeans of their land and herds. Many were also killed either by European bullets or diseases. As a result, most of the Cape's Khiosan were reduced to a status of servitude. Gradually, the servant and slave populations, with a considerable admixture of European blood, merged to form the core of the so-called Coloured group.

At the beginning of the nineteenth century, the Cape Colony reverted to British control. During the 1830s the British abolished slavery and extended legal rights to servants. But, as with the American South, emancipation did not end racial barriers to the political and economic advancement of nonwhites. Nonetheless, even the limited reforms that were introduced upset many of the white "Cape Dutch" (or "Boers"), whose society was evolving its own "Afrikaner" identity. (Today some 60 percent of the whites and 90 percent of the Coloureds in South Africa speak the Dutch-derived Afrikaans language.) During the mid-nineteenth century, thousands of Afrikaners, accompanied by their Coloured clients, escaped British rule by migrating into the interior. They established two independent republics, the Transvaal and the Orange Free State, whose constitutions recognized only whites as having any civil rights.

(United Nations photo)

The system of apartheid makes it impossible for most black South Africans to share in South Africa's economic prosperity.

The Afrikaners, and the British who followed them, did not settle an empty land. Then, as now, most of the people living in the area beyond the borders of the old Dutch Cape Colony were blacks who spoke languages that are linguistically classified as Bantu. While there are 9 officially recognized Bantu languages in South Africa, all but 2 (Tsonga and Venda) belong to either the Sotho-Tswana (Pedi, Sotho, Tswana) or Nguni (Ndebele, Swati, Xhosa, and Zulu) subgroupings of closely related dialects.

Throughout the eighteenth and nineteenth centuries, the indigenous populations of the interior and the eastern coast offered strong resistance to the white invaders. Unlike the Khiosan of the Cape, these communities were able to preserve their ethnolinguistic identities. However, the settlers eventually robbed them of most of their land, as well as their independence. Black subjugation served the economic interests of white farmers, and later industrialists, who were able to coerce the conquered communities into providing cheap and forced labor. After 1860, many Asians, mostly from what was then British-ruled India, were also brought into South Africa to work for next to nothing on sugar plantations. As with the blacks and Coloureds, the Asians were denied civil rights.

The lines of racial stratification were already well entrenched at the turn of the twentieth century, when the British waged a war of conquest against the Afrikaner republics. During this South African, or Boer, War, tens of thousands of Afrikaners, blacks, and Coloureds died while interned in British concentration camps. The camps helped to defeat the Afrikaner resistance but left bitter divisions between the resistance and pro-British English-speaking whites. However, it was the nonwhites who were the war's greatest losers. A compromise peace between the Afrikaners and the British Empire paved the way for the emergence, in 1910, of a self-governing Union of South Africa, made up of the former British colonies and Afrikaner republics. In this new state, political power remained in the hands of the white minority.

"GRAND APARTHEID"

In 1948 the Afrikaner-dominated Nationalist Party (NP) was voted into office by the white electorate, on a platform promising apartheid; the party has remained in power ever since. Under the apartheid system, existing patterns of segregation were reinforced by a vast array of new laws. *Pass laws,* which had long limited the movement of blacks in many areas, were extended throughout the country. Black men and women were required to carry "passbooks" at all times to prove their right to be residing in a particular area. Under the Group Areas Act, more than 80 percent of South Africa was reserved for whites, who now make up no more than 15 percent of the population. In this area, blacks remain confined to townships or white-owned farms, where, until recently, they were considered to be temporary residents. If they lacked a properly registered job, they were subject to deportation to one of the 10 "homelands."

Under apartheid, the homelands—poor, noncontiguous rural territories that together account for less than 13 percent of South Africa's land—were the designated "nations" of South Africa's blacks, who make up more than 70 percent of the population. Each black was assigned membership in a particular homeland, in accordance with ethnolinguistic criteria invented by the white government. Thus, in apartheid theory, there was no majority in South Africa but, rather, a single white nation, which in reality has remained divided between speakers of Afrikaans, English, and other languages, and 10 separate black nations. The Coloureds and the Asians were consigned a never clearly defined intermediate position as powerless communities associated with, but segregated from, white South Africa. The apartheid "ideal" was that each black homeland would eventually become "independent," leaving white South Africa without the "burden" of a black majority. Of course, black "immigrants" could still work for the "white economy," which would remain reliant on black labor. To assure that racial stratification was maintained at the workplace, a system of job classification was created, which reserved the best positions for whites, certain middle-level employments for Asians and Coloureds, and unskilled labor for blacks.

Until recently the Nationalist Party ruthlessly pursued their ultimate goal of legislating away South Africa's black majority. Four homelands—Bophutatswana, Ciskie, Transkie, and Venda—were declared independent. The 9 million blacks who were assigned as citizens of these psuedo-states, which have not been recognized by any outside country, do not appear in the 1989 South African Census, even though most live outside of the homelands. Indeed, despite generations of forced removals and influx control, today there is not a single magistrate's district (the equivalent of a U.S. county) that has a white majority.

While for whites apartheid has been an ideology of mass delusion, for blacks it has meant continuous suffering. During the 1970s alone, some 3.5 million blacks were forcibly relocated because they were living in "black spots" within the white area. Many more have at some point in their lives fallen victim to the pass laws. Within the townships and squatter camps that ring the white cities, families have survived from day to day not knowing when the police might burst into their homes to discover that their passbooks are not in order.

Under apartheid, blacks are as much divided by their residential status as by their assigned ethnicity. In a relative sense, the most privileged are those who have established their right to reside legally within a township like Soweto. Township dwellers have the advantage of being able to live with their families and seek work in a nearby white urban center. Many of their coworkers live much farther away, in the periurban areas of the homelands. Some in this less-fortunate category spend as much as one-third of their lives on Putco buses, traveling to and from their places of employment. Still, the periurban homeland workers are in many ways better off than their male colleagues, who are confined to crowded worker hostels for months at a time while their families remain in distant rural homelands. There are also millions of female domestics who generally earn next to nothing while living away from their children in the servant quarters of white households.

Further down the black social ladder are those living in the illegal squatter camps that exist outside the urban areas. Without secure homes or steady jobs, the squatters have been frequent victims of nighttime police raids. When caught, they are generally transported back to their homelands, from whence they will usually try once more to escape. The relaxation, since 1986, of influx control regulations has eased the tribulations of many squatters, but their lives remain insecure. Yet even the violent destruction of squatter settlements by the state has not stemmed their explosive growth. For many blacks, living without permanent employment in a cardboard house is preferable to the hardships of the rural homelands. Nearly half of all blacks live in these areas, where unemployment tops 80 percent and agricultural production is limited by marginal, overcrowded environments.

Recent changes have tended to accentuate the importance of these residential patterns. Although their wages on average remain only a fraction of those enjoyed by whites, many township dwellers have seen their wages rise over the past decade, partially due to their own success in organizing strong labor federations. At the same time, life in the homelands has become more desperate as their populations have mushroomed.

Apartheid was a totalitarian system. Today an array of security legislation still gives the state vast powers over individual citizens, even in the absence of a state of emergency such as existed throughout much of the country between 1985 and 1990. Control is also more subtly exercised through the schools and other public institutions. An important element of apartheid has been "Bantu Education." Beyond being segregated and unequal, black educational curriculums have been specifically designed to assure under-achievement, by preparing most students for only semiskilled and unskilled occupations. The schools are also divided by language and ethnicity. A student who is classified as Zulu is taught in the Zulu

language to be loyal to the Zulu nation, while his or her playmates may be receiving similar instruction in Tsonga or Sotho. Ethnic divisions are also often encouraged at the workplace. At the mines, ethnicity generally determines the job and hostel to which one is assigned.

LIMITED REFORMS

During 1982 and 1983 there was much official publicity about reforming apartheid. Yet the Nationalist Party's moves to liberalize the system were limited and were accompanied by increased repression. Some changes were simply semantic. In official publications, the term "apartheid" was replaced by "separate development," which was subsequently dropped in favor of "plural democracy."

A bill passed in the white Parliament in 1983 brought Asian and Coloured representatives into the South African government—but only in their own separate

chambers, which remained completely subordinate to the white chamber. The bill also concentrated power in the office of the presidency, which eroded the oversight prerogatives of white parliamentarians. Significantly, the new dispensation completely excluded blacks. Seeing the new Constitution as another transparent attempt at divide-and-rule while offering them nothing in the way of genuine empowerment, most Asians and Coloureds refused to participate in the new political order. Instead, many joined together with blacks and a handful of progressive whites in creating a new organization, the United Democratic Front (UDF), which opposed the Constitution.

In other moves, the NP has gradually done away with examples of "petty" apartheid. In many areas, signs announcing separate facilities have been removed from public places; but, very often, new, more subtle signs have been put up to assure continued segregation. Gas stations

(United Nations photo)

Millions of black South Africans have been forcibly resettled in villages. The formation of these so-called black "homelands" represents the largest forced movement of people in peacetime history.

			Shaka develops	
			the Zulu nation	
			and sets in	
Migration of	The first		motion the wars	The Boer War:
Bantu speakers	settlement of		and migrations	the British fight
into Southern	Dutch people in	The British gain	known as the	the Afrikaners
Africa	the Cape of	possession of the	Mfecane	(Boers)
1000–1500	Good Hope area	Cape Colony	**1820s**	**1899–1902**
	1652	**1815**		

in the Transvaal, for example, now have their facilities marked with blue and white figures to assure that everyone continues to know his or her place. Another example of purely cosmetic reform was the legalization of interracial marriage. Although it is no longer a crime for a man and a woman belonging to different racial classifications to be wed, under the Group Areas Act, it remains an offense for such a couple to live in the same house. In 1986 the hated passbooks were replaced with new "identity cards." Unions were legalized, but in the Orwellian world of apartheid, their leaders were regularly arrested. The UDF was not banned but, rather, was forbidden from holding meetings. Although such reforms were meaningless to most nonwhites living within South Africa, some outsiders, including the Reagan administration, were impressed by the "progress."

BLACK RESISTANCE

Resistance to white domination dates back to 1657, when the Khiosan first attempted to counter Dutch encroachments on their pastures. Throughout the first half of the twentieth century, the African National Congress, which was founded in 1912 to unify what until then had been regionally based black associations, and other political and labor organizations, attempted to wage a peaceful civil-rights struggle. An early leader within the Asian community was Mahatma Gandhi, who pioneered his strategy of passive resistance in South Africa while resisting the pass laws. During the 1950s the ANC and associated organizations adopted Gandhian tactics on a massive scale, in a vain attempt to block the enactment of apartheid legislation. Although ANC President Albert Luthuli was awarded a Nobel Peace Prize, the NP regime remained unmoved.

The year 1960 was a turning point. Police massacred more than 60 persons when they fired on a passbook-burning demonstration at Sharpeville. Thereafter the government assumed emergency powers, banning the ANC and the more recently formed Pan Africanist Congress. As underground movements, both turned

to armed struggle. The ANC's guerrilla organization, the Umkonto we Sizwe ("Spear of the Nation") attempted to avoid taking human lives in its attacks. Poqo ("Ourselves Alone"), the PAC's armed wing, was less constrained in its choice of targets, but also proved less able to sustain its struggle. By the mid-1960s, with the capture of such figures as Umkonto leader Nelson Mandela, active resistance had been all but fully suppressed.

A new generation of resistance emerged during the 1970s. Many nonwhite youths were attracted to the teachings of the Black Consciousness Movement (BMC), led by Steve Biko. The BMC and likeminded organizations rejected the racial and ethnic classifications of apartheid by insisting on the fundamental unity of all oppressed black peoples (that is, all nonwhites) against the white power structure. Black consciousness also rejected all forms of collaboration with the apartheid state, which brought the movement into direct opposition with homeland leaders like Gatsha Buthelezi, whom they looked upon as sellouts. In the aftermath of student demonstrations in Soweto, which sparked months of unrest across the country, the government suppressed the BMC. Biko was subsequently murdered, while in detention. During this crackdown, thousands of young people fled South Africa. Many joined the exiled ANC, helping to reinvigorate its exiled ranks.

Despite heavyhanded repression, internal resistance to apartheid continued to grow. Hundreds of new and revitalized organizations—community groups, labor unions, and religious bodies—emerged to contribute to the struggle. Many became affiliated through coordinating bodies such as the United Democratic Front, the Congress of South African Trade Unions (COSATU), and the South African Council of Churches (SACC). SACC leader Archbishop Desmond Tutu became the second black South African to be awarded a Nobel Peace Prize for his nonviolent efforts to bring about change. But, in the face of continued oppression, black youths, in particular, became increasingly willing to use whatever means necessary to overthrow the oppressors.

The year 1985 was another turning point. Arrests and bannings of black leaders led to calls to make the townships "ungovernable." A state of emergency

(United Nations photo)

Resistance groups have gained international recognition in their struggle against the South African regime.

was proclaimed by the government in July, which allowed for the increased use of detention without trial. By March 1990, some 53,000 people, including an estimated 10,000 children, had been arrested. Many detainees have been tortured while in custody. Stone-throwing youths have, nonetheless, continued to challenge the heavily armed security forces sent into the townships to restore order. By 1993 more than 10,000 people had died in the unrest.

PROSPECTS FOR A NONRACIAL SOUTH AFRICA

Despite the government's ability to marshal the resources of a sophisticated military-industrial complex to maintain its totalitarian control, the Nationalist Party has been forced to consider giving up apartheid along with its 4-decade monopoly of power. Throughout the 1980s South Africa's advanced economy was in a state of crisis due to the effects of unrest and, to a lesser extent, due to sanctions and other forms of international pressure. Under President P. W. Botha, the NP regime stubbornly refused to offer any openings to genuine reform. However, Botha's replacement, in 1989, by F. W. de Klerk opened up new possibilities. The unbanning of the ANC, the PAC, and the South African Communist Party was accompanied by the release of many political prisoners. As many observers had anticipated, after gaining his freedom in March 1990, ANC deputy leader Nelson Mandela emerged as the leading advocate of a nonracial South Africa. More surprising has been the de Klerk government's willing-

ness to engage in serious negotiations with the ANC and other groups. By August 1990, the ANC felt that the progress being made justified the formal suspension of its armed struggle.

Many obstacles continue to block the transition to a postapartheid state. For one thing, although the government seems prepared to accept some form of power-sharing, it remains opposed to the concept of one-person, one-vote in a unified state. Instead, de Klerk's NP appears to favor some form of dispensation that will preserve major elements of white privilege and power. The ANC, UDF, COSATU, and SACP, which are loosely associated as the Mass Democratic Movement (MDM), are loyal to the nonracial principles of the 1955 Freedom Charter. While there exist possibilities for a future compromise between the NP and Charterists, after more than 2 years of negotiation, the two sides remain far apart.

Other groups are opposed to negotiations. The PAC and other critics of the ANC fear that the apartheid regime is not yet prepared to agree to its dismantlement and that the ongoing talks can only serve to weaken black resistance. On the opposite side of the spectrum are powerful elements in the white community who remain openly committed to their continued racial supremacy. In addition to the Conservative Party, the principal opposition in the white Parliament, there are a number of militant racist organizations, which are prepared to resort to terrorism to block reforms. At least some within the South African security establishment are also seeking to sabotage the prospects of

peace. In March 1992 these far-right elements suffered a setback, when nearly 70 percent of the white voters approved continued negotiation for democratic reform.

Another wild card is Buthelezi's Inkatha Freedom Party (IFP) and other, smaller black groups that have aligned themselves in the past with the South African state. Thousands have been killed in ongoing clashes between Inkatha and MDM supporters, which allegedly have been encouraged by the police. Others identified with the MMD have been murdered by so-called third-force death squads, who have been linked with reactionary elements in the security establishment and others opposed to the MMD. In the aftermath of one anti-ANC massacre at the Boipoteng Township, the ANC in June 1992 suspended its talks with the government and announced that it would embark on a campaign of "mass action" until effective steps were taken to end the violence.

Perhaps the greatest barrier to the creation of a nonracial South Africa will not be in reaching a consensus in its favor but, rather, finding a means to translate the vision into reality. Even under the best of circumstances, it will not be easy for South Africans to dismantle the legacies of apartheid.

DEVELOPMENT

In anticipation of a new, postapartheid, economy, the debate between advocates of various economic approaches has become increasingly serious. Many believe that the state must play a major role in righting the economic injustices of apartheid. Others believe that only a freer private sector can best create the necessary economic opportunities.

FREEDOM

Under apartheid, nonwhites have been systematically denied basic freedoms, and even white critics of the state have faced severe restrictions. The political opening in 1990 has created in some respects a freer atmosphere. However, police repression and death squad activities continue.

HEALTH/WELFARE

State health and educational facilities remain segregated. Those reserved for whites are far superior on average than those for nonwhites. Black schools have been periodically hit by politically motivated student boycotts, but since 1987 most students have opted to remain in the classroom.

ACHIEVEMENTS

As government-selected black leaders step down and security and services are reduced in the black townships, local "people's governments" are emerging. At risk to their lives, black representatives join in larger committees to make decisions for the townships, and communities attempt to educate the youth.

Swaziland (Kingdom of Swaziland)

GEOGRAPHY

Area in Square Kilometers (Miles):
17,366 (6,704) (slightly smaller than
New Jersey
Capital (Population): Mbabane
(administrative) (52,000); Lobanta
(legislative)
Climate: temperate; subtropical;
semiarid

PEOPLE

Population
Total: 859,000
Annual Growth Rate: 2.7%
Rural/Urban Population Ratio: 74/26
Languages: official: English, Siswati;
others spoken: Zulu, Sesotho, Nguni

Health
Life Expectancy at Birth: 51 years
(male); 59 years (female)
Infant Mortality Rate (Ratio):
101/1,000
Average Caloric Intake: 97% of FAO
minimum
Physicians Available (Ratio): 1/9,731

Religion(s)
60% Christian; 40% traditional
indigenous

Education
Adult Literacy Rate: 55%

COMMUNICATION
Telephones: 15,400
Newspapers: 2

TRANSPORTATION
Highways—Kilometers (Miles): 2,853
(1,769)
Railroads—Kilometers (Miles): 297
(184)

Usable Airports: 22

GOVERNMENT
Type: monarchy
Independence Date: September 6,
1968
Head of State: King Mswati III
Political Parties: banned
Suffrage: none

MILITARY
Number of Armed Forces: n/a
*Military Expenditures (% of Central
Government Expenditures):* n/a
Current Hostilities: none

ECONOMY
Currency ($ U.S. Equivalent): 2.85
emalangenis = $1
Per Capita Income/GDP: $670/$575
million
Inflation Rate: 13%
Natural Resources: iron ore; asbestos;
coal; timber
Agriculture: corn; livestock;
sugarcane; citrus fruits; cotton; rice;
pineapples
Industry: milled sugar; cotton;
processed meat and wood; tourism;
chemicals; machinery, beverages;
consumer goods; paper milling;
mining

FOREIGN TRADE
Exports: $543 million
Imports: $651 billion

NCWALA

Visitors to Swaziland are frequently impressed by the pageantry associated with many of its state occasions. The most important ceremonies take place during the lunar *Ncwala* month, in December and January. This is a time when the nation reaffirms its bonds with the royal house. As the month begins, runners are sent to collect water from the ocean and various rivers, thus reestablishing their historic association with the Swazi. The main festival lasts for 6 days and includes the king's tasting of the first fruits, blessings to the ancestors, and prayers for rain. During the entire period there is ritual dancing, the most important of which is performed on the fourth day by the king and other members of royalty.

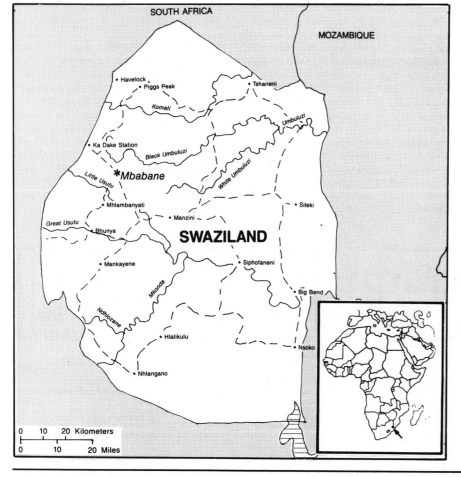

Zulu and South African whites encroach on Swazi territory **1800s**	A protectorate is established by the British **1900**	Britain assumes control over Swaziland **1903**	Independence is restored **1968**	Parliament is dissolved and political parties are banned **1973**	King Sobuza dies; efforts to annex South African Homeland territories collapse

1980s–1990s

King Mswati III is crowned, ending the regency period marked by political instability

The People's United Democratic Movement, Swaziland United

Front, and Swaziland National Front defy the 1973 ban on political parties

SWAZILAND

Swaziland is a small, landlocked kingdom sandwiched between the much larger states of Mozambique and South Africa. Casual observers have tended to look upon the country as a peaceful island of traditional Africa that has been immune to the continent's contemporary conflicts. This image is a product of the country's status as the only precolonial monarchy in sub-Saharan Africa to have survived into the modern era. Swazi sociopolitical organization is ostensibly governed in accordance with age-old structures and norms. But below this veneer of timelessness lies a dynamic society that has been subject to internal and external pressures.

From 1903 until the restoration of independence in 1968, the country remained a British colonial protectorate, despite sustained pressure for its incorporation into South Africa. Local white settlers, who at the time made up only 2 percent of the population but controlled more than two-thirds of the land, largely favored such a transfer.

Throughout the colonial period the ruling Dlamini dynasty, which was led by the energetic Sobuza II after 1921, successfully served as a rallying point for national self-assertion on the key issues of regaining control of alienated land and opposing union with South Africa. Sobuza's personal leadership in both struggles contributed to the overwhelming popularity of his royalist Imbokodvo Party in the elections of 1964, 1967, and 1972. In 1973 Sobuza, faced with a modest but articulate opposition party, the Ngwane National Liberatory Congress, dis-

solved Parliament and repealed the Westminster-style Constitution, characterizing it as "un-Swazi." In 1979 a new, nonpartisan Parliament was chosen; but authority remained with the king, assisted by his advisory council, the Liqoqo.

Sobuza's death in 1982 left many wondering if Swaziland's unique monarchist institutions would survive. A prolonged power struggle increased tensions within the ruling order. Members of the Liqoqo seized effective power and appointed a new "Queen Regent," Ntombi. However, palace intrigue continued until Prince Makhosetive, Ntombi's teenage son, was installed as King Mswati III in 1986, at the age of 18. The new king approved the demotion of the Liqoqo back to its advisory status and has ruled through his appointed prime minister and cabinet.

One of the major challenges facing any Swazi government is its relationship with South Africa. Under Sobuza, Swaziland managed to maintain its political autonomy while accepting its economic dependence on its powerful neighbor. The king also maintained a delicate balance between the apartheid state and the forces opposing it. During the 1980s this balance became tilted. A Swazi-South African non-aggression pact resulted in a greater degree of cooperation between the two countries' security forces in curbing suspected African National Congress activists.

Swaziland's economy, like its politics, is the product of both internal and external initiatives. Since independence the nation has enjoyed a high rate of economic growth, led by the expansion and diversification of its agriculture. Success in

agriculture has promoted the development of secondary industries, such as a sugar refinery and a paper mill. There has also been increased exploitation of coal and asbestos. Another important source of revenue is tourism, which depends on weekend traffic from South Africa.

Swazi development has relied on capital-intensive, rather than labor-intensive, projects. As a result, disparities in local wealth and dependence on South African investment have increased, while only 16 percent of the Swazi population, including migrant workers in South Africa, were in formal-sector employment by 1989. Until recently the economy was boosted by international investors looking for a politically preferable window to the South African market. An example is Coca Cola's decision to move its regional headquarters and concentrate plant from South Africa to Swaziland; the plant employs only about 100 workers but accounts for 20 percent of all foreign-exchange earnings. The current reform process in South Africa, however, is reducing Swaziland's attraction as a center for corporate relocation and sanctions-busting. It has also increased pressure for greater democracy.

DEVELOPMENT

Much of Swaziland's economy is managed by the Tibiyo TakaNgwana, a royally controlled institution established in 1968 by Sobuza. It is responsible for the financial assets of the communal lands (upon which most Swazi farm) and mining operations.

FREEDOM

The current political order restricts many forms of opposition, although its defenders claim that local councils, *Tikhudlas*, allow for popular participation in decision-making. The leading opposition group is the People's United Democratic Movement, which calls for democratic reforms and is sympathetic to the ANC.

HEALTH/WELFARE

Swaziland's low life expectancy and high infant mortality rates have resulted in greater public-health allocations, which in 1989–1990 accounted for 15% of recurrent expenditures. There has also been a greater emphasis placed on preventive medicine.

ACHIEVEMENTS

Education accounts for a 28% share of government spending, the largest item in the budget. Enrollment is currently 100% for the primary-school and 43% for the secondary-school age groups. The University of Swaziland was established in the 1970s and now offers a full range of degree and diploma programs.

Zambia (Republic of Zambia)

GEOGRAPHY

Area in Square Kilometers (Miles):
752,972 (290,724) (slightly larger than Texas)
Capital (Population): Lusaka (818,000)
Climate: tropical to subtropical

PEOPLE

Population
Total: 8,446,000
Annual Growth Rate: 3.5%
Rural/Urban Population Ratio: 45/55
Languages: official: English; others spoken: Bemba, Nyanja, Tonga, Lozi, others

Health
Life Expectancy at Birth: 55 years (male); 58 years (female)
Infant Mortality Rate (Ratio): 79/1,000
Average Caloric Intake: 90% of FAO minimum
Physicians Available (Ratio): 1/7,150

Religion(s)
51% Christian; 48% traditional indigenous; 1% Hindu and Muslim

---

THE H-P WOMAN'S DEVELOPMENT CORPORATION

The H-P Woman's Corporation is an entirely female-owned and -run company aimed at helping women to get ahead by starting self-sustaining small businesses. Named after its founder, women's-rights lawyer Tsitsi Himuyanga-Phiri, it loans small amounts of money to women who lack the necessary collateral or male permission to get ordinary bank loans. In addition to money, H-P provides project-assessment, accounting, market-research, legal, and record-keeping facilities. Its Mother's Aid program provides such services as child care, house cleaning, and home nursing to allow its loan recipients to devote themselves to their businesses. Successful entrepreneurs have become shareholders; H-P has survived since 1989 without any government or donor-agency assistance. With only 350,000 jobs currently available in Zambia's unproductive formal sector, innovative grass-roots initiatives like the H-P Development Corporation could play a key role in the nation's economic reconstruction.

Education
Adult Literacy Rate: 73%

COMMUNICATION
Telephones: 71,700
Newspapers: 2

TRANSPORTATION
Highways—Kilometers (Miles): 36,370 (22,549)
Railroads—Kilometers (Miles): 1,266 (785)
Usable Airports: 106

GOVERNMENT
Type: multiparty republic
Independence Date: October 24, 1964
Head of State: President Frederick Chiluba
Political Parties: Movement for Multiparty Democracy; United National Independence Party; Democratic Alliance; Democratic Party
Suffrage: universal at 18

MILITARY
Number of Armed Forces: 18,500
Military Expenditures (% of Central Government Expenditures): n/a
Current Hostilities: none

ECONOMY
Currency ($ U.S. Equivalent): 122.6 kwachas = $1
Per Capita Income/GDP: $580/$4.9 billion
Inflation Rate: 80%
Natural Resources: copper; zinc; lead; cobalt; coal
Agriculture: corn; tobacco; cotton; peanuts; sugarcane
Industry: foodstuffs; beverages; chemicals; textiles; fertilizer

FOREIGN TRADE
Exports: $1.1 billion
Imports: $1.1 billion

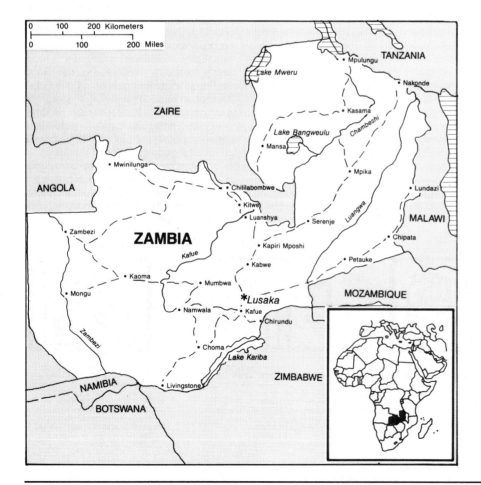

| Rhodes' South African Company is chartered by the British government **1889** | Development of the Copperbelt **1924–1934** | Federation of Northern Rhodesia, Southern Rhodesia, and Nyasaland is formed; still part of British Empire **1953–1963** | Zambia celebrates independence **1963** | Nationalization of 51% of all industries **1969** | Zambia becomes a one-party state under the United National Independence Party **1972** | |

1980s–1990s

South African military raids on Zambia

In the face of mounting unrest, President Kenneth Kaunda agrees to internationally observed multiparty elections

Kaunda is defeated and Frederick Chiluba is immediately sworn in as the nation's second president

ZAMBIA

In October 1991 Zambian voters rejected their long-serving first president, Kenneth Kaunda, and his United National Independence Party (UNIP), in the country's first multiparty elections in more than 2 decades. The landslide victory of Frederick Chiluba's Movement for Multiparty Democracy (MMD) touched off mass rejoicing that, finally, "the hour has come." But the celebrations were tempered by the widespread recognition that the bankrupt country's problems have not disappeared.

Kaunda had been in power for Zambia's entire 27-year history. During much of this period the nation's economy, along with the well-being of its citizenry, steadily declined. The former leader consistently blamed his country's setbacks on external forces rather than on his government's failings. There was some justification for his position. Until 1975 the high rate of return on exported copper made the nation one of the most prosperous in Africa. Since then fluctuating, but generally depressed, prices for the metal—and the disruption of landlocked Zambia's traditional sea outlets as a result of strife in neighboring states—have had disastrous economic consequences. Nonetheless, it has long been apparent that internal factors have also contributed to Zambia's decay, while creating barriers to its recovery.

From the early years of independence Kaunda and UNIP showed little tolerance for political opposition. In 1972 the country was legally transformed into a one-party state in which power was concentrated in the hands of Kaunda and his fellow members of UNIP's Central Committee. After 1976 the government ruled with state-of-emergency powers. Although Zambia was never as repressive as such neighboring states as Malawi and Zaire, torture and political detention without trial were common.

In its rule, UNIP was supposedly guided by the philosophy of "humanism," a term that became synonymous with the thoughts of Kaunda. The party also claimed adherence to socialism. Although it was once a mass party that had spearheaded Zambia's struggle for majority rule and independence, UNIP came to stand for little other than the perpetuation of its own power.

An underlying economic problem has been the decline of rural production, despite Zambia's considerable agricultural potential. The underdevelopment of farming is rooted in the colonial policies that favored mining to the exclusion of other sectors. Since independence the rural areas have continued to be neglected in terms of infrastructural investment. Until recently Zambian farmers were paid little for their produce, while the urban diet was maintained through government subsidization of imported food. The result has been a continuous influx of individuals into the towns, despite a lack of jobs, and falling food production. Today 55 percent of all Zambians are urban, one of the highest figures in Africa.

Zambia's rural decline has severely constrained the government's ability to meet the challenge imposed by the depressed international price of copper. Copper, along with its by-product cobalt, has consistently accounted for more than 90 per-

cent of Zambia's export earnings. Falling prices have thus resulted in severe shortages of foreign exchange and mounting indebtedness—$7 billion by 1992. After years of relative inertia, the government, during the 1980s, devoted greater attention to rural development. Agricultural production rose modestly in response to increased incentives. But the size and desperate condition of the urban population discouraged the government from decontrolling prices altogether; rising maize prices in 1986 set off riots that left at least 30 people dead. The new MMD government has ended the subsidies.

By 1990 the government's continuing economic crisis dovetailed with rising agitation for a return to multiparty democracy. Despite the president's attempts to label multiparty advocates as "misfits, malcontents, drug-peddlers and dissidents," the movement grew, with the support of Zambia's major labor federation, its powerful Catholic Church, and a number of prominent UNIP backbenchers. In June and July of 1990 severe riots culminated in a coup attempt, which, although unsuccessful, exposed the weakness of Kaunda's regime, forcing it finally to agree to free and fair elections.

DEVELOPMENT

Higher producer prices for agriculture, technical assistance, and rural-resettlement schemes are part of government efforts to raise agricultural production. The agricultural sector has shown growth. However, financial inputs are needed, and much maize is smuggled over the border to Zaire, reducing Zambia's potential for recovery.

FREEDOM

The MMD's victory has been seen as a great victory for democracy. But some, fearing a continuation or revival of the bad habits of its predecessor, are demanding that the new government honor its election commitments to privatize the media and reform the security services.

HEALTH/WELFARE

Life expectancy rates have increased in Zambia since independence, as a result of improved health care facilities. In 1986, 80% of primary-age children attended school; about 1 out of 4 went on to at least some secondary education. AIDS increasingly looms as a critical hazard.

ACHIEVEMENTS

Zambia has long played a major role in the fight against white supremacy in Southern Africa. From 1964 until 1980 it was a major base for Zimbabwe nationalists. Namibia's SWAPO and South Africa's ANC have also had headquarters in Zambia's capital of Lusaka.

Zimbabwe (Republic of Zimbabwe)

GEOGRAPHY

Area in Square Kilometers (Miles): 390,759 (150,873) (slightly smaller than Montana)
Capital (Population): Harare (730,000)
Climate: subtropical

PEOPLE

Population

Total: 10,720,000
Annual Growth Rate: 2.9%
Rural/Urban Population Ratio: 75/25
Languages: official: English; others spoken: (Chi)Shona, (Si)Ndebele, others

Health

Life Expectancy at Birth: 60 years (male); 64 years (female)
Infant Mortality Rate (Ratio): 61/1,000
Average Caloric Intake: 86% of FAO minimum
Physicians Available (Ratio): 1/6,700

Religion(s)

75% Christian; 24% traditional indigenous; 1% Muslim

AGRICULTURAL SURPLUSES AND FOOD SECURITY

During Zimbabwe's first decade of independence, farmers on both small communal farms and large commercial estates enjoyed great success in boosting local food production. Peasant farmers boosted their marketed maize surpluses by as much as 1,000 percent, while their statistical share of agricultural production rose from 8 percent to 64 percent. Large-scale commercial farmers were able to triple their output. Government loans and investment in infrastructure, an end to wartime dislocations, and the modest efforts to resettle landless Zimbabweans contributed to this growth in productivity.

Unfortunately, the very success of Zimbabwean agriculture encouraged complacency regarding the need to assure food security. Allegedly encouraged by international financiers, record agricultural exports in 1990 and 1991 left Zimbabwe without adequate emergency stocks to cope with the severe 1992 drought, a painful lesson for when the rains return.

Education

Adult Literacy Rate: 67%

COMMUNICATION

Telephones: 247,000

Newspapers: 2

TRANSPORTATION

Highways—Kilometers (Miles): 85,237 (52,964)
Railroads—Kilometers (Miles): 2,743 (1,704)
Usable Airports: 415

GOVERNMENT

Type: paramilitary democracy
Independence Date: April 18, 1980
Head of State: Executive President Robert Mugabe
Political Parties: Zimbabwe African National Union and Zimbabwe African People's Union (merged); Zimbabwe Unity movement
Suffrage: universal over 18

MILITARY

Number of Armed Forces: 68,500
Military Expenditures (% of Central Government Expenditures): 6.2%
Current Hostilities: none

ECONOMY

Currency ($ U.S. Equivalent): 5.06 Zimbabwe dollars = $1
Per Capita Income/GDP: $540/$5.8 billion
Inflation Rate: 13%
Natural Resources: gold; chrome ore; coal; copper; nickel; iron ore; silver; asbestos
Agriculture: tobacco; corn; sugar; cotton; livestock
Industry: mining; steel; textiles

FOREIGN TRADE

Exports: $1.7 billion
Imports: $1.4 billion

ZIMBABWE

Zimbabwe achieved its formal independence in April 1980, after a 14-year armed struggle by its disenfranchised black African majority. Before 1980 the country was called (Southern) Rhodesia; a name that honored Cecil Rhodes, the British imperialist who had masterminded the colonial occupation of the territory in the late nineteenth century. For its black African majority, Rhodesia's name was thus an expression of their subordination to a small minority of privileged white settlers whose racial hegemony was the product of Rhodes' conquest. The new name, Zimbabwe, was symbolic of the greatness of the nation's precolonial roots.

THE PRECOLONIAL PAST

By the fifteenth century, Zimbabwe had become the center of a series of states that prospered through their trade in gold and other goods with Indian Ocean merchants. These civilizations left as their architectural legacy the remains of stone settlements known as *zimbabwes*. The largest of these, the so-called Great Zimbabwe, lies near the modern town of Masvingo. Within its massive walls are dozens of stella, topped with distinctive carved birds whose likeness has become a symbol of the modern state. Unfortunately, early European fortuneseekers and archaeologists destroyed much of the archaeological evidence of this site, but what survives confirms that the state had trading contacts as far afield as China.

From the sixteenth century the Zimbabwean civilizations seem to have declined, possibly as a result of the disruption of the East African trading networks by the Portuguese. Nevertheless, the states themselves survived until the nineteenth century, while their cultural legacy is very much alive today, especially among the approximately 80 percent of Zimbabwe's population who speak (Chi)Shona.

Zimbabwe's other major ethnolinguistic community are the (Si)Ndebele speakers, who today account for about 15 percent of the population. This group traces its local origin to the mid-nineteenth century conquest of much of modern Zimbabwe by invaders from the south under the leadership of Umzilagazi, who established a militarily strong Ndebele kingdom, which subsequently was ruled by his son.

WHITE RULE

Zimbabwe's colonial history is unique in that it was never under the direct rule of a European power. In 1890 the lands of the Ndebele and Shona were invaded by agents of Rhodes' British South Africa Company (BSACO). During the 1890s both groups put up stiff resistance to the encroachments of the BSACO settlers, but eventually they succumbed to the invaders. In 1924 the BSACO administration was dissolved and Southern Rhodesia became a self-governing British Crown colony. "Self-government" was, in fact, confined to the white settler community, which grew rapidly but never numbered more than 5 percent of the population.

In 1953 Southern Rhodesia was federated with the British colonial territories of Northern Rhodesia (Zambia) and Nyasaland (Malawi). This Central African Federation was supposed to evolve into a "multiracial" dominion, but from the beginning it was perceived by the black majority in all three territories as a vehicle for continued white domination. As the Federation's first prime minister put it, the partnership of blacks and whites in building the new state would be analogous to a horse and its rider; no one had any illusions as to which race group would continue to be the beast of burden.

In 1963 the Federation collapsed, as a result of local resistance. Black nationalists established the independent "nonracial" states of Malawi and Zambia. For a while it appeared that majority rule would also come to Southern Rhodesia. The local black community was increasingly well organized and militant in demanding full citizenship rights. However, in 1962 the white electorate responded to this challenge by voting into office the Rhodesia Front (RF), a party determined to uphold white supremacy at any cost. Using already existing emergency powers, the new government moved to suppress the two major black nationalist movements: the Zimbabwe African People's Union (ZAPU) and the Zimbabwe African National Union (ZANU).

RHODESIA DECLARES INDEPENDENCE

In a bid to consolidate white power along the lines of the neighboring apartheid regime of South Africa, the RF, now led by Ian Smith, made its 1965 Unilateral Declaration of Independence (UDI) of any ties to the British Crown. Britain, along with the United Nations, refused to recognize this move. In 1967 the UN imposed mandatory economic sanctions against the "illegal" RF regime. But the sanctions were not fully effective, largely due to the fact that they were flouted by South Africa and the Portuguese authorities who controlled most of Mozambique until 1974. The United States for a number of years continued openly to purchase Rhodesian chrome, while many states and individuals engaged in more covert forms of sanctions-busting. The Rhodesian economy initially benefited from the porous blockade, which encouraged the development of a wide range of import-substitution industries.

With the sanctions having only a limited effect and Britain and the rest of the international community unwilling to engage in more active measures, it soon became clear that the burden of overthrowing the RF regime would be borne by the local population. Beginning in 1966, ZANU and ZAPU, as underground movements, began to engage in armed struggle. The success of their attacks initially was limited, but from 1972 the Rhodesian Security Forces were increasingly besieged by the nationalists' guerrilla campaign. The 1974 liberation of Mozambique from the Portuguese greatly increased the effectiveness of the ZANU forces, who were allowed to infiltrate into Rhodesia from Mozambican territory. Meanwhile, their ZAPU comrades launched attacks from bases in Zambia. In 1976 the two groups became loosely affiliated, as the Patriotic Front.

Unable to stop the military advance of the Patriotic Front, which was resulting in a massive white exodus, the RF attempted to forge a power-sharing arrangement that preserved major elements of settler privilege. Although rejected by ZANU or ZAPU, this "internal settlement" was implemented in 1978–1979. A predominantly black government took office, but real power remained in white hands, and the fighting only intensified. Finally, in 1979, all the belligerent parties, meeting at Lancaster House in London, agreed to a compromise peace, which opened the door to majority rule while containing a number of constitutional provisions designed to reassure the white minority. In the subsequent elections, held in 1980, ZANU captured 57 and ZAPU 20 out of the 80 seats elected by the "common roll." Another 20 seats, which were reserved for whites for 7 years as a result of the Lancaster House agreement, were captured by the Conservative Alliance (the new name for the RF). ZANU leader Robert Mugabe became independent Zimbabwe's first prime minister.

THE RHODESIAN LEGACY

The political, economic, and social problems inherited by the Mugabe government were formidable. Rhodesia had essentially been divided into "two nations": one black and the other white. Segregation prevailed in virtually all areas of life, with

| Heyday of the gold trade and Great Zimbabwe **1400s–1500s** | The Ndebele state emerges in Zimbabwe **1840s** | The Pioneer Column: arrival of the white settlers **1890** | Chimurenga: rising against the white intruders, ending in repression by whites **1895–1897** |

those facilities open to blacks being vastly inferior to those open to whites. The better half of the national territory had also been reserved for white ownership. Large commercial farms prospered in this white area, growing maize and tobacco for export as well as a diversified mix of crops for domestic consumption. In contrast, the black areas, formally known as Tribal Trust Lands, suffered from inferior soil and rainfall, overcrowding, and poor infrastructure. Most black adults had little choice but to obtain seasonal work in the white areas. Black workers on white plantations, together with the large number of domestic servants, were particularly impoverished. But, until the 1970s, there were also few opportunities for skilled blacks as a result of a de facto "color bar," which reserved the best jobs for whites.

Despite its stated commitment to revolutionary socialist objectives, since 1980 the Mugabe government has taken an evolutionary approach in dismantling the socioeconomic structures of old Rhodesia. This cautious policy is, in part, based on an appreciation that these same structures support what, by regional standards, is a relatively prosperous and self-sufficient economy. Until 1990 the government's hands were also partially tied by the Lancaster House accords, wherein private property, including the large settler estates,

could not be confiscated without compensation. In its first years, the government nevertheless made impressive progress in improving the livelihoods of the Zimbabwean majority by redistributing some of the surplus of the still white-dominated private sector. With the lifting of sanctions, mineral, maize, and tobacco exports expanded and import restrictions were eased. Workers' incomes rose, and a minimum wage, which notably covered farm employees, was introduced. Rising consumer purchasing power initially benefited local manufacturers. Health and educational facilities were expanded, while a growing number of blacks began to occupy management positions in the civil service and, to a lesser extent, in businesses.

Zimbabwe had hoped that foreign investment and aid would pay for an ambitious scheme to buy out many white farmers and to settle African peasants on their land. However, funding shortfalls have resulted in only modest resettlement. Just over 4,000 white farmers own more than one-third of the land. In 1992 the government passed a new bill that allows for the involuntary purchase of up to 50 percent of this land at an officially set price. While enjoying overwhelming domestic support, this new land redistribution measure has come under considerable

external criticism for violating the private property and judicial "rights" of the large-scale farmers. Others have pointed out that, besides producing large surpluses of food in nondrought years, many jobs are tied to the commercial estates. The government is thus expected to move cautiously in making use of its new powers.

While gradually abandoning its professed desire to build a socialist society, the Zimbabwean government has continued to face a classic dilemma of all industrializing societies: whether to continue to use tight import controls to protect its existing manufacturing base or open up its economy in the hopes of enjoying a takeoff based on export-oriented growth. While many Zimbabwean manufacturers would be vulnerable to greater foreign competition, there is now a widespread consensus that limits of the local market have contributed to stagnating output and physical depreciation of local industry in recent years.

POLITICAL DEVELOPMENT

The Mugabe government has since independence promoted reconciliation across the racial divide. Although the reserved seats for whites were abolished in 1987, the white minority, who now make up less than 2 percent of the population, are well

(Oxfam America photo)

As in many African institutions, decisions in Zimbabwean organizations are often made by consensus, arrived at after long discussions.

Local government in Southern Rhodesia is placed in the hands of white settlers
1924

Unilateral Declaration of Independence
1965

Armed struggle begins
1966

Elections following cease-fire bring victory to ZANU-PF and an end to the war

1980s–1990s

Government forces brutally suppress unrest in Matebeleland

ZANU and ZAPU merge and win the 1990 elections

Severe drought in 1992 leads to widespread suffering and economic depression

represented within government as well as business. Unfortunately, Mugabe's ZANU administration has shown less tolerance of its political opponents, especially ZAPU. ZANU had originally been a breakaway faction of ZAPU. At the time of this split, in 1963, the differences between the two movements had largely been over tactics. But elections in 1980 and 1985 confirmed that the followings of both movements have become ethnically based, with most Shona supporting ZANU and Ndebele supporting ZAPU.

Initially, ZANU agreed to share power with ZAPU. However in 1982 the alleged discoveries of secret arms caches, which ZANU claimed ZAPU was stockpiling for a coup, led to the dismissal of the ZAPU ministers. Some leading ZAPU figures were also detained. The confrontation led to violence that very nearly degenerated into a full-scale civil war. From 1982 to 1984 the Zimbabwean Army, dominated by former ZANU and Rhodesian units, carried out a brutal counterinsurgency campaign against supposed ZAPU dissidents in the largely Ndebele areas of western Zimbabwe. Thousands of civilians were killed—especially by the notorious Fifth Brigade, which operated outside the normal military command structure. Many more fled to Botswana, including, for a period, the ZAPU leader, Joshua Nkomo.

Until 1991 Mugabe's stated intention was to create a one-party state in Zimbabwe. With his other black and white opponents compromised by their past association with the RF and its internal settlement, this largely meant coercing ZAPU

into dissolving itself into ZANU. However, the increased support for ZAPU in its core Ndebele constituencies during the 1985 election led to a renewed emphasis on the carrot over the stick in bringing about the union. In 1987 ZAPU formally merged into ZANU, but their shotgun wedding has made for an uneasy marriage.

With the demise of ZAPU, new forces have emerged in opposition to Mugabe and the drive for a one-party state. Principal among these is the Zimbabwe Unity Movement (ZUM), led by former ZANU member Edger Tekere. In the 1990 elections, ZUM received about 20 percent of the vote, in a poll that saw a sharp drop in voter participation. The election was also marred by serious restrictions on opposition activity and blatant voter intimidation. The deaths of ZUM supporters in the period before the election reinforced the message of the government-controlled media that a vote for the opposition was an act of suicide.

Mugabe initially claimed that his 1990 victory was a mandate to establish a one-party state. But in 1991 the changing international climate, the continuing strength of the opposition, and growing opposition within ZANU itself caused him to shelve the project. While more moderate elements have long favored the preservation of multiparty politics, many radicals have also come to see the establishment of a one-party state as a final step in the betrayal of the Zimbabwe revolution by an authoritarian government. That these and other views continue to be the subject of vigorous debate underscores the fact that

there has developed within Zimbabwe a strong civil society that is increasingly resistant to the centralization of power.

In 1992 public confidence in the government was greatly eroded by the outbreak of the worst drought in a century. Despite warning signs of the impending catastrophe, little attempt had been made to stockpile food. This has resulted in widespread hunger, dependence on expensive imported food, and severe dislocations to the already troubled economy. Long-neglected waterworks, especially those serving Bulawayo, the country's second-largest city, are proving to be inadequate. Unless the rainfall significantly improves soon, hundreds of thousands will have to be resettled. With idle factories and farms and record-high unemployment and inflation, the country is being pushed to the brink. Yet, notwithstanding its current crisis and recurrent political and economic controversies, the welfare of most Zimbabweans has improved during the last dozen years. Nonracial policies are helping to overcome the legacy of the "two nations."

DEVELOPMENT

Peasant production has increased dramatically since independence, creating grain reserves and providing exports for the region. The work of communal farmers has been recognized both within Zimbabwe and internationally.

FREEDOM

Since the 1990 lifting of the state of emergency that had been in effect since the days of the Federation, Zimbabwe's human-rights record has generally improved. Institutions of government, especially the Central Intelligence Organization, are still accused of extrajudicial abuses.

HEALTH/WELFARE

Public expenditure on health and education has risen dramatically since independence. Most Zimbabweans now enjoy access to medical facilities, while primary-school enrollment has multiplied fourfold. Higher education has also been greatly expanded. But the advances are now threatened by downturns in the economy, and school fees have been reintroduced.

ACHIEVEMENTS

Zimbabwe's capital city of Harare has become an arts and communications center for Southern Africa. Many regional as well as local filmmakers, musicians, and writers based in the city enjoy international reputations. And the distinctive malachite carvings of Zimbabwean sculptors are highly valued in the international art market.

Articles from the World Press

Annotated Table of Contents for Articles

Topic Guide to Articles

TOPIC AREA:	TREATED IN:	TOPIC AREA:	TREATED IN:
African National Congress (ANC)	24. Of Peace and Hope	Economy	3. Nation Building in Black Africa 11. The CFA Franc
Agriculture	17. Africans Push More Ambitious Environment Goals 18. Kenya's Green Belt Movement 21. Namibia's Land Reform	Environment	17. Africans Push More Ambitious Environment Goals 18. Kenya's Green Belt Movement
		Family	12. The African Woman Today
Apartheid	24. Of Peace and Hope 25. Democracy in the Balance	Famine	7. Myths of African Hunger
Arts	13. Literature in Postcolonial Africa 14. BaKongo Cosmology 23. A Nation of Poets	Foreign Aid	4. Africa: The Scramble for Existence 9. Uses and Abuses of African Debt
Civil War	15. A Traveller's Notebook 19. America's Lost Stepchild 22. How Somalia Was Left in the Cold	Foreign Investment	4. Africa: The Scramble for Existence 9. Uses and Abuses of African Debt 10. Why Africa Stays Poor, And Why It Doesn't Have To
Class	8. Black Africa's Open Societies 12. The African Woman Today 24. Of Peace and Hope 25. Democracy in the Balance	Foreign Relations	10. Why Africa Stays Poor, And Why It Doesn't Have To 22. How Somalia Was Left in the Cold
Cultural Roots	1. Promise and Uncertainty 2. Ethnic Loyalties Are on the Rise 8. Black Africa's Open Societies 13. Literature in Postcolonial Africa 14. BaKongo Cosmology 20. Three Days in Timbuktu 23. A Nation of Poets	History	1. Promise and Uncertainty 2. Ethnic Loyalties Are on the Rise 3. Nation Building in Black Africa 14. BaKongo Cosmology
		Human Rights	12. The African Woman Today 24. Of Peace and Hope 25. Democracy in the Balance
Current Leaders	1. Promise and Uncertainty 5. Africa's Turn 10. Why Africa Stays Poor, And Why It Doesn't Have To 22. How Somalia Was Left in the Cold 24. Of Peace and Hope	Independence	4. Africa: The Scramble for Existence 10. Why Africa Stays Poor, And Why It Doesn't Have To
		Land Reform	17. Africans Push More Ambitious Environment Goals 18. Kenya's Green Belt Movement 21. Namibia's Land Reform 26. The Dynamic Nature of Land Reform
Debt	9. Uses and Abuses of African Debt 10. Why Africa Stays Poor, and Why It Doesn't Have To		
Economic Development	3. Nation Building in Black Africa 5. Africa's Turn 9. Uses and Abuses of African Debt 11. The CFA Franc 16. Ethiopia Rebuilds Ruined Economy	Literature	13. Literature in Postcolonial Africa
		Natural Disasters	18. Kenya's Green Belt Movement
Economic Investment	9. Uses and Abuses of African Debt 10. Why Africa Stays Poor, And Why It Doesn't Have To	Natural Resources	7. Myths of African Hunger 17. Africans Push More Ambitious Environment Goals
Economic Reform	10. Why Africa Stays Poor, And Why It Doesn't Have To 16. Ethiopia Rebuilds Ruined Economy 26. The Dynamic Nature of Land Reform	Philosophy	8. Black Africa's Open Societies 14. BaKongo Cosmology

TOPIC AREA:	TREATED IN:	TOPIC AREA:	TREATED IN:
Political	2. Ethnic Loyalties Are on the Rise 3. Nation Building in Black Africa 5. Africa's Turn 10. Why Africa Stays Poor, And Why It Doesn't Have To 16. Ethiopia Rebuilds Ruined Economy 24. Of Peace and Hope 27. Zambia: A Model for Democratic Change	**Refugees** **Religion** **Science** **Turmoil**	22. How Somalia Was Left in the Cold 14. BaKongo Cosmology 14. BaKongo Cosmology 15. A Traveller's Notebook 16. Ethiopia Rebuilds Ruined Economy 19. America's Lost Stepchild 20. Three Days in Timbuktu 22. How Somalia Was Left in the Cold
Political Reform	3. Nation Building in Black Africa 4. Africa: The Scramble for Existence 5. Africa's Turn 24. Of Peace and Hope 27. Zambia: A Model for Democratic Change	**Violence**	15. A Traveller's Notebook 16. Ethiopia Rebuilds Ruined Economy 19. America's Lost Stepchild 22. How Somalia Was Left in the Cold
Political Unrest	4. Africa: The Scramble for Existence 15. A Traveller's Notebook 19. America's Lost Stepchild 25. Democracy in the Balance	**Women**	12. The African Woman Today 17. Africans Push More Ambitious Environment Goals 18. Kenya's Green Belt Movement

Article 1   *Unesco Courier*, November 1992

Promise and Uncertainty

Elikia M'Bokolo

Elikia M'Bokolo, Zairean historian, is Director of Studies at the Ecole des Hautes Etudes en Sciences Sociales in Paris. He has published many books on African history and civilizations, including L'Afrique au 20ᵉ siècle, le continent convoité *(Le Seuil, Paris 1985) and* Afrique Noire, Histoire et Civilisation, 19ᵉ–20ᵉ siècles *(Hatier, Paris, 1992).*

During the pre-colonial period, those political units in Africa that had no developed state structures were gradually absorbed, in an increasingly brutal way, into larger groupings that had. African societies thereby learned that any authority tends to arrogate to itself as much power as it can, and that every state, if left uncontrolled, tends to abuse its power.

Secession was one of the oldest forms of protest. Dissident individuals or groups would switch their allegiance to rulers renowned for their tolerance, or more often would set up new units that responded better to the people's aspirations to liberty and autonomy.

Forms of political control varied between cultures, but one characteristic common to most traditional societies was the sanctity of kingship. A connection was made between on the one hand the welfare of the world and the community and on the other the physical and moral state of the king, who was held accountable for every economic, political or ecological crisis. Royal failings, such as erratic and antisocial behaviour, were punishable. The holder of supreme power would pay the supreme penalty. These practices seem to have functioned in many parts of the continent and tempered many abuses.

In the nineteenth century a more complex form of state organization came into being. Most states opted for a federal rather than a centralized system, at least until belated attempts were made to enforce unification on the eve of colonization. Once they had proclaimed their allegiance to the king and had accepted such obligations as paying taxes and providing soldiers for the army, the local units—villages, ancient kingdoms or tribes—kept their own laws, customs, language and religious practices.

There are indications that this political model still lingers in people's memories. It is remarkable that one factor in current demands for democracy has been the desire to set up—or restore—federal structures in many states. This may reflect a departure from the centralization inherited from the colonial era (in the French- and Portuguese-speaking countries) or its immediate aftermath (primarily in the English-speaking ones), but perhaps it also suggests a determination to return to older traditions.

With the coming of colonialism, collective resistance began to express itself in new fields—against foreign domination and harsh exploitation. For too long a heroic, elitist vision credited this resistance to modern political parties, intellectual leaders and administrators produced under colonization, and to the future "fathers of the nation". In fact the most enduring resistance came, throughout the colonial period, from "stateless societies" that opposed the forces of occupation and the new forms of subjection imposed by the Europeans in much the same way as they had resisted pressure from the great nineteenth-century African state structures.

The most perceptive colonialists were aware that societies of this type were unfailingly hostile to all forms of oppression. Governor Gabriel Angoulvant, who was responsible for the "pacification" of the Ivory Coast, noted that "One of the greatest difficulties we have encountered in establishing our influence lies in the attitude of the natives or, to put it bluntly, in the moral condition of the country.... The previous state of anarchy, which had real advantages for savage populations, is still too persistent among the natives of the centre of the colony and the lower Ivory Coast. It has left profound traces everywhere, and its gradual disappearance is causing too many regrets for all its effects to disappear."

By the late nineteenth century, the political struggle of educated Africans and the urban working classes was beginning to make an impact in Senegal, South Africa, Ghana and Nigeria. At first the colonial authorities contained the agitation within the bounds of a mild reformism, and opposition only really took off after the Second World War, when the rural population began to rally to the new political parties. It was then that the colonizers reluctantly agreed to reform the colonial system—before being forced to wind it up altogether.

Many forms of resistance helped to shatter the colonial edifice: opposition from the syncretic churches and Messianic movements; workers' strikes and mutinies among the police; insurrections in rural areas and armed rebellions, almost always led by self-proclaimed religious revivalists; communist ideologies and methods imported from Europe (notably into South Africa, French West Africa and the Portuguese colonies); and non-violent resistance, which was particularly widespread in Ghana.

The diversity of these home-grown and imported forms of opposition illustrates the extent of resistance within African societies, as well as their capacity for invention. They contained the demands for democracy that were a feature of this phase of history and are in many cases re-emerging today. Overt and covert forms of racism were rejected. So too were all kinds of discrimination based on ethnic or religious criteria or on a so-called respect for cultural sensibilities which was nothing more than racism in a subtle and shameful disguise. Demands for sovereignty were made. There was a desire to replace unapproachable bureaucracies in distant capitals with effective participation in public affairs. In material terms Africans aspired to enjoy a minimum of available wealth. Culturally they sought the richest possible experience of modern artistic creation and knowledge.

The most sincere and clear-sighted leaders of the independence movements, men such as Patrice Lumumba and, later, Amilcar Cabral, expressed all these aspirations. More often, however, the politicians who rose to head (or were placed at the head of) these movements emphasized the legal and political side of the struggle. Kwame Nkrumah, one of the most fervently nationalistic of them all, told his followers "Seek ye first the political kingdom, and all other things shall be added onto it".

In practice, the citizens of the new nations rarely found the political kingdom, still less what was to be added onto it. One-party systems proliferated in the post-independence period. In many lands, the old colonial set-up was re-established under a new name and on different pretexts. Everywhere the people grew poorer at a time when most of the leaders were feathering their nests.

The notion of "second independence" sometimes used to describe the demands and struggles of today neatly expresses the continuity between past and present discontent. Continuity does not, however, imply that slogans, aspirations or political programmes are necessarily the same. On the contrary, it seems that unsatisfied earlier aspirations have been absorbed into fresh ones. This suggests that the present situation is serious and that irreversible processes are now under way in a group of states which are all, as it were, several revolutions behind and pregnant with major reforms that have yet to be born.

A LONG HISTORY OF INTERNAL DISSENT

The actors who now dominate the African political scene and are imposing a long overdue process of democratization are merely going through a crucial stage in what J. Copans has called a "long march", the first steps of which can be traced back to the disillusionment that followed independence. Since the 1960s, peasants, young people, intellectuals, women, the urban working classes, and professional politicians have all, with varying degrees of intensity at different times and in different countries, tried to change the course of events.

Specialists in African history and political sociology have tended to pay little heed to these counter-movements and voices of dissent. It is only in the last decade that they have begun to pay attention to grassroots politics and popular dissidence, and by that time the bandwagon was already moving at speed.

In the early 1960s, the Congo (today Zaïre) was engulfed in peasant rebellions against a state that was identified with bureaucratic centralization, technocratic and authoritarian modernization, neo-colonialism, fiscal extortion and corruption.

Disturbances in the towns and cities, whether organized by workers (as in the case of the resignation of Abb Fulbert Youlou in Congo in 1963) or by school students like those which led to the downfall of Jean Bedel Bokassa in the Central African Empire in 1979, brought down a number of regimes that exemplified the worst features of the post-colonial period.

Even supposedly stable regimes, which were for that reason attractive to Western investors, had to cope with endemic protest in forms ranging from student and teacher discontent, to remonstrations from Christian and syncretic churches and from Muslim brotherhoods, and repeated criticisms from intellectuals and artists, who have had a greater impact than is often thought.

A number of artists have done much to instill in young people the spirit of radical criticism that is widespread today. The songs of the Nigerian musician Fela, with their vitriolic descriptions of the acquisitive lifestyle of the Nigerian middle class, are one example. Another is the Congolese singer Zao, whose less overtly political works nonetheless praise such forbidden notions as antimilitarism and pacifism, describe the difficulties of city life, and deduce from the equality of all people in the face of death the same equality for the living.

The movement towards democracy accelerated rapidly in the 1980s, for reasons that have yet to be fully analysed. Many commentators have pointed to the wind blowing at gale force from Eastern Europe or to factors such as the "Gorbachev effect" or the "Ceausescu effect".

But why not look at events in Africa itself? On the positive side, for instance, there was a "Senghor effect", proving that a one-party regime could move without mishap towards multi-party democracy. There was also a "Mandela effect". On the other side of the coin were the "Bokassa effect", which showed how a regime actively supported by a great power could be brought down by a movement triggered by students, and the "Idi Amin effect", the toppling of an archetypal bloodthirsty dictatorship by a long civil war.

The autocratic oligarchies are on the defensive. But though they may be shaky, they are still on their feet. And so the extraordinary diversity of current forms of struggle illustrates two things: the inventiveness of the champions of democracy, and also the resilience and adaptability of the existing regimes.

The number of civil wars and latent civil wars shows that, for many leaders,

the current situation is no more than a repeat of earlier forms of agitation. At worst it is a transitional period to be got through with a minimum of damage by means of a judicious combination of intransigence and vague promises.

PATHS OF TRANSITION

The increasingly hard line taken by several governments may be the swan-song of dying regimes. Nevertheless these regimes are one of the great question marks hanging over the transition to democracy in Africa. Others are trying to prolong their hold on power by means of a constitutional facelift.

One course that was followed in the late 1970s with the support of the Western powers, which had no desire to lose partners with a reputation for reliability, was for countries to "liberalize" their ruling parties without calling into question the principle of the one-party state or the quasi-dynastic nature of the regimes. In some cases, however, this provided an opportunity for part of the political class to detach itself permanently from government. Moreover, the revelation of all kinds of scandal entailed many risks. By the start of the 1980s, most regimes had abandoned this experiment.

Another model entails the imposition from above of a multi-party system controlled by those in power. African statesmen who choose this model seem to think that controlled democratization paying lip-service to the principle of multi-party choice can protect the long-term interests of the ruling oligarchy more securely than thorough-going authoritarian rule. But there have been surprises, as we saw recently in Cape Verde, where President Aristides Pereira and the African Party for the Independence of Cape Verde, which had been in power since independence in 1975, went over to a multi-party system in 1990 and lost a general election held in January 1991.

Another phenomenon is to use a "national conference" as an original framework for a painless transition to democracy. National conferences, the first of which was called to extricate the rulers of Benin from a political and economic crisis caused by a wave of strikes that had brought the country to a halt, subsequently spread like wildfire throughout Africa. Two were held in 1990 (in Benin and Gabon) and five in 1991 (in Congo, Mali, Togo, Niger and Zaïre). In other countries, notably Cameroon and the Central African Republic, the call for a national conference is the main plank in the opposition platform.

The first of its kind, the Benin national conference was hastily organized and was dominated by a technocratic emphasis on legal formalities and economic detail. Its chief business was to neutralize a corrupt and worn-out ruling group, so as to have access to credit from the International Monetary Fund, the World Bank, and France. A similar process took place in Gabon and possibly in Mali.

In Congo, on the other hand, the conference lasted three whole months, against the wishes of the international financial organizations. Regarded by some as an interminable African talking shop, in many ways the Brazzaville conference set an example for others. The French historian Jean Chesneaux recently pointed out, correctly, that any truly participatory democracy is time-consuming.

The time taken from coping with economic emergencies and from the efficient despatch of business was devoted to an in-depth scrutiny, unprecedented in Africa, of the nation's history. In Africa's present state of moral, political and economic bankruptcy, there is a need for stock-taking. Here, for the first time, a whole country uncompromisingly examined the most recent, and hence most shadowy and controversial, phase of its history, one during which a one-party state had decreed a monopoly over information and its interpretation.

In my view, if democracy is the nonconflictual resolution of social conflicts, it requires a certain minimum of consensus to achieve that end. No consensus has as much force as one based on lucidity and a common interpretation of crucial moments in a nation's history. It is still too early to appreciate the full significance of the new symbolism used at the conference, which mingled Christian concepts of forgiveness with the specifically African pagan rite of "the washing of hands" above the tomb of the ancestors after making confession. This act traditionally sanctioned the renewal of social bonds and the establishment of a new social contract enabling the members of the community to continue to live together and respect clearly stated common values.

But many obstacles lie ahead. Perhaps they are part of Africa's economic and social situation. What should be a cause for anxiety is not so much the economic crisis, which by definition cannot last for ever, as the structure of economies long shaped by the demands of an unequal division of labour and earnings. The working people of Africa drew no profit from economic growth during the 1960s and 1970s. They know that the supposed reforms devised by the International Monetary Fund and the World Bank have not solved any of Africa's development problems, since their aim is to redress the external imbalances of the African economies. Their social effects, on the other hand, have been very serious for most of the population.

A COMMON LABORATORY

There is therefore a serious short-term risk that almost before the gulf separating the people from the authoritarian oligarchs has been bridged, another one will open between a ruling class committed to technocratic modernization and the mass of the population. If it does, the people will feel that they have again been denied their "revolution".

Another major obstacle is the territorial structure of the African states, which were shaped a century—in some cases only decades—ago, at the whim of Western diplomats, to suit the interests of the great powers. Ethnic and regional problems are everywhere in evidence.

In the 1960s, the Katanga and Kasai dramas in Zaïre and the Biafra trauma in Nigeria, all of them involving outside intervention, led African political and intellectual elites to wholeheartedly condemn "regionalism" and "tribalism". Things are very different today. Frantic centralization in the name of the nation-state has been one of the foundations of the dictatorships that are now embroiled in crisis. Ethnic and regional discontent in Ethiopia, Angola, Congo, Zaïre and Togo has, on the other hand, stimulated calls for democracy. Ethnic parties represent a considerable risk, but so does a form of Jacobinism that in Africa as elsewhere would represent the triumph of a technocratic bureaucracy over a participatory democracy that would invest at least a minimum of power and responsibility in local hands.

The struggles, achievements, difficulties and questions described above indicate that Africa today is not so much a confused battlefield as a laboratory. Will it be a laboratory which will concentrate on its own specific and intractable situation, while others look on or at best offer encouragement? Or, in the heat of events, will Africa become a forum where new questions of universal importance can be addressed and where democratic demands and formulae of universal relevance can be worked out?

Many people both within and outside Africa rend to look upon the continent as a unique case. How convincing are their arguments?

Now that the foreign loans raised by the post-independence governments have been exhausted, at devastating cost for the peoples of Africa, it looks as if African countries are becoming introverted, turning back again to their own political cultures, and testing the powers of creativity and invention of both urban elites and villagers. There is a desire for mutual exchange and contact among African countries. From Cotonou to Kinshasa, from Douala to Antananarivo, from Brazzaville to Niamey, from Monrovia to Addis Ababa, from Bangui to Johannesburg, the similarities seem striking: in each place the cast in the social drama is the same, there are the same forms of mobilization, confrontation and negotiation.

However, I should like to correct this impression of an introverted Africa and to put this appearance of total originality into perspective. Africa is currently experiencing problems that both the old democratic states and the many countries of the "South" and "East" which are now coming to democracy also have to solve. There are three main problems. The first is that of the relationship between formal representative democracy (with all the attendant risks of the confiscation of power by experts, technocrats and politicians, all of whom are nonetheless necessary to the process) and the indispensable role of citizens in controlling and participating in power. The second is that of achieving a balance between centres of power, such as parliaments and governments, and the places where life is lived (businesses, residential neighbourhoods, villages and regions). Here the settling of the ethnic question is paramount. Thirdly, there is the question of harmonizing, in the exercise and guarantee of democracy, "national" territories and wider community-type groupings.

But Africa also needs to establish new bonds to strengthen a democratic world order. This will only come about on two conditions. On the one hand, colonial practices which have always played into the hands of the African dictatorships must be repudiated. On the other, aggressive and insidious forms of ideological and political paternalism must be done away with.

Article 2   *The Christian Science Monitor,* December 28, 1992

Ethnic Loyalties Are on the Rise Globally

There is no justification for calling the phenomenon 'tribalism' in Africa and 'nationalism' or 'ethnopolitics' elsewhere.

Herbert S. Lewis

Herbert S. Lewis is a professor of anthropology at the University of Wisconsin at Madison.

There are no fewer than 1,000 distinct "ethnic groups" among the more than 50 countries on the African continent. There is no way to give an exact accounting because these categories are dynamic ones, as people define themselves and their ethnic boundaries in response to changing circumstances.

These groups rest on language, religion, precolonial social and political divisions ("tribes," chiefdoms, kingdoms), region, and, sometimes, modes of subsistence (farmers versus herders, for example). More than 500 languages are said to exist in Nigeria alone, and Ethiopia has more than 75. Each one can be the basis for an ethnic identity and a self-conscious group. Many of today's African states—such as Nigeria, Ghana, Uganda, Ethiopia, and South Africa—contain the still-remembered loyalties, and perhaps the structures, of older kingdoms.

It is popular to blame the European colonial powers that ruled most of Africa from the 1890s to the early 1960s for creating these divisions, but while they certainly exacerbated many situations, the bases for most of the groups were there before they came. Ironically, rather than dividing groups (though they certainly did split some between two or more countries), the major impact of the colonial enterprise was to bring peoples together for the first time in sustained interaction within single political entities. This often had the effect of forcing people who might previously have had no direct contact with each other into economic, political, and social competition.

The colonial powers created the boundaries of today's African states and enclosed within them populations that are supposed to live together regardless of differences, enmities, and conflicting interests. The colonial officials drew the boundaries of the political units they created in order to maximize their own power and glory. And the peoples within those borders must now get on as best they can. The more people become educated and involved in the "modern sector"—studying, teaching, participating in the military and government service, in commerce and political activity—the more reasons there seem to be for ethnic conflict.

From the time Africans began regaining their independence at the end of the 1950s, the threat of "tribalism" (as ethnicity is too often called in the African context) has been haunting the leaders of all these new nations. Even though their borders were drawn by the colonial rulers, no matter how many actual or potentially feuding groups each state contained, no African leader would countenance the loss of any land, no matter how "troublesome" the groups that lived on that land might be. From the beginning, African leaders, through the Organization of African Unity, declared their opposition to changes in their borders.

Often they tried to deny that any problem existed, that there were ethnic inequalities or antagonisms. They usually insisted on unitary states and, very often, single-party rule. "Tribalism" was not only a threat to the integrity of virtually every African state, it also seemed to represent a backward and embarrassingly "primitive" force. In the 1950s and 1960s, politicians, social theorists, and ideologues all over the world widely believed that "parochial" loyalties to ethnic and religious groups, to anything other than "nations" (i.e. "states") or "classes," was "primitive," and "atavistic."

For liberals these narrow, primordial loyalties were not only destructive of progress and national unity but ethnic chauvinism was also seen as belonging to an earlier "premodern" era that would be transcended naturally as a result of "modernization." But the theories have been proven, so far, to be grossly oversimplified if not plain wrong.

For those inspired by Marx, ethnic loyalties represented "false consciousness," blinding working people to their true class interest and preventing "international proletarianism." Socialism or communism—in the USSR and Yugoslavia, in Ethiopia and Somalia—would overcome these differences. These states had rulers who worked toward this end and pretended they were succeeding. Of course, they normally forwarded the interests of their own groups, while feigning neutrality.

The "scientific socialist" rule of Mengistu Haile-Mariam that succeeded the monarchy of Emperor Haile Selassie in Ethiopia continued to impose the rule of the same group in that multi-ethnic empire. While President Mohamed Siad Barre of Somalia suppressed all talk of "tribes," he single-mindedly furthered his own ethnic relations at the expense of their rivals. It was obvious that the Russians were doing something similar in the USSR.

By 1992, however, it has become apparent that ethnic nationalism is one of the most up-to-date and powerful factors in current world politics. Both the left and the liberals underestimated the power of ethnicity. These loyalties and interests have not disappeared but have become heightened at the end of the 20th century. We can now see "tribalism" in various forms in such "primitive" countries as Canada, Belgium, the lands of the Czechs and Slovaks, Spain, France, the United Kingdom (and not only Northern Ireland), not to mention the former USSR, Yugoslavia, Iraq, Lebanon, India, Burma, Guatemala, Peru, Ecuador, Brazil—and the United States.

In the light of events since the 1960s, a re-evaluation of the meaning and nature of ethnicity is in order. If African countries are presented with some special problems because of the sheer numbers of groups and the arbitrary way in which their borders were drawn, the core phenomenon is very much the same all over the world. There is nothing more or less "primitive" about it on the African continent. (There is also no justification for calling the phenomenon "tribalism" in Africa and "nationalism" or "ethnopolitics" elsewhere.)

The root of the problem is that ethnic loyalties and identities are powerful bases for social and political life in the world today, despite earlier theories to the contrary. Far from being atavistic, residual, or "merely circumstantial," they may serve as the basis for social relations, the development of new patterns of culture, and as political interest groups. Ethnic groups are proving to be far more easily mobilized than were "classes" because they can combine a broad range of social, cultural, economic, and political interests with a real sense of identification, loyalty, and emotion. Individual and group identities are tied up in ethnicity in ways they are not in class, and appeals to ethnic pride and to grievances over unequal economic opportunities, discrimination, suppression of language, history, and cultural heritage serve increasingly to mobilize peoples.

The idea is spreading throughout the world that ethnicity is a legitimate basis for political organization and protest, and that ethnic groups no longer have to accept domination by others. The surprise is not that there is "tribalism" in Africa but that so few of its many states are in imminent danger of disintegration.

Nevertheless, where major fault lines based on ethnicity exist—as in Sudan, Kenya, Ethiopia, Nigeria—they should not be ignored, simply deplored, or set aside by blaming the former colonial powers. Ethnicity today can be the basis of powerful human feelings, interests, and motivations. It cannot be wished away by either politicians or analysts.

Article 3   *The World & I,* March 1992

NATION BUILDING IN BLACK AFRICA

Robert I. Rotberg

Robert I. Rotberg is president of Lafayette College in Easton, Pennsylvania.

The process of creating nations in black Africa is still not concluded—more than three decades after many were created and most of the continent south of the Sahara became free. Each state has a flag, an anthem, stamps, a state television and radio service, one or more official languages, and an identity. But each still contains a mlange of peoples, often uncomfortably yoked together in parliaments, cabinets, armies, and all aspects of official life.

When the colonial overlords retreated, beginning with Britain in the Sudan and Ghana in the 1950s, France in West and Equatorial Africa at the end of that decade, Britain, France, Belgium, and Italy in the great transfer of 1960, and then Britain and Portugal's settler areas of eastern and southern Africa throughout the succeeding decades, they left behind great geographical accidents and anomalies. The three-hundred-mile-long sliver that is Malawi makes no more sense historically than the outline of today's Togo or the larger and more rational-appearing shape of Zimbabwe. All, even obscure Djibouti or Equatorial Guinea, Spain's remnant, are products of the nineteenth century, when the nations of Europe occupied the shores and then the interior of black Africa.

Sea captains and slavers led the way, but it took an era of exploration from the

PRÉCIS

Partly because of its colonial legacy, black Africa continues to struggle with the problem of nation building. Each country is composed of a mlange of languages and cultures, often artificially bound together. This results from a period during the nineteenth century in which European imperialists carved up the continent, leaving behind major political anomalies.

The conquering Western powers, however, were not concerned with the problems that this would leave in their wake after they departed. Partially as a result, postindependence Africa has a dismal record of massive economic and political failures. In the period from 1965 to 1970, there were fifty coups, and many more later. Dictatorship has followed dictatorship, some benevolent, some not. A few have been infamous. Idi Amin in Uganda and Jean-Bedel Bokassa in the Central African Republic were exceptionally brutal. Except in Botswana and a few of the Anglophone states in eastern and southern Africa, most African rulers have been corrupt and often ruthless.

But there are also potential signs of hope here and there. Tribalism and strife are not inevitable. In South Africa there is potential for nation building because the African National Congress wants control of South Africa as a unitary whole and a powerful nation-state. Moreover, there are many black professionals in South Africa who disdain ethnic exclusiveness. Hopefully, they will recognize that everyone must have equal access to power and prosperity. Only then can viable nationhood be achieved.

late eighteenth century through three-quarters of the nineteenth century for the continent's opportunities and obstacles to become known. Then, to oversimplify vastly, imperialism and the scramble for black Africa followed. Most often, especially in Britain's case, the European conquest occurred more in order to keep others out than from naked greed. British finance ministers knew how horribly expensive conquest (and subsequent administration) could be. But their foreign ministers were nervous that French or German advances would adversely affect British hegemony worldwide. So preemptive competition prevailed, and the resulting carve up of black Africa followed the lines of easy access, momentary advantage, the feints of adversaries, accessible rivers, or the tracks of traders and explorers.

The Germans and French raced to see which one would control the Islamic strongholds of northern Nigeria, but the British Won. Britain and Germany competed for the interior west of Zanzibar and eventually divided it. Cecil Rhodes, the South African mining magnate, competed with Belgium's King Leopold for the copper riches of Katanga (Shaba), and Leopold—using the armed might of a battalion led by a Nova Scotian mercenary—killed a major chief and bested Rhodes. The Portuguese fought Rhodes for control of central Mozambique and, after British official intervention on behalf of the Portuguese, Rhodes' attack was repulsed. But the Germans took what is now Namibia despite British and South African fulminations. Eventually, by an accumulation of these individual actions, the borders of the

colonies and protectorates of black Africa became established, were certified by treaty, and formed the basis for twentieth-century nations.

There was a long colonial interlude, from the 1890s to the 1950s, 1960s, and up through 1980 in the case of Zimbabwe. But that period of consolidation and administration did little to change the arbitrary nature of the borders, and of what those borders enclosed. By the end of World War I, the occupiers had conquered and begun to tax even the last holdouts—ethnic groups hiding away in the hills or deserts of the new territories. Official languages had been established—English, French, Portuguese, Spanish, Italian, and German (and Swahili). But in only the French case, where the colonizers focused on and tried to educate a tiny elite, and in scattered portions of the older colonies, was assimilation a conscious policy.

BLACK POSTCOLONIAL AFRICA

Black Africa emerged from the colonial era much more Westernized and urbanized than it had been in the nineteenth century. The veneer of nonindigenous political culture was thin, but serious and significant, and many of the Africans who had been educated well by white missionaries and many of the leading, politically modern nationalists who had forced the pace of self-government and independence expected to follow the Western democratic models and use the Western political institutions that had been bequeathed to them.

Nationalist movements were ceded power as successors to the whites. There

were elections. And then—not everywhere but in most places—black Africa's inability to pay more than lip service to Western canons of multiparty democracy became apparent. Even the earliest and most promising experiments turned sour as presidents banned oppositions, defended single-party rule as peculiarly African, flirted with Marxism, and further rationalized state centralism and the disfranchisement of the masses as being a manifestation of something peculiarly African.

Dictatorship, often tempered and benevolent (but in the cases of Idi Amin of Uganda, Jean-Bedel Bokassa of the Central African Republic, and Macias Nguema of Equatorial Guinea, pathological) became common. There were fifty military coups, too, between 1965 and 1970, and many more since. The young securocrats in small countries (and in Nigeria, too) felt that they could do better than the usually corrupt politicians and that they deserved to share the spoils of rule. For, except for Botswana and a few of the Anglophone states in eastern and southern Africa, extracting riches from the populace became the prime underlying purpose of government in much (but never all) of black Africa by the 1970s. Like the Amins and lesser figures, the rulers preyed on their peoples and used the coffers of the states (and special concessions and licensing arrangements), to enrich themselves and their families. President Mobutu Sese Seko of Zaire, the archetypical predator, is reputed to control billions of dollars while his country somehow also owes foreign lenders $8 billion and the country itself remains starved of services and largely impoverished.

Parties have always functioned in Botswana, where there have regularly been elections and where the first leaders of the country imbued an ethos of tolerance and fair play. But Botswana is more homogeneous than most other colonial artifacts, having been created largely as a protectorate for people speaking Setswana and owing allegiance to a single paramount chief.

In neighboring Zambia, by contrast, there are seventy different ethnic groups and four major and at least two minor languages. President Kenneth David Kaunda, who ran Zambia almost single-handedly from 1964 to 1991, was born and brought up within the country and speaks Cibemba, one of its four key languages. But he is not a Zambian by family (his father was a Presbyterian evangelist from neighboring Malawi), and being an "outsider" contributed to his political strength. He managed to rise above language and tribe and to be the "father" of all Zambians. But he decreed a one-party state in 1972 in order to prevent the opposition from being "divisive" and precipitating ethnic rivalries. Within his authoritarian but comparatively gentle state, President Kaunda carefully balances appointments (making sure that all groups were represented) to the ruling party's central committee, to the cabinet, and to the military and the civil service. Except for occasional ethnic or linguistic violence, his leadership kept the lid on potential ethnic explosiveness, but did little to advance the economy.

Nigeria, Sierra Leone, Uganda, the Sudan, Ethiopia, and Benin are much more volatile. In those countries and elsewhere, the years of independence have seen episodes of extreme ethnic antagonism and religious enmity as well. Nigeria is vast, incorporating as it does about a quarter (110 million) of the population of black Africa and three hundred of black Africa's seven hundred identifiably separate ethnic and language groups. So it is no wonder that violence between sections of the country has been common during the postcolonial period, and that intranational battles escalated into the Biafran war. The Ibo, the most entrepreneurial of the larger peoples of Nigeria, believed themselves denied their rightful share of the wealth of the country and precipitated an unsuccessful but bloody secession conflict (1967–1970).

SOMALIA AND ETHIOPIA

Northern Somalis last year successfully battled southern Somalis for autonomy in or separation from a country brought together only in 1960, when the Italians and British withdrew. Coastal Eritreans sought their freedom from up-country and larger Ethiopia since 1961, and finally obtained it in 1991. The Christian and animist southern Sudanese are locked in a bitter battle with Islamic northern Sudanese, and in Uganda there were echoes of the northern-southern war that engulfed Amin's country in the 1970s and 1980s.

What is and was common to these internecine rivalries is the abuse of entitlement. During the colonial period such abuses were either ignored or subsumed in the indigenous struggle for freedom. Also, the colonial rulers were rarely corrupt and only in a few areas discriminated blatantly against whole ethnic congeries. They were outsiders, too, and could therefore attempt to brush aside or deal evenhandedly with ethnic envy. After independence, however, there was much more to be gained and lost from the spoils of victory. Those spoils were nowhere (except in Botswana) divided equally. Whether verifiably or not, minorities (or in some cases, majorities) felt excluded from civil service jobs or other employment possibilities by their new governments. Merit and equity were denied. Favoritism became endemic (at least in the minds of the aggrieved). Africans understood family loyalties, old-boy networks, and the role of personal enrichment from public office, but they eventually objected to their excesses and the lack of a sense of proportion. Coups often followed, but almost invariably the process of unholy favoritism was resumed.

Dictatorship, often tempered and benevolent (but in the cases of Idi Amin of Uganda, Jean-Bedel Bokasa of the Central African Republic, and Macias Nguema of Equatorial Guinea, pathological), became common.

All Somalis speak the same language but are driven into clans that have long vied for power. When the colonial powers went home, local politicians at first took their place and competed with one another across a national spectrum. But after Siad Barre led a coup in 1969 and asserted his individual authority, Somalia's opportunities favored Siad's family and his clansmen. Northerners, believing themselves better educated (and in English), resented southern hegemony and southern privilege as well as Siad's arbitrary and corrupt rule. From 1988 they used violent means to express their discontent. Now, within southern Somalia clans vie bitterly for control of Mogadishu, the capital, and what is left of the country.

In Ethiopia, Eritreans had been educated and colonized by the Italians, whereas the highlanders loyal to the indigenous monarchy had repulsed imperialist invasions. When the United Nations "returned" the former Italian area to Emperor Halle Selassie in 1950, Eritreans demanded autonomy within the empire. Largely Muslim and Westernized, the Eritreans feared being dominated by backward Christians loyal to the feudal Monophysite Coptic Church. When Selassie was overthrown by Marxist soldiers in 1974, it seemed that the long civil war might have ended. But the ethnic and cultural divide remained too strong, and Mengistu's tactics of terror reassured few of the dissidents. Indeed, as the regime led by Mengistu became more and more intolerant of dissent and more brutal internally, so it began to forfeit any possibility of reconciliation in Eritrea. Tigre, a northern province of Ethiopia bordering on Eritrea, also turned to revolt in 1975. Putting the empire back together is probably impossible, since after decades of war there are so many competing self-interests, personal and ethnic. Moreover, the peoples of the periphery resent and feel disfranchised by the perpetuation in military hands of the long dominance of the Ethiopian imperial center. Once again, there is no sense of a collective nationality.

SUDAN

The haphazard results of imperially determined geography can be seen with particular clarity in the Sudan. The northern third of the country for many centuries has been controlled by Muslims. The southern two-thirds, especially in and around the great rivers, has been the domain of several large groups of blacks—Dinka, Nuer, and Azande—who still

■ **Digging a well in a dry riverbed in Ethiopia.**

ARILD VOLLAN / COURTESY OF THE UNITED NATIONS

the harsher aspects of Islamic law not only on the Arab north, but also on the south. The civil war followed.

Sudan's General Gaafer al-Nimeiry attempted to impose the harsher aspects of Islamic law not only on the Arab north, but also on the south. The civil war followed.

Even after Nimeiry was overthrown in 1985, the war in the south continued unabated. Now that the Sudan is ruled by an alliance between an army junta led by Lt. Gen. Omar Hassan Ahmed al-Bashir and fundamentalist Muslims aided by Iran, the divide between Non-Muslim and Muslim has grown sharper and more bitter. Bashir and his government, furthermore, rule harshly, give no quarter to opponents in the north, much less to rebels in the south, and seem determined to continue the Sudan's precipitous slide beyond bankruptcy into penury. Famine stalks the west and the south, too, despite the efforts of worldwide human assistance organizations.

The Sudan is 2,000 miles long and about 1,200 miles wide. Its 967,500 square miles make it Africa's largest country. Given its limited communications, its lack of all-weather roads, and a long history of animosity between north and south, it is no wonder that differences developed into war. But tumult was almost always likely since the geographical construct called the Sudan had never been consolidated into even the early beginnings of a nation. Only the use of English as one common tongue (but Arabic was dominant) brought south and north together. Otherwise there was no glue, especially when the services provided by the government became less and less with the spread of economic despair under Nimeiry. From the southern point of view, there was no nation to which its people could belong. Yet Col. John Garang's secessionist Sudan People's Liberation Army is suing for autonomy—it wants to be left alone to arrange its own political and economic

worship in traditional ways or have become Christians under missionary inspiration. In pre-colonial times, Arabs from Egypt and what is now northern Sudan raided the black peoples of what is now southern Sudan for slaves, thousands of whom were shipped across the Red Sea to Arabia in the century before Britain helped end the nefarious trade midway through the nineteenth century. North and south were linked by the White Nile and its tributaries, and by the slave trade and its cessation. Yet the Sudan began as an Anglo-Egyptian condominium, in large part as an administrative device meant to help secure the flow of the Nile northward (essential for agriculture in the Egyptian delta) and thus Britain's hegemony over the Suez Canal and the shortest route to India.

After the reconquest of the Sudan by Britain in 1898, a fine Anglo-Arab civil service was created and the vast territory

was ruled benevolently by dedicated British governors and their Sudanese staffs. The Sudanese bureaucrats were predominantly Arab, since the peoples of the south were undereducated and inexperienced in the ways of the West. In 1954, Britain eventually transferred power, with very little fuss, to nationalists who were Arab. From then on, through elected and military regimes, the north both dominated and economically neglected the south. As the Sudan gradually became more and more bankrupt, thanks to the improvidence of its military rulers and the massive shift in terms of trade against the Sudan after the Arab oil embargo of 1973 (and the fall in the world price of cotton), there was less and less for the south. Yet prospectors found signs of oil in the south, which a rising crop of Western-educated southerners sought to keep for themselves. Then General Gaafer al-Nimeiry attempted to impose

GLOBAL STUDIES: AFRICA

affairs—without pressing the more difficult case for independence. In a sense, Garang wants what the south experienced during the decades of British rule: different rules and a destiny of its own.

The case of the Sudan does not imply that all the colonially derived geographical expressions are absurd. That case can be made, for borders still divide peoples of the same language and culture and tie strangers together under a "national" government everywhere except Swaziland, Lesotho, Botswana, and (theoretically but not actually) Somalia. Yet what is apparent, and more and more so each year, is that black Africans in plural societies have found it harder and harder to share fairly—to give equal or reasonable stakes in their countries to all of the peoples within their derived borders. Some have done much better than others and avoided fratricidal strife, like Tanzania and Malawi, but the Liberian and Ugandan cases demonstrate that only the wisest and fairest government, with a broad sharing of perquisites, employment opportunities, military preferment, and other potential riches, can persuade peoples divided by language and sometimes by color, culture, and religion that they are just as privileged as those whom they envy. Alternatively, all the peoples of a country could feel that they participate equally in the national political process, but only in Botswana is that sense of full participation at all widespread.

UGANDA

In Uganda, the British favored the peoples of the five Bantu-speaking kingdoms of the south and west and located the protectorate's capital and main trading center within Buganda. Comparatively, they showered less attention on the non-Bantu-speaking, non-Christian north, but they recruited soldiers there and missionaries educated young people. A. Milton Obote, a northerner, led Uganda's nationalist movement to independence in 1962 and gradually became more authoritarian and more antagonistic to the Bantu-speaking southerners and their opposition party. What had been a small, model colony with a good educational system and a robust agricultural economy suddenly became a land where ethnic ties became more important than Western kinds of achievement. Obote was corrupt, too, and with him and Amin, his general who took over in 1971 and proceeded to brutalize Uganda, the long nightmare of civil convulsion began.

Amin was from the far north, had little education, and had no sense of or belief in

Uganda as a nation. Only today, after Tanzania's invasion of Uganda and the crushing of Amin, a brief period of further decay under Obote, and a perpetuation of the south-north civil conflict, has Uganda emerged on the edge of peace under Yoweri Museveni. But the ethnic tensions are not and will not for many years be reduced. The years of attrition and destruction have left an indelible mark. Only long periods of peace and a gradual redevelopment of something called Ugandan nationalism can recreate the Ugandan nation that almost was in 1962. Moreover, the question still remains very open: Given the failure of seventy years of colonial rule to create a true, enduring nation, can Uganda ever become what it was intended to be? Uganda is an amalgam of Bantu and Nilotic speakers, plus others. Agriculturalists live next to pastoralists. Nationally, there are many cultures, possibly a dozen, and Islam and varieties of Christianity vie with traditional worship. Some of its peoples live by cattle raiding, others by watching banana trees grow. And the reborn state is pitifully poor as a result of war. Only extraordinary economic management and strong, fair leadership over many years can begin the process of creating the new Uganda.

Building nations in black Africa depends on prosperity, otherwise the capital has no goods to distribute to the provinces or to the various ethnic groups who are not in power or who might otherwise wonder to what entity they belonged. Prosperity can build roads, telephone networks, clinics, and schools, and it can pay teachers to glorify the nation in outlying communities. But this difficult and problematic process is made almost impossible (or meaningless) in less developed countries like the Central African Republic or Mali, where there is almost nothing to share and the government in the capital largely leaves the periphery alone. Much of the countryside is neglected and not so much ill-governed as not governed at all. Such absence of attention stirs no dissatisfaction, provided that no part of the periphery is favored by the president's men, but it also inculcates no nationalism. The state is a void, and rulers in the most underdeveloped territories preside over no more than rudimentary geographical expressions.

NAMIBIA

Now that it will soon celebrate its second year of independence, can Namibia also achieve nationhood? Given its unusual geographical, ethnic, and historical mix,

as well as the attitudes of the new government of President Sam Nujoma, the auguries are far better than in many African countries. Namibia's peoples have lived within the same borders for more than a hundred years and were subject to the same South African administrative influence from 1915 to 1990. Before 1915, Namibia was a German colony. English, German, and Afrikaans are understood everywhere, and so are the languages of the Ovambo and Herero. All indigenous Namibians share the common adversity of having fought for freedom first against the Germans and then against the South Africans (from 1966 to 1990). Most Namibians also share a common ecological experience, for much of the desertlike land of the country is harsh and intractable.

Most important, Namibia's leadership has understood that favoring one ethnic group over another unnecessarily would prove a recipe for internal conflict. The seven branches of the Ovambo comprise about 800,000 of the country's 1.4 million inhabitants. The new government of President Nujoma is led by Ovambo, but certainly not exclusively. Some—but not all—of the other ethnic entities of the country are represented in the corridors of power. The Herero (about 90,000 people) have significant influence through individuals, as do the Damara (100,000), whites (75,000), Coloureds (50,000), and Nama (49,000). The Kavango (110,000), Caprivians (47,000), San (35,000), Basters (29,000), and Tswana (9,000) may perceive that they have less influence, but such issues have not yet bedeviled the new government.

So far President Nujoma and his cabinet officials have not rushed pell-mell to redress the past in ways which have discomforted minority groups. The Ovambo leadership has not privileged Ovambo. Wise leadership has prevailed, as it did in neighboring Botswana where Sir Seretse Kgama, the first president, incorporated the admittedly less powerfull and numerically fewer minorities of his country into the body politic, the civil service, and the ruling party. If Namibia develops enough wealth to treat its citizens well, or at least continues to find ways to make all its peoples feel a part of the new nation, then the creation of more than another postcolonial geographical expression has a fighting chance of success.

SOUTH AFRICA

When South Africa achieves majority rule, the exacerbation of ethnic differences is always possible, but the equal or greater tendency will be for South Africa to build upon its past and develop a nation more enduring than many others in black Africa. Given white South Africa's attention to ethnicity, separation, and division, this might seem a paradoxical expectation. Knowledge of the recent history of bantustans or homelands, and the prominence of M. Gatsha Buthelezi's ethnic experiment in KwaZulu (and now his regional importance in Natal) might lead skeptics to expect only bitter battles between language and ethnic groups after the accomplishment of majority rule. Buthelezi has mobilized seven million Zulu, South Africa's largest ethnic category, behind his Inkatha movement and watched as Zulu battled non-Zulu throughout Natal and the Transvaal for several years. Moreover, even if the mobilization of Zulu has been carried to a successful extreme, there are other examples of the state's arousal of repressed ethnic consciousness: Venda, Ndebele, Shangaan, Pedi (northern Sotho), and southern Sotho are more aware of their minority status within the black majority and keenly conscious of the ambitions of Zulu politicians. So are Xhosa, the country's second-largest linguistic group and the main antagonists of Zulu in the Transvaal and elsewhere. Within the single-sex compounds that house the majority of South Africa's gold mines, there are still clashes between largely uneducated and unskilled Zulu workers and non-Zulu. The power of the tribe—of language, culture, and imagined or real disputes—can certainly be aroused in South Africa as it has been brought to the surface in so many other parts of Africa since the end of colonial rule. When the rewards of victory are limited, competition will take ethnic forms if those are the perceived avenues of power and wealth.

Fortunately for South Africa and for black Africa, the disease of tribalism and ethnic irredentism is not inevitable. In an era when almost weekly another new nationality seeks release from the clutches of what was the Soviet Union, far-from-homogenous entities like South Africa might appear to have no chance. Nevertheless, the African National Congress (ANC) and the other leading movements

of indigenous nationalism seek control of South Africa as a rich, powerful nation, not a collection of bantustans. The pressure of past struggles places a high premium on the integrity of the state. Unlike SWAPO in Namibia, too, the ANC is not identified primarily with a single ethnic entity.

But the most formative difference between a majority-ruled South Africa and many of its northern neighbors is its depth of education and urbanization. South Africa's mixed and segregated universities graduate hundreds of Africans each year. Many black professionals are third and fourth generation. More than half of the country's black population is urbanized, and has known cross-tribal marriages for a century. In the cities, children are educated together, irrespective of ethnic origin. In corporate and bureaucratic life, urban Africans work alongside each other without more than passing regard for ethnic background. English and Afrikaans are the mediums of most discourse, even within professional black families. Police forces are mixed. Only on the mines and in the homelands is there ethnic and linguistic segregation.

Fortunately for South Africa and for black Africa, the disease of tribalism and ethnic irredentism is not inevitable.

True, politicians have used and will continue to employ ethnic slogans. They will seek advantage, as they have so often in black Africa, by appealing to the worst instincts of their linguistic compatriots. In Bantu languages, where proverbs are so much a mark of in-group sophistication, they will employ the telling parable that

encourages kith to combine only with kin. Xenophobia, no more primeval or primordial in Africa than anywhere else, will be encouraged for the worst reasons. Nevertheless, with the spread of urbanization and with the rise in all of black Africa of mixed marriages, cross-ethnic education, and a middle-class mentality that disdains (or at least sees through) crude appeals to ethnic exclusiveness, there is hope for Africa and for the building for new nations.

The citizens of the cities—thirty years ago, black Africa boasted three cities of 500,000 or more; now there are twenty-eight—are able at last to think of themselves as Kenyans, not Kikuyu; as Zairese, not Luba; as Sierra Leoneans, not Mende; as Central Africans, not Banda. Doing so is hardly universal, and only possible for the young or the well-educated. But purely tribal institutions and tribal chiefs are dying commodities in the more modern states. Prosperity or aspirations for wealth breed contempt for what some regard as "primitive" culture and backward ideologies.

The fastest accomplishments of successful nation building have come in those parts of Africa where strong and wise leaders have refused to employ the easy political ploys of ethnic division. As black Africa abandons the false gods of Afrosocialism, the single party state, and military rule, and turns under the pressure of the modern middle class to broader forms of political participation, so will nations finally have a fuller chance to emerge from the dissonance of ethnicity. Africans can overcome their various internal linguistic divisions, their differences of culture and sometimes of color, and their divergent histories of preference and discrimination if, and only if, corporate and governmental power is shared generously, and exclusivity is regarded as disagreeable. Accepting the fact that all groups should have access to power and privilege through the political process is basic to the major shift that is both required and, because of an awareness of the dissatisfaction with the economic and political results of the last three decades of independence, on the way.

Article 4   *Time*, September 7, 1992

Africa: The Scramble for Existence

Lance Morrow

The Great Rift Valley can be seen from space. It shears down the eastern shoulder of Africa, a vast geological gash, one of the mysteries of the continent's power. Human life began in the Rift, as if it were gleaming up through a crack in the world.

Africa has a genius for extremes, for the beginning and the end. It seems simultaneously connected to some memory of Eden and to some foretaste of apocalypse. Nowhere is day more vivid or night darker. Nowhere are forests more luxuriant. Nowhere is there a continent more miserable.

Africa—sub-Saharan Africa, at least—has begun to look like an immense illustration of chaos theory, although some hope is forming on the margins. Much of the continent has turned into a battleground of contending dooms: AIDS and overpopulation, poverty, starvation, illiteracy, corruption, social breakdown, vanishing resources, overcrowded cities, drought, war and the homelessness of war's refugees. Africa has become the basket case of the planet, the "Third World of the Third World," a vast continent in free fall.

In the face of political instability and disintegrating roads, airports and telephone networks, and other disincentives, investors from Europe, America and Japan are withdrawing from sub-Saharan Africa and looking elsewhere; Africans too are pulling out their money. Why risk expropriation or failure in a continent with a weakness for one-party kleptocracy, where drainage by corruption often equals or exceeds the legitimate intake?

Cynics in Kenya refer to President Daniel arap Moi's mining interests as "That's mine! That's mine! And that's mine! . . ." Expatriate businessmen estimate that wealthy Nigerians have enough money in personal deposits abroad to pay off the country's entire foreign debt, more than $36 billion. Zaïre's President Mobutu Sese Seko has a personal fortune that has been estimated from $4 billion to $6 billion, not far below the level of the country's external debt. He has isolated himself from his people—and from gathering political unrest—aboard a luxury yacht that cruises the Zaïre River.

If it is to recover, Africa in the coming years will need all its mystical powers of resilience. AIDS is devastating the continent's population. It has hit as hard among the cosmopolitan, educated élite as among the villagers, a fact that threatens continuing development. If the rate of infection continues to increase, the effect could be like that of World War I upon the youth of Britain, France and Germany. Yet in the strange arithmetic of apocalypse, AIDS will not serve as an ultimate check on overpopulation. According to World Bank projections, sub-Saharan Africa's population will rise from 548 million today to 2.9 billion by the year 2050. The huge increase in mouths to be fed threatens to swamp any foreseeable economic growth and force living standards ever downward.

There are 160 countries on the United Nations' annual development index, a measure of comparative economic and political progress: 32 of the lowest 40 are in Africa. Between 1960 and 1989, Africa's share of the world's gross national product dropped from 1.9% to 1.2%. Since 1980, sub-Saharan Africa's external debt has tripled to about $174 billion.

For decades, Africa could count on the cold war as an economic resource. The U.S. and the former Soviet Union

---

HURTING

Sub-Saharan Africa's economic growth rate, 1.5%, is the world's lowest. The region's 530 million people have a combined GNP of less than $150 billion, roughly the same as Belgium and its 10 million people.

Food production is 20% lower than it was in 1970, when the population was half the size it is now.

Only 37% of sub-Saharan Africans have clean drinking water. There is one doctor for every 24,500 people.

Population is growing at a rate of 3.2% annually, vs. 2.1% for Latin America and 1.8% for Asia.

Average life expectancy is 51 years—12 fewer than for Indians or Chinese.

Half the world's refugees are African, most of them fleeing drought or civil war or both.

---

muscled each other through African proxies, pouring in money to prop up pro-Western or pro-Communist surrogates. Now the big powers' priorities have gone elsewhere. Russia's most prominent expert on African economies, Sergei Shatalov, devotes his attention to his own country's debt problems. Europe's available investment capital is being diverted to Eastern Europe and the former Soviet states.

Americans are thinking more about their own problems as well. Says Herman Cohen, the Assistant Secretary of State for African Affairs: "What the Africans really have to worry about is not competition for our resources from the former Soviet Union but from Los Angeles and the Third World that lives in the U.S."

Business investors make hard calculations. Companies building plants to take advantage of cheap labor, an African plus, look for other assets as well: a reliable infrastructure, basic security and some hope for good returns. Capital and operating costs in African countries are 50% to 100% higher than in South Asia, where the return on investment is nine times as great; 25 years ago, the regions were even.

The external world's interest in Africa threatens to become merely charitable—a matter of humanitarianism, a moral test for the West. Should the wealthy nations allow Africa to drift further and further into the margins? Says Larry Diamond, a senior fellow at the Hoover Institution: "I don't think we could live with ourselves, or would want to, if we sat by while millions of people of a different color are condemned to misery and death."

But even doom has nuances, and like Africa it has a thousand layers of meaning. The "margin" of one thing is also the center of something else. Africa has its own "centers," its resources of vitality and resilience. It operates by its own inner dynamics and metaphysics. Africa looks hopeless, but it is not. In many ways the continent is headed in the right direction for the first time in centuries. Real changes for the better are occurring. Africa is evolving African solutions.

The continent's inner rhythms of development were shattered 400 years ago by the intrusion of Europeans, who brought in alien controls, boundaries and forms of government. But for the first time since 1444, when the Portuguese sailed into the "land of the blacks" to establish slaving forts, Africa is mostly free from outside interference. Despots are falling; here and there, democracy precariously takes hold. Improvised alternative economies flourish.

The continent remains connected to its powerful and—to outsiders—mysterious genius. Africa is different, still an inchoate self. There is a Europe, with its shared history, shared culture, shared economies—all accomplished the hard way, over many centuries. There is not—yet—an Africa of defined, stable boundaries and economies, not yet a sense of shared destiny.

Jung once wrote, "Different people inhabit different centuries." Something in the African clock of development got smashed when Europe broke into the continent. And when the colonialists pulled out, they left the economic, political and cultural infrastructure reconfigured in such a way that the new countries served Europe better than they served one another. This result was not necessarily intentional but was profoundly damaging nonetheless. Robert Ruark touched on the cultural destruction in his novel Something of Value: "If you change a man's way of life, you had better have something of value with which to replace it."

Who knows what Africa would have become had it been left alone? In any case, Africa today is changeable and still shattering into new configurations. There is now a Burkina Faso, an Ivory Coast, a Kenya, a Nigeria, but the nation-state has been an imposition from the West, and a sometime thing. Once there was a Liberia (founded in the early 19th century by freed American slaves); now Liberia is splintered in feudal fashion. There are two Sudans, each at war with the other.

The nation-states were dictated more by a European cartography of power than by any internal dynamic of allegiances. What is often missing is a social contract between the governing and the governed. In fact, millions of Africans have found that their economic energy, their sanity and even their survival depend on how they succeed in outmaneuvering the state.

Zambia, called Northern Rhodesia in its colonial incarnation, has begun to work hard in forming a social contract with its people. The country's story is a synopsis of some of the things that have gone wrong—and something of an object lesson.

At the time of its independence from Britain in 1964, Zambia was the richest black country in Africa south of the Sahara. It had $1.1 billion in foreign reserves, plus the world's second largest copper-mining industry. It also had emeralds, other gemstones and immense fertile areas. It had the potential to become southern Africa's breadbasket, and President Kenneth Kaunda promised every Zambian a pint of milk and an egg a day by 1970.

Arriving in Lusaka today, a visitor might think Zambia is a country emerging from war. Stretches of road in the capital look as if they have been under mortar bombardment. Buildings are dilapidated, vehicles rattletrap. Thousands live in tin-shelter shantytowns. Unemployment and crime are running high. Zambia has become one of the poorest nations anywhere, with one of the world's highest per capita foreign debts—nearly $1,000 for each of its 8 million people; average annual income per person is less than $290. As in many African countries, a small layer of extremely wealthy people flourishes above the impoverished mass.

Kaunda ruled for 27 years, then gambled on elections last year and lost. When the Movement for Multiparty Democracy government took over last November, its members were stunned by the decay and confusion they found. Morale among civil servants was abysmal, corruption pandemic. The new Minister of Agriculture found his office building vandalized; employees had stolen not only the light bulbs but also the lighting fixtures.

What happened to Zambia? Complex things, most of them bad. Kaunda took some principled stands against Ian Smith's white-dominated Rhodesia, which later became Zimbabwe, and against South Africa, but these acts vastly increased the cost of transporting Zambia's copper. In 1968 Kaunda announced the nationalization of 20 foreign companies; in 1969 he began a takeover of the copper industry. Nationalization undermined the confidence of private companies and discouraged foreign investment.

Assistant Secretary of State Cohen argues that African independence leaders were often close to European left wingers, "who implemented in Africa the biggest socialist fantasies that they weren't able to implement in their own countries—mainly government ownership of everything and government engineering of the economy at every level." Here formed a destructive paradigm: the state came to own and manage 80% of the formal economy. Senior managers were appointed for political reasons, not for competence; the enterprises, incompetently run, lost money. Tribalism, provincialism and nepotism flourished and led to overemployment—along with resentment and low morale. Kaunda, like other African leaders, used the bloated public sector to keep politicians happy and to balance rival tribes.

Then the arrangement began to collapse. In the early '70s OPEC multiplied the price of oil severalfold, and world copper prices tumbled—a disaster for Zambia, since copper exports had never accounted for less than 90% of foreign exchange earnings. Foreign debt began to mount. In the end, copper production dropped from 700,000 tons at independence to less than 450,000 tons today, partly because of serious underinvestment; equipment is old and inefficient.

The Kaunda regime, for political reasons, neglected to diversify, especially to encourage agriculture. Today, with only 5% of its arable land cultivated, Zambia is still considered one of the world's few real farming frontiers. But to stay in power and appease the urban masses, Kaunda kept food prices low, thereby encouraging rural people to come to the towns while discouraging those who remained in the countryside from growing crops for sale. Result: Lusaka's population has increased tenfold to 1.2 million since independence.

In the Ivory Coast the surface is much different. For years it was one of Africa's success stories, an exception,

President Félix Houphouët-Boigny's French-veneered miracle.

Step off a plane at Abidjan's international airport into the liquid heat of an African morning, and the veneer still seems to be there. An advertisement framed in a distinctive aluminum-and-glass case beckons: BENSON & HEDGES. *decouvrez l'or.* The two hands languidly reaching for a cigarette in the ad are white.

It is a glimpse of a country caught between Europe and Africa, with a certain dead-end, alienated aping of French élites, something that does not work anymore—if it ever did. The Ivory Coast is still charming and agreeable, with an endearing—to foreigners—Frenchness. Almost everyone speaks French in Abidjan. Paris has Le Drugstore; so does Abidjan, along with a café named La Rotonde and the Charles de Gaulle Bridge.

But the Gallic lamina is thin. The Ivory Coast's population, 13 million, consists of 80 ethnic groups, each of which speaks a different dialect. The miracle country is growing somewhat threadbare. Throughout most of the 1970s, the Ivory Coast enjoyed annual economic-growth rates of 6% to 7%, the most vibrant in former French West Africa. The trend has reversed since coffee and cocoa prices collapsed in the 1980s. High oil prices mean a gallon of gasoline sells at $5. From 1986 to 1989, export earnings dropped from $3.2 billion to $2.5 billion, while costs continued to rise. Total debt, $12 billion, rose from 37% of gross domestic product in 1979 to 130% in 1991, effectively crowding out the private sector's ability to tap into domestic credit sources. "They mortgaged their soul to the West," says a diplomat. Now, with an integrated European market about to become reality, the attention of French businessmen is being distracted away from Africa. And a unified European Community may force Paris to adopt a Europe-first policy, denying the Ivory Coast its privileged position within France.

Billboards picturing Houphouët-Boigny, 86, are everywhere. They show *Le Vieux* in a charcoal-gray leisure suit surrounded by enthusiastic young Ivory Coasters, the camera angle chosen to make the tiny President look as tall as everyone else. Houphouët is regarded as a master politician. Says a Western diplomat: "When the Ivory Coast won a regional soccer game, everyone was convinced it was because Houphouët managed to buy off the other teams. They feel he is capable of anything."

But *Le Vieux,* many Ivory Coasters believe, is surrounded by corrupt advisers. Although his policies helped make the country richer than its neighbors, he also stripped his government of credible economic alternatives and virtually guaranteed that the politicians who come after him will not be able to sustain the prosperity.

One symbol of the Ivory Coast's profound cultural disjunction is a huge edifice that rises from flat green fields at Yamoussoukro, Houphouët's native village: the Basilica of

Our Lady of Peace, which cost some $175 million, a gesture of lifeless grandiosity. Amid the grazing goats and the lagoons, the basilica looks like an ill-shapen mushroom, massive from a distance and strangely sterile up close. Ismail Serageldin, director of the technical department at the World Bank, observed during a recent Cairo lecture dealing with culture shock that there were "certain symbols of a society dissociated from its own people." The most spectacular of all, said Serageldin, "may be the basilica in the Ivory Coast. In all the mosaics, the only black person is the portrait of the President." Yet a young local woman asks a Westerner, "Do you think a poor country like this shouldn't have the right to something that grand?"

Houphouët-Boigny is old. Forty-three percent of his country's population is age 15 or younger, and most are uneducated. Last year university students rioted, and an elite military assault team attacked their dormitories. The army sees the students as pampered rich kids. Class differences are rising. The future may belong to the educated young—or it could be dictated by the embittered, uneducated masses from which the army and the gendarmerie draw their recruits. As elsewhere in Africa, there are two deadly races: economic growth against population, and basic education against ignorance.

There was much optimism in Africa in the 1970s, in the first full decade or two after the granting of independence. Africa had its Golconda of commodities—cocoa, coffee, copper and palm oil—and their prices were high. Africans borrowed against those prices; the world happily lent. Unlike other countries now heavily indebted, African nations owe the bulk of their debt to First World governments, the International Monetary Fund and the World Bank rather than to commercial banks and other private creditors.

The cheerleading slogan for Africa, coined by Tanzania's Julius Nyerere shortly after his country won its independence, was "We Must Run While They Walk." It caught the mood of euphoria and ambition, the dash of social heroism. Now the sense of heroic hope is mostly gone. Vast stretches of Africa are in worse shape than when they became independent. People routinely live at subsistence levels. Says Denys Lawrie, a mining consultant who works in West Africa: "Africans have wasted 20 years." The world's attention has gone elsewhere, and African leaders know their rations of aid will be smaller.

What is the danger if the industrialized world withdraws all help? Senegalese President Abdou Diouf has warned that allowing Africa to fall apart could lead to a population surge toward Europe and the U.S. Perhaps. On the other hand, neglecting Africa carries no immediate, urgent threat to the rest of the world. Black Africa has no nuclear powers. Why pour in more money to be misspent or rerouted to private Swiss accounts?

Perhaps in reaction, a new sense of realism has become the vogue in Africa, and the slogan for the continent's chastened 90s might be "Learn to Walk Before You Try to Run." In 1989 the World Bank issued a landmark report titled *Sub-Saharan Africa: From Crisis to Sustainable Growth.* It warned that if Africa's slide into underdevelopment continued, some countries would soon find themselves in worse poverty than the most stricken Asian lands in 1900.

Today Africa is changeable and still shattering into new configurations

The assessment marked the end of the era of Mau-Mauing Westerners into a chic guilt. The World Bank, the IMF and the so-called donor countries made it clear they wanted to wean African countries from thinking of aid as a permanent fact of life. Part of the trend, especially in West Africa, has been to move African executives trained at the World Bank into key decision-making posts within national governments. The Ivory Coast's Prime Minister, Alassane Ouattara, for example, worked for the IMF for nearly two decades before taking a post at home.

The World Bank report looked at the African regression: modest development after independence in the '60s, stagnation in the '70s, decline in the '80s. Factors such as drought and the oil crisis obviously played a role. But the principal cause of the continent's wasting disease was seen as a fundamentally wrong approach to economics. Instead of developing and diversifying agriculture, most African countries tried, often ineptly or corruptly, to industrialize at a time when much of the world was already on its way into the postindustrial age. African industrial products never had a chance to compete in a high-tech world. Farmers who could not overcome unrealistic price controls, or simple neglect, moved into overcrowded cities. That meant enormous quantities of food had to be imported and paid for in hard currency.

Ingenious capital schemes were concocted to finance new projects. Socialized, centrally directed economies—dressed up in ideological pretensions and encouraged by guilt-ridden sympathizers in the First World—enabled Africa's traditional grafters to operate on an industrial scale.

The World Bank's Serageldin draws a fascinating graph. The vertical y line represents bonding—quite literally the ties that bind a society together. The horizontal x axis represents options and opportunities—freedom. Each society and each individual must make a trade-off, represented by an oblique line that angles up between the x and y coordinates. Someone who opts for traditional social bonds loses opportunities, but someone who chooses total freedom risks losing the social ties that give his life meaning. The U.S. and other developed countries rank high on options and opportunity, low on social bonds. Traditional societies like Africa's usually rated strong on bonding, are low on options and opportunities. "We have visions of reality that are different," says Serageldin. Therein lies the problem. "Bonding, imposed on a modern, institutional structure, becomes nepotism"—a universal African practice. The worst outcome, he says, is to have neither one nor the other: "If we trade bonds for options but do not succeed economically, we risk catastrophe"—precisely what has happened in the American big-city ghettos.

Despite 30 years of failure in Africa, many of the social ties still exist. How long they can endure is another question. "There is a mood of Afro-pessimism," says Serageldin. "It is sustained by press images of famine and slaughter that tend to swamp the positive achievements."

Much of the real energy of Africa, and its future, lies outside present government structures. Africans have been even quicker than Western donors to cut themselves off from corrupt government and nonfunctioning states. They simply ignore their governments because they have their own economy. Variously called the "informal sector" or the "parallel" economy, it is the real engine of life.

The U.N. International Labor Organization has estimated that the informal sector employs 59% of sub-Saharan Africa's urban labor force. If this sector is included, the size of Zaïre's economy increases threefold. In many respects Africa is ahead of the former Soviet Union and Eastern Europe when it comes to free markets and regional economic ties.

Salaries in Africa become living wages only by unofficial dealing—by baksheesh, bribing, finagling, operating off the books, bartering, finding a thousand intricate routes around the occlusions of law and bureaucracy. A telephone company repairman in Lagos earns $60 a month. Therefore, the only way one can get a phone repaired is to "offer him a little something" on the side; in one day the repairman can pocket his official pay. No tip, no repairs—which may be why most phones in Lagos do not work.

Kaunda, like other leaders, used the bloated public sector as an instrument of tribal balancing

The second economy is endlessly inventive. It embraces everything from street vendors selling cigarettes and candy in a Dar es Salaam market to the intricate border smuggling of Zambian gemstones. At least 10 million of 26 million Kenyans make a living from small-scale cashcrop farming, carpentry, metalworking, tailoring, illicit brewing and running private transport. Secondhand clothes are imported from Europe and America and sold by the roadside. Packing cases are fashioned into furniture. Oil drums are made into roofing sheets, frying pans, barbecues, stoves, knives and lamps. Cars that cannot be repaired are salvaged piecemeal and turned into donkey carts. Much of this unofficial labor is carried out in the open air and is called *jua kali*—"hot sun." As multinational companies are driven away by government policies and demands for kickbacks, as state enterprises fail and lay off workers, the *jua kali* economy is booming.

The official minimum monthly wage is 5,000 shillings ($17) in Tanzania, where a loaf of bread costs 190 shillings and a pair of trousers 4,000 shillings. "Nobody in Tanzania expects to survive on his salary," says Thomas Mrima, a truck driver who plies between Tanzania, Rwanda and Zaïre. "Everybody makes money with everything he can lay his hands on. They steal government stores and sell them over the border. They use government machinery for private building contracts." Ripping off the government has become a popular sport: it is thought of as stealing from thieves.

So Africa improvises its own unofficial social contract, one deal at a time. People are brilliant at adapting to the impossible conditions created by their governments. That is the difficulty: such adaptation has allowed ramshackle government practices to continue too long, postponing the catharsis the continent needs to purge itself of corruption and incompetence.

Frustration over Africa has led some outsiders to the conclusion that Africans are hopeless at organizing anything. The reverse is true: they are ingenious organizers and able businessmen. The problem is bad government.

The trouble has arisen in part because of the gap between national aspirations and the practical problems of putting together a working government. Says Cyrus Reed, head of the African Studies Center at the American University in Cairo: "These countries were extremely fragile, yet they set goals that even the most organized governments would have had trouble fulfilling." Nearly all African leaders realized the first challenge of government is keeping the loyalty of the people; the solution was patronage. As that became more expensive and resources dwindled, the leaders turned toward the World Bank and the IMF to bail them out. So the countries went deeper into debt and dependence.

Now they are beginning to find ways out. If the '80s were the lost decade, the '90s show signs of hope. In 1990 more African nations introduced multiparty politics than in all the previous 25 years. When the Berlin Wall fell in

1989, 38 of Africa's 47 states were ruled by one party or by military juntas; today about half those countries have held free elections or adopted democratic reforms. Many Africans are talking about a second revolution.

Mali, Liberia and Congo have announced legal moves to recover assets they say were stolen under previous one-party regimes. In the case of Mali, the Swiss Foreign Ministry has decided to reroute part of its country's aid to Mali to pay for Swiss lawyers—clever rerouting—to investigate whether Swiss aid money was wrongfully deposited in Swiss banks during the 23-year reign of deposed President Moussa Traore. Nigerian President Ibrahim Babangida has a bolder if unrealistic idea: he suggested last year that African states might demand reparations from the West for the damage done by the slave trade. The estimated cost: $130 trillion in loss of people and production potential over the centuries. The estimated chance of success: zero.

Europeans, as the historian Basil Davidson writes, destroyed the moral universe of the continent. Colonialism imposed a different cultural universe with its alien definitions of God and progress and the rule of law. Now postcolonial Africa is defined as being on "the margins" of that universe. But, says Babacar N'Diaye, the president of the African Development Bank, "even if marginalization is true, it is not my concern. What I have to do is to create my self-respect. To create my self-respect is to put my house in order. There is a tremendous venue for intra-African trade we have not developed. We can cut our military expenditures and develop health and education. I don't like the word marginalization because Africans are using it to make demands from the developed world to pay attention to Africa. I think we must pay attention to ourselves."

Ugandan President Yoweri Museveni, by contrast, embraces the word. "A little neglect would not be bad," he says. "The more orphaned we are, the better for Africa. We will have to rely on ourselves. We have to go back to the year 1500, where we left off building an economy integrated in itself, able to produce its own food, its own tools, its own weapons."

It seems a plausible, even indispensable vision: Africans reunited at last with themselves, with their cultures and governments, brought home after centuries of terrible alienation. But then Museveni goes on, "Today 50 out of 100 Ugandans can't read or write. If 90 out of 100 can read and write and start to be guided by science and rationality, that's the day of liberation."

It may be a long swoop from Africa's year 1500 to European-sounding formulas about "science and rationality." In 1961, with civil war erupting around him and his own assassination only days away, Patrice Lumumba, the newly independent Congo's first Prime Minister, wrote a letter to his wife in which he conjured a splendid vision: "History will one day have its say, but it will not be the history that is taught in Brussels, Paris, Washington or in the United Nations. . . . Africa will write her own history, and . . . it will be a glorious and dignified history."

Perhaps. For the moment, African glory lies around a historical bend of the river, in some unseeable future.

—Reported by William Dowell/Abidjan, J. F. O. McAllister/Washington and Marguerite Michaels/Nairobi

---

Article 5   *World Monitor*, February 1992

Africa's Turn

Since the Berlin Wall Fell in 1989, Eight African Nations Have Had Multiparty Elections.

Robert M. Press

Robert M. Press has been covering East, West, and Central Africa for The Christian Science Monitor and Monitor Radio since 1987. He lives in Nairobi, Kenya, with his wife, photographer Betty Press.

Dossouvi Logo remembers clearly the night in August 1990 when his secret efforts to help bring democracy to the tiny West African nation of Togo were discovered. His story, and Togo's, are part of what is happening across Africa today.

Many African dictators are on the run, for the first time since the heady days of African independence. Freedom is on the upswing. A wave of democracy is gathering momentum. Under the very noses of the dictators, antigovernment movements are gaining strength. Some times it's a risky game, as Logo recalls: "I was at home. It was about 7 p.m. Four people came in wearing civilian clothes and handcuffed me. They had no identity papers. They searched my home for seven hours. They turned everything upside down. They found nothing."

But they took Logo to a secret torture house in Lomé, the capital. "They beat me. They tied my hands behind me. Twenty policemen beat me with sticks and kicks."

Then police jailed him and 12 others suspected of working against the government. Logo was tortured for three days with electric shock. The police wanted him to name the people he had been working with clandestinely to print and deliver antigovernment literature.

"I said nothing," he told me, with a steely-eyed look of conviction.

He was held in a small cell, where he had to sleep on the cold cement floor. He and his cellmate did exercises to warm up. "We prayed a lot," Logo says.

On Sept. 21, 1990, he was taken to court. Police may have assumed that by then he was subdued—but instead he told the court he had been tortured. He was, nevertheless, found guilty. Then Togolese lawyer Djovi Gally, another in a small band of people struggling to bring freedom to Togo, made a clever move. He won a delay in sentencing. That gave activists enough time to organize a public protest—the first major one in Togo against the dictatorial regime of President Gnassingbé Eyadéma.

Several thousand people showed up, jamming the courthouse and the area around it. Security forces were surprised, but soon waded in, bashing heads. Now a taboo had been broken—people had demonstrated against the government. And they were not afraid to do so again, and did. More street protests, strikes, and confrontations with police—some of them deadly—followed. By early June 1991, Eyadéma had agreed to sign a document endorsing a national conference of opposition and government leaders to form a transitional government.

The conference, held last August, quickly claimed it had sovereign authority over the country—and over the Army. Later, on Nov. 26, the transitional parliament abolished the military-backed political party of Eyadéma, claiming it was blocking rallies by newly formed opposition parties—and the Army struck back.

On Dec. 3, 1991, the Army used heavy artillery and tanks to attack the official residence of the man the conference had named transitional prime minister, Joseph Kokou Koffigoh. At least 17 people were killed. Koffigoh survived and was taken by the Army to President Eyadéma, who ordered him to form a new transitional team with more representatives of the president's supporters.

Despite Eyadéma's dictates, reform is far from dead in Togo. The Togolese people are still determined to shake off a long dictatorship. And the United States has told Eyadéma that a military government in Togo cannot expect to have good relations with the US. Nor are many other Western nations likely to support continued dictatorship in Togo. So change is likely to come, though more gradually than the reformists wanted.

Democracy is not entirely new to Africa. Botswana, Senegal, and a handful of other African states have had competitive elections and varying degrees of democracy for a number of years. Namibia, which became independent in March 1990, is now generally considered a multiparty democracy. Several of the big African nations are also starting to upset one-party rule. Zambia emerged from 27 years of one-man domination in 1991, when the opposition assumed power in an open election. Angola, after 16 years of bloody civil war, is scheduled to hold elections between the two sides' leaders in the second half of this year. Nigeria, black Africa's most powerful state, is beginning to emerge from a tradition of military coups; it recently held "guided" elections and is headed for a similar presidential contest later this year. In Zaire and Kenya, opponents of long-time dictators are braving bully tactics in an effort to dislodge corrupt regimes.

Questions hover over all these courageous efforts: Will the publics who have struggled for these political reforms have the patience to endure the economic upheaval democratization inevitably brings? Will they give their new leaders time to overcome the damage done by past corruption? Whether their patience will hold is the next big question for Africa—one that I'll come back to below.

But for now Africans in many countries are showing unprecedented determination to gain the same basic freedoms people everywhere want. Among those: the right to speak their minds, the right to attend a meeting, and the right to live without fear of government attack. Most want multiparty democracies to replace one-party, often one-man, regimes—a phenomenon they know is sweeping South America and parts of Eastern Europe and East Asia.

Since the Berlin Wall fell in 1989, eight African nations have had multiparty elections—in most cases their first since independence—according to Freedom House, a democracy watchdog organization in New York.

Another 13 countries are undergoing democratic reforms, many of which will lead to multiparty elections, and 17 have started democratic transitions that are currently stalled, according to Freedom House. But some nations, including Malawi and Equatorial Guinea, so far are in the eddies, unmoved by the swelling stream of democracy in Africa. Others, such as Sudan, Somalia, and Liberia, have been embroiled in civil wars.

THE ROLE OF BRAVERY

Why is Africa moving toward democracy now, some three decades after independence? African and Western experts cite several factors: (1) In most countries, other systems had failed to bring freedom or economic well-being; (2) the end of the Cold War left dictators more exposed—less propped up by Western or East-bloc aid; (3) the examples of South Africa's liberalization, and to a lesser degree, the fall of communism in Eastern Europe, encouraged proponents of change—though the struggle predates these two events.

But two intangibles are also making a difference in the democratization movement. First, individual activists such as Logo (who was then working as a part-time tourist guide) are brave—braver than most of us could be expected to be. Second, invisible barriers of fear of government are falling. In Togo, they fell during the courthouse demonstrations.

The fear barrier broke in Kenya Nov. 16, 1991, according to many Kenyans. Activists campaigning for multiparty elections to replace Kenya's one-party, practically one-man rule, had scheduled a public rally that day in an open field near a downtown slum, the site of some of Kenya's pro-independence speeches during British colonial rule.

Kenyan President Daniel arap Moi had launched his usual bombastic warnings about "anarchists" trying to upset Kenya's stability, and, predictably, had banned the meeting.

Such warnings had led activists to cancel planned rallies in July 1990 and October '91.

But this time the activists didn't blink. Despite the nighttime arrest of some of the organizers 36 hours before the rally, several others escaped, going underground. From hiding, they issued calls to attend the rally, and several thousand Kenyans did just that—or at least tried. They filled the streets near the rally site. Hundreds of armed police and other security agents filled the site itself, and with guns and clubs began bashing the heads of anyone who came too near. Police then spread out into neighboring residential areas, ordering even small groups to disperse and clubbing them if they did not.

Yet something amazing happened on the streets that day. Despite their understandable fear of getting hit by police, people lost their usual fear of the government. Some ran, but some also walked back—to taunt police and shout peace and democracy slogans. The police, for their part, did not shoot into the crowds, as they had in July 1990.

Then on Nov. 18, 1991, the miracle of diminishing fear spread: Thousands more Kenyans cheered openly, defiantly, even in the rain, as the arrested rally organizers appeared at rural courthouses, where they had been sent by the government to get them out of the capital, Nairobi.

From that week on, many Kenyans stopped looking over their shoulders to spot the often-present police informant and began to openly criticize the Kenyan government. Even President Moi came under criticism in public conversations, though not in the still-controlled press.

Then on Nov. 26 another load fell on Moi's shoulders. At a meeting in Paris chaired by the World Bank, major Western donors agreed to withhold new aid to Kenya for six months, pending both economic and human rights reforms.

Six days later, Moi caved in to this domestic and international pressure, endorsing multiparty politics in Kenya. The opposition quickly split, then made up, and prepared to challenge the monopoly hold on power of Moi's party, the Kenya African National Union.

PEOPLE SPEAK THEIR MINDS

Fear finally broke, to a lesser degree in Ethiopia, during the final year or two of the brutal dictatorship of Mengistu Haile Mariam, who was chased into exile in May 1990 by approaching—and soon victorious—rebels. I recall an Ethiopian government journalist standing in an empty hallway in the capital, Addis Ababa, complaining about the regime. I was more worried than he that he might be overheard. But, in his own way, he was doing what others even in public group taxis began doing in the final year of Mengistu: expressing their disgust with the dictator, and their longing for freedom. When Mengistu fled (to Zimbabwe), people rushed to tear down the huge poster of him at Revolutionary Square, as well as a giant statue of Lenin.

Ethiopia's former rebels set up a government based on sharing power with the nation's many ethnic groups. That's more democracy than Ethiopia has ever seen. There have been some ethnic clashes in parts of the country as a result. But after 30 years of war (mostly over the question of secession of Eritrea), most Ethiopians were willing to try something new.

In Benin on the equatorial west coast, following months of strikes, and some confrontations with the police, dictator Mathieu Kérékou came out of a national conference in early 1990 nearly powerless. In tears, he told delegates at the conference that he was the victim of a "civilian coup d'état." The delegates named an interim prime minister: Nicéphore Soglo, a former World Bank official. Kérékou surprised many by running for president a year later. But the last

laugh was not his: Soglo won. Benin's national conference has turned out to be precedent-setting. Congo and Mali have each held one, and the convening of a national conference has also been demanded by opposition groups in Cameroon, Central African Republic, Guinea, and Ivory Coast.

Togo's national conference marked the public emergence of the nation's opposition. A year earlier I had gone to Togo and met, secretly, with a variety of opponents of the Togolese government. At some risk to themselves, in homes, cars, and back rooms of restaurants, they told me of government abuses of power, including torture, arbitrary arrests, and Eyadéma's facade of public support. Eyadéma liked to tell visitors he had been ready to step down from power several times but each time the "people took to the streets to say 'no.'" Togolese critics claim the pro-government demonstrations were staged.

Among the delegates and observers at the national conference were the same people I had met privately the year before—now openly attacking the government and laying plans for a new administration. Logo was there. So were some of the police who had tortured him. He even shook hands with them.

On the final day of the national conference, Eyadéma called out troops, cut off Togo's phone and telex lines to the rest of the world, and proclaimed an end to the transition effort. The delegates at the national conference ignored him, however. With troops nearby, the meeting went on to select human rights leader Koffigoh as interim prime minister.

The military's intervention since then may mean that the Togolese won't achieve their goal of replacing Eyadéma in multiparty elections in mid-1992. But in Togo, as in many other African countries, ordinary people are taking to the streets in protests to claim their democratic rights when these rights are threatened.

Though they may lose a battle now and then, and though a country may slip back into totalitarian control, the genie of hope for freedom is out of the bottle in Africa. And, as Nigerian diplomat Joe Garba says, "It will be very difficult to subdue black Africans again."

Africa's move toward democracy "can only be delayed—it can't be stopped," predicts Zambian Mark Chona, special assistant to former Zambian President Kenneth Kaunda from 1968 to 1980.

But Africa's remaining dictators have their bags of tricks. In Zaire, President Mobutu Sese Seko, whose supporters credit him with keeping the country from

splitting apart, is a master trickster. While agreeing in 1990 to multiparty politics in the face of growing unrest, he allowed so many parties to form that the political landscape became confusing. Scores of parties popped up, including some his critics say Mobutu helped finance. When opposition to him kept growing, he tried another trick: Co-opt your enemy by making him your ally. Mobutu named first one, then another opponent as prime minister. Zaireans were not fooled, however, and opposition continued.

In Kenya, Moi's tactic was to preach the danger of multiparty elections, claiming they would lead to multitribal conflicts. Many Kenyans reject the argument, but some, especially those in minority tribes, contend that larger tribes such as the Kikuyu will use multiparty politics to try to establish control at the expense of smaller tribes. Moi's supporters say smaller tribes have done better under Moi than during the rule of Kenya's only other president, the late Jomo Kenyatta, a Kikuyu.

Tribalism is a factor in all the equations in Africa's march toward greater political liberty. But it works both ways. Moi is Kalenjin, a cluster of minority tribes. Critics charge him with stacking government posts with Kalenjin.

In Madagascar, President Didier Ratsiraka withstood months of massive public demonstrations against him in the capital, Antananarivo. Hundreds of thousands of protesters tried to form a rival government, while Ratsiraka sought a formula to stay in power. But in Benin and Zambia, the dictators stepped down gracefully—leaving their successors to face enormous challenges. For example, Benin's President Soglo is finding civil servants want back pay. Journalists hound him about why he hasn't made much progress uncovering the corruption of the previous regime. Businessmen resent his slow customs procedures on imports. And the poor, like "taxi" driver Doe Marcos, wonder when democracy will translate into a better life.

"Democracy is better," he says. "Now you can talk, no matter where. You can criticize even the government. No one arrests you." But life is still tough, he adds. "I've been out of work since 1989. Meanwhile, I drive a motorcycle as a taxi. Some days I earn 2,100 [West African francs, or about $7], some days 2,400. It's very difficult. In the rain, the sun, I'm out here, almost all day, without rest. I start at 7 in the morning and finish at 10 p.m. I have two children."

Zambia's new democratically elected president, Frederick Chiluba, might have been thinking about Zambia's poor when he gave his inaugural speech Nov. 2, 1991. Taking over from Kenneth Kaunda, who had ruined the economy during his 27 years of rule, Chiluba said: "The Zambia we inherit today is destitute, ravaged by the excesses, ineptitude, and corruption by a party and a people who have been in power for too long."

He challenged Zambians to bear with him through hard times of economic recovery: "On this inaugural day, I say, let us not have false pride, let us work."

Work is something many Africans are willing—eager—to do; but many are jobless. Figures for unemployment (and the much larger problem of underemployment) are unreliable. But at best, only 10% to 15% of Africans entering the job market each year find wage employment, according to the United Nations.

ONE OF WORLD'S TOUGHEST JOB MARKETS

I know a man in Nairobi, Kenya, who looked for a job for three years before finding one. A hopeful, newly trained secretary in Nairobi has sent out more than 100 applications-without a single reply so far. And Kenya is a bit better than many countries in terms of jobs. But most African economies have been poorly run for decades. Periods of infatuation with government-run economies have slowed progress in many countries, though sometimes providing needed social services.

Reviving these economies may take years. Michael A. Priestley, a UN official, says restoring Ethiopia's war-wracked and environmentally damaged economy could take 30 to 40 years of sustained foreign aid—and peace.

It remains to be seen how often money-withholding pressures will be used on African leaders.

According to the World Bank, sub-Saharan Africa is the only region in the world where the number of poor people is increasing. The total of poor people, the bank reports, is likely to rise from an estimated 180 million in 1985 to 265 million by the year 2000—only eight years away. Continent-wide, Africa's population is

growing at an average of 3% a year—faster than any other region of the world and enough to almost double from an estimated 677 million in mid-1991 to nearly 1.2 billion by 2010, according to the Population Reference Bureau in Washington.

Such data pose a serious question for Africa: If economic progress is slow, will the freedoms accompanying democracy satisfy people enough to keep them from turning again to autocratic leaders?

Pauline Baker of the Aspen Institute in Washington has spent years studying Africa and has lived in Nigeria. "I think there's going to be a short honeymoon" for multiparty, democratic politics, she says, with "lots of turmoil in the next decade." Some democratic governments may be replaced by military ones as people insist on quick fixes to impoverished lives, Baker says, then democratic governments will take power yet again as disillusionment sets in.

Nigeria has gone both ways. The current military government pledged to concede power to elected civilian leaders in late 1992, under a two-party system designed by the military.

"A man comes in on a white horse and says, 'Let me save you,' " says I. William Zartman, director of Johns Hopkins University's African studies program. But when demands outstrip the ability of a leader to deliver results, he may simply deliver words, Zartman adds.

"We have no illusions; we know there are tough times ahead" for African democracies, says George Nzongola-Ntalaja, a Zairean and a professor of African studies at Howard University in Washington. Nzongola, past president of the African Studies Association in the US, adds: "We know simply having elections is not enough and that democracy does not automatically bring about development and a better life." But, he says, "democracy is a fundamental human right." And there's probably a better chance at economic progress with a democratic government because people will be free to be watchdogs on how government funds are spent, he argues.

"We've tasted colonialism: It didn't work." says Zambian Mark Chona. "We've tasted military regimes: They didn't work. We've tasted civilian dictatorships: They all simply haven't worked." At least with Zambia's new, democratically elected president, he says, "We'll have a new approach, a better vision than in the past. As long as that hope exists, people will cooperate."

Professor Nzongola admits it will take time for African democracies to blossom,

pointing out how long it took France, Britain, and the US to arrive at their versions of democracy.

For a Kenyan friend of mine, the sooner the process of democratization begins, the better. He insists there can never be democracy in a one-party state, and he dreams of the day when he can run for parliament and be a voice of constructive criticism in his country.

This friend is a university graduate, a thinker, an analyzer. But what about the Zairean farmer I met who calls Zairean dictator Mobutu "Papa" and says it's up to him (Mobutu) to do with the country what he wants? In that village, old men wait for the news and views of young men returning from the city, where the political battles are being fought. And in Nigeria, a village chief told reporters that people will "vote the way I tell them to vote." In November, Nigerian officials annulled a number of state governorship primary elections because of rigging.

But the presidential election in Zambia apparently was fair, according to former US President Jimmy Carter, one of the international observers. His presence at the election raises another question about the movement toward democracy in Africa: What role does the rest of the world have in encouraging the trend?

One answer is that money still talks. After more than a year of talk about using aid as leverage to get more democratic reforms, Western donors finally drew the line—across Kenya—when they declined new aid for six months until Kenya made more economic and political reforms.

Scott Spangler, assistant administrator for Africa of the US Agency for International Development, told me at that time, speaking of Africa as a whole: "We are definitely going to make how much aid, and whether aid continues, to be conditional on good governance—human rights, freedom of speech, free and fair elections, and an independent judiciary."

It remains to be seen how often money-withholding pressures, such as those against Kenyan President Moi, will be used on other African leaders who balk at democratization. But realities are clear: Africans must bid for aid alongside Eastern Europeans and everyone else. "The competition has increased for the pot of funds," says Spangler.

Some money is likely to continue flowing to reward Africa's new democratic leaders. But probably not much, compared to Africa's needs. The burden—and the future—of democracy in Africa is likely to remain mostly on the shoulders of Africans themselves.

What aid does come must not be used too bluntly or too quickly to force economic changes, argues Zambian analyst Chona. Sometimes the future of democracy in Africa depends on the price of bread, or cornmeal.

Chona says, for example, that if the donors press too hard and force a quick cutback on Zambia's costly subsidy for mealymeal—cornmeal—the new Zambian government could face popular riots that threaten the country's democracy.

Like an army, democracy's supporters travel on their stomachs. They are challenging dictators because they cannot live on bread alone. But they also will not hesitate to let new leaders know they cannot live without it. WM

Article 6

Current History, May 1992

Finding Peace through Democracy in Sahelian Africa

The Sahelian countries in West Africa have been plagued by ethnic turmoil and military governments. But the growing trend toward democracy in Africa seems to have begun to gain ground in this volatile and ecologically scarred region.

Richard L. Sklar and Mark Strege

Richard L. Sklar is a professor of political science at the University of California at Los Angeles and a former president of the African Studies Association. His latest book, coauthored with C. S. Whitaker, is African Politics and Problems in Development *(Boulder, Col.: Lynne Rienner, 1991). Mark Strege is currently completing his master's degree in African studies at the University of California at Los Angeles. He has previously served with the Peace Corps as an agricultural extension agent in Mali.*

Africa today is tormented by the scourge of war. At the beginning of 1991, 15 African wars took their daily toll of casualties.[1] These included civil wars in Ethiopia, Sudan, Chad, Liberia, Angola, Mozambique, and South Africa; clan and factional warfare in Somalia; an invasion of armed exiles into Rwanda; ethnic insurrections in northern Uganda; revolts by the Tuareg people in Mali and Niger; an insurrection by separatists in the Casamance region of Senegal; armed resistance to government-sanctioned violence against the non-Moorish, African minority in Mauritania; and the war in Western Sahara, where the Sahrawi are fighting for the region's independence from Morocco. All these conflicts were basically internal wars,

yet their crossboundary ramifications embittered relations between neighboring states. In the somber view of Jacques Delors, president of the Commission of the European Community, Africa was on the verge of becoming "a zone of fundamental instability."[2]

While recent, current, and impending warfare in Africa underscores Delors's dire forecast, some conflicts on the continent have been resolved, and the manner in which they were concluded offers pathways to end ongoing disputes. No fewer than eight major military conflicts have ended since the Burkina Faso–Mali war of December 1985. They include the intermittent war between Chad and Libya, which appears to have ended in 1987; the western Zimbabwe insurrection, at its peak during the early 1980s and finally resolved through political negotiations in 1987; South Africa's attempts to destabilize Angola between 1975 and 1989; the Namibian war of independence from South Africa, concluded in 1989; the African National Congress's armed struggle against South Africa, which was suspended by the ANC in 1991 as part of a process designed to result in a nonracial democracy; a 30-year civil war in Ethiopia, which concluded with the fall of Addis Ababa in 1991 and led to negotiations for the resolution of sundry disputes; a 16-year civil war in Angola, ended in 1991 as a result of negotiations sponsored by the United

States and the Soviet Union as well as Portugal; the Liberian civil war of 1989–1991, which resulted in military intervention by the Economic Community of West African States (ECOWAS) and subsequent, albeit as yet inconclusive, political negotiations.

During 1991, several smoldering wars in the Sahelian region of West Africa appear to have been mitigated by conciliatory attitudes arising from a regional—and continental—movement for political democracy. In Mali and Niger, increased political freedom, representative national conferences, and transitional governments with democratic objectives have reduced the intensity of domestic conflicts. In Mauritania, political reforms, including multiparty elections in January 1992, may help reduce crossborder violence in the Senegal River Valley. However, in Chad, ethnic and factional violence continues to complicate a proclaimed transition to democracy.

The simultaneous mitigation of these low-intensity conflicts provides an opportunity to assess comparatively the relationship between democratization and international conflict resolution in a single region. It has often been remarked that, in modern times, democracies have hardly ever waged wars against one another. Yet this obvious relationship between democracy and peace appears to have been discounted and largely overlooked by students of African international relations.

A causal relationship between democracy and peace in Africa was nearly acknowledged in the report of a 1990 Conference on Security, Stability, Development and Cooperation in Africa, organized by the African Leadership Forum in collaboration with the secretariats of the Organization of African Unity (OAU) and the United Nations Economic Commission for Africa. While the conferees specified the existence of a "link between development and democracy," they did not identify a similar link between democracy and peace.[3] The discussion that follows examines the presumptive relationship between democratization and the collective security of the states in Sahelian Africa.

The Tuareg Insurrection in Mali and Niger

The Tuareg, a Berber people who number between 1 million and 1.5 million, inhabit the northern regions of Mali and Niger. Their main urban settlement in Mali is in the city of Timbuktu, which was founded by Tuaregs in the twelfth century; in Niger their historic capital is Agadez. French colonial rule terminated an era of predation by the "blue men," so named for the Tuaregs' flowing indigo robes. By the time of Niger's and Mali's independence in 1960, the Tuareg were a relatively small minority of less than 10 percent in countries governed by those who had once been their victims. The sins of their forebears were

visited on present-day Tuaregs in 1964, when a Tuareg rebellion was brutally subdued by the Malian armed forces.

During the 1980s, periodic episodes of drought and famine led to an exodus of Tuaregs from Mali to Algeria, Libya, and other neighboring countries. Many of those who have since voluntarily returned or have been expelled as illegal immigrants live miserably in refugee camps in both Niger and Mali. Protests against alleged maltreatment in those camps set the stage for armed attacks against government installations in both countries during 1990. One group of Tuareg dissidents plotted to overthrow the one-party regime of General Moussa Traoré; others have been secessionist. The counterinsurgency methods of the Malian army have been condemned for their brutality by Amnesty International and France's Socialist party. In turn, Traoré's regime alleges that the rebels are Libyan proxies and that many of them belong to the Libyan Islamic Legion. To be sure, many able-bodied Sahelian émigrés have soldiered for Libya, as they have for Iraq and the Afghan resistance. And the flames of Tuareg separatism are fanned by a belief that the French promised to create an independent Tuareg state in return for Tuareg participation in the French force fighting in colonial Indochina.

In 1990, a United Nations Development Program report found that Niger and Mali were the two most deprived countries in the world. The report based this assessment on a new "human development index," which reflects "life expectancy, literacy and command over the resources to enjoy a decent standard of living." Neither country has experienced effective economic management; at the same time, the two have faced recurrent drought and relentless ecological deterioration.[4] In March 1991, after 23 years in power, the unpopular Traoré regime was toppled by the Malian army. Lieutenant Colonel Amadou Toumani Touré, advised by representative civilians, began a political reform process designed to result in the establishment of a constitutional democracy. Although elections were to be held in January 1992 but then were postponed until April, partly because of unrest in the Tuareg regions, few observers doubt that a transition to civilian government will occur soon. Significantly, the interim government includes two traditional Tuareg leaders, who represent the insurrectionist Azaouad Popular Movement and the separatist Azaouad Islamic Arab Front.

In Niger, a national conference convened at the end of July 1991 promptly proclaimed its sovereign authority. Chaired by Professor André Salifou, dean of the faculty of education at Niamey University, the conference was attended by delegates from the Federation of Labor Unions, the Teachers' Union, the government itself, 24 registered political parties, and 69 other associations. In November the conference installed an interim government pending democratic elections after a 15-month transition period. Meanwhile, President Ali Saibou has resigned as president of the former ruling party, the National Movement for a Developing Society, which has been shorn of its special status. The president's own powers as head of state also have been sharply curtailed.

Democratic reforms in Niger and Mali could provide an attractive alternative to warfare for the Tuareg people. Despite the troubled history of African-Berber relations, there are also many ties that bind. Like the Kurds, a Muslim people divided among several states in western Asia, the Sahelian Tuaregs could realize freedom for themselves as a transnational people if democratic governments were established in those sovereign states that contain their principal homelands.

Both Mali and Niger have said Libya is the principal supporter of Tuareg separatism. Although Tuareg sources try to minimize the extent of Libyan involvement, Colonel Muammar Qaddafi's role as champion of the Tuaregs is unmistakable. If the insurrections continue, Libya may be expected to provide sanctuary for Tuareg noncombatants, just as Algeria has provided sanctuary for both the Western Sahara independence movement and embattled Tuareg combatants and refugees in the past.

Neither Mali nor Niger is able to resolve its Tuareg problem unilaterally or in concert with the other at present. In September 1990 the governments of those two countries along with Algeria and Libya established an "interministerial committee" on the Tuareg question. Subsequently, in January 1991, bilateral negotiations between the Malian government and Tuareg rebels were held in Tamanrasset, Algeria. The government agreed to withdraw troops from Tuareg areas in northern Mali, to devolve federal-type powers to the largely Tuareg regions of Gao and Timbuktu, and to allocate a substantial portion of the national budget to develop those regions for the next six years. In return, the rebels agreed to a cease-fire. Assassinations, banditry, and summary executions have since marred the implementation of these accords.

Since the Tuareg people inhabit several adjacent areas in Mali, Niger, Algeria, Libya, and Burkina Faso, the problems of displacement, rebellion, and resettlement are clearly regional in scope. Three regional international organizations may be able to cope with the various issues relating to the Tuaregs more readily than individual states. The three groups are the Agreement on Nonaggression and Defense (ANAD), which includes Mali and Niger as well as Benin, Burkina Faso, Ivory Coast, and Togo; the 16-member ECOWAS; and the newly formed Arab Maghreb Union, consisting of Algeria, Libya, Mauritania, Morocco, and Tunisia.

Although ANAD was used effectively to settle the Burkina Faso–Mali conflict of 1985, its functions are strictly political and initiated by heads of state, none of whom represent Tuareg interests. In contrast, ECOWAS is primarily an economic organization and can address a major

aspect of the Tuareg problem—nomadic pastoralism as an economic activity and a way of life. Free passage across national boundaries, a necessary part of any political settlement that might satisfy the Tuaregs, implies at least some kind of free-trade zone. The current activities of the ECOWAS Monitoring Group (ECOMOG) in Liberia show that its political potential is far greater than had been previously believed. Moreover, ECOWAS can enlist Nigeria as a guarantor of any agreements reached. The Arab Maghreb Union, whose goals include the creation of a fiscal union and the economic integration of its member-states, offers a way to contain Qaddafi's ambitions by harmonizing Libyan policies with those of its neighbors. ECOWAS and the Arab Maghreb Union could conceivably resolve the Tuareg problem.

Storm Over Mauritania

Mauritania is a sparsely populated country of some 2 million people that has been impoverished by desertification and endemic ethnic conflicts.[5] The Moors, a people of mixed Arab-Berber descent, constitute two-thirds of the population. They are divided into two main groups: the Beydanes and the Haratines. The Haratines were originally slaves of the Beydanes. Although slavery has been abolished formally on three occasions in Mauritanian history, most recently by legislative action in 1980, Africa Watch, a human rights group, alleges that in 1990 there were at least 100,000 slaves in the country.[6] The remaining one-third of the population consists largely of small ethnic groups who live mainly in the south.

Near the end of his 18 years in power, Mauritania's first president, Moktar Ould Daddah, struggled with the burning question of Spanish Western Sahara. In 1975, he agreed to divide the former colony with a potentially menacing neighbor, Morocco, in order to create a land buffer between that powerful kingdom and Mauritania's northern-based mineral industry. However, the Mauritanian armed forces were unable to protect the mining operations against attacks by the Popular Front for the Liberation of Saguia el-Hamra and Río de Oro (Polisario), the guerrilla group fighting for the territory's independence, nor were they able to secure territory claimed by the Polisario as its own. Rising military expenses coupled with economic decline as a result of recurrent droughts and a dispirited army resulted in a 1978 coup and the eventual assumption of power by a pro-Polisario, or "Algerian," faction of the army that then renounced Mauritania's claim to Western Sahara.

In 1984, after another military coup, Colonel Maaoûya Ould Sid Ahmed Taya became president of Mauritania. Taya sought to maintain good relations with both Morocco and the Polisario-Algerian alliance. But the consensual basis of his regime was shattered in 1987 when the government alleged it had thwarted a coup attempt by officers from the southern Toucouleur and Soninke ethnic groups. Tensions increased to the point of rupture along the country's main cultural dividing line that ranges the Moor majority against the non-Moorish minority. While the minority, like the majority, is Muslim, it firmly rejects the policy of cultural and linguistic Arabization that Taya's regime has aggressively pursued.

Taya's ruling Military Committee for National Salvation consists of two principal political factions: the dominant Nasserites, or Qaddafists, who tend to support the Polisario-Algerian alliance; and the minority Baathists, who adhere to the pan-Arabist Iraqi movement and were pro-Moroccan until relations between Iraq and Morocco deteriorated in 1990–1991 during the Persian Gulf crisis. However, the main thrust of Mauritanian Baathist strategy has been Arabization at the expense of the non-Moorish minority, which is made up of people who have grand imperial traditions of their own and resent the imposition of cultural hegemony by the Moorish state. Furthermore, the Moors adhere mainly to the Islamic Qadiriyya brotherhood, while most of the southerners are adherents of the rival Tijaniyya brotherhood.

In 1989, conflicts over grazing land (a result of relentless desertification) involving villagers in the Senegal River Valley ignited the tinder of ethnic tensions in the capitals of both Mauritania and Senegal. When angry mobs looted the shops of Mauritanian merchants in Dakar in Senegal, Senegalese and other non-Moors were killed in Nouakchott. In all, hundreds of people died and more than 1,000 injured in reciprocal spasms of urban violence. According to one report, "During the ensuing months an estimated 170,000 Mauritanians fled Senegal while Mauritania reportedly expelled 70,000 Senegalese and 40,000 other nationals (the expulsion of the latter group underlining the schism between Arab and Black Mauritania)."[7] Diplomatic relations between the two countries were severed, and "a brief, but bloody exchange of artillery fire" was reported in January 1990.[8] Subsequently, attacks by an African guerrilla organization, the African Liberation Forces of Mauritania, have provoked reprisals in Mauritania.[9]

Meanwhile, Moors have occupied land and villages abandoned by non-Moors in the valley. Mauritania has also demanded $1 billion from Senegal as compensation for economic losses and has alleged Senegalese government complicity in a coup plot against the Taya government. In turn, Senegal has threatened to assert a land claim north of the Senegal River, and has also alleged that arms have been sent from Mauritania to separatist rebels in the Casamance region of Senegal.

This latter complaint indicates that particular Arab-"African" alliances complicate the picture of an Arab-"African" racial conflict in the region. The most significant

transcultural tandem is the firm alliance between Senegal and Morocco. Before the Persian Gulf war in early 1991, Morocco's monarch, King Hassan II, was disturbed by the growth of Iraqi influence in Mauritania, which funneled weapons from Iraq to Polisario guerrillas.[10] Pro-Iraqi Baathists in Mauritania are foremost in both the Arabization campaign and the organization of violence against non-Moors. It was not surprising that Senegal, like Morocco, contributed a contingent of troops to the United Nations (UN) coalition that forced Iraq to withdraw from Kuwait during the war.

Soon after the UN victory in the Gulf, Taya announced a political reform program, including constitutional changes and multiparty competition. However, opponents of the regime denounced this maneuver as a subterfuge designed to consolidate the ruling group's power, and they disputed official reports of overwhelming approval of the new constitution in a later referendum. The opposition demands included the installation of an interim government pending the convocation of a sovereign national conference—a process similar to the one carried out in Niger. Taya's subsequent election as president, in January 1992, was sharply disputed by the legal opposition, which includes the leadership of Mauritania's sole labor union as well as dissident Haratines. However, non-Moorish voices of dissent have been silenced or driven into revolutionary channels by severe repression. Amnesty International has reported that as many as 339 political prisoners may have died, many of them under torture, in military or police custody between November 1990 and March 1991.[11] Meanwhile, the army continues to enforce an undeclared policy of expelling non-Moors, who live in the valley, from their homes.

Despite the turn toward reform, Taya's regime appears to contemplate prolonged managed conflict with Senegal rather than a genuine settlement of critical disputes. Expulsion of the non-Moors from southern Mauritania, often on the dubious ground that they are not citizens, is a demagogic technique that diverts attention from pressing economic problems. Indeed, the problems caused by ecological deterioration and political disruption have been compounded by the loss of revenues that had been remitted by the prosperous Mauritanian merchant community in Senegal, as well as the loss of foreign aid previously given by Arab opponents of Iraq. Historically, the Moors have disdained farming in favor of pastoralism. Hence a general exodus of southerners would wreak havoc in the agricultural sector.

Northern elites have exploited the issue of cultural differences between Moors and non-Moors since it allows them to contain a potentially divisive tension between the black and white sections of the Moorish community. The policy of Arabization, in particular, is designed to bind the Haratines to the Beydanes, who are aware of their exclusively Arab and Berber heritages. Left to themselves, the so-called white Moors would be vulnerable to Arab versus Berber conflicts and conflicts between clans. For all these reasons, the Nouakchott regime would not want to create a purely Moorish nation. Instead, its policy is to marginalize non-Moors within a multicultural political system. The fearful implication of this practice is continued internal warfare with potentially dangerous external consequences.

Chad: A State of War

In Mauritania, Mali, and Niger, particular ethnic groups (Moors, Bambara, and Hausa respectively) are large enough to dominate the country's political life. In the vast expanse of Chad, with its total population of nearly 5 million, only one group, the Christian-influenced Sara of the southern part of the country, numbers more than 1 million people. Outside the relatively fertile south, there are two other centers of political gravity. First, in northern Chad, the Toubou, adherents of the Islamic Sanusiyya brotherhood, overshadow a more numerous group of nomadic Arab clans that have not exercised political influence. Second, in eastern Chad, Islamic peoples such as the Hajeray and Zaghawa are culturally oriented toward western Sudan.

Chad has been torn by war ever since Quaddafi's regime in Libya extended support to northern insurgents against the southern-based government of President François Tombalbaye in 1971. Tombalbaye's assassination in a 1975 coup ushered in a period of instability that lasted until 1982, when Hissène Habré, a northerner yet a sworn enemy of Qaddafi, seized control of the Chadian government and summoned French military assistance to counteract Libyan intervention. Habré's consolidation of power culminated in the expulsion of Libyan forces from northern Chad in 1987.[12]

Habré's regime was based mainly on collaboration between three highly politicized ethnic groups: Habré's own Gorane faction of the northern Toubou plus two eastern groups, the Hajeray and the Zaghawa. A Hajeray defection in 1984 reduced the number of groups to two. In 1989, the Zaghawas, sensing an erosion of their power, withdrew support from Habré and organized an insurgent armed force, with Libyan backing, in western Sudan. Habré tried to negotiate a settlement with Qaddafi at a "summit" attended by the leaders of Algeria, Gabon, Libya, Mali, and Nigeria in the Malian capital of Bamako in July 1989. Shortly thereafter, Chad and Libya agreed to submit a territorial dispute over the mineral-rich Aozou Strip in northern Chad to the International Court of Justice for arbitration. Habré continued to authorize the military training of Libyan dissidents in Chad, financed by Saudi Arabia and conducted by teams of American and Israeli instructors, while Libya continued to supply anti-Habré force in Sudan.

In November 1990 the insurgent army, led by Colonel Idriss Déby, a well-regarded military commander, crossed into Chad, defeated the Chadian national army (forcing Habré into exile), and seized control of the government. Habré's fall was, at first, widely perceived to be a setback for the United States, which supported his seizure of power in 1982 as a stroke against Libya. However, after France, Habré principal source of financial and military aid at the time of his fall was Iraq. Libya and Iraq are rivals in Chad, where Déby's assumption of the presidency marked a setback for Iraqi President Saddam Hussein. (In Sudan the two countries continue to compete for favor with the military government of Brigadier General Omar Hassan Ahmed al-Bashir.)

Initially, Déby's regime, based mainly on eastern elements—specifically his own Zaghawa ethnic group and the neighboring Hajeray—was unstable and liable to come apart.[13] In the past, Chadian regimes based on coalitions of rival claimants to power have been notoriously unstable; Déby's own coalition has already been strained by Hajeray-Zaghawa conflicts as well as struggles among Zaghawas themselves. Then, in January 1992, supporters of former President Habré crossed the border from Nigeria into western Chad; more than 100 people were killed before they were driven back.

Despite recurrent rebellions and incursions, the fragmented polity of Chad may yet facilitate democratic reform, since this would prevent the monopolization of power by any one political bloc. Although Déby is himself a product of Chadian warlordism, he appears to have renounced that legacy by calling for a 30-month transition to a democratic government. A commission, representing diverse political views as well as the organized labor movement, has been asked to frame a legal code for the regulation of political parties. Déby has also pledged to convene a national conference, with sovereign authority, to draft a constitution no later than May 1992. Meanwhile, he is attempting to consolidate numerous independent military factions into a single national army. His two-track policy of democratization with discipline has generated new hope for the future of this deeply divided country.

Reinforcing the Effects of Freedom

In each of the four conflicts examined, an internal war, either ongoing or recently suspended, threatens to precipitate international warfare. The currently stilled border war between Mauritania and Senegal could restart at any time. In Senegal, Mali, and Niger the government views outbursts of civil strife in Mauritania with grave concern. The

Berber Tuaregs of Mali and Niger are ethnic cousins of the Arab/Berber Moors and could be incited to violence by the racial and cultural conflict in Mauritania. Mali, in particular, is endangered by the potential transborder effects of that conflict. It would be logical to consider Mauritania's security problems in conjunction with those of Mali and Niger in multinational initiatives for peaceful solutions.

Similarly, the wars in Chad are unlikely to be concluded until the regional sovereigns, including all six states with which Chad shares a border, agree to a collective security arrangement. Without exception, the principal rivals for power in Chad have been utterly dependent on foreign patrons. Chad differs from the other Sahelian countries in its extreme degree of political fragmentation and the amorphous character of the Chadian state. An escape from the ravages of warlordism in Chad may come through the development of representative government based on multiparty democratic elections. Democratization may also help resolve the recurrent internal wars of Mauritania, Mali, and Niger, which are far more cohesive nation-states than Chad. In every case, the advance of democracy would facilitate the resolution of disputes and the maintenance of peace in a society where insecurity has been rife.

It should not be assumed that African countries will deviate from the rule of thumb that modern democracies rarely if ever wage wars against one another. That proposition can be tested by looking at the transborder relationships of democratizing countries in the Sahel, such as the formerly troubled borderlands of Mali, and either Algeria or Burkina Faso. It could also be tested by examining the relationship between Mauritania and either Mali or Senegal, provided the process of proclaimed democratization in Mauritania becomes more genuine than it has thus far appeared to be.

The democratization process in Mauritania could be driven off course by the winds of war in neighboring Western Sahara. Both Morocco and its antagonist, the Polisario Front, expect to win a showdown referendum, previously scheduled to be held under UN auspices in January 1992, but postponed pending the resolution of procedural questions and a dispute over who should be eligible to vote. (Morocco contends that its own citizens who are "born of a Saharan father" should be registered.) The choice before voters will be either independence for a Sahrawi republic or integration into Morocco. If a free and fair vote can be held, and if a credible result is obtained and accepted by the losing side, then Mauritania's own evolution toward democracy would be strongly promoted. Conversely, a state of war in sparsely settled Western Sahara would strengthen the hand of Mauritanian militarists who sympathize with their Hassaniyyan-speaking compatriots of the Polisario. Similarly, reconciliation through democracy in Chad or Niger could be undermined by threats to their security by Libya and Sudan, whose regimes are not accountable to the inhabitants of the two countries.

These observations indicate that it would be difficult to test the hypothesis of a causal relationship between democracy and peace in the Sahelian region. Governments that have chosen the path of democratic reform are vulnerable to intervention from neighboring dictatorial states. Moreover, the probability that a few dictatorships will continue in this part of Africa implies that diplomatic initiatives and other precautions are required to minimize threats.

At present, peacekeeping services, including conciliation and mediation, are provided in the Sahel by several intergovernmental organizations. They include the OAU, the Arab League, the Arab Maghreb Union, ANAD, ECOWAS, and special purpose groups, such as the "interministerial committee" on Tuareg issues. There is no apparent need for new intergovernmental organizations to secure peace among the Sahelian nations. However, the potential contribution of nongovernmental organizations (NGOs) to the cause of peace in this region has not yet been explored.

While the African Leadership Forum, itself an illustrious NGO, has recognized the important role of NGOs in relation to development problems, it has overlooked the potential utility of such bodies in resolving international conflicts.[14] Yet NGOs have attempted to mediate armed conflicts in Africa in the past. Most have been identified with religious groups and the results of their efforts, which have been recently summarized by David R. Smock, are mixed.[15]

The World Council of Churches and the All Africa Conference of Churches jointly served as principal mediator in the 1972 Addis Ababa agreement on Sudan. Leading Mozambican clerics along with the Santo Egidio Community in Italy are playing central mediation roles in the negotiations between the Mozambican government and the Mozambican National Resistance (also known as Renamo). Smock also draws attention to the unsuccessful, yet constructive, attempts by former United States President Jimmy Carter and the Carter Center at Emory University during 1989 to mediate both the Ethiopian and the Sudanese conflicts.

A few institutions comparable to the Carter Center, designed to study political and social problems, such as the Nigerian Institute of International Affairs, already exist in Africa. Many more similar institutions are needed to critically examine the issues of war and peace. Their functions could encompass crisis prevention as well as mediation. Independent study centers could issue early warnings of potentially dangerous conflicts by means of objective analyses and scholarly communications. Respected NGOs could convene meetings, attended by diplomats, political actors, publicists, scholars, and others who could make positive contributions, to consider questions such as conflict resolution for disputes that have resulted in violence; existing or impending threats to the maintenance of peace between nation-states; and chronic causes of war, which require complex analyses and prescient remedies. The arrival of Africa's own peace movement may soon be at hand. Its emergence in war-torn countries and regions would be the logical consequence of increasing political freedom and allowing greater democracy.

Notes

1. For a concise summary, see Raymond W. Copson, "Peace in Africa? The Influence of Regional and International Change," in Francis M. Deng and I. William Zartman, eds., *Conflict Resolution in Africa* (Washington, D.C.: The Brookings Institution, 1991), pp. 22–24.
2. Quoted in *Le Monde* by Jacques de Barrin, "Africa—A Zone of Fundamental Instability?" *Manchester Guardian Weekly*, November 18, 1990, p. 16.
3. "Report of a Brainstorming Meeting for a Conference on Security, Stability, Development and Co-operation in Africa," Addis Ababa, Ethiopia, November 17–18, 1990, pp. 7–8.
4. On Niger, see Robert B. Charlick, *Niger: Personal Rule and Survival in the Sahel* (Boulder, Col.: Westview Press, 1991). On Mali, see Joseph Roger de Benoist, *Le Mali* (Paris: Harmattan, 1989), and Pascal J. Imperato, *Mali: A Search for Direction* (Boulder, Col.: Westview Press, 1989).
5. For general background, see Virginia Thompson and Richard Adloff, *The Western Saharans* (Totowa, N.J.: Barnes and Noble, 1980).
6. *Africa News*, July 23, 1990, p. 16.
7. Arthur S. Banks, ed., *Political Handbook of the World: 1990* (Binghamton, N.Y.: CSA Publications, 1990), p. 413.
8. Ibid.
9. *West Africa* (London), December 17–23, 1990, p. 3065.
10. *Africa Confidential* (London), August 24, September 22, and October 12, 1990.
11. Amnesty International (London), Amnesty International Index: AFR 38/07/91.
12. For succinct, incisive accounts of Chadian politics and international relations, see René Lemarchand, "The Crisis in Chad," in Gerald J. Bender, James S. Coleman, and Richard L. Sklar, eds., *African Crisis Areas and U.S. Foreign Policy* (Berkeley, Cal.: University of California Press, 1985), pp. 239–256; and William J. Foltz, "Chad's Third Republic: Strengths, Problems, and Prospects," *CSIS Africa Notes*, no. 77 (October 30, 1987).
13. Hugo Sada, "Les grandes manoeuvres d'Idriss Déby," *Jeune Afrique* (Paris), November 28–December 4, 1990, pp. 24–25.
14. "Report of a Brainstorming Meeting," op. cit.
15. David R. Smock, "Conflict Resolution in Africa: The Mediation of Africa's Wars (Paper presented at the annual meeting of the American Political Science Association, Washington, D.C., August 30, 1991), p. 19.

Article 7   *Institute for Food and Development*, revised edition, 1987

Myths of African Hunger

Kevin Danaher

Africa has vanished from our TV screens and the front pages of our newspapers. The widespread starvation that swept the continent during 1984–85 has receded. But a hunger crisis continues. The United Nations reports that of the seven million children worldwide who die each year of malnutrition-related causes, five million are African children.

In the public discussion of African hunger many myths and misconceptions have been created about why so many Africans go hungry. For those of us who want to put an end to needless suffering, it is important to understand the real causes of hunger in Africa.

MYTH ONE:
Nature is the main cause of famine in Africa.

Drought in many parts of Africa has intensified hunger, but poverty is the real cause of famine. It is only the chronically impoverished who die from the effects of drought. And Africa's impoverishment has been several hundred years in the making.

As European countries colonized Africa, they disrupted African farming and herding systems that for centuries Africans had adapted to changing environmental conditions. Ecologically balanced food systems were undermined; the best agricultural lands were seized for growing coffee, sugar cane, cocoa, and other export crops that would benefit Europe. Private and government investment went into developing these cash crops, while food production for the poor majority was neglected.

Colonial cash cropping ravaged the soil, reducing large areas to desert and semidesert. Millions of acres of brush and trees were cleared, robbing the soil of organic replenishment. Export crops such as cotton, peanuts, and tobacco absorbed large amounts of nutrients from the soil. After each year's harvest the soil was left bare and unprotected.[1]

Seizing the best land for export agriculture not only degraded the environment; it also impoverished the peasants, forcing many to either work on the plantations or crowd into the cities seeking employment. This gave the plantations and other commercial interests a large labor force that could be paid low wages, thus ensuring high profits.

Poor rainfall is troublesome for farmers throughout the world. It pushes people into famine, however, where farmers and pastoralists have been made vulnerable by economic and political structures that impoverish the many while enriching the few.

MYTH TWO:
African hunger is caused by overpopulation.

Contrary to popular opinion, hunger is not caused by extreme population density. If it were, we would expect to find widespread hunger in densely populated countries like Japan and the Netherlands.

And we would expect to find little or no hunger in sparsely populated countries like Senegal and Zaire where, in fact, malnutrition is widespread.[2]

Africa is not densely populated. Compare Africa's 18.2 persons per square kilometer to Europe's 101 and Asia's 102.4.[3] Only about one-fourth of Africa's potentially arable land is now under cultivation.[4] But of all continents, Africa ranks last when it comes to the use of irrigation, fertilizer and tractors.[5] The problem is not a shortage of land but a shortage of money, training and technology to develop the land.

It is true that Africa's population growth rate (3.1% per year) is higher than that of any other continent. But having large families is a logical response to the conditions of poverty under which most Africans live. On the small family farms that produce most of Africa's food, the most important factor of production is family labor. The high birth rate is partly a response by parents to this need for farm labor.

A woman in Burkina Faso (formerly Upper Volta) reported: "It takes me four hours every day to fetch water, and another four hours to collect firewood. Then there are the cattle to care for. I need children to help with the chores. They can also work for other people, and eventually earn and contribute to our income."[6]

With the world's highest rate of death for children aged 0–4, African mothers must give birth to three children to ensure the survival of two.[7] This is not to say the question of family size is always answered "the more the better." For some mothers the burden of raising another child under difficult circumstances outweighs the eventual benefits of another laborer in the family.

Data from all over the world show a close connection between raising living standards and lowering birth rates.[8] If African parents were assured their children would survive, they would not need to have so many. If parents could earn enough from their own labor, and were assured of support in old age, they would see it in their own interest to limit their number of children. And if women were empowered as equal members of society, they would be able to make full use of family planning technology.

Africans use a very small percentage of the globe's resources: It is the populations of the rich countries who are the real drain on world resources. For example, Africa's 500 million people consume just 2.5 percent of the world's commercial energy, while the USA's 250 million people consume 25.5 percent.[9]

The key problem is not too many people, it is too much inequality.

MYTH THREE:
African governments bear the main responsibility for declining food production.

To lay all the blame on African governments is to imply that they alone control the destiny of their countries. The forces that have institutionalized hunger in Africa are made up of African elites, transnational corporations, western governments, and international agencies. Together they form a "transnational elite coalition" whose lifestyle and interests are very different from those of Africa's rural majority.

Over the years this elite coalition implemented policies that undermined food crops. Prices paid to farmers for food crops were kept artificially low, thus providing cheap food to people in the cities. This reduced the likelihood of urban unrest and allowed urban employers to pay lower wages, but it also stifled incentive for increased food production.[10]

The elite coalition directs most agricultural assistance to cash crops, mainly benefiting large commercial interests. For example, between 1975 and 1980 the countries along the Sahara Desert's southern border received $7.45 billion from international aid agencies such as the World Bank. But even though nearly all the region's food production comes from rainfed agriculture, only eight percent of the aid went to rainfed crops.[11] The bulk of the aid further expanded export production.

The peasants are too dispersed, poor, and unorganized to wield much political clout. The fact that policymaking is dominated by men, while most food is produced by women, also helps explain the low priority given to food crops. The elite coalition directs most agricultural training and development assistance to men, neglecting women farmers.

But food production can be increased, as developments in Zimbabwe show. After years of guerrilla war against a white minority government, Zimbabwe achieved independence in 1980. Since then the government of Robert Mugabe has raised the price paid for food crops, and has given small farmers credit so they can purchase seeds, fertilizer, and tools. Though these programs do not reach all the family farmers in need, they have led to a massive increase in food production. In 1985, despite several years of drought, small farmers not only fed their families, but they also marketed twice as much corn as ever before.[12]

Africa is a diverse continent with over 50 governments ranging from blatantly antifarmer to those genuinely trying to help the poor majority. But in every nation it can be said that only when the majority gain control of their country's resources will we see an end to policies that systematically impoverish people, leaving them vulnerable to natural disasters.

MYTH FOUR:
The "free market" holds the solution to Africa's food problems.

Most people fail to realize that the world market is Africa's worst enemy. Most African countries are dependent on exporting minerals and cash crops. World market prices for these raw materials have declined during the post–World War II period. But the prices of manufactured imports from industrial countries averaged *annual increases* of 5.4 percent during 1965–73 and 11 percent during 1973–80.[13]

Africa's earning power has been crippled by new synthetic substitutes for many of its raw material exports. For example, communications equipment that formerly used tons of copper wire now requires only pounds of glass fiber optics, and sugar exports are being replaced by cyclamates and Nutrasweet. These new industrial processes have undermined the theory of "comparative advantage" whereby third world countries were supposed to benefit by concentrating on raw material exports.

Another problem is protectionism. As the World Bank notes, the same industrial countries preaching the wonders of the free market "have erected high barriers to imports . . . from developing countries and then have subsidized their own exports."[14] This is particularly significant given that 75 percent of Africa's exports go to industrial capitalist countries.[15]

The deterioration in Africa's terms of trade means that most African governments have been forced to spend more in the world market than they earn. They have filled the gap by borrowing.

By 1986, external debt for Sub-Saharan Africa was conservatively estimated at well over $100 billion. The debt of the semi-arid, low-income countries equals more than 90 percent of annual Gross Domestic Product.[16] The World Bank concludes that Africa's debt service payments have risen to "unsustainable levels."[17] Sudan, for example, would have had to pay more than 100 percent of its export earnings in 1985 if it had not rescheduled its debt payments.

The world financial system is a greater cause of hunger in Africa than is bad weather. If African governments were not so deeply in debt, they could buy food on the world market. They would not be forced to wait for unreliable shipments of donated food while millions go hungry.

Markets allocate food according to monetary wealth, not nutritional need. The handful of large corporations that control 85 to 90 percent of world grain shipments are concerned with profits, not malnutrition. Thus we are confronted with the cruel irony that world grain reserves are at their highest levels in history, while widespread hunger afflicts millions of Africans.

Within African countries, small farmers are often victimized by private speculators. These traders buy up the food crop at harvest time when plentiful supplies push down prices. Later in the year, during what they call the "hungry" season, small farmers run out of savings and are forced to borrow at exorbitant interest rates from local merchants just to survive until the next harvest.

Even when overall supplies are adequate, markets dominated by wealthy speculators work against the majority. "The 1982 rains were poor in many parts of the Sahel, but private traders had large stocks of millet available throughout the year. But by June and July, Oxfam field staff were reporting that the poorer villagers were all telling the same story: they did not have the money to buy grain at the traders' high prices."[18]

The Reagan administration claims that economic progress will be achieved if African governments refrain from intervening in markets. But the problem is not that African governments intervene in the marketplace, rather it is the way they intervene: against the interests of the poor majority, in favor of the rich and powerful.

Markets can be tamed to serve the interests of the majority. But this can only be achieved by governments genuinely committed to the poor.

MYTH FIVE:
U.S. foreign aid is
helping Africa's hungry.

During the recent African famine the United States donated large amounts of emergency food. But while it is essential to help people in need, we must remember that food aid, at best, only treats the symptoms of poverty, not its causes.

Food aid can undermine local food production by flooding local markets and depressing food prices. It can also create dependence on foreign aid or be used by recipient governments to manipulate the poor. During a 1985 fact-finding trip to the Horn of Africa, Food First cofounder Joseph Collins saw the Ethiopian government using food as a weapon, withholding it from people for political reasons.

As we point out in our books, *Aid As Obstacle* and *Betraying the National Interest*, most food aid from the U.S. government is not even intended for the hungry. It is purchased by foreign governments using money loaned by the United States. These governments then sell the food on the open market, which means the poor do not benefit.

The concentration of U.S. aid on only a few countries shows that its objectives are strategic rather than humanitarian. Of all U.S. aid to Africa, 63 percent goes to just one country: Egypt. Of U.S. aid to African countries other than Egypt, nearly half (48 percent) goes to just five countries (Sudan, Somalia, Kenya, Zaire and Liberia).[19] These countries contain only 12 percent of Africa's population, and their governments do not follow policies favoring the majority, but they have naval bases, CIA listening posts, or other strategic assets.

Between 1981 and 1985 the Reagan administration oversaw a 136 percent increase in security assistance to Africa (from $248m to $586m) while development assistance increased by only 17 percent (from $300m to $352m).[20] Both Washington and Moscow have been more interested in militarizing Africa—using it as a battleground in the cold war—than in fostering economic development.

The U.S. government uses foreign aid as a political tool. In 1981 when the government of Mozambique expelled several U.S. officials for spying, the Reagan administration cut off $5 million of food aid even though thousands of Mozambicans were facing starvation. Washington slashed aid to Zimbabwe by nearly one-half after Robert Mugabe's government differed with the United States on two U.N. votes dealing with the Soviet downing of a Korean airliner and the U.S. invasion of Grenada, and then eliminated the remaining aid when a junior Zimbabwean official criticized U.S. policy toward South Africa.

While punishing these governments which have demonstrated a commitment to helping the poor, Washington lavishes aid on corrupt regimes such as that of Mobutu Sese Seko in Zaire. Mobutu is one of the richest men in the world, but most Zaireans live in desperate poverty, suffering from malnutrition, lack of health care, and high infant mortality. Despite his mismanagement of Zaire, Mobutu has received billions of dollars from U.S. banks and the U.S. government because his country has important mineral reserves and he is staunchly anticommunist.

Nearly all U.S. foreign aid is directed to repressive elites who have enriched the few while impoverishing the many. They use U.S. aid money to strengthen their hold on power. Given the undemocratic nature of these regimes, U.S. aid is more likely to perpetuate poverty than eliminate it.

WHAT YOU CAN DO

1. **Educate yourself and others about the root causes of hunger in Africa.** Understanding the real causes of Africa's economic crisis can build hope and increase the chances for a lasting solution to widespread hunger.

In the Food First book, *Fighting the Famine*, photographer Mike Goldwater provides 70 dramatic photos, and Africa expert Nigel Twose gives a clear analysis of the causes and possible cures for hunger in Africa. Food First is distributing a book by our Issues Analyst, Kevin Danaher, *In Whose Interest: A Guide to US–South Africa Relations*, which covers all aspects of US involvement in South Africa. We also distribute an excellent curriculum on South Africa (*Strangers in Their Own Country*) suitable for high school and college classrooms.

Food First Action Alerts on hunger in South Africa and South Africa's aggression against neighboring countries are useful organizing tools.

A reliable weekly that covers all of Africa is *Africa News*, P.O. Box 3851, Durham, NC 27702.

2. **Work to end all U.S. military aid for elite-controlled governments that impoverish their people.** The U.S. government could set an example by cutting back weapons sales and challenging other arms exporters such as the USSR, France, Britain and Israel to do the same. Only if your representatives in Congress hear from you will they work to cut military aid to Africa.

3. **Oppose hunger in South Africa.** The white minority government has purposely impoverished the black majority to ensure a docile work force willing to work for low wages. This forced impoverishment has resulted in widespread hunger among black South Africans (see the Food First Action Alert, "South Africa: Hunger in a Land of Plenty"). South Africa also launches military attacks on neighboring countries, targeting their

food systems for destruction (see our Action Alert, "Hunger as a Weapon: South Africa's War Against Its Neighbors").

There is much Americans can do about this problem. Through trade, investment, intelligence cooperation, and diplomatic support, the United States is the key international ally of South Africa's apartheid regime. By working to cut all U.S. support for the apartheid regime, we can hasten the arrival of a democratic South Africa. Groups to contact on how to get involved include: the Washington Office on Africa, 110 Maryland Ave. NE, Washington, DC 20002 (202) 546-7961; TransAfrica, 545 8th St. SE, Washington, DC 20003 (202) 547-2550; and the American Committee on Africa, 198 Broadway, New York, NY 10038 (212) 962-1210.

4. **Support democratic development projects in Africa.** For those Americans who feel a need to donate money to direct assistance, we recommend two groups who do exemplary grassroots development work in Africa: Grassroots International, Box 312, Cambridge, MA 02139 (617) 497-9180; and Oxfam America, 115 Broadway, Boston, MA 02116 (617) 482-1211. For information on groups in Africa and elsewhere doing grassroots development work, write to Food First's Positive Developments program.

NOTES

1. See Chapters 3 and 4 of Richard W. Franke and Barbara H. Chasin, Seeds of Famine: Ecological Destruction and the Development Dilemma in the West African Sahel (Montclair, NJ: Allanheld Osmun, 1980).

2. For a more detailed analysis of the relationship between population growth and hunger, see Frances Moore Lappé and Joseph Collins, World Hunger: Twelve Myths (New York: Grove Press Food First Books, 1986), Chapter Three.

3. World Resources Institute, World Resources, 1986 (New York: Basic Books, 1986) p. 256.

4. "Africa's Development Crisis: Looking Beyond the Famine," Overseas Development Council, 1984, p. 4.

5. World Resources 1986, pp. 264–265.

6. Oxfam America, "Hunger and Population," Facts for Action, No. 7, p. 2.

7. UNICEF, State of the World's Children, 1984 (Oxford: Oxford University Press, 1983).

8. World Bank, World Development Report 1984, p. 162.

9. World Resources 1986, p. 292.

10. For details see Robert H. Bates, Markets and States in Tropical Africa: The Political Basis of Agricultural Policies (Berkeley: University of California Press, 1981).

11. Alan Grainger, Desertification: How People Make Deserts, How People Can Stop, and Why They Don't (Washington, DC: Earthscan, 1982), p. 48.

12. U.S. Department of Agriculture, Sub-Saharan Africa: Outlook and Situation Report, RS-85-10, July 1985, p. 27.

13. World Development Report 1986, p. 25.

14. World Development Report 1986, p. 11.

15. UNCTAD Statistical Pocket Book (New York: United Nations, 1984) p. 39.

16. Kathie L. Krumm, The External Debt of Sub-Saharan Africa (Washington: World Bank, 1985), p. 20.

17. World Development Report 1986, p. 52.

18. Why the Poor Suffer Most: Drought and the Sahel (Oxford, England: Oxfam, 1984), p. 12.

19. Agency for International Development, Fiscal Year 1987, Summary Tables, March 1986.

20. Agency for International Development, Congressional Presentation, (Main Volume) Fiscal Year 1983 (p. 481) and Fiscal Year 1987 (p. 666).

Article 8

Unesco Courier, June 1992

Black Africa's open societies

Iba Der Thiam

Iba Der Thiam, Senegalese historian, politician and diplomat, is involved in a wide range of activities both in his own country and internationally. A former Minister of Education of Senegal (1983–1988) and member of UNESCO's Executive Board (1978–1983), he is the author of a number of books on history and civics, including Histoire du mouvement syndical africain 1799–1929 (Paris, 1991), *and of many articles. He is also co-editor of the two volumes of UNESCO's* History of Mankind: Cultural and Scientific Development, *covering the 19th and 20th centuries.*

Tolerance has always held a preeminent position in the thought of many African peoples. In West Africa, for example, it is the fundamental principle on which the entire social life of the Senegambian region is built, governing the interaction between individuals and ethnic groups as well as international relations.

Nothing illustrates this better than the central place the concept of peace occupies in the region's moral thinking. The Wolof saying, "*Ci Jaam la yeep xeej*", which signifies that peace bears innumerable promises, implies that peace is the necessary precondition for social stability, political equilibrium, economic prosperity and moral and material progress.

Even before the experience of the slave trade and colonial oppression, the aspiration for peace was a deeply-felt need in a society exposed for centuries of its long history to the vicissitudes of wars fought in the name of conquest or in defence of local aristocracies. It has left its mark on the most anodyne details of daily life. When two people meet, one says as a greeting, "Are you at peace?" "Nothing but peace," the other replies, as if the harmony born of universal accord, whatever the philosophical, religious or moral starting-points or choices of the people involved, could bring an inner calm and sense of hope more valuable than anything else life has to offer.

The same leitmotif of an aspiration for peace and security reappears in the prayer offered by each family to call down God's blessings on its members and on all things. In the words of one traditional Guinean supplication, "Let peace reign in the world! May the pot and the calabash not fall out! Let the beasts live in harmony! May every bad word and unbecoming thought be rooted out and packed off to the back of beyond, to the depths of the virgin forest!"

As the principal element regulating relations between people and between communities, tolerance is the imperative that governs all social life. In some African societies it means refusing to mistrust other people and rejecting both fear and preconceptions in dealing with whatever is new, unknown, unusual or out of the normal pattern.

The Human Dimension

Professor Cheikh Anta Diop suggested that in the Cayor region of Senegal the election of the king was a traditional perquisite of what he called the "governing council". All the social groups that made up the nation were represented in this institution. The aim was not merely to make the body representative but also to encourage collegial participation and friendly social relations in an atmosphere of mutual tolerance and respect.

Although the diawerigne m'boul, the officer presiding over the council, was always chosen from among the geer or aristocracy, the lamane diamatil, the bataloupe ndiob and the badie gateigne, all of whom were governors of important provinces as well as council members, had to come from the gmegno, the ranks of the people of caste, while the diawerigne boule represented the house-slaves.

For traditional societies of this sort, humankind may be one in essence but it is nonetheless diverse in its ways of living and thinking and in the manner in which its constituent groups come to terms with themselves and other peoples. Consequently they made the nitt or human being their principal frame of reference. This human essence was seen as a generic concept, independent of time and place, the supreme embodiment of the divine presence on Earth. Stripped of all moral, philosophical or political connotations, it became a sublimated ideal to which everyone owed consideration and deference.

It is in this light that the treatment of strangers in some African societies must be considered. Newcomers are wel-

comed with kindliness and generosity, no matter what language they speak or what their sex, age, religion or social or political condition may be, for they are human beings first and foremost. As such, they have a right to food and shelter. Their person, goods and health will be protected, and they will be given a decent burial if they die.

In some Wolof communities, it is quite common for the head of a family to give up his own house and bed, or that of his wives or children, to strangers, without giving a thought to his own state of health. Among the Bassari, custom dictates that the tribal chief may even graciously put a female companion at the newcomer's disposal, in the hope that the possible seed sown by their relationship may revivify and strengthen the community.

Following this logic, the differences between peoples, far from being stressed as barriers separating humankind, are minimized to such an extent that they finally lose much or all of their meaning and their divisiveness, and are blurred and blunted until they become harmless. Integration of this sort involves not a denial of the foreigner's identity—and here I have in mind those insidious processes of assimilation that are really more like mutilation—but a profound and freely accepted awareness of the symbiotic complementarity linking the individual to other people. Unbreakable bonds are forged in this fusing of essences.

Renewing The Tradition

This was the state of mind in which Africa, from the dawn of history, opened itself to the outside world. From the time of Queen Hatshepsut's expedition from her native Egypt to the land of Punt in the years between 1493 and 1490 BC until the nineteenth-century explorers, there is no lack of witnesses to the African spirit of tolerance and unfailing hospitality.

It was as a result of the prevailing peace that Habib ben Unada and al-Fazari, around 800 AD, were able to compile their chronicles, the first to mention the existence of the empire of Ghana; that Ibn Hawqal was free to visit the lands south of the Sahara; that al-Bakri, al-Idrisi, Yakut Ibn Sad and al-Umari, between the eleventh and the fourteenth centuries, could give us precious descriptions of the kingdoms of the so-called Sudanic belt from Senegal to the Nile; that Ibn Battuta could visit Mali and Leo the African Timbuktu. Free of dogmatism and sectarianism, the spirit of tolerance encouraged dialogue and the exchange of ideas.

The same phenomenon was at work on the West African coast. Gomes Eanes Zurara's chronicles of Guinea, and the travel writings of Diogo Gomes, Duarte Pacheco Pereira, Joo de Barros and of the Venetian Ca'da Mosto all bear witness to the open-mindedness of the peoples of Cayor, Baol and Sine Saloum, whose humanity would also be attested to by other Western visitors from the seventeenth to the nineteenth centuries. Tolerance extended to colour, language, religion and ethnic and social origin as well as to sex and philosophical or moral views. This atmosphere enabled Christian missionaries to carry out their work without risk wherever traders had set up bases and colonizers had raised their flags.

Despite long-held views to the contrary, these were in effect open societies where freedom and justice reigned. Dare one say that democracy and tolerance flourished

there until the slave trade and colonial conquest and all that went with it—native status, taxes, military conscription, land seizure, forced labour—created an endemic state of violence that corrupted social habits and ways of life to the point at which they were no longer recognizable.

So a precious heritage lies buried beneath the still-smouldering ruins of colonial imperialism. Contemporary Africa must rediscover it quickly, to create worlds of freedom, peace and social harmony in which all its children can find fulfilment.

Article 9   *Dissent*, Summer 1992

Uses and Abuses of African Debt

The International Squeeze on Poor Countries

Susan George

Susan George, an American who lives in France, is an associate director of the Transnational Institute, Amsterdam.

No phenomenon lasting for a decade deserves to be labeled a "crisis." It has thus become acutely embarrassing to speak in 1992 of the third-world debt "crisis." Certainly a chronic condition; arguably a cancer; some even say a conspiracy—but a crisis, no.

The longevity of Africa's debt is particularly worrisome. It is also bizarre. There seem no valid economic reasons whatever for the rich world to have made Africa drag its debt burden so far, for so long. One can, perhaps, understand why the banks are prolonging the agony in Latin America: they still have some $250 billion in shaky loans outstanding there.[1] Banks spent the eighties disengaging from the southern hemisphere, off-loading a significant portion of their dubious debt onto public institutions, diluting their portfolios, cashing in debt against tangible foreign assets ("debt-for-equity" swaps) and generally finding their way out of the Latin American woods that they entered with such enthusiasm in the 1970s. Meanwhile, however, they have made so many *other* stupid loans (for instance, to the U.S. energy or property development sectors) that one can see why they are trying to squeeze every

last penny out of the likes of Argentina, Mexico, or Brazil.

But Africa? What logic can there be for grinding down a whole continent in the name of an insignificant debt? Before proceeding further, we'll specify which "Africa" we're talking about. The whole of the African continent owes its public and private creditors $283 billion, but a large chunk of that ($119 billion or 42 percent) has been lent to North African countries, including heavies like Egypt, Algeria, and Morocco. The debt of Egypt alone amounts to about one-sixth of the African continent's entire debt burden—at least it did until Mr. Mubarak received spectacular debt relief as a reward for fighting on the "right" side in the Gulf War. To say "Thanks, Hosni," the United States reduced Egypt's debt stock in one grand gesture from $51.2 to $39.9 billion, a drop of 24 percent, and one that no other third-world country has come close to meriting.

Since lumping North Africa with the rest of the continent badly skews reality, we will deal from now on only with Sub-Saharan Africa (SSA), whose debt, at the end of 1990, amounted to $164 billion. A mere $28 billion (17 percent) of that sum was owed to private banks, nearly all of them European. This relatively small exposure was furthermore concentrated in just a handful of countries (Nigeria and Côte d'Ivoire stand out). In other words, 83 percent of Sub-Saharan Africa's total debt—and virtually all the debt of the

very poorest SSA countries—is owed to public sources: either to OECD country governments or to multilateral agencies like the World Bank and the International Monetary Fund (IMF).

Herein lies the mystery: $136 billion worth of debts reimbursable to public lending sources represents a crushing load for Africa, but for the said public lending sources the same $136 billion is, frankly, peanuts. Yet these agencies have kept a strict watch on Africa, holding its figurative and collective nose to the grindstone. Those who say offhandedly that the level of Africa's debt doesn't really matter because Africa isn't paying back anyway have not looked seriously at the figures. Since 1982, the continent has been bled dry in order to reimburse its wealthy northern creditors.

Between the beginning of 1982 and the end of 1991, every month, for one hundred and twenty months, SSA somehow scraped together an average of nearly a billion dollars for purposes of debt service. In 1990 and 1991, for example, total service payments (interest and principal) represented a shade over 7 percent of total outstanding debt. Latin America provides a more usurious rate of return, true, and for northern governments and multilateral institutions 7 percent may not be the most lucrative imaginable return on capital, but for the world's poorest continent, it's not bad. The question most people would ask, hearing yet another report of hunger in Africa, is why such countries should be required to provide a return on capital *at all.*

In addition, most normal people would assume that in exchange for this Herculean effort, the continent had at least reaped a substantial reward. Unfortunately, this is not the case. "Herculean" is also the wrong adjective to describe the effort, better labeled "Sisyphean." In spite of a decade of sacrifices, in spite of well over one hundred billion dollars sent northward in debt service alone, by the end of 1990 Sub-Saharan Africa's debt had more than doubled. From $77 billion in 1982, it had risen to $164 billion, an increase of 113 percent.

Seen from the African point of view, then, debt is ever more intolerable. Yet seen from a global perspective, SSA's debt can only be called insignificant. We can measure its importance in a variety of ways. For example, in 1990, Africa's share of total third-world debt was only 11 percent. We will abstain from comparing Sub-Saharan African debt to the total public debt of the United States so as not to provoke hilarity among the readers of a serious journal. Taking a different yardstick, Africa's debt accumulated over many years amounts to only 16 percent of the losses sustained (at least on paper) in a single afternoon of October 1987 when world stock markets crashed. It also represents less than 5 percent of the total annual sales of the world's top two hundred transnational corporations.

In other words, Africa's debt is so modest as to be no threat to anyone except to Africans. Even in the most unlikely event that all forty-three SSA countries suddenly and collectively decided to stop servicing their debt, the world financial system would just keep trundling along, its computer screens registering scarcely a blip.

Because Africa's debt is minuscule by global standards, because it is mostly owed to public creditors, because it causes such obvious hardship, you might think that it would be particularly amenable to a political solution. You would be wrong. At the end of 1991, the United Nations's optimistically titled publication *Africa Recovery* wanly reported, under the headline "Donors stalled on 'Trinidad' relief," that "discussions under way for over a year among Western creditors offer only the prospect of a watered-down version of the so-called 'Trinidad' proposals which . . . would significantly help a number of African countries."[2]

The wine being thus "watered down" was pretty insipid to begin with. The

"Trinidad Terms," as first proposed by British Prime Minister John Major, could *at best* reduce Africa's debt by $34 billion (if all low-income African countries were to be made eligible for relief, which is highly unlikely). These terms would probably touch only $18 billion of SSA's total debt—this, in any case, is the amount being "watered down." Even if the higher figure were lopped off the total, it could change little or nothing with regard to the actual payments required. This may sound odd, but is easily explained. Today, although making unprecedented sacrifices including the literal starvation of millions of its people, Africa as a whole is still paying only about half of the debt service theoretically due. If the stock of debt were to be reduced only marginally, that is, by much less than half, this could serve mainly to free up cash for increasing other interest payments.

The "Trinidad Terms" follow the "Toronto Terms," which follow—well, never mind, since no proposal to reduce African debt has ever made much headway. Under the "Toronto Terms," the most debt-distressed countries, alter protracted negotiations, finally obtained agreements saving them all of one hundred million dollars annually in actual cash outflow. Even these minor savings were painfully arrived at, because each of the debtors had to negotiate separately with the so-called "Paris Club," which represents all the creditors. Not only must the debtor face the gang of its creditors alone; it is also subjected to what one well-placed observer has called the Paris Club's "arcane protocols and procedures which are profoundly inimical to the interests of debtors or indeed to the achievement of sensibly negotiated outcomes"—this from a man who until recently had spent most of his career as a high-ranking official at the World Bank![3]

If we keep on going at this rate, the World Bank estimates that Africa's actual annual cash savings in debt service could reach a breathtaking $310 million by the year 2000.[4] Every summer when the G-7 are about to hold their annual jamboree summit, there is a flurry of rumors that African debt will at last be seriously dealt with. Just as regularly, nothing happens and everyone goes home. The United States is invariably singled out as the chief stonewaller: the U.S. Treasury takes a hard line on debt—anybody's debt— with the possible exception of its own. The only hopeful sign for Africa so far on this front is that in 1991, the United Kingdom for the first time broke free of the U.S. iron debt-management grip, an-

nouncing that it would apply the Trinidad terms by itself even if nobody else did. This could be a valuable precedent for other European countries, which have, to date, shown a remarkable unity in their craven deferral to their American partner.

Reimbursement of Africa's debt has led to unimaginable human suffering. African economies have been wrenched by "structural adjustment" measures dictated by the World Bank and the International Monetary Fund. Thirty of the forty-three SSA countries have in place formal adjustment agreements with the Fund, while most of the others have instituted policies so close to the usual IMF prescriptions as to be undistinguishable. The purpose of structural adjustment is to generate "surplus" cash so that debt can be serviced. It is not an exaggeration to state that the IMF and the Bank now act as collection agencies for the creditor countries.

The effects of their policies are well known. In all these countries, real wages have plummeted by anything from 30 to—in extreme cases—90 percent. Most people don't have paid jobs anyway and rely heavily on the so-called "informal sector"—about 60 percent of the urban work force is not "employed" by anyone. Rural-urban migrants gravitate to the "informal sector" as well in an attempt to make ends meet, but as the International Labor Organization has pointed out, "[T]he informal sector is a labor sponge with a finite capacity of absorption."

Under structural adjustment programs, admittedly bloated public administrations have also massively sacked personnel, adding to the ranks of the unemployed. Public investment has virtually ceased. Hospitals and schools are dilapidated, without drugs or books. The social gains of the sixties and seventies, where they existed, have been eroded or destroyed. For example, the number of children enrolled in primary school increased dramatically in the 1970s, but declined from 1980 onward. Women have, as elsewhere, borne much of the brunt of adjustment, and their workload has increased.

One positive point: UNICEF has made considerable progress in vaccinating African children and is not averse to pointing out that a greater proportion of children has been immunized against preventable diseases in parts of Africa than in the Bronx. But this does not mean that the vaccinated children are healthier. The World Food Program reports that malnutrition now strikes about 40 percent of African children compared to 25 percent in 1985. Recent harvests have been good in most of Africa, but production still does not keep pace with population growth.

In 1986, 46 percent of all World Food Programs (WFP) emergency food aid operations were destined for Africa; in 1990, 85 percent of them were. The WFP estimated that in 1991, at least thirty million Africans required emergency food aid. Overall food import needs are projected at thirty to forty million tons by the year 2000—at prices no one can foresee today. So structural dependency on food aid will continue. Today, three-quarters of all food aid to Africa is in the form of wheat, which cannot be grown in Africa. A lot of it is sold on ordinary markets at ordinary prices, with the "counterpart funds" of these sales supposedly benefiting the hungry. Sometimes they may, but meanwhile, people with purchasing power acquire a taste for bread and other wheat products, driving imports up further.[5]

Poverty, hunger, illness, illiteracy—the litany is familiar. Nor is Africa's plight improved by the maintenance of costly military machines or by leaders whose priorities include the purchase of multiple mansions abroad or the construction of outsized replicas of Saint Peter's and four-story statues of themselves at home. Whatever indicator one cares to choose, the African disaster of the past decade is, or should be, obvious to all. That the debt crisis has been a major factor compounding this disaster should be equally obvious.

So the crucial question really is, Why does the "crisis" endure and the cancer fester? Why do creditors continue to demand their pound of flesh? At first glance, the situation is indeed wholly confounding—Africa can't afford to pay, and the West doesn't need the money. So why the unremitting bloodletting? Creditors have major responsibility for the impasse, but in their own way, so have the debtors.

One reason the cancer is metastasizing is that African governments have never seriously sought to unite under a single debt-negotiating banner although they have had every reason to do so—and this is what bodies like the Organization of African Unity are supposed to be for. This inability to arrive at a common stance has made it even easier for creditors to isolate and browbeat individual debtors when they take the Paris Club witness stand. (Note, however, that this incapacity to unify is not peculiar to Africa. Latin American debtors owe three times as much as Africans and are far fewer in

number, but they too have remained divided and therefore conquered.)

The consequences of this failure are grave and have proved that disunity is a luxury Africa can ill afford. Many African governments still appear to be under the illusion that their countries are more important in the world scheme of things than they are. They also seem to believe that their legitimate concerns are genuinely taken into consideration by the industrialized countries. Sadly, neither is true. Yet many Africans, when told this bluntly by people who are basically on their side, still protest vehemently, insisting that they *are* important because the rich world cannot do without their raw materials and their cheap labor.

This view may have been valid in the 1960s, but the world of the 1990s is a very different place. Naturally, those who run this world are interested in safeguarding whatever parts of Africa contain strategic materials unobtainable elsewhere, but these parts make up an astonishingly small portion of the continent. The overwhelming majority of African countries rely for their foreign exchange earnings on run-of-the-mill commodities, increasingly produced in Latin America and especially Asia as well, and often obtainable with less fuss and bother than in Africa.

Prices for these raw materials have lately dropped to the lowest levels on record since the 1930s. Many respected authorities, including the World Bank, have claimed to see light at the end of the tunnel, repeatedly announcing that the commodities situation is about to take a turn for the better. All the figures belie this optimism. Nineteen-ninety was a bad year, 1991 was dire. Of fourteen commodities monitored by the United Nations in 1991, only one—iron ore—showed a modest gain in price. Sugar, in perpetual doldrums, fell by a further 27 percent, bauxite and groundnuts by nearly 20. Coffee and cocoa, traditionally two of Africa's most important exports, seem destined to remain on the down escalator: their prices have been in continual decline for five and seven years, respectively.

International officials *must*, in a sense, voice optimism, because the whole point of the structural adjustment programs they have devised is to improve countries' export earnings. Without exports there's no hard currency, and without hard currency there's no debt service. Thus the best efforts of the Fund and the Bank are concentrated on what economists call "tradeables"— anything you can sell abroad—while "non-tradeables" are neglected. Non-

tradeables aren't just whatever local people eat, live in, and so on, but are roads and public transport, sewage and water systems, schools and hospitals, and anything else that, by definition, cannot be uprooted and exchanged for dollars, francs,etc.

The export-led strategy in Africa is, however, a dismal failure. According to a study undertaken by the Transnational Institute (TNI), to be published in 1992, Africa simply cannot hope to emerge from the current crisis so long as it continues to rely on exports of traditional products. The TNI research team looked at all the usual factors determining demand, but also interviewed commodity traders, promising them anonymity. These traders, who are the actual purchasers of African raw materials, paint a gloomy picture indeed. With the single exception of tea, TNI found that the present practices and future intentions of these purchasers are highly unfavorable to Africa.

This is all the more serious because trade is, on the whole, thriving. GATT (the General Agreement on Tariffs and Trade) labeled the 1980s "a dynamic decade for world trade." Perhaps so, but during this dynamic decade, Africa's trade of goods and services regularly declined—the only region in the world where this was the case. Asia's annual trade growth, in contrast, was close to 8 percent.[6] Where would Africa be if we were in a period of world trade recession?

Probably so low as to be statistically insignificant. Already, by 1989, Africa's share of world trade was down to a mere 2½ percent. Roughly 60 percent of even that tiny figure can be ascribed to trade transactions carried out by South Africa and the North African countries, which GATT lumps in the "Africa" totals.[7] This means that the whole of the rest of Africa currently represents no more than 1½ percent of world trade. One can almost hear the sound of SSA sliding off the world map. As for the presumed advantages of cheap African labor, international business seems unimpressed. It is investing little in the continent and is sometimes withdrawing altogether. In 1982, private sources invested a total of $2.2 billion in Africa. Though not a princely sum as these figures go, it turned out to be the best one of the decade and was followed by two years of disinvestment. By the end of the eighties, the annual inflow of investment had crept back up to about a billion dollars, but this was still only 3 percent of total annual private investment in "developing countries." Again, Asia took the lion's share.[8]

Africans themselves seem to have little confidence in the economies of their own countries, structural adjustment or no structural adjustment. Although the Bank and the Fund always claim that their programs will reverse the trend, the OECD (under?) estimates flight capital from the region at some $40 billion. To date, wealthy Africans show no signs of bringing their money home.[9]

Only foreign Non-Governmental Organizations (NGOs) have taken pity on Africa. They have increased their contributions from six hundred million dollars at the outset of the 1980s to a billion dollars at the end of the decade. Their grants now equal total private investment. Today, Africa has to count more on aid and less on trade.

Events in Eastern Europe haven't helped. Although one cannot make the case—at least not yet—that aid to the former Eastern bloc has "diverted" funds from Africa, as many African leaders claim it has, it is true that "Sub-Saharan Africa [is] the only major developing region not to have experienced an increase in overall financial flows," according to the OECD. In 1990, the United States increased its aid to SSA (to $985 million) and so did France (to $4.4 billion), but Germany, Italy, and the United Kingdom all reduced theirs.[10]

In calculations of available aid, people sometimes forget that the former USSR and Eastern Europe used to be donors themselves—modest ones, perhaps, but donors all the same. They gave significant amounts of aid to Ethiopia, Angola, and Mozambique. In a not atypical year before the demise of the communist bloc, Tanzania received $21 million from the USSR while Zambia and Sudan had all their outstanding debt to East bloc countries rescheduled on highly favorable terms.[11]

There could be a hidden advantage for Africa in the liberalization of Eastern Europe if these countries begin to consume significant quantities of African products. When the Berlin Wall was first breached, Western Europeans sat spellbound watching television pictures of East Germans devouring bananas as if they were nectar and ambrosia. But these economies won't be genuinely affluent for several years at best, and, meanwhile, the cheap and highly skilled workers and the astonishing investment opportunities in the former communist countries are likely to make investment in Africa appear even less attractive, if not insane.

Thus one important reason that SSA's debt crisis has dragged on and on is simply that Africa hasn't the economic voice to make itself heard or the commercial clout to make its presence felt. Economically and commercially, it occupies too little space to force the world system to take much notice of its problems. Africa's *potential* is indeed enormous, as many African leaders never tire of pointing out. But the real questions remain: Who needs this potential? For what? And when?

Another answer to the enigma of enduring debt is a political and ideological one. The debtors' collective failure to confront the creditors has given the latter an unprecedented opportunity to carry out the most enormous, ideologically driven economic experiment ever devised in history. On behalf of the creditors, the Terrible Twins of Bretton Woods—the Fund and the Bank—are forcibly applying orthodox, neoclassical, unfettered market economy doctrine to most of the southern hemisphere and to the African continent in particular.

The existence of significant debts, or in the case of small and weak countries, even of insignificant ones, provides outsiders with huge leverage over economic and political management. Governments have no choice but to give up much of their sovereignty to their creditors and their creditors' proxies. These "lenders of last resort" hold the keys of the entire world economic and financial system and are thus in a position to make offers impossible to refuse.

It's not that all the measures the Twins impose are, in and of themselves, harmful. No reasonable person denies that some form of "structural adjustment" is necessary in Africa and elsewhere. Except for the United States, which is privileged to print and mint the world's standard unit of account, countries cannot live beyond their means forever any more than individuals or families can. The problem with adjustment as now practiced, however, is the simultaneous and dogmatic application of an identical model to dozens of countries at once. Every country must devalue its currency (thus largely canceling out the supposed benefits of devaluation, since everyone's goods become cheaper on world markets at once). Everyone must attempt to export the same limited range of raw materials or slightly more sophisticated products to shrinking markets.

No one denies either that the state probably has no place in the direct production of goods and that markets should be allowed to do what they do well. What

they do not do well is protect the weaker and more vulnerable members of society. Adjustment measures theoretically designed to help, say, small farmers and food production in Africa turn out on closer inspection to have the opposite effect. As the International Labor Organization points out,

> [O]ne of the reasons for the growing extent of malnutrition in Sub-Saharan Africa is related to the policy of price liberalization for agricultural commodities . . . an improved pricing policy does not automatically alleviate rural poverty. The majority of farmers in the region cultivate small plots of land and do not produce sufficient marketable surplus to benefit from higher producer prices. In some cases, food-deficit farmers may actually become worse off.[12]

But such measures are part of the economic canon, and damn the consequences. The whole continent has become a laboratory for an experiment *en grandeur nature*.

Although the near-universal imposition of the free-market model is, from the creditors' point of view, a major achievement, politically, too, the debt crisis has its uses. One need not subscribe to conspiracy theory to recognize the political advantages that debt has conferred on the creditors. Although these creditors almost certainly did not plan on these advantages when the debt crisis first began to assume major importance, this does not mean that they are now prepared to throw them away.

Debt is used as a weapon of what I have called elsewhere "Financial Low Intensity Conflict," or FLIC, a new kind of warfare far better adapted to the late twentieth century than traditional forms of warfare like invasion and occupation.[13] These more "primitive" techniques—unless they are exceptionally quick and "clean," as in the Gulf War—are no longer accepted by most Western public opinion.

Nor can "primitive" warfare achieve the aims of today's sophisticated aggressor. What, after all, is the objective of war? As Karl von Clausewitz put it in his classic work *On War*, "War is an act of violence whose goal is to force the adversary to do our will." Debt provides a powerful lever for forcing the third-world "adversary" to submit to the will of the creditors. We have already mentioned several of the advantages they may find in maintaining the debt burden:

They can obtain raw materials on the cheapest possible terms. As noted above, dozens of debtor countries are competing to unload primary commodities. Glut and structurally depressed prices result as the debtors attempt to export even more in the vain hope of at least keeping revenues stable. The system is self-perpetuating. Northern industry benefits, although the savings are rarely passed on to the consumer.

Through debt-for-equity swaps, one can take over assets and infrastructure, although this technique has rarely been applied in Africa because the continent offers few attractive targets for takeover. On the other hand, there are obvious financial advantages in continuing to receive interest payments.

Financial low-intensity conflict is also preferable to more naked intervention because it is so low profile. Most people in the creditor countries know little and care less about third-world debt. It seems boring and gets no television coverage. The connections between debt and marginally "sexier" subjects—epidemics, food crises, and the like—are almost never made.

Debtors dependent on the good will of creditors are also unlikely to challenge the dominant—or new, if you will—world order. The decade of crisis has put a stop to whatever attempts the South once made to obtain collective advantages through the United Nations and other forums. The "Group of 77" leads a nominal existence. Gone are the demands for a New International Economic Order, for binding codes of conduct for transnational corporations, or transfers of technology under favorable terms. The only items on the North-South agenda are privatization, competitiveness, and structural adjustment. This change of vocabulary in the discourse of international relations reflects one of most important and least noticed phenomena of recent years. Debt makes debtors timid and creditors bold.

The not-so-subtle formulae for making the third world shut up and abandon its long-standing demands are accompanied by a de facto assault on the very notion of the state. The ascendancy of the World Bank and the IMF includes a substitution of their own power for the traditional powers of the state. Among the prerogatives now being dictated from outside are

• Control over the currency. Indebted countries must devalue when instructed to do so. This is supposed to make exports more competitive but the effects are often negligible because so many countries are devaluing at once.

• The fixing of macro-economic policy. The framework is set by the structural adjusters; only the details are left to the government.

• The choices of foreign policy. The classic case is the carrot/stick approach applied to Egypt during the Gulf War.

• The "monopoly of legitimate violence." At the Bank-Fund annual meeting in Bangkok in October 1991, the managing director of the Fund, Michel Camdessus, for the first time made clear that his institution would henceforward look much more closely at the military expenditures of its "clients." In his view the cessation of cold war hostilities made such expenditures obsolete. While we may welcome any measures leading to disarmament anywhere, the ability to make war and peace and to defend itself have always been essential to the nature of the state.

The indebted state is thus left with its judicial functions and, above all, the maintenance of *internal* public order. This is one crucial state function the creditors want nothing to do with. Austerity measures—particularly the doubling or tripling of prices for basic staples—have led to riots in over two dozen debtor countries and have caused at least four thousand deaths with many thousands more wounded or detained.[14] Outside managers do not want to be seen as involved, much less as interfering in such circumstances, and leave local police forces to put down rioters. Thus the real causes of the protests may never become visible to the outside world.

Just as the state is undermined, so are those parts of the United Nations system that could be most useful to the debtor countries. The Bank and the Fund have much more influence over, say, health and education than the World Health Organization and UNESCO.

How—if at all—might Africa escape debt bondage and begin to emerge from the depths? Here we enter the realm of utopia. Realpolitik seems to militate almost entirely against an equitable solution for Africa, and only the extremely guarded optimism of the French belief that the worst is not always certain can be of some comfort. Assuming the worst indeed isn't absolutely certain, what should Africa aim for? African leaders should make clear to anyone who will listen that the continent simply cannot survive, much less develop, on the basis of "export-led growth." The needs of Africans must come before those of outsiders, who, in any event, are buying fewer and fewer African products.

The Economic Commission for Africa has published a detailed diagnosis, analysis, and economic plan, which is at once more logical and more humane than the Bank-Fund austerity scenario. Titled The African Alternative Framework to Structural Adjustment Programmes for Socio-Economic Recovery and Transformation, it provides the necessary macro-economic guidelines that we do not intend to summarize here.[15]

It is, however, important to recall that pure and simple debt cancellation could lead to cutting Africa out of the world system altogether, and that African leaders should beware any Greeks bearing gifts of this kind. Debt relief must be linked to a coherent development plan, including much greater popular participation and genuine democracy. Unless African nations, singly or jointly, can propose a plan bold enough to capture the imagination and the attention of the industrialized countries' governments and citizens, they will be forgotten in the New World Order.

Africa's leadership must above all give their creditors credible guarantees that African peoples will be full partners in the enterprise. If the leaders promise that freedom of association and popular organizations will be encouraged and nurtured, that human and democratic rights will be fully respected, then they can propose a solution to debt based on a new social contract. The creditors, who claim that democracy is all-important, would look foolish and hypocritical if they refused to listen.

SSA should propose to stop paying debt service to public creditors (83 percent of the total) in hard currency. They should contract to pay in local currency over a long period and to put their payments into national or regional development funds whose purpose would be threefold.

First, such funds would provide financing to popular organizations for their own projects and for which they were prepared to supply the labor (building schools or clinics, improving village water supply, feeder roads, and so on).

Second, such funds would provide a basis for revolving credit funds granting small loans to farmers and would-be entrepreneurs. An excellent model for this kind of popular credit scheme is the Grameen Bank of Bangladesh, where repayment rates run over 99 percent. Participants are given training in basic numeracy and accounting, and they must also adhere to certain basic development principles. The African traditional "tontine" (common fund) provides a similar model where social pressure to reimburse is strong because the existence of the group depends on it.

Third, such funds would provide wages for workers engaged in environmental rehabilitation and renewal. Ecological destruction in Africa is widespread and growing. So long as people cannot be paid to plant trees, build terraces, shore up dunes, and so forth, the destruction will spread, because people are too busy surviving to be able to work without pay.

For the creditors, such a scheme would be equivalent to debt cancellation, but would keep Africa inside the system. Creditor countries, through their aid programs, should "anchor" such funds with hard currency and should monitor the agreements so that inflation does not en-

sue from injection of too much local currency into the system. "In-kind" payments could be accepted as well. For example, X trees planted, Y schools built, could lead to Z dollars of debt forgiveness.

Such a plan would have many advantages. It would free hard-currency export earnings for more useful purposes than debt service and would simultaneously reduce the pressures to export, thus gradually allowing commodity prices to rise. Since a substantial part of the hard currency thus freed would be used to purchase products from northern industries, creditors would receive much the same income as before. But instead of sterile inflows to governments and multilateral agencies, the money would create some jobs in the North and Africans would get something in exchange for it.

The continent would then participate in the world trading system as a partner, not a beggar. Popular energies for genuine development would be mobilized, making thousands of communities and individuals more self reliant. Environmental ruin could be halted and reversed.

At present, genuine political will to cure the debt cancer is lacking on both sides and imagination is at an even lower ebb. If at least a few African leaders had the courage to declare publicly that they are, given the means, prepared to share full responsibility for development with their own civil societies, we could move into a new phase. If they are not, and we do not, then the 1990s risk being for Africa not just another lost decade, but a deadly one.

NOTES

1. Unless otherwise noted, all debt figures are derived directly or calculated from OECD, *Financing and External Debt of Developing Countries, 1990 Survey*, OECD, Paris 1991. I prefer this source to the World Bank's better known *World Debt Tables* because the OECD relies on creditors' reports, not on the "debtor reporting system" of the Bank. Rightly or wrongly, I believe that creditors are more likely to report accurately how much they are owed and what service payments they have received than debtors are to say how much they owe and what they have paid. The OECD's figures also include short-term debt whereas the Bank's do not; short-term debt usually represents at least 15 percent of a country's total obligations. The OECD and the Bank keep promising to "harmonize" their debt reporting systems and their fig-

ures: for example, the OECD estimates total third-world debt at $1450 billion, the Bank at "only" $1300 billion. This would greatly facilitate the task of the researcher, but so far it hasn't happened.
2. *Africa Recovery*, United Nations, December 1991, p. 3.
3. Percy S. Mistry, *African Debt Revisited: Procrastination or Progress?* Forum on Debt and Development (FONDAD), The Hague, 1991, paragraph 4.10.
4. Mistry, ibid., paragraphs 4.16 and 7.09.
5. World Food Programme *Journal*, No. 19, January–March 1992 and Solagral, *Courrier de la Plante*, No. 4, February 1992, passim.
6. GATT, *International Trade 89–90*, Vol. I, p. 15 and chart 5, p. 19.
7. GATT, ibid. Vol. II, Table III.39 and (calculated from) Table III.43.

8. OECD, op. cit., Table III.6.
9. *Africa Recovery*, op. cit., Note 2, p. 9.
10. Ibid., pp. 8–9.
11. OECD, *Development Cooperation 1987 Report*, Paris 1988, section on CMEA Countries, from p. 153.
12. International Labour Organization, *African Employment Report 1988*, Jobs and Skills program.
13. Susan George, *A Fate Worse Than Debt* (New York: Grove Press, 1988).
14. The Franco-Peruvian researcher Denis Sulmont has made a tally of these riots and their consequences, relying mostly on Western press sources for the numbers of casualties. It is thus entirely possible that these figures are underestimates.
15. ECA, AAF-SAP, /ECA/CM.15/6/Rev.3, United Nations, 1989.

Article 10   *The Humanist*, March/April 1993

Why Africa Stays Poor

And Why It Doesn't Have To

David Aronson

David Aronson grew up in Nigeria and the Ivory Coast and spent a year in Zaire on a fellowship. He is a graduate of Wesleyan University and the University of Florida and is currently working on a book about Zaire.

The images are so familiar that we have become all but inured to them: starving African children outlined against a broad expanse of empty sky; ragged, impover-

ished families huddled together on a stony steppe. They could be Biafrans in 1968, Sahelians in 1973, or Ethiopians in 1985. The most recent pictures are from Somalia, a barren stretch of East African coastland that juts into the Indian Ocean. Once a consolation prize in the Cold War (the real trophy in the Horn was Ethiopia, a richer and more populous nation), Somalia has since disintegrated into fiefdoms of grizzled warlords armed with Kalashnikovs and AK-47s. Now 2,000 Somalis die every day from hunger and its attendant dis-

eases, and reports from elsewhere in Africa suggest that Somalia is only the beginning; according to the United Nations, 20 million to 60 million people are at risk of starvation throughout the eastern and southern parts of the continent.

The news out of Africa has been so grim for so long that the continent seems hopeless, its problems ineradicable. Yet this perception—though it has been reinforced by endless images of famine, disease, and warfare—is both untrue and unnecessarily fatalistic. There are some good reasons, I will argue, for hoping that Africa's next 30 years will be better than the last three decades.

It must first be acknowledged, however, that Africa is in a dismal state. Though statistics cannot convey the miseries of living in a shantytown outside Lagos, or the hardships of wresting a subsistence from the leeched landscape of the Sahel, they can suggest the dimensions of Africa's problems. In the 1980s, per capita African gross national product declined by nearly 25 percent. African farmers produce 20 percent less food today than they did in 1970, and there are twice as many mouths to feed. (At its current rate, Africa's population will reach nearly three billion by the year 2050.) Direct private investment in Africa constitutes 2 percent of the world's total, and experts predict that much of that miniscule figure will be siphoned off as Eastern Europe and Asia rebuild. One French diplomat has written: "Economically speaking, if the entire black Africa, with the exception of South Africa, were to disappear in a flood, the global cataclysm would be approximately nonexistent."

By the late 1980s, most of Africa's states were facing outright financial ruin. The 1990 World Bank annual development report listed 27 African countries among the world's 40 poorest. It seemed to matter very little what path to economic growth these countries were ostensibly pursuing; political scientist Crawford Young argued as much in his book *Ideology and Development in Africa*. "Does ideology matter?" he asked. "My reading of the evidence does not lead to a single unambiguous conclusion." "Socialist" Zambia, Tanzania, and Ghana; or "capitalist" Zaire, Kenya, and Nigeria; the still verdant Congo or the desertified Mali—by 1990, all were mired in economic and political stagnation.

Africa's troubles are not just economic. Civil war and ethnic strife have erupted in over a dozen African countries. Liberia and Somalia have followed Chad and Mozambique into Hobbesian anarchy. Even Kenya and the Ivory Coast—long touted as the two "success" stories of black Africa—have been jolted by a series of anti-government demonstrations. Meanwhile, the AIDS pandemic looms over Africa like a modern-day bubonic plague; the World Health Organization estimates that the disease will kill *20 percent* of Africa's working adults by 1996, including disproportionate numbers of the educated and successful. Perhaps the most sobering aspect of the AIDS crisis is the attitude of resignation that many Africans seem to have taken toward it. In a

continent where 12,000 children die every day of hunger and hunger-related causes, that attitude is depressingly easy to understand: what to us is some horrific medieval plague to them is simply one more deadly infectious disease.

In the West, newspaper editors came up with the term *compassion fatigue* to describe their audiences' reactions to Africa's problems (and, one suspects, to justify their meager coverage of them). A famine in Mozambique, civil war in the Sudan, a slaughter of innocents in Burundi, chaos in Zaire and elsewhere—in the post-Band Aid era, the litany of Africa's woes was buried in the back pages of the press. The impression to be gleaned from this coverage was that Africa's problems were monolithic, insurmountable, and utterly alien—and therefore, presumably, not of pressing concern to us.

Though examples of African success are admittedly few, they provide much-needed evidence that the continent's current woes are not insurmountable. A few African countries made it through the 1980s with their economies and political systems reasonably intact: the Gambia and Botswana are islands of democracy; the Cameroon's economy grew by 8 percent per year through much of the decade; and Mauritius' economy grew by over 5 percent per head. And though Africa's problems seem nearly universal, they are far from monolithic.

Zambia provides an instructive example of the continent's shifting fortunes. In 1964, when Zambia achieved independence under the leadership of Kenneth Kaunda, it was one of Africa's brightest prospects, with a highly developed infrastructure and abundant copper reserves that gave it some of the highest income levels on the continent. Kaunda himself was genial and charming, his political rhetoric an eloquent blend of socialism, pacifism, and pan-Africanism. Zambia became one of the world's largest per capita recipients of foreign aid. However, from 1965 to 1988, Zambia's average annual rate of growth was minus 2.1 percent, and today it is one of the poorest countries in the world—ranked eighteenth from the bottom in per capita GNP.

Belying his oft-proclaimed "humanistic philosophy," Kaunda officially declared Zambia a one-party state in 1972. Under the infamous Emergency Powers Act—a holdover from the colonial era—he regularly had dissenters jailed, beaten, or sent into exile. Kaunda also came to enjoy a life-style that few Zambians could have imagined, playing golf several times

a week on a course adjoining his presidential estate and stocking his private zoo with peacocks and deer.

It was not, however, the gap between his professed idealism and his actual politics that brought Kaunda down —after all, any number of governments have survived telling more risible lies. Nor were Zambia's problems the result of outside pressures, though Zambia respected the African trade embargo against South Africa at considerable cost to its own economy. Rather, Kaunda's downfall was the result of economic policies that eventually boxed him in—policies that left him unable to fulfill the social contract he had established with his urban population.

Kaunda relied upon his nation's copper reserves to create a huge bureaucracy; at one point, nearly 40 percent of Zambia's wage earners received their checks from the government. At the same time, Kaunda poured money into the cities at the expense of the countryside. Schools, medical facilities, and subsidized housing were all available to the urban population; farmers had to make do with rigged, artificially low prices for their produce.

The economic consequences were as devastating as they were predictable. The rural poor moved to urban areas, where they came to rely upon subsidized food as part of the social contract; declining food production forced the government to spend an ever-greater percentage of its earnings on imported grain. Zambia borrowed heavily in the 1970s and early 1980s on the strength of its copper reserves and used the money to support urban consumption, to import food, and to keep afloat its bloated civil service. But as copper reserves dwindled and international commodity prices dipped, the government could no longer afford its part of the social contract. In 1990, rioting erupted in several cities, forcing Kaunda to allow elections. The results were overwhelming: in Kaunda's home seat of Nchanga, the vote went 20,680 for his opponent to only 637 votes for Kaunda himself.

In Zaire, Zambia's giant neighbor to the north, the pro-democracy opponents of President Mobutu Sese Seko have had a far rougher time of it. Mobutu has ruled Zaire since 1965, when he seized power in a CIA-sponsored coup after the conflicts of Zaire's early years. It is frequently claimed that, whatever Mobutu's sins, he at least brought unity to a war-torn country; in fact, the government in place at the time had already made peace with all but one minor rebel group when Mobutu staged his coup. If Mobutu brought unity to Zaire, it is a unity born of Zairians' near-universal hatred of his regime.

Under Mobutu, Zaire's economy fell through the floor. In 1990, per capita annual income was $170; real wages had plummeted to one-tenth their 1960 levels. In Mobutu's 27 years in power, not a single hospital has been built. The road network that linked Zaire together in 1960 has crumbled; the country is larger than the United States east of the Mississippi, yet there are now fewer miles of paved roads in all of Zaire than there are in Toledo, Ohio. Only 3 percent of the central government's budget goes to health and education; 23 percent goes to the military, and 50 percent to lining the pockets of Mobutu and his ruling elite. Mobutu Sese Seko—his adopted name means "the cock that leaves no hen untouched"—has accumulated a dozen French and Belgian chateaux, a Spanish castle, and a 32-bedroom Swiss villa. His net worth is variously estimated at $3 billion to $7 billion. Meanwhile, one out of every two children born in Zaire dies before the age of five.

Mobutu pillaged his country with scarcely a murmur of dissent from his Western sponsors—particularly the United States. There were two reasons for this: first, Zaire is an important supplier of minerals, including industrial diamonds, copper, and cobalt (needed for the alloys used in military aircraft); and second, Mobutu allowed his country to be used as a base for covert American military and diplomatic expeditions into Angola and Chad. His stature as one of America's most important assets in the region was underlined in 1988 when Mobutu became Africa's first head of state to meet with President George Bush.

In 1990 and continuing through most of 1991, pro-democracy agitators put Mobutu on the defensive. Led by the popular long-time dissident Etienne Tshisekedi, they forced him to convene a national conference on the future of the country's leadership. Mobutu did all he could to disrupt the proceedings of the conference; in the ensuing riots, scores of people in various cities were killed by the military. Mobutu himself fled to a luxury yacht cruising the Congo River but retained control of the elite' army troops and his security forces. Meanwhile, Zaire's economy and its political institutions have collapsed.

During the Cold War, diplomats and politicians in the West frequently justified their support for Mobutu by arguing that the alternative was a return to the chaos of Zaire's early years. This argument is founded, as I've indicated, on a willful

misreading of history; it ignores the fact that the situation in Zaire was well past its crisis point when Mobutu took power, and it also implies that Western support for Mobutu was motivated, at least in part, by a humanitarian concern for Zairians. "We care," the diplomats seemed to be saying, "that Zairians not be forced to suffer again the internecine warfare that accompanied the birth of their nation." But since the confrontation between the national conference and Mobutu reached a stalemate, the West has done almost nothing to help resolve the situation; in the absence of Cold War exigencies, we seem to have lost interest in the country. What remains, as political scientist Rene Lemarchand has written, "is a country teetering on the brink of chaos—a devastated economy, an empty treasury, a peasant sector reduced to subsistence agriculture, an urban population at the edge of starvation, and hundreds of thousands of unemployed youth for whom life has nothing to offer." For years, we heard from our politicians and diplomats that it was "Mobutu or chaos." Now it is both.

Finally, there is Uganda, once known as the "pearl" of East Africa. No longer. The rolling green hills and fertile soil that so pleased the colonists are still there, but since the 1971 coup that brought Idi Amin to power the country has lurched from one disaster to the next, bloodier one. Consider: there are half a million internally displaced people and over a quarter-million foreign refugees living in Uganda; it is probably the one country most hard-hit by AIDS in the world; its economy is in a shambles, with tea and other agricultural exports down to one-fifth or one-tenth of 1970 levels; and it has suffered from more or less continuous political unrest and warfare. Even by African standards, Uganda is a basket case.

The reasons for this startling decline are complicated. Before 1963, Uganda boasted a flourishing economy, a well-trained populace, extraordinarily fertile land, and a highly developed infrastructure. Makerere University was one of the best in Africa, and Kampala was among Africa's most cosmopolitan cities. For several years after its independence, Uganda seemed poised to fulfill the immense potential that was perceived for it. The economy flourished under the moderate leadership of Prime Minister Milton Obote, and with the *kabaka*, or king, of Buganda assuming the largely ceremonial role of president, the political situation seemed remarkably stable.

In fact, however, Uganda was built on the most fractured of foundations.

Buganda was only one (albeit the principal one) of several traditional kingdoms the British had lumped together into one protectorate; and with independence came not only heightened ethnic rivalries but also religious, regional, and ideological tensions. To be sure, the challenges to nation-building represented by these divisions were to be found throughout the continent: the jigsaw puzzle of national boundaries the colonial powers left behind bore little relationship to pre-existing ethnic or linguistic identities. But in Uganda, these divisions were never overcome. No central authority ever managed to impose a national identity on the disparate groups competing for power, and the result was that no one group or party was ever seen as legitimate. The tensions within the polity could be submerged, but they could never be resolved.

Uganda's political history probably reached its nadir during the eight-year reign of Idi Amin, the notoriously brutal army sergeant turned international buffoon. But Uganda's problems neither began nor ended with Amin. Obote, Uganda's first prime minister, had spent most of his time in office trying to contain the forces that were tearing the country apart. In 1966, for example, he ousted the *kabaka* under pressure from radical youth groups in the capital; to keep the army happy, he tripled its share of the nation's budget. That did not prevent factions from developing within it, and eventually one of them—led by Amin—secured the patronage of Great Britain and Israel, who were dissatisfied with Obote's growing radicalism.

Amin's 1971 coup brought an end to Uganda's economic growth. During his bloody rule, coffee, tea, and cotton production fell to one-third their earlier levels, and industrial performance dropped 85 percent. Amin was finally overthrown in 1979, after an attempted invasion of Tanzania turned into a rout of the Ugandan army by the better-trained, better-led Tanzanian troops. But a succession of leaders proved unable to stop the anarchy that had characterized Amin's final years, and the economy continued to sputter. Under Uganda's current leader, Yoweri Museveni, there has been a modest economic recovery, and aid from the major donor nations has also begun to trickle in. But though a semblance of order prevails, it seems only a matter of time before the next political tremors erupt.

Are there any observations to be made, any lessons to be distilled, from the divergent experiences of these three countries? The first is that it pays not to live near one of Africa's hot spots. Zambia respected the boycott against South Africa at enormous cost to its own economy. Other countries, particularly Mozambique and Angola, endured South African-sponsored terrorism and civil war that effectively blocked any possibility of their own development. And though guerrilla movements in these countries have now acquired a momentum of their own, support from the apartheid regime was critical in launching them. Much the same could be said of the Libyans in Chad and the Ethiopians in Djibouti.

The second observation to be made is that it was the misfortune of certain African nations to come of age during the intellectual heyday of a certain kind of nondemocratic socialism. It is true that, with few exceptions, Soviet and Chinese ties to Africa were always considerably weaker than the cold warriors would have had us believe. Thus, Herman Cohen, the outgoing American Assistant Secretary of State for African Affairs, has now blamed *European left-wingers* for implementing in Africa "the biggest socialist fantasies that they weren't able to implement in their own countries." But Cohen's is a simplistic rendering of history—a piece of Reaganite revisionism. African countries like Ghana, Tanzania, and Zambia "went" socialist not from any affection for the leaden Stalinists (Soviet advisers were despised wherever they went), nor from European left-wingers' denunciations of their own bourgeoisie (we should be so lucky, thought the Africans), but for complex reasons of their own. Socialism represented the opposite of capitalism, the system of Africa's colonizers. It offered a blueprint for social and political mobilization that seemed more coherent and plausible to some African leaders, and, with its hazy vision of a utopian future, it fed into a hallowed conception of Africa's past—a vision of a prelapsarian (read: precolonial) Eden whose traditions contained all the promises of Western political thought but none of its painful contradictions.

Nothing, alas, could have been more impractical for these fledgling nations. To work at all, socialism requires an educated bureaucracy and a vigorous, disciplined central government—precisely the conditions that did not exist in post-colonial Africa. After 30 years, the verdict is unequivocal: capitalism's record is mixed, but socialism—at least of the sort practiced by Kaunda in Zambia, Nyerere in Tanzania, or Nkrumah in Ghana—has been an utter failure.

The third observation to be made is that it was disastrous for Africa to come of age during the Cold War. Both the United States and the Soviet Union helped to install and maintain tyrants whose records are a blot upon the human race. America's support for Mobutu in Zaire and the Soviets' for Mengistu in Ethiopia may (or may not) have been justified by the superpowers' national-security needs, but the price that ordinary Zairians and Ethiopians paid for that security lies beneath the gravestones of countless children. It is important to be blunt about this: we have a moral duty to acknowledge how much of our own putative security has been purchased with the blood of others.

A fourth observation concerns the extent of corruption in Africa. From the governor who pockets half the state's budget for public works to the nurse at the local clinic who demands a bribe before changing a bandage, corruption is so deeply entrenched and so endemic that it requires an explanation. Peter Wanyande, a Kenyan political scientist at Kenyatta University in Nairobi, suggests that corruption flourishes in Africa in part because there are few institutions aside from the state through which the gifted and the capable can rise. But in contrast to the tribe or the extended family, the state remains an abstraction, commanding neither loyalty nor affection. The dispensation of favors and the profitable manipulation of alliances thus become the *modus vivendi* for Africans on the make. In Nigeria, in Zaire, and increasingly in Kenya, corruption is not so much the grease that keeps the wheel turning as it is the wheel itself.

This is not to justify the flagrant abuses of a Mobutu but, rather, to put them into context. The powerful in Africa steal because they can; the poor steal to survive. Corruption in Africa, then, was born of the structural weaknesses of African political and civil society, and it is now a cause as well as a consequence of African poverty.

A fifth observation is that, like the former Yugoslavia, many African countries are still wrestling with the demon of tribalism (a polluted term, no doubt, but more accurate than its euphemisms). Tribal conflicts simmer in Uganda, Rwanda, Burundi, Kenya, and Zaire, and they have boiled over in Chad and the Sudan. Tribalism hurts countries not only when blood is spilt; the energy expended on keeping the peace between rival ethnic groups represents a considerable distraction from the business of economic, political, and cultural development.

The culminating lesson is that, in Africa as elsewhere, the prerogatives of history are impossible to deny. Lumped arbitrarily into geographic units at the Berlin Conference of 1885 and launched toward independence 80 years later in entities that corresponded in no way to African realities or experience, the continent has limped behind the rest of the world—not because Africans are stupid or lazy or incapable of collective action, but because they are caught in structures that negate their strengths and frustrate their efforts. Africans remain poor because the states in which they live are artificial constructs, unmoored to the societies or people they govern, largely free of any constraint from civil institutions, and subject all too often to fracture along the substantive divisions of class, religion, and ethnicity.

Are there any grounds for hope, any reasons to believe, that Africa will do better in its next 30 years than it has in the last three decades? Certainly, there has been a veritable sea-change in African attitudes toward development. Nigerian statesman Olusagen Obasanjo is among the most eloquent:

I believe that for us in Africa, our salvation lies in our own hands and nowhere else. Only we can be the architects of our future; as we have been the architects of our misfortune by and large for the past quarter of a century.

Then, too some countries—most notably Ghana—have embarked on ambitious economic restructuring programs to eliminate waste, corruption, and mismanagement and to encourage private industry. The World Bank has been the driving force behind much of this movement, and there is, naturally, considerable debate about how fair these programs are and whether or not they will work. To a certain extent, the programs represent recolonization of Africa by Western technocrats. This is not necessarily bad, some argue: at the helms of central banks, it is better to have the gnomes of Zurich than the kleptocrats of Kinshasa. But these programs also represent the third or fourth generation of development initiatives sponsored by the World Bank, and they share with the Bank's earlier initiatives a refusal to acknowledge the political environments in which they operate. In fact, economic policies prescribed with little regard for such realities may exacerbate—as they have in the past—both the political and the economic problems confronting Africans. This is an age-old criticism of the Bank, but one that, despite an abundance of evidence, it seems constitutionally incapable of attending. The Bank's charter, argue its defenders, is properly economic and deliberately apolitical. Zairians—who have seen the results of such "aid" in the Mercedes-Benzes driven by the political elite through that country's corroded streets—might be excused for wondering whether the intention has not been improperly political and deliberately uneconomic. Their president could, after all, pay off the country's entire national debt.

The end of the Cold War ought to be a tremendous spur to African political and economic development; the West no longer needs to support dictators simply because they happen to be *our* dictators. Smith Hempstone, the American ambassador to Kenya and a conservative of long standing, has not hesitated to agitate on behalf of Kenya's fledgling democrats, even though he has irked Kenyan President Daniel arap Moi considerably in doing so. Significantly, in the past three years, a half-dozen African countries have followed Eastern Europe into democracy, and another dozen or so are struggling to achieve it. It is no exaggeration to say that the democracy movement represents the most important political shift in Africa since independence. It is clear, moreover, that the democracy movement has far deeper roots than many observers could have imagined. "Throughout the continent, independent political and social forces have emerged to challenge moribund, authoritarian patrimonial regimes of many varieties," says Peter Lewis. "The result has been a succession of movements pressing for fundamental political change." At every level of government, indigenous institutions are evolving as a response to popular demands. The shape and future direction of these institutions are still difficult to determine; all that can now be said is that they belong to Africa in a way that the pre-fab parliaments and constitutions left behind by the colonialists never did. Kwame Nkrumah's famous injunction—"Seek ye first the political kingdom"—is at last being realized.

The news out of Africa has been grim for so long that one hesitates to conclude on a dispiriting note. However, the battle between democratic and despotic governments in Africa is by no means won: in Togo, for example, the former dictator is back on his throne, and in Kenya, President Daniel arap Moi seems to have survived the recent election. Moreover, the United States continues to send the bulk of its economic assistance to tyrannical regimes. Randall Robinson, executive director of Trans-Africa, points out that, in the last fiscal year, the United States gave $130 million to Kenya, Zaire, and Malawi—"states where there is massive corruption, broad repression, and little if any appreciation of democratic values." On the other hand, countries like Benin, Botswana, and Namibia, which are now fully democratic, received just $30 million. (Namibia, with the most liberal and democratic constitution on the continent, received $500,000.)

What is to be done? Let me conclude by listing several things the West can and should be doing to help Africa. I use the word *should* advisedly—not to insist on Western culpability but, rather, on Western responsibility, which should derive from a decent regard for humankind.

First, Western nations—particularly the United States—can send more aid more selectively. The U.S. budget for all of sub-Saharan Africa is about $800 million, roughly one-third of what we give to better-off (but more "strategic") countries such as Egypt or Pakistan. We ought, furthermore, to be giving our aid to those countries which are making genuine political and economic reforms; whatever else aid does, it bestows official approval on a Third World country's government. There's no longer any reason (if there ever was) for the United States to support tyrants.

The largest incentive the West can offer Africa's reformers is the prospect of debt relief. Compared to Latin America's debt burden, Africa's has been ignored. The numbers involved are much smaller and don't pose a threat to the world banking system; yet, according to the *Economist*, Africa's burden is 50 percent greater as a percentage of gross domestic product than Latin America's, and the continent remains "profoundly, unsustainably indebted." Swapping debt for political and economic reform is one of the best and least costly ways for the West to help out.

Second, there should be more contact between Africa and the West: more student exchanges, more artistic conferences, more sister-cities and business conventions, and more professional colloquia. Ties between newspapers, universities, and community or religious groups should be strengthened. The West can and must find a way to encourage the institutions of African civil society; their continuing development represents the best hope for the continent's future.

Third, the early-warning system that is supposed to signal the potential for famine in Africa needs to be strengthened. Cobbled together by the United Nations after the Sahelian famine of the mid-1970s, it has not been an effective agency; it predicted major famine-related deaths in 1991, and when these failed to materialize, it lost much of its credibility. It needs a better intelligence network on the ground and more effective links to the wider community of Africanist scholars, diplomats, and journalists.

Fourth, U.N. troops ought to be empowered as a peace-making force, not just as peace-keepers. As in the case of Somalia and Yugoslavia, difficult decisions about the conflicting claims of various groups and issues of international law and human rights will need to be addressed. At what point does a regime so violate the accepted standards of international law that it forfeits its claims to sovereignty? How feasible or desirable is direct intervention in another country's affairs? What price is the West willing to pay to save the innocent victims of a murderous regime? My bias here is plain.

Finally, the press could do a far better job than it has covering African issues. It is one of the sadder ironies of our time that famines in Africa only make headlines when thousands have already died. Unlike earthquakes or typhoons, famines can be spotted months and even years in advance—when the rains fail, crops wither, and prices for grain shoot up. All these things take time and can be monitored. Given their pervasive influence, the media have a moral responsibility to alert the world to the potential of famine and to agitate aggressively, if need be, to ensure that the matter is attended to before people die.

Beyond the issue of famine, however, is the more mundane issue of poverty. In its quiet way, poverty—of the day-to-day sort that millions of Africans are mired in—is more destructive than the occasional spectacular famine. Every day, some 12,000 children in Africa die because their parents are too poor to buy them the food or medicine they require. Though the press duly takes note of Africa's rebellions, civil wars, coups d'etats, and corruption, the biggest story in Africa—the quiet struggle of ordinary people to survive against grim odds—has hardly been told at all. The media should find a way to bring this story home. In its global ramifications, the gap between the rich and the poor countries of the world is certainly one of the most important stories of our time—and yet, it is being largely ignored.

Article 11   *Finance & Development*, December 1992

The CFA Franc: Zone of Fragile Stability in Africa

The CFA franc zone is a currency union linked to the French franc. If viewed as a monetary union alone, it does not appear to be close to an optimal currency area. When viewed as part of a wider franc zone, however, its viability and its benefits become clearer.

James M. Boughton

James M. Boughton, a US citizen, is the IMF Historian in the Secretary's Department. He was previously an Advisor in the Research Department and holds a PhD from Duke University.

Most of the more than 50 countries in Africa are poor, and all have faced enormous challenges during the past decade. Their economic performance and policies have nevertheless been quite diverse. Output per capita in 1989 ranged from less than $100 in Mozambique to more than $5,300 in Libya. The annual inflation rate for the 1980s ranged from negative 1 percent in Chad to 108 percent in Uganda. The percentage of output derived from manufacturing in 1989 ranged from 4 percent in Tanzania to 25 percent in Zimbabwe. Total external debt at the end of 1989 ranged from the equivalent of seven months' export receipts in Mauritius to 270 months in Somalia. And the average annual rate of change in the exchange rate against the SDR for the 1980s ranged from nearly 135 percent depreciation in Uganda to 1.7 percent appreciation in Rwanda.

This last statistic—the behavior of the exchange rate—may be the most esoteric, but it illustrates a key difference in the way countries have responded to the difficulties of the past decade. The exchange rate plays two very important but conflicting roles in economic policy. It can serve as an anchor for financial stability: If a country can run financial policies so as to be consistent with exchange rates that are stable against key currencies, then that country will gain credibility and will promote confidence in its economy. However, the exchange rate is also an instrument of external adjustment. If a country that has allowed wages and prices to get too high can reduce their real value through exchange rate depreciation, then that country will gain international competitiveness. Because these linkages are complex and uncertain, and because financial stability and competitiveness are both prerequisites for sustainable real economic growth, there is no single "right" approach to exchange rate policy.

Roughly two thirds of all developing countries in the world have chosen to favor stability over flexibility by pegging their exchange rates to a single currency or to a basket of currencies, or (in a few cases) by intervening in exchange markets so as to limit flexibility against a currency. Africa is a microcosm of that choice: 34 out of the 50 countries for which data are available have some sort of pegging arrangement. Two peg to the South African rand, five to the US dollar, 13 to the SDR or other basket, and 14 to the French franc. It is this last phenomenon that is of interest here: Does it make sense today for a large and diverse group of African countries to peg firmly to a single European currency, or is that arrangement a historical accident that could unduly constrain economic policy?

What Is The CFA Franc Zone?

The CFA franc zone is an outgrowth of the economic and financial arrangements under which France administered its colonies. Prior to World War II, French colonies typically maintained their own currencies at parities that were firmly linked to the French franc. After the war, the system was simplified by consolidating the currencies of colonies in the Pacific region into a single currency known as the CFP franc ("le franc des Colonies Françaises du Pacifique") and all others (most of which were in Africa) into CFA francs ("le franc des Colonies Françaises d'Afrique"). In each case, the currencies were fully convertible into French francs at the fixed parity. Each participating central bank established an "operations account" at the French Treasury, into which it deposited most of its foreign exchange. Convertibility was guaranteed through rules permitting overdrafts on these accounts, if necessary. This system permitted the free mobility of capital throughout the zone, and it encouraged the growth of international trade by instituting common trade and financial policies. These principles continue to govern the CFA franc zone.

The most remarkable feature of the CFA franc zone is that the exchange rate against the French franc has not changed for more than 40 years. There was some initial instability immediately after the war, and the rate was then set at 0.5 CFA franc per French franc. In 1958, France effected a currency reform and issued new francs at the rate of 1 per 100 old francs; the value of the CFA franc was left unchanged, so the exchange rate became 50 CFA francs per new French franc, where it remains as of 1992.

There have been some important institutional changes over the years, however, reflecting the political and economic turbulence that this region of the world has experienced. First, the number of member countries has fluctuated. In the first 30 years, several countries—mostly those that are not contiguous to the others—such as Madagascar and Djibouti—left the zone to establish independent currencies or to adopt the French franc. In the 1980s, however, the trend in membership was reversed, as Mali rejoined in 1984 after an absence of 22 years, and Equatorial Guinea in 1985 became the first member country without colonial (or even close economic) ties to France. Since then, there have been 13 member countries in the zone, forming a contiguous group across the equatorial region of west and central Africa. (The 14th African country pegged to the French franc is the Comoros, which has an independent currency fixed at the same parity as the CFA franc; elsewhere, French Polynesia, New Caledonia, and Wallis and Futuna Islands use the CFP franc, with a different fixed parity.)

A second principal change is that the system has become less dependent on France. The member countries gradually achieved independence in the late 1960s and early 1950s, and major "Africanization" reforms were implemented in 1974. These reforms strengthened the control of the member countries over their central banks, while retaining a participatory role for central bank directors appointed by France. Reflecting these changes, the concept of the CFA franc as a colonial currency was abandoned.

Today there are two separate currencies, both of which are known as the CFA franc, but whose full names have changed. The seven member countries in west Africa—Benin, Burkina Faso, Côte d'Ivoire, Mali, Niger, Senegal, and Togo—use currencies known as the "franc de la Communauté financière d'Afrique." They have formed a regional association, the West African Monetary Union (WAMU), and have vested authority to conduct monetary policy in a common central bank, the Banque Centrale des Etats de l'Afrique de l'Ouest (BCEAO). The six members in central Africa—Cameroon, the Central African Republic, Chad, the Congo, Equatorial Guinea, and Gabon—use the "franc de la Coopération financière en Afrique centrale," and have their own central bank, the Banque des Etats de l'Afrique Centrale (BEAC).

Along with these political and institutional changes has come an increasing degree of economic diversification. From the mid-1960s to the mid-1980s, the portion of the zone's international trade that was with France dropped

from nearly 50 percent to around 30 percent, with other European countries taking up much of the difference. Over the same two decades, the share of food products and agricultural materials in the zone's exports dropped from 75 percent to less than 50 percent, with petroleum and other mineral products taking up the difference. Nine different products constitute the dominant export commodity for the 13 countries. For seven countries, minerals are the largest export, and for five others, agricultural materials (cotton and timber). For only two countries were food products the dominant export in the mid-1980s: cocoa from Côte d'Ivoire and fish from Senegal. With this diversity have come disparities in per capita output, ranging from less than $200 a year in cotton-producing Chad to more than $3,000 in petroleum-rich Gabon.

There are three basic mechanisms for controlling monetary growth in the CFA franc zone. First, interest is charged on overdrafts in the operations accounts (and interest is paid on credit balances). Second, when the operations account balances fall below specified target levels, the central bank concerned must implement policies restricting credit expansion. These restrictions focus on raising the cost of rediscounting paper with the central bank and restricting access to rediscount facilities; this emphasis on rediscounting reflects both the limited development of domestic financial markets and the absence of bank reserve requirements. In order to implement the credit restriction rules, each central bank's operations account balance is nationally allocated among the member countries, with a residual allocated to the bank itself. Third, credit from the central banks to the public sector of each country is limited to a maximum of 20 percent of the previous year's fiscal revenue. These rules do not dictate a strict ceiling on total domestic credit growth, but they do impose a strong measure of financial discipline.

How Well Does The System Work?

The effectiveness of the zone's arrangements has been subjected to much scrutiny in the past few years, owing to the severe and prolonged deterioration in economic performance since the mid-1980s. The currency has on occasion come under speculative attack in the form of capital flight, in response to rumors of impending devaluation. The countries concerned have responded, most recently in meetings at both ministerial and head-of-state level during the summer of 1992, by seeking to strengthen rather than abandon the arrangements. Notable proposals to emerge from those meetings include plans to establish intergovernmental councils for coordination of monetary, fiscal, and related macroeconomic policies and to promote real (in addition to monetary) integration of the region. Such efforts will succeed in the long run only if the zone itself is a sensible response to economic condition.

One way of analyzing the effectiveness of the CFA franc zone is to ask how well it fits the usual criteria for a successful currency union. These criteria include factors such as the degree of flexibility of wages and prices; the degree of labor mobility; the similarity between countries in the effects from external disturbances; and the degree of intraregional trade. There are positive aspects on each front, but on none of these economic grounds would the zone appear to be a natural candidate for a common currency area.

Downward flexibility of prices and wages is inherently limited in all parts of the world economy. If prices and wages were highly flexible, the optimum arrangement would be to promote financial stability and the growth of international trade by fixing exchange rates, leaving any required adjustment to individual markets. Studies of CFA franc countries have shown some evidence of downward flexibility of real wages during inflationary periods, but there have been notable examples of failed attempts to cut nominal wages—especially in the public sector—during deflationary periods. In addition, when coffee prices plummeted by half in the mid-1980s, the prices paid to coffee growers held firm throughout the zone.

Labor mobility between countries is significant in certain parts of the region. One recent study estimated that in 1975, 25 percent of employed people in Côte d'Ivoire were foreign nationals, and that labor migration was correlated with economic conditions. This type of migration enables unemployed workers in one country to move to areas where jobs are relatively plentiful; in the absence of such migration, exchange rate changes might provide an alternative means of restoring equilibrium between labor markets. The potential for migration to serve as a flexible response to shifts in economic conditions is limited, however, by the vast distances between cities, the limited transportation network, and restrictive policies in some member countries.

The absence of country-specific shocks would be another consideration that could limit the need for exchange-rate adjustment. Unfortunately, this is one area where the CFA franc zone was hit hard in the 1980s. The major adverse shock in this period was a sharp deterioration in the terms of trade, in the form of a large decline in world market prices of many of the commodities exported by these countries. But the declines were far from uniform. From 1980 to 1990, prices of palm oil, cocoa beans, and uranium fell by 50 percent or more; prices of petroleum, fish meal, phosphate rock, cotton, and beef dropped by 20 percent or less; and timber prices rose slightly. As noted earlier, the structure of exports differs greatly between countries across the zone; these diverse price movements thus have translated into sizable differences in terms-of-trade shifts.

Finally, intraregional trade is quite limited. In contrast, the high degree of intraregional trade in Europe is one of the key arguments cited by advocates of European monetary union: Use of a common currency reduces the cost of making transactions within the union, and the higher the portion of covered trade, the greater the benefit. For example, 57 percent of France's international trade was with other members of the European Community in 1985–87. In the CFA franc zone, just 7.5 percent of trade was within the region during the same period. This very low portion results from the same factors that limit labor mobility, plus the limited markets for many products in low-income countries.

The Zone As A Monetary Standard

Another perspective on the effectiveness of the zone is whether it makes sense as a monetary standard. An important feature of the CFA franc zone is that it combines the use of a common currency by a group of countries with a firm peg against an outside anchor currency, with the active cooperation of the anchor country. This feature conveys potential benefits, via the establishment of a strong independent central bank, the imposition of fiscal discipline, and the maintenance of currency convertibility—as well as potential costs, via the loss of the exchange rate as an adjustment instrument. On balance, the net benefits on this perspective are rather more favorable.

Perhaps the key to the remarkable persistence of the zone is the benefit from the financial discipline that it imposes and the credibility that it conveys to financial policies. For the 1980s as a whole, all of the CFA franc countries recorded inflation rates that were close to or below France's inflation rate, in sharp contrast to the highly inflationary experiences of many of the other countries in the region. The unweighted average for inflation in consumer prices in the zone was 4.2 percent (1980–89), compared with 6.5 percent in France. More important, this price stability was achieved at no apparent cost in long-term growth: The mean annual growth in real output was around 2.5 percent, compared with 2 percent in France and somewhat less than 2 percent in neighboring African countries. These simple cross-country comparisons do not imply that growth would have been lower under a more flexible exchange rate regime, but they do indicate that the member countries have done at least as well as their neighbors (all of whom have had somewhat more flexible regimes).

A more direct way of judging the effectiveness of the zone's hard-currency arrangements is to examine the strength and stability of international competitiveness. Even though inflation has been relatively low, member countries could have lost competitiveness through changes in exchange rates between other countries or through terms-of-trade shocks. In this regard, attention has focused on a few notable cases of appreciation of real effective exchange rates: 36 percent appreciation in Côte d'Ivoire from 1985 to 1988, and the same magnitude in Cameroon from 1982 to 1987. These movements, however, have tended to be reversed over time, and there has been no systematic tendency toward appreciation. Real effective exchange rate indexes are published in the IMF's *International Financial Statistics* for five of the CFA franc countries. From 1980 to 1990, only Cameroon showed a net appreciation (just over 10 percent); Togo depreciated by more than 20 percent, Gabon by 10 percent, and Côte d'Ivoire and the Central African Republic by 3 to 4 percent.

These data do not imply an absence of competitive problems. Owing to the deterioration in the terms of trade, the real exchange rate indexes should have declined just to maintain the initial position in external trade, and the magnitude of the external deficit that has resulted is indicative of serious structural imbalances. Like many other developing countries in the 1980s, most members of the zone have experienced rising current account deficits, declining output, depleted net foreign assets, and recourse to rescheduling agreements on external indebtedness. But to the extent that these problems resulted from external traumas rather than from financial mismanagement, the ability of exchange rate flexibility or other shifts in macroeconomic policies to deal with them is inherently limited.

In The Final Analysis . . .

Making the case for the CFA franc zone depends on viewing it in broad terms: as a combination of a currency union and a monetary standard. The countries in the zone are economically diverse, and there is relatively little trade among them. They do, however, have very strong trading links with Western Europe. Consequently, the zone has become part of a wide area of currency stability comprising the CFA franc countries, France, and other western European countries. Fully 70 percent of the trade of the CFA franc countries is conducted within this broad zone. By persisting with the currency union in the face of the shocks of the past decade, these countries have traded away the exchange rate as an instrument for external adjustment and in some cases have been forced to resort to protectionism and other price-distorting measures. Overall, however, they have gained a measure of financial stability that has proved elusive elsewhere in the region. In addition, they have maintained and even strengthened their trade and financial linkages with Europe. Whether this trade-off will reap dividends in the long run is one of the key questions facing Africa in the 1990s.

For a more detailed study, see "The CFA Franc Zone: Currency Union and Monetary Standard," by James M. Boughton, IMF Working Paper (WP/91/133), available from the author.

Article 12   *Dissent*, Summer 1992

The African Woman Today

Ama Ata Aidoo

Ama Ata Aidoo, former minister of education of Ghana, is one of Africa's leading writers.

"In most countries of Africa whole sectors of the economy, such as internal trade, agriculture, agro-business and health care, are in the hands of women."

West Africa (September 9–15, 1991)

It might not be fair to blame as well-intentioned an event as Bob Geldof's Band Aid,[1] which was staged to raise awareness of the plight of drought victims in Ethiopia, and even raise funds for them. But there is no doubt that since then the image of the African woman in the mind of the world has been set. She is breeding too many children she cannot take care of, and for whom she should not expect other people to pick up the tab. She is hungry, and so are her children. In fact, it has become a cliché of Western photojournalism that the African woman is old beyond her years; she is half-naked; her drooped and withered breasts are well exposed; there are flies buzzing around the faces of her children; and she has a permanent begging bowl in her hand.

This is a sorry pass the daughters of the continent have come to—especially when we remember that they are descended from some of the bravest, most independent and innovative women this world has ever known. We speak of the Lady Tiy of Nubia (ca. 1415–1340 B.C.E.),

the wife of Amenhotep III and the mother of Akhenaton and Tutankhamen, who is credited with, among other achievements, leading the women of her court to discover make-up and other beauty-enhancing processes. Her daughter-in-law was the incomparable Nefertiti, a black beauty whose complexion was nowhere near the alabaster she is now willfully painted with. Again from the pharonic era, we evoke Cleopatra, about whom "more nonsense has been written . . . than about any African queen . . . mainly because of many writers' desire to paint her white. She was not a white woman. She was not a Greek . . ." says John Henrik Clarke with the impatience of painstaking scholarship.[2] According to C. W. King, of Julius Caesar, Mark Antony, and Cleopatra, the last was "the most captivating, the most learned, and the most witty." Among the many languages she spoke fluently were "Greek, Egyptian, Latin, Ethiopian, and Syrian." Yet Shakespeare, heralding Western racism, could only dismiss Cleopatra as a "strumpet."[3]

COLLISIONS

Modern Africa came into collision with Europe with the journey of Vasco da Gama from Portugal southward to find Asia. He passed what became known to the West as the Gold Coast (Ghana) in 1492, and the Cape of Good Hope in 1496. Since then Africa has never known peace. First there was the slave trade. Then the end of the slave trade was celebrated with the conquest and colonization of Africa in the mid-nineteenth century. From then on, various Western groups considered Africa their happiest hunting ground. The energies of the people, the wealth on and in the land, everything that could be taken was taken by European powers, with complete abandon. The people resisted—to the best of their abilities. But it could not have been an even match, since one side fought with spears or bows and arrows, while the other used guns.

Less known is that in response to Europe's insistence on conquering the continent, Africa over five centuries produced countless women soldiers and military strategists, many of whom died in the struggles. A famous example was Nzingha (1582–1663), who tried to prevent the Portuguese from overrunning Angola. She died without achieving her objective, but only after showing them what she was made of. For their part, the Portuguese demonstrated that they had not come to Africa on a mission of chivalry. They fought Nzingha with uncompromising viciousness. When she suffered serious setbacks in 1645–1646, they captured her younger sister Fungi, beheaded her, and threw her body into the river.

In fact, in precolonial times, fighting women were part of most African armies, a well-known example being the all-female battalions of Dahomey (ancient Benin, early nineteenth century), who sought to protect their empire against invaders and internal treachery.

The Nzingha/Portuguese pattern was to be repeated in several areas of the continent over the next centuries. Queen after queen rose against the invaders. In the last years of the nineteenth and early twentieth centuries, Yaa Asantewaa, an Asante (Ashanti, Ghana) queen led an insurrection against the British. Although her armies were defeated, "it is safe to say

that she helped to create part of the theoretical basis for the political emergence of modern Africa."

True, all these women were reigning monarchs who found it relatively easy to organize armies against foreign occupation. But history is also replete with accounts of insurgencies organized by women from nonmonarchical traditions. One example is the women of Aba in Eastern Nigeria, who in the 1920s so successfully harassed the British that the colonial administration had to move its headquarters from Calabar to Lagos. Around the same time in Rhodesia (Zimbabwe), Mbuya Nehanda (Nyakasikana) was accused of fomenting an insurgency against the British. In the end, the conquerors decided that the only way to get rid of this frail woman was to hang her. And they did.

STRUGGLES FOR INDEPENDENCE

After the Second World War, many women stayed in the forefront of the agitation for independence. Some, like General Muthoni (of the Mau Mau Rebellion) became guerrilla leaders whom the enemy feared even more than their male counterparts. Others, like Mrs. Ransome-Kuti of Western Nigeria, were mainly nationalists of bourgeois and petit-bourgeois backgrounds. But then, so were the majority of the men who were their companions in such struggles.

Today, we know that the story of South Africa's fight against the institutionalized horrors of conquest would be different if women had not been prepared to get actively involved. And they paid the price. They were killed, maimed, incarcerated, and exiled. For instance, Sibongile Mkhabela was a student leader at the time of the Soweto riots. The only woman charged in the June 7th (1978) trials, she was jailed for three years and then banned after serving the sentence. Countless others like Winnie Mandela, Albertina Sisulu, and Zodwa Sobukwe survived the hounding of their men, only later to show an awesome readiness to assume leadership with all the sacrifices such decisions entailed.

Given such a heroic tradition, it is no wonder that some of us regard the docile mendicant African woman of today as a media creation. But if she does exist, she is a result of the traumas of the last five hundred years' encounter with the West, the last one hundred years of colonial repression, the current neocolonial disillusionment, and of a natural environment that is now behaving like an implacable enemy.

In 1992, the African woman must cope with a "structural adjustment program" imposed by the International Monetary Fund (IMF) and the World Bank that is removing subsidies from her children's education, from health care, from food. Transportation to and from vital areas of her life have either broken down or never existed.

In 1992, there is a drought and the world is phenomenally hot. And the African woman has already given up on the season's crops. She is now wondering whether there will be enough water to last her and her children through this year for drinking, for cooking nonexistent food, and to keep the body minimally clean.

In 1992, the African woman is baffled by news of a "plague that has come to end all human hopes."[4] And she is afraid that she and her children might not survive this disease whose origins no one seems to know, and for which there is yet no cure.

Africa is the second largest continent, covering an area of over thirty million square kilometers. In spite of centuries of exploitation by its conquerors, it is still, potentially, the richest piece of earth in the world, with 60 percent of all known exploitable natural resources. And in spite of the vicious campaign about an African population explosion, Africa is not the most populous place on this earth. China is. In fact, given its size, and its current population of around five hundred million, the continent is *underpopulated.*

BURDENS AND RIDDLES

Three major factors have influenced the position of the African woman today. These were indigenous African societal patterns; the conquest of the continent by Europe; and the apparent lack of vision, or courage, in the leadership of the post-colonial period. "Leadership" in this context does not refer to the political leadership exclusively. We speak of the entire spectrum of the intellectual, professional, and commercial elites in positions to make vital decisions on behalf of the entire community.

From ancient times, the majority of societies around the world were either matrilineal or patrilineal. It is now clear that most African societies were matrilineages lasting millennia, from the prepharonic period all the way down to a micronation like the Akans of Ghana. What changed the pattern in some areas were, first, Islam and, later, Christianity, since both religions were obviously patriarchal in orientation. The African societies that retained vestiges of their matrilineages were also the ones that met both Islam and Christianity with the greatest resistance. These areas—for instance, coastal West Africa—are also where one finds some of the least oppressed women.

Today, it is not at all easy to imagine the *coastal* West African woman bearing with any equanimity even the thought of the heavy black veil, the burden of purdah, circumcision, infibulation, and so forth. But even for the West African Moslem woman, the veil is no more than a couple of meters of an often pretty gossamer fabric. This she normally and winsomely drapes over the back of her head and her shoulders. Indeed, the effect of this type of veil is to make its wearers look more attractive and decidedly unhidden. In this, West African women seemed to have more in common with Islamic women in faraway places like the Indian peninsula and the rest of Asia than with their "sisters" to their immediate north.

What seems to separate the woman "south of the Sahara" from the Arab-Islamic woman of the north is not so much the latter's "closeness to Europe" and "civilization," as the former's relative freedom to create herself, economic and political dynamics permitting.

But then, according to Nawal El Saadawi, "There are many misconceptions [in the West] about the identity, character and diversity of Arab women." This Egyptian writer asserts that although the North African-Islamic-Arab woman *is* veiled and circumcised, to know nothing more than that about her "borders on racism." Maybe African women share more commonalities than we are aware of.

In any case, some tenets presumed to be "Islamic" may not sound so strange to women in Southern Africa who have had nothing to do with Islam. For instance, in precolonial Zimbabwe as well as in colonial Rhodesia, the woman was regarded as a permanent minor, first her father's ward, then her husband's. If she outlived her husband, then as a widow she became the ward of some male in either her husband's home or her own home. Sometimes a woman became a ward of her own son(s)! This meant that she could never own property or be granted a bank loan. The situation was so bad that a conscientious and sensitive ZANU (PF) government (in Zimbabwe) attempted a corrective measure by passing the Legal Age of Majority Act in 1982. This law stipulated that at age eighteen a young woman became an adult, with all the attendant rights and privileges.

To a certain extent, African women are some sort of riddle. This is because, whether formally educated or not, "traditional" or "modern," they do not fit the accepted notion of them as mute beasts of burden. And they are definitely not as free and equal as African men (especially some formally educated ones) would have us believe. In fact, they fall somewhere between those two concepts.

To some West African men, the way West African women struggle to be independent "is really quite bad." They think that "these women are all over the place." Wherever men meet, you can be sure to hear jokes and stories about women, all of which are supposed to show how "terrible" we are. One solid piece of "advice" any growing boy is likely to pick up along the coast of West Africa is: "Fear women." And if there really is a Fon (Gabon) proverb that translates as "Woman is the root of all evil, only our souls can save us [from her]," then women have been in trouble for a long time in Africa!

The colonial period did not help women either. It is true that some of the "civilizing" missions did not want their policies to run counter to any patterns in the "natives" that were tolerant of women's development. So they gave a few girls some opportunities for formal education. Some of the girls' secondary schools in the area go as far back as 1837. But the missions came with their own ideas on how females should be educated to be "proper women." While the boys in colonial elite schools were being prepared to go to England to become professionals (mostly lawyers), girls in the equivalent schools were being taught needlework and needlepoint, crochet, and baking. This was to make sure that they became wonderful wives and great mothers. And many turned out exactly as programmed. Even they were only a few women from either traditionally royal or nouveaux riches families. For the great majority of West African women, colonialism meant unmitigated suffering.

A few women managed to squeeze some advantages out of the neocolonial era, and excelled in areas where women would not normally be expected to. The emphasis is on "few," because educational policies in Africa have never been democratic. Today, the pyramid is a symbol of what is happening to young women in the education systems of West Africa: a massive base and a needle-thin top. At the primary levels, girls and boys get equal opportunities to enter the system, or almost. But by the time a given age group gets to the universities, the ra-

tio of girls to boys is as low as one to ten or worse. Apart from impossibly poor environments, this is a result of a number of negative forces in young women's lives, such as becoming pregnant and getting expelled from school, while the offending male—whose identity no one cares to know—is left free,[5] or receiving discouraging career counsel from sexist teachers and school authorities as well as schoolmates and well-meaning but reactionary relatives.[6]

HIGH-POWERED TOKENS

Given the chance, a number of young women show their independence and courage in choosing careers, and in most cases do brilliantly, but women in high-powered positions are still hostages to tokenism. Certainly as "tokens" many of them have attained the top of their professions. Some even got there as early as other women from some of the most technologically advanced regions of the world. So that for a long time some countries in Africa have produced women doctors, lawyers, judges, university lecturers, and professors. There have been women in "rarified" professional areas such as imaginative writing, publishing, geology, architecture, engineering, transportation ownership and management, and music conducting. When we talk of African women today, we speak of over two hundred million people, some of whom are commercial and air-force pilots, engineers (electrical and mechanic), primary and secondary school teachers, telephone operators, and nurses. These professional African women are the exception rather than the rule—but that is how it is throughout much of the world today.

However, there is one group of women almost peculiar to West Africa. These women are in trade and commerce. Mostly, such women are referred to as "market women" or "market mammies" by non-West Africans. But of course, not all of them actually work from the markets, although the great majority do. Their activities range from gem dealing and high finance to "petty" trading. Therefore, their workplaces also range from highly sophisticated modern office complexes to the pavements of the cities where their kiosks stand.

For these women, the market is both a business arena and a home away from home. From early morning when they occupy their stalls they conduct their commercial business *and* their business as homemakers, including the day's cooking for husband and children. Indeed, many people who grew up in urban places (for example, in Ghana, Nigeria, Togo, and Benin) could confirm that much of the time they went after school straight to the market to be with their mothers. The market was where they ate lunch and supper, did their homework, and had their baths from buckets and bowls. Such people recall, often with a great deal of nostalgia, that during the weekday, home was the market: a house was only for sleeping in. Meanwhile, these women make money to feed, clothe, and educate their children, and sometimes support their men.

For most West African women, work is a responsibility and an obligation. This idea is drummed into us from infancy. We could never have fought for the "right to work"—a major concern of early Western feminists. In West Africa, virtually no family tolerates a woman who doesn't work. So that today, there may not be too many homes in the region, including traditionally Islamic areas, where girls are encouraged to think they needn't have ambitions because one day they'll grow up to marry and be looked after by men.

Yet, Africa's women farmers may get the rawest deal of all.[7] Although it may now be fashionable to admit that women have been the backbone of the continent's agriculture, that is a very recent trend. Earlier on, their existence was not even acknowledged. Governments never mentioned women in agricultural policies. So the burden of constant poverty, of working on the farm from sunup to sundown and then coming home to take on dozens of other roles, was added to the deprivation of being invisible to policy-makers.

DEBATING FEMINISM

Currently, the debate about African women and feminism is hot. It is common to hear feminism dismissed as a foreign ideology, imported into Africa "with . . . crusading zeal" (A. N. Mensah, 1990) to ruin good African women. It is also easy, and a trap we all fall into every now and then, to feign a lack of interest in this discourse, or to airily maintain that "we don't need feminism" because we had strong women for antecedents. Many of us have declared at one time or another that "African women were feminists long before feminism." Certainly from the male camp, the cacophony is that African women do not need "feminism." Even though in many modern African states grown-up women are expected to crawl on their knees to offer food and other services to their husbands, their in-laws,

and others in authority generally, most men still maintain that in their country, "women are not oppressed. There are roles which women and men have to play"—including crawling, obviously. The latest and most interesting front in the discourse was opened by Alice Walker, when she proposed that we substitute the term "womanist" to describe the global African woman's particular concerns.

When people ask me rather bluntly every now and then whether I am a feminist, I not only answer yes, but I go on to insist that every woman and every man should be a feminist—especially if they believe that Africans should take charge of our land, its wealth, our lives, and the burden of our own development. Because it is not possible to advocate independence for our continent without also believing that African women must have the best that the environment can offer. For some of us, this is the crucial element in our feminism.

On the whole, African traditional societies seemed to have been at odds with themselves as to exactly what to do with women. For although some of them appeared to doubt gender and biology as bases for judging women, in the end, they all used gender and biology to judge women's capabilities. Otherwise, how was it that men ruled by proxy for women from those nationalities, like the Akan of Ghana, among whom inheritance and succession, and therefore power, were vested in the matrilineage and not the patrilineage?[8]

Some of us are convinced of something else: that much of the putting down of women that educated African men indulge in and claim is "African culture" is a warmed-up leftover from colonization. European colonizing men (especially Victorians) brought with them a burden of confusion: first about their own women, and then about other women. All of which was further muddled up by the colonizers' fantasies about the sexual prowess of both African men and women.

In the meantime, no one wants to hear African women discuss their problems. In Harare, a journalist recently wrote an incredible outburst that began with "Women, women, women, will they ever stop moaning?" He then went on to ask "whether [our] women will ever stop weeping to find solutions to their problems so they won't weep again?" He ended by declaring grandly that "it serves no purpose trying to convince each other that women are oppressed. *There are better issues to focus on.*"[9] (Emphasis

mine.) A full comment on this piece could make a sizable book.

A way to appreciate some of the contradictions in the position of African women today is to adopt a bifocal mode of looking at them. One view would be from inside their own environments. This would reveal that in relation to their men, they were just as badly off as women everywhere. But viewed from outside, internationally, the picture changes somewhat. "For years, some of us have been struggling to get the world to look at the African woman properly. Hoping that with some honesty it would be seen that in actual fact, vis-à-vis the rest of the world, the position of the African woman has not only *not* been that bad, but in some of the societies . . . she had been far better off than others."[10] And this should include the self-congratulatory West.

This much is evident about the majority of African women today, from the Cape of Good Hope to Cairo. They live in the rural areas of the continent and its urban shanties. They have had only the most minimal education or none at all. They are married, monogamously or polygamously. They have had between two and six children. They are involved in peasant farming and petty trading. Their lives are ruled locally by men who speak in languages they do not understand and from abroad by alien men who speak languages they could not possibly understand.

All this should be enough to make the African woman want to fold her arms, keel over, and just die. But she is doing anything but that. She is still pushing. The African woman today is a real heiress of her past. We need to intensify our struggle. For instance, instead of letting ourselves be "lulled into a false sense of security through tokenism and processes of 'de-feminization' which in most cases is a prerequisite for performing certain functions," we need to be able to challenge "gender and class oppression, imperialism and exploitation" and seek "access to policy-making positions, legal reforms, equal rights in education, employment and credit facilities."[11]

In the meantime, if, like men around the world, African men harbor any phobias about women moving into leadership positions, then they had better get rid of them quickly. After all, men have monopolized leadership positions in Africa over the last five hundred years, and still overwhelmingly do. If they alone could save us, they would have done so by now. But instead, every decade brings us grimmer realities. It is high time African women moved onto center stage, with or without anyone's encouragement. Because in our hands lies, perhaps, the last possible hope for ourselves, and for everyone else on the continent.

NOTES

1. Also sometimes referred to as Live Aid, it was organized by Geldof in 1985. It galvanized the world. Among the honors Geldof received was an honorary knighthood bestowed by the Queen of England, and the 1986–87 Third World Prize. The Western media fell over itself paying him well-deserved homage, calling him "Santa Bob," "Sir Bob," and "St. Bob."
2. See, among others, Cheikh Anta Diop, *Cultural Unity of Negro Africa* (1980); Ivan Van Sertima, ed., *Black Women in Antiquity* (1981), and any of the volumes in *The Journal of African Civilizations* series by the latter.
3. In Act One of *Antony and Cleopatra*, Shakespeare was unbelievably crude about Cleopatra. But then the Bard's racism is a great source of acute embarrassment. See *The Tempest, The Merchant of Venice,* and *Titus Andronicus.*
4. Line from my poem: *These Days: II.*
5. The story is so heartbreaking that no aspect of it bears telling. *The Herald* (Harare, Feb. 20, 1992) reports the most terrifying example of this to have come to the continent's notice in recent times. In an incident between boys and girls in a co-educational secondary school in Kenya that left "*19 female students*" *dead*, and during which, according to doctors, "71 girls were raped," "*only two schoolboys were charged with the offense!!!*" (Emphasis added.) Some of us keep talking about the problem, albeit to deaf ears. For example, "Profile: Remembering Tomorrow—A Conversation with Ama Ata Aidoo," by Sarah Modebe, *Africa World Review* (October 1990–March 1992), London; *African Woman* (Autumn 1991), London.
6. One stock advice to a young schoolgirl who plans on having higher education is that she should be careful. Otherwise she would never find a husband. The harm done is never less because such "advice" is often well-meant or based on the common knowledge that "men are scared of smart women."
7. According to Anthony Yudeowei of West Africa Rice Development Association, "over 80 percent of the small holder rice farmers of West Africa are women."
8. Of course, this shows why it is dangerous to assume that because a society is matrilineal, it is also a *matriarchy.* Certainly, the Akans are one very good example of a people with a matrilineal base and an obvious patriarchal superstructure. (Freudian symbols unintended.)
9. Cephas Chitsaka in the *Sunday Mail*, November 24, 1991.
10. Quotation from my letter to Mineke Schipper to explain why I felt unhappy at the title and subtitle of her book, *Source of All Evil—African Proverbs and Sayings On Women.*
11. Page 176, *West Africa* (3–9 February, 1992). Bisi Adeleye-Fayemi was reacting to a letter from K. Asare in a previous issue of the weekly. From my rather brief experience as cabinet minister (Education in Ghana, January 1982–June 1983), I fully endorse the view that in order to function as tokens women defeminize. Or we fall into the trap of being overly feminine. But then either way, we are rendered ineffective. Because on one hand we alienate the public (?) and on the other, our male colleagues refuse to take us seriously.

Article 13   *Dissent* Summer 1992

Literature In Postcolonial Africa

Repression, Resistance, and Reconfigurations

Biodun Jeyifo

Biodun Jeyifo teaches African and African-American literature and Marxist and postcolonial critical theory at Cornell University.

Underdevelopment, as we now know, is the presence of absence in the present, the mythical character in a debased drama named neocolonization which fills the stage of today's events with both actors and scenery. . . . It is a mysterious force whence issue the Delphic emanations of external exploitation, the matrix from which fetishes are endlessly turned out. Every African brought into its service like Caliban by Prospero's wand is working only to accomplish its desires. Therefore, since in Africa there is no reality except through this savage fiction, the extraordinary resilience of which [Aimé] Césaire spoke and which all of us wish for can only come about through the projection over Africa—the whole of Africa—of unbridled entities which, spreading to infinity, liberate new energy.

—Stanislas Adotevi, "Negritude Is Dead: the Burial"

Historical co-ordinates don't fit any longer, new ones, where they exist, have couplings not to the rulers, but to the ruled. It is not for nothing that I chose as an epigraph for my novel July's People *a quotation from Gramsci: "The old is dying, and the new cannot be born; in this interregnum there arises a great diversity of morbid symptoms."*

—Nadine Gordimer, "Living in the Interregnum"

Only that historian will have the gift of fanning the spark of hope in the past who is firmly convinced that even the dead will not be safe from the enemy if he wins. And this enemy has not ceased to be victorious.

—Walter Benjamin, "Theses on the Philosophy of History"

Literature has been an extraordinarily influential institution in postcolonial Africa, and African writers have been prominent in the struggles to build modern democratic societies on the ruins of the colonial state and against the brutalities of the many dictatorial post-independence regimes of the continent. (I shall be talking of literature from sub-Saharan Africa in this piece, with only passing references to writers from North Africa. This is less a matter of ideological persuasion than, alas, of professional ignorance.) A great number of African writers have had their works banned by these regimes, many have been jailed for long terms, and not a few have been killed or hounded into involuntary exile. (Among the prominent African writers who have suffered detention or been forced into exile are Mongo Beti, Breyten Breytenbach, Dennis Brutus, Nurrudin Farah, Bessie Head, Festus Iyayi, Abdelatif Laabi, Jack Mapanje, Micere Mugo, Keorapetse Kgositsile, Maina wa Kinyati, Ngugi wa Thiong'o, Nawal El Saadawi, and Wole Soyinka.) The South African apartheid state, Idi Amin's Uganda, Kamuzu Banda's Malawi, and Daniel arap Moi's Kenya have been the most repressive for the arts and the life of the imagination, but literature has also been embattled in the most "benevolent" or paternalistic regimes, like those of Houphet-Boigny's Côte d'Ivoire, Kenneth Kaunda's Zambia, and Robert Mugabe's Zimbabwe.

Literature in postcolonial Africa is thus deeply political, just as it had been in colonial Africa. This calls for a careful explanation, one that transcends the narrow conception of the relationship of politics and literature represented in its extreme form by Stendhal's famous remark that politics in a novel is like a pistol shot in a concert hall. Certainly, the politics of literary expression in Africa includes forms like protest, agitprop, satirical sketches in street theater performances, prison notes and journals (often smuggled out while the writer is still incarcerated), pamphlets and manifestoes, all of which have been used to defy postindependence African dictatorial regimes. However, beyond these "instant" forms of political literature—which, we must never forget, often require great courage—some of the finest writings of postcolonial African literature involve a sophisticated *testamentary* tradition that taps the deepest democratic aspirations of the continent and its peoples. Surely, this connects African writing with some of this century's great literature from around the world.[1] In the most powerful of these works the voices of postcolonial

African literature mingle with those of other writers of this century who have made of literature the nemesis of state terrorism and a light in dark times, from Bertolt Brecht to Aleksandr Solzhenitsyn, from Primo Levi to Gabriel Garcia Marquez.

The finest of these writings belong to the great body of political literature of this century whose provenance lies in the confrontation of gifted imaginations with the most monstrous political systems of the century: European fascism, the Stalinist gulag, the mythical world of the ferocity and corruption of the Latin American military strongman, the *caudillo*. This gives us a simultaneously depressing and exhilarating dialectic: great political writing, it seems, always requires unspeakable crimes and barbarities; but at the same time, let evil be so awesome that it seems to spring from the very depths of nature and history, it will always meet, through great writing, a resistance that calls forth the spirit of all the victims of present and past crimes and injustices against humanity. Thus, to the surpassing evil of the Voerwoods and Bothas, the Idi Amins and the Mobutus, the Nguemas and the Bandas, the most powerful literary imaginations of the continent have responded with momentous works imbued with the spirit of the human will to freedom. And only an appreciation of this explains the otherwise baffling point that although so much of the greatest works of postcolonial African writing is so profoundly pessimistic, even melancholic, much of it is also, to borrow the title of one of Neruda's volumes of poetry, "fully empowered," full of verbal vigor, innovative narrative, brilliantly original forms and techniques.

A few examples might serve to illustrate this point. In Wole Soyinka's *Madmen and Specialists*, evil and genocide are on the loose, creeds, families, and nations are broken up, and even the individual psyche is penetrated and colonized by this omnipresent evil. But the play derives its *texture* from the brilliant deconstructive wit of its protagonist, the Old Man, a Sade-like genius, and his acolytes, four beggar-vagrants who have been trained to perform like vengeful itinerant circus artists out to confront humanity. Ngugi's *Devil on the Cross* is a literary primer on the cruelties of neocolonialism. The text, however, comprises a stunning melange of Aesopian fables, poetic songs and chants, dramatic inserts, Kikuyu proverbs and legends, savage Swiftian satirical cartoons, and incorporations of biblical materials. Bessie Head's acclaimed novel *A Question of Power* is suffused by the gloom of the writer's discovery, upon her arrival as an exile in Botswana from South Africa, that black Africans inflict on one another the kind of cruelties and degradation that whites inflict on blacks in her apartheid homeland. However, the writing moves back and forth between expressionist refraction of the protagonist's descent into schizophrenia and madness, philosophical disquisitions on gender and the institutional determinations of the moral and spiritual guidance of humanity and society, and a diary-like detailing of work on the collective self-help projects in the village in which the novel is set. In these works, and others like Marechera's *Black Sunlight*, Fugard's *The Island*, Coetzee's *Waiting for the Barbarians*, and Armah's *Fragments*, thematic pessimism is leavened by the force and originality of the rendering, and this becomes in itself a metaphor of indomitable will against apartheid and the neocolonial nightmares to the north.

I have stressed a continuity between the literature of colonial Africa, especially in its declining phase, and that of postindependence Africa, but to this I would add three qualifying observations.

First: in this essay I shall be engaging only the most significant postcolonial African writing. I shall not be concerned with some of the problems that affect the production and circulation of literary work *in* Africa, problems deriving from economic backwardness and the failures of autonomous development. Although these effects will not be explored here, some can be succinctly stated: it is much easier to obtain the works of African writers in Europe and North America than in Africa itself; and the most insightful criticism of this literature is mostly published in foreign journals and magazines.

Second: much of Africa's important writings have sprung from wars, political turmoil, and the tyranny of many of the postindependence regimes of the continent. Thus, those who might wonder at how quickly postcolonial African writing attained political and moral maturity would do well to remember that the lessons were learned in the womb of colonialism, against the negations and tyranny of colonial rule. Colonialism, in virtually all parts of Africa, did not enter its "liberal" phase until after the Second World War, And even then the battles *had* to be fought to expand the civic and human rights of Africans, to regain independence, and to exorcise dependency and inferiorization by challenging racially determined Eurocentric constructions of truth, rationality, and moral agency. Nationalist and radical social thought and literature in colonial Africa were invaluable intellectual and cultural "fronts" of these battles.

Thus the social thought of Pan-Africanists like Blyden, Casely-Hayford, Sekyi, and Diop, and revolutionary nationalists like Kwame Nkrumah, Amilcar Cabral, Frantz Fanon, and Eduardo Mondlane had literary counterparts in works like Casely-Hayford's *Ethiopia Unbound*, Sekyi's *The Blinkards*, David Diop's *Hammer Blows*, Neto's *Stubborn Hope*, and Oyono's *Houseboy* and *The Old Man and the Medal*. A volume like *When Bullets Begin to Flower*, Margaret Dickinson's collection of patriotic and revolutionary Angolan anticolonial poetry, is a vivid illustration of this point, since "patriotism" in this volume is defined as much in reinventing the nation as in ending the foreign usurpation of sovereignty that colonialism represented; it is defined as much by exorcising racist, denigrating images of Africa and Africans as by drawing upon the varied poetic, rhetorical, and expressive traditions of the Angolan peoples. Hence the slogan that runs throughout the poetry in this volume as an underlying motif: *Vanos Descobir Angola!* (Let us Discover Angola!)

The third point derives logically from this complex interplay between colonialism and the postcolonial condition. Between the extremes of those who deny any relationship between the colonial past and the postcolonial present and those who absolutize the connection between them, there is a great variety of views. This point is crucial to perceptions of tradition and identity in African literature. Thus, those who insist that colonialism was entirely and unambiguously evil and injurious to African cultural traditions and creativity also take the view that postcolonial African literature should abandon Western literary influences. Among major proponents of this view are the late Ugandan poet, cultural anthropologist, and theorist Okot p'Bitek and the Nigerian critic and cultural journalist Chinweizu. The opposite view is expressed by people like the Zairean philosopher and novelist V. Y. Mudimbe and the Ghanaian philosopher and cultural critic Kwame Anthony Appiah, who hold that reassertions of literary tradition, even when they are based on precolonial sources, cannot be pure products unaffected by colonialism, but are indeed *re-inventions* overwhelmingly shaped by colonialism; correspondingly, they speak of syntheses between African forms and sources and Western influences.

In between these two positions, other commentators take more flexible, perhaps theoretically and ideologically weaker positions. Ali Mazrui, for instance, talks of a "triple heritage," which unproblematically includes precolonial African, Arab-Islamic, and Western traditions. Another view, very widely held, involves simple empiricist accounts of the chronological supersession of colonial Africa by postcolonial Africa, with the attendant and inevitable pains of modernization and Westernization. In African literary criticism, this view is best exemplified by the editorial texts of the important journal *African Literature Today*.

In the opinion of this writer, the most useful accounts of this relationship come from a composite group of social theorists, philosophers, writers, and cultural critics, mostly of the revolutionary or democratic left, a group that includes names like Amilcar Cabral, Frantz Fanon, Samir Amin, Paulin Hountondji, Marcien Towa, Stanislas Adotevi, Chinua Achebe, Omafume Onoge, Omolara Ogundipe-Leslie, Ayi Kwei Armah, Wole Soyinka, Abiola Irele, Ousmane Sembene, Agostinho Neto, Ngugi wa Thiong'o, Mahmoud Mamdani, Ama Ata Aidoo, and Bessie Head. There is within this group a great diversity of ideas about postcolonial African critical thought and literature, but I extrapolate some common themes: that colonialism profoundly affected Africa, but in complex ways that simultaneously involved both exploitation, inferiorization and condescension, and mostly, but not entirely unintended transformative, positive processes; that the aftereffects of colonialism continue to plague Africa; that modernization in Africa is part of the alienating, global modernity of the capitalist epoch; that while much of postcolonial African literature and critical thought involves the exploration of Africa's place in the world, the most important issue in African cultural politics is the relationship of Africa to itself, the encounter of African nations, societies, and peoples with one another.

All of this points to the fact that the idea of a *colonial* line of descent for postcolonial African literature is not a mere given fact of political and cultural history; it is a construct of great consequence for both the production and the reception of the literature. The postcolonial does not come merely adventitiously *after* colonialism. Complex and ambiguous historical dynamics link the two and link both to precolonial Africa. For the rest of the essay I wish to explore the most important literary manifestations of this postcolonial cultural space. For this, it is important for us to bear in mind Achebe's characteristically lucid admonition:

> It is the very nature of creativity, in its prodigious complexity and richness, that it accommodates paradoxes and ambiguities. But this, it seems, will always elude and pose a problem for the uncreative literal mind. The literal mind is the one-track mind, the simplistic mind, the mind that cannot understand that where one thing stands another will stand by it.

Consider the first epigraph at the head of this essay. There the ethnologist and philosopher Stanislas Adotevi, the author of *Negritude et Negrologues*, perhaps the most brilliant and radical critique of Senghorian Negritude, calls for the projection over all of Africa of "unbridled entities" that would "liberate new energy" by exceeding the scope set by Prospero for Caliban. Moreover, Adotevi deliberately portrays both colonialism and neo-colonial dependence as witches' cauldrons from which phantasms and fictions about Africa and Africans are brewed, thus necessitating the need for counter fictions and "entities."

In Prospero and Caliban, Adotevi is alluding to perhaps the most widely deployed tropes of postcolonial literature. No pair of symbolic figures from the European literature of empire and colonization has had the same suggestiveness. The central factor in the resonance of *The Tempest* seems to have been the way that the play sees both colonial conquest and resistance to it as predicated on language—its power of establishing definitions of truth, reason, and

reality and its corresponding power to disestablish and delegitimate. Prospero absorbs Caliban into the universe of his totalizing order of language, knowledge, and power; but Caliban revolts.

In contemporary African literature and criticism, much has been made of the Prospero-Caliban complex, mostly in terms of expanding Shakespeare's text and making of Caliban the "native" artist, intellectual, or critic who uses Prospero's language to revolt against Prospero and to wrest political control over the island or the colonized territory. By this reckoning, Caliban's revolt is successful to the extent that in appropriating Prospero's language he defamiliarizes it, makes it undergo an estrangement such that Prospero can no longer recognize himself, his world, his projects, his supercilious racial and cultural pretensions in the "de-formed" language. This indeed was one of the main ideas in Jean-Paul Sartre's famous 1948 essay "Orphée Noire" in its celebration of the poetry of Negritude in the French language. This view implies that postcolonial literary expression *within* a European-based linguistic medium, within *Francophone, Anglophone,* or *Lusophone* literatures, are not so much local variants of metropolitan European literatures as new counter-hegemonic *national* literatures in their own right.

This view rests on premises radically opposed to positivist accounts of language as human social practice, accounts incapable of grasping the complex alchemies that shape languages when they meet and collide. We need a comparative critical discourse that will astutely deploy Achebe's warning against literal-mindedness: "Where one thing stands, another will stand by it."

The most significant postcolonial African writing comes from this conceptual universe. And for this, the metaphor of Caliban's linguistic revolt, for all its resonance, clearly falls short of grasping the issues involved, since its implication of inversions of Prospero's language to estrange Prospero cannot admit of one thing standing where another one stands. For there are vast differences between European and African languages, and in yoking together their accumulated resources, postcolonial African writers are able to achieve transmutations impossible outside a postcolonial context. And it bears repeating that *this* context, this *space* involves the uneven coexistence of cultural forms from the precolonial, the colonial, and the postcolonial social formations.

The most accomplished postcolonial writers draw upon structures of feeling perhaps once treasured in pre-industrial European culture but long vanished from either the present-day living stock of ordinary speech or its incorporations into literary language. The examples are legion: the Ghanaian poet and novelist Kofi Awoonor draws extensively on the funeral dirges, the songs of ritual abuse and contests of the Ewe-speaking peoples, and achieves cadences otherwise unimaginable in English; Amos Tu-

tuola's characters and narratives come from an exuberant Yoruba metaphysical universe worked over by colonial and postcolonial influences, and this gives his writings their celebrated haunting, enigmatic quality; the black South African poet Mazizi Kunene reinvents a new heroic, epic poetry in English by drawing on ancient Zulu poetic, chanted modes.

Perhaps the greatest practitioners of this quintessentially postcolonial literary practice are Chinua Achebe and Wole Soyinka. In Soyinka's plays like *A Dance of the Forests, The Road, Madmen and Specialists,* and *Death and the King's Horseman,* autochthonous rites jostle with sensibilities produced by the contradictions of colonial capitalism or postcolonial alienation; the presiding spirit, the muse here, is not Caliban but Ogun, the ancient Yoruba god of creativity and destruction. Achebe draws on the brooding myths of the Igbo within novelistic frames that are utterly realistic and an ideational universe that is relentlessly rationalist and skeptical. Indeed, one of the most illuminating observations on postcolonial writing is provided by Achehe himself.

> In one sense then [there] is a travelling away from its old self towards a cosmopolitan, modern identity while in another sense [there] is a journeying back to regain a threatened past and selfhood. To comprehend the dimensions of this gigantic paradox and coax from it such unparalleled inventiveness requires ... the archaic energy, the perspective and temperament of creation myths and symbolism.

This notion of paradox and ambiguity as fundamental to the situation of postcolonial African literature finds noteworthy instantiations in two particular strands of postcolonial African writing: white South African authors who challenge apartheid and its intellectual foundations and writings by women and their challenge to the assumed normative *male* ground of postcolonial African literature. Let us turn first to the former.

If, as we have seen, the metaphor of Caliban's revolt has only limited application to postcolonial writing by *black* African writers, surely it has an even lesser application to *white* African authors, who may metaphorically be called Prospero's "African" progeny, for it is Prospero himself who is Africanized, who must now invent a new cultural identity for himself free of superciliously ethnocentric Enlightenment universalism. The limits etched here go back to Shakespeare's play: at the end of *The Tempest,* Prospero goes back to his beloved kingdom, his idealized Europe. This of course obscures the historic and cultural dynamics of *settler colonialism,* which, in a different scenario, would have Prospero stay on in the island, in the colonized African, South American, or Caribbean country. This indeed is the central plot element in Aim Csaire's adaptation of Shakespeare's play in his *A Tempest,* a play that finds a

historic limit in the founding moment of settler colonialism. Meanwhile, however, *this* form of colonization, represented in its most evil expression in the apartheid system, has run its full course and has been unraveling in the last two decades at least, undone by its indefatigable internal opponents and by the pressure of external forces.

The sense of this unraveling pervades the works of South African white authors and establishes a line of demarcation from their black compatriots within the community of apartheid's literary naysayers. This unraveling of apartheid in works by white authors is overwhelmingly marked by the sense of apocalypse but also of redemption. It is this double articulation that is conveyed in the otherwise bleak vision of Gordimer's notion of "morbid symptoms" in the second epigraph to this essay. Thus, it seems that the discourse of civilization, empire, and colonization, which had an ambiguous provenance in classic European texts like Shakespeare's *The Tempest,* Defoe's *Robinson Crusoe,* Conrad's *Heart of Darkness,* and Gide's *The Immoralist* has run its full course in postcolonial African literature of white South African extraction. This point is given a great variety of thematic, representational, and moral inscriptions in works like André Brink's *A Dry White Season* and *Writings in a State of Siege;* Breyten Breytenbach's *A Season in Paradise, Confessions of an Albino Terrorist,* and *In Africa, Even the Flies are Happy;* J. M. Coetzee's *Waiting for the Barbarians, The Life and Times of Michael K,* and *Foe;* Athol Fugard's *Statements After an Arrest for the Immorality Act* and *A Lesson for Aloes;* and Nadine Gordimer's *The Late Bourgeois World, July's People,* and *The Essential Gesture.* Listen to the accents of one particular expression of this historical unraveling, in Breyten Breytenbach's *A Season in Paradise:*

> And in this night we now enter, the fires of nationalism will be fanned, will flare up even brighter and more destructive. It will be said that it is "us" or "them"—without our knowing who "us" is, without our knowing "them." That side which we are going to have to choose, is it going to be a knowing choice, or a desperate tribal choice? Will we even have a choice? The expectation will be that something will be defended. What? A Western civilization? What Western civilization, and whose? The white man's sole right to decision-making? The white skin? Only death's skin is an unblemished white. Afrikaans? Whose Afrikaans? ... One would like to believe that it could be possible to write in this country for and about people as people. But the poison of racism flows so deeply in our veins. Even in our language, our beautiful language, our wonderful vehicle. We speak of man and woman, of boy and girl. And when these are not pale enough? Kaffir, nigger, coolie, blockhead, "Uncle," ayah, kwedin, maid, wog, munt.... Some of these terms were dropped under

the pressure of growing consciousness, but will we accept the full and equal, self-evident humanness of the "others"? . . . Do we later want it said then—in this land of sunshine, there were two species of homo sapiens—man, and white man?

"Man, and white man"—even in uncovering and undermining the racist, Eurocentric roots of apartheid, patriarchal tropes contaminate Breytenbach's attempt to imagine a humanist, universalist discourse purged of its inherited ethnocentricism and bigotry. It is for this reason that many African women writers and critics—and some men—speak of a *double*, and not a single, colonization. One colonization engenders the resistance of nationalism; the other engenders a resistance that questions both colonialism and nationalism, since both are predicated on "man" as the ground and sign of all reality, imagination and creativity and "woman" as the passive complement of this male power to name and control all things and relationships.

The range of perspectives in this strand of postcolonial African literature is considerable and often follows regional and generational differences. Thus the vision of a female supersession of the double colonization of classical colonialism and nationalism seems to be simultaneously deeper *and* less separatist in the works of South African writers like Nadine Gordimer and Bessie Head than in the works of their counterparts in the north. Furthermore, older writers like Flora Nwapa of Nigeria, Grace Ogot of Kenya, and Efua Sutherland of Ghana espouse a more conservative, "traditionalist" view of women and gender relationships than writers of a second wave of postcolonial African women's writings represented by authors like Buchi Emecheta, Werewere Liking, and Tsitsi Dangarembga. However, transcending these demarcations of region, generation and ideology are the works of writers like Ama Ata Aidoo, Nawal El Saadawi, Bessie Head, and Nadine Gordimer in their all-encompassing evocative power and moral authority. To give only one illustration of this, Ama Ata Aidoo's brilliant play *Anowa* uncovers the genealogies of African women's oppression in precolonial institutions, the internal slave trade, and colonial capitalism, and at the same time engages the great subjects of nationalist postcolonial African literature: foreign domination, the reinvention of tradition, the oppression of the laboring classes, the struggle for personal autonomy. The implication of works like *Anowa* is that women will no longer be marginalized by an agenda of national liberation set by unexamined patriarchal values, nor will they be ghettoized into a tolerated "women's writing" enclave.

Some aspects of contemporary Western critical thought and literary theory, stemming from Lyotard and others, makes a distinction between two forms of knowledge: on the one hand, "stories" and "narratives," and on the other hand, scientific abstraction. This follows a putative global division of knowledge production: the non-Western, peripherally capitalist nations and societies have "story" and "narrative"; the Western, developed societies have "science." This seems to be supported by trends in world literature whereby the most exciting and vigorous forms of writing are emerging from the developing world. For instance, of the last six Nobel laureates in literature, three have come from Africa: Wole Soyinka (1986), Naguib Mahfouz (1988), and Nadine Gordimer (1991). And this year's winner of the Booker prize, Britain's most prestigious literary award, is the young Nigerian novelist Ben Okri. This view of contemporary world literature and intellectual relations, however, has a twist that has been brilliantly articulated by, among others, Fredric Jameson:

> What this formulation does very sharply achieve . . . is the radical differentiation between the consumption of the past in narrative and its storage, hoarding and capitalization in "science" and scientific thought: a mode of understanding that, like the first surplus on the economic level, will little by little determine a whole range of ever more complex and extensive institutional objectifications—first in writing; then libraries, universities, museums; with the breakthrough in our own period to microstorage, computerized data, and data banks of unimaginable proportions, whose control or even ownership is . . . one of the crucial *political* issues of our own time.

The vitality of the literary arts in postcolonial Africa seems pertinent here. The narrative arts, the cultural value of telling a good story and of reclaiming a threatened past through fictions all remain relatively unchallenged in Africa and the developing world by the technological and social revolutions of knowledge production and consumption that are decisive phenomena of the cultural scene in the developed world. This is an enormous cultural asset, and it does underscore the vitality and growth of African writing against so much that is dismal in the continent at the present time. But as the third epigraph to this essay from Walter Benjamin warns us, we must beware "an enemy who has never ceased to be victorious." Against this grim but realistic pessimism, the long, historic, and optimistic view is that the world will never lose the desire for "story" and "narrative"; and the present systemic and institutional divisions of knowledge production that consign "story" to the South and "science" to the North are not immutable.

Note

1. From a long list of works that, although they share a common vision of human possibilities stunted but ultimately unquenchable, exhibit a

great diversity of styles and technical resources, the following texts stand out: Chinua Achebe's *Anthills of the Savannah* and the book of essays *Hopes and Impediments*; Ayi Kwei Armah's *The Beautyful Ones Are Not Yet Born* and *Fragments*; Ama Ata Aidoo's *Anowa*; Mariama Ba's *So Long a Letter* and *Scarlet Song*; Breyten Breytenbach's *A Season in Paradise*; J.M. Coetzee's *The Life and Times of Michael K* and *Waiting for the Barbarians*; Athol Fugard's *Boesman and Lena, Sizwe Bansi Is Dead*, and *The Island*; Nadine Gordimer's *July People, The Late Bourgeois World*, and the book of

essays *The Essential Gesture*; Bessie Head's *A Question of Power* and *Maru*; Ahmadou Kourouma's *The Suns of Independence*; Dambudzo Marechera's *House of Hunger* and *Black Sunlight*; Ngugi wa Thiong'o's *Petals of Blood, The Barrel of a Pen*, and *Matigari*; Niyi Osundare's *The Eye of the Earth*; Femi Osofisan's *Another Raft* and *Esu and the Vagabond Minstrels*; Nawal El Saadawi's *Woman at Point Zero* and *God Dies by the Nile*; Ousmane Sembene's *Xala* and *The Last of the Empire*; Wole Soyinka's *The Man Died, A Play of Giants, A Shuttle in the Crypt*, and *Madmen and Specialists*.

Article 14   *The World & I, September 1988*

BaKongo Cosmology

Complex ideas of the universe from the heart of Africa were little recognized until recent decades

Wyatt MacGaffey

Wyatt MacGaffey is John R. Coleman Professor of Social Sciences at Haverford College.

European visitors to Africa have often been reluctant to credit the people they meet with the capacity for abstract or systematic thought. In the 1880s, travelers and missionaries with experience of the Lower Congo believed "the ideas of the natives" amounted to no more than "a ruinous heap." Said one, "There is no coherence in their beliefs, and their ideas about cosmogony are very nebulous." Anthropologists have concurred: "One would seek in vain in [Kongo] culture for large and coherent conceptions and structures such as would give the human reality they incarnate the prestige accorded in Africa and elsewhere to other civilizations."

Yet, some African civilizations have indeed earned prestige for the complexity of their cosmologies and the refinement of their moral and symbolic systems. The ideas of the Dogon of Mali and the related Bamana (Bambara), noted also for their sculptures, have been studied for decades by a school of anthropology founded by Marcel Griaule. The Dogon had a graded series of initiation lodges in which wisdom was progressively revealed to a religious elite. In the best-known of his publications, *Conversations with Ogotemmeli*, Griaule describes how the Dogon assigned a learned elder to explain the origin and mysteries of the universe to him.

But where no hierarchy of religious elite existed—such as in the Lower Congo—there was no social basis for the development and authentication of cosmological knowledge. We also expect to learn about a cosmology from myths and to recognize myths by the miraculous events that occur in them, in which sacred beings and divine heroes shape the world. But in Lower Congo we find no narratives of this kind.

Instead of asking whether the BaKongo or any other people have a cosmology, we could assume that they must have one, because all social interaction necessarily presupposes some ordering of the world in space and time, specifying the place of human actors within it. If two Americans meet, for example, they are usually unaware that they think anything about "cosmology" or that, if they did, it would have any relevance to their interaction. Nevertheless, to interact at all, they must know or assume certain fundamental things about each other. It is necessary to know, for example, whether the person one is addressing is alive or dead. Usually that is no problem, though it is possible to be mistaken; comedies and thrillers both exploit the shock value of such mistakes. The difference between life and death also has serious public consequences, since a live person has civil rights and legal responsibilities that a dead person does not.

The difference between life and death is not a given in nature, however; that is, it is not in all cases a simple matter of observation. In the last two decades, Americans have repeatedly asked their

courts and legislatures to decide just what the difference is. The beginning of life is as difficult to identify as the end and has given rise to as many controversies. The language used by parties to these disputes is often overtly religious, in a denominational sense, but even if it is not, their emotional tone and their feeling that these issues are fundamental tell us that we are in the domain of religion.

Cosmological distinctions about the order of the universe, the place of humankind within it, and the nature and varieties of human beings vary from one society to another. They may or may not be true in some scientific sense. Since they are fundamental to social life and experience, it is difficult if not impossible for the members of the society to step outside their assumptions, which they take to be given realities, or to imagine what life would be like in a different universe.

KONGO COSMOLOGY

The BaKongo, who live in the western Zaire province of Lower Zaire (called in colonial times Lower Congo) and in adjacent parts of both northwestern Angola and the People's Republic of Congo, may number some three million people. Their territory, on the Atlantic threshold of the Zaire basin—the heart of Africa—has been deeply influenced by relations with Europe going back more than five hundred years to the first arrival of Portuguese ships on the coast in 1483. After the creation of the colony of the Belgian Congo in 1908, most Kongo men, and many women, went to school, became

Traditional BaKongo wood carvings.
A crouching figure on a round bell.

Carved head for an ivory staff.

Catholics or Protestants, and entered wage labor. Their political party, Abako, led by Joseph Kasa-Vubu, was one of the most effective forces in the fight for national independence, obtained in 1960. In Zaire today they are among the best educated and most influential groups.

In 1970, most BaKongo believed that the universe is divided into the two worlds of the living and the dead, separated by water and related to each other in such a way that when the sun sets among the living it rises among the dead. The movement of human life resembles that of the sun, in that after being born into this world and spending a lifetime in it, the soul passes into another existence in the alternate world. The other world is very much like this one. In fact, it is in a sense identical to it, since after dark, when the living go to sleep, the dead wake up and go about their daily occupa-

tions in what they think of as day, in the same houses that the living use, cultivating the same fields and cooking at the same hearth. There are also differences, however; in some ways the dead contrast with the living. Since they are older and can see in our world as well as their own, they are more powerful. They do not suffer from disease as we do, and they have become white rather than black.

Kongo cosmology is in fact more complex than this, but the sketch suffices to suggest that the fundamental concepts of time, life, death, and race are entirely different from those taken for granted by Americans or Europeans. In this cosmology, since the land of the dead is like another village, and not really very far away, it is remarkable rather than epochmaking that individuals may be able to go there and return to this world, to die and rise again from the dead.

The land of the dead is the village cemetery in the adjacent forest, but it can also be entered through certain caves and deep pools. The water that divides the worlds may be any pool or stream—the Zaire River or the Atlantic Ocean. In one of the most powerful applications of this cosmology, America, the land on the other side of the ocean, is the land of the dead to which Africans go when they die, changing their skins and becoming white.

The cosmology of divided worlds is an abstract model that enables the BaKongo to comprehend and interpret the facts of history and geography, human social experience, and relations of power. As we shall see, they use it to understand international relations, a dispute between two villages, or their own dreams. As the grammar of their thinking, it has not itself, until recently, been the object of their intellectual scrutiny. As an interpretive

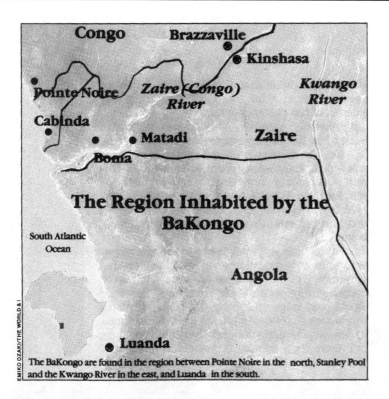

The BaKongo are found in the region between Pointe Noire in the north, Stanley Pool and the Kwango River in the east, and Luanda in the south.

schema, it is mobilized when the urgencies of events demand it, and it may be applied differently by different individuals, drawing different conclusions.

The Kongo cosmology was first set out in print by Fu-kiau kia Buneeki in 1969, in a short work entitled *The MuKongo and the World in Which He Circulates*, written in KiKongo and published with a French translation. Fu-kiau, a young man with a good secondary education, was prompted to write by his conversations with the anthropologist J. M. Janzen. Fu-kiau was not a hoary Ogotemmeli steeped in tradition, but a man whose contact with outsiders was such that he could appreciate their problem in understanding the Kongo perspective. A diagram of the universe, similar to Fu-kiau's and labeled in KiKongo, has been found in use among Afrocubans in Cuba.

Fragmentary elements of Kongo cosmology have long been discussed, only to be relegated to footnotes as oddities instead of being taken seriously as parts of the missing system of Kongo religion. Europeans, representing a civilization that sees itself as obviously superior to all others in its moral, scientific, and political achievements, have naturally been reluctant to admit that they were seen by Congolese as spirits of the dead, their morality as witchcraft, their science as magic, and their politics as cannibalism. It is still more difficult to admit that there may be some truth to this perspective.

PERSONAL EXPERIENCES

Kongo cosmological thinking was brought home to me personally when my wife and I lived in Matadi, the main port of Zaire, situated at the head of navigation on the Zaire estuary. It had about 180,000 inhabitants in 1970, many of them sailors who regularly traveled to Antwerp, New York, Houston, and even Japan on Belgian and Zairean merchant ships. Many more worked in the docks, and most of them had opportunities for contacts of various sorts with the crews of foreign ships. The town was also the seat of Protestant and Catholic missions established there since its founding in the 1880s. My host was a relatively prosperous man, an electrician, who could afford to keep a substantial household, including two wives and twelve children.

As I walked across the marketplaces of the town, I would be followed by a murmur of explanation from one marketwoman to another. "*Ndombe kena!* He's black!" People would tell the story: My host, the electrician had formerly owned a bar. To raise money for it, he had sold me his nephew, by witchcraft, to persons unspecified (missionaries, perhaps), who had transported me to America. I had become white in the land of the dead, had made good to the point of being able to marry a white lady, and had now come back to demand a reckoning; that explained why I was living in my "uncle's"

house without paying any rent, why I was willing to eat local food, spoke authentic KiKongo and asked all those questions about local tradition—I was trying to recover my roots.

Sometimes people would put the question to me directly, in French or KiKongo: "Monsieur, is it true that you are black?" Others brought me photographs of recently deceased relatives to ask how they were getting on in the States. I had to reply that unfortunately we had so many immigrants arriving in America every day that it was hard to keep track of them all. Not everybody thought the same way. My host and his wives insisted to their friends that I was a *real* white man, and students from the secondary school, upwardly mobile all, noting my nondescript clothes and the fact that I went about on foot, would sometimes sneer at me as a bankrupt, poor white.

Even these skeptics had not really abandoned the traditional cosmology; the land of the dead has its native population, people whose ancestors were always white, in addition to those who have been imported as slaves by witchcraft. "Monsieur, were your ancestors black or white?" A matter of common puzzlement is the skin-change: Does it happen immediately or gradually? A black American evangelist visiting Kinshasa was asked about his light-brown color; how did he get that way? Embarrassed to recall a presumptive history of plantation miscegenation, he said that it came gradually, and his questioner went away satisfied.

The view of myself that I encountered in Matadi was not new to me. Five years before, I had lived in the village of Mbanza Manteke which, though rural, is no more remote from contact with Europe than is Matadi. A famous Protestant mission was established there in 1879, and since the turn of the century its male inhabitants have worked in cities like Kinshasa or Matadi. It gradually became clear that people expected me to take a siesta at noon, not just because that had been the habit of the missionaries when they lived there, but because for white people, as the BaKongo saw it, noon was really midnight, so of course they needed to sleep. Likewise, the European custom of sea-bathing was understood as a means of restoring one's health by contact with home base, as it were, the land beyond the water. My neighbors would call me "dead man" and laugh, somewhat uneasily.

At that time—1964—the U.S. government saw itself as engaged in a struggle with the Russians for the hearts and minds of the Congolese. The United States Information Agency took care to provide local newspapers with accounts, in French, of the presidential elections, in order to demonstrate the virtues of democracy. Some of the villagers read these accounts with great interest and asked me questions to further their understanding. It turned out that they interpreted what they read in terms of their cosmology, in which not only the universe but any part of it may be thought of as divided into two opposed worlds. They gathered that Mr. Johnson, representing North America and therefore a white man, was contending with Mr. Goldwater, a black man, the leader of South America.

At the same time, they knew all about Sputnik, alerted by radio, and they would draw my attention to satellites passing overhead. They greatly admired both the Russians and the Americans, who could produce such marvels. But they had no use for communists, such as the Belgians, who were nothing but witches and incapable, they were sure, of building so much as a railroad locomotive. Later, the Americans were to be congratulated on flying to the moon, something Kongo magicians could also do, but the trouble with magicians was that one was never sure they were not up to mischief with their remarkable feats. Just what were the Americans doing on the moon, anyway? I was never able to answer this question satisfactorily.

RITUALS AND DREAMS

Cosmology is revealed not only in such personal experiences but also through the analysis of rituals. Kongo rituals proceed in a space that has first been laid out as a microcosm, sometimes by drawing a diagram on the ground. The simplest and most common diagram is a cross, not to be confused with the Christian cross. A person taking an oath, for example, may mark a cross in the dirt with his finger, then stand on it to swear. The transverse line corresponds to the boundary between the worlds; the intersecting one, to the path of forces moving between them. In some of the complex rituals performed in precolonial times, initiates were described as spending several days, weeks, or even months in the land of the dead under the water. What in fact they did was to spend the time in a specially built enclosure or distant camp. When they emerged from seclusion, they were considered to have been reborn, able to speak the secret languages of the dead and endowed with miraculous powers.

Their cosmology is so necessary to the organization of their culture and so taken

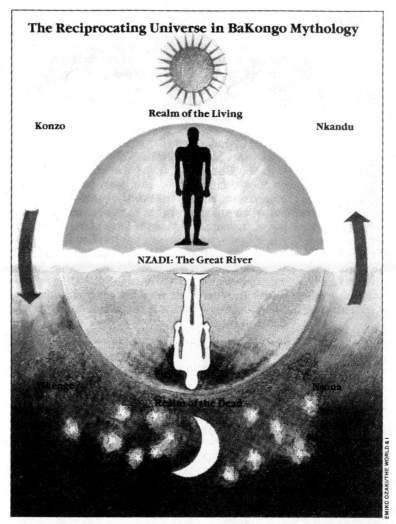

The Reciprocating Universe in BaKongo Mythology

Konzo

Nkandu

Realm of the Living

NZADI: The Great River

Nkenge

Ngona

Realm of the Dead

EMIKO OZAKI/THE WORLD & I

for granted by them that the BaKongo do not recognize it as a topic or "problem." Conversely, once we have been alerted to it, the evidences of it are everywhere. The cosmology that the foreigner finds surprising is treated merely as the setting for transitory ingenuities, as in the riddle, "What black man went to Europe and became white?" Answer: a manioc root left soaking in the water for three days (to remove the acid) and then peeled.

In dreams, the soul may see something of the other world, so dreams are taken seriously as glimpses and warnings of the occult forces at work in our lives. To dream of trucks, trains, or ships is a sinister warning that someone will be "traveling." In the 1930s, when trains were new to the country, people would go down to the station to watch for recently deceased relatives passing through on their way to Matadi and beyond. Only people with special sinister powers, however, are actually active in the night world, while their bodies lie asleep in bed. They include witches, and also chiefs, who must

have powers like those of witches in order to be able to defend the community against them.

KONGO HISTORY THROUGH KONGO EYES

The BaKongo tell no stories of the kind that the Western ear recognizes immediately as myths. In a cyclical or reciprocating universe such as Fu-kiau describes, one would not expect to find an account of its origin. What one does hear, in many hotly contested versions, are the stories of the origins of the clans in Mbanza Kongo. Mbanza Kongo, located in what is now northern Angola, was the capital of the Kingdom of Kongo when the Portuguese visited it at the end of the fifteenth century. The kingdom disintegrated after the battle of Mbwila in 1665, the capital itself being reduced to no more than an important village to which the legendary majesty of the past still faintly clung.

In modern Kongo, everyone derives his or her social position from membership

A typical inland BaKongo village.

in his or her mother's descent group or clan. Clan membership specifies the range of partners it is possible to marry and indicates where one has rights to land and residence. In asserting a claim to land or to political office, the head of a clan recites its tradition of origin, in which it usually appears that the founding chief left Mbanza Kongo, crossed the great river (*nzadi*), and arrived at the clan's present territory where, there being no other inhabitants, he "swept up the droppings of the elephant" and founded his own *mbanza*, or central place. The story tells his magical deeds, such as crossing the river on a raffia mat. It reports what clans he met along the way, whose sister he married, and so on. The representatives of other clans are supposed to be able to confirm the truth of these events and thus the property rights that the story legitimates.

Since, in a general sense, such stories might well be true, historians have generally treated them as accounts of actual migrations in which the BaKongo dispersed over their present territory from their original home. Scholars assumed that the river was the Zaire (Nzadi) and dismissed the magical events as accretions on a historical core. In fact, the supernatural references are among a number of clues showing that the stories are the missing myths, that they are narrative versions of the model of the divided worlds of the Kongo universe. In

both the stories and the model, the essential movement in time is a crossing from one world to the other across the water that divides them.

THE SLAVE TRADE AND THE CHRISTIAN MISSIONS

From the mid-seventeenth century to about 1890, the history of Kongo is bound up with the slave trade. Trials for ritual offenses, often violations of cult rules specially designed to trap the unwary, fed a thriving internal trade in slaves. Political losers and troublemakers could be sold to another village nearer the coast, with replacements acquired from further inland. At the coast, European slave traders established depots by treaty with chiefs who could guarantee orderly conditions of business and a steady supply of slaves in exchange for guns, cloth, liquor, and other goods.

This trade is understood by modern BaKongo as witchcraft; or rather, "witchcraft" is, among other things, what the BaKongo call slave trading. Witches, who are one's evilly intentioned neighbors, acquire sinister powers from the other world that enable them to operate "at night," that is, in unseen, occult ways. They steal the souls of victims, often relatives, who in the daylight world will be seen to die shortly afterwards. These souls may be eaten by members of the witch's coven, each of whom is obliged to

provide a meal for the others in turn. This belief is the basis for stories interpreted by foreigners as cannibalism; there was never any actual cannibalism among the BaKongo.

Instead of being "eaten," stolen souls may be sold for an unholy profit, which explains, in Kongo eyes, why some people get rich. Victims should be sold, like slaves, at some distance, so that they cannot make their way home. Most victims of witchcraft end up in America, where they are supposedly put to work in factories making textiles and automobiles. Their souls would go to America anyway, after a normal death, but witchcraft sends them there prematurely.

Described and understood as witchcraft, the slave trade is believed to have persisted into the twentieth century. All relations with Europe and America, collectively referred to as *Mputu*, are understood in the same way. When Protestant missionaries arrived in the 1880s, they were seen as practicing a new form of the same trade. To be converted meant to be initiated into a magical conspiracy, similar to the traditional cults, in which the initiates learned how to become powerful and wealthy. In exchange, as in other cults offering sinister competitive advantage over one's neighbors, the converts had to hand over the souls of one or more relatives. These victims the missionaries kept stored, it was believed, in attics, trunks, or boxes, until the time came to ship them to America. In 1912, when a certain Swedish missionary began to build a brick house, the local people said, "It's all over, he's building a warehouse for souls." And when schoolchildren began to learn the French terms for parts of the body, many people fled as far away as Brazzaville.

Despite this dubious reputation, the Protestants did win many converts. So did the Catholics, who came later, so that since the 1930s virtually all BaKongo have been Christians. Nevertheless the reputation exists. In 1980, in Kisangani, about one thousand miles northeast of Kongo territory, rumor explained the recent arrival of Baha'i missionaries in that area by saying that the government had incurred an enormous foreign debt in building the new international airport there and had had to allow a new group to harvest souls in order to pay it off.

THE ECONOMICS OF IMPERIALISM

The production of export goods by local labor, organized by the Belgians in the earliest stages of colonial rule, continued the same extortion of souls by other means. I was told in 1970 that ivory and rubber, the principal exports at the turn of the century, were merely the containers for souls being shipped overseas. Later on, when the cultivation of urena was introduced (and required), the fact that some people's bundles of fiber weighed surprisingly heavy when sold to Belgian traders proved that the victims of witchcraft had been stowed in them. Amid the nationalist fervor of 1960, a Kongo newspaper published an article, in French, demanding the immediate return of all Kongo people who had been transformed into a chemical product as merchandise.

It was believed in 1970, in Matadi and elsewhere in Lower Congo, that some individuals, willing to do anything to get to America and become rich, would volunteer for this traffic. They would enter into an agreement with a foreign technician about to go home on leave and eager to do a little business on the side, such that he would take them with him to sell in Mputu. Industrial accidents in the port of Matadi were popularly explained in this way. Elsewhere I was told of certain deep pools into which ambitious persons anxious to reach the land of the dead would throw themselves, to return later as newly arrived but "locally made" white technicians or managers.

In the office of a certain magical healer, I was told a whole colonial history. The office was a murky little shed in Matadi; around the walls hung various obscure bundles, a small stuffed crocodile, a turtle shell, and a calendar from the Dime Savings Bank of Brookline. On the healer's desk stood a glass full of ballpoint pens awaiting medication so that their schoolboy owners would be able to pass their examinations. The story:

This trade was not created by black people but by the Catholic missionary. From the time of our ancestors it was our custom to sell people, but they did not die entirely. They were sold to the Portuguese, who stuffed them into ships for transportation to Belgium. When they arrived there, the Belgians sent out a notice to all the nations, saying, "What shall we do with these people? for they are worthless." Then the Protestant missionary said, "It is not proper to kill them; they should be sent to an island with water on every side, where they will die of hunger, and that will be the end of them." So they signed an agreement and put the people on ships and cast them away on an island where there was a forest with no food in it, and the sea on every side.

A symbolic power-figure made of wood and iron nails.

But truly God does not sleep. He gave them civilization, and skyscrapers sprang up, and food appeared, and every needful thing. When the Belgians came to see what had happened, they found nothing but skyscrapers, with no room anymore to plant food. And so it is to this day.

So the Catholic priest considered that something else should be done, saying, "This time, when we buy someone, we had better finish him off for good." When a man dies he has no means of knowing he is going to Belgium. Lots of people when they have been traded have the idea that now they are going to be rich, they will have their own magic. But when one has gone to Europe, that's where his name is; as for a return here, there is none—he wants the white man's ways.

Later the priest, seeing how things were, sent a message to the colonial government, saying, "The medicines the people use, which give them power, should

be taken away." So now in Belgium they have a whole house full of our things, though they have no idea how to use them.

It would be a mistake to treat this story as fantastic or even simply wrong. Despite the unfamiliar idiom, we can recognize in it references to both Manhattan and the Royal Museum of Central Africa at Tervuren in Belgium. More importantly, the story conveys a far more accurate picture of the extraction of labor from Africa for the benefit of the developed world than does the usual self-serving account of Europe's "civilizing mission" and the white man's burden.

THE SOURCES OF COSMOLOGY

A system of belief does not descend ready-made from the sky, nor can we explain either its origin or its present strength by saying that it is a relic of the traditional past. Their cosmology seems real to the BaKongo because they live it; their daily experience confirms it. If we examine that same life sociologically, we find that the sociological models of political organization and marital alliance exhibit the same structure as the cosmology.

Every free man or woman belongs to a matrilineal clan, a group whose members trace their descent from an original female ancestor. The group is exogamous, meaning that everyone must look to some other group for a spouse. In practice, the members of any one clan marry into many other clans, but if we were to construct a model of the marriage system, it would be necessary to show only one other clan in order to demonstrate the principle. The marital alliance extends into other matters as well. For example, every group needs at least one other to testify to the truth of its traditions and its property claims. Though every individual belongs with his mother in one group, his father necessarily belongs to the other, where he has certain religious and political functions to fulfill, and so on.

This simple, egalitarian model is well established in Kongo thought and expressed in a variety of proverbs, such as "Where the needle goes, the thread follows, and "Whence the pig escaped, they return the piglet." It is also embodied in a number of figures of speech, found among many Central African peoples, that describe the relationship between two clans as being like the two banks of a river. The role of a married woman in linking them is compared to that of a canoe going to and fro. The similarity to the model of the reciprocating universe is clinched by the term *nzadi*, which means not only "large river" but "in-law." Hence the riddle, "What large river is full to overflowing, but we don't fail in?"

The reciprocating universe is thus real to BaKongo because they literally live it.

In 1921, Simon Kimbangu arose as a prophet in Lower Congo, preaching the Gospel, healing the sick and casting out witchcraft. So began one of the best-known African religious movements of modern times, surviving Belgian repression through several decades and giving rise to many variants. One of the strongest Kimbanguist themes concerns the expected return of the "King of the Americans." A hymn says, "When the King of the Americans comes, to announce the King of Kongo, our sufferings will have been noticed."

Not understanding Kongo cosmology, the Belgians took this millenarian expectation literally, attributing it to the nefarious influence of Marcus Garvey or of the American government, eager to take over the Belgian colony. In fact it meant that BaKongo expected the hand of God, working through his prophet Kimbangu, to turn the world upside down, so that the ancestors from across the water (the Americans) would return, and disease and oppression would end. Similar ideas guided popular understanding as national independence approached in 1960.

Many people thought they would become white, and some of them knocked politely on the doors of European residences asking to see the kind of accommodations they would be moving into. The Europeans thought them naive, as no doubt in a sense they were, though not in the sense that was attributed to them.

A longer discussion would show that the whole cosmology is intriguingly more complex than I have shown here. Like other cosmologies, Kongo ideas of the universe are not in a simple sense either true or false. Component propositions may be refutable, but the system, as part of the fabric of a way of life, is self-confirming. As that way of life changes, so will it become implicit in the cosmology. Such a process happens not because of any universal tendency but because of particular local events. More and more BaKongo individually live urban, bureaucratic lives to which the clan system is becoming irrelevant. More radically, the government of Zaire has taken legal, economic, and political steps to destroy local social structures such as the one described here.

ADDITIONAL READING

Wyatt MacGaffey, *Religion and Society in Central Africa*, Chicago, 1986.

Robert Farris Thompson and Joseph Cornet, *The Four Moments of the Sun: Kongo Art in Two Worlds*, Washington, 1981.

Article 15   *New Internationalist*, December 1992

A traveller's notebook

War has been the only steady diet for the people of northern Ethiopia and Eritrea. But NI editor Richard Swift finds grounds for hope of better fare in the future.

The Toyota land cruiser screeched to a halt. Two strange men jumped out and pointed their odd machines at the boy in the purple shirt and his sister. The little nomad girl leaped off the camel and ran screaming up the hill. The two strange men were me and my colleague Mel from Oxfam-Canada and the odd machines were Japanese cameras. Our driver Walde called out in the Tigranya language to reassure the girl that there was no danger. But in a land like Eritrea where the countryside is still pock-marked with trenches it is hard to get used to the fact that 30 years of war are finally over. The girl's reaction was perfectly understandable—death could easily come at the whim of strangers in large vehicles pointing odd machines in your direction. Peace will take a bit of time to get used to.

Travel anywhere in the Horn of Africa and one reality becomes obvious. War is contagious. Its consequences—

Ethiopia

POPULATION: 50 million.

HISTORY: The only country in Africa that was never colonized. The royal family—Haile Selassie was the last monarch—traced its lineage back to biblical times and the Queen of Sheba. Their original seat was the Tigrayan highland town of Axum, where they were closely linked to the spiritual power of the Orthodox Church. The centre of power slowly shifted southward to Addis Ababa where the Amharic people of Shoa province dominated government and economy. Colonel Mengistu seized power in a military coup in 1974, promising socialism and equality but delivering war and economic stagnation.

ECONOMY: Primarily agricultural. Most people are either smallholders or nomadic pastoralists. The rate of inflation is low for Africa and the public sector remains important. Any industry is concentrated in pockets around Addis Ababa and a few other centres. During Mengistu's rule military spending increased from one-quarter to one-third of the government budget—this in a country where income per head is $120 a year and the third lowest in the world. The emphasis on the commercial production of cash crops, particularly coffee, has hurt domestic food production.

POLITICS: When the coalition forces of the Ethiopian People's Revolutionary Democratic Front entered Addis Ababa in May of 1991 it marked the end of a bitter war of resistance against Colonel Mengistu Haile Mariam's military government. The new transitional government under Meles Zenawi has promised elections and a radical decentralization of power from Addis to the different ethnic regions. In June 1992 the first local elections were held. But there is armed conflict between the Government and the Oromo Liberation Front.

BASIC NEEDS: Life expectancy for Ethiopians is just 45 years. Some 84 per cent of the population cannot get safe water. Half are without access to health care and 40 per cent of all children are malnourished. In 1991 more than eight million Ethiopians suffered from serious shortages of food.

HUMAN RIGHTS: Under Mengistu arbitrary arrest, torture and execution were commonplace. During the 'Red Terror' of the 1970s thousands of students and opposition activists were slaughtered in Addis Ababa. In 1983 more than a million people were forcibly resettled from the northern highlands, resulting in at least 100,000 deaths. The situation has improved under the present government, which has gone some way towards restoring the rule of law, although force is still used against political opponents.

refugees, weapons, ecological destruction, fear and oppression—overflow borders and infect the entire region. Weapons from Ethiopian wars are now in the hands of young gunfighters who make survival on the streets of Mogadishu—which used to be the capital of Somalia—a matter of firepower or just plain luck. Refugees from southern Sudan caught in the crossfire of civil war flee in terror across the Ethiopian border. Not too long ago Ethiopian refugees fled across the Sudanese border for exactly the same reason.

But if war and instability can overflow borders, how about peace and a commitment to meet people's basic needs? As I travelled through Eritrea and the northern Ethiopian province of Tigray I got at least the hint that this is possible, which would be all the more remarkable given the startling conditions in the region. Few illusions are possible about this part of the world—it is poor in almost every sense of the word. It has few natural resources, no surface water, badly degraded soil and very little rain. The highlands of both Eritrea and Tigray are rolling hillscapes of endless rock interspersed with spindly trees or the odd clump of green. Here and there the vegetation takes on the

regularity of crop lines that farmers have managed to coax out of the stingy ground, still using the same ox-drawn iron plow that they have for centuries. Women stagger under huge loads of firewood that must have taken the better part of a day to collect given the scarcity of mature trees.

For me this country has a vaguely Biblical feel. Nomadic people such as the Rashida or the Beja still wander these hills with camels, donkeys and goats in tow trying to survive in an era where modern states with their penchant for regimentation make nomadic life increasingly difficult.

Cars are rare and transportation is hard to find, making hitchhiking a highly evolved art form involving anything from hand gestures and beseeching looks or cries to feigning authority or simply acting as a human roadblock. The roads are in dreadful shape but then so is the rest of the infrastructure. The relatively new hospital in Massawa, Eritrea's Red Sea port, is a case in point. It was so badly damaged by Ethiopian bombing that only a small outpatient clinic on the bottom floor remains open. And this is certainly not due to lack of business in a coastal area plagued by malaria and dengue fever.

Still the mood in Eritrea is remarkably upbeat. After 30 years of almost constant warfare the Eritrean People's Liberation Front (EPLF) has expelled all Ethiopian forces and is on the brink of achieving the long cherished Eritrean desire for independence. The streets of the capital Asmara are remarkably clean and safe (for both sexes) and everyone you talk to is infected by a quiet optimism about the future. Time and again I was told 'finally we will see what we can do for ourselves'.

There is an acute awareness about the pitfalls that have plagued development in the rest of Africa. A spokesperson at the Ministry of Foreign Affairs was blunt about the penchant for states in post-colonial Africa to build up a centralized and remote bureaucracy in the comfort of Western-style capital cities. Such bureaucracies have too often been an expensive dead weight on the development aspirations of the rural majority.

With this in mind, the new government of Eritrea has already embarked on a radical decentralization, shifting some of its most talented people out of Asmara to run provincial administrations. The dedication of Eritreans to the success of their new country is not hard to see. All upper-level civil servants installed after the collapse of Ethiopian rule are working for 60 birr ($30) a month in order to give the fledgling treasury some breathing space before the formal ratification of independence by referendum in early 1993. It is hard to imagine any other society in the world where the upper levels of the civil service (and most of the army as well) would work as virtual volunteers for nearly two years.

Although Eritrean Peoples Liberation Front leader Isaias Afwerki is hugely popular you cannot find his picture in any of the restaurants or bars that dot Asmara's streets. The EPLF has always eschewed the cult of personality to which even the most progressive Third World leaders seem susceptible.

As you make your way down the windy roads that run west out of Asmara to Eritrea's second city, Keran, the national obsession with terracing and reforestation is quickly apparent. Hill after hill shows the fruits of food-for-work programs (a staple of famine relief in this part of the world): regularly interspersed neat stone lines and young saplings to help hold the precious highland soil in place. The sheer variety and ingenuity of water catchment systems is another pillar of Eritrean agricultural policy—micro-dams, settling ponds, handpumps, hand-dug or machine-dug wells, and even elaborate home-made irrigation systems to trap precious water during the rainy season.

As we travel further south into the Ethiopian province of Tigray the story is very much the same—what so much of the world (even the African world) takes for granted is a matter of constant effort throughout these northern highlands. One Tigrayan village is appropriately named Kilishi

Inni, which roughly translated means 'too many stones'. Here the women are very careful not to shout or talk too loudly when they are near the well for fear they will scare the water away. This seems like good sense in an area where nature is more whimsical than bountiful.

In Tigray as in Eritrea a mood of determined optimism about making the best of a difficult situation is never far from the surface. Heshe Lemma of the Relief Society of Tigray (REST) can barely contain his enthusiasm when he talks of the agricultural outreach programs that are being made available in rural Tigray for the first time. Farmers here have historically been neglected. Emperor Haile Selassie concentrated wealth and power in Addis Ababa and the Amharic regions of Ethiopia, leaving the poor north to its own devices and hiding its famines from the outside world. And the Dergue that overthrew him was little better: its dreams were of massive state farms churning out export crops to pay for the weapons systems that were so dear to their hearts and so essential to their survival.

'Only now,' says Heshe, becoming very animated, are agricultural extension services being made available to the poor peasant farmers who are the backbone of our society.' This could of course be just an official line—but the evidence of our own eyes proves its truth.

Remote Tigrayan villages give new meaning to the word 'outreach'. It's only 30 bone-jarring kilometres between the highland town of Adwa and the little farming village of Mia Kinetal yet it takes us more than two hours. At several points along the road I give up hope that the land cruiser is up to the task, not least when we teeter on two side wheels as we struggle to ford a particularly difficult stream bed.

Once in the village Heshe takes us to its seedbank. As we drink large cups of murky sua—the local brew—REST's agricultural extension officer explains how things work. The system is simple enough. Farmers borrow seeds from the bank the first year and repay it with good seeds from their crops after harvest time. REST's original grant in 1989 provided 4,300 of the 8,000 local farmers with seeds. The extension officer shuffles through a box of carefully maintained records to show that there have been remarkably few defaults despite the poor rainfall last season. The seedbank is particularly important in reducing the vulnerability of the rural population. Hungry farmers are no longer faced with the impossible choice of eating their seeds or being too weak to work in the fields.

Another REST program is the oxen bank—an idea also being tried in Eritrea. This is crucial because oxen are not only essential for animal traction but the main source of capital in cash-poor northern Ethiopia. The cyclical droughts of the 1980s have meant many farmers have been forced to sell their animals or the animals have died of starvation.

The commitments of the Eritrean and Tigrayan liberation movements to the peasant population are understandable. It was these farmers who provided the backbone of resistance to the Dergue. Without their support the military regime in Addis could never have been defeated. But anyway development in these highlands cannot be about mega-projects or dreams of industrial take-off. It must be about survival. Its success or failure will be measured by its effect on the rhythms of everyday life—how long it takes to get water from the new well or if there are enough healthy oxen to plow the fields for the whole village.

But commitments to the peasant smallholders can only be guaranteed if the political system gives them real power to shape their own fates. The hope for both Eritrea and Tigray lies in the promise of a grassroots democracy that allows the majority of people a direct say over the decisions that shape both their communities and their lives. But there are risks here. In Eritrea there is no opposition party on the horizon and it would be quite easy to take bureaucratic shortcuts or confine meaningful discussion of policy options to inner circles of the Eritrean Peoples Liberation Front. Dissent might be taken as subversion. Without a formal political opposition complete freedom of speech, assembly and the press will be essential if democracy is to evolve—as well as grassroots organizations free of party control.

In Tigray the task is even more complex. The Tigrayan People's Liberation Front (TPLF) is not only responsible for Tigrayan affairs but is a key component of the transitional Ethiopian government in Addis Ababa. The transition to a democratic system in a society like Ethiopia with no such traditions is never easy. It will be made more complicated if the government with its strong Tigrayan roots is seen as favouring Tigray over the other regions of the country. The new government in Addis must deal with the thorny problem of balancing the claims of all Ethiopia's different nationalities and their often quarrelsome political organizations.

Already armed conflict has broken out in southern and eastern Ethiopia between government forces and those of the Oromo Liberation Front—who claim to represent the majority Oromo population. The rights and wrongs of this situation are difficult to work out but the willingness of both parties to resort to military means to solve their disagreements bodes ill for a land badly in need of peace.

Still, both the EPLF and TPLF have shown a willingness to rely on compromise and negotiation rather than administrative decree to solve political problems. Also the democratic expectations of the peoples of Eritrea and Tigray are very high. Zemichael Gebremedhin, who is responsible for social affairs in Tigray, is blunt on this point. He seems somewhat ill at ease sitting over a hotel meal in Mekele—Tigray's lively but very poor capital. 'We have only been out of the bush for a few months,' he says, 'so we are bound to make some mistakes. But one thing is certain: the people of Tigray will never accept an undemocratic system again.'

Article 16   *The Christian Science Monitor,* January 13, 1993

Ethiopia Rebuilds Ruined Economy

Early market reforms win Western support, but farmers still may not own their land

Robert M. Press

Staff writer of the Christian Science Monitor

ADDIS ABABA, ETHIOPIA

In celebration of Christmas Jan. 7 in accord with the Ethiopian calendar, priests at the Balewold Orthodox Church, wearing elegant robes and hats and shaded by umbrellas, slowly circled the outside of the building three times.

In another old ritual, beggars, some deformed, made their way slowly through the dense crowd of faithful men and women gathered around the church, collecting coins in their open palms.

Against a background of rich traditions, and a mix of extreme poverty and relative affluence, Ethiopia's new rulers are trying to modernize this ancient country.

Thirty years of war and 17 years of Marxist policies have left Ethiopia one of the world's poorest countries. Infrastructure is in tatters. But while many serious problems remain and urban residents complain life is getting harder, the young Ethiopian government has accomplished major reforms in the past 20 months, according to the World Bank and United States diplomats.

Despite their history of advocating Marxism and Socialism prior to taking power, the rebels who in May ousted dictator Mengistu Haile-Mariam have steered Ethiopia toward a free market economy.

Some of the initial market reforms target:

•Agriculture. Farmers for the first time are now free to sell crops anywhere, at any price. Previously, they had to sell a significant share of their harvest to the Mengistu government, usually at below-market prices. The new government also offers farmers the option of a minimum guaranteed crop price.

The United Nations Food and Agriculture Organization says higher crop prices have led farmers to plant more acres. This, along with the end of the civil war and good rains, have produced what is likely to be a record crop, now being harvested.

•Transportation. Truckers for the first time may travel anywhere and charge any price, without the hindrance of tariff- and bribe-collecting road barriers and other state restrictions.

Though in the short run this may push up transportation prices, in the long run, US officials say, prices are likely to fall again as the number of truckers competing for business increases. Free movement of trucks is seen as a key to moving food quickly from fields to markets in a country where people have starved in one region while there were surpluses in another.

In a vote of confidence for the economic reforms already made and additional ones planned, Western donors held a joint meeting on Ethiopia in Paris in November, their first since 1974, approving $1.2 billion in aid for use by June 1994.

The aid will help pay for imports and development and recovery projects, and will help to ease a "very precarious budget situation," says one Ethiopian economic official.

Senior officials in the ruling Ethiopian People's Revolutionary Democratic Front (EPRDF) say the first economic priority is development—the rebuilding of roads, schools, clinics, and hospitals destroyed during the war.

The government is planning to sell off some of the many state-owned companies, and is trimming its bloated civil service.

"In some offices there were 60 type-writers and 300 secretaries," says Gilma Kidane, an Ethiopian Red Cross official working on a government program to re-build war-damaged areas.

"These are extraordinary changes," says Willard Pearson, director of the US Agency for International Development program in Ethiopia.

But existence is still difficult for the more than 80 percent of the population who are farmers, typically earning only about $100 a year on less than three acres of land, Mr. Pearson says.

Many Ethiopians grumble over higher living costs resulting from the Oct. 1 de-valuation, by 58.6 percent, of the birr. Import prices shot up, but so did the price of domestic food and other items trans-ported with imported fuel.

Laid-off government employees find it difficult to feed their families. Many of the 500,00 former soldiers of the Mengistu Army, now demobilized, are jobless and landless.

The government also has not moved completely to a market economy. The EPRDF has retained state ownership of land and key industries, including min-ing and communications.

Alemseged Amlak, a senior govern-ment official, says this reflects the reality of the EPRDF's broad mix of people, "from priests to communists."

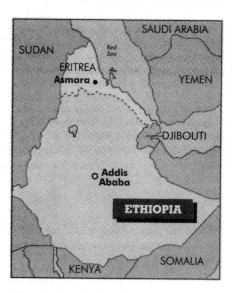

Mr. Alemseged says the government wants to avoid continued economic domination by "the old ruling class,"— the elite Amhars of central Ethiopia, who governed for about a century.

"We should create real change in the life of the peasant," Alemseged says.

The government retains title to land, he says, to prevent the Amhars from buying up farmland and forcing landless farmers to flood the cities, and thus increasing urban joblessness.

"We want to get rid of [economic] re-strictions without hurting the social fab-ric," says Teffera Shaiwl, acting head of press and information in the Ministry of Foreign Affairs.

Article 17   *AfricaNews*, June 8—June 21, 1992

Africans Push More Ambitious Environment Goals

The slogan "Think globally, act locally," coined by envi-ronmental groups in the wealthy, industrialized countries of the northern hemisphere, is becoming a way of life for more and more people in the poor nations of the south. From mountain farmers protecting a nature reserve in Cameroon to Kenyan scientists developing environment-friendly pest controls, Africans are part of the trend.

No one person better personifies the environmental movement in developing countries than biologist Wangari Maathai of Kenya, who says that awareness of the need for urgent collective action is spreading. "People have personalized the message," she says, "because they have seen the need to take care of their immediate environment, and by participating they have been able to reap some of the benefits."

At the same time, the growing numbers of people trying to eke out a living on fragile tropical soils is putting unprecedented pressure on local resources. Trees are cut for fuel. Water is polluted by agricultural chemicals. Wildlife is killed by farmers shielding their crops.

That reality has spawned a view evident in environmental discussions and press reports in the north, that people in poorer countries have less vested interest in protecting the environment than those in more developed nations. *Newsweek* magazine quotes a Western diplomat who characterized the view of many poor countries this way: "If there's a decision to be made between development and environment, they'll go for development."

Presenting the case for financial assistance to help poorer countries develop in ecologically sound ways, *Newsweek* says the world will reap the benefit. People in developing countries, the magazine says, "might someday look at a tree the way people do in Marin County as the handiwork of God, rather than a big piece of firewood stuck in the ground."

Tell that to Wangari Maathai! The Greenbelt Movement she founded 15 years ago has mobilized 50,000 women who already have planted millions of trees and are still going strong.

As Maathai sees it, the debate over development versus the environment is a false one. The more pressing issue is one of power: who wields it and who benefits? As long as poor-country dictators are installed, supported or tolerated by powerful international interests, she argues, the global environment is at risk. Only democratic structures that empower ordinary people—especially women—can save the world.

"When we plant trees in Kenya," Maathai says, "we know that we will eventually have our hands on politics, on economics, on culture, on all aspects that either destroy or create a sustainable environment. And in countries like ours, where there is a lot of poverty, you eventually have to address that issue and ask: 'Why is here so much poverty?' "

Maathai and other developing-country environmentalists acknowledge that rural peasants around the world will chop trees or kill animals to survive the next day. On the other hand, the activists argue, poor people—when given the slightest margin to act in their own behalf—become the world's most vociferous conservationists.

To even the most zealous North American activist, issues like global warming are several removes from daily survival. Living closer to the edge, people in developing

countries can reap immediate tangible benefits from environmental protection and reclamation. A road not built through a coastal mangrove swamp spares the habitat upon which the day's fishing depends. A rain forest exempted from logging will provide culls for vital cooking fuel. A river saved from pollutants can be the difference between life and death for entire communities.

The spreading realization that rich and poor are united in their long-term dependence on a shared global heritage is the impetus behind the "Earth Summit" in Rio de Janeiro, Brazil. The hundreds of world leaders and thousands of concerned citizens who have converged on the summit have begun, at least superficially, to speak a common language.

"Sustainable development," the concept that economic growth must be pursued in a way that preserves the ability of future generations to meet their own needs, is being championed in the halls of the World Bank, the mines of Zambia, the deserts of north Africa and the streets of Nairobi.

But how to achieve the goal remains a bitterly divisive question. One of the problems, says American economist Winifred Armstrong, is that governments remain committed to an obsolete model of economic growth. "As I see it," she says, "neither the North nor the South is sustainable under the present economic framework. Trying harder, using current economic premises, is clearly not working."

Armstrong, who derives her perspective from applied experience, including years of work for a major U.S. mining company with extensive international interests, recently returned from seven months of travel across Africa. She says both individuals and governments need to move beyond the restrictive framework of both capitalist and socialist economic models.

Like Armstrong, Wangari Maathai sees a multiplicity of factors constraining healthy economic growth, including the massive debts encouraged by international lenders and incurred by corrupt or inefficient authoritarian governments. Africa has the largest proportional debt burden by far, and repayment obligations consume the bulk of many countries' resources. The need to earn foreign currency to repay those debts has intensified the drive to abandon subsistence agriculture and clear forests in order to grow cash crops for export. "It is ordinary men, women and children who pay," Maathai says.

"Most people I talked to in Africa," says Winifred Armstrong, "believe they can live primarily on what their countries produce. But under the prevailing export model of growth, most African countries can't even survive."

Maathai believes that foreign aid, whether in the form of loans or grants, has played a direct role in stifling African development. "We have seen a lot of aid flowing into Africa," she told Charlayne Hunter-Gault of the "Mac-

Neil/Lehrer Newshour." "But a lot of that aid was in the form of arms that were used to sustain dictators that we are now desperately trying to get rid of. And this was done with the full knowledge and support of the super powers."

African activists are insisting that shared power, not only within individual countries but also among the world's nations, is an essential ingredient of global progress.

"Certain actions by the industrialized countries indicate that developing countries will have problems being taken seriously in Rio," says Tendai Msengezi of the Southern African Research and Documentation Center (SARDC) based in Harare, Zimbabwe. "Developing countries fear that the industrialized countries are determined to dictate to them."

Economists and environmentalists from poor countries worry that—despite the hoopla surrounding the Earth Summit in Rio de Janeiro—developed nations will push ineffective half measures: insisting that poor countries remove tariffs on imports, while retaining their own barriers against competition from the developing world; insisting on debt repayment, while paying bottom dollar for the commodities that poor countries produce; demanding protection of wildlife in tourist-frequented game parks, but encouraging roads through rain forests housing endangered species; financing reforestation on the one hand and backing mining projects that denude vast tracks on the other.

Korinna Horta of the Washington DC-based Environmental Defense Fund, maintains that "on the ground, it's business as usual." She cites a $10 million grant by the Global Environment Facility—a sort of environmental superfund launched in 1990 and administered by the World Bank—to project in Congo, whose stated aim is to "bring forestry exploitation back to life." The United Nations Development Program and the World Rain Forest Movement are among the groups who have questioned whether renewed logging will benefit the area the grant is intended to protect.

The Bush administration's announcement that the United States will oppose the biodiversity treaty negotiated last month by 98 nations in Nairobi has further fueled doubts that northern governments are willing to do more than talk tough about the environment. The treaty, which was to have been a major achievement of the Rio meeting, along with an agreement on global warming, aims to protect threatened plants, animals and natural resources around the world.

In a SARDC report last month, Tendai Msengezi wrote that at the final preparatory meeting in New York prior to the Summit, northern governments balked at any conference follow-up "that is not dominated by the G7 countries [the United States, Canada, Britain, France, Germany, Italy and Japan]."

"Britain led an opposition group from the industrialized countries," Msengezi wrote, "which refused a proposal made by 40 developing countries for a sustainable development commission to monitor the performances of both the North and the South in implementing decisions that would have been arrived at in Brazil."

So the image of wealthy nations pressing for environmental safeguards and poor nations resisting strict standards, in the interests of their own development, may be turned topsy-turvy in the months after Rio. If the representatives of grassroots groups, green movements and non-governmental organizations forge a global network, as many hope, their voices may become the chorus that drowns out the established tune equating economic health with conventional growth models.

"Am I optimistic that we *will* do it? Not necessarily," says Winifred Armstrong. "Am I optimistic that we *can* do it? Yes."

Article 18   *Unesco Courier*, March 1992

Kenya's Green Belt Movement

A community-based project created and directed by women

Wangari Maathai

Wangari Maathai, of Kenya, is the founder and co-ordinator of the Green Belt movement. She has received many awards for her work, most recently the 1991 Africa Prize.

Thousands of Kenyan women are today playing an active part in a nationwide environmental protection campaign which takes the tree as a symbol of hope and an indicator of what must be done to conserve the environment and ensure development that meets today's needs without jeopardizing the world of tomorrow.

The campaign is being waged by the Green Belt Movement, which was launched in 1977 under the auspices of the National Council of Women of Kenya

(NCWK) as a grassroots struggle against desertification, deforestation, soil loss and fuelwood scarcity. Its main practical objective is to halt desertification by encouraging tree planting and soil and water conservation in rural communities. At the same time it is committed to increasing public awareness of the relationship between environmental degradation and such issues as poverty, unemployment, malnutrition and the mismanagement of natural resources, and the impact of these problems on the political and economic situation throughout Africa.

The story of the Green Belt Movement began in 1977 when a small group of NCWK members launched a tree-planting project called "Save the Land Harambee", (Harambee is a Swahili expression which means "let's all pull together"). We had no tree nursery, no staff and no funds, only a conviction that there was a role for ordinary country people in efforts to solve environmental problems.

We held our first tree-planting ceremony in Nairobi on 5 June 1977, World Environment Day. From then on interest in the project grew rapidly, and soon people from all over the country were asking us where they could find tree seedlings.

To help them we approached the Department of Forestry in the Ministry of Environment and Natural Resources, which has a national network of tree nurseries. The head of the Department

Seven steps to conservation

In our 15 years of field experience in Kenya, we have developed a procedure for spreading the conservation message that has produced good results. The elements of this procedure, listed below, may also work in other developing countries.

• **The message should respond to a local need.**

Most people in developing countries are poor and concerned about basic needs such as food, water, firewood and clothing. Conservation cannot be presented to them as a luxury issue. The Green Belt Movement introduces the idea of environmental conservation through trees because trees meet many basic needs of rural communities. We encourage small farmers to plant trees to meet their own needs, and as we work with them we try to help them appreciate that trees also do a lot for their communities and for the country as a whole.

• **The message must make good sense.**

How is it possible to explain the importance of protecting genetic resources to members of a women's group, most of whom are illiterate?

We explain that trees which have survived in a certain part of the country since time immemorial are better suited to our environment than recently introduced foreign trees. We often ask members of women's groups to list the ways in which they or their parents use local trees—as a source of medicine, perhaps, or as pest-resistant wood, or in traditional ceremonies. This type of discussion helps to make the environment seem a real and living part of their community life.

• **The project must be honest.**

If the members of a community feel that a project is honestly run and designed specifically to benefit them, they will support it.

• **The project should work patiently to motivate communities.**

Spreading the conservation message is a slow process. It is not easy to motivate rural communities, but if they come to believe in your own motivation they will begin to walk along with you and eventually to work on their own for the message.

• **Ensure that the project offers some short-term successes.**

It is important for people to see some success stories within a reasonable period of time. Developing both short-term and long-term objectives will create momentum for a project. When a Green Belt nursery is set up, for example, the first crop of tree seedlings are released to the community within three to six months. The women's group responsible for the nursery then receives compliments and gains respect from the community.

• **Try to reach the decision-makers as well as reaching the rural communities.**

Decision-makers in the developing world often pay lip service to conservation. Without their support, however, it is impossible to take the conservation message effectively to rural communities. Decision-makers must realize that they will benefit if the masses work to prevent desertification.

The message should thus be taken to the powerful and to the communities almost simultaneously. Even though it may take a long time before the support of decision-makers is more than rhetorical, it is essential that they should give a verbal commitment to the project. Rural communities will be even more enthusiastic about the project if their leaders are supportive.

• **Create a forum for continuous dialogue.**

In taking the message to rural communities, the teachers must also become the pupils. We all have much to learn from each other. There must be continuing dialogue until people believe that the protection of our world is for the benefit of all.

laughed when we told him that we intended to plant a million trees, and without hesitation promised us all the seedlings we needed. Less than a year later he had to go back on his decision when he found that we had distributed more seedlings than he could afford to give away. From then on we had to pay for seedlings from government nurseries—fortunately at low prices and with useful guidance and support from government foresters.

The project grew by leaps and bounds. In the last fourteen years over a thousand nurseries have been established at which women grow seedlings that are then released to small farmers and to public institutions such as school and churches. The women are paid for the seedlings they grow, and many jobs have been cre-

ated, mostly in the rural areas. To date some 10 million trees have been planted and have survived—a survival rate of about 70–80 per cent. Up to 80,000 women are today involved in work at nursery sites.

The trees have been planted to meet immediate community needs—to provide fuelwood and material for fencing and building, and to give shade. Gradually, however, people learned that trees also prevent soil erosion and the consequent loss of soil fertility. They came to see the link between loss of soil fertility, poor crop yields and famine.

The Green Belt Movement harnesses local expertise and resources and encourages communities to stand on their own feet. We deliberately discourage direct participation by high-powered techni-

cians and managers from outside. We want to create confidence in local people who are often overwhelmed by experts and come to think that they are incapable and backward.

The aims of the Green Belt Movement are inspired by the needs and problems of Kenya—we encourage, for instance, the use of indigenous trees and shrubs in order to help protect the genetic resources of Kenya's different ecological zones (see box). Four years ago, however, our Movement entered a new phase of its activities when it approached a number of other countries in eastern and southern Africa and launched what will, it is hoped, become an All-Africa Green Belt Movement Network. Our objectives are valid for many other countries, not only in Africa but elsewhere in the world.

Article 19   *World Monitor*, February 1993

America's Lost Stepchild

Liberia is a kind of Somalia West—ravaged by civil warfare. But US aid to this earliest haven for freed slaves has backfired. Will Clinton help?

Dayle E. Spencer

Dayle E. Spencer, a lawyer/negotiator, was an observer at the heads of state summits on Liberia and has traveled throughout West Africa meeting with leaders on Liberia's interim government and the warring factions. As Director of the Conflict Resolution Program of the Carter Center of Emory University, she collaborated with former President Carter to develop the International Negotiation Network, known for its work in Ethiopia, Sudan, and elsewhere.

The Firestone Rubber Plantation at Harbel, Liberia, has a long winding driveway to a mansion like something from "Gone With the Wind." Tall white columns grace the two-story front porch. The second level has a panoramic view of the rolling hillside—a million acres of rubber trees in orderly rows. As a visitor from Georgia, I could easily imagine being back home, if cotton were substituted for rubber. But—just as it did in "Gone With the Wind"—civil strife threatens the pastoral scene. In early November cluster bombs rained down on Harbel

as it became just another in a long line of devastating casualties felt by America's forgotten stepchild, Liberia, over the past three years.

Most Americans aren't aware that this West African country had its origin in the efforts of several US philanthropic societies to establish freed slaves (or Americo-Liberians as they came to be called) in a colony long before the US Civil War and the Emancipation Proclamation. In 1822 a settlement was formed near the spot where the capital city of Monrovia now stands. On July 26, 1847, the state was constituted as the Free and Independent Republic of Liberia.

The US government has maintained a close relationship with the country. Some key cities are named for American presidents, e.g. Monrovia (Monroe) and Buchanan. Liberia is the closest the US ever came to having a colony, rivaled only by its relationship to the Philippines.

Liberia has some 16 distinct ethnic groups, such as the Krahn, Mano, Gio, and Mandingo. Historically their relations were peaceful and even included intermarriage. Perhaps this peacefulness was only on the surface, owing to almost total political and economic domination by the Americo-Liberians, a small percentage of the population, which is now about 2 1/2 million.

There were signs of trouble as early as the late 1970s. Riots broke out when the government raised the price of rice, the country's most important staple product, at a time of recession. A year later Samuel Doe (no, it is not an alias) staged a coup, executing more than two dozen of the country's top leaders on the sands of one of its prettiest beaches.

Doe was a master sergeant in the Liberian Army and a Krahn. His coup was initially seen as a people's revolution, and was met with dancing in the streets. It was also widely believed that the uneducated and unsophisticated Doe would not entrench himself but allow a quick transition to true democracy. Like his predecessors, however, he was quickly seduced by the power of the autocratic presidency.

From 1980 until the start of the civil war in 1989, Doe's administration was marked by widespread abuse of human rights. When members of the Mano and Gio groups staged a coup attempt against Doe, his response was a total crackdown and still harsher treatment of ethnic groups other than his own.

In 1985, in response to international pressure, Doe allowed national elections to be conducted. Most observers would agree that the processes leading up to the elections, though not perfect, were basically fair. But there was little doubt that Doe stole the election as the votes were being counted. Many ballots cast in anti-Doe areas were burned, and newspapers published photographs of them still smoldering.

Still, Doe's hand-picked election officials certified that he had won by 51%. And a highly placed US State Department representative testified to Congress that, despite some shortcomings, "election day went off very well."

Liberians knew better. Within a month one of Doe's former colleagues, Thomas Quiwonkpa, a Gio, attempted a coup. He was arrested, tortured, mutilated, and killed. According to a human rights monitoring group, the post-coup reprisals "brought ethnic tensions to a boil."

The Doe regime's abuses ranged from the detention and firing of university faculty and student leaders to closing prominent newspapers and refusing to investigate allegations of abuse. As a result, large numbers of Liberia's most prominent intellectuals fled the country.

One might have expected US aid to Liberia to be cut, sanctions employed, or other drastic action taken. The US Congress did pass a nonbinding resolution for suspension of security assistance until genuinely free and fair elections were held. The House of Representatives also contended that further economic aid should be conditioned on release of all prisoners and other steps toward democracy. Doe complied with none of these terms.

Yet the Reagan administration took no action in response to the congressional recommendations. In the first five years of Doe's rule, US aid to Liberia was half a billion dollars—more than to all other sub-Saharan countries combined. The US had a Cold War interest in using Liberia's soil to monitor communications, so it looked the other way as Doe violated international law.

"US assistance is having the unintended effect of providing [Doe's] tribe, the Krahn, with the means by which it is able to dominate all the others," concluded a human rights analyst at the time. "Thus, it is argued, the United States, far from promoting stability, may be unwittingly sowing the seeds of further conflict by aggravating ethnic divisions."

Three years after this assessment was made, the Liberian civil war began. Charles Taylor, trained in Libya and largely equipped by Libya, began his revolution against Doe on Christmas Eve of 1989. Within six months he had advanced to the capital. Along the way a splinter group was formed under a former Taylor officer, Prince Johnson. The Taylor and Johnson forces engaged in heavy fighting with each other and with remnants of the Doe army.

The combat was most intense in Monrovia, where almost no buildings were left undamaged. Traveling around the city in the past two years I have seen large mortar holes still unrepaired in the sides of most buildings. Some 600 people, mostly women and school children, were massacred inside the sanctuary of St. Peter's Lutheran Church. Their mass grave in the front yard resembles an Indian burial mound. Across the street many people were shot down in the United Nations complex when they tried to flee the killing.

One building was noticeably unscathed—the presidential headquarters. It was spared, because it was the prize. It would be occupied by whichever group could defeat the other two. Schools, churches, homes, shops, hospitals, legislative buildings—all these were expendable.

More than 20,000 people lost their lives in six months. Half of Liberia's population was displaced, with tens of thousands pouring into neighboring countries like Ivory Coast and Sierra Leone.

Doe sent out urgent calls for help to traditional allies such as the United States. No US Marines landed on the beaches. However, in response to Doe's pleas, leaders of neighboring states took a step unprecedented in African diplomacy. They saw the civil war was having a very negative impact on regional economies. They knew both the Organization of African Unity and the UN were forbidden from becoming involved in the internal affairs of sovereign nations. So they sent in their own multinational peacekeeping force under the auspices of the Economic Community of West African States (ECOWAS). These troops landed in Buchanan on Aug. 24, 1990, and began fighting their way into Monrovia. They wanted to isolate and neutralize the three warring parties until a political settlement could be reached. The Taylor forces, owing in part to a request from the US, withdrew to the outskirts of Monrovia, remaining in control of some 95% of the country.

Samuel Doe escaped the worst of the fighting in Monrovia, only to be kidnapped on Sept. 9, 1990, by Prince Johnson. Doe's torture and death were videotaped for international distribution.

A cease-fire came on Nov. 28, 1990. For two years there was relative peace, with the political puzzle frozen in place. ECOWAS leaders launched an all-out effort to negotiate a solution allowing Liberians the option of ballots instead of bullets to determine who would occupy those unscathed presidential offices. The leaders convened a series of summits at the boyhood home of Africa's longest-serving head of state, President Houphouet-Boigny of Ivory Coast. Finally, on Oct. 31, 1991, they agreed to call for national elections and for disarmament of all warring parties to be completed by Jan. 14, 1992.

That date has long since passed, and the situation is as bad as it was in early 1990, if not worse. There are now two additional armed factions: the United Liberian Independence Movement and, representing the interim government, a freshly trained batch of soldiers referred to as the Black Berets, Secret Army, or Medusa Group.

The West African coalition that held the peacekeeping forces together seems to be dissolving, with reports that the Senegalese troops may be withdrawing completely. Without the Senegalese the delicate balance between English-speaking and French-speaking nations as peacekeepers may be upset. Consequences could be grave for the entire region.

Many opportunities for peace were missed during the two-year hiatus in fighting. Taylor would sign agreements at the heads-of-state summits and repudiate them before the participants could even travel home to announce them. Once he complained that he signed an agreement under duress by the African leaders. He even used a child-like scrawl instead of his usual grandiose, scorpionlike signature to demonstrate his lack of agreement to what he was signing.

Nigeria contributed the largest contingent and bore the principal financial responsibility for the peacekeeping operations. From Taylor's perspective, these troops were his enemy. They battled his troops and forced them back from the city in 1990, with many casualties on both sides. Taylor felt that Nigerian President Babangida had motives other than altruistic ones for his presence in Liberia.

No matter what justification Taylor gave for his delays, the regional leaders came to see him as untrustworthy and intransigent. Maintaining troops on Liberian soil was taking a large economic and political toll on the West African members of the economic coalition. Over time, momentum began toward finding a military solution to somehow end the standoff.

Meanwhile, in Sierra Leone, remnants of the old Doe army began to gather into a new force. In September 1992, this force made an incursion into Liberia, advancing easily through border areas that were supposed to be secured by the peacekeepers. This led the Taylor group to claim that the peacekeepers were not neutral. At about the same time, the interim government of Liberia—which had dispatched its own soldiers to a neighboring country for military training—returned them to the streets as the new Black Berets.

With such an assortment of armed factions, tension building with the peacekeeping troops, and patience wearing thin on the part of the West African leaders, it did not require a crystal ball to foresee a renewal of fighting in Liberia. There is some dispute about how it started, but Liberians are living in a state of dj vu. Rockets scream overhead. Children run for cover from the random bullet or the stray bomb. Women are killed, as were five American nuns in a highly publicized incident last fall. Soldiers in all the factions fight and die believing that their cause is just.

If America has any influence remaining with Liberians, perhaps it can best be used to support democratic elections as a means to end the fighting. This will be an important challenge for the Clinton administration.

The last I heard, the presidential offices were still standing in Monrovia, although almost everything else is damaged or in ruins.

Article 20   *The Christian Science Monitor, April 14, 1992*

Three Days in Timbuktu

Despite civil tensions, hospitable people make a visit to Mali's once-thriving caravan city a memorable desert sojourn

Robert M. Press

Staff writer of The Christian Science Monitor

TIMBUKTU, MALI

You've probably heard the name of this town. But when? Why? It's just a dusty little town far from everywhere else. Yet it's one of the best-known and least-visited towns in the world.

To many non-Africans, Timbuktu is a word for far away, end-of-the-earth, mystery, desert. It's all of that.

Like many people, I grew up knowing the name of this place without knowing where in the world it was.

Or that one day my wife, Betty, and I would walk its sandy streets, swatting flies, greeting adults while trying to elude the more pesky of the kids demanding *cadeaux* (gifts of money).

As you walk, history pops out at you. Plaques mark the residences of early European explorers. Mud mosques somehow survive after hundreds of years, their framework-support poles poking out of their minarets like toothpicks in hors d'oeuvres. But mostly, Timbuktu is people.

We meet Aissata Sangare, a secretary, who dreams of traveling to see the world; George and Baraka, two of the many young, self-appointed Malian guides who wait and wait at the two nearly empty hotels for tourists who seldom come; a policeman who welcomes us, then speaks angrily about Tuareg rebels in this region.

There are few signs of modernity in Timbuktu, though wealthier families enjoy home videos and electricity from the town generator. And there is an airport. But with just a bit of effort, you can imagine yourself far back in a time without cars and electricity—a time of Sahara-crossing camel caravans, of swords, and turbans—all of which are still here.

Some things are changing. Our three-day visit coincided with an election day: Timbuktu's—and Mali's—first free election after a long history of kings and a more recent history of dictators. Casting their paper ballots (white for *oui* or yes, pink for *non*) are women in long, robe-like dresses and head scarves, men in full-length robes and, often, turbans that can be pulled up to cover all but the eyes, protection against wind-blown sand.

Turnout was low. Many people hadn't received their voter-identification cards in time. And there was stiff competition from a radio broadcast of an international soccer game. The votes, some of them counted by kerosene lamp in mosques, were nearly unanimous in favor of a new constitution allowing more than one political party.

Salem Ould el Hadj, an Islamic scholar at the Ahmed Baba Center here, says, "We've had several administrations [in Mali] that left no freedom to people. This is the first time in our history that the people, freely expressing their will, have drawn up a constitution. And with no force. Everyone is voting. So it's a historic day: important for multiparty [elections] and democracy."

In a corner room of the Ahmed Baba Center, a modest collection of small, one-story buildings on a sandy side street, researcher Ali Ould Sidi opens a glass case displaying books in Arabic dating back 500 and 600 years. He says the dry climate helps preserve them. The pages look almost new.

Timbuktu, he explains, was begun around A.D. 1080 by Tuareg, the nomads of the desert known in the French-speaking world as *les hommes bleu*, or blue men, for their indigo-colored turbans.

By around 1600, according to Ali Ould Sidi, Timbuktu was a thriving trade and academic center, with some 100,000 people, including a large enrollment at the University of Sankore. Some students came from as far away as Spain. Camel caravans arrived from the Sahara, bringing salt and other items for trade.

Today, Timbuktu has only about 23,000 people, he says. The caravans still come, but only a few. Until the rebellion by the Tuaregs flared up a couple of years ago, truck traffic was the most common mode of transportation. Since then, rebel attacks on travelers have limited access primarily to boats on the Niger River and planes.

Timbuktu, long isolated from most of the outside world by distance, found itself isolated by politics. But a recent treaty between the government and the autonomy-seeking Tuaregs in Mali brings hope of a lasting settlement.

The rebellion has not only disrupted travel and tourism, it has affected daily life here as well.

"People are afraid," says Suliman Traore, an English teacher, who invited us for meals at his home. "Before the rebellion . . . there were really good relationships between [local Tuaregs and non-Tuaregs]."

BUT when a well-known Tuareg resident was killed in December, in reprisal for a Tuareg rebel attack on Timbuktu, many Tuaregs fled the town. Non-Tuaregs feared traveling outside the city, especially at night. A curfew was imposed.

Ms. Sangare found herself feeling more isolated here than ever. "I really dream of going overseas. The United States would be nice, or France. I really dream of traveling. But I don't have the money. I want to discover the world," she says.

Her father, a retired civil servant who farms, explains that despite years of drought, people manage to get enough to eat because of foreign-financed irrigation systems near Timbuktu that were built more than a dozen years ago.

"People are able to produce, so agriculture is doing well now," he says, as sheep bleat loudly in his courtyard.

His house, like most here, is built of mud brick, abutting its neighbors. Furnishings in most homes are sparse. They are even more sparse in the stick and reed-mat-covered homes of the few Tuaregs who have not fled and continue living on the sand dunes outside of town.

Many Tuaregs displaced by the rebellion and facing drought are suffering in the desert today. Those still nearby are apprehensive, even the children.

"I'm afraid, I'm afraid," says little Fidi, a young Tuareg girl, as we walk toward a non-Tuareg settlement amid nearby dunes.

That afternoon, I walked out of town in another direction, just to feel the solitude of the desert. From atop a dune, Timbuktu was a faint dark ridge on the horizon. The sun filtered through the smudgy-gray, dust-filled air. For me, Timbuktu would soon fade from sight. But never again would it be just a name: It would now be people.

Article 21   *International Agricultural Development*, March/April 1992

Namibia's Land Reform: Who Will Benefit?

Namibia is less dependent on agricultural commodities than many African countries and can afford to be more even handed on land reform, writes Martin Adams

Martin Adams

Martin Adams is a rural development planner.

When Namibia came to independence in 1990, the South West Africa People's Organisation (SWAPO) announced its intention to "transfer some of the land from those with too much of it to the landless majority". Yet, two years later, more than half the agriculturally usable land in the country is still occupied by some 4200 commercial ranchers, mainly white. The rest provides a home and, in varying degrees, a source of subsistence for about 120,000 black rural households scattered through the communal areas, the former ethnic homelands.

Namibia is a mostly pastoral country; only relatively small areas in the north are suitable for crops and these are frequently stricken by drought. In the south and west, where mean annual rainfall ranges from 50 to 200mm, small stock predominate. In the centre and north, which receive up to 600mm, cattle are more important. Meat is exported to South Africa and the European Community.

The country is finding out that land reform—that is, the redistribution of property or rights in land for the benefit of small farmers and agricultural labourers—is a very difficult change to carry through, especially in a ranching country with strong interests in the preservation of the status quo.

National Conference

As the government began to consider the practicalities of land reform, it became evident that a great deal of information and consultation was required. Supported by the opposition parties, it decided to conduct a national consultation on the land question culminating in a national conference, held in Windhoek in June 1991. In addition to buying time, the objective was to achieve the greatest possible consensus on the major issues and to make recommendations to government.

The conference, chaired by the Prime Minister, brought together all the major political organizations and interest groups. Specialists on land-related topics from Namibia, as well as from Zimbabwe and Botswana, were engaged to inform the debate. The views of rural people were expressed in a video based on a survey of opinions on land issues.

Ancestral Land Rights

In the run up to the conference, political groups, representing different ethnic interests, pressed for the restitution of their ancestral lands. These had been lost to the German colonisers at the turn of the century and were now occupied by white-owned freehold farms in the central parts of the country. The passion with which these competing claims were prosecuted threatened to wreck the conference and the fragile process of national reconciliation.

However, after three days of debate, the Prime Minister obtained broad agreement that the restitution of particular areas of land to specific groups was not feasible. This was because ancestral land rights of the various ethnic groups in central and southern Namibia had been super-imposed on one another for centuries, if not for millennia, and could not be identified with accuracy.

The conference then moved on to debate the present inequity of land ownership. It recommended to government, among other things, that foreigners should not be allowed to own farmland, that the land of absentee land-

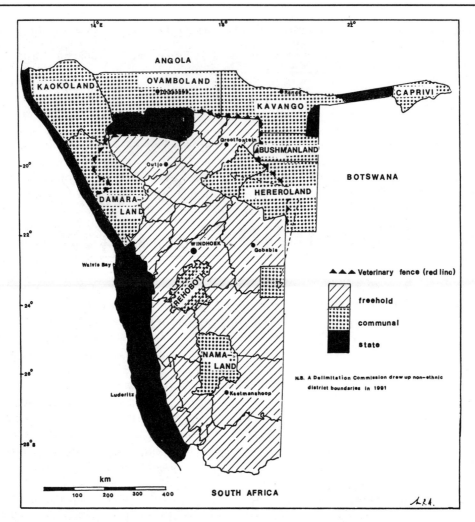

Namibia land tenure, 1990

lords should be expropriated and that very large farms, and/or ownership of several farms should not be allowed. Other resolutions related to the need to improve the conditions of farmworkers and to resolve land-related problems in the overcrowded communal areas.

For the organisers and the majority of participants, the conference met its immediate objectives, namely to reach a consensus on the land question; this satisfaction was reflected in the media and the mood of the public. Bearing in mind the wide gulf which separated the various factions at the beginning of the conference, the level of agreement reached among participants was remarkable. Can consensus be obtained also on the speed and direction of implementation?

It is still too early to draw conclusions on the implementation of land reform. Land policy has yet to be formulated by the government which is still trying to decide what should be done. Several of the conference resolutions raise fundamental issues with which neighbouring African countries have long been grappling. In retrospect, it can be seen that it was easier for the conference to recommend

who should lose land than it was to decide who should gain it. Land for the landless was barely discussed at the conference, despite the vivid pleas in the video.

Widening Ownership

The view which received the most attention at the conference was that freehold farms should be made available on financially favourable terms to black farmers. The pressure for this reform comes from a number of quarters. It comes from white politicians who are keen to recruit rich and politically influential black farmers into their ranks; from black businessmen and government officials who wish to own farms themselves, and from small farmers in the communal areas who resent the pressure on communal grazing exerted by the large herds and flocks of wealthy stock owners. These small farmers are supported by officials of the Ministry of Agriculture who argue for the transfer of the large herds to commercial farms on environmental grounds. (It should be noted, however, that both environmental and equity arguments for moving larger livestock owners to fenced farms were advanced in Botswana in 1975. The result was negative on both counts).

It was noteworthy that the owners of large herds in the communal areas were not themselves in favour of moving their stock to commercial farms. In the communal areas they enjoy free grazing, water, drought relief and various services without having to pay income tax.

The level of demand for freehold farms will clearly depend on the credit terms available. At current interest rates—18 percent a year—demand is expected to remain negligible. The problem will be to target the larger farmers in the communal areas and discourage applications from urban businessmen and officials.

Even a programme of assistance for communal area farmers to buy freehold farms would reach only a fairly small number. It would provide only temporary and partial relief to the crowded communal grazing where the environmental benefits of the programme would be difficult to detect.

Land For The Landless

By comparison with the attention given to the relocation of large farmers, the technical and socio-economic problems of providing poor families, landless people, farm labourers and war returnees with land received very little attention at the conference. Namibia is generally dry, and the land is mostly unsuitable for arable cropping.

The proposal to settle peasants from overcrowded communal areas on former commercial ranches raises a number of difficult practical issues. In the light of experience with pastoral settlement schemes elsewhere in Africa, neither the subdivision of ranches into family livestock farms, nor group or cooperative ranching are likely to be viable options.

The cost of settling farmers with small herds and flocks on individual farms, with reasonable standards of social and economic infrastructure, would be very high and the economic return almost certainly negative. In addition to the economic consequences of subdivision there are likely to be far-reaching environmental effects. Small herds, of 50 to 100 head of cattle, are difficult to manage as commercial units. Offtake is much lower (less than half) than from a commercial herd. Initially, herd growth rates would be fast, assisted by the relatively better grazing and by low offtake.

But in the narrow confines of the family farm, grazing pressure would be intense and continuous, to the detriment of the herbage and, in some areas, of the soils.

The only viable solution would be to amalgamate several farms, takedown internal fences and retain only the minimum number of water points needed for the herds and flocks. If the farms in question are adjacent to an existing communal area, the boundary fence between the two could be removed and the communal range simply extended. This solution tends to be favoured by the majority of stock owners. In their experience, there is no substitute for space to move in. Communal grazing has many virtues, which are often ignored, but the more confined the space, the more destructive it becomes.

However the evidence from neighbouring Botswana is that efforts to improve communal grazing systems by subdividing communal land into separate camps, or by transferring herds from communal land to individual camps on commercial farms, have generally resulted in the accelerating rate of environmental degradation, even if stock numbers are not increased.

Any proposal to extend the communal area is highly controversial. As elsewhere in Africa, official thinking on the development of communal rangeland has for long been characterised by an approach to land use derived from the commercial farming sector.

Agricultural progress, as envisaged by development agencies and African governments, has been confined to transforming traditional stock keepers into commercial farmers and replacing customary forms of communal tenure with individual title. This formula is based on the assumption that "traditional" techniques of pastoral and livestock management are environmentally destructive and that improvements in husbandry and land management can only be achieved on private farms, a view which has led to widespread landlessness in Africa.

Until now, African politicians and businessmen wishing to acquire ranches with government loans have found allies in mainstream range management theory. However, in the recent words of an authoritative paper, these views "are fundamentally flawed in their application to certain types of rangeland systems. They require not minor adjustment but a thorough reexamination."

Agriculture in Namibia employs 60 per cent of the population, but generates only 10 per cent of GDP. With its mineral wealth, Namibia is much less dependent than other postcolonial territories on white farmers and on the export of agricultural commodities to earn foreign exchange. Namibia can probably afford to be more even handed when it comes to land reform. Whether it will be will emerge in the coming months.

Article 22   *The New York Times*, February 6, 1993

How Somalia Was Left in The Cold

S. J. Hamrick

S. J. Hamrick, a former State Department diplomat, served in Somalia and Ethiopia in the 1970's.

MARSHALL, VA.

The cold war is over and so are its intrigues, now buried in the diplomatic archives, forgotten except by those who suffer its legacy, as they do in Somalia. The tragedy in Somalia is well-known, but not the diplomatic tale of misperception, näiveté and duplicity that brought it about.

In early 1977, Jimmy Carter hoped to build constructive new relationships with third world countries alienated from the U.S. by cold war hostilities. Somalia seemed a promising candidate, and the opportunity wasn't by chance. President Mohammed Siad Barre let it be known through covert diplomatic channels that he was searching for an escape from Moscow's orbit, if only the West would hold out its hand. Mr. Carter was intrigued.

The problem jeopardizing Soviet-Somali relations was Ethiopia, where Lieut. Col. Mengistu Haile Mariam had toppled Haile Selassie in 1974 and declared the country a socialist state. The core issue was the Ogaden, Somali-occupied pastoral lands that Western colonial powers had ceded to the Selassie empire in 1948.

As a member of the world socialist community, Somalia believed the subjugated Ogaden would soon win its freedom from an Ethiopia in chaos. A historic opportunity was at hand but denied by the Russians, who insisted socialist solidarity must prevail over national liberation. The Ogaden Somalis would be sacrificed to Colonel Mengistu's revolution.

So long as his Soviet alliance had worked to Somalia's advantage, President Siad Barre was able to maintain his socialist polity, but not when it began to fail. Renunciation of the Ogaden was anathema to all Somalis. By 1977, the Ogaden was their unifying cry.

The first Soviet-Ethiopian arms agreement was signed in 1976. The 1977 Somalia overture to the U.S. was President Siad Barre's warning to the Soviet Union to limit its collusion with Ethiopia. Moscow refused.

Most significantly, the Soviets hadn't yet moved decisively to rescue Colonel Mengistu's armies, who were struggling against various rebel insurgencies. The Soviets supported strength, not weakness, a characteristic President Siad Barre often noted in comparing the Russians with the less resolute U.S. He'd seen how swiftly the Soviets had projected power in Angola. And the lack of a decisive Soviet response on behalf of the Ethiopians convinced the Somali leader that the Russian alliance with his enemy lacked depth.

> ## Siad Barre played off the Soviets against the U.S. and lost.

Thus, President Siad Barre increased his covert support for the Ogaden guerrillas while his diplomats warned of the imminent danger of "Soviet imperialism." Meeting with President Carter in June, Somalia's ambassador claimed the Soviet Union was compelling the country "to accept Soviet hegemony in the Horn." President Carter said the U.S. would consider supplying defensive weapons but had no intention of competing in an arms race.

On July 15, the U.S., along with Britain and France, agreed in principle to meet Somalia's defensive needs. President Siad Barre was now persuaded he could free the Ogaden and force Moscow's hand. If, as he expected, the Soviets conceded Colonel Mengistu's weakness and remained faithful to their true socialist ally, acceptance of the Ogaden fait accompli would be negotiated between Somalia and Ethiopia under Moscow's auspices.

If not—the Somali leader doubted the Soviet Union would favor disintegrating Ethiopia over progressive Somalia— he would retain his Ogaden victory with old and new arms. Already supporting 12,000 Ogaden guerrillas, he sent his army into the Ogaden on July 21, 1977. Within days the Ethiopians had been routed.

On July 23, U.S. satellite intercepts of Somali Army radio transmissions suggested Somali Army units were in the Ogaden. On Aug. 8, the U.S. offer was suspended. On Aug. 18, it was withdrawn. Refusing to admit his army was in Ethiopia, President Siad Barre flew to Moscow on Aug. 28 to strike a deal. President Leonid Brezhnev didn't receive him; Foreign Minister Andrei Gromyko, Prime Minister Aleksei N. Kosygin and Mikhail A. Suslov, the party ideologue, told him to first remove his troops.

For President Siad Barre retreat was politically impossible. The army and guerrillas had overrun 97 percent of the Ogaden and the country was jubilant and fiercely united. By September, Cuban armored troops had reinforced the Ethiopian Army; the offensive would go no further. As the stalemate continued, President Siad Barre continued to bargain for U.S. arms, offering on Oct. 13 to abrogate the 1974 Soviet friendship treaty in exchange for U.S. weapons. The U.S. refused.

With nowhere to turn, the Somali leader continued to drift and so did the Russians. Finally, on Nov. 13, 1977, he denounced the Soviet treaty and expelled the Russians. Freed of its own indecision, the ideological impasse of two client states killing one another and the Somali leader's endless intrigues, the Soviets mounted an enormous air and sea lift to rescue Colonel Mengistu. It was the show of strength President Siad Barre had never expected the Soviets to offer Ethiopia.

Although Somali troops wouldn't withdraw from Ethiopia until the following spring, the war was over. Despite the Somali leader's warnings of a Soviet-supported Ethiopian invasion, no U.S. arms were forthcoming.

Today's chaos in Somalia began with the 1974–1976 Ethiopian revolution, which demolished the de facto U.S.-Soviet détente in the Horn and brought on the bloody Ogaden war of 1977–1978. The defeat smashed the clan coalition President Siad Barre had ruled for eight years and bred the anarchy that followed.

Somalis in victory, they were rebels in defeat: first the Merjeteen, then the northern Isaqs and soon others broke with the Somali leader. President Siad Barre met the rebellions with increasing repression. By 1989, the Hawiyas around Mogadishu had joined the battle, and in 1991 he was overthrown. The two Hawiya warlords in Mogadishu, Gen. Mohammed Farah Aideed and Ali Mahdi Mohammed, are the brutal result. The rest the TV cameras have told us.

Article 23

AfricaNews December 21, 1992—January 3, 1993

A Nation of Poets

Tami Hultman

Africa News Service

Americans know Somalia as a land of gaunt children and marauding gunmen. But for centuries, those familiar with the wedge-shaped piece of land jutting into the Indian Ocean have called it "A Nation of Poets."

Somalia's poetic tradition differs markedly from Western practice. Somali scholar Said Sheikh Samatar, in an essay to accompany a 1986 exhibit at the Smithsonian's Museum of African Art, wrote that it is difficult for Westerners to appreciate the role of poetry in Somali culture. "Whereas in the industrialized West, poetry—and especially what is regarded as serious poetry—seems to be increasingly relegated to a marginal place in society," he said, "Somali oral verse is central to Somali life."

Samatar wrote that "even a casual observation" of Somali society reveals "the remarkable influence of the poetic in the Somali cultural and political scene."

English explorer Richard Burton, who traveled through Somalia in 1854, noted the prevalence of the art. "The country teems," he wrote, "with 'poets, poetasters, poetitoes, poetaccios': every man has his recognized position in literature as accurately defined as though he had been reviewed in a century of magazines—the fine ear of this people causing them to take the greatest pleasure in harmonious sounds and poetical expressions, whereas a false quantity or a prosaic phrase excite their violent indignation."

Somali poetry has been the country's chief means of mass communication, substituting for history books, broadcasting and newspapers. In recent decades, after the Somali language was written for the first time, and cheap radios and tape recorders began to spread into rural as well as urban areas, there was an expectation that oral poetry might decline as a societal force.

In fact, modern communications and transportation have spread the art more efficiently from one area to another. Distinguished poets began to travel from area to area, leaving behind tapes of their work to be passed around and evaluated. After World War II, literary productions on Somali national radio and the Africa Service of the BBC attracted huge audiences.

"Thus, it is a common, if amusing, thing," Samatar wrote, "to come upon a group of nomads huddled excitedly over a short-wave transistor, engaged in a heated discussion of the literary merits of poems that have just been broadcast while they keep watch over their camel herds grazing nearby."

But to say that poetry permeates Somali society is not to say that everyone is a poet. Somalia is no exception to the rule that artistic genius is a scarce commodity anywhere. There is keen competition among talented poets, and a nation of poetry connoisseurs demands a high level of skill and persuasiveness from its practitioners.

Poets who win public favor are a privileged class, socially and politically. At the same time, though, they assume the burden and responsibility of preserving history and shaping current events. Historically, Somali bards have mobilized public opinion in support of war or peace, as they saw the need.

Sayyid Muhammad Abdille Hasan—who was immortalized in British history as the "Mad Mullah"—used his verse to unify Somalis in the fight against British colonialism.

And the Somali Dervish Movement, a religious-based resistance to foreign domination in the first two decades of this century, produced a body of work that pitted the Dervishes not only against the European powers who were carving up the country, but also against their Somali collaborators. Since the Somalis on both sides were skilled poetic gladiators, the verse of the period is filled with appeals to opponents to change sides and with pleas to neutrals to join the battle.

"Although most of the poets, on both sides of the conflict, were concerned mainly with the conduct of the war," writes B. W. Andrzejewski in an essay for the Smithsonian exhibit, "they remained faithful to their calling as artists." The formal skills and devises, such as poetic diction and figurative language, continued to be cultivated. Even the most practical of poems, such as those designed to communicate military strategy, were full of lyrical passages.

Dervish leader Sayid Maxamed Cabdulle Xasan, whose rise to power depended heavily on his talent as an epic poet, was a master of the genre. In a poem warning his followers about the perfidy of an ally who changed sides when threatened by enemy reprisals, there is a preamble about the loyalty and bravery of the Dervish "reciter," who carries the poetic message and transmits it to others. Although the alliteration—a key component of Somali verse—is lost in translation, the evocative images remain.

You did not leave me when the ignorant
stampeded. . .

You loaded your camels and came over to me when
they defected to the British generals . . .

And I count on you during the dry season of the
year.

A rosy cloud, a scud of white vapor, precipices of
cloud flashing with lightning,

Resounding thunder, flood water running over the
parched earth,

The past night's repeated showers,
noisy as the jibin bird

The heavy rain which fell, the longed-for rain of
the spring,

Ponds brimming over, old campsites luxuriant,

Thorns become as tall as grass, thick undergrowth
crackling—

I shall satisfy your needs as when one pours out
salty water for a she-camel

And I shall entertain you with a poem as precious
as a jewel.

The poetry of Salaan Arrabay, on the other hand, became an anti-war weapon. His best-known work, "O Kinsman,

Pierce the Sky

Somalis have long debated the merits of a nomadic, pastoral existence versus those of a settled agricultural community. In this excerpt from a Somali poem, a nomad explains his decision to return to his herd after a brief try at farming:

It is said that one cannot pierce the sky to get rain for one's garden,

Nor can one drive the farm, as one drives animals, to the place where the rain is falling.

Worst of all, one cannot abandon one's farm, even though barren, because all one's efforts are invested in it.

The farmer, in counter argument, replies:

A man with no fixed place in this world cannot claim one in heaven.

Stop the War," was an appeal to end a long-standing feud between two rival sections of the Isaaq clan in northern Somalia. "Tradition has it," says Samatar, "that the poet on his horse stood between the massed opposing forces and, with a voice charged with drama and emotion, chanted the better part of the day until the men, smitten with force of his delivery, dropped their arms and embraced one another."

The collapse of the Dervish resistance in 1921 set the stage for Somalia's current tragedy. The legacy of the conflict was poverty and destruction among the vanquished Somalis. "The situation was made worse," says Andrzejewski, "by the fact that large quantities of firearms had found their way into the nomadic interior and were now used in fratricidal warfare devoid of any ideological aspect." Poetry again played a role, whether inciting local feuds, "or counseling peace and appealing to the sentiments of a common culture and religion."

The colonial and post-colonial period saw a change in Somali poetic traditions. The 1940s gave birth to a romantic species of verse that avoided the hazards of political and social commentary. But politics continued to intrude, sometimes covertly. "The metaphoric and allusive language," says Andrzejewski, "was well suited to fooling the foreign censors who at that time were trying to check the activities of those Somalis who were working toward independence, and it sometimes happened that an apparently harmless love lyric was easily decoded by Somali listeners into an attack on the authorities."

During the two-decade dictatorship of Mohamed Siad Barre, who ruled Somalia from 1970 to 1991, poetry became a tool of an authoritarian regime. While verse helped mobilize the population for such social programs as national immunization and literacy campaigns, it also was employed to consolidate Siad Barre's power.

At the same time, Somali writers began to explore prose fiction. But the poetic tradition infused the new form, as in a 1981 serialized story by Cismaan Caliguul. The tale of two young lovers, whose relationship is opposed by their families, glows with poetic imagery in the heroine's accounts of her elopement.

We rode on and on through the night in complete darkness—darkness which knew nothing of our troubles. I turned my head and there was the dawn pursuing us. We listened and the birds were chirping and twittering—they were pleased with the new day that was running toward them. How different was their situation from ours! They wanted the dawn to break quickly so that they could begin picking berries, and we wanted the dawn to linger behind so that we could escape beyond the territory of my clan under the cover of night....

The grass on which the rain had fallen the night before now spread its blades towards the sun for which it had been waiting, and the dew resting on the leaves of the trees took on the color of gold. The trees were pleased with the growing warmth and the sunshine, but all this was of no benefit to us, travelers who were passing by.

Now, in a break with centuries of history, Somalia's poets have fallen silent.

Before Siad Barre's overthrow last year in a mass uprising, oral traditions were already in decline. The combined pressures of increasing poverty and political repression sapped energies, dampened creativity and curbed the free expression upon which poetry had thrived.

Andrzejewski predicts that in the future, poetry as a living art will be confined mainly to texts of work and dance songs, anecdotal narratives, and children's lore. But in a more optimistic mood, he believes that an improvement in Somalia's material situation will permit a flowering of written literature, including poems, short stories, novels and literary scholarship.

For the moment, though, Somalia's rich civilization is obscured by images of human suffering. In the language of modern media, Somalis are either victims or thugs, passive or drug-crazed. And the exquisite sound of poetry has been drowned by the vulgar thunder of guns.

For more information about Somalia's verbal and visual arts, see *Somalia in Word and Image*, a 1986 publication of Indiana University Press. Prepared for an exhibition mounted by the Foundation for Cross Cultural Understanding, the book is available at the National Museum of African Art of the Smithsonian Institution, Washington, DC.

Article 24   *The Wall Street Journal* October 29, 1992

Of Peace and Hope

A South African Town Embodies A Struggle Central To Nation's Fate

Whites Make Concessions, Expect Calm; Blacks Say Not Till Equality Comes

Two Very Different Worlds

Ken Wells

Staff Reporter of The Wall Street Journal

VREDE, South Africa—Carel van den Heever, a white merchant and entrepreneur, is trying to be an optimist. "Black and white can coexist here," he says. "We need each other. If only cooler heads can prevail, we will make it. If not. . . ."

Mr. van den Heever, an energetic, 50ish man, pauses, then manages a smile. The root fear—a race war—is too awful to contemplate. "I have to be optimistic," he says. "Besides, there's no turning back."

On Vrede's rim, in the ramshackle black township of Thembalihle, Bheki Radebe, a 26-year-old high-school teacher, dreams of coexistence, too. But the road there, he thinks, will be a long one marked with confrontation to jar whites out of "racism and complacency."

He practices what he preaches: So far, Mr. Radebe's chapter of the African National Congress has plotted a string of crippling boycotts—seven in two years—of Vrede's white merchants. The boycotts have come with a list of demands, including a Thembalihle sewer system and fairer access to Vrede's health clinic.

LITTLE IN COMMON

"Whites here still do not respect blacks," says Mr. Radebe. "The apartheid laws have been repealed, but the attitude of apartheid is alive."

Vrede, a town of 2,000, and Thembalihle, a township of 18,000, share a common boundary yet little common ground. Vrede is white, manicured, relatively prosperous. Thembalihle is black, and a jumble of official neglect: potholes, open sewers and acute unemployment.

As the country stumbles toward majority rule in what President F. W. de Klerk calls "the New South Africa," the fortunes of Vrede and Thembalihle must inevitably fuse. The struggle here—whether it ends in wary accommodation or war—is a microcosm of the hope and gloom gripping all of South Africa.

Vrede (pronounced FREER-dah) is an Afrikaans word meaning "peace," while Thembalihle (Tim-bah-LEE-lay) is Zulu for "good hope." But there is no peace now in Vrede. And the hopes of Thembalihle's ANC majority give Vrede's white business community scant hope that peace will come soon.

CLOSING SHOPS

Indeed, the ANC's eighth boycott against Vrede is scheduled for Nov. 15. Five shops have closed so far, and white merchants are growing desperate. Avowals of optimism aside, "these boycotts," says Mr. van den Heever, "are killing us."

Vrede, 100 miles southwest of Johannesburg, seems a place plucked from the American Midwest. Pickup trucks crowd its compact main street. Neat rows of modest homes nestle around the town center.

There are four churches, two hotels, a farm-implement shop and an air of order and bustle about the place. Most roads empty into a sea of rolling, big-sky ranch land; one road tumbles into Thembalihle.

For Ann and Fred Harington, looking to invest a nest egg and eventually retire, Vrede was the perfect spot. Ten years ago, they put their savings into a combination cafe and grocery store "hoping to take it easier," says Mrs. Harington. "Of course, we've never worked so hard in our lives."

They also wonder if they've made a mistake.

THE TRANSITION

By South African standards, the Haringtons are moderate whites: solid members of the National Party, among the 80% of white voters who approved Mr. de Klerk's move last March toward multi-racial elections. It is no small thing to them that, since then, blacks have been welcomed into their cafe.

They admit their drift to the center mirrors the reality that Mr. de Klerk acknowledged when he set about to dismantle apartheid. This is a strategy to circumvent bloody revolution, a gamble by whites, who are just 14% of South Africa's population, to buy peace on favorable terms.

"We realized we were in for a transitional period," says Mr. Harington. "We didn't realize it would be this difficult."

Five years ago, Vrede had a population of 2,000 whites and Thembalihle 5,000 blacks. Vrede's economy ran on agriculture. But the unraveling of apartheid has stood the town on its head. With the abolition of the nation's influx control laws—the so-called pass laws—Thembalihle's black population swelled to 18,000. At the same time, the nation's farm economy began to slide toward recession—and Vrede's followed.

Now, Vrede is Thembalihle's economic servant. "Our business is probably 60% black," says Mr. Harington. For other merchants, the percentage is closer to 80% or 90%.

Political winds were stirring, too. In 1990, the predominantly black ANC, the nation's dominant opposition party, was dropped from the government's list of illegal organizations. Thembalihle, in the heart of the Afrikaans-controlled Orange Free State—South Africa's equivalent to America's old Deep South—seemed a poor candidate for ANC organizing.

But soon a group of young academics, led by Mr. Radebe, arrived to rouse the township. For the ANC organizers, who call each other "comrade," talk with the whites is cheap until blacks win the right to vote.

Vrede's whites, ironically, were moving toward the center, slipping from the long grip of the Conservative Party, the haven of the white minority still clinging to notions of white dominance here. In the town's latest elections, National Party centrists, led by Mr. van den Heever, swept all the town council seats.

Vrede finally had a government willing to at least listen to black concerns. If things go badly here, history is likely to declare it was a government that simply arrived too late.

Mr. Harington is keenly aware of this irony as he sits at a table in the rear of his cafe chain-smoking and regretting the damage of apartheid. What he regrets most is the educational chasm into which many blacks have sunk—especially in the last generation. It is from this pool of dispossessed blacks that ANC radical factions gain their strength.

At the moment, Mr. Harington wishes everyone would "join the real world and stop living in the past." His is the common white lament: Apartheid is wrong; it is being repealed; sensible whites are reaching out to make amends. But nothing will be achieved unless blacks meet them halfway, move forward instead of brooding over old wounds. Majority rule is just, but the road to democracy should not be a white suicide pact.

This argument also holds a kernel of white backlash, since in Vrede, and throughout South Africa, the great white

middle is growing impatient. It expects rewards for its move toward the center. So far, in its view, it has seen few.

Recent events have been stirring white fears. Four blacks are being sought in the shooting of a white Vrede farmer. Firebombs have exploded in a white town not far to the north. Just as Mr. de Klerk and Nelson Mandela seemed to have agreed to restart talks on forming a new government, the black homelands of KwaZulu and Ciskei are calling such bilateral agreements a sham.

But Fred Harington asks: "What good will it do blacks here if whites are driven out of business? We will pick up and go, but where will the blacks who work here go?"

Mr. Harington's question rings hollow for Alfred Selepe, Plaatjie Booysen and thousands of Thembalihle's chronically unemployed blacks. Theirs is a world of unpaved streets, unlovely shacks, unmet expectations. Mangy dogs, raw-ribbed goats and scrawny chickens all share the landscape.

"Everyone here is poor," says Mr. Selepe. He is 40ish with a quick, toothy grin. Jobless for 10 years, he finds it hard to imagine—short of famine and slaughter—that his life will get any worse.

It's not that he doesn't think there are whites who are serious about ending apartheid. But in his view whites have come to this position only because their welfare is threatened: Before the ANC came to town, Thembalihle's concerns didn't concern them.

Mr. Selepe echoes a common refrain when he says blacks still don't feel they are human in the eyes of most white South Africans. "Whites do not understand us. Whites lean on us," he says. To these things "the ANC came here to open my eyes." He thus supports the boycotts, and will do so until "there is a correct situation in the town."

Mr. Booysen, who is in his 20s, chronically sick and unemployed, fully agrees. He lives for the ANC—and worries there will be violence. "Sometimes I think there is no solution," he says.

Yes, he's heard of the efforts by Vrede's whites to negotiate. Yes, there's been some progress: Thembalihle's first water and sewer system is being installed. But he recalls two years ago when blacks finally tried to use Vrede's white swimming pool after the repeal of the Separate Amenities Act. First, the town raised prices to keep blacks out, he says. And when some persisted, they were harassed and driven off with whips.

It was that incident that spurred the first ANC boycott; it stopped the thrash-

ings, but didn't change attitudes. "Apartheid here is still too strong. How many days must we wait for it to end?" says Mr. Booysen.

'THE OLD SYSTEM'

Such impatience is beginning to manifest itself in ways that seem illogical and destructive to Vrede's whites. The ANC is demanding construction of a new recreation center in Thembalihle—this after its youthful cadres recently tore down the walls of a center that had long served the township.

"It was of the old system," Mr. Selepe explains. "It had to go."

For Mr. van den Heever, the foundations of the new South Africa have already been formed; if only the politics would just catch up. On a reservoir just out of town, Mr. van den Heever has put one million South African rand (about $350,000) into a hotel and marina. There's a bar, pool, boat launch and lots for sale on which to build weekend cottages. It's open to all, black or white.

But while blacks may be welcomed by Mr. van den Heever, they may not be by some of the people they may meet there. One night at the bar some local farmers are quaffing copious amounts of Castle beer and lamenting the passing of the world they knew. They tell racist jokes and use racial slurs. A black waiter stands silently nearby.

"There are extremists on both sides," Mr. van den Heever says later. "It's like these boycotts. Eighty percent of the blacks here don't want them. . . . but they are too intimidated to speak."

Mr. van den Heever goes over a list of ANC demands. "Many of the things they ask are reasonable," he says: Sewer and water systems, an ambulance for the township, a full-time social worker, full access to the health clinic.

THE TOWN CLERK

But as an illustration of the gulf between "moderate" whites and blacks here, Mr. van den Heever calls the demand for firing the town clerk "ridiculous." ANC officials contend that Vrede's town clerk has verbally abused blacks while drunk at his desk, brought in a shotgun to intimidate blacks and neglects black business to play golf on Wednesdays. This demand has been at the core of many of the boycotts.

On this day, the town clerk isn't around to speak for himself, but Mr. van den Heever happily speaks for him. He doesn't drink at work; he brought the gun, a broken antique, into his office so that a colleague who repairs guns could look at it; he works many nights recording various committee meetings; he gets Wednesday afternoons off to compensate.

"And besides, he's protected by civil service—we can't fire him," Mr. van den Heever says. The ANC knows this, he says, and is pushing the issue knowing that "it's a demand we can't meet."

Abram Mohomane sits in a tiny brick shack in Thembalihle. He is a university-educated teacher of Afrikaans—the language of his old enemies, the Boers. Rain—the first in a year—beats upon a tin roof that seeps light in several places.

Mr. Mohomane, 47, is both bewildered and awed by the new South Africa. Nelson Mandela is his hero, but Mr. Mohomane dislikes the local ANC leadership passionately. Whites have treated blacks cruelly in the past, yet some whites, like Mr. van den Heever, seem genuinely interested in change.

At least now, says Mr. Mohomane, "there is hope for blacks"—as well as a chance for disaster. He wishes the young cadres of the ANC would tone down their rhetoric. He says there are many in Thembalihle like him, but they are reluctant to speak.

Soon, Mr. Mohomane will be doing a remarkable thing. Others march, boycott and picket, but he has saved and scrimped and bought a house in Vrede. He is moving into the new South Africa. "I will be welcome there," he says.

Article 25

Financial Times, July 5, 1992

Democracy In The Balance

The transition to multiracial rule is proving difficult and slow as whites battle to preserve power and privilege. Patti Waldmeir assesses the prospect for establishing freedom and stability in one of the most divided societies in the world.

What will replace apartheid in South Africa?

Will South Africans rise above their 350-year history of division and exploitation to build a liberal, multiracial democracy, a model to divided societies worldwide? Will they experiment with democracy, but fail, leaving black domination to replace white oppression? Or will the country's politicians, black and white, do an unholy deal to stifle dissent and restore civil order, jointly imposing authoritarian rule?

After two years of horrifying political violence, tortuous negotiations which have yielded little obvious progress, an accelerating decline in black living standards, and an explosion of crime, many South Africans are suffering from a crisis of confidence about their future.

The tremendous sense of relief and elation which greeted the release from prison two years ago of Mr Nelson Mandela, African National Congress (ANC) president—and the vision of a brave new egalitarian future which he inspired—has proved difficult to sustain under the pressures of political transition.

The historical imperatives which drove white and black to the negotiating table remain the same—in spite of the failure of last month's plenary session of the Convention for a Democratic South Africa (Codesa), the constitutional negotiating forum. Codesa is floundering, and the installation of a multiracial interim government, which had been expected within weeks, now seems likely to be delayed.

But the reality remains that neither the ANC, the largest black group, nor the ruling National Party, the most powerful white party, can run South Africa on its own. They need each other, and sooner or later, they will strike a deal. What is not certain is whether it will be a fully democratic deal.

"There is nothing inevitable about a democratic outcome to transition in South Africa," says Professor Frederik van Zyl Slabbert, a former liberal politician who has stimulated debate on future political systems. "I think we have the capacity to become democratic, but if I have to be very frank, I cannot see us approaching it within the next 10 years. . . . The dynamics of the transition may precipitate undemocratic options."

None of the 19 parties to Codesa exhibit truly democratic instincts. They all pay lip service to democracy. But the National Party has only recently discovered the need for political tolerance—now that its own interests are at risk—and the ANC permits dissent only so long as it does not threaten unity. Both are deeply suspicious of the press, intolerant of criticism, dirigiste in their economic policies and authoritarian by nature.

Indeed, the two sides have already largely agreed that a multi-party interim government should retain similar emergency powers to those exercised so brutally by the National Party, which detained 40,000 people in the late 1980s. In a passage chillingly reminiscent of the bad old days of apartheid, a working document agreed to by all the Codesa parties notes that "special measures are necessary to deal with the threat to public order during the transitional period", including detention without trial (subject to unspecified "procedural controls"), and powers to declare a state of emergency on the advice of an unelected interim executive appointed by Codesa.

Senior National Party officials admit privately that they envisage a period of authoritarian rule until the end of the decade—imposed in the interests of stability and economic growth—and the ANC, worried about its ability to control its own constituents, seems likely to agree.

Both have already agreed to rule by coalition, in a government of national unity aimed at reconciling all South Africans to a new constitution. The duration of the coalition is still in dispute: the government wants coalition government to be entrenched in an interim and a permanent constitution. If the National Party has its way, South Africa will be governed for decades by a coalition which would guarantee the political role of whites.

The ANC, for its part, is intent on achieving majority rule—though it favours voluntary coalition for the first two to five years of the new regime. Some moderate ANC officials believe the government of national unity should last until the end of the century. For the National Party, though, coalition government on its own will not be enough to prevent abuse of power by the (black) majority. It wants a constitution which devolves power substantially to regional and local government—making it impossible for central government to dominate.

The party's position is that South Africa's fragmented and fractious society cannot be governed peacefully from the centre. That may well be so, but the drive for regionalism has a more immediate goal: to accommodate the political ambitions of Zulu Chief Mangosuthu Buthelezi, who would be guaranteed power in his ethnic base of Natal. He would never compete as a national politician but he would resist—perhaps violently—being sidelined under a unitary constitution.

Strong regional government would achieve another cherished National Party goal. It would ensure that the Western Cape, the only region where blacks do not form the majority, would become, in the words of one junior minister, a kind of "haven for civilised western values". (This assumes that whites and coloureds (mixed-race peoples) would make common cause together against Africans, probably a realistic assumption.)

The ANC, with its ideal of non-racialism, finds such notions abhorrent but its officials are realistic enough to admit that ethnicity cannot simply be wished away, and that devolution can help accommodate it. In a recent paper entitled "Rooting Democracy on African Soil", ANC constitutional lawyer Zola Skweyiya argues: "It is necessary to consider the challenge that ethnicity poses to democratic transformation and the way in which this challenge may be diffused.

"The experiences of independent Africa, Yugoslavia, Bulgaria, and the former USSR have demonstrated clearly how difficult it is to replace individual ethnic identities by a commitment to a single overarching nationalism."

But Mr Skweyiya acknowledges that his view is not received wisdom within the ANC and many tough battles lie ahead before the new government's structure is agreed.

Indeed, the next few months could prove the most difficult so far in the transition. Codesa must resolve the central question of who wields power in the new South Africa. Will whites have an effective veto, through an upper house packed with political minorities? Will they exercise a veto over the new constitution, by insisting that all clauses are passed by three-quarters majority? How much power will devolve to regions?

The ANC will not easily relinquish its demand for a majority-rule constitution, but this is incompatible with the National Party's bottom line—a large political role for whites, guaranteed indefinitely. The movement will be tempted to exercise its own veto over the process of reform, by calling for a general strike and other forms of mass protest.

Meanwhile, economic growth—which is so crucial to stability—will continue to be sabotaged by political upheaval.

But given South Africa's peculiar legacy of apartheid and ethnic diversity, poverty and isolation, nation-building was never going to be easy. With any luck, the inter-racial goodwill which persists against all the odds, the Christian commitment of most South Africans, and the desire for economic advancement will ensure that South Africa avoids the risk of social disintegration. It remains to be seen whether democracy will survive the strains of the transition.

Article 26   *International Agricultural Development*, March/April, 1992

The Dynamic Nature of Land Reform

John Cusworth looks at the issues arising from the land resettlement programme in Zimbabwe

John Cusworth

John Cusworth works for the Development and Project Planning Centre at the UK's University of Bradford.

In the struggle for independence the land issue was of fundamental significance in Zimbabwe; a programme of land redistribution started soon after independence. After ten years and the resettlement of over 50,000 families on more than 3.1 million hectares of acquired land, the motivation for continuing resettlement remains strong. Given the growing population pressure in the Communal Areas (CAs), pressure to proceed faster with resettlement is increasing.

The broad aims of Zimbabwe's Land Resettlement Programme are to redress the historical imbalance in access to land between the races, and to create an opportunity for alleviating the economic plight of some of the poorest rural people, whilst maximising the economic potential of the land.

Resettlement has been slow. If it were simply a matter of land transfer between different groups of people with an equal capacity to utilise it, then the rate of resettlement would probably have been much faster. But the current programme involves the transfer of land between people with a fundamentally different approach to land utilisation and with very different resource bases.

The Large Scale Commercial Farm sector consists of a relatively small number (around 4,500) of very large holdings (average size 2,200 ha.) deploying relatively capital intensive, technically modernised farming methods. The sector contributes significantly to exports with practically all coffee, tea and tobacco, and half the cotton crop, being produced on commercial farms. Practically all the sugar cane,

soya and wheat crops are produced by the commercial sector, also about half the marketed staple maize crop—although this is declining.

On the other hand the small scale CA farmers who are intended to be resettled under the programme come from a sector of the agricultural industry that employs relatively little modern technology, produces primarily for family subsistence and concentrates on the production of food crops—although CA farmers are now producing more cotton and sunflower.

The significance of the contribution to the national economy of the large-scale farming sector, and the uncertainties over whether small producers could sustain this contribution under resettlement in the short to medium term, lay at the heart of the problem faced by government.

The issue of settler selection is particularly important when considering how to increase productivity. It has been generally acknowledged that many people resettled under the programme are those least likely amongst the CA farming community to be able to make full use of the productive potential of the resources being allocated to them. Had better-resourced and experienced farmers, with a greater capacity to bear the risks of innovation, been selected for resettlement, then current productivity levels would almost certainly have been higher.

"Pressure to proceed faster with resettlement is increasing"

More productive settlers, earning higher incomes, might reasonably have been expected to make some contribution

to the development and running of the schemes from which they were benefiting. As it is, settlers make no contribution to the upkeep and maintenance of schemes. Increased production, and any contribution to the sustaining of the social infrastructure, would have the effect of creating more resources for government to invest in the CAs where the benefits would be more widely spread.

Additionally, given that most settler households occupied little or no land in their former CAs, resettlement has had little impact on the intensity of CA land use, as the programme has not resulted in any significant release of land.

SERVICES

It was recognised from the inception of the programme that settlers would need substantial assistance in the early years of settlement if they were to take full advantage of the resources allocated to them. Consequently settlers were provided with a range of productivity services such as extension, credit, veterinary services, etc.

For many settlers these services have proved a profound disappointment. While the establishment phase of the programme was conducted relatively smoothly, with the implementation of resettlement fully in line with organisational objectives, it was a different matter over services. Input supply, marketing and credit systems singularly failed to provide the settlers with the required level of services. This is not a new phenomenum—virtually all over Africa such support services fail to meet the needs of small farmers.

The institutions required to service the productive needs of the settlers found that resettlement provided them with nothing but extra administrative work for no financial benefit. Institutions had been orientated mainly towards dealing with a relatively small number of mainly commercial farmers. They were required to reorientate their operations towards several hundred thousand clients in communal and resettlement areas. It was not surprising that such institutions experienced difficulties coping with such a dramatic organisational change.

On resettlement, each settler is granted three permits. One to de-pasture a certain number of livestock on a communal basis, one to cultivate an arable plot, and one to reside on a specific residential plot. These permits are for no specific duration and there is currently no prospect of them being upgraded to leasehold or freehold status.

Whilst there is no substantial evidence that settlers feel particularly insecure under resettlement, there is evidence that settler households are reluctant to cut their ties completely with the CAs from which they came and in particular to release their right to cultivate land there.

This feature of settler attitudes frustrates one of the objectives of resettlement which is to release land in overcrowded CAs and may also act as a disincentive for settlers to invest in the medium and long term future of their holdings. Again if the objective is to reduce the uncertainty of settlers being able to match the output and productivity of former commercial farm land it would seem appropriate to provide an added incentive for settlers to better husband the land by providing them with an increased stake in its long term future.

One of the key factors in determining the success of any land reform programme as an economically viable development initiative will be the extent to which land is utilised. Two main factors relate to the utilisation of land—the degree to which land is being utilised at the planned level of intensity, and the appropriate intensity of land use for the particular area. Ministry of Agriculture survey data in Zimbabwe suggests that there is no substantial under-utilisation of

arable land in resettlement areas in terms of aggregate land area cultivated.

The issue remains as to whether the planned intensity of arable cultivation under resettlement is appropriate. This issue cannot be treated in isolation to that of livestock stocking rates and draught power. The level of utilisation of grazing will, to a great extent, determine the overall intensity of land use on the schemes. Surveys show that more than half of settler households own no cattle, with a further 21 per cent having less than the planned number. At the same time 28 per cent of settler households own herds greater than the planned number and own 78 per cent of the cattle. This highly skewed pattern of cattle ownership has resulted in considerable under-utilisation of the grazing resources in some resettled areas.

The result appears to be both under- and over-utilisation of land in resettlement areas. As schemes mature, the problem of over-utilisation will become more intense, as richer settlers keep more than the allocated number of cattle and over-cultivate their plots. The conclusion to be drawn is that there is a certain dynamic nature of land reform programmes that almost always lead to an inequitable distribution of economic benefits amongst the settlers and a varied pattern of land utilisation.

A number of the issues raised by land resettlement in Zimbabwe are relevant to Africa as a whole. If productivity levels could be sustained regardless of ownership, or mode of production, then the need for land reform could be argued simply on equity grounds. Some studies, including the resettlement evaluation in 1988 of the British's government's Overseas Development Administration, support the view that transfer of land from large scale farming to smallholders increases productivity.

However the cost of such reform is beyond the capacity of most governments and there is also a considerable amount of

evidence to suggest that the capacity to utilise land productively varies enormously according to the resource and technology base of the individual smallholder.

THREE OPTIONS

There are basically three main options for reforming land tenure arrangements in Africa—"individual title allocation", "leasehold ownership with conditions" and "communal control of land allocation and land use".

The arguments in favour of the first include that of the need to provide an incentive for investment and conservation over the long term. It is also argued that land titles will provide collateral for credit transactions which will stimulate investment. The arguments against are that only title holders will benefit over the short term and that anyone not currently occupying land for any reason would be excluded from doing so forever. Furthermore whilst title deeds may prove valuable as collateral this may encourage reckless borrowing and indebtedness leaving title owners no option but to sell out to bigger and richer farmers.

The conditional leasehold option has the attraction of providing the land user security of tenure. It would also limit the potential for fragmentation of land holdings. It may also ensure maximum use of the land. However the drawback to this type of tenure system is that it requires a massive institutional infrastructure to administer it. This is expensive and may ultimately be unworkable in many areas.

The communal control of land allocation and land use is closer to the systems that operate more generally in most of Africa today. It has the advantage of giving local communities the responsibility for this important function; it means developing ways in which the less powerful members of the community, that is, women and the poorest, are able to have a say.

Article 27   *Current History,* May 1992

Zambia: A Model for Democratic Change

Zambia's multiparty elections in late 1991 saw the end of single-party rule and the emergence of a freely elected government. Richard Joseph, who took part in monitoring the elections, examines the new government and finds that "Zambia stands a good chance of becoming a beacon of political liberty" in Africa.

Richard Joseph

Richard Joseph is a professor of political science at Emory University and director of the African Governance Program at the Carter Center at Emory. He helped administer the international observer mission for the Zambian elections and recently took part in a postelection mission. This article has benefited from the research assistance of Kathleen Hansel.

Certain dates stand out in the democratic upheaval that has swept the African continent since 1989.* Among them is October 31, 1991, when Kenneth Kaunda's 27-year rule over the Republic of Zambia was brought to an end by a free and fair vote by the Zambian people. Zambians chose trade union leader Frederick Chiluba to replace Kaunda as president, while giving the insurgents' party, the Movement for a Multiparty Democracy (MMD), 125 of the 150 seats in the country's unicameral parliament.

Zambia thus joined Benin and the island nations of Cape Verde and São Tomé and Príncipe in ousting an incumbent government through elections in the current wave of political renewal in Africa. Only the Indian Ocean island of Mauritius had experienced such a reversal in the three decades of postcolonial government in Africa. And of these events, the defeat of Kaunda and his ruling United National Independence party (UNIP) was surely the most momentous.

Kaunda belonged to the pantheon of African leaders—including Kenya's Jomo Kenyatta, Tanzania's Julius Nyerere, and Ghana's Kwame Nkrumah—who had wrested independence from the colonial authorities. Over the course of his almost 30 years in power, he had twice served as chairman of the Organization of African Unity (OAU)

and was a respected leader of the black-ruled "frontline" states in their confrontations with South Africa. Kaunda had become a symbol of African determination to resist racist regimes, whether the Rhodesia of Prime Minister Ian Smith or the South Africa of Presidents H. F. Verwoerd and P. W. Botha.

The Disintegration of The Single-Party State

The relentless decline of the Zambian economy in the 1980s and the collapse of world prices for Zambia's primary export, copper, resulted in the emergence of opposition to Zambia's single-party state. Although Zambia was one of the wealthiest African nations at independence, stagnant agricultural growth and government mismanagement of the country's vast copper deposits led to a sustained deterioration in the standard of living. By 1990 basic social services had crumbled, schools lacked books, and hospitals were spurned by all but the indigent. Food riots erupted in the capital, Lusaka, in June 1990 after a government effort to decontrol the price of maize meal, the country's staple food, brought large price increases.

On June 30 an army officer burst into a radio station and announced that the Kaunda government had been overthrown. Thousands of Zambians poured into the streets to celebrate. Although the coup attempt quickly fizzled, it sent an unmistakable signal: the people were tired of the government, and they wanted change.

The MMD's broad-based coalition of trade unions, businesses, and civic groups, established in July 1990, pressed for a referendum on a future government for Zambia. Increasing support for the MMD forced the initially unyielding Kaunda to relent, and a date was set for the vote. Challenged by enormous opposition rallies, however, the president canceled the referendum and amended the constitution to permit the legal registration of other parties. The MMD—whose slogan "The hour has come!" came to represent popular demands for a return to accountable

---

* For a general overview of democratization in Africa, see Richard Joseph, "Africa: The Rebirth of Political Freedom," *Journal of Democracy,* vol. 2, no. 4 (Fall 1991); additional information on Zambia can be found in Michael Bratton, "The Rebirth of Political Pluralism in Zambia," *Journal of Democracy,* vol. 3, no. 2 (Spring 1992).

government—officially registered as a political party shortly after the amendment was approved by parliament in December 1990. Continued controversy culminated in a meeting between Kaunda and Chiluba in July 1991, at which Kaunda agreed to take account of some opposition demands in a new constitution.

The opposition also insisted on the need for international observers to monitor forthcoming multiparty elections, since the government's overwhelming control of material resources, including the electronic and print media, provoked fears that the elections would not be fair. Although he initially disparaged the notion of observers, Kaunda was once again made to reverse himself—and not only because of popular pressure.

The country was by now in receivership to a host of international and bilateral lending agencies. Successive International Monetary Fund stabilization plans had been agreed to, but not implemented. Zambia was in arrears on its repayment schedules and spending millions of dollars monthly to subsidize maize sales while failing to pay agricultural producers an attractive price. It was an extreme case of an economy in need of adjustment. The government's ability to resist political opposition was sapped by the increasing reluctance of foreign creditors to keep bailing it out.

It is to the advantage of Zambians that Kaunda has never been averse to changing his position when confronted by overwhelming force of numbers or argument. Although autocratic, he never became a brutal dictator like President Mobutu Sese Seko of Zaire. Kaunda yielded on the issue of election observers, and issued invitations to several world leaders and international organizations. Leading an array of groups that took on the task was a joint operation of the Carter Center at Emory University and the National Democratic Institute of International Affairs. Two Zambian umbrella groups were also formed: the Zambia Independent Monitoring Team and the Zambia Elections Monitoring Coordinating Committee (ZEMCC). Together with delegations from the British Commonwealth and the OAU, they provided effective surveillance of the balloting and vote-counting on October 31 and November 1. In acknowledgment of the MMD's landslide victory Chiluba was inaugurated as the first president of the Third Republic on November 2, even though no official tally had been announced.

Although several other opposition parties emerged as soon as multiparty politics was legalized, the MMD was able to retain the bulk of its organizers and supporters when it transformed itself from a movement to a party of the same name. To the surprise of many observers, Chiluba, for 17 years the leader of the Zambian Congress of Trade Unions, defeated several seasoned politicians to become the MMD's leader and later the party's presidential candidate. Chiluba's ascent was aided by the visibility he

had gained from opposing the Kaunda regime over the years. In 1980, Chiluba's expulsion from UNIP resulted in wildcat strikes in the Copperbelt, which were joined by bank workers. In 1981, Chiluba and four colleagues were detained by the government before being released on an order from the High Court. Over the course of his political career, Chiluba has gradually converted from socialism to capitalism.

Promised Transformations

After decades of state-directed experimentation in Zambia that left the country saddled with inefficient state-owned corporations in almost every sector of the economy, the MMD was determined to embark on a thoroughgoing program of privatization. It was also determined to wean Zambians from the subsidization of basic consumer items, especially maize meal, which the country could no longer afford.

The new government's program of reforms was intended to be comprehensive. There was, first of all, the issue of corruption. The extensive public sector in Zambia, the sprawling structures from years of single-party rule, and the pocketing of much of the country's foreign exchange earnings from the sale of copper had created fertile conditions for the growth of corrupt practices. One of the Chiluba government's first acts was to order the sealing of the offices of Zambian Consolidated Copper Mines, the country's huge corporation for copper sales, to prevent the destruction of evidence needed for an investigation of the corrupt use of the company's proceeds over many years.

The freedoms to assemble, to organize, and to express grievances, which had been reasserted during the campaign for multiparty democracy, were also given new force. Civic groups that took part in election monitoring, especially under the umbrella of the ZEMCC, are determined to continue working to further civic education, political liberties, and human rights. They should help broaden the process of democratization beyond the deliberations in parliament and the jousting of political parties.

The most promising sign for the future is that the new government is resolved to implement its challenging economic program. Sharp increases in producer prices for maize have been introduced, and government subsidies have been reduced, without propelling Zambians into the streets to protest, as would certainly have been the case under the previous government. Unfortunately, one of the most severe droughts in recent memory struck the region while the new policies were being put into effect, forcing the government to seek emergency assistance. Nevertheless, bureaucratic barriers to private investment are being stripped away, and (the government is quickly preparing a recovery program that will set guidelines for domestic and foreign investors.

Some old habits that appear to infringe human rights and to belie Zambia's commitment to the highest international standards have resurfaced in certain ministries. Questionable actions under ministerial sponsorship have included a roundup of hundreds of aliens, many from West Africa, who have been accused of taking part in illegal mining and the smuggling of gemstones. In some cases the police have entered mosques to seize their quarry. But Zambia's minister of legal affairs, Rodger Chongwe, is a strong advocate of human rights who has not hesitated to bring to the attention of errant fellow ministers the standards of civil liberties and human rights that the government has pledged to uphold. Combined with the significant degree of judicial independence that was the norm under Kaunda, Zambia stands a good chance of becoming a beacon of political liberty on the continent.

In the rush to eliminate public ownership and government control of industry and commerce, however, the redressing of social inequities in Zambia appears to have been postponed. It will be interesting to see how long the government can continue on such a course before the pain of economic adjustment and the generally meager living standards for most of the population prompt calls for more immediate relief.

Lessons From Zambia

The message of the Zambian transition that has come through most loudly and clearly is that Africa is ready for multiparty democracy. To cite just one indication of the Zambian model's influence, examine the case of Cameroon, where the opposition has been locked in a struggle with the government of President Paul Biya over demands for an open political system. In the January–March 1992 issue of *Cameroon Monitor*, it is argued that

> despite the scaremongering which predicted chaos and general instability in Zambia were free elections to be held there, now that these are a fait accompli, Kenneth Kaunda has had the decency to bow to popular will and has made his exit from the political arena in a quiet and dignified way. The Zambian case has illustrated that a peaceful transfer of power from an unpopular government to a free and universally elected one is possible.

All the usual arguments that leaders such as Daniel arap Moi of Kenya were making to justify denying people the right to decide who should govern them lost much of their force as Zambia democratized without any loss of life. Those acts of violence that occurred were confined to particular areas and did not affect the generally peaceful

conduct of the electoral campaign, the voting, or the ballot-counting.

Zambia has also sent a message to those countries that have embarked on more convoluted transition processes, especially through the agency of a national conference that brings together various social forces to establish a transitional government to prepare for national elections. This Jacobin model of civil revolution seemed at first to be an effective means for uprooting entrenched autocracies. But as more of these transitions have been derailed or halted by embattled regimes, for example in Togo and Zaire—or become trapped in prolonged struggles for such a conference, as in Cameroon and Burkina Faso—the Zambian route of a modified revision of the constitution immediately followed by free and fair elections seems to hold clear advantages.

The key element is free elections. Most authoritarian African governments will not permit them. Thus the opposition is usually forced to boycott those elections that are held, as in Burkina Faso, or to take part only under protest, as in Ivory Coast, thereby yielding governments that lack legitimacy. Dissatisfaction among forces that feel cheated of the opportunity to effect genuine political renewal could lead to continued instability in such countries.

The international community is deeply involved in these processes and will remain so for many years. Cold war politics has left deep marks on the political psyche of African countries accustomed to being kept afloat by their patrons in the Western or Eastern bloc. Most countries in Africa are in economic distress and survive only through an array of development loans and grants from more affluent countries and international organizations.

In 1989 and 1990 several Western governments sent unmistakable warnings to Africa's rulers that they could no longer rely on external financial and military support in facing popular unrest, which was likely to continue. This tilt in favor of the burgeoning opposition has played a major role in hastening the transformations in Africa that have already occurred. However, the attention spans of Western governments may not be long. France, for example, has already shown a lack of resolution when longtime clients such as President Gnassingb Eyadéma in Togo and Biya in Cameroon opted to use force against opponents. As this pattern of behavior is replicated elsewhere—for example in Burkina Faso—opposition forces are likely to move to direct confrontations, knowing that they cannot depend on France to pressure the regime to make it more responsive. In the case of the other major former colonial power in Africa, Great Britain, lofty ideals frequently expressed in London by ministers in support of democratization are seldom reflected in concrete action in Africa, even in countries such as Kenya, with which Britain enjoys strong economic ties.

Fortunately, other countries have become more resolute in supporting democratic transitions in Africa, notably the Scandinavian countries, the Netherlands, and, increasingly, Germany. As for the United States, for the first time in the postcolonial history of Africa it is implementing policies toward Africa that reflect the principles for which the American government stands. Whatever the outcome of the 1992 presidential election in the United States, it does not appear that this refreshing change in official behavior is at risk.

The democratic movement in Africa, however, cannot count too much on foreign goodwill. The future, Chiluba has emphasized to the Zambian people, is up to them. As he declared in his inaugural address, "In our time of need, we will look to the world not for handouts, but for help to stand on our own feet again." The new president has repeatedly admonished Zambians to reestablish traditions of hard work and honesty that were eroded during the years of single-party dominance.

If Zambia succeeds, many other countries in Africa can be induced to follow its lead; if it falters, the remaining autocrats will feel that they can ease a few controls on their societies and win sufficient respite from external pressures for change. The Zambian government and people are fully aware of the national, continental, and international implications signaled by October's new beginning. Zambia's courageous battle to add economic recovery to political renewal should command as much attention as the precarious experiments now under way in eastern Europe.

Credits

Glossary of Terms and Abbreviations

Acquired Immune Deficiency Syndrome (AIDS)   A disease of immune-system dysfunction assumed to be caused by the human immunodeficiency virus (HIV), which allows opportunistic infections to take over the body.

African Development Bank   Founded in 1963 under the auspices of the United Nations Economic Commission on Africa, the bank, located in Côte d'Ivoire, makes loans to African countries, although other nations can apply.

African National Congress (ANC)   Founded in 1912, the group's goal is to achieve equal rights for blacks in South Africa through nonviolent action. "Spear of the Nation," the ANC wing dedicated to armed struggle, was organized after the Sharpeville massacre in 1960.

African Party for the Independence of Guinea-Bissau and Cape Verde (PAICG)   An independence movement that fought during the 1960s and 1970s for the liberation of present-day Guinea-Bissau and Cape Verde from Portuguese rule. The two territories were ruled separately by a united PAIGC until a 1981 coup in Guinea-Bissau caused the party to split along national lines. In 1981 the Cape Verdean PAIGC formally renounced its Guinea links and became the PAICV.

African Socialism   A term applied to a variety of ideas (including those of Nkrumah and Senghor) about communal and shared production in Africa's past and present. The concept of African socialism was especially popular in the early 1960s. Adherence to it has not meant governments' exclusion of private-capitalist ventures.

Afrikaners   South Africans of Dutch descent who speak Afrikaans and are often referred to as *Boers* (Afrikaans for "farmers").

Amnesty International   A London-based human-rights organization whose members "adopt" political prisoners or prisoners of conscience in many nations of the world. The organization generates political pressure and puts out a well-publicized annual report of human-rights conditions in each country of the world.

Aouzou Strip   A barren strip of land between Libya and Chad contested by both countries.

Apartheid   Literally, "separateness," the South African policy of segregating the races socially, legally, and politically.

Arusha Declaration   A document issued in 1967 by Tanzanian President Julius Nyerere, committing the country to socialism based on peasant farming, democracy under one party, and self-reliance.

Assimilado   The Portuguese term for Africans who became "assimilated" to Western ways. Assimilados enjoyed equal rights under Portuguese law.

Azanian People's Organization (AZAPO)   Founded in 1978 at the time of the Black Consciousness Movement and revitalized in the 1980s, the movement works to develop chapters and bring together black organizations in a national forum.

Bantu   A major linguistic classification for many Central, Southern, and East African languages. Also, a derogatory term for Africans, used by the South African government.

Bantustans   Areas, or "homelands," to which black South Africans are assigned "citizenship" as part of the policy of apartheid.

Basarawa   Peoples of Botswana who have historically been hunters and gatherers.

Berber   The collective term for the indigenous languages and peoples of North Africa.

Bicameral   A government made up of two legislative branches.

Black Consciousness Movement   A South African student movement founded by Steve Biko and others in the 1970s to promote pride and empowerment of blacks.

Boers   See *Afrikaners*.

Brotherhoods   Islamic organizations based on specific religious beliefs and practices. In many areas, brotherhood leaders and their spiritual followers gain political influence.

Cabinda   A small, oil-rich portion of Angola separated from the main body of that country by the coastal strip of Zaire.

Caisse de Stabilization   A marketing board that stabilizes the uncertain returns to producers of cash crops by offering them less than market prices in good harvest years while assuring them of a steady income in bad years. Funds from these boards are used to develop infrastructure, to promote social welfare, or to maintain a particular regime in power.

Caliphate   The office or dominion of a caliph, the spiritual head of Islam.

Cassava   A tropical plant with a fleshy, edible rootstock; one of the staples of the African diet. Also known as manioc.

Chimurenga   A Shona term meaning "fighting in which everyone joins," used to refer to Zimbabwe's fight for independence.

Coloured   The South African classification for a person of mixed racial descent.

Committee for the Struggle Against Drought in the Sahel (CILSS)   A grouping of eight West African countries, formed to fight the effects of drought in the region.

Commonwealth of Nations   An association of nations and dependencies loosely joined by the common tie of having been part of the British Empire.

Congress of South African Trade Unions (COSATU) Established in 1985 to form a coalition of trade unions to press for workers' rights and an end to apartheid.

Copperbelt   A section of Zambia with a high concentration of copper-mining concessions.

Creole   A person or language of mixed African and European descent.

Dergue   From the Amheric word for "committee," the ruling body of Ethiopia after the revolution in 1974.

East African Community (EAC)   Established in 1967, this organization grew out of the East African Common Services Organization begun under British rule. The EAC included Kenya, Tanzania, and Uganda in a customs union and involved common currency and development of infrastructure. It was disbanded in 1977, and the final division of assets was completed in 1983.

Economic Commission for Africa (ECA)   Founded in 1958 by the Economic and Social Committee of the United Nations to aid African development through regional centers, field agents, and the encouragement of regional efforts, food self-sufficiency, transport, and communications development.

Economic Community of Central African States (CEEAC, also known as ECCA)   An organization of all of the Central African states, as well as Rwanda and Burundi, whose goal is to promote economic and social cooperation among its members.

Economic Community of West Africa (CEAO)   An organization of French-speaking countries formed to promote trade and regional economic cooperation.

Economic Community of West African States (ECOWAS)   Established in 1975 by the Treaty of Lagos, the organization includes all of the West African states except Western Sahara. The organization's goals are to promote trade, cooperation, and self-reliance among its members.

Enclave Industry   An industry run by a foreign company that uses imported technology and machinery and exports the product to industrialized countries; often described as a "state within a state."

Eritrean Peoples' Liberation Front (EPLF)   The major group fighting the Ethiopian government for the independence of Eritrea.

European Community (EC, or Common Market)   Established in 1958, the EC seeks to establish a common curency and a common agricultural policy as well as uniform trade and travel restrictions among its members.

Évolués   A term used in colonial Zaire (the Congo) to refer to Western-educated Congolese.

Food and Agricultural Organization of the United Nations (FAO)   Established in 1945 to oversee good nutrition and agricultural development.

Franc Zone   This organization includes members of the West African Monetary Union and the monetary organizations of Central Africa that have currencies linked to the French franc. Reserves are managed by the French treasury and guaranteed by the French franc.

Freedom Charter   Established in 1955, this charter proclaimed equal rights for all South Africans and has been a foundation for almost all groups in the resistance against apartheid.

Free French Conference   A 1944 conference of French-speaking territories, which proposed a union of all the territories in which Africans would be represented and their development furthered.

French Equatorial Africa (FEA)   The French colonial federation that included present-day Congo, Central African Republic, Chad, and Gabon.

French West Africa   The administrative division of the former French colonial empire that included the current independent countries of Senegal, Côte d'Ivoire, Guinea, Mali, Niger, Burkina Faso, Benin, and Mauritania.

Front for the Liberation of Mozambique (Frelimo)   Liberation forces established in 1963 to free Mozambique from Portuguese rule; the dominant party in independent Mozambique after 1975.

Frontline States   A caucus supported by the Organization of African Unity (consisting of Tanzania, Zambia, Mozambique, Botswana, and Angola) whose goal is to achieve black majority rule in all of Southern Africa.

Green Revolution   Use of Western technology and agricultural practices to increase food production and agricultural yields.

Griots   Professional bards of West Africa, some of whom tell history and are accompanied by the playing of the kora or harp-lute.

Gross Domestic Product (GDP)   The value of production attributable to the factors of production in a given country regardless of their ownership. GDP equals GNP minus the product of a country's residents originating in the rest of the world.

Gross National Product (GNP)   The sum of the values of all goods and services produced by a country's residents at home and abroad in any given year, less income earned by foreign residents and remitted abroad.

Guerrilla   A member of a small force of irregular soldiers. Generally, guerrilla forces are made up of volunteers who make surprise raids against the incumbent military or political force.

Harmattan   In West Africa, the dry wind that blows from the Sahara Desert in January and February.

Homelands   See *Bantustans*.

Horn of Africa   A section of northeastern Africa including the countries of Djibouti, Ethiopia, Somalia, and the Sudan.

Hut Tax   Instituted by the colonial governments in Africa, this measure required families to pay taxes on each building in the village.

International Monetary Fund (IMF)   Established in 1945 to promote international monetary cooperation.

Irredentism   An effort to unite certain people and territory in one state with another, on the grounds that they belong together.

Islam   A religious faith started in Arabia during the seventh century A.D. by the Prophet Muhammad and spread in Africa through African Muslim leaders, migrations, and wars.

Jihad   A struggle, or "holy war," waged as a religious duty on behalf of Islam to rid the world of disbelief and error.

Koran   Writings accepted by Muslims as the word of God, as revealed to the Prophet Mohammed.

Lagos Plan of Action   Adopted by the Organization of African Unity in 1980, this agreement calls for self-reliance, regional economic cooperation, and the creation of a pan-African economic community and common market by the year 2000.

League of Nations   Established at the Paris Peace Conference in 1919, this forerunner of the modern-day United Nations had 52 member nations at its peak (the United States never joined the organization) and mediated in international affairs. The league was dissolved in 1945 after the creation of the United Nations.

Least Developed Countries (LDCs)   A term used to refer to the poorest countries of the world, including many African countries.

Maghrib   An Arabic term, meaning "land of the setting sun," that is often used to refer to the former French colonies of Morocco, Algeria, and Tunisia.

Mahdi   The expected messiah of Islamic tradition; or a Muslim leader who plays a messianic role.

Malinke (Mandinka, or Mandinga)   One of the major groups of people speaking Mande languages. The original homeland of the Malinke was Mali, but the people are now found in Mali, Guinea-Bissau, The Gambia, and other areas, where they are sometimes called Mandingoes. Some trading groups are called Dyoula.

Marabout   A Muslim saint or holy man, often the leader of a religious brotherhood.

Marxist-Leninism   Sometimes called "scientific socialism," this doctrine derived from the ideas of Karl Marx as modified by Vladimir Lenin; it was the ideology of the Communist Party of the Soviet Union and has been modified in many ways by other persons and groups who still use the term. In Africa, some political parties or movements have claimed to be Marxist-Leninist but have often followed policies that conflict in practice with the ideology; these governments have usually not stressed Marx's philosophy of class struggle.

Mfecane   The movement of people in the nineteenth century in the eastern areas of present-day South Africa to the west and north as the result of wars led by the Zulus.

Mozambique National Resistance (MNR, also known as Renamo)   A South African-backed rebel movement that attacks civilians in attempting to overthrow the government of Mozambique.

Muslim   A follower of the Islamic faith.

Naam   A traditional work cooperative in Burkina Faso.

National Youth Service   Service to the state required of youth after completing education, a common practice in many African countries.

National Union for the Total Independence of Angola (UNITA)   One of three groups that fought the Portuguese during the colonial period in Angola, later backed by South Africa and the United States and fighting the independent government of Angola.

Nkomati Accords   An agreement signed in 1984 between South Africa and Mozambique, pledging that both sides would no longer support opponents of the other.

Non-Aligned Movement (NAM)   A group of nations that chose not to be politically or militarily associated with either the West or the former communist bloc.

Non-Governmental Organization (NGO)   A private voluntary organization or agency working in relief and development programs.

Organization for the Development of the Senegal River (OMVS)   A regional grouping of countries bordering the Senegal River that sponsors joint research and projects.

Organization of African Unity (OAU)   An association of all the independent states of Africa (except South Africa) whose goal is to promote unity and solidarity among African nations.

Organization of Petroleum Exporting Countries (OPEC)   Established in 1960, this association of some of the world's major oil-producing countries seeks to coordinate the petroleum policies of its members.

Pan Africanist Congress (PAC)   A liberation organization of black South Africans that broke away from the ANC in the 1950s.

Parastatals   Agencies for production or public service that are established by law and that are, in some measure, government organized and controlled. Private enterprise may be involved, and the management of the parastatal may be in private hands.

Pastoralist   A person, usually a nomad, who raises livestock for a living.

Polisario Front   Originally a liberation group in Western Sahara seeking independence from Spanish rule. Today, it is battling Morocco, which claims control over the Western Sahara (see *SADR*).

Popular Movement for the Liberation of Angola (MPLA)   A Marxist liberation movement in Angola during the resistance to Portuguese rule; now the governing party in Angola.

Rinderpest   A cattle disease that periodically decimates herds in savanna regions.

Saharawi Arab Democratic Republic (SADR)   The Polisario Front name for Western Sahara, declared in 1976 in the struggle for independence from Morocco.

Sahel In West Africa, the borderlands between savanna and desert.

Sanctions Coercive measures, usually economic, adopted by nations acting together against a nation violating international law.

Savanna Tropical or subtropical grassland with scattered trees and undergrowth.

Senegambia A confederation of Senegal and The Gambia signed into agreement in December 1981 and inaugurated on February 1, 1982.

Sharia The Islamic code of law.

Sharpeville Massacre The 1960 pass demonstration in South Africa in which 60 people were killed when police fired into the crowd; it became a rallying point for many antiapartheid forces.

Shengo The Ethiopian Parliament.

Sorghum A tropical grain that is a traditional staple in the savanna regions.

Southern African Development Coordination Conference (SADCC) An organization of nine African states (Angola, Zambia, Malawi, Mozambique, Zimbabwe, Lesotho, Botswana, Swaziland, and Tanzania) whose goal is to free themselves from dependence on South Africa and to cooperate on projects of economic development.

South West Africa People's Organization (SWAPO) Angola-based freedom fighters who have been waging guerrilla warfare against the presence of South Africa in Namibia since the 1960s. The United Nations and the Organization of African Unity have recognized SWAPO as the only authentic representative of the Namibian people.

Structural Adjustment Program (SAP) Economic reforms encouraged by the International Monetary Fund which include devaluation of currency, cutting government subsidies on commodities, and reducing government expenditures.

Swahili A widespread *lingua franca* in East Africa; an African-based Afro-Arab language and culture.

Tsetse Fly An insect that transmits sleeping sickness to cattle and humans. It is usually found in the scrub-tree and forest regions of Central Africa.

Ujamaa In Swahili, "familyhood"; government-sponsored cooperative villages in Tanzania.

Unicameral A political structure with a single legislative branch.

Unilateral Declaration of Independence (UDI) A declaration of white minority settlers in Rhodesia, claiming independence from the United Kingdom in 1965.

United Democratic Front (UDF) A multiracial, black-led group in South Africa that gained prominence during the 1983 campaign to defeat the government's Constitution, which has given only limited political rights to Asians and Coloureds.

United Nations (UN) An international organization established on June 26, 1945, through official approval of the charter by delegates of 50 nations at a conference in San Francisco, California. The charter went into effect on October 24, 1945.

United Nations Development Program (UNDP) Established to create local organizations for increasing wealth through better use of human and natural resources.

United Nations Educational, Scientific, and Cultural Organization (UNESCO) Established on November 4, 1946, to promote international collaboration in education, science, and culture.

United Nations High Commission for Refugees (UNHCR) Established in 1951 to provide international protection for people with refugee status.

United Nations Resolution 435 Voted in 1978, this resolution calls for internationally supervised elections and independence for South African-ruled Namibia.

Villagization A policy whereby a government relocates rural dwellers to create newer, more concentrated communities.

World Bank A closely integrated group of international institutions providing financial and technical assistance to developing countries.

World Health Organization (WHO) Established by the United Nations in 1948, this organization promotes the highest possible state of health in countries throughout the world.

Bibliography

RESOURCE CENTERS

African Studies Centers provide special services for schools, libraries, and community groups. Contact the center nearest you for further information about resources available.

African Studies Center
Boston University
270 Bay State Road
Boston, MA 02215

African Studies Program
Indiana University
Woodburn Hall 221
Bloomington, IN 47405

African Studies Educational Resource Center
100 International Center
Michigan State University
East Lansing, MI 49923

African Studies Program
630 Dartmouth
Northwestern University
Evanston, IL 60201

Africa Project
Lou Henry Hoover Room 223
Stanford University
Stanford, CA 94305

African Studies Center
University of California
Los Angeles, CA 90024

Center for African Studies
470 Grinter Hall
University of Florida
Gainesville, FL 32611

African Studies Program
University of Illinois
1208 W. California, Room 101
Urbana, IL 61801

African Studies Program
1450 Van Hise Hall
University of Wisconsin
Madison, WI 53706

Council on African Studies
Yale University
New Haven, CT 06520

Foreign Area Studies
The American University
5010 Wisconsin Avenue, N.W.
Washington, D.C. 20016

African Studies Program
Center for Strategic and International Studies
Georgetown University
1800 K Street, N.W.
Washington, D.C. 20006

REFERENCE WORKS, BIBLIOGRAPHIES, AND OTHER SOURCES

Africa South of the Sahara (updated yearly) (London: Europa Publications, Ltd.).

Africa on Film and Videotape 1960–1961, A Compendium of Reviews (East Lansing: Michigan State University, 1982).

Africa Today, An Atlas of Reproductible Pages, rev. ed. (Wellesley: World Eagle, 1987).

Scarecrow Press, Metuchen, NJ, publishes *The African Historical Dictionaries*, a series edited by Jon Woronoff. There are more than 40 dictionaries, each under a specialist editor. They are short works with introductory essays and are useful guides for the beginner, especially for countries on which little has been published in English.

Colin Legum, ed., *Africa Contemporary Record* (New York: Africana) (annual). Contains information on each country for the reporting year.

Africa Research Bulletin (Political Series), Africa Research Ltd., Exeter, Devon, England (monthly). Political updates on current issues and events in Africa.

Chris Cook and David Killingray, *African Political Facts Since 1945* (New York: Facts on File, 1983). Chronology of events; chapters on heads of state, ministers, parliaments, parties, armies, trade unions, population, biographies.

MAGAZINES AND PERIODICALS

African Arts
University of California
Los Angeles, CA
Beautifully illustrated articles review Africa's artistic heritage and current creative efforts.

African Concord
5–15 Cromer Street
London, WCIH 8LS, England

Africa News
P.O. Box 3851
Durham, NC 27702
A weekly with short articles that are impartially written and full of information.

Africa Now
212 Fifth Avenue, Suite 1409
New York, NY 10010
A monthly publication that gives current coverage and includes sections on art, culture, and business, as well as a special series of interviews.

Africa Recovery
DPI, Room S-1061
United Nations
New York, NY 10017

Africa Report
African American Institute
833 UN Plaza
New York, NY 10017
This bimonthly periodical has an update section, but most of each issue is devoted to broad-based articles by authorities giving background on key issues, developments in particular countries, and U.S. policy.

Africa Today
Graduate School of International Studies
Denver, CO 80208

The Economist
P.O. Box 2700
Woburn, MA
A weekly that gives attention to African issues.

Newswatch
62 Oregun Rd.
P. M. B. 21499
Ikeja, Nigeria

UNESCO Courier
UNESCO, Place de Fontenox
75700 Paris, France
This periodical includes short and clear articles on Africa, often by African authors, within the framework of the topic to which the monthly issues are devoted.

The Weekly Review
Agip House
P.O. Box 42271
Nairobi, Kenya

West Africa
Holborn Viaduct
London, EC1A Z FD, England
This weekly is the best source for West Africa including countries as far south as Angola and Namibia. Continent-wide issues are also discussed.

NOVELS AND AUTOBIOGRAPHICAL WRITINGS

Chinua Achebe, *Things Fall Apart* (Portsmouth: Heinemann, 1965).
This is the story of the life and values of residents of a traditional Igbo village in the nineteenth century and of its first contacts with the West.

___, *No Longer at Ease* (Portsmouth: Heinemann, 1963).
The grandson of the major character of *Things Fall Apart* lives an entirely different life in the modern city of Lagos and faces new problems while remaining committed to some of the traditional ways.

Okot p'Bitek, *Song of Lawino* (Portsmouth: Heinemann, 1983).
A traditional Ugandan wife comments on the practices of her Western-educated husband and reveals her own life-style and values.

Buchi Emecheta, *The Joys of Motherhood* (New York: G. Braziller, 1979).
The story of a Nigerian woman who overcomes great obstacles to raise a large family and then finds that the meaning of motherhood has changed.

Nadine Gordimer, *July's People* (New York: Viking, 1981).
This is a troubling and believable scenario of future revolutionary times in South Africa.

___, *A Soldier's Embrace* (New York: Viking, 1982).
These short stories treat the effects of apartheid on people's relations with each other. Films made from some of these stories are available at the University of Illinois Film Library, Urbana-Champaign, IL and the Boston University Film Library, Boston, MA.

Cheik Amadou Kane, *Ambiguous Adventure* (Portsmouth: Heinemann, 1972).
This autobiographical novel of a young man coming of age in Senegal, in a Muslim society, and, later, in a French school, illuminates changes that have taken place in Africa and raises many questions.

Alex LaGuma, *Time of the Butcherbird* (Portsmouth: Heinemann, 1979).
The people of a long-standing black community in South Africa's countryside are to be removed to a Bantustan.

Camara Laye, *The Dark Child* (Farrar Straus and Giroux, 1954).
This autobiographical novel gives a loving and nostalgic picture of a Malinke family of Guinea.

Ousmane Sembene, *God's Bits of Wood* (Portsmouth: Heinemann, 1970).
The railroad workers' strike of 1947 provides the setting for a novel about the changing consciousness and life of African men and women in Senegal.

Joyce Sikakane, *A Window on Soweto* (London: International Defense and Aid Fund, 1977).

Wole Soyinka, *Ake: The Years of Childhood* (New York: Random House, 1983).
Soyinka's account of his first 11 years is full of the sights, tastes, smells, sounds, and personal encounters of a headmaster's home and a busy Yoruba town.

Ngugi wa Thiong'o, *A Grain of Wheat* (Portsmouth: Heinemann, 1968).
A story of how the Mau-Mau Movement and the coming of independence affected several individuals after independence as well as during the struggle that preceded it.

INTRODUCTORY BOOKS

A. E. Afigbo, E. A. Ayandele, R. J. Gavin, J. D. Omer-Cooper, and R. Palmer, *The Making of Modern Africa,*

vol. II, *The Twentieth Century,* 2nd ed. (London: Longman, 1986).
An introductory political history of Africa in the twentieth century.

Gwendolen Carter and Patrick O'Meara, eds., *African Independence: The First Twenty-Five Years* (Midland Books, 1986).
Collected essays surrounding issues such as political structures, military rule, and economics.

Basil Davidson, *The African Genius* (Boston: Little, Brown, 1979). Also published as *The Africans.*
Davidson discusses the complex political, social, and economic systems of traditional African societies, translating scholarly works into a popular mode without distorting complex material.

___, *Let Freedom Come* (Boston: Little, Brown, 1978).
A lively and interesting history of Africa in the twentieth century.

___, *Africa in History* (Macmillan, 1991).
A fine discussion of African history.

John Fage and Roland Oliver, *Cambridge History of Africa,* 6 vols. (New York: Cambridge University Press, 1975).
Comprehensive descriptions of regional histories.

___ *A History of Africa, 2nd ed.* (Unwin Hyman, 1989).
A comprehensive look at the historical evolution of Africa.

Bill Freund, *The Making of Contemporary Africa: The Development of African Society Since 1800* (Bloomington: Indiana University Press, 1984).
Recent African history from an economic-history point of view, with emphasis on forces of production.

Adrian Hastings, *A History of African Christianity, 1950–1975* (Cambridge: Cambridge University Press, 1979).
A good introduction to the impact of Christianity on Africa in recent years.

Goren Hyden, *No Shortcut to Progress: African Development Management in Perspective* (Berkeley: University of California, 1983).
An assessment of development in relation to obstacles, prospects, and progress.

John Mbiti, *African Religions and Philosophy* (Portsmouth: Heinemann, 1982).
This work by a Ugandan scholar is the standard introduction to the rich variety of religious beliefs and rituals of African peoples.

Phyllis Martin and Patrick O'Meara, eds., *Africa,* 2nd ed. (Boomington: Indiana University Press, 1986).
This collection of essays covers history, culture, politics, and the economy.

J. H. Kwabena Nketia, *The Music of Africa* (New York: Norton, 1974).

The author, a Ghanaian by birth, is Africa's best-known ethnomusicologist.

Chris Searle, *We're Building the New School: Diary of a Teacher in Mozambique* (London: Zed Press, 1981; distributed in the United States by Laurence Hill & Co., Westport).
A lively book that shows that the lives of students and teachers in the nation of Mozambique are both exciting and difficult.

Timothy Shaw and Adebayo Adedeji, *Economic Crisis in Africa: African Perspectives on Development Problems and Potentials* (Boulder: L. Rienner, 1985).

J. B. Webster, A. A. Boahen, and M. Tidy, *The Revolutionary Years: West Africa Since 1800* (London: Longman, 1980).
An interesting, enjoyable, and competent introductory history to the West African region.

Frank Willett, *African Art* (New York: Oxford University Press, 1971).
A work to read for both reference and pleasure, by one of the authorities on Nigeria's early art.

COUNTRY AND REGIONAL STUDIES

Tony Avirgan and Martha Honey, *War in Uganda: The Legacy of Idi Amin* (Westport: Laurence Hill & Co., 1982).

John E. Bardill and James H. Cobbe, *Lesotho: Dilemmas of Dependence in Southern Africa* (Boulder: Westview Press, 1985).

Gerald Bender, *Angola Under the Portuguese: The Myth and the Reality* (Berkeley, University of California Press, 1978).

William Bigelow, *Strangers in Their Own Country* (a curriculum on South Africa), 2nd ed. (Trenton: Africa World Press, 1989).

Allan R. Booth, *Swaziland: Tradition and Change in a Southern African Kingdom* (Boulder: Westview Press, 1984).

Marcia M. Burdette, *Zambia: Between Two Worlds* (Boulder: Westview Press, 1988).

Gwendolen Carter, *Continuity and Change in South Africa* (Gainesville: African Studies Association and Center for African Studies, University of Florida, 1985).

Christopher Clapham, *Transformation and Continuity in Revolutionary Ethiopia* (Cambridge: Cambridge University Press, 1988).

Maureen Covell, *Madagascar: Politics, Economy, and Society* (London and New York: F. Pinter, 1987).

Toyin Falola and Julius Ihonvbere, *The Rise and Fall of Nigeria's Second Republic, 1979–1984* (London: Zed Press, 1985).

Robert Fatton, *The Making of a Liberal Democracy: Senegal's Passive Revolution, 1975–85* (Boulder: L. Rienner, 1987).

Foreign Area Studies (Washington, D.C.: Government Printing Office). Includes country-study handbooks with chapters on history, politics, culture, and economics, with maps, charts, and bibliographies. There are more than 20 in the series, with new ones added and revised periodically.

Marcus Franda, *The Seychelles: Unquiet Islands* (Boulder: Westview Press, 1982).

Sheldon Gellar, *Senegal: An African Nation Between Islam and the West* (Boulder: Westview Press, 1982).

Joseph Hanlon, *Mozambique: The Revolution Under Fire* (London: Zed Press, 1984).

Tony Hodges, *Western Sahara: The Roots of a Desert War* (Westport: Laurence Hill & Co., 1983).

P. M. Holt and M. W. Daly, *A History of Sudan: From the Coming of Islam to the Present Day* (Boulder: Westview Press, 1979).

Allan and Barbara Isaacman, *Mozambique from Colonialism to Revolution, 1900–1982* (Boulder: Westview Press, 1983).

Richard Joseph, *Democracy and Prebendel Politics in Nigeria: The Rise and Fall of the Second Republic* (Cambridge: Cambridge University Press, 1987).

Michael P. Kelley, *A State in Disarray: Conditions of Chad's Survival* (Boulder: Westview Press, 1986).

David D. Laitin and Said S. Samatar, *Somalia: Nation in Search of a State* (Boulder: Westview Press, 1987).

J. Gus Liebenow, *Liberia: Quest for Democracy* (Bloomington: Indiana University Press, 1987).

Tom Lodge, *Black Politics in South Africa Since 1945* (New York: Longman, 1983).

David Martin and Phyllis Johnson, *The Struggle for Zimbabwe: The Chimurenga War* (Boston: Faber & Faber, 1981).

Norman N. Miller, *Kenya: The Quest for Prosperity* (Boulder: Westview Press, 1984).

Malyn Newitt, *The Comoro Islands: Sturggle Against Depencency in the Indian Ocean* (Boulder: Westview Press, 1984).

Julius Nyerere, *Ujamaa: Essays on Socialism* (Dar es Salaam: Oxford University Press, 1968).

Thomas O'Toole, *The Central African Republic: The Continent's Hidden Heart* (Boulder: Westview Press, 1986).

Jack Parson, *Botswana: Liberal Democracy and the Labor Resource in Southern Africa* (Boulder: Westview Press, 1984).

Deborah Pellow and Naomi Chazan, *Ghana: Coping with Uncertainty* (Boulder: Westview Press, 1986).

Bereket Habte Selassie, *Conflict and Intervention in the Horn of Africa* (New York: Monthly Review Press, 1980).

Study Commission on U.S. Policy Toward Southern Africa, *South Africa: Time Running Out* (Berkeley and Los Angeles: University of California Press, 1981).

Rachid Tlemcani, *State and Revolution in Algeria* (Boulder: Westview Press, 1987).

Michael Wolfers and Jane Bergerol, *Angola in the Frontline* (London: Zed Press, 1983).

Rodger Yeager, *Tanzania: An African Experiment* (Boulder: Westview Press, 1983).

Sources for Statistical Reports

U.S. State Department, *Background Notes* (1992).

C.I.A. *World Factbook* (1992).

World Bank, *World Development Report* (1992).

UN *Population and Vital Statistics Report* (January 1993).

World Statistics in Brief (1992).

Statistical Yearbook (1992).

The Statesman's Yearbook (1992–93).

Population Reference Bureau, *World Population Data Sheet* (1992).

World Almanac (1993).

Demographic Yearbook (1992).

Index